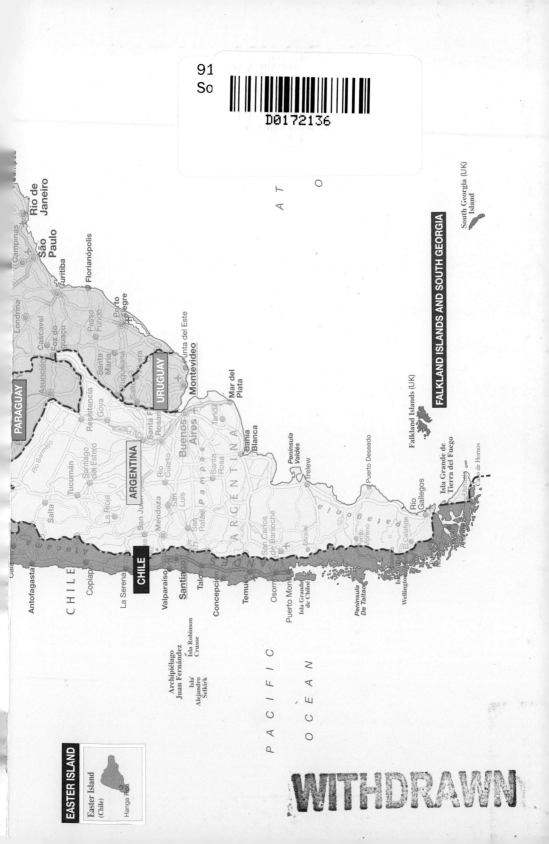

PARAGUAY

URUGUAY

ARGENTINA

CHILE

EASTER ISLAND

Easter Island
(Chile)

Hanga Roa

FALKLAND ISLANDS AND SOUTH GEORGIA

South Georgia (UK)
Island

Falkland Islands (UK)

Rio de
Janeiro

São
Paulo

Curitiba

Florianópolis

Londrina

Campinas

Cascavel

Foz do
Iguaçu

Passo
Fundo

Santa
Maria

Porto
Alegre

Asunción

Resistencia

Goya

Santiago
del Estero

Tucumán

La Rioja

Salta

Antofagasta

Copiapó

La Serena

Valparaíso

Santiago

Talca

Concepción

Temuco

Osorno

Puerto Montt

Isla Grande
de Chiloé

CHILE

Archipiélago
Juan Fernández

Isla
Alejandro
Selkirk

Isla Robinson
Crusoe

Mendoza

San
Rafael

San
Luis

San Juan

Río
Cuarto

Santa
Rosa

Buenos
Aires

Rosario

Santa Fe

Salto

Paraguaná

Punta del Este

Montevideo

Mar del
Plata

Tandil

Bahía
Blanca

Península
Valdés

Trelew

Puerto Deseado

Río
Gallegos

El Calafate

Puerto
Moreno

Esquel

San Carlos
de Bariloche

Península
De Taitao

Wellington

Isla Grande de
Tierra del Fuego

Cabo de Hornos

Río Bermejo

Río Paraná

Pampas

ARGENTINA

Patagonia

ANDES

Atacama

CHILE

PACIFIC
OCEAN

ATLÁNTICO

A T   O

INSIGHT GUIDES
SOUTH AMERICA

APA PUBLICATIONS L
Part of the Langenscheidt Publishing Group

The first Insight Guide pioneered the use of creative full-color photography in travel guides in 1970. Since then, we have expanded our range to cater for our readers' need not only for reliable information about their chosen destination but also for a real understanding of the culture and workings of that destination. Now, when the internet can supply inexhaustible (but not always reliable) facts, our books marry text and pictures to provide those much more elusive qualities: knowledge and discernment. To achieve this, they rely heavily on the authority of locally based writers and photographers.

Insight Guide: South America is structured to convey an understanding of the region and its people as well as to guide readers through its attractions:

The **Best of South America** at the front of the guide helps you to prioritize what you want to see and do.

The **Features** section, indicated by a pink bar at the top of each page, covers the political, cultural, and social history of the continent and includes illuminating essays on music and dance, arts and crafts and outdoor adventures.

The main **Places** section, indicated by a blue bar, is a complete guide to all the sights and areas worth visiting. Places of special interest are coordinated by number with the maps.

The **Travel Tips** listings section, with a yellow bar, starts with an overview of useful information applying to the whole of South America, then provides tips for each individual country: how to get there and get around, and an A to Z section of essential practical information.

The **photographs** are chosen not only to illustrate the South American landscapes, and the beauty of its cities, national parks, nature reserves, archeological sites and beaches, but also to convey its cultural diversity.

The contributors

This new edition of *Insight Guide South America* was commissioned and edited by **Alexia Georgiou** at Insight Guides' London office.

The entire book was comprehensively updated by **Stephan Kueffner**, a Quito-based journalist who writes for several English-language publications including *The Economist* and *Time Magazine*. Kueffner also wrote the Best of South America feature, as well as new essays on the rise of populist leaders, eco-tourism, and the

uncontacted Amazon tribes. He also compiled the redesigned Travel Tips at the back of the book, assisted by researcher **Pamela Ibarra**.

This version builds on previous editions produced by **Tony Perrottet** and **Natalie Minnis**. The original history chapters were written by specialist Latin American analyst **Nick Caistor**. Natalie Minnis wrote about the people of South America, and the music and dance chapter was contributed by **Shannon Shiell**. The arts and architecture chapters were contributed by **Mike Gonzalez**, Professor of Latin American Studies at University of Glasgow. The outdoor sports chapter was written by **Jane Letham** and **Mark Thurber**, who run their own trekking and mountaineering tours around Peru and Ecuador.

Other past contributors include **Claire Antell** (The Guyanas), **Ruth Bradley** (Chile), **Dominic Hamilton** (Venezuela), **Gabi Mocatta** (Peru), **Christopher Pickard** (Brazil), **Janet Santamaria-Fox** (Ecuador), **Liz Tremlett** (Bolivia), **Luisa Urueña** and **Susan Wunderli** (Colombia).

Many of the images are the work of three experienced travel photographers: **Eduardo Gil**, **Abe Nowitz**, and **Corrie Wingate**. **Penny Phenix** compiled the index.

Map Legend

▬▬ ▬ ▪	International Boundary
▬ ▬ ▬ ▬	State Boundary
⊖	Border Crossing
▬ ▪ ▬	National Park/Reserve
▬ ▬ ▬ ▬	Ferry Route
✈ ✈	Airport: International/Regional
🚌	Bus Station
❶	Tourist Information
✝ ✝ ✝	Church/Ruins
✝	Monastery
🏰 🏚	Castle/Ruins
☾	Mosque
✡	Synagogue
∴	Archaeological Site
∩	Cave
𝟏	Statue/Monument
★	Place of Interest
⊠	Post Office
Ⓜ	Metro

The main places of interest in the Places section are coordinated by number with a full-colour map (eg ❶), and a symbol at the top of every right-hand page tells you where to find the map.

Contents

THE BEST OF SOUTH AMERICA: TOP ATTRACTIONS

From the peaks of the Andes to the beaches of Brazil, here is a rundown of South America's most spectacular attractions.

△ **The Lake District.** Crossing from Chile to Argentina not only has numerous lakes and beaches, but ski slopes and beautiful forests. See pages 298, 343.

△ **Iguazú Falls.** More than 250 waterfalls form the Iguazú Falls straddling the jungle border between Argentina and Brazil. See pages 259, 342.

▽ **The Amazon.** Approach the Amazon basin, home to the greatest diversity of animal and plant species on the planet, from jungle lodges in several countries. See pages 165, 212, 260.

▽ **Rio de Janeiro.** A *cidade maravilhosa* – the marvelous city – Rio de Janeiro is cosmopolitan, vibrant, and completely Brazilian, with a stunningly beautiful cityscape. See page 237.

▽ **Easter Island.** The earth's most remote inhabited area is home to the unresolved mystery of the giant moais. See page 309.

△ **Angel Falls.** Deep in the Venezuelan jungle, the world's highest waterfall is still a pristine destination in a prehistoric landscape. See page 126.

△ **Lake Titicaca.** Split between Bolivia and Peru, the world's highest waterway is surrounded by snow-capped peaks and is the birthplace of two ancient empires. See pages 164, 172, 184.

▷ **Machu Picchu.** Marvel at the masonry and remote location of South America's finest archeological wonders in Peru's Sacred Valley and Machu Picchu. See page 162.

▽ **Old Quito.** The historic old town of Quito, one of the biggest in the Americas, is studded with Baroque churches. The city snakes through the Andes at the foot of volcanoes, almost touching the Equator. See page 205.

△ **Torres del Paine.** Sculpted by time, ice, and wind, it rises from Chile's azure lakes and Patagonian plains to form an unforgettable landscape. See page 305.

◁ **Cusco.** Navel of South America's greatest native empire, Cusco in Peru is a monument to the artistic creativity of both the Incas and the Spanish Conquerors. See page 156.

▽ **Ouro Preto.** Preserved in time but very much alive, Baroque colonial gem Ouro Preto clings to the hillsides in the Brazilian interior. See page 249.

◁ **Buenos Aires.** Argentina's capital isn't the Paris or Madrid of South America, it is a non-stop, world-class city in its own right. See page 331.

△ **Andean Desert.** Shared by Argentina, Chile and Bolivia, the Andean Desert holds beautiful oasis villages, spectacular wildlife, and more particularly the world's largest salt flats, Uyuni. See page 195.

◁ **Avenue of the Volcanoes.** Conical peaks along Ecuador's Andean spine form this avenue where you can hike at the top of the world (as measured from the earth's center). See page 209.

△ **Tierra del Fuego National Park.** Trails lead through southern beech forests to hidden lakes in this huge coastal reserve, which can be reached from Ushuaia on the Tren del Fin del Mundo. See page 349.

△ **Colonia del Sacramento.** Partly because little has happened here since the Portuguese founded it as a rival to Buenos Aires in 1680, this Uruguayan city retains more of its original flavor than most in the region. See page 320.

◁ **Otavalo.** Culture does not get more Andean than in Otavalo, with its excellent textile market. Nearby lakes, haciendas, and colonial Ibarra round off the experience. See page 208.

△ **Cartagena.** Bathed by the Caribbean and protected by great walls and a massive fortress, this is also a Colombian city of brightly painted houses, narrow streets and romantic corners. See page 107.

◁ **Rupununi Savannah.** This area in Guyana is a birdwatcher's and naturalist's dream and the highly endangered red siskin, a brightly colored finch, can be seen here. See page 133.

THE BEST OF SOUTH AMERICA: EDITOR'S CHOICE

From cosmopolitan capitals to deserts, and churches to parties... here, at a glance, are our recommendations.

Vermelha Beach near Parati, Brazil.

BEST WILDLIFE WATCHING

Península Valdés. Argentina's Península Valdés has both marine wildlife – whales, sea lions, elephant seals, penguins – and Patagonian wildlife including guanacos, ostrich-like ñandus and hare-like maras. See page 347.

The Pantanal. On the borders of Brazil, Bolivia and Paraguay is one of the world's biggest wetland areas. Wildlife is easier to spot there than in the dense Amazon Rainforest. See pages 258, 280.

Mindo, Ecuador. The tropical cloud forests around Mindo to the west of Ecuador's capital, Quito, offers birdwatchers

Whale watching.

the chance of spotting hundreds of bird species. See page 207.

Llanos, Venezuela. The vast savannahs of Venezuela's Llanos allow the viewing of giant anacondas, capybaras (the world's biggest rodents) and caimans on foot or horseback. See page 125.

Galápagos Islands. Beyond its unique birdlife and namesake giant turtles, the Galápagos Islands are also one of the world's best diving destinations. See page 217.

Torres del Paine, Chile. One of the best places in the world to spot the elusive puma, the park also has condors, guanacos, and Patagonian foxes. See page 305.

BEST MUSEUMS

Museo Tumbas Reales del Señor de Sipán, Lambayeque, Peru. This museum showcases and recreates the multilayer tomb of the "Lord of Sipán" in a superb display of Mochica craftsmanship. See page 171.

Museo del Oro, Bogotá, Colombia. Houses a vast collection of gold expertly worked by more than a dozen indigenous cultures in Colombia. See page 99.

Museo Fundación Guayasamín, Quito, Ecuador. Showcases the Ecuadorian artist's world-famous works, particularly his paintings, along with his personal collection of pre-Hispanic and colonial art. His *Capilla del*

Hombre is perhaps the most stunning and complete example of Modernist Latin American art on the continent. See page 205.

Museo Paleontológico Egidio Feruglio, Trelew, Argentina. One of the world's best collection of dinosaur bones and other fossils is on display in this modern museum in Argentina's Patagonia. See page 347.

Pre-Columbian artifact on display in the Señor de Sipán Museum, Lambayeque, Peru.

BEST OUTDOOR ADVENTURES

Whitewater rafting expedition in Chile.

Hiking the Inca Trail to Machu Picchu, Peru. Despite the crowds, no trek in the Andes equals the 4-day hike from near Cusco to Machu Picchu for the unparalleled landscape and imperial Inca architecture.See page 160.

Climbing Cotopaxi, Ecuador. The 5- to 8-hour ascent over ice and snow takes you to the top of one of the world's highest active volcanoes. See page 207.

Skiing the Andes. Resorts dot the Andes from central Chile and Argentina to Tierra del Fuego, with some of the world's steepest runs, sunny slopes and deep powder, suiting all skill levels. See page 75.

Rafting in Futaleufú. Some of the planet's best rafting is on the wild waters of Chile's Futeleufú River. See page 75.

Mountaineering in Parque Nacional Fitzroy. This national park in Argentina features glacier treks and challenging mountaineering on the sheer face of Mt. Fitzroy. See page 349.

BEST RUINS

Cusco and the Sacred Valley, Peru. Groups together one of the world's greatest series of archeological sites, culminating in the mountaintop marvels of Machu Picchu and Huayna Picchu. See page 155.

Nazca lines, Peru. One of the world's greatest archeological mysteries. Southern Peru's Nazca lines, best appreciated from the air, are geo-metric designs, forming huge animal figures in the desert – some over 200 meters (660ft) across. See page 154.

San Agustín, Colombia. Huge stone sculptures of animals and human beings, some 12ft (4 meters) tall, form Colombia's most important archeological site. See page 102.

Chan Chan, Peru. Near Trujillo, built by the Chimú, lasted for 600 years until conquered by the Incas. Remains of the vast adobe city are remarkable for the intricate carvings of sea animals in its walls. See page 169.

The massive carved adobe wall at Chan Chan.

BEST CUISINE

Peruvian blend. Peruvian blend is at the culinary vanguard of South America, mixing Chinese recipes, Pacific Coast seafood and Andean staples into a refined bouquet of tastes. See page 402.

Manabi, Ecuador. Manabí specializes in a delightful mix of seafood and heavier ingredients, producing varied tastes. Typical dishes include lobster in beer sauces, dishes with corn and peanuts, as well as tropical staples such as cooked bananas and coconut sauces. See page 387.

Salvador de Bahía, Brazil. This is the heartland of Brazil's Africa-influenced cuisine where there is a great love of red peppers and acarajé – peeled black-eyed peas fried in palm oil and stuffed with spice pastes including shrimp or vegetables and substantial moqueca fish stews. See page 373.

Beef. Buenos Aires and Montevideo take the hearty rural food of the gaucho – beef and more beef – to cosmo-politan palates on both sides of the Río de la Plata. See pages 330 330, 364, 409.

Juicy beef on the grill, Jujuy Province, Argentina.

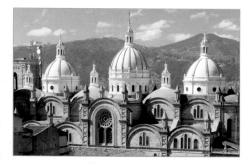

The center of Cuenca, a city founded on the site of the Inca city of Tomebamba.

BEST COLONIAL CITIES AND TOWNS

Cuenca, Ecuador. Perched on a cliff above a river, Cuenca is at once very Spanish, cosmopolitan, and indigenous. Numerous hotels have been restored and the number of restaurants and bars keeps growing. See page 211.

Cajamarca, Peru. This is still relatively off the beaten track but well worth the detour from the coast into the Andes to see the intricately carved church facades, whitewashed adobe houses, and Atahualpa's prison. See page 170.

Olinda, Brazil. This pretty flower-filled hilltop town above the Atlantic Ocean is a maze of cobblestone streets. The blue-tiled interiors of the monasteries take you back in time. See page 254.

Villa de Leyva, Colombia. Preserved as if time hadn't passed since the Viceroys of New Granada, it looks and feels as if you stepped onto the movie set of *The Mission*. See page 105.

Parati, Brazil. Like a relic of what Rio de Janeiro must once have been, the palm-fringed port where tropical mountains meet the Atlantic would be stunning even without its Portuguese colonial architecture and cobblestone alleys. See page 244.

Taking a ride on the beach is good family fun.

BEST FOR FAMILIES

Búzios, Brazil. This resort town has 20 beaches and plenty of activities for children of all ages, including horseback riding and skating. See page 244.

Máncora, Peru. Near Peru's border with Ecuador. The white sands, warm water, dolphins playing offshore, and small-town atmosphere make it a good place for children. See pages 76, 171.

Montevideo, Uruguay. Excellent yet recognizable food makes Uruguay easy on children's palates. The capital has numerous attractions for kids and a long string of beaches. See page 317.

Galápagos Islands, Ecuador. Close quarters with exotic and curious wildlife, warm weather and multi-colored beaches make the archipelago an excellent family destination. See page 217.

Ski resorts, Chile. Santiago de Chile's easily accessible ski resorts – El Colorado, La Parva, and Valle Nevado – hold plenty of activities for skiers and snowboarders as well as a snowboard park for teenage energies. See pages 75, 292.

Laughing kids at Arraial d'Ajuda, Bahia, Brazil.

BEST NIGHTLIFE NEIGHBORHOODS

Palermo, Buenos Aires, Argentina. An amalgam of quiet streets, trendy culture and counterculture with chic and rebel boutiques and bars, particularly in the "Palermo Soho" and "Palermo Hollywood" areas. See page 336.
Lapa, Rio de Janeiro, Brazil. Under the giant former aqueduct, enough bars, rock, jazz, samba, and dance clubs have sprung up to outshine the more famous Ipanema. See page 241.

Parque 93 and Zona Rosa, Bogotá, Colombia. Dozens of rock bars, trendy lounges, and discos make for a raucous celebration of Colombia's vastly improved security. See page 384.
Bellavista, Santiago de Chile, Chile. From grimy to classy, cheap beers to sushi and cocktails, arts and theater, Santiago's center of Bohemian life is here, almost round the clock. See page 289.

La Compañía de Jesus in Quito took 163 years to finish and is the most ornate church in Ecuador.

BEST CHURCHES

La Compañía de Jesus, Quito, Ecuador. With an elaborate facade, tiled towers, gold-plated walls, and vaulted ceilings, this Jesuit church is one of the most impressive in Latin America. See page 206.
Cusco cathedral, Peru. Set on a beautiful square, this ornate, red-stone cathedral combines Renaissance and Baroque architecture and holds the finest collection of paintings from the Cusco School. See page 157.

São Francisco de Assis, Ouro Preto, Brazil. Aleijadinho's masterpiece, flanked by twin round towers, has a dramatically painted, red and blue ceiling. See page 250.
Monasterio de Santa Catalina, Arequipa, Peru. Includes a unique Baroque hamlet inside Peru's White City. Continuously built over two centuries, Monaserio de Santa Catalina is a masterpiece of the fusion of Spanish and indigenous art. See page 163.

Party at Bombordo club, Porto Seguro, Brazil.

TOP TIPS FOR TRAVELERS

Cowboy cultures. In many countries, rural farms (haciendas, *hatos*, and *estancias*) offer a unique way to get away from it all and immerse yourself in untainted local culture and active vacations.
Pray and party. Even Carnival has religious origins, but South America has hundreds more religious festivals to offer – with solemnity and celebration.

Happy haggling. Markets are still the place where millions of locals shop not just for food but for arts and crafts and where real bargains, from jewelry to clothes to antiques, can be found.
Andean Spanish classes. Ecuador, Peru, and Bolivia are the best countries in South America to learn Spanish and there are dozens of language schools in popular tourist destinations.

Cheap eats. Find some of the best food on the subcontinent in the flavorful local markets from the Asian spices in Guyana through the hearty meals in the Andes to the seafood of Chile and beef of Uruguay.
Cheap seats. See some of the world's best soccer players at second-division prices during South America's grueling, two-year FIFA World Cup qualifiers.

Market day in Ecuador.

Iguaçu Falls.

Train journey along the Devil's Nose, Avenue of Volcanoes, Ecuador.

THE UNDISCOVERED CONTINENT

From the Andes to the Amazon, from dense
forests to alluring beaches, South America's
diversity is extraordinary.

Esmeraldas boy, Ecuador.

According to Colombian novelist Gabriel García Márquez, foreigners see South America as "a man with a mustache, a guitar, and a revolver." South America has long been the victim of stereotypes and misconceptions. Many see it as one huge, mysterious jungle, a mountainous wasteland or a backward world lost in an eternal *siesta*.

But these images fail to capture even a fraction of the reality. There are mighty rivers, and vast wilderness, but also ancient civilizations and vibrant new cultures. The Amazon Basin and its remote outposts grab the imagination of novelists, screenwriters, and adventure seekers, while the elegant cafés of Buenos Aires and the stylish resorts along the Caribbean attract a less vocal following. The Andes are home to communities that have preserved traditions for centuries, while life in the enormous metropolises of Brazil and Argentina is so modern and energetic it will leave you breathless.

Rafting on the Maipo River, Chile.

The countries of South America share a common history – thousands of years of indigenous cultures broken by European intrusion over 500 years ago; colonial rule followed by bitter wars of independence; then an unsteady progress at the fringe of world events – yet each country retains its own character.

On the north coast are Colombia, Venezuela, and the Guayanas, racially mixed and geographically divided between rugged mountains, Caribbean coastline, and dense Amazon rainforest. Peru, Bolivia, and Ecuador form the Andean heartland. They have the largest native populations on the continent, clustered around the highlands where the mighty Inca Empire once reigned. The east is dominated by Brazil, separated from its neighbors by a Portuguese heritage and vast untamed jungle. In the cooler southern zones are Chile, Uruguay, and Argentina, the most European-influenced of the republics, with vast empty spaces from the spine of the Andes to the last stop before Antarctica: Tierra del Fuego.

Featherwork tabard dating from 700BC–AD 1000, when the Nazca and Huari cultures were prominent along the coast of southern Peru.

20,000–4500 BC

PRE-COLUMBIAN TIMELINE

Human settlement in South America began with nomadic hunter-gatherers traveling

Pre-Columbian artifacts, Museo Banco Central, Quito, Ecuador.

southward, and reached its peak with the Inca Empire at the time of the Conquest.

EARLIEST ORIGINS

The first humans arrived in South America in around 20,000 BC, and were related to

hunter-gatherers who crossed the Bering Straits "ice-bridge" between Asia and the Americas, following herds in search of food.

SETTLING DOWN

Cave remains and shell mounds (*sambaquis*) in Brazil and stone tools in Peru

3000–400 BC

POTTERY AND METAL

The first production of ceramics in South America began around 3000 BC, according to carbon-dated remains found in Colombia and Ecuador. These earliest ceramics were fashioned by hand, and were mostly utensils, but highly sophisticated ornamental and ceremonial items were soon being produced, from the

Andes to the mouth of the Amazon. Gold was the first metal known to be worked in the Andes, with remnants found in central Peru dating from around 2000 BC. The practice soon spread

Fan made from natural feathers, Paracas necropolis period, Peru.

to Bolivia and later to Ecuador and Colombia. Gold and silver items of incredible beauty and technical quality were produced in huge quantities, as symbolic decorations of the ruling classes of the emerging state societies.

400 BC–AD 1100

MASTER WEAVERS

The earliest textiles, found in central Peru, have been dated from as early as 8600 BC. Around 400 BC, the Nazca and Paracas cultures rose to prominence

Ceramic vessel, Chavín culture, Peru, c.900BC.

along the coastal desert of southern Peru. These people were masters at weaving and pottery, much of which has survived in the dry air of the funeral chambers. Some of these

textiles have over 200 threads to the square inch – finer than most modern materials. The Nazca culture also produced the lines on the desert floor, which still mystify visitors and archeologists alike – with interpretations ranging from an astronomical calendar to an extraterrestrial landing strip.

AD 1100–1569

LEGEND OF THE INCAS

AD c.1100, Manco Capac, rising out of Lake Titicaca, was hailed to be the Sun god and divine leader of the chosen Inca race. According to legend, he founded Cusco. The Inca state was called Tawantinsuyu, the "Land of the Four

Quarters," with Cusco at its center, as the "Umbilicus of the Universe."

AD c.1430, the Incas defeated Chancas and extended their empire across a huge

area of South America, based on military efficiency, road networks, terracing, irrigation, and stone architecture.

Artifacts from the tomb of the Lord of Sipán.

suggest that the earliest humans lived here from c.17,000–5000 BC. But the most reliable evidence of the first human settlement is at Monte Verde in Chile, where remains have been dated at 12,500 BC.

Woollen poncho with animal motifs, Paracas necropolis period, Peru.

FISHING AND FARMING

Between 7500 BC and 4500 BC Andean peoples began the seasonal cultivation of crops, including potato, maize, manioc, and sweet potato; and the domestication of dogs, llamas, alpacas, and guinea pigs. Coastal tribes from present-day Ecuador to

SOCIAL SKILLS

From about 2800 BC, societies began to form in the central and northern Andes. The earliest of these were the Chavín in northern Peru, the Tiahuanaco to the south of Lake Titicaca, and the San Agustín culture in southern Colombia. They built massive ceremonial urban centers in stone, and produced highly sophisticated ceramics, textiles,

northern Chile harvested the rich marine life of the Pacific, enriched by the Humboldt Current. The fishermen made hooks from shell, bone, and cactus spines.

Pre-Columbian artifact from the Gold Museum, Bogotá, Colombia.

and religious artifacts. They formed large populations of up to hundreds of thousands, organized in complex social hierarchies and covering large administrative regions. Amazonian societies also flourished at about this time, if not earlier. Aruak-speaking people inhabited a region near to present-day Manaus from as early as 3000 BC.

IMPERIAL EXPANSION

Based in the deserts of northern Peru, the Moche culture built an empire from about AD 100–800 that covered much of the country's north. Military and commercial influence was aided by their road building and irrigation works, skills later picked up by the Incas. Above all, the Moche were superb

artisans, producing fine metal and precious stone ornaments. The Moche Empire disappeared dramatically and mysteriously, around AD 700. From about AD 600–1000 the religious Tiahuanaco culture combined with the militaristic Huari of the central Andean highlands to form an empire that at its peak spread into present-day Bolivia.

Atahualpa, the last Inca emperor, in chains after capture by the Spaniard Pizarro.

PEAK AND FALL

Around the mid-1400s, the Inca Empire surged under Pachacutec and later under his son, Topa Inca. The Chimu Empire in northern Peru was defeated by the Incas AD c.1466. The Spanish conquistadors

arrived in Peru in AD 1532; Inca Atahualpa was executed a year later. In 1572, Tupac Amaru, the Last Inca, was killed by the Spanish, completing the Conquest.

Gold ornament, Sinu culture, Colombia, AD 1100–1600.

THE FIRST PEOPLES

Pre-Columbian South America was a place of cultural diversity where enduring traditions and unique lifestyles were forged, and great empires were built.

The first colonization of South America is shrouded in mystery. Knowledge of those early times has had to be pieced together from archeological finds and linguistic evidence. Experts now believe that the first Americans arrived from the Asian continent, crossing the Bering Straits when they were solid with ice during the last Ice Age, some 40,000 years ago. Genetic research shows several periods and sources of immigration, gradually spreading south; some sites in Patagonia show the far south was inhabited by around 9,000 BC. Remains of mastodon, giant sloth, and other animals that have since disappeared, found together with arrowheads, demonstrate that these people were hunter-gatherers, but little else is known about their way of life.

Over several thousand years, these small groups turned from hunting to a more settled farming existence. According to archeological evidence, some lived close to the seashore and subsisted on a diet of fish and shellfish; some settled in the Andean highlands, and others adapted to the tropical lowlands of the Amazon. These early settlers appear to have grown beans and peppers, and to have used domesticated dogs to help them hunt small game. Maize is thought to have been cultivated from Peru down to Argentina by 3,000 BC, and some of the highland groups also began to herd llama and other camelids. The first pottery remains found date from about 5,500 years ago.

First societies

As these groups became based around seasonal agriculture, population increased, and more complex societies emerged, with officials, including chieftains and priests or shamans.

The astronaut figure, one of the ancient geoglyphs in southern Peru's Nazca Desert.

Some of the earliest ceramic remains discovered are from **Valdivia** in Ecuador, dating from *c*.3500–1500 BC. The earlier Chinchorro culture in northern Chile was one of the outstanding neolithic sites. Here, mummies from 7,000 BC indicate a high degree of social organization, with religious ceremonies and complex burial rites.

Over the centuries, these small villages grew into larger regional units, with ceremonial sites that have yielded a great deal of information. In some cases, such as the **Taironas** of the northeastern highlands of Colombia, it is thought that up to 250,000 people lived on one site; by now, the main buildings were made of stone, and gold, emeralds, and other precious stones were used both for ornament and for trade.

The great edifices

In Peru and in the Andean highlands of Bolivia, there is evidence that settled occupation began as early as 5,000 BC. Caral, north of today's Lima, is believed to be the oldest city in the Americas, from 2,700 BC. One of the most significant of these early centers grew up around 1,200 BC in the **Moche Valley** near the northern Peruvian coastline. It is known as the **Chavín** culture, after the archeological site at **Chavín de Huántar**, about 3,000 meters

Their imposing capital at **Moche** is dominated by two large structures – the **Huaca del Sol** and the **Huaca de la Luna** – temples of the sun and moon, built around a large plaza or central square. In around AD 500 natural disasters probably forced them to move from Moche; their later center at **Pampa Grande** shows that the culture continued to thrive until the 8th century. Later, the **Chimu** culture, based at **Chan Chan**, showed a continuity of development in these coastal sites.

At the same period in the south of Peru, the **Nazca** culture came to the fore. The Nazca people are best known for the extraordinary lines

The pyramid at Caral, Peru.

(10,000 ft) up in the Andean mountains. The most impressive structure here is a platform of earth and rock with a hollow interior, known as **El Castillo** or The Castle, probably used for religious ceremonies.

The Chavín culture, which also produced fine pottery and intricate stone stelae, is believed to have gone into a decline around 500 BC. It was superseded in northern Peru by the **Moche** culture, which flourished in AD 100–600. The Moche are known for their prolific production of beautiful stirrup-spouted pottery, which depicted every aspect of their lives, from violence and erotica to medical treatments. They also produced fine gold, silver, and copperwork.

THE MYTH OF EL DORADO

One of the early Colombian cultures, Chibcha, gave rise to perhaps the most enduring South American legend, that of El Dorado. The Chibchas were divided into two kingdoms who worshiped the sun as their chief deity, and practiced human sacrifice. The ceremony for appointing a new Chibcha ruler apparently involved throwing gold statues into a lake, covering the new leader in gold dust and immersing him in the water until it had washed off. This made him El Dorado – the Golden One, giving rise to the legend of a golden city. Driven by a desire for gold, numerous versions arose, each putting the legendary city in a different potential location.

they drew in the desert, which from the air can be seen to represent hummingbirds, monkeys, or fish, but do not make sense from ground level. The size and complexity of the lines gave rise to the hypothesis that extraterrestrials must have visited South America in ancient times. As yet there is no convincing explanation as to why a farming community should have spent so much time making such an immense display.

Farther inland, near Lake Titicaca in northern Bolivia, the **Wankarani** people, who lived by fishing, herding llama, and growing potatoes, gave rise to the **Tiahuanaco** culture.

Viracocha. In 1438 his son Yupanqui defeated the Tiahuanaco people around Lake Titicaca, and Yupanqui's son Tupac Yupanqui defeated the Chimu to the north, so that in two generations the Incas succeeded in taking over the most important Andean centers. The Incas continued to extend their rule – south into Chile and north into what is now Ecuador, where Huayna Capac set up a second imperial center in Quito. By 1525, the Inca empire extended 4,000 km (2,500 miles) from southern Colombia to central Chile. Between 6 and 12 million people are estimated to have lived in

The Gateway of the Sun, Tiahuanaco, Bolivia.

Their main center, or *pukara*, was 3,600 meters (12,000 ft) up on the Altiplano of the Andes. Some 40,000 people are thought to have lived in this city, with an impressive ceremonial complex at its heart. The people of Tiahuanaco are among the first in South America to use stone to create large permanent buildings; about 1,200 years ago their power reached as far as the Atacama Desert in Chile.

The Incas

The last and most impressive of these Andean highland cultures was the **Inca** empire. This was based in the valley of Cusco, in what is now Peru, and only emerged around AD 1400, during the rule of the semi-mythical leader

the empire known as **Tawantinsuyu** or "Land of the Four Quarters."

At the top of the Inca hierarchy was the emperor, Cápac or Sapa Inca, thought to be a descendant of the sun god Inti. The emperor was married to his sister, but had many other wives as well. Beneath him was a complicated priestly and administrative system, designed to control the empire. Communications were based on a 30,000-km (18,640-mile) network of paved roads, many of which still exist, along which relays of runners carried messages.

The imperial language, Quechua, was imposed throughout: the sons of royalty among the conquered peoples were taken to Cusco to learn it along with other important elements of Inca culture. The Incas had no writing as we know it, but used knotted pieces of string to record important dates and numbers, which were memorized by a special group of officials. The Inca ceremonial centers at Machu Picchu, Cusco, and elsewhere show their mastery of architecture, based on cutting and fitting large blocks of stone together without mortar.

First peoples

Estimates as to how many people lived in South America before the Europeans arrived vary from 5 to 50 million; discoveries in the

The Inca empire is believed to have encompassed around a third of South America's population and was by far the largest indigenous state.

Tierra del Fuego, where they were hunted to extinction as late as the early 20th century.

The European attitude toward these peoples is illustrated in an extract from Charles Darwin's journal when he sailed down these coasts on HMS *Beagle* in 1832: "I could not have

Doorway of Inca temple at Machu Picchu.

Artifact from the Gold Museum, Bogotá.

Amazon region have led archeologists to think there may have been several million inhabitants there. Over the centuries these peoples have been absorbed into the dominant system, or persecuted and their way of life destroyed. This process began in the 1530s, when the Inca empire was conquered by Francisco Pizarro. Lacking resistance to European diseases, millions were wiped out, and the survivors pushed to the bottom rung of society.

The Mapuche people of Chile and Argentina resisted the longest, living independently until the end of the 19th century. Other indigenous groups in Argentina were wiped out in the so-called Wars of the Desert in the 1870s, or pushed to the remote coasts of Patagonia and

believed how wide was the difference between savage and civilized man: it is greater than that between a wild and domesticated animal…"

Such attitudes led to the extermination of indigenous groups in the 20th century. Although there are some groups in the Amazon who have had no contact with the outside world, their way of life is under threat, while the Yanomami in Brazil and the Ashaninka in Peru have had to organize to defend their rights. Elsewhere, descendants of the Inca and other highland groups, the Mapuche in Chile, and the Tairona and others in Colombia and Ecuador, live as part of the mixed heritage of Latin America. But they also stand apart, with many of their beliefs and traditions still powerful below the surface.

LOST EMPIRES AND DISCOVERED TREASURE

What was life like in South America before the Europeans arrived? It's a mystery that continues to enthrall, and there are some intriguing clues.

As no writing has been found from pre-Columbian South America, the artifacts left behind are likely to remain mere clues, giving us exciting glimpses into the lives of a host of very different communities that flourished and declined through various times and locations. The central Andes is by far the richest region for finding artifacts of the ancient past – partly because the dry desert conditions prevalent in the area are much more suitable for preserving ancient remains than the humid climate of the Amazon rainforest. But there is no doubt that the central Andes, especially the region that is now Peru, was a center for skilled activity of all kinds for centuries, producing numerous advanced communities long before the great Inca civilization arrived on the scene. Some ancient finds have echoes in the modern cultural practices of local communities, while others, such as the mysterious people who built the megaliths of San Agustín, Colombia, seem to have disappeared without a trace.

Trying to remember all the names of the pre-Columbian groups can be an implausible task. Most were named by archeologists after the locations where their remains were found, and grouped according to type, location, and dating. Their complexity can be confusing, but the visitor with enough time to go to the excellent museums and archeological sites from Colombia to Chile will gain a picture of a fascinating era when civilizations waxed and waned, fought and conquered one another, and exchanged goods, skills, and ideas.

Ingapirca ruins, Southern Sierra, Ecuador.

Archeological exhibits at the Museo Antropologico y de Arte Contemporaneo, Guayaquil, Ecuador.

Original pottery from the Moche culture that flourished on Peru's coast from 200 BC to 700 AD.

Carved and erected around 1900 BC, the ancient Sechín complex, north of Lima, is decorated with extraordinary wall carvings showing bellicose warriors and their hapless, dismembered victims.

LIFE AND TIMES OF THE MOCHE

If the Incas were master architects and empire builders, the much earlier Moche culture must be one of the most artistic and intriguing in South America. The Moche settled near the modern city of Trujillo in northern Peru, and flourished for a few centuries before and after the time of Christ. What sets the Moche apart is the high quality and quantity of the artifacts they left behind; from adobe pyramids to finely crafted gold jewelry. The 1987 discovery of the tomb of the Lord of Sipán was one of the most important finds ever in the area, displaying Moche mastery of metallurgy. The vast collection of Moche ceramics found provides a remarkably accurate and detailed record of life 2,000 years ago; some superb textiles have also been found.

Pre-Incan woven artifact at the Brüning Archeological Museum in Lambayeque, Peru.

Gold and turquoise earrings depicting the Lord of Sipán himself, at the Museum of the Royal Tombs of Sipán, Peru. The Lord was discovered in a remarkably preserved burial chamber in 1987, covered in layers of clothes sheathed in turquoise and lapis lazuli, and crowned in gold.

Pre-Colombian Manabi pottery, Banco Central Museum, Bahia de Caraquez, Ecuador.

THE EUROPEAN CONQUEST

In the 16th century, most of South America
quickly fell to Spain and Portugal,
except for Patagonia, which would remain
unconquered for three centuries.

At the end of the 15th century, Christopher
Columbus explored the shores of Central
and South America. Soon afterward
another Italian sailor, Amerigo Vespucci, was
to give the new continent its name. Both these
Italian explorers were in the pay of the Spanish
crown, and before long, numerous Spaniards
were arriving. From their bases on the islands
of Hispaniola, Puerto Rico, and Cuba, they
started to explore Central America and the
South American mainland.

Gold was the lure that enticed most of them
into the unknown territories. El Dorado was
the legendary paradise where everything was
made of gold. In 1532 Francisco Pizarro set out
to find these fabled riches in the Inca Empire,
which then stretched from north of Quito (in
present-day Ecuador) south through the areas
now known as Peru, Bolivia, and northern
Chile and Argentina. With only 150 followers,
Pizarro took control of the entire Inca Empire
in just two years. This was achieved with ruth-
less determination aided by the fear struck
into the indigenous armies by the Spaniards,
mounted on horseback and using firearms.
Also, after years of centralization and uniform-
ity, the Inca Empire was severely weakened at
the very moment Pizarro began his conquest.

Downfall of the Incas

Before the Spaniards arrived, the Incas had
expanded their empire from Cusco, Peru, to
Pasto, Colombia, in the north. The Inca Tupac
Yupanqui had founded the magnificent city
of Tomebamba (now Cuenca) after brutally
subduing the Cañari people. His son, Huayna
Capac, married the daughter of the local ruler
to consolidate their kingdoms.

*Francisco Pizarro, Spanish conqueror of the Incan Empire
and founder of Lima.*

Their son Atahualpa was to become Huayna
Capac's favorite, but Atahualpa's half-brother
Huascar, descended from Inca lineage on both
sides, was the legitimate heir. In 1527, Huascar
ascended the Cusco throne, dividing the empire
for the first time between Quito and Cusco.
Atahualpa won the ensuing five-year civil war,
killing his brother and establishing the new
capital of Cajamarca in northern Peru. But the
war had severely weakened both the infrastructure and the will of the Incas.

The Spanish arrived in Cajamarca in 1532.
At a prearranged meeting, Atahualpa and
several thousand followers – many unarmed
– entered the great square, where a Spanish

priest called on them to embrace Christianity and accept the sovereignty of the Spanish king, Charles V. When Atahualpa refused, the Spaniards ambushed the Incas, hundreds of whom were killed. Pizarro took Atahualpa prisoner, demanding a room full of gold to pay his ransom. This was done, but the Inca was not freed. After nine months, the Spaniards accused Atahualpa of treason, and garrotted him. The Spaniards then marched on the Inca capital, Cusco, and used Inca bureaucracy and administrative divisions for their own ends. The Incas put up a valiant fight but were outmatched by the conquerors' superior technology and mili-

ended completely in 1572, when Tupac Amaru was defeated and killed. Farther north, Gonzalo Jiménez de Quesada set out to explore New Granada (Colombia). He quickly subdued the Chibcha kingdoms, and in 1538 Santa Fé de Bogotá was founded.

The birth of Brazil

Europeans were soon busy exploring the Atlantic seaboard of South America and the Orinoco and Amazon river systems. This brought the Spanish and Portuguese crowns into conflict over who should own the new territories. The dispute was theoretically set-

The meeting of Pizarro and Atahualpa at Cajamarca.

tary zeal and by 1533, Pizarro was in command of the entire Inca Empire.

The Spaniards founded the city of Lima in 1535 as their colonial capital. The city grew and prospered, as did its religious zeal, prompting some to dub it the "Rome of South America." Churches and monasteries sprang up, each more ostentatious than the next. Nuns, bishops, priests, and monks flocked to Lima, and with them, eventually, came the Holy Inquisition, which meted out its frightful tortures in Peru from 1570 to 1761.

Lima was the seat of the Spanish Empire in South America for several centuries. Vilcabamba was the last redoubt of Inca rule, which

tled at the Treaty of Tordesillas in 1494, which established that Portugal should have the right to all lands east of the mouth of the Amazon – which meant the whole of the Brazilian coastline. Pedro Alvares Cabral claimed Brazil for Portugal in 1500. For many years, its most important export was its namesake dyewood or Brazil wood, but European settlement was slow, as the Portuguese preferred to trade with their new colony rather than to settle it. Eventually, a system of captaincies was set up, in which ownership of the land was granted by the Portuguese crown to individuals. Many of these people, such as Martim Afonso, brought in cattle and began to cultivate sugar, using enslaved native peoples initially, and then slaves shipped from Africa.

The new settlements of the south

In the far south, explorers were still seeking a sea route from Europe to Asia. Between 1519 and 1522, Ferdinand Magellan's fleet rounded Cape Horn and sailed into the Pacific Ocean, making them the first Europeans to land in Patagonia and Chile. Sailors like Antonio Pigafetta enhanced the mystery of the new lands to wide-eyed Europeans, with lurid descriptions of the strange beings encountered there: giants, men with heads under their arms, or tails like pigs.

Ancient gold model of a raft and figures depicting a scene from the myth of El Dorado, on display at the Gold Museum in Bogotá, Colombia.

THE HORRORS OF DISEASE

According to received wisdom, diseases carried by European conquerors wrought more devastation on the native peoples of South America than the weapons they brought. Indigenous populations, who had evolved without developing immunity to infectious diseases such as smallpox, cholera, and even malaria, fell by 95 percent in some regions. Further disease followed the arrival of African slaves. But recent research suggests that native diseases spreading from Mexico were at least as lethal as imported ailments. Better nutrition among Europeans, then as now, helped them survive the epidemics at higher rates than indigenous people.

Another wave of Spaniards set out to explore the Rio de la Plata network. Pedro de Mendoza founded Buenos Aires in 1536, and Asunción de Paraguay the following year. But the settlers were soon driven out of Buenos Aires by local tribes. It was not until 1580 that colonists sailed down from Asunción and successfully set up a fort on the south bank of the River Plate.

On the Pacific Ocean side, Pedro de Valdivia pushed south from Inca territory into Chile, and established the capital city of Santiago in 1541. The Incas had exacted tribute only as far south as the Bíobío River; Valdivia fared little better when he marched south of the river, meeting his match in the Araucanian (Mapuche) warriors, for whom death in battle constituted a supreme honor. In 1554, they captured Valdivia, bound him to a tree, and beheaded him. Legend has it that the executioner ate Valdivia's heart.

The south (now Patagonia) belonged to the Araucanian, and other indigenous peoples well into the 19th century. They organized a cavalry and learned to use firearms. The Spanish had to make do with maintaining garrison towns on the coast, and making marauding slave runs into indigenous territory.

A Spanish treasure trove

This first wave of conquest lasted for two generations. From then until the beginning of the 19th century, the Spanish and Portuguese crowns sought to administer their vast empires. Economic activity was based on mining – first for gold, then silver, which by the middle of the 16th century became the most valuable export.

Agriculture was developed, with Spaniards being awarded large tracts of land and "given" large numbers of indigenous people to work them, under the *encomienda* system, a feudal method of securing plantation labor in exchange for a subsistence living. Taxation in the form of animals and produce was exacted from the natives, and labor was unrewarded.

But the power in South America was firmly located in the growing towns and cities. It was here that Spanish authority was rooted. Most of South America became a viceroyalty based in Lima and its port at Callao. From here, Spain attempted to impose a commercial monopoly on all its colonies, whose inhabitants were only permitted to sell their products to Spain, and could only purchase products from the mother country. A Council of the Indies was set up in

Seville in southern Spain to administer the territories. The riches of South America were dispatched to Europe in annual fleets, which soon attracted the interest of pirates.

A new society

Through the 16th and 17th centuries, the Spaniards consolidated their rule. In each country there was a small number of Spanish-born administrators and clergy. Below them in rank were the *criollos*, people born in South America but claiming both parents as having Spanish blood. But the fastest-growing sector of the

Cravings for precious metals drove the conquest, with deposits in Potosí in Bolivia and Minas Gerais in Brazil rewarding the conquerors. The outflow of colonial gold and silver was so great that it caused inflation in Europe.

in from west Africa and Angola, rising to a million by the 18th century.

When the demand for sugar fell, the discovery of gold and diamonds in Minas Gerais led to a further boom, and Rio de Janeiro became

Woodcut of Potosí from 1555, the earliest known drawing of a New World mining enterprise.

colonial population were the mestizos, mixed-race people, most born of a Spanish father and an indigenous mother. One of the conquerors of Chile, Francisco de Aguirre, claimed 50 such children, and proudly affirmed that "the service rendered to God in engendering mestizos is greater than the sin incurred in so doing."

Many indigenous groups remained outside Spanish society, or were forced to work in slavelike conditions. As more labor was needed, the trade in slaves from Africa grew; they were brought mostly to the Caribbean coast of Venezuela and Colombia, and the coast of Peru, but it was in Brazil where African slaves made most impact on society. As the Brazilian sugar plantations grew in importance, so did the numbers of slaves shipped

increasingly important as a port. In 1763 it was made the capital, and had expanded further by the end of the century, with the growth of Brazil's new treasure crop, coffee. As Brazil's economic strength grew, so relations with Portugal became more difficult. Brazilian merchants wanted to be free to trade with other countries, and local politicians wanted more control over their own affairs. A similar situation arose in the Spanish colonies. Most of the treasures shipped back to Spain had been used to finance wars in Europe, but by the end of the 18th century, Spain had fallen behind France and Great Britain as an industrial and colonial power. By the 19th century, European wars were to lead to the loss of its South American empire.

INDEPENDENCE

The end of the Spanish and Portuguese empires in
South America came about after bitter struggles,
but brought neither peace nor prosperity.

General José de San Martín crossing the Andes with his army towards Peru during the Latin American Wars of Independence
(1810–1824).

When the Emperor Napoleon invaded
Spain in 1808, the consequences were
felt all over Spanish America, as locally
born *criollos* (creoles) took advantage of Spain's
weakness to free themselves from the demands
of the Spanish Empire. In previous decades,
republican ideas from the revolutions in the US
and in France had been taken up by many Latin
Americans, who wanted to trade with countries
other than Spain, and to pick their own leaders.

Rebellions in the south

Spain's gradual decline as a European power
after 1600 was recognized by rivals, the crown
itself, and the creoles in its colonies. The new
Bourbon dynasty after 1714 sought to reassert
economic control through a series of reforms
during the 18th century that, while increasing
revenue for the crown, bred resentment in the
Americas. Military losses in the Seven Years'
war led to a militarization of creole elites as
they were recruited to reinforce the teetering
empire. Revolts against colonial elites, rather
than against the king himself, occurred in several locations, including Paraguay, Venezuela,
Quito, and Peru. Alexander von Humboldt's
expedition revealed a continent with its own
economic strengths and intellectual life, but also
harsh political and social conflicts. The expulsion of British forces by local militias in 1807

gave Buenos Aires residents (known as *porteños*) confidence in their ability to govern themselves.

Napoleon's conquest of Spain triggered the uprisings that led to the independence of most of Spain's American empire by replacing King Ferdinand VII with his brother Joseph in 1808. As in the mother country, the creoles rejected the new king imposed by France and created self-governing juntas in several colonial administrative centers, including Mexico City, Montevideo, and Quito, professing allegiance to Ferdinand. Initially, none of these demanded outright independence, in part because the elites feared a repeat of the social upheaval that took hold in Haiti during that country's push for independence. By 1810, these juntas had spread to many parts of Spanish South America, from Venezuela to Chile. Friction soon surfaced, however: the more radical leaders demanded full independence, while most initially favored greater political autonomy and economic freedom. Many Spanish officials clung to their posts and sought to impose the will of the Bonapartiste crown, which they generally achieved by 1812. This, however, radicalized many creoles.

When Ferdinand returned to the throne in 1814, he sought a full restoration of the absolutism in force until 1808. He rejected a liberal constitution drawn up two years earlier in Cádiz that would have improved the rights of the colonies' citizens, and moved to reassert Spanish authority.

El Libertador

In the northern part of South America, the independence struggle was led by El Libertador (The Liberator) Simón Bolívar. The struggle began in his native Venezuela, where he successfully fought off Spanish loyalists to become dictator. He was successful at first, winning six battles against royalists in 1813, but with the defeat of Napoleon in 1815 and the restoration of the Spanish monarchy in Europe, Spain became resurgent and the fight to recover the colonies began in earnest, with the independence movements supported by Great Britain, which sought to replace Spain's economic hegemony and open its American ports to British products. Bolívar was forced to retreat to Haiti and Jamaica: letters he wrote from exile were to become the fundamental ideology behind the independence struggle. Three years

later, he was back on the mainland, leading a force of Venezuelans and European mercenaries, many of them veterans from the Napoleonic Wars. Amid fierce royalist resistance, he promised social progress to Venezuela's fierce mixed-race savannah warriors, known as the *llaneros*, along with other marginalized groups.

The Battle of Boyacá in northern Colombia on August 17, 1819, marked the end of royalist resistance there, and not long afterward Bolívar entered Santa Fé de Bogotá in triumph. In 1822, his General José Antonio de Sucre won the battle of Pichincha, a skirmish with far-reaching

General Simón Bolívar, El Libertador.

FALLING FROM FAVOR

Except for Paraguayan dictator José Rodríguez de Francia, the independence leaders swiftly fell out of favor with the elites of the newly independent countries. The coalitions that fought for independence disbanded amid the grab for spoils, and warring factions led Bolívar's dream of unity to collapse. He died on his way to exile, Sucre was murdered, San Martín, O'Higgins, and Artigas all forced into exile. Only decades later did they return to favor, and today's leaders extol their virtues to an extent that portrays them more like saints than warriors. Every country in South America now has statues, streets, cities, and even currencies named after them.

consequences as it ended Spanish rule in Ecuador and set the stage for the conquest of Upper Peru, Spain's last important stronghold.

José de San Martín and Manuel Belgrano led the war in the south. Most of the battles there focused on what is now Argentina's Andean northwest between Jujuy and Tucuman, where the La Plata provinces – Argentina – declared their independence in 1816. The situation shifted to a stalemate as troops from Argentina and from Spain were each unsuccessful in driving the other out of their respective territories. San Martín shifted his view east to an invasion

> Simón Bolívar was an inspiration to many foreign romantics. The English poet Byron named a boat after him and planned to sail it to Venezuela.

the contents of their discussion, San Martín left for Argentina, leaving the final push for Upper Peru to Bolívar and Sucre. Sucre defeated a Spanish army at Ayacucho in 1824 in the last major battle for independence and the provinces of "Upper Peru" were declared a new republic

The first flag of Argentina is presented to the revolutionary army by General Belgrano on 27 February, 1812.

of Chile and then of Lima, the viceregal capital, from the sea. In 1817 he led his army across the Andes – a tremendous feat of organization – to help the Chileans in their struggle. He was joined by exiled Chilean revolutionaries including Bernardo O'Higgins, who became Chile's first president after the battle of Maipú in 1818. Two years later, with loans from Great Britain, San Martín and the Chileans organized a flotilla that carried some 1,600 men – including about 600 (mostly British) foreigners – to attack Peru. After landing at Pisco in late 1820, he declared Peru's independence in Lima in 1821. San Martín in 1822 met Bolívar at Guayaquil, incorporated into the northern leader's ephemeral Great Colombia. While neither leader revealed

named in honor of the Liberator: Bolivia. With nothing in common, these disorganized territories, stretching from the Amazon to the icy sierra, were now forced to fuse and develop as a nation.

The years following independence were in many ways more difficult than the struggle itself. Bolívar dreamt that the newly emerging countries could stay united as La Gran Colombia, but within a decade, Ecuador, Venezuela, and Colombia had gone their separate ways after a war with Peru. Chile and Argentina were in disarray, the latter's woes allowing Paraguay to assert its independence. Uruguay survived as an independent state only after warring with Brazilian forces in 1825–8 and surrendering territory to the Portuguese colony.

In 1830, disillusioned and dying, Bolívar spent his last days at Santa Marta in Colombia. Argentina's San Martín, discovering the new generation of politicians had no place for a troublesome general, went into exile in France.

Rise of the dictators

For several decades after independence, there was virtual civil war in most of the emerging republics. The fight for control was usually between those from the interior who wanted some kind of loose federal political arrangement, and those from the cities who traded ruled from overseas, Brazil became a dominion in its own right. João returned to Portugal in 1821, leaving his son Dom Pedro in charge. Portugal then tried to reinstate Brazil's colonial status and recalled Pedro in 1822, leading him to rebel and declare Brazilian independence on September 7. He became Emperor Pedro I.

In the early 19th century, Brazilian society comprised about a million people of European ancestry, the local indigenous groups, and some 2 million black slaves. In 1831, Pedro returned home to take on the Portuguese throne, abdicating in favor of his son, Pedro II. Brazil was

Following the Brazilian War of Independence, Don Pedro I is acclaimed as the first constitutional emperor of Brazil, 12 October 1822.

more with the outside world and wanted strong central control of the new nation. Those groups were usually identified with conservatives and liberals, allegiances that survive to this day. Often the struggle for power was only settled by the emergence of a strong autocratic leader, which hindered the growth of democratic rule. By the mid-19th century, many South Americans found the tyranny of rule from Spain had been replaced by a more brutal local variety.

Brazil: independence without war

Portugal, Brazil's imperial power, was also invaded by Napoleon's troops. The Portuguese king Dom João VI fled and moved his entire court to Brazil in 1808. While Portugal resented being dominated by the large estate owners of the north, who used huge numbers of slaves to grow sugar and other crops, with little concern for efficiency or social progress. Pedro II encouraged European immigrants to settle in the south, in Rio Grande do Sul, where they made São Paulo a focus for development. There were increasing tensions between these two power groups, with slavery at the center of the debate. Pedro II fell out of favor with both liberals and conservatives as he was unable to reconcile his opposition to slavery and support for the separation of Church and State with demands for faster development. In 1889, he was deposed by the military and went into exile, ending South America's only monarchy.

Brazilian dancers during the closing ceremony of the 2012 London Olympic Games; Rio de Janeiro will host the 2016 Olympic Games.

INTO THE 21ST CENTURY

The republics of South America have trodden
a rocky road to stability, failing to prosper
despite – or because of – natural wealth.

Much of Latin America has just turned the page on bicentennial independence celebrations, but it took until 1827 for Portuguese and Spanish colonial rule to have come to an end. Years of war took their toll on local economies. Blacks and mestizos, lured into the fight with promises of freedom, soon saw these hopes dashed as, for the most part, the same wealthy families and military leaders refused to relinquish power. Except for Brazil, ruled by Dom Pedro, crown prince and later king of Portugal, most countries descended into virtual anarchy as disputes over the spoils arose among the victors. Many of the latino clichés emerged at this time as the caudillos, the quintessential strongman leaders, fought each other for the presidency. Ecuador and Venezuela broke away from Colombia but became embroiled in internal struggles. Argentina, still without Patagonian territories, was dominated by caudillo Juan Manuel de Rosas, but risked falling apart too as Buenos Aires temporarily and Paraguay permanently seceded. Debt to Britain and myriad border disputes rounded out their troubles, and only in the 1850s did a semblance of order return.

19th century unrest

Most wars – both civil and international – were brief affairs. Two major conflicts erupted in the second half of the 19th century however. In the southeast, Paraguay gambled and took on Brazil, Argentina, and Uruguay. The Triple Alliance War ended after five long years in a crushing defeat in 1870, with 90 percent of Paraguay's men dead. The aftermath was troubling for the victors too as Paraguay's long resistance discredited military officers of Argentina and Brazil. On the Pacific Coast, Chile in the 1879–1883

A crowd gathers in support of Evita and Juan Domingo Peron during Labour Day, Buenos Aires, 1940s.

BUYING BRITISH

Before the emergence of the United States as a great power, Britain did brisk trade with South America. The newly independent nations quickly racked up debt with London that they were still repaying in the 20th century. In the 1850s the British Consul in Argentina wrote about the gauchos: "Take his whole equipment, examine everything about him – and what is there not of hide that is not British? If his wife has a gown, ten to one it is from Manchester. The camp kettle in which he cooks his food, the common earthenware he eats from, his knife, spoon, bits and the poncho which covers him – are all imported from England."

Saltpeter War wrested control of rich mineral deposits from Peru and Bolivia, leaving the latter without a coastline and a traumatized Lima sacked. But before Chile could extricate itself from the war, it suffered from guerrilla attacks in occupied Peruvian territory.

Toward the end of the century, the US replaced Britain as the most influential power. It intervened far less in the region than in Mexico and Central America, but it imposed the separation of Panama from Colombia in 1903 as it coveted the isthmus for the canal. In the far south, by 1900, Chile and Argentina had conquered the

The newly completed Panama Canal heralds the entrance of the first boat, the tug 'Gatun', through the Gatun lock in 1913.

whole of Patagonia, finally subduing and largely destroying the indigenous cultures in the process. In Argentina, General Julio Roca's "Conquest of the Wilderness" in the 1870s opened up the pampas and Patagonia. Any native standing in his path was killed, the rest herded into reservations. The land was used to raise cattle for European markets, taking advantage of new methods of freezing meat. Chile in the 1880s subdued the Mapuche, which the Spanish had never managed to conquer. But unrest continues to this day as the Mapuche attempt to defend their rights.

The haves and have-nots

In much of the region, agricultural and mineral products became a new boon to the old elites. Coffee in Colombia, cocoa in Ecuador and Venezuela, *guano* – fertilizer – and rubber in Peru, tin in Bolivia, and saltpeter in Chile, all filled the pockets of wealthy families, but also helped link South America to the global markets. Banks emerged, amid gradual modernization, including new railroads. Slavery had by then ended in the region, last in Brazil, but indigenous peoples and many mixed-race workers continued to suffer widespread abuse.

Argentina and Uruguay meanwhile saw the greatest influx of immigrants in relation to the resident population in world history. Immigrants however usually arrived penniless, and did not get to share in the country's wealth, as the great landowning families refused to break up their massive holdings. The immigrants received small plots, but only to work for three to five years before moving on. Unlike North America, which was settled by millions of small landowners, Argentina remained the property of around 200 close-knit families referred to simply as "the oligarchy." Nevertheless, it blistered ahead and became synonymous with wealth. In 1905, it was one of the world's richest countries. Uruguay became one of the first countries to create a national welfare system. Other countries failed to match their pace, but struggles for increased political rights became common to all as liberals wrestled with conservatives over the right strategy to emulate the wealthy nations of the north. US companies played a huge role in many countries, from railroads to banana production and banking, often breeding resentment that continues to the present.

Countries made some progress, like the separation of church and state and the introduction of women's right to divorce and vote in Ecuador in the early 20th century. In Argentina, Chile, and Peru, unions demanding workers' rights including an eight-hour workday emerged at the same time. But most rights expanded only slowly, and violent struggles – along with the *caudillos*' perennial disputes over power – marked the last century. A military coup ended Brazil's monarchy in 1889 and South America's giant began to politically resemble its crisis-prone neighbors more closely.

The Great Depression marked a watershed as prices for South American exports and their markets collapsed. Saltpeter and rubber had already been replaced by synthetic products that hit the economies of Brazil, Chile, and Peru. Great upheaval began in 1930, breaking down the oligarchic order and, with halts and starts, leading to a deep modernization mostly unrecognized by the clichés. Middle classes expanded and received a share of political power. Non-whites began to ascend in the military. Populist leaders, sometimes influenced by European fascists, appealed to the disenfranchised masses. They could be military leaders like Brazil's Getulio Vargas or Argentina's Juan Domingo Perón. They could also be civilians like Raúl Haya de la Torre in Peru and José María Velasco Ibarra in Ecuador, both of whom suffered military opposition.

In return for favors bestowed on the archbishop, Venezuela's dictator Juan Vicente Gómez was given special dispensation to eat meat on Good Friday.

Vargas' fall, a long period of constitutional rule followed. Brazil's economy and population grew rapidly, a growth symbolized by the construction of Brasília as the country's new capital in the late 1950s. Still, South Americans failed to reach consensus on economic and

The bombing of La Moneda, Santiago, Chile, during the 1973 coup.

Trade unions were permitted, albeit sometimes under strict rules.

Industrialization progressed haltingly however, and often failed under state control and protectionist policies that protected inefficient companies. Argentina, reeling from the Great Depression, never recovered and rejoined the region as a developing country. While better health contributed to a population explosion, unemployment remained rife. But the 1950s brought some stability. The Bolivian revolution of 1952 brought real empowerment for the indigenous majority. In Brazil, during his 15 years in power, Vargas built up a strong state and promoted Brazilian industry, in ways reminiscent of Benito Mussolini in Italy. After

social progress. Nowhere was the violence greater than in Colombia.

The Cuban Revolution of 1959 inspired a radicalization of social demands that often led to a violent backlash, particularly in the formerly stable countries of the Southern Cone and Brazil that saw tens of thousands die in the "dirty wars" unleashed by anti-communist military rulers. Only Colombia and Venezuela went through the last third of the 20th century without military dictatorships, and civilian rule didn't allow Colombia to escape continued strife.

Emerging democracies

Military rule has had a mixed track record. Even until the present, some foreign and domestic analysts continue to laud them as having safe-guarded the region from communism during the Cold War, even over their mostly appalling human rights records. But their economic policies, often run by civilian officials, even in Chile, weren't particularly successful. General Augusto Pinochet held on to power there until 1989 even amid a wrenching economic crisis that saw most military rulers forced to step down elsewhere. Sadly, the fledgling democracies, too, for the most part were saddled with the economic troubles – particularly, debt the dictators had amassed – that coined the term

Confiscation of 11 tons of cocaine in Colombia.

"lost decade" for Latin America in the 1980s. Stricken by guerrilla insurgencies, Colombia teetered near the brink of becoming a "failed state." Peru recovered from its 1980s civil strife but suffered the iron-fisted rule of Alberto Fujimori. Bolivia, Ecuador and Venezuela once again became unstable as their export prices plummeted, helping set the stage for the present crop of populist leaders. Argentina grappled with hyperinflation, a 1990s boom, followed by yet another bust in 2000 that has since seen a major recovery but many unsolved social, political, and economic problems. Crime has emerged as a huge problem throughout the region, particularly in the shantytowns and poor neighborhoods of the vast urban areas.

Still, almost everywhere, civil empowerment has made vast progress since the 1970s, and even the semi-authoritarian populist regimes must at least pay lip service to human rights. Since the turn of the century, fast economic growth has helped millions escape poverty. Even if politics still lags behind, companies have created international networks of white-collar jobs, while South Americans have begun to discover each other through travel and the entertainment industry. Internet is available almost everywhere through grids and mobile phones.

Economic boom

New generations of well-trained professionals from all parts of society, including Afro-South Americans and indigenous peoples, have brought the region much closer to a point where it could finally escape the political and economic pitfalls that have for so long held it back. Although once again high commodities prices spurred the most recent economic boom, some countries have developed significant industries, particularly Brazil and Colombia. Even Bolivia has joined the rank of middle-income nations. The world is noticing, too, as soccer's FIFA World Cup 2014 returns to the region for the first time since 1978 and Rio de Janeiro prepares to host the Olympic Games in 2016, the first time they will go ahead in South America. Through new regional organizations like UNASUR and the Pacific Alliance including most countries from Chile to Mexico, the region is stepping out of the shadow of the "backyard of the US." For all the remaining caveats and inequality, the subcontinent's prospects look brighter than they have in a century.

A DIRTY TRADE

Chewing coca leaves does not have the same effect as taking the powdered drug, with massive amounts needed to make cocaine. Since the late 1960s, the spectacular growth of the export of refined drugs to the US and Europe has made drugs and drug trafficking a huge problem for the region. Irrespective of the US-led "war on drugs", tons of coca leaves are made into the paste for cocaine in remote hideouts in the Andean foothills. Throughout South America, the trade is a huge if largely invisible presence. Laundered drug money has financed new banks, hotels, and buildings from beach resorts in Chile to high-rises in downtown Bogota.

Rise of Populist Leaders

After Hugo Chávez' inauguration as president of Venezuela, almost all of South America's elected leaders are promising to eradicate poverty.

Privatizations in the 1980s and 1990s left a bitter aftertaste in much of South America as half-hearted neoliberalism failed to make a real difference to the underemployed majority. Racked by foreign debt and a decline in the price of the region's raw materials and agricultural products, government services evaporated and debt rose as foreign lenders – above all, the International Monetary Fund – demanded austerity packages to keep the credit lifeline going. Corrupt and incompetent governments from Venezuela to Argentina failed to present viable – and speedy – answers to the despair that affected middle-class voters who lost their life savings as banks and currencies collapsed. Corrupt leaders were voted out or thrown out in Brazil, Argentina, Ecuador, Peru, and Venezuela.

In 1992, Hugo Chávez, a lieutenant colonel from a poor rural background, attempted to overthrow President Carlos Andrés Pérez. The coup failed, but Chávez became a folk hero in Venezuela. Pérez was soon forced to resign amid accusations of corruption, while Chávez prepared his legal entry into politics. He won the presidency in late 1998 running on a left-wing platform, and took office in early 1999. A year later, a very different socialist, Ricardo Lagos, was sworn in, in Chile. Álvaro Uribe, a staunch conservative, became president of Colombia in 2002, and political forces in the rest of the subcontinent over the next decade became marked by the triangle formed by these three leaders. All three became highly popular, with Chávez and Lagos confronting the wealthy "haves," while Uribe fought down the Marxist FARC rebels. Both Chávez and Uribe reformed constitutions to allow them to stand for re-election and, while pursuing different economic agendas, concentrated political power.

Constitutional reform

Similarly anti-establishment leaders soon followed. In Brazil, labor leader Luiz Inácio "Lula" da Silva was elected in 2002, and in Argentina, Néstor Kirchner, a left-leaning Peronist took office in 2003. In 2006, Michelle Bachelet, an unconventional socialist, succeeded Lagos in Chile, the same year that in Bolivia, Evo Morales, an Aymara union leader of the coca planters, became that country's first indigenous president. Tabaré Vázquez in Uruguay, Rafael Correa in Ecuador, and Fernando Lugo in Paraguay rounded out the lurch to the left.

Chávez meanwhile had embarked upon massive reform, changing the constitution, ramping up social spending, controlling the exchange rate, and nationalizing companies. He survived a coup attempt and general strike in 2002 and aligned himself with Cuba and Asian adversaries of the US, the biggest buyer of Venezuelan oil. Even in rela-

Hugo Chávez with Luis Inácio Lula da Silva.

tively moderate Chile, Chávez' anti-imperialist stance found support on the left. In Ecuador and Bolivia, Correa and Morales copied the Chávez model of constitutional reform and both easily won re-election to new terms. But while higher social spending has benefitted the poor, corruption and attacks on freedom of expression have marred these leaders' track records. Chile, Brazil and Peru are more democratic, while personal differences between leaders remain great. Amid the boom in commodity prices, most governments spent liberally, and when the global economic crisis hit in 2008, the state-centric economic policies shook off some of the criticism they had suffered earlier. If the global economy continues to wilt, the populists might find their days are numbered.

Bahian woman in traditional dress,
Salvador, Brazil.

Gauchos in Patagonia, Argentina.

Peruvian mother and son with vicuña.

A LAND OF MANY FACES

The people of South America are as diverse as the countries many of them came from, yet they also share a distinctive Latin American heritage.

Ever since Colombus landed in what is now the Bahamas and thought he had arrived in the East Indies, the indigenous peoples of the Americas have been lumped together and collectively termed "Indians." The number of terms used to describe ethnicity in South America today may daunt the visitor – it's an indication not just of the continent's racial diversity, but also of the importance of ancestry here.

In Brazil, mestizo or *mameluco* describes someone who is part indigenous, part European. Mulatto means someone whose origins are African and European, while *cafuso* describes someone of indigenous and African heritage.

All this complex ethnic terminology probably grew out of people's attempts to define their identities in a continent that has seen so much immigration in the past 500 years, and where national boundaries were only defined in the 19th and 20th centuries and may yet be in dispute. This is a continent where people from the world's most diverse nations and cultures meet, mix, and intermarry. Nationalities include the Welsh in Patagonia, Croats in southern Chile, Koreans in Paraguay, and Japanese in Peru and Brazil. Yet the surface multiculturalism of South America hides a complex mesh of social and racial hierarchies.

In addition, national characteristics and patriotic pride are very strong, although outsiders tend to group South Americans together as "Latins." Inhabitants of neighboring countries such as Venezuela and Colombia can be very different from each other, while Brazil offers a special world of its own. One of the pleasures of traveling through the continent is to discover the variety and individuality each country

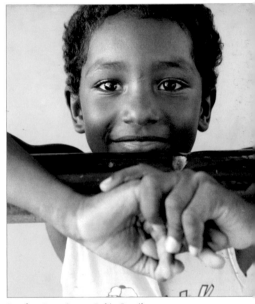

Boy from Porto Seguro, Bahia, Brazil.

offers, expressed in food, dress, and music, and the versions of the languages that are spoken.

The new arrivals

South America's ethnic make-up changed dramatically after the arrival in the 16th century of Europeans, who were predominately Spanish and, in Brazil, Portuguese. They initially arrived as single men, intermarried with indigenous women, and brought in slaves from Africa. By 1888, when slavery was finally abolished in Brazil, immigration from Europe was being actively encouraged, particularly to Brazil and Argentina. Most of the immigrants initially came from Spain and Italy, but there were also

Germans, eastern Europeans, Syrians, Lebanese, Japanese, and Chinese.

The people of the Andes – from eastern Venezuela south to Argentina and Chile – are predominately mestizo. These areas also have the highest pure indigenous populations, partly because there were a lot of native people there at the time of the Conquest, and partly because of the large-scale destruction of the indigenous societies outside the mountain chain.

People of African descent are concentrated in northern Brazil and the coastal regions of Colombia, Venezuela, Ecuador, Peru, and the

Two boys from the Ecuadorian Andes.

Guyanas, places where their ancestors were taken as slaves. Argentina, Uruguay, and southern Brazil are predominately Caucasian, and Chile is roughly 20 percent European.

Guyana, Suriname, and French Guiana, on the north Caribbean coast, have a particularly interesting ethnic make-up, due to their histories as crop-producing outposts of three world empires – Dutch (Suriname), British (Guyana) and French (French Guiana). African slaves were brought in to work the sugar, coffee, and cotton plantations, and many then fled into the rainforest to form their own "Cimarron" or "Maroon" communities, retaining many of their African traditions.

After the abolition of slavery, indentured labor was imported from other parts of the empires, leaving all these countries with highly mixed populations composed of Asians, natives, Africans, Portuguese *mulattos*, and Europeans.

New communities

The Cimarrons are not the only group to have taken advantage of South America's formidable territory in order to pursue their chosen lifestyle. This continent has a number of discrete independent communities that often transcend national boundaries, such as the gauchos and the Protestant Mennonite groups. Don't be surprised if you come across lederhosen on the Caribbean coast, or Welsh hats in Patagonia – these are the legacies of groups of immigrants who may have felt their way of life restricted in their country of origin, or who just wanted to build a new life in a new country.

The continent's racial diversity is reflected in its languages. Although Spanish is by far the dominant language, and Portuguese the official language of Brazil, many other languages are spoken. Native languages are frequently spoken in the Andean regions, and in Bolivia, Spanish, Quechua (or Quichua), and Aymara are all official languages. In Peru, Spanish and, since 1975, Quechua, are both official. In Paraguay, Spanish is the official language, but most people also speak Guaraní. The Guyanas also follow a colonial pattern, with English the main language of Guyana, Dutch mainly used in Suriname, and French the language of French Guiana.

The racial hierarchy

In many areas the melting pot has been blended so completely that local people are

---

BRAZILIAN HOLOCAUST

In 1639 the Spanish Jesuit Cristóbal de Acuña wrote: "Amazon Indian settlements are so close together that one is scarcely lost sight of before another comes into view." But this was not to last – 17th-century officials in Brazil boasted that they killed 2 million natives in the lower Amazon. *Bandeirantes* hunted indigenous people to use as slaves in vast territories, and even crossed into Spanish-held areas. Brazil's indigenous population was estimated at 2.5–6 million at the time of the Conquest. Numbers fell by a third in the 20th century, but grew again in recent years, and people of indigenous origin now are estimated at about 520,000.

unexpectedly homogeneous. In the cities of northern Chile, Bolivia, and Peru, for example, pale European tourists are distinctive enough to turn heads, as are people with darker skin coloring, who will frequently hear themselves described as *moreno* or *negrita*.

In many South American countries, skin color and racial origins have a distinct bearing on status. The palest people are frequently concentrated in the professional establishments or in front of television cameras. One can often detect a striking color difference between the faces that appear on the television screen and

America are overwhelmingly Catholic (except for Guyana, formerly a British colony). Yet many communities have incorporated their religious traditions into Catholicism, producing hybrid religions in some areas, like *Macumba* in Brazil.

In the years following the Conquest many indigenous societies were forced to adapt or be obliterated. The Andes and the low-lying Amazon regions were devastated by European disease and violence. Native heritage long remained a stigma, to the extent that most people prefer to describe themselves as white rather than mestizo, particularly in urban areas

In Lumaco, Chile, community chiefs and representatives of the Mapuche communities from Araucania hold a meeting.

Women in local traditional dress and wearing Cabana hats, which are painstakingly embroidered.

those watching it, with the few dark or black on-screen faces relegated to servile roles. But this is changing, and even being spoofed in more recent television dramas and comedies.

Off the screen, indigenous people – particularly in the Andes region – are usually seen laboring in the fields or behind market stalls. Many have steadfastly continued to practice their ancient customs and traditions, often in the face of strenuous opposition. The distinctive dress of Bolivian *campesina* women is believed to have developed as a response to the conquistadors' prohibition of traditional dress. The death penalty was imposed in many cases for natives who resisted conversion to Christianity, so it's not surprising that the countries of South

– although the opposite also happens. However, in recent years, Peru and Bolivia have elected presidents of indigenous origin, and there is a new pride in being able to relate to traditional societies. Despite this, it is still the more "European" groups who wield the power and dominate the economy almost everywhere.

Lifestyles under threat

People who live in South America's urban regions may feel economically and socially under pressure to deny their indigenous ancestry, but for many tribal peoples of the Amazon, their heritage and distinctive traditions are among the few resources left in the struggle for the survival of their communities. Many of these lifestyles are constantly evolving and adapting in response to their changing environment, which is particularly vulnerable to the encroachments of the technological age.

In some areas, tribal groups are benefiting from increased tourist interest, which brings in some income while encouraging the continuity and development of their way of life. Some such schemes are criticized as creating tribal theme parks, but there is reason to believe the alternative for the tribes concerned could be oblivion.

Many indigenous groups, like the Mapuche of Chile, have found it necessary to take political

Yanomami woman with facial wood stick piercing.

THE YANOMAMI

The Yanomami of northern Brazil and Venezuela were undiscovered by the rest of the world until the 1960s, when "civilization" began to encroach on their Roraima rainforest home. Like other Amazon basin peoples, they practiced limited, slash-and-burn agriculture along with hunting and gathering. A gold rush in the 1970s attracted tens of thousands in a mostly futile attempt to escape poverty. In 1993, 20 Yanomami were massacred. The Yanomami have managed to publicize their plight, but attempts to do something about it have been unsuccessful, notably since the rainforest fires in 1998, that destroyed an area the size of Belgium.

action to ensure their survival. Increasingly, since the commemoration of the fifth centenary of European arrival in 1992, indigenous groups have organized themselves politically to have their voice heard. This has led to upheavals in Ecuador and Bolivia, where these groups are large, but almost everywhere the pressure has produced a new awareness of this distinct element within South American society.

Growing pains

The middle classes are becoming more influential, and education is expanding opportunities for many ethnic groups. But South America continues to be the most unequal part of the world. Modernization begs the question of what kind of society and political model these countries should aspire to. More often than not, aspirations have transformed into aggressive consumerism. Consumer debt is on the rise even as wages remain low amid poor productivity. Even candy sellers in the street are counted as semi-employed. Social cohesion and respect for the environment remain rare as many of the wealthy lock themselves into gated communities and new immigrants from the countryside fight for turf in the poor quarters. Nasty driving habits and omnipresent littering are only two examples of civic problems. Others are widespread corruption and, as prohibition of some drugs continues, the spread of violent crime, to which these societies have yet to find a solution.

Women's changing role

In recent years, South American women have been playing an ever more prominent role in political and professional life. In 2006, Chile elected its first woman president, Michelle Bachelet, while most other countries have women ministers. As doctors, lawyers, and in civil society pressure groups, women are to the fore. Young women are often the best and most enthusiastic students in many academic disciplines.

Yet in this mainly Catholic continent, there is still a general assumption that a woman should above all be a good wife and mother. The word machismo was, after all, coined to describe the Latin male; and there are frequently activities and attitudes that reject women. Often they are expected to combine motherhood with a full day's work, although they are rarely paid as much as their menfolk.

There may be 350 indigenous language groups in South America – maybe just a third of the number that were spoken when Europeans arrived. Catholic priests expanded the use of Quechua as lingua franca.

Young people

At all levels of society, it seems, children are the focus of South American life. Families are large, contraception is often frowned upon, and women tend to start producing children at an

forced to carry the burden of their parents' poverty and low social position. People both within and outside South America have worked hard to publicize and alleviate the situation, but for many children of poor families in South America, life can be a very hard slog indeed.

Music and dance is an outlet for all levels of society in exuberant South America. Youth is celebrated and indulged, and recaptured throughout life at fiestas and in the dance clubs, where anyone can dress up in tight Lycra and get away with it. Youth brings romance, often rapidly followed by procreation and more chil-

A young Brazilian girl brushes her teeth in a Rio de Janeiro favela.

earlier age than in Europe and North America.

Some visitors might be alarmed at the incessant noise of children's exuberant shouts, which will often continue late into the evening – these playful noises are indulged and encouraged, with the adults often joining in. The best thing to do is to shrug your shoulders, join in, and put off any quiet-time activities you may have planned until the next day's siesta. Or invest in a good pair of earplugs.

The importance of children in South America makes the plight of the street children, orphaned and abandoned to scavenger lifestyles on the streets of big cities like Rio de Janeiro, seem all the more shocking. This is another case of social status coming into play, with children

dren. But there is nothing perfunctory about this eternal cycle. Try to count the number of times you hear the words "*mi corazón*" (my heart) in popular songs. South American men may have a reputation for machismo, but it may be partly a front to disguise the very obvious passion for romance that pervades this emotionally charged part of the world.

Fun, pleasure, and romance are of the highest priority, and can transcend the boundaries of religion, race, politics, and social status. Everyone, whatever their background, is expected to indulge in the lighter side of life occasionally. In music, dance, and a determination to enjoy life whatever the burden, the diverse people of South America are linked with a common bond.

THE IRRESISTIBLE LURE OF THE UNKNOWN

From gold-crazy conquistadors to modern eco-adventurers, South America has attracted a long line of explorers in pursuit of elusive dreams.

The earliest Spanish and Portuguese explorers were primarily concerned with charting the length and breadth of the newly discovered continent. In 1520, the great ocean navigator Ferdinand Magellan rounded the globe, giving his name to the stormy straits he passed at the southern tip of present-day Chile. In the same era, conquistadors Gonzalo Pizarro and Francisco de Orellana led arduous expeditions into the Amazon jungle in search of the mythical city of gold, El Dorado. They never found much gold but, in 1541, Orellana's expedition sailed down the Amazon to the sea, becoming the first Europeans to cross South America.

In the 18th century, the Age of Enlightenment in Europe sparked off a new, scientific interest in the little-known South American wildlife.

One of the foremost explorers was Alexander von Humboldt, a Berlin-born student of botany, chemistry, astronomy, and mineralogy. With his companion, French botanist Aimé Bonpland, Humboldt in 1799 set off on an expedition from Venezuela to Ecuador, Peru, and Cuba, charting the link between the Orinoco and Amazon rivers. He assembled meticulous lists of plants and animals, which led to the publication of *Essays on the Geography of Plants*, pioneering studies into the relationship between a region's geography and its flora and fauna.

Humboldt and Bonpland were reduced to a diet of ground cacao beans and Amazon River water when damp and insects destroyed their supplies.

While on the Galápagos Islands, Charles Darwin observed marine iguanas. These unique reptiles have a breathing system that has adapted to life in the ocean.

Despite the harsh realities met on arrival, expeditions were often well-funded and publicized, to considerable popular enthusiasm.

Early explorers endured long, mosquito-ridden journeys, with little food, and fear of attack by fierce beasts, and violent natives.

THE ORIGINAL INDIANA JONES

In 1906, a British army officer, Colonel Percy H. Fawcett, went to South America, contracted by the Bolivian and Brazilian governments to help demarcate their jungle borders.

Fawcett had his own plan, however, which was to locate the fabled continent of Atlantis. He arrived armed with an 18th-century Portuguese document, and a stone idol thought to be of Brazilian origin and identified by psychics as having come from Atlantis.

On Fawcett's second expedition in 1925, he was accompanied by his son Jack and a man called Raleigh Rimell. The three men all vanished without trace in the Matto Grosso area of the Amazon – the predators swallowed up by their prey. (The dog that had accompanied them returned unharmed.)

But the story did not end there. Tales of Fawcett's quest attracted more explorers over the years, several of whom sent back reports of white men living with jungle tribesmen; none, however, succeeded in finding him. Fawcett's mystery and fame still live on today, and he is credited with being the inspiration behind the Hollywood hero, Indiana Jones.

Tango dancers in the San Telmo neighborhood of Buenos Aires, Argentina.

MUSIC AND DANCE

South America pulsates to the beat of many rhythms as, through music and dance, people express their joys, their struggles, and often their longing for home.

Abus journey in South America can be a whole new experience: a bumpy ride from somewhere you can't remember to somewhere you can't pronounce. Your driver will probably make numerous unscheduled stops to pick up passengers, call over a friend or jump out on an errand, and may also want to demonstrate his DJ skills to his captive audience. As your bus pitches and thunders down perilous mountain trails or bleak, dusty stretches, local musical delights blare at deafening volume from crackling speakers. For the driver, savoring the delights of his playlist, staying on the road is not always top priority.

Music is considered a staple in the South American diet, being as important as food itself, feeding and replenishing the soul. Popular Latin music is laden not just with passion, sentiment, happiness, and anguish, but with history and nostalgia. Just as early musical expression symbolized resistance for slaves and fueled struggles for independence in the 17th and 18th centuries, music and dance are revered by the underdogs of modern South American society. They are a tonic to counteract the harsh realities of everyday life.

Dancing serves as a pressure valve, a reprieve from life's chaos, or a celebration because tomorrow is Friday and you feel lucky.

Dancing for everyone

To understand the evolution of musical and dance forms on the subcontinent is to attempt to fathom the tremendous demographic upheaval that took place over 500 years. The richness and diversity of Latin music is a reflection of the many colonizing and colonized forces present over the centuries. Along

Glitz and glitter is an intrinsic part of the Carnival show.

with native South American elements, Africa, Europe, and the United States all had a hand in the shaping of this magical music.

Music grew from a brutal and loveless relationship, out of enslaved indigenous people and Africans, European settlers, and colonial power brokers. Often oceans away from their homelands, these early inhabitants all had their music and dances. These were a way of remembering home and who you were in an uncertain landscape. Thrown together in an ethnic melting pot, many traditions were either discarded or bonded together.

Out of this struggle was born regional and national musical traditions that, in a sense, represent different colonial experiences and development. So there are historical reasons for the tango belonging to Argentina, the samba to Brazil and the *cumbia* to Colombia.

A spicy mix

Arguably the most international of all Latin American rhythms is what we now call **salsa**. The term itself is really nothing more than a marketing ploy adopted by the US music industry in the late 1960s, which assumed that people could not cope with the many different types of music Latin America had to offer. *Son*, mambo, guitar, and claves or sticks tapping out the beat. The beat is syncopated and loaded with poly-rhythms of regular pulses provided by the clave (two sticks that beat at a 2–3 or 3–2 tempo), the *campana* (cowbell), and accents that are offbeat (piano, bass, and brass). This is all useful to know if you want to blame your partner for messing up when he or she is clearly the better dancer.

If salsa means sauce, then the musical ingredients in these complex arrangements need a master chef to work with them. As music is food for the soul to Latin Americans, culinary references in the lyrics are compulsory.

Folklore dancers, Mitad del Mundo, Ecuador.

Dancers compete during the Fiesta de la Marinera in Trujillo, Peru.

guaracha, and many other styles were lumped together so that they could be easily packaged for consumption. Salsa means "sauce" and the name was inspired by many musicians who would scream "Salsa!" at a pulsating audience to excite them even further. This artificial grouping of many different styles means that most discussions about the origin of salsa become as hot and spicy as the dancing the music inspires. Most unbiased opinion, however, takes the view that today's salsa is really a jazzed-up version of *son*, whose origins date back to eastern Cuba in the 1880s.

Son intermingled African rhythms with Spanish verse forms, and its early means of expression were drums, maracas, Cuban *tres*

Modern *son* and salsa, predominant in Colombia, Venezuela, and throughout Central America, have been enhanced by the addition of piano, bass, and heavy brass sections. A disproportionate number of famous names continue to be from the Antilles, but Colombia and Venezuela in particular have produced some important salsa acts, including the Colombians Los Niches, Joe Arroyo, and Son de Cali. Oscar d'Leon, Javier Plaza, and La Dimensión Latina are among the main Venezuelan exponents of salsa.

The accompanying dance may look easy but it is as intricate and erratic as the music, fluctuating between regular and counter movements. Salsa is electrifying, sensual, and dynamic, yet it can be cheeky and passionate at the same time. Don't be discouraged by the stylish, fast footwork, for much of the rhythm is contained within set steps. You will get as much of a kick out of observing the rhythmic exchange between the couples spinning and strutting their stuff or caught in a swaying embrace as from actually taking part.

A crisp, frothy beat

Merengue came to South America via the Dominican Republic in the Caribbean. It comes, as you might expect, from the French

other, as in salsa, and when dancing close together, the woman places her right foot in between the man's feet. The couples resemble palm trees swaying in the breeze as they move to the beat.

Recent adaptations have seen *merengue* embracing North American crazes such as rap, hip-hop, and techno music. This has proven highly popular among the youth in Dominican and Caribbean *barrios* (neighborhoods) in the United States, who see hip-hop *merengue* as a Latin expression of the "brotherhood" practiced by their African-American counterparts. The

Quechua men playing guitar in Maimara, Argentina.

meringue, meaning "whipped egg whites and sugar." Both the dessert and the dance are a frothy, exciting mix. From its origins in the formalized 18th-century dances of the French court, *merengue* acquired African influences as it settled in the Dominican Republic. It also provided the beat for many protest marches against foreign intervention during the 20th century, as well as being a vehicle for addressing social problems.

The dance that complements *merengue* is easily picked up compared to salsa. The basic version consists of bending one knee then the other forward and then back in clockwork alternate movements while not lifting your heels off the ground. Couples mirror each

adaptability of the rhythm and the facility of the dance has given it the upper hand over salsa in many Latin communities in the US, and in Andean South America.

Music from Spain

The bolero is a melodic, guitar-laden form of music born in Spain in the 18th century and adapted in numerous Caribbean and South American countries. You will find men of all ages ably strumming guitars and singing these historic songs in squares and traditional restaurants throughout Spanish-speaking South America, appealing to the patrons' sense of nostalgia. Boleros preceded pop songs as immensely popular themes.

The samba danced at Carnival differs from one city to the next. Its proper name is samba enredo. First introduced in the 1930s, this is the form that most associate with the phenomenal footwork and bottom-shaking of this dance.

Leading singers included Julio Jaramillo of Ecuador, Colombia's Alci Acosta, and Chile's Huasos Quincheros, a group still playing but originally founded in 1937. More recent pop singers also regularly include boleros in their romantic repertoire.

A dance for lovelorn men

The **tango** is closely associated with Argentina. To many people, this is the most sensual and erotic of all South American dances, and its origins lie in the Buenos Aires slums of more than a century ago. There, lovelorn male migrants, bereft of female company, would re-enact the intimacy of man and woman. Hence, the tango was initially a dance of men. One male would play the part of the female coquette while the other represented the rough wooer.

The upper classes looked with initial disdain on the immodest hip movements and swift footwork of a dance whose all too obvious sexual connotations could only arouse dismay and moral approbation. In fact, it wasn't until tango caused a sensation in the dancehalls of pre-World War I France that it gained acceptance both internationally and in Argentinian high society.

Today, tango is enjoying an extraordinary resurgence. Following on from the dance form's global appeal, a whole new generation of young Argentinians is ensuring the survival of tango in the steaming cafés and clubs of Argentina.

Samba-mania

If the tango is Argentinian, the samba belongs to Brazil. **Samba** comes from an African word, *sembu*, a type of belly dance. It originated in Africa as a reel dance and is first recorded in the 1875 festivals in Bahia in northeast Brazil. Samba today takes many forms. Ballroom, Carnival, and *pagode* (a slower São Paulo version) are just a few. It is universally popular and has influenced the **bossa nova** musical form, the first recording of which was made by Elizabeth Cardosa in the 1950s.

Samba dancers are reminiscent of leaves quivering violently in the wind as they are driven along by the feverish beat of the *bateria* (rhythm section) of drums and percussion.

Brazil's biggest show

It was the Portuguese who brought the practice of Carnival to Brazil at the end of the 17th century as a festivity to mark the end of worldly indulgence before the start of Lent, and celebrated by people pelting each other with flour and water bombs. The music and dance is essentially African in origin. Carnival

Tango, the passionate dance for two.

NEW LATIN RYTHYMS

South American music has adopted styles from many countries to produce a hybrid of dance rhythms. Traditional *cumbia* sounds, enhanced with synthesizers, produce *techno-cumbia*, popular in the Andes. Hip-hop and rap from the US is big, while *Reggaeton*, a fusion of hip-hop and reggae, is danced to all over the continent. Similarly, garage music has influenced tango experiments in Argentina, while *bailanta*, based on traditional folk rhythms, can be found in many nightclubs. Rock groups singing in Spanish and Portuguese are also popular. The most influential was Argentina's Soda Stereo until its singer suffered a stroke in 2010.

is undoubtedly one of the biggest displays of modern Brazilian popular culture, blending festivity with show, and art with folklore, as everyone takes to the streets in extravagant and colorful costume.

The excitement starts to escalate from the Christmas period and New Year celebrations. In the run-up to Lent, an eerie hysteria hangs heavily in the air like the tension before a monsoon. The observer is washed along by a wave of infectious anticipation and then buffeted by relentless musical elements for four days and nights as this tropical storm sweeps over the

In recent years the Bahia carnival, which is held in the colorful northeastern city of Salvador, has grown in popularity. Held as a massive street party, *trios eléctricos* – floats that transport deafening speakers pumping out 100,000 watts of samba, **axé** (the fast-paced marching form originating in Recife), and **frevo** (a fusion of frevo and other local genres with reggae and electronic sounds) music – lead the processions through the winding cobbled streets. The air dances and heads undulate. The smell of *vatapá* – a maize and shrimp dumpling dish – forms a haze, served

Carnival parade at the Sambodrome, Rio de Janeiro, Brazil.

country. It is a test of stamina that leaves you feeling numb, exhausted, and giddy, whether you participate or are kept awake by it.

Carnival in Rio is distinct from the rest of the country, with its purpose-built Sambódromo stadium and world-famous samba schools of up to 4,000 participants each, who jealously compete for the title of champion. Each presentation must have a central theme, and is judged by a government-appointed jury. The din filling the huge Sambadrome comes from the samba percussion *baterias*, and sounds like torrential rain beating down on a tin roof. Scantily clad women shake violently as if possessed, and a chorus of several hundred voices chant responses to the samba caller.

by mountainous Baiana women swathed in traditional white dresses.

Home to Brazil's acclaimed writer Jorge Amado, who died in 2001, and international musical exports Olodum, with their army of drummers who played with Michael Jackson and Latin music superstars Daniela Mercury and Caetano Veloso, Bahia is the bastion of Africanism in Brazil. It is also home to the Santería religion known as *candomblé* and the African martial-arts dance *capoeira*. Bahia is considered the center of musical innovation in Brazil, and draws heavily on its African roots. Many dance crazes originate in the northeast before being eagerly snapped up by the rest of the country.

The plaintive panpipes

A world away from the samba drums and salsa tambours is the haunting, plaintive sound of the Andean panpipe, an instrument that dates back at least 2,000 years, and was developed independently in Europe and Asia, as well as the Andes. Panpipe music – *peña* – is played in such countries as Ecuador, Bolivia, and Peru. Drums, rattles, flutes, panpipes, and the famous *charango* (a miniature guitar sometimes made from an armadillo shell) characterize it. *Peña* is a mixture of pre-Columbian and Spanish instrumentation, which traditionally involves

Songs of struggle

Used by dictatorial powers as a propaganda tool, traditional music has, nevertheless, also been a useful source of social revolution and protest. The *Nueva Canción* (New Song) movement that emerged in Chile in the 1960s and 1970s put music at the forefront of the struggle in South America. One of the leading lights of *Nueva Canción* was the musician and poet Violeta Parra, who received little recognition in her own country, Chile, until after her death by suicide in 1967. *Nueva Canción* was designed to voice the struggle and suffering of those

Capoeira performance in Salvador, Brazil.

no lyrical accompaniment – but this has changed recently. The music is now accompanied by ballads sung most often in Quechua, Aymara, or Spanish. These plaintive yet raucous songs record the daily lives, romances, and ribald interludes of rural indigenous communities.

It is music to dance to. Andean music is a foot-stomping version of a barn dance – and it is very moving. It shakes the soul and makes the air jump. The rhythm can accelerate from that of a ballad to a frenetic dance. The pitch becomes feverish and your feet seem to move of their own accord. This kind of indigenous folk music attests to the survival of the complex history of local populations. Music is, in a sense, the last place to hide what is left of yourself.

Chileans who were persecuted during the dictatorship of the 1970s and 1980s. Cuba's equivalent, *Nueva Trova*, produced Silvio Rodríguez and Pablo Milanés, two of Latin America's most respected musicians.

General Pinochet was well aware of the danger that *Nueva Canción* posed to his regime, and had its leading exponent, Victor Jara, incarcerated in the notorious football stadium in Santiago shortly after the September 1973 coup. There, the inspirational Jara sang to his fellow prisoners, for which Pinochet had his hands smashed and his tongue cut out, and then had him murdered.

Another important Chilean dance style is *la cueca*. It began as a pantomime; a game of

> Throughout South America dance is viewed as a right, to be expressed freely at any hour or occasion. It is refreshingly different from attitudes in many northern hemisphere countries, where dance has been exiled to nightclubs.

coy evasion and rebuttal by women and playful conquest by men, in which the woman holds a white handkerchief. It was at one time a dance of remarkable restraint. There was no physical contact between the pair until the point of the *vacunao*, when the man claims the woman with a pelvic movement, gentle kick or swat.

What is more moving about *la cueca*, however, is that it was employed by women to protest against the mass disappearances of their sons and husbands under Pinochet's regime during the 1970s and 1980s. *La cueca* became a dance of anger and grief. The women danced alone, their partners lost, disappeared. Their plight was brought to world attention when the British artist Sting paid tribute to them in his song *They Dance Alone*.

Dances of the countryside

On a more cheerful note, the giddy *cumbia* is a popular coastal dance from Colombia, which has become immensely popular throughout the Andes. It consists of a rousing, regular beat with a steady "molasses" bass line and brassy horns.

Urban myth has it that the movements to the *cumbia* reflect gender-based rural activities. The man makes a sweeping movement with his hand that mimics the machete cutting a path through the bush. The woman, with one hand, raises her petticoats, and with the other hand, holds a candle. This purportedly alludes to her guiding the man through the wilderness.

There is a close relationship between the *cumbia* and *vallenato*, as both come from the Caribbean coastal regions of Colombia. Traveling *vallenato* musicians would move from one small town to another. They were gossips who shamelessly grafted local scandal and intrigue into their songs. The lyrics were built piece by piece from the feckless lives of isolated communities. Crowds would gather and eagerly devour the news brought by these musicians. This was before the advent of telephones, and the gossip was juicier.

In recent years *vallenato* has enjoyed a surge in popularity. Carlos Vives spirited this revival with his modern sound. He appeared in a Colombian television soap opera as a wide-eyed *campesino* called upon to defeat Lucifer in a singing contest. The fate of a village lies in his hands. At first things don't look good for Vives. You worry about the village – and about his dubious wardrobe. Still, Vives and his accordion manage to deal a fatal blow to the devil by striking an original chord, thus securing the future of the village and the *vallenato*. As is so often the case in South America, it seems, music conquers all.

Get into the rhythm at the Cali salsa club, Colombia.

FURTHER STEPS

Major music retailers stock Latin music, and it is also sold online and at specialist shops in many cities. The Tumi Latin American Music Sampler (Tumi music label) offers good introductions, featuring panpipes, cumbia, salsa, merengue, and son. The more adventurous may wish to attend dance classes specializing in salsa, samba or merengue. Informal classes offering tuition for beginners are best. They are great fun but, being little advertized, may be hard to locate. Inquire at a Latin American restaurant or bar or check out the internet for Latin American dance websites. Salsa clubs also tend to offer free lessons early in the evening.

Di Cavalcanti painting at Brazil's national museum of fine arts, the Museu Nacional de Belas Artes.

ARTS AND CRAFTS

Visitors to South America will find art all
around them – indigenous crafts, pre-Columbian
treasures, colonial Baroque art, and powerful
modern paintings.

For more than five centuries, South Americans
saw themselves through the eyes of others. In
1492 Spain conquered a continent it had not
known existed; within a few short years it had
overwhelmed the population that already lived
there – the 30 million or so indigenous peoples
of South America – and made them "disappear."
Those 20 percent or so who were not killed or
assimilated were pushed into the background,
perceived as barbarians and savages.

The native population of South America
and the black African communities imported
as slaves were rarely depicted by painters after
the Flemish artist Theodore de Bry produced
his famous engravings of the Conquest. When
they did appear it was usually as curiosities,
exotic figures in the landscapes of European
travelers documenting this New World after
Spain finally lost its South American empire
in the early 19th century – artists like Jean-
Baptiste Debret in Brazil, or Camilo Fernández

Traditional crafts in the making in the Uros Islands, Peru.

*The growth of tourism has contributed to the
resurgence of traditional crafts – in the
Ecuadorian community of Otavalo, for example. But it has changed them, too, integrating
communities into the global tourism market.*

in Colombia (his watercolors can be seen in
Bogotá at the Biblioteca Nacional).

Occasionally you can catch glimpses of the
work of anonymous indigenous artists – in the
paintings of the Cusco School in Peru, for example, with its black Madonnas and curious indigenous faces painted in the background or carved
into the frames. Yet the arts of the native and

black population did survive, in what we now
call craftwork or folk arts – papier-mâché figures,
painted gourds, fine weaving, etc. Contemporary
crafts represent a continuous line from the past,
although they have also changed beyond recognition from their original models.

A new consciousness

It was not until the mid-19th century that South
American painters began to see their own world
as worthy of attention. José Correia de Lima
painted Brazil's black people for the first time
(Museu de Belas Artas, São Paulo), while in
Peru, Pancho Fierro recorded the native and
mestizo people on Lima's streets (Museo de

Arte de Lima). In the Museo Nacional de Artes Plásticas in Montevideo, Uruguay, the paintings of Juan Manuel Blanes record the inhabitants of the pampas, the open grasslands where the gauchos lived. Pedro Figari, painting in the first half of the 20th century, created delicate and evocative images of a life of poverty in a similar world.

Change was coming – and it exploded upon South America at the beginning of the 20th century. After a century of political independence, the ties of external domination were still strong. Any bid to find real freedom meant turning the artistic gaze inward and rediscovering both the

A depiction of Creole dance, before 1927 (oil on card).

CHECK YOUR SOUVENIRS

It is not difficult to find good reproductions of the featherwork of Paracas or the fine beaten gold of the Inca highlands. But it is illegal to take authentic historical artifacts out of most South American countries. So many have already been spirited away and hoarded in Europe and North America that visitors are strongly discouraged from continuing the depletion of the historical past – and there are stiff penalties for those who are caught doing so. It is also illegal – as well as highly irresponsible – to export certain materials, such as the feathers of protected bird species, which are sometimes found in handicrafts at local markets.

reality and the traditions that were authentically South America's own.

Ironically, the new cultural nationalists were often artists who, as their contemporaries so often did, first traveled to Europe in search of culture. Many became involved in the new modernist movements there and brought the avant-garde back to South America, where it came face to face with a different and dramatic reality. South America's modern art movements were born out of those encounters.

The past rediscovered

The 1910–20 period was a time of political and social upheaval – and of nationalism above all. Every country in Latin America began to rediscover – unearth, almost – its past; Hiram Bingham's "rediscovery" of Machu Picchu in Peru in 1911 was a signpost to the *Indigenismo* movement of the 1920s. In 1910 the Mexican Revolution reverberated around the whole continent, influencing university students, who began to demand an art and an education that reflected their own reality.

The *Semana de Arte Moderna*, a famous exhibition that took place in São Paulo in 1922, announced the new movement in music, literature, and all the arts. Most representative of its extraordinary innovations was the work of the artist Tarsila do Amaral. Her famous painting *Central Railway of Brazil*, like much of her work, marries bright colors and geometric forms set in a primitive landscape, it is on display in the Museu de Arte Contemporânea of the University of São Paulo. Amaral, along with contemporaries such as Anita Malfatti, represented one face of the new movement; beside them Emílio de Cavalcanti and Cándido Portinari used the media of etching, woodcutting, and engraving to portray the experience of the ordinary people of Brazil. Portinari's War and Peace fresco adorns the UN building in New York.

European Influences

Joaquín Torres-García, like his contemporary Rafael Barradas, returned from Europe and the United States to his native Uruguay in 1932, and began to generate his own version of the geometric three-dimensional designs he had learned from the Constructivists. The exciting and inventive MADI group (Movimiento de Arte Concreto-Invención), founded in Buenos Aires in 1945, developed that work in entirely new directions.

The extraordinary purity of Armando Reverón's paintings clearly owes its origins to Manet and the post-Impressionists, searching as it does for the perfect expression of light and color that led him finally to the blinding whites of his last canvases. Reverón's claim was to have captured the essential atmosphere of his own coastal town in Venezuela – an achievement far removed from the innovative and daring new directions for which his country earned an international reputation. For in the capital, Caracas, the architect Carlos Raúl Villanueva was building a new university and inviting a younger generation of

gardens and landscapes full of color and menace. He and Peruvian Fernando de Szyszlo (born 1925) are key figures in the introduction of abstract painting in South America.

The *Indigenismo* movement

Even the most non-representational kind of painting in Latin America has wrestled with the past, the "invisible" South America. The powerful *Indigenismo* movement that began in the late 1920s in Peru, Ecuador, and Bolivia sought out the indigenous communities in all its artistic expressions – in music, literature, and painting.

Brazilian artist Candido Portinari's two-mural painting, 'War and 'Peace', which normally adorns the UN building in New York.

exciting new artists to participate in the design of new and very modern spaces. This invitation was eagerly accepted by artists like Alejandro Otero, Jesús Rafael Soto, and Carlos Cruz Díez, whose disturbing optical games with light, movement, and geometric form can be seen in their settings in Caracas Central University.

In the late 1950s the Neo-Concretist movement was formed by several like-minded Brazilian artists – Lygia Pape, Lygia Clark, and Helio Oiticica among others – and explored space and color in several dimensions in the museums and streets of Rio de Janeiro, where much of their work may still be found. In Chile, Roberto Matta (1911–2002), an artist with a strong social conscience, drew on European surrealism to create a universe of mysterious

José Sabogal was the doyen of *Indigenismo* in the visual arts, influencing a whole generation in Bolivia and Ecuador. But for some he was too close to an exaggerated Socialist Realism that owed much to the Mexican muralists.

A newer generation of artists took that brute realism in new directions – particularly the controversial Ecuadorian artist Oswaldo Guayasamín (1919–1999), who moved toward a kind of primitive abstraction, his paint piled on the canvas as if the physical gesture of painting itself conveyed the emotions it contained. His enormous popularity and commercial success invited the accusation that he painted to pander to the metropolitan world's vision of the south. Many of his paintings and sculptures can be seen in the Museo Guayasamín in Quito.

Satires on complacency

The satirical portraits of a plump and complacent South American bourgeoisie have brought Colombian artist Fernando Botero (born 1932) both success and the enmity of some of his subjects.

This variety of individual expression has its counterpoint in movements whose object is to create art that is collective in its nature. The radicalization of Chilean political life between 1968 and 1973 produced a mural art reflecting a movement in the streets. This movement was founded by the group Brigada Ramona Parra, named after a young art student who was killed

El Mestizaje, a painting by Oswaldo Guayasamín in the Capilla del Hombre, Quito.

in a demonstration. Elsewhere, that impulse took art into the realms of sculpture and performance – art as a public statement, ranging from Chilean Eugenio Dittborn's poignant "airmail paintings," mailed to exhibitions around the world, to Argentine Antonio Berni's provocative and highly political collages.

Since the 1990s, artists of international renown have continued to transcend national borders, leaving the old idea of local "schools" behind. In the early 21st century, Latin American art has won over collectors' fancy and enjoys a fast-growing scene. Galleries abound in the main cities of the region, presenting painting both steeped in tradition and ultra-modern

that seeks to break free of stereotype. Miami is the hub for the market in "Latin" art, foremost through its version of the Art Basle fair, but Buenos Aires hosts its important ArteBA. But biennales in Cuenca, Ecuador, Havana, and, most recently, Porto Alegre in Brazil have joined Sao Paulo as key showcases of contemporary art.

Artists who've made international names for themselves in the past generation include Argentine painter Guillermo Kuitca. Doris Salcedo of Colombia, Chilean Alfredo Jaar, Vik Muniz and Cildo Meireles are known for their installations that immerse viewers into current political and social issues of their countries, all influenced by Marcel Duchamp.

A meeting of art and crafts

In another direction, art left the studio to reconnect with a completely different, popular tradition – colorful, naïve, passionate. It had its representatives in Brazil, and in Chile in the work of Luis Herrera Guevara.

It was here that art met "craft." In the aftermath of the Chilean military coup of 1973, for example, groups of women began to make *arpillerías* – patchworks – that employed traditional skills to make powerful symbolic statements about freedom, pain, and the search for the "disappeared." Of course, these crafts had evolved and changed from their origins in pre-Columbian America or in Africa, yet they remained the property of the poorest sections of South American society.

Craftsmen and women often produced useful items – beautifully woven *ponchos* in Ecuador, sweaters of llama or alpaca wool in Peru, and woolen ponchos, hats, and gloves in the Andes – all functional as well as beautiful.

Handmade clay sculptures with enormous hands and feet can be bought everywhere in Peru – their faces are those of the highland peoples. The beautifully painted scenes inside bamboo stalks or hollowed-out nuts are survivals of authentic skills as well as attractive mementoes for sale to tourists.

In markets across the continent, plastic items and tacky electronic goods cohabit on blankets laid out on the street with delicate paper-lace cut-outs or fine ceramics. This coexistence of dramatically different ways of life and methods of production is part of the contradictory reality of South America.

The Otavaleño Weavers

Otavalo is a modern miracle of economic achievement but it grew out of colonial oppression and inhuman working conditions.

Forced by their colonial Spanish masters to become weavers, about half of Ecuador's Otavaleño people are today involved in the craft, which has made them the most prosperous indigenous group in Ecuador, possibly in all of South America. They export their fine-quality textiles to the United States, Canada, and Europe, while the bulk of their business remains in South America.

Otavalo lies between Ecuador's capital, Quito, and the Colombian border. Today's Otavaleños are probably descended from the Cara tribe, which expanded from Colombia to the Ecuadorian sierra about 1,000 years ago. The Cara established trade links with neighboring tribes, and traded cotton and blankets, along with dogs and salt, in exchange for *achiote* (a plant from which dyes are extracted), parrots, and monkeys.

The arrival of the Incas in the late 1400s marked the beginning of 500 years of colonization and imposed both labor duties and a system of beliefs. After 17 years of fighting, the Inca Huayna Capac took Caranqui, the Cara capital, and massacred thousands of its inhabitants. Many Cara were transported to Peru, while loyal Inca subjects were settled on Cara territory. The Incas introduced coca and llamas, an excellent source of wool, but their rule was too shortlived to seriously influence Otavaleño culture. In fact, it may be that the area of Inca control ran along the eastern side of Imbabura volcano alone after the Otaveleños stopped them at the Mojanda lagoons, leaving their unique culture intact.

Weaving workshops

Under the Spanish, the *encomienda* system was established in Otavalo, putting Spanish settlers in control of an area and its indigenous inhabitants. The first weaving *obraje* (workshop) was set up in the 1550s with 500 workers, some as young as nine years old. Modern tools were introduced and within 50 years the Otavalo *obraje* was the most productive in Ecuador. Otavaleños labored 14 hours a day manufacturing cloth, woolen blankets, and rope for export. In 1648 an *obraje* in Peguche had to be closed, because the number of suicides among workers had grown to alarming proportions.

The Otavaleños were forced to learn Spanish to facilitate their conversion to Christianity, although their Catholicism today incorporates a number of ancestral beliefs.

Land reforms enacted in Ecuador in 1964 abolished the *wasipungo* system, based on enforced indigenous labor. The first store selling woven products opened in Otavalo in 1966, and within a dozen years there were 75 such stores. Weaving has now decentralized and become a cottage industry. Over the years, the ingenuity

Poncho Plaza market wares in Otavalo, Ecuador.

of the Otavalo weavers has brought them worldwide fame.

Every Saturday morning, the usually quiet streets of the town teem with life. By 9am the main textile market, known as Poncho Plaza, is a feast of colors and textures: rolls of cloth, thick blankets, tapestry wall hangings, chunky sweaters, long patterned belts or *fajas*, and *cintas* – ribbons or tapes the women use to bind their long hair. Most *Otavaleño* textiles are made of sheep's wool, although some alpaca sweaters can be found. The mechanization of the modern textile industry, potentially disastrous for the Otavaleños, has been compensated for by tourism and an emphasis on quality goods produced naturally.

ARCHITECTURE

South American cities have been at the forefront of modern architectural movements with their innovative designs, but there are also much older monumental wonders to be seen, from Inca temples to colonial cathedrals.

W e do not know the names of those who built the extraordinary Inca cities – Cusco and Machu Picchu – or the magnificent fortress of Sacsayhuamán, forming the pinnacle of pre-colonial architectural skill. But whoever they were, their constructions were built to last forever. In Cusco and Quito, the Spanish colonialists built their houses on the foundations of the Inca city. Cusco was built at what the Incas saw as the center of the world, and to symbolize this, it is divided into four districts, representing each corner of the empire, surrounding a central square.

There are still older, monumental remains stretching from Colombia to Bolivia. Elsewhere, the ancient indigenous peoples of what are now Argentina, Chile, and Brazil left less grand signs of their passing.

The Spanish influence

When the Spanish conquered Latin America, they brought their own values, their own religion, and their own forms of artistic expression. But they preserved the structure of the cities, since Spain built its colonial cities on a grid system around a central square as did the Incas. For in a real sense, Spain's was an urban culture and, apart from the great plantation houses, rural building was left to the communities who lived there, relying on their skill in using local materials.

For more than 300 years, Latin America's building styles originated in Europe – first with some late Renaissance reminiscences, later shifting to the typically Spanish *plateresque* style, along with other Baroque influences from other parts of Europe. Elaborate decorated surfaces and cascades of gold and mirrored glass reflected the confidence of a colonial order, but were influenced by the tastes and beliefs of

The Compañía de Jesús church on Cusco's Plaza de Armas, Peru.

MASTERS OF MASONRY

Hundreds of sites throughout their vast empire display the outstanding masonry skills of the Incas, from the famous Twelve-Angled Stone at Cusco and the *intihuatana* at Machu Picchu, the "hitching post of the sun," to the gigantic stones used to build Sacsayhuamán. The Incas were expert at earthquake-proofing their buildings, inserting strips of smaller, narrower stones amid massive rock in Ollantaytambo to offset the earth's movements. Over the centuries Inca foundations have proved far more resistant to earthquakes than later Spanish constructions. Ruins stretch from Ibarra in Ecuador south to La Puerta near Copiapó in Chile.

native and mestizo craftsmen. In Colombia and Ecuador, churches could be exuberant – sometimes blue and red washes were added to the swirling gold; sometimes they were influenced by *Mudéjar* (Moorish) styles, and incorporated wooden beams, carved closed balconies, and geometrical patterns, despite the codes of austerity that were imposed from Madrid.

The native influence

Indigenous craftsmen in Bolivia left their mark on Sucre Cathedral and the churches of San Lorenzo in Potosí and San Francisco in La Paz,

and idiosyncratic are the statues of the Prophets at Congonhas do Campo.

Looking to Europe

Landscape and geology affected construction, too, as South America's western viceroyalties lay across an earthquake zone, which toppled many of Lima's colonial buildings – though, all too often, contemporary architects and politicians have blamed earthquakes for the dereliction of colonial town centers, when in fact they have been victims of mindless bricks-and-mortar modernization. The Torre Tagle Palace (now Peru's

The Inca Twelve-Angled stone in Cusco.

and in Peru in the carved soft lava stone used in Arequipa. Bright colors, animals and plants, and occasional dark-skinned faces carved into the stone are testimony to their presence, for example in the facade of the old Jesuit University in Cusco's central square. And in Brazil, where the imported Portuguese style encountered no local architecture to stand in its way, the reality of the tropics found its way into the Baroque facades of Pernambuco and the extraordinary São Francisco da Penitencia churches of Recife and Bahia.

The most outstanding expression of this "tropicalized" Baroque is the work of sculptor-architect Aleijadinho on churches and other buildings in Minas Gerais – his most enduring

Ministry of Foreign Affairs) is one of the most important colonial buildings to have survived in the city. La Moneda, the famous presidential palace in Santiago, Chile, now restored after being destroyed by bombing during the 1973 military coup against Salvador Allende, was Spain's last major construction project in South America.

Once freed from Spain, the leaders of a newly independent subcontinent turned their attention to other parts of Europe. The 19th century produced an imitative grandeur, mimicking the wide boulevards and grand palaces of France and London, and their new enthusiasm for neoclassical styles. In Buenos Aires, growing to dominance in the latter half of the 19th century, the newly wealthy bourgeoisie used architecture to emphasize their European roots, producing their own versions of the grand boulevards of the Champs-Elysées. In Lima this change was exemplified by the demolition of the old city walls to make way for the new avenues.

Outside the planned, structured heart of Latin American cities, buildings tend to be somewhat improvised and transient. By the late 19th century the spaces between the grand houses and tenements had themselves become living places for a poor immigrant population. In the 20th century these areas swelled spreading like mushrooms (*callampa*, the name for

> *"I created my work with courage and idealism, but also with an awareness that what is important... is attempting to make this world a better place in which to live."*
> Oscar Niemeyer, The Curves of Time

21st century by gilding its new urban spaces with the most daring "machines for living." Le Corbusier's lecture tour of Argentina and Brazil galvanized local urban planners, and Brazil's 1930 revolution, which was led by young mili-

The statue of prophet Jeremiah by Aleijadinho at the Basílica do Bom Jesus de Matosinhos, Minas Gerais, Brazil.

a shanty town in Chile, means mushroom) around and through the burgeoning metropolises. The hillside *favelas* of Rio are extreme examples of this phenomenon.

Beacons of the technological age

South America – in particular Brazil and Venezuela – has been at the very center of innovation in architecture since the 1930s. The architects responsible for the modernist revolution in Brazil traveled to Europe and brought back new and experimental ideas. They seized on the ideas of the great Swiss-French architect Le Corbusier and the German Ludwig Mies van der Rohe as they imagined great modern cities. They hoped the subcontinent would be catapulted into the

tary officers promising to modernize and industrialize, provided the opportunity.

The Ministry of Education and Health in Rio was the landmark of the new movement. Completed in 1937 by a team that included Lúcio Costa and Oscar Niemeyer, it was the center of an urban utopia. Not just buildings, but whole cities would be built like efficient machines, with clean lines, and open, flexible spaces set in planned landscapes like those designed by Brazilian architect and landscape designer Roberto Burle Marx. The high blocks along Rio's Copacabana beach are one such example; the recreational complex at the suburb of Pampulha another. The church of São Francisco de Assis at Pampulha, decorated by

Candido Torquato Portinari, symbolized the marriage of painting, sculpture, and the constructive arts.

The triumph was Brasília, the new capital and the most ambitious of several new cities purpose-built in the late 1950s that illustrate the meeting of architecture and sculpture. Niemeyer, the principal architect, imagined a city that would create a way of living. In just 10 years the Brazilian movement transformed architecture everywhere, as the 1943 "Brazil Builds" exhibition at New York's Museum of Modern Art testified.

construction of which began in the early 1950s, expressed the confidence of a newly oil-rich country. Villanueva created more than buildings – this was a landscape where natural lines and plants and trees were represented in concrete and metal.

In Argentina, where the neoclassical forms persisted longer than elsewhere, the Teatro Colón expressed both the high point and the end of the movement. The next generation of architects was equally responsive to the modern movement as the country began its process of industrialization. Clean, sharp lines and open

The unmistakable style of Oscar Niemeyer is seen in the Museu de Arte Contemporânea, Rio, Brazil.

Modern icons

Less well known abroad, but equally significant, was the movement led by Carlos Raúl Villanueva in Venezuela, and in particular in Caracas. Villanueva's first major projects – the El Silencio (Silence) and El Paraíso (Paradise) workers' housing complexes, built in the 1940s – symbolized a utopian and optimistic modernism. As in Brazil, the mass housing projects represented the promise of an organized and smooth transition to urban growth; the concrete and glass that were its chief materials were not indigenous but they were cheap and readily available. Like the Brazilians, Villanueva saw architecture as a meeting point between spatial and visual arts. The Central University,

space characterized the work of new architects like Amancio Williams, whose house in Mar del Plata for his brother, the composer Alberto, was entirely functional and without artistic pretensions. In Chile the long, low buildings of Emilio Duhart and Alberto Piwonka reflected an adaptation of the same ideas to the earthquake-prone Santiago.

In the 1980s and 1990s, architectural innovation took place largely in the commercial sphere. However, in 1996 Niemeyer completed the Museu de Arte Contemporânea in Niterói, across the bay from Rio – a stunning, sculptural flying saucer, perched on the edge of a cliff. Not least, the Rio Olympics 2016 will provide an opportunity for even newer gems.

ADVENTURES IN SUN, SNOW, AND WATER

Only Asia can rival South America for natural diversity – and economic growth has helped fuel a boom in new outdoor sports, from sandboarding to paragliding.

South America is a paradise for outdoor enthusiasts. Down the spine of the continent is the Andes, the longest continuous range of mountains in the world. This lofty landscape has snowcapped peaks for mountaineering, trekking, horseback riding, mountain biking on remote trails through isolated villages, and world-class kayaking and river rafting.

Within the Amazon basin to the east lie thousands of square miles of virgin rainforest best explored by dugout canoe. Beaches offer excellent surf and the northern Pacific and Caribbean reefs are great for scuba diving. Adrenaline sports such as snowboarding, paragliding, and bungee jumping are on the increase. But there is little regulation of the adventure travel business, so choose your travel company with care.

National parks

Nahuel Huapi, the first national park in South America, was created in Argentina in 1903. Since then hundreds of parks have been established throughout the continent, protecting beautiful wilderness. Access to parks is becoming easier with improved transportation and infrastructure. In the more developed countries, notably Chile and Argentina, the parks have established trail systems with visitor centers.

Cusco in Peru is the Mecca for outdoor adventure, the most popular excursion being the Inca trail trek to Machu Picchu. Cusco's surrounding mountains are also perfect for mountain biking. There is a popular ride to the Inca terracing and salt ponds at Moray. Instead of taking a bus tour, the Sacred Valley can now be experienced by rafting the Urubamba River, going on horseback, or paragliding from the cliffs.

Farther south, the spectacular alpine and coastal wilderness of southern Chile brings in

The Andes seen from the dirt road linking San Alfonso to El Morado National Park.

visitors from October through April. The town of Pucón is a good base for hikes, climbs, river rafting, mountain biking, and horseback riding into the nearby national parks of Huerquehue and Villarrica. Even farther south is spectacular Torres del Paine National Park.

Mountaineering

The high peaks of the Andes attract high-caliber international climbers. Acclimatization, proper equipment, and preparation are paramount. The highest of these peaks is Aconcagua (6,962 meters/22,841 ft) in Argentina. In northern Peru, from June through September, the small town of Huaraz is filled with climbers organizing expeditions to the glaciated peaks in the Cordillera Blanca, the highest being Huascarán (6,768 meters/22,205 ft). Ecuador's volcanoes can offer the novice a taste of high-altitude mountaineering.

Skiing and snowboarding

The world's highest ski run, at 5,420 meters (17,780 ft) near La Paz, Bolivia, on the slopes of Chacaltaya, sadly evaporated along with the glacier that supported it. The views, however, are fantastic. Reliable ski areas have been developed in Chile and Argentina, with Cerro Catedral near Bariloche in Argentina, and Portillo in Chile near

Tierra del Fuego, often taking detours off the Pan-American Highway, up into Cajamarca or the Cordillera Blanca in northern Peru, for the best views and to avoid traffic. For the less serious cyclist there are one-day cycle tours coasting down the flanks of the active Cotopaxi volcano or pedaling from the mountains of Baños to the jungle town of Puyo in Ecuador.

Rafting and kayaking

Beginners can descend the fun and safe Class III rapids of the Upper Napo River, near Tena, Ecuador. More experienced rafters can run the

Mountain biker in Patagonia, Argentina.

Aconcagua considered the most prestigious. The resorts near Santiago, such as Valle Nevado and El Colorado, also have challenging slopes. Smaller resorts dot both sides of the Andes all the way down to Tierra del Fuego, the most modern being Cerro Castor near Ushuaia. Some resorts also offer snowboard parks and cross-country skiing, and tiny El Mirador near Punta Arenas is the only resort in the world where the ocean is visible from the slopes. The season runs from June to October, though hiking and mountain biking are available for much of the rest of the year.

Cycling

Every year a few serious cyclists pedal the length of the Andes to the southern tip of the continent,

Colca River rapids in southern Peru in a canyon twice as deep as the Grand Canyon. Condors soar above, and sheer cliffs tower hundreds of meters on either side. Futaleufú in Patagonia is Chile's hub for rafting. Its namesake river has Class V rapids, making it one of the most difficult to raft or kayak anywhere. For novices, much tamer trips are also available. The Bío Bío River in central Chile has excellent whitewater, spectacular gorges and waterfalls, and Mapuche settlements, making it one of the most exciting rivers in the Andes.

Paragliding

In Rio de Janeiro, Brazil, you can paraglide tandem over Atlantic rainforest, soaring above the skyscrapers and landing on the beach.

Paragliders are often seen off the coastal cliffs of Miraflores in Lima, Peru. The craze has also hit Mérida in Venezuela and Tucumán in Argentina. You can also have a go at ballooning in Rio from the Autodromo de Jacarepaguá.

Beach and watersports

Crazy *buggeiros* (buggy drivers) will take you out on their buggies along the beaches and sand dunes of Brazil. Some of the most popular areas are the Natal beaches of Río Grande do Norte. The massive sand dunes in the desert of Huacachina near Ica in southern Peru offer a different kind of fun. All you need is a board (cheap to rent) for sliding down the sand, and to be prepared to walk to the top of the dunes.

The Humboldt current brings constant surf to the west coast. Various towns along the Pacific coast such as Montañita, Ecuador and Máncora, northern Peru, have become hip places for foreign surfers to hang out. Puerto Chicama, set in the arid coastal desert of northern Peru, has become famous for its long left point break.

You can snorkel with hammerhead sharks, rays, starfish, seals, and penguins off the Galápagos

White water rafting on the Maipo River, Chile.

SANDBOARDING

Sandboarding is the summer alternative to snowboarding and has spread to many countries in the region, particularly Argentina, Chile, and Peru. It is still very much an adventure sport. Sharp-tipped, shorter boards are sold in Brazil; in Chile, handmade wooden boards are sold, and can be rented in San Pedro de Atacama for use in nearby Valle de la Muerte, a short bike ride away. Other locations in Chile include the dunes at Concón near Viña del Mar, while in Argentina, boards can be rented in Puerto Pirámide on the Península Valdes. The best dunes are at Cerro Blanco in Peru and Valizas, Uruguay. Take plenty of water and sunscreen.

Islands, Ecuador. Along the Caribbean coast, palm-fringed beaches offer the perfect start for snorkeling and scuba diving. The coral islands of Los Roques, off the coast of Venezuela, are teeming with marine life. Morrocoy National Park is also a popular center for snorkeling and scuba diving off Venezuela's coastline.

Jungle trips

Canoe trips along small tributary rivers are far more exciting than floats along the Amazon, which is too wide for wildlife viewing. Trips into the Cuyabeno Nature Reserve in Ecuador, Manu National Park in southern Peru, and from Rurrenabaque, Bolivia offer real jungle experiences.

Ecotourism

Sensible tourism can offer ancient cultures a way to value and regain pride in their culture amid the pressures of globalization.

South America's native cultures aren't closed to outside influences. In fact, many – particularly among those from the Amazon that last came into contact with the West – immediately desire manufactured status symbols from cellphones to pickup trucks. In many areas, however, ecotourism and community tourism have opened up alternatives to migration to the shanty towns of the big cities – and not just in the rainforest.

Myriad projects have sprung up since the 1990s, from luxurious rainforest lodges like the award-winning Napo Wildlife Center in the Ecuadorian Amazon to tiny inns at the end of the road in Chilean Patagonia. Amazon and fly-fishing lodges are among the most expensive of these opportunities to get into close contact with nature. Others are at the cheap end of the spectrum, and an option for those really interested in roughing it.

Some projects, however, offer nothing more than a label and may, in fact, provide an entry point for mass tourism. Uncontrolled access to remote native people can be devastating for their societies. National Geographic's Center for Sustainable Destinations and the International Ecotourism Society offer guidelines for choosing a destination properly. There are local certificates, although international standards like the Blue Flag for beaches are more reliable. It is also good to check whether claims of certification are actually true.

On the other hand, other projects are controversial for the opposite reason, ie they stand in the way of industrial development. US clothing entrepreneur Douglas Tompkins – founder of The North Face and Esprit – has bought tens of thousands of hectares of native forest in Chile and Argentina to protect them from destruction, and has created several private nature preserves, Pumalín in Chile being the most famous. A follower of the "Deep Ecology" movement, his vocation for conservation has, however, made him a rival of business interests in the forestry and electricity industries. Chilean conservatives are critical that a foreigner was allowed to buy land stretching from the Pacific to the Andes, cutting off parts of the country. Tompkins and his wife, Kristine McDivitt,

are also vocal critics of the plan to build several dams to generate electricity in Chilean Patagonia. Conservation groups like the Wildlife Conservation Society, which has established a vast preserve at Karukinka on the Chilean side of Tierra del Fuego, have recognized that under no circumstances will schemes work that don't engage local people.

Economic pressures

Even so, conflicts arise as companies run by natives – some of whom have only come in contact with mainstream society in the past few decades – face the same economic pressures as all tour operators, and not everyone can find work. One of the most

Pataxo Indian man walking at the Reserva Indigena da Jaqueira, Bahia, Brazil.

famous Amazon lodges, Kapawi in Ecuador, has had to invest much time and diplomacy in defusing conflicts with the Achuar rainforest warriors who staff the lodge and live in nearby hamlets. Visitors should also have no illusions about ecotourism being able to replace the billions of dollars pouring in from oil, mining, and agro-industry. Salaries in those industries will always be higher than in tourism. Ecotourism does, however, offer jobs for many people that these mechanized industries don't. Properly run, even oil production can co-exist with rainforest lodges. For travelers, ecotourism is the best way to get an in-depth experience they won't find in the homogenous beach resorts or hotel chains.

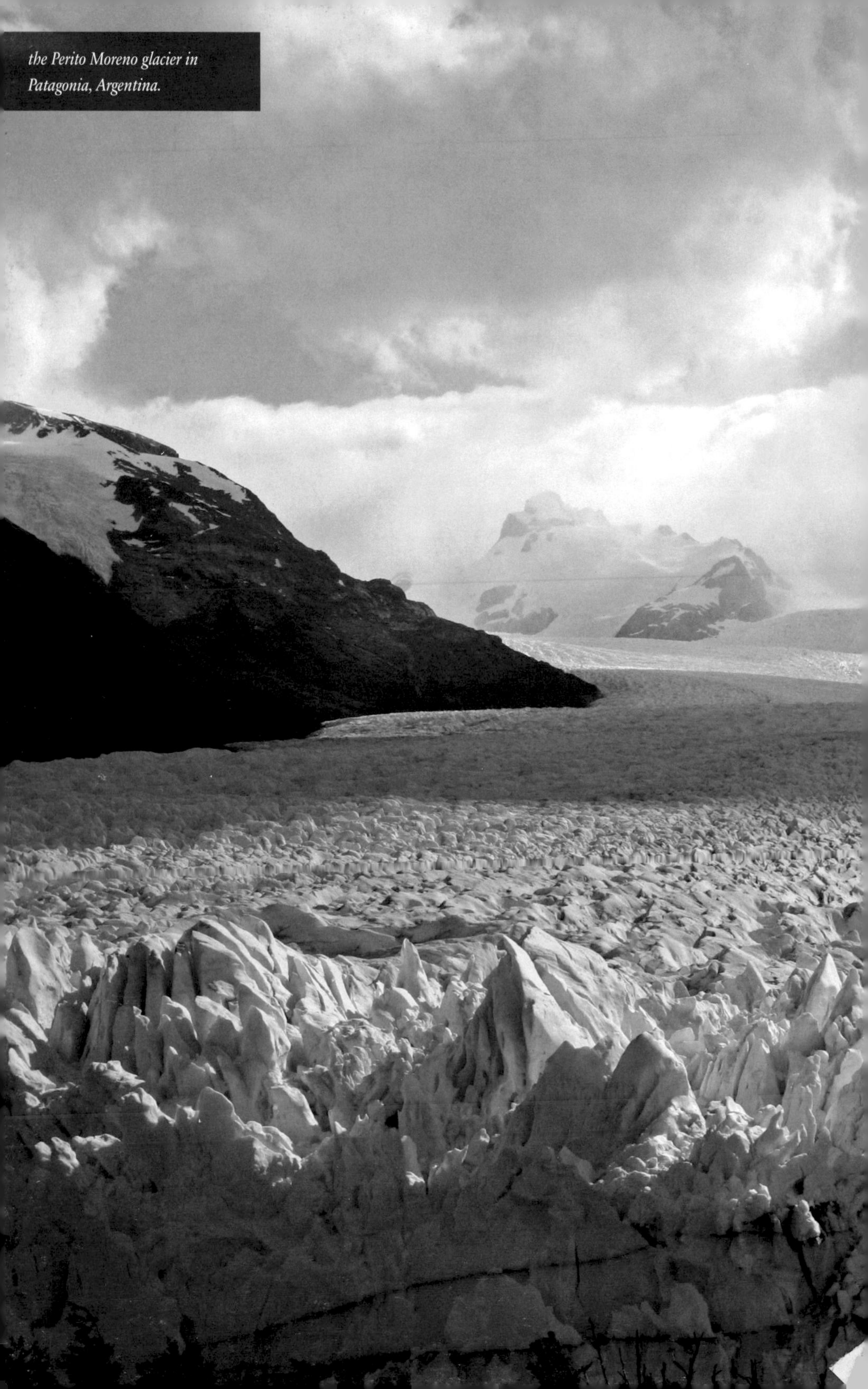

the Perito Moreno glacier in Patagonia, Argentina.

The colonial streets of Cuñeca,
Southern Sierra, Ecuador.

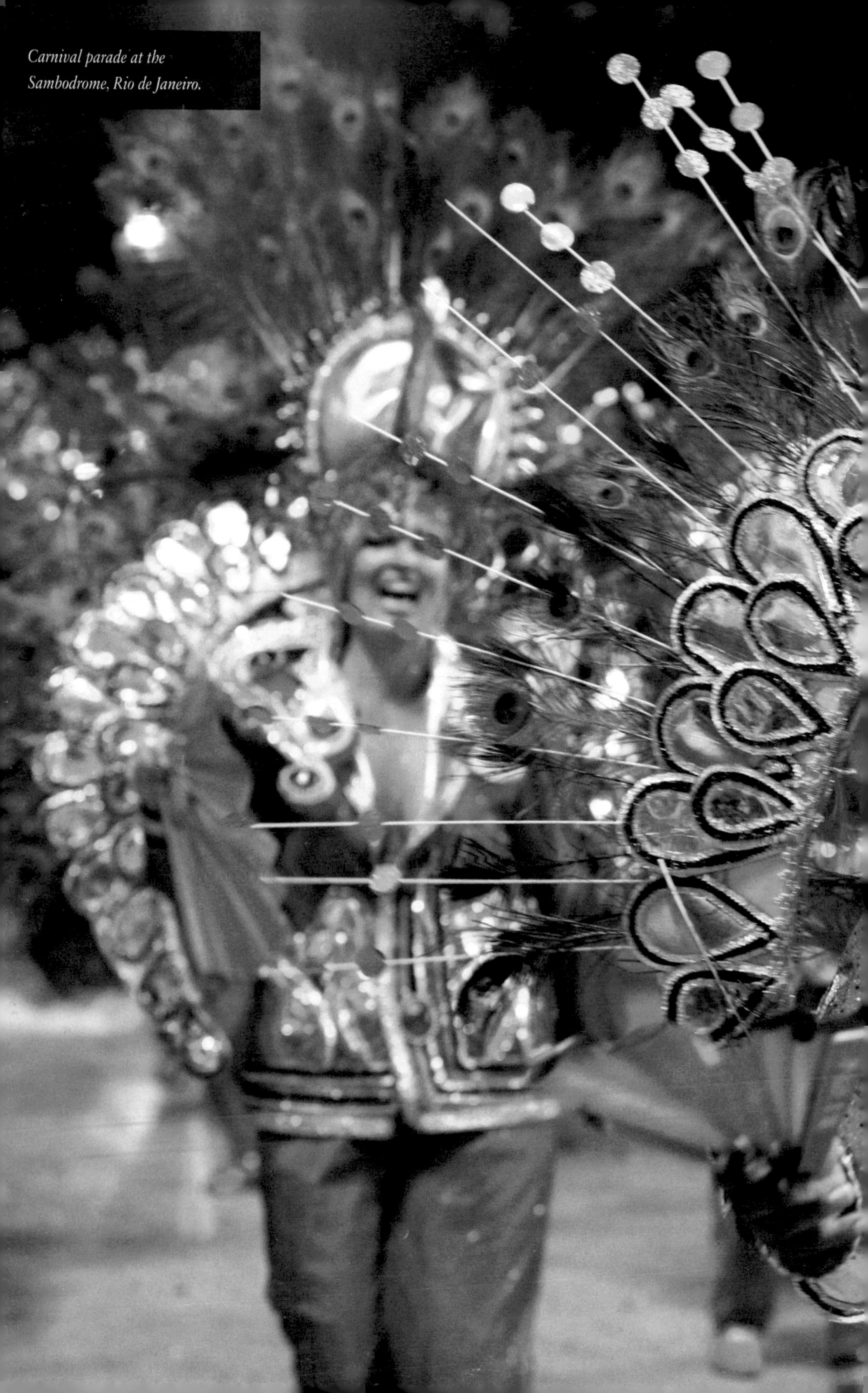

Carnival parade at the Sambodrome, Rio de Janeiro.

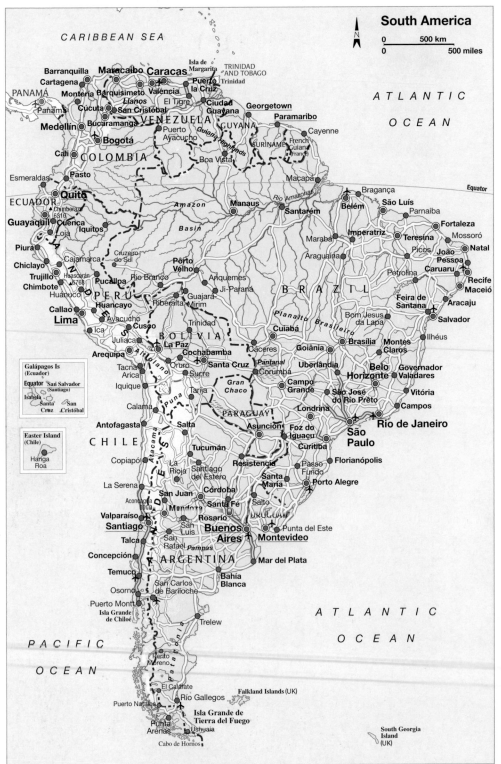

South America

0   500 km

0   500 miles

CARIBBEAN SEA

Barranquilla
Cartagena
Monteria
PANAMÁ
Panamá
Medellín
Cali
BOGOTÁ
Pasto
Esmeraldas
Quito
ECUADOR
Guayaquil
Cuenca
Loja
Piura
Chiclayo
Trujillo
Chimbote
Huánuco
Callao
Lima
Ica

Maracaibo
Cúcuta
Bucaramanga

Caracas
Barquisimeto
Valencia
San Cristóbal
VENEZUELA
Puerto
Ayacucho

Isla de
Margarita
Puerto
la Cruz
El Tigre
Ciudad
Guayana
Llanos

TRINIDAD
AND TOBAGO
Trinidad

Georgetown
Paramaribo
GUYANA
SURINAME
Cayenne
French
Guiana
(France)

ATLANTIC
OCEAN

COLOMBIA

Boa Vista

Guiana Highlands

Macapá

Equator

Chimborazo
6310
Huascarán
6768
Cajamarca
Pucallpa
Huancayo
Ayacucho
Cusco
PERÚ

Iquitos

Amazon

Basin

Cruzeiro
do Sul

Rio Branco

Manaus

Rio Amazonas

Santarém

Belém

Bragança

São Luís
Parnaiba

Fortaleza
Mossoró
Natal
João
Pessoa
Recife
Maceió
Aracaju

Teresina
Picos

Marabá
Imperatriz
Araguaina

BRAZIL

Caruaru
Petrolina

Pôrto
Velho
Ariquemes
Ji-Paraná
Guajará-
Mirim
Riberalta
Trinidad

BOLIVIA
La Paz
Cochabamba
Oruro
Sucre
Tarija
Tacna
Arica
Iquique
Calama

Juliaca
Arequipa
Altiplano
Puna

Cuiabá
Cáceres
Corumbá
Pantanal
Gran
Chaco

Goiânia
Uberlândia
Campo
Grande

Brasília
Planalto Brasileiro
Bom Jesus
da Lapa

Montes
Claros
Belo
Horizonte
São José
do Rio Prêto
Londrina

Governador
Valadares
Vitória
Campos

Feira de
Santana
Salvador
Ilhéus

Antofagasta
Copiapó
La Serena
CHILE
Atacama
ANDES

Salta
Tucumán
La
Rioja
Santiago
del Estero
San Juan
Aconcagua
6960
Mendoza
Valparaíso
Santiago
Talca
Concepción
Temuco
Osorno
Puerto Montt
Isla Grande
de Chiloé

PARAGUAY

Asunción

Resistencia
Santa
María
Córdoba
Santa Fé
Salto
URUGUAY
Rosario
San
Luis
San
Rafael
Pampas
ARGENTINA
Bahía
Blanca
San Carlos
de Bariloche

Foz do
Iguaçu
Curitiba
Passo
Fundo
Porto Alegre

Florianópolis

São
Paulo
Rio de Janeiro

Montevideo
Punta del Este

Buenos
Aires
Mar del Plata

ATLANTIC
OCEAN

Galápagos Is
(Ecuador)
Equator
San Salvador
(Santiago)
Isabela
Santa
Cruz
San
Cristóbal

Easter Island
(Chile)
Hanga
Roa

Patagonia

PACIFIC
OCEAN

Perito
Moreno
El Calafate
Puerto Natales
Punta
Arenas
Ushuaia
Cabo de Hornos

Trelew

Río Gallegos
Falkland Islands (UK)

Isla Grande de
Tierra del Fuego

South Georgia
Island
(UK)

INTRODUCTION

A detailed guide to the whole of South
America, with major sites cross-referenced
by numbers to the maps.

*Thursday market in
Guamote, Ecuador.*

Because of the diversity of sights and adventure
activities on offer in South America, for a short
visit, it's best to confine yourself to a limited geographical area, or to certain types of experience, from
rainforest expeditions and archeological tours, tropical
beach life to subantarctic forays, music and nightlife,
and much more.

Starting in the north, Colombia, Venezuela, Guyana,
Suriname, and French Guiana run from west to east.
Colombia and Venezuela have an abundance of tropical
white-sand beaches as well as large modern
cities. Their densely forested interiors are home to exotic species and some of the world's most traditional communities.

Next, we come to the countries of the Andean highlands,
Peru and Bolivia, linked by Lake Titicaca, and Ecuador,
which preserve remains of fascinating ancient civilizations, as well as the distinctive living cultures of the Andean
people. Their natural diversity includes mountains, tropical lowlands, and desert. Wildlife enthusiasts flock to the
famous Galápagos Islands, 970km (600 miles) off the coast
of Ecuador.

Rio de Janeiro's Ipanema beach.

From the Andes we move east to Brazil, which sprawls
over an area nearly half the size of all South America.
Everything in Brazil seems to be on a giant scale: its massive
Amazon rainforest in the north, the huge and vibrant cities of the east
coast, its world-famous *Carnaval*, and Iguazú Falls in the south. It is now
gearing up to host the two mega-events of the 2014 soccer FIFA World
Cup and the 2016 Rio de Janeiro Olympics.

In the Southern Cone, long, narrow Chile lines the Pacific from
tropical to subantarctic latitudes. The Atlantic coast is covered by small
Uruguay and huge Argentina, while Paraguay is landlocked. These countries share a strong rural heritage and vast wilderness, but Buenos Aires
and Santiago are among the region's most dynamic cities. Tiny Easter
Island, a colony of Chile since 1888, lies 3,790km (2,355 miles) west of
the coast, one of the most isolated inhabited islands in the world. Some
500km (300 miles) east of Argentinian Patagonia lie the chilly Falkland
Islands (Islas Malvinas), Great Britain's most far-flung colony.

THE NORTH COAST

Great adventures start here – on the balmy Caribbean
coast, or in the remotest reaches of the rainforest.

*Family of the Guambino
tribe near Silvia, Colombia.*

Hot palm-fringed beaches, languid lifestyles, and fast nightlife characterize South America's northern Caribbean coast, but just inside the coastal belt are miles of tropical rainforest, and mountain ranges high enough to provide cool respite in these equatorial zones. Both Colombia and Venezuela attracted gold-seekers in colonial times, and later fortunes were made from Venezuela's oil, or "black gold," while in Colombia it was drugs that made fortunes – and unfortunate headlines. Today, the search for minerals continues in both countries, but fortunes have reversed, with Colombia safer and much easier to travel than Venezuela.

The people who live in the highland regions are mostly mestizos – mixed European and indigenous – while on the coast, African heritage bears testimony to the slavery of colonial times. In Guyana, Suriname, and French Guiana, fascinating communities of African descent have settled in the interior, living in the traditional manner. There are also native communities who still cling to their rainforest ways.

Colombia, in the northwest, is notorious for its guerrilla networks and urban violence, but most of the country is safe for visitors, and is becoming an increasingly popular destination, for its friendly people, breathtaking scenery, and exciting dance culture. It has some remarkable historical sites, includ-

Blue Morpho butterfly.

ing the ancient ruins of San Agustín, the Spanish fortress city of Cartagena, and the finest gold museum on the continent *in* Bogotá, the capital.

Venezuela sports beautiful beach resorts, many on the paradise island of Margarita. It is also a naturalist's dream, with some magnificent wildlife and dramatic scenery. The remote Guayana region, where the world's highest waterfall, Angel Falls, cascades, is characterized by enormous, sheer rock formations, golden savannah, and dense jungle.

East of Venezuela lie sparsely populated Guyana, Suriname, and French Guiana, with extensive rainforest hinterlands. All five inhabited continents are represented in the people of these countries, due to their histories as outposts for three different world empires.

Women in colorful dresses sell plates of sliced fruit (caimito) in Plaza Santo Domingo.

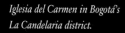
*Iglesia del Carmen in Bogotá's
La Candelaria district.*

COLOMBIA

Despite its notoriety as the drugs capital of the world, this is a beautiful, friendly country of enormous natural diversity and historical treasures.

Colombia has gained a fearsome reputation as the world's foremost producer of cocaine (though Peru topped it in 2010), and for relentless violence and civil unrest. This, however, tells only part of the story of a country where myth and modernity mingle to produce a vast diversity of cultures. This is where the myth of El Dorado and the lure of untold riches caught the imagination of the Spanish conquistadors. Miners still pursue this dream, now in search of emeralds as well as gold. Although the society is modern and outward-looking on the surface, the legacy of Spanish colonial rule is here for all to see, as are the remains of some of the great pre-Columbian civilizations.

Geographically, Colombia is the fourth-largest country in South America, and is unique in having lengthy Pacific and Atlantic coasts. Three *cordilleras* (mountain ranges) stretch north from the southern border with Ecuador to meet the lowland plains of the Caribbean. Most of the country's 45 million inhabitants live in the central region, which incorporates the capital, Santa Fe de Bogotá, set high amid the mist and rain of the eastern *cordillera*, and Medellín and Cali. The population is predominantly mestizo, but there are sizable Afro-Caribbean populations on the Caribbean and Pacific coasts and around Cali, and more than 50 indigenous groups.

In between the mountain ranges lie the valleys of the Cauca and Magdalena rivers, the most fertile agricultural areas. Eastern Colombia is made up of vast, largely uninhabited grasslands known as *los llanos,* and forbidding Amazon jungle.

The turbulent past

Colombia's 19th century was marked by 50 insurrections, eight civil wars and several constitutions. The most

Main Attractions

Bogotá and its Gold Museum
(Museo del Oro)
Zipaquira Salt Cathedral
Cali and Popayán
Tunja and colonial towns
Cartagena and Mompóx

Cartagena street musician.

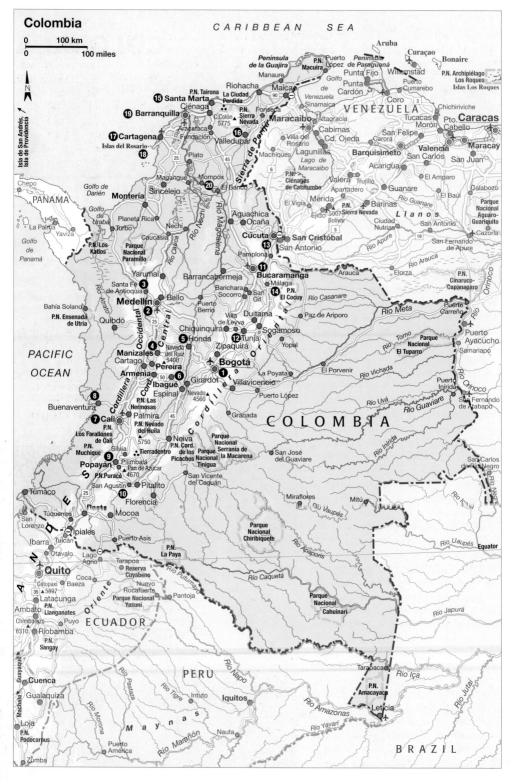

Colombia

0 — 100 km
0 — 100 miles

N

CARIBBEAN SEA

Aruba
Curaçao
Bonaire

Península de la Guajira
P.N. Macuira
Puerto López
Manaure
Punta Fijo
Península de Paraguaná
Willemstad
Punta Cumarebo
P.N. Archipiélago Los Roques
Islas Los Roques

Golfo de Venezuela
Puerto Cardón
Coro
Chichiriviche

Riohacha
Maicao
Fonseca
Sinamaica

15 Santa Marta
P.N. Tairona
La Ciudad Perdida
Ciénaga

19 Barranquilla
C. Colón 5775
P.N. Sierra Nevada
Valledupar
Maracaibo
Altagracia
Villa del Rosario
Cabimas
Cd. Ojeda
San Felipe
Tucacas
Morón
Pto. Cabello
Caracas

17 Cartagena
Islas del Rosario
18
Aracataca
Fundación
16
Machiques
Lago de Maracaibo
Lagunillas
Barquisimeto
Valencia
Maracay
San Carlos
San Juan

Plato
Magangue
Mompox
El Banco
20
Ciénagas de Catatumbo
El Vigía
Mérida
Ejido
P.N. Sierra Nevada 5007
Trujillo
Apartadero
Valera
Ciudad Nutrias
Guanare
Barinas
Acarigua
El Amparo
El Baúl
Calabozo
Parque Nacional Aguaro-Guariquito
Cazorla

PANAMA
Golfo de Darién
Montería
Sincelejo
Aguachica
Ocaña
San Cristóbal
San Antonio
Pamplona
Llanos
San Antonio
San Fernando de Apure
Cazorla

Chepo
La Palma
Yaviza
Golfo de Urabá
Planeta Rica
Nechí
Caucasia
13
Cúcuta
Arauca
P.N. Cinaruco-Capanaparo
Rio Arauca
Elorza
Rio Apure

Turbo
Parque Nacional Paramillo
Barrancabermeja
11
Bucaramanga
Málaga
P.N. El Cocuy
Paz de Ariporo
Puerto Carreño
Rio Meta

P.N. Los Katíos
Yarumal
Baricharas
Socorro
San Gil
Rio Casanare
Rio Meta

Bahía Solano
Santa Fé de Antioquia
3
Bello
2
Medellín
Puerto Berrío
Duitama
Villa de Leyva
Sogamoso
Yopal
El Porvenir
Rio Vichada
Puerto Ayacucho
Samariapo

P.N. Ensenada de Utría
Quibdó
5
Honda
Chiquinquirá
12
Tunja
Rio Tomo
Parque Nacional El Tuparro
Puerto Inírida

PACIFIC OCEAN
4
Manizales
Cartago
Nevado del Ruiz 5400
Zipaquirá
1
Bogotá
La Poyata
Rio Guaviare

8
Buenaventura
Pereira
6
Armenia
Ibagué
Girardot
Villavicencio
Puerto López
El Porvenir
Rio Uvá
Puerto Inírida
San Fernando de Atabapo

7
Cali
P.N. Los Farallones de Cali
Espinal
Nevado 4560
Granada
Rio Guaviare

Palmira
P.N. Las Hermosas
COLOMBIA
San Carlos de Río Negro

P.N. Muchique
9
Popayán
P.N. Nevado del Huila 5750
Neiva
P.N. Cord. de los Picachos
Parque Nacional Tinigua
San José del Guaviare
Miraflores
Rio Inírida
Rio Negro

Silvia
Tierradentro
Parque Nacional Serranía de la Macarena
Mitú
Rio Vaupés

Tumaco
P.N. Puracé
Pan de Azúcar 4670
San Agustín
Pitalito
San Vicente del Caguán
Parque Nacional Chiribiquete
Rio Vaupés
Equator

10
Florencia
Rio Apaporis

San Lorenzo
Túquerres
Pasto
Mocoa
Rio Caquetá

Ibarra
Ipiales
Tulcán
Puerto Asís
P.N. La Paya
Rio Putumayo
Parque Nacional Cahuinari
Rio Japurá

Otavalo
Lago Agrio
Tarapoa
Reserva Cuyabeno
Coca
Nuevo Rocafuerte
Parque Nacional Yasuní
Pantoja

Quito
Cotopaxi 5897
35
Baeza
Latacunga
P.N. Llanganates
Puyo
Rio Napo

Ambato
Chimborazo 6310
Riobamba
ECUADOR
P.N. Sangay

PERU
Iquitos
Rio Amazonas
Leticia
P.N. Amacayacu
Tarapacá
Rio Ica
Rio Jutaí

Guayaquil
Machala
Cuenca
Gualaquiza
Intuto
Nauta
Rio Yavarí
Rio Marañón

Loja
P.N. Podocarpus
Zumba
Maynas
Puerto América
Rio Morona
Rio Pastaza
Rio Tigre
Rio Napo

BRAZIL

Isla de San Andrés, Isla de Providencia

violent civil war, the War of the Thousand Days, began in 1899, and cost 130,000 lives but wrought few changes. The government remained in the hands of a white minority that paid scant attention to the mestizos, mulattos, blacks, and natives who formed the bulk of the population.

Meanwhile, the United States took advantage of Colombia's chaos to foment a secessionist movement in Panama, which was then part of Colombia, to build the Panama Canal. Colombia grudgingly accepted the loss in 1921.

The Boston-based United Fruit Company created huge banana plantations along the coast, paying starvation wages to the workers and, in 1928, ending a long-running strike by using the Colombian Army to machine-gun unionists. As the banana boom came to an end, coffee became the new hope for the economy, but the pattern of large plantations repeated itself, and small fluctuations in the world price would devastate whole areas of the countryside.

Unprecedented brutality

In 1948, Jorge Eliécer Gaitán, a popular Liberal politician who had been pushing for real political change, was gunned down in the streets of Bogotá. A spontaneous explosion of frustrations led to the period known as *La Violencia* (The Violence), bringing angry crowds to the streets of the capital; widespread riots ensued (the *Bogotazo*). Civil war followed, with fighting between peasants, police, and soldiers reaching unprecedented levels of brutality. At least 300,000 people lost their lives in the struggle. By 1953, armed peasant groups had begun to develop a clear revolutionary philosophy, forming the Revolutionary Armed Forces (FARC).

Fearful of a Communist advance, the Liberals and Conservatives quickly united, and in 1957 they agreed to share power for the next 16 years, thus ensuring that there would be no real change.

Meanwhile, the various peasant armies in the countryside dragged on their battle with the armed forces, a fight that continues to this day, giving the FARC the extremely dubious title of the oldest guerrilla force in the continent.

Drug economy

The presidency of Virgilio Barco (1986–90) opened the way for full competition in democratic elections but the government now had to battle against a new force – the Medellín drug cartel, headed by Pablo Escobar, that controlled 80 percent of the world traffic in cocaine.

Escobar died in a hail of bullets in 1993, and the rival Cali cartel was put down during the 1990s. However, this fragmented the drug business rather than ending it, as the trade shifted to left-wing guerrillas, right-wing paramilitaries, and Mexican drug lords. Andrés Pastrana won the presidency in 1998, promising economic regeneration and peace. After peace talks with the FARC failed, he introduced the $7.5 billion, military-oriented drug smuggling crackdown,

Colombia's President Juan Manuel Santos delivers a speech during the opening ceremony of the VI Summit of the Americas, 14 April 2012.

Plan Colombia, largely backed by the United States.

In 2002, right-wing lawyer Alvaro Uribe won a landslide victory, vowing to get tough on the FARC. In 2005 reduced jail terms were offered to paramilitaries who turned in their arms. Uribe was re-elected in 2006 following an amendment to the Constitution allowing presidents to serve up to two consecutive four-year terms. His former defense minister Juan Manuel Santos succeeded him in 2010, moving to more moderate policies and improving ties with Ecuador and Venezuela. Since Uribe, improved security has led to growing investment and economic growth. Although safety has improved dramatically, observe caution and seek official advice before visiting what is otherwise a beautiful and fascinating country.

Bogotá, capital and intellectual hub

Shrouded by clouds amid the Andes (and beset by air pollution), the city of **Bogotá** ❶ grew 20-fold in

REGIONAL DIVERSITY

While Bogotá is the cultural center of the country, each region has developed a distinct identity, aided by geographical diversity, that is reflected in almost every strand of life. Colombia is the fourth-largest nation in South America by territory and has the third-largest population in all of Latin America, with about 45 million people. The northern coast is Caribbean, much of the center Andean; the east is split into a plains section – the llanos – and Amazon rainforest, and the west is stretched out along the Pacific coast. Geography and historic difficulties in integrating the vast country via roads and railroads have helped distinct regional cultures to evolve. Along with the backdrop of numerous indigenous cultures, several regional cultures also exist, and can be identified by the people's accents. The *Cachacos* are people from Bogotá and the surrounding areas, including the northeast Andes. *Paisas* live in the coffee-growing center of the country and in Antioquía around Medellín. *Costeños* are the people along the Caribbean, heavily influenced by Afro-Caribbean culture. The *Llaneros*, related to the similar Venezuelan cowboy culture across the border, live in the eastern savannahs. Around Cali live the *Vallunos*, named after the Cauca Valley. These regional cultures have their own distinct festivities, dances, and other traditions, as well as their own dialects of Spanish.

the second half of the 20th century. Layers of history peel away like the rings of an onion: outlying slums give way to towering skyscrapers of polished steel and glass; grand government palaces tower over quaint English mansions. The center is colonial Spanish with flower-covered courtyards and regal monuments of stone and weathered brass.

This Andean city, 2,642 meters (8,670ft) above sea level, is often viewed with incomprehension by people of the Colombian coast, who see its inhabitants as cold and aloof. Reflecting a popular view, writer Gabriel García Márquez once described Bogotá as "a gloomy city where on ghostly nights the coaches of the viceroys still rattled through the cobbled streets."

The image has never worried *Bogotános*, who see themselves as cultured and cosmopolitan. Anything and everything can be found in Bogotá's chaotic avenues: opulent restaurants, homeless children, vendors selling emeralds, peasants in ponchos, endless traffic jams, and walls covered with graffiti. Above all, it is the intellectual hub of Colombia, a place where the Festival Iberoamericano de Teatro, the largest theatrical festival of its kind in South America, is held on even-numbered years. In the streets of Bogotá you will find dozens of theaters, vibrant university life, classic museums, bookshops, and avant-garde art galleries, all joined in a creative tumult.

Orientation

Bogotá's El Dorado airport, west of Downtown, is surrounded by miles and miles of greenhouses that grow some of Colombia's most important exports – flowers.

The best view of the city is from the top of **Cerro de Montserrate**, which can be reached by funicular railway and cable car. On weekends, *Bogotános* stroll to the summit to enjoy the view, join Mass, and pray to the statue of

El Señor Caído (the Fallen Christ). Below, the city is arranged in a grid pattern, with numbered *calles* running east–west and *carreras* running north–south. On the way down, call in at the **Quinta de Bolívar** (Tue–Fri 9am–5pm, Sat–Sun 10am to 4pm), a magnificent colonial mansion with expansive gardens, once the home of "The Liberator" Simón Bolívar, after whom Bolivia is named. It is full of paintings depicting Bolívar's life, as well as many of his personal effects.

To the west of the city are are the nation's botanic gardens, the **Jardín Botánico José Celestino Mutis** (Mon–Fri 8am–5pm, Sat–Sun 9am–5pm). The extensive grounds have an impressive collection of Colombian flora. The garden is named after an 18th-century Spanish botanist who spent most of his life in Colombia.

The city center

In 1538, three conquistadors met at what is now the heart of the old city, the **Plaza de Bolívar**, to found a town in the fertile lands of the native Muisca. The plaza has a statue of Bolívar at its center. To the south, the **Capitolio Nacional**, where Congress sits, looks like a classic Greek temple. Beyond it is the **Casa de Nariño** (President's Residence), sacked in 1948 during the *Bogotazo* uprising.

On the western side of the plaza is the **cathedral**, which was begun in 1565, destroyed by an earthquake two centuries later and only completed after Colombia became independent. Alongside it are the **Capilla del Sagrario** (chapel) and the sumptuous **Teatro Colón**, the city's principal theater, which can only be visited on a guided tour (Tue–Sat on the hour, except during performances).

The colonial quarter

A short stroll from the Plaza de Bolívar takes you to Bogotá's colonial quarter, **La Candelaria**. Single-story whitewashed buildings seem to creep up a hillside, their red tile roofs and decaying cupolas stretching out towards the city center.

Like all of South America's colonial cities, Bogotá has a wealth of religious art. **Iglesia de Santa Clara** (Calle 9/

The majesty of the mountains surrounding Bogotá, Colombia.

Restored colonial houses in the historical center of Bogotá.

A Golden Heritage

Although less well known than the art of the Incas, the mastery of metalworking by Colombia's pre-Hispanic peoples was unsurpassed.

Protected almost like Fort Knox, the **Museo del Oro** (Carrera 6a No. 15–88; tel: 01-343 2222; www.banrepcultural.org/museo-del-oro; Tue–Sat 9am–6pm, Sun 10am–4pm) in the heart of Bogotá is one of the world's finest treasure troves. Run by the Banco de la República, Colombia's central bank, the museum is on the Parque de Santander. The permanent collection is housed on the three top floors of a museum building inaugurated in late 2008. The website offers an online tour. Its collection of bracelets, earrings, masks, statues, and rings runs to more than 36,000 pieces from a dozen pre-Columbian cultures, all revealing a mastery of technique that leaves modern jewelers astounded.

The museum seeks to immerse visitors in the totally different view of gold the early Colombians held, compared with contemporary values and usage. Extracted from the ground, it was worked on through a plethora of methods, and found

Anthropomorphic pendant made by the 'lost wax' process, Tolima Archeological area.

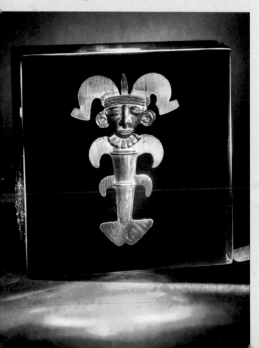

utilitarian and ceremonial use, only to be returned to the ground again as an offering to the gods.

Even before many of its pieces were revealed to be false, the Gold Museum in Lima was a pale collection in comparison to this one. This is largely due to the impatience of the gold-crazed Spanish conquistadors, who were too busy plundering the Inca empire to the south to search deep below the surface of the earth for the occasional piece of jewelry from long-forgotten cultures. Thus the great art of the Incas and other Peruvian cultures, easily robbed by the Spaniards, was melted down into gold bars to be shipped back to the royal coffers, while the jewelry of the Colombian cultures was left to be discovered by the archeologists of later years and also, sadly, by the ever-present *huaqueros* (grave robbers) who have scoured ruins for generations.

The development of metalwork

The metalworking tradition of the Americas developed from the middle of the 2nd millennium BC up to the 16th century. The gold technology of ancient Colombia is remarkable, embracing all the known techniques then available in the New World. Its diversity is extraordinary: each of the 12 cultures described in the museum developed its own style, isolated by the country's wild and inhospitable geography.

Hammering was the most primitive technique for making gold objects, although great skill is required to manage the metal. Sometimes bones or wood were used as forms to give the objects their shape. Some cultures developed smelting, using combinations of alloys to strengthen the gold. Joining techniques were perfected to connect sheets of gold to more complex figures, and it is probable that the technique of lost-wax casting – using molds of wax models which dissolve on contact with the alloy – was first developed in Colombia.

Pre-Columbian people used gold for decoration and religious rites, recognizing the value of a metal that did not tarnish. Clear guidelines were laid down as to who could wear the metal, while in some areas it was also used as an item of trade.

One of the museum's prize possessions is a tiny boat created by the Muisca people, showing the ritual of throwing gold into Lake Guatavita as an offering to the gods, while the chief gilded himself with gold, giving rise to the myth of El Dorado. Other highlights include a golden trumpet from Calima, a platinum-beaked bird of prey emerging from a golden ornament from Tumaco, and earrings and necklaces from Nariño, adjacent to Ecuador.

Carrera 8), built during the 17th century, has a sumptuous interior with works by the most famous of Bogotá's painters at the time, Gregorio Vásquez de Arce y Ceballos. On a less sublime note, history records that the church became notorious for the kidnapping of several novices – on one occasion Vásquez himself was implicated and imprisoned.

The **Museo de Botero** (Calle 11, No. 4–41; Mon–Sat 9am–7pm, Sun 10am–5pm), right next to the **Luís Angel Arango Library**, offers a large collection of the masterpieces of Fernando Botero (the figurative artist born in the city in 1932), as well as works by Monet, Renoir, Dalí, Matisse, and other European artists.

To get a taste of the flourishing emerald business, head for the corner of Avenida Jiménez and Carrera 7. Colombia controls 60 percent of the world's production of these precious gems, and well-fortified shops sell them to travelers with a few thousand dollars to spare. Emeralds are graded by their brilliance, color, and purity, but beware of fakes.

Bogotá's top museum is the **Museo del Oro**. The **Museo Nacional** (Tue–Sat 10am–6pm, Sun 10am–5pm, tel: 381 6470) is housed in the Panóptico building, which was designed as a prison by Englishman Thomas Reed in the early 19th century (following philosopher Jeremy Bentham's original design), and built so that the 200 cells could be observed from a single vantage point. It was used as a prison until 1946, and has been meticulously restored. Each corridor displays a different episode from Colombian history. The lower level is devoted to art.

Cathedral of salt

Traveling from Bogotá along the North Highway through 48km (30 miles) of lush countryside, an excursion can be made to the **cathedral of Zipaquira** (Mon–Fri 9am–4.30pm, Sat–Sun 9am–5pm, Sun mass at 1pm), carved out of salt. The salt mines had been worked for centuries by the local people by the time the Spanish took over. By the 1920s, such a large cavern had been dug that the Banco de la República decided to

'Horse' statue by Fernando Botero, one of the 23 sculptures by the artist in Medellín's streets.

Inside the salt cathedral of Zipaquira.

build a cathedral inside. Cut from a mountainside above the small town of Zipaquira, a tunnel leads into a sulfur-laden darkness. Finally an altar appears silhouetted in the distance: the cathedral is 25 meters (78ft) high and has held more than 10,000 people at one time, but the walls are black, giving the unsettling sensation of walking through space. Despite the color, they are 75 percent pure salt – as can be affirmed by a quick taste – and mining is still going on elsewhere in the mountain.

The other side of Medellín

Four hundred kilometers (250 miles) northwest of Bogotá is **Medellín ❷**, Colombia's second-largest city and the capital of Antioquia province. The city has done its best to shed its infamous image as murder and kidnap capital of the world and the home of the country's main drug cartel. Violence is much less common than it was, but it is still a place where foreign visitors should be careful. More happily, Medellín is sometimes known as the "city of eternal spring"

Hacienda de Guayabal coffee plantation.

due to its pleasant climate. Residents have a reputation for being passionate about most things, including business, food, and enjoyment.

One of the best ways to see the city is on the metro, much of which runs above street level. Medellín is, above all, a modern city, but the red-brick cathedral on **Parque Bolívar** is interesting. There is a permanent exhibition of the work of Colombia's best-known contemporary sculptor and artist, Fernando Botero, in the **Parque San Antonio** (Calle 46/Carrera 46).

Bananas and coffee

For a more relaxed pace, head northwest on the road toward **Turbo** to **Santa Fe de Antioquia ❸**. Set among rolling hills, Santa Fe is a beautifully preserved colonial town. Two-story houses with brightly painted balconies line the streets. From Santa Fe the road continues northward to the port of **Turbo** in the banana-growing region of **Urabá**. Unless you are going to the World Heritage Site of **Parque Nacional Los Katíos**, this dangerous area is best avoided.

South of Medellín lies the main coffee-growing region, the *zona cafetera*. Coffee remains Colombia's biggest export and almost all the hillsides around here are dotted with small coffee farms. **Manizales ❹**, some 270km (168 miles) south of Medellín, is the capital of the coffee-growing zone, a modern city founded in the mid-19th century when Antioquian farmers migrated south in search of new agricultural land. The city suffered several fires and earthquakes in the early 20th century, but its huge cathedral survived. Its streets are built on steep hills, so walking can be tiring. Nearby is the **Parque Nacional Los Nevados**. This is a trekker's paradise, but do take local advice about routes. The park's highest peak is the **Volcán Nevado del Ruíz**, which erupted in 1985, wiping out the town of Armero on the other side of the cordillera.

From Manizales, the road to Bogotá passes through **Honda ❺**, a picturesque colonial town and weekend resort on the Río Magdalena. Directly to the south of Honda lies **Ibagué ❻**, a rapidly expanding, but still pleasant, industrial city.

Salsa city

Going west from Ibagué the main road ascends steeply to cross the central cordillera. The pass can be freezing cold and for much of the year it is shrouded in mist. The Pan-American Highway then heads south and descends into the fertile valley of the Río Cauca where sugar, rice, and cotton are grown, providing important sources of income for **Cali ❼**, Colombia's third-largest city. Cali was founded in 1536 but remained relatively small until the early 20th century when, with the arrival of the railroad and the growth of the sugar industry, the city expanded at an unprecedented rate. Today it is the most important commercial center in southeast Colombia. When the drug cartels of Cali were partly broken up during the mid-1990s, the city declined somewhat, as unemployment and crime soared.

There are several interesting colonial churches here, such as **San Francisco** (Carrera 6/Calle 10) and **La Merced** (Carrera 4/Calle 7), as well as **La**

The city of Cali.

Ermita, built in Gothic style but dating only from the 1930s, the star of numerous postcards of the city. A short walk north from the center is the church of **San Antonio**, built in the mid-18th century on a hill, the **Colina de San Antonio**, with good city views. In the main square, **Parque Caicedo**, tall, arching palm trees can provide shade from the heat and humidity that smothers the city during the day. At night, fanned by cooling winds, the city really comes alive and its numerous dance clubs can be heard from miles away.

For a more relaxing pace, visit one of several haciendas (farm estates) north of the city. One of the most interesting is **El Paraíso**, a beautifully preserved colonial mansion where local writer Jorge Isaacs (1859–95) wrote *María*, a highly regarded work of romantic realism. The house and its garden have been turned into a museum (Tue–Sun 9am–4pm). Nearby is the hacienda of **Piedechinche** with a sugar refinery and sugar museum (Mon–Fri 9am–4pm, Sat–Sun 9am–4.30pm). The haciendas can be visited on a tour with a Cali travel agent, or you can take a bus

to Amaime on the road between Buga and Palmira and walk from there (but don't travel alone).

Traveling northwest from Cali for 120km (75 miles) you reach the Pacific coast port of **Buenaventura** ❽. The town is fairly ramshackle, but some of the country's best salsa musicians were born here, so there is usually something going on at night. From here, launches run up the coast to the fishing villages of **Juanchaco** and **Ladrilleros**, which both have dark sandy beaches.

A few hours south of Cali by road is the city of **Popayán** ❾, founded in 1536. The town prospered in colonial times due to its location on the road between Lima, Quito, and Cartagena. In 1983 its Holy Week processions ground to a halt when a massive earthquake struck the region, reducing most of the city's oldest buildings to rubble. Almost all of them have been painstakingly restored, including the white cathedral on the main square, the **Parque Caldas**. Other churches worth visiting include **La Encarnación** (Calle 5/Carrera 5), **San Agustín** (Calle 7/Carrera 6), and **Santo Domingo**

Holy Week penitents in a procession through Popayán.

(Carrera 5/Calle 4). Popayán's Holy Week processions are famous throughout the Catholic world.

Silvia, a small village in the hills north of Popayán, is home to the culturally distinctive Guambiano, who come to sell their goods at the market on Tuesdays. Just northeast of Popayán, near **San Andrés de Pisimbalá**, is the National Archeological Park of **Tierradentro**. This World Heritage Site is made up of a number of pre-Hispanic stone statues and burial chambers, some of which have motifs and figures carved onto the walls. Little is known about the culture that built the tombs, but the statues are believed to have been carved at a later date, probably around the same time as those further east at San Agustín.

Natural beauty and ancient wonders

From Popayán a poor road goes east to **Parque Nacional Puracé**, an outstandingly beautiful spot with volcanoes, lakes, waterfalls, thermal springs, and wildlife, including bears, condors, and tapirs. The park's altitude, from 2,500 to 4,800 meters (8,200 to 15,750ft), accounts for the natural diversity. There are tourist facilities at **Pilimbalá**, at the northern end of the park.

Southeast of Popayán is **San Agustín** ⑩, a village famous for its ancient stone statues, mysterious remnants of a lost culture, from one of the most important archeological sites in South America. Layers of red-tiled roofs lead past a church tower to the surrounding hills, covered with banana plants. The mountains beyond are a rich green because it rains every day for nine months of the year in a light, erratic drizzle. The village, with its laid-back atmosphere and beautiful surroundings, has long attracted tourists. Transport is mostly by horse: on every corner, cowboys in ponchos and wide-brimmed hats stand beside their trusty steeds.

Baffling figures

The statues of San Agustín have continued to baffle archeologists. Around 500 figures have been found in the surrounding Magdalena Valley: some resemble masked monsters, others

Mysterious statue in the San Agustín Archeological Park.

A SPORTING NATION

Soccer is by far the most popular sport. The most famous teams are América de Cali, Millionarios, and Atlético Nacional, each with at least 10 national championships to their credit. The country has also produced several world-class cyclists including Mauricio Soler, the best mountain cyclist in the 2007 Tour de France. Along the Caribbean coast, baseball is the favorite sport, where four professional teams compete in annual competitions between October and January. Colombia, however, doesn't participate in baseball's Caribbean Series. Colombia has also had several speed skating (on inline roller skates) world champions. Bullfighting, a colonial tradition, is held Saturdays and Sundays during Bogotá's January bullfighting season; Colombian César Rincón is among the best toreros (matadors) in the world.

TIP

Every August a festival of kites takes place in Tunja's main square, and in December there is a festival of lights. The city is worth a trip for its colonial architecture.

eagles, jaguars, or frogs. Nobody knows who carved the statues or for what reason. Even today, investigators can only date the civilization to between the 6th and 12th centuries.

Some of the statues are arranged neatly in archeological parks near the village. Within walking distance are the **Bosque de los Estatuas**, where there are more than 35 figures, and the **Alto de los Idolos**, where the largest statue is 7 meters (23ft) high. Nearby are four *mesitas*, ancient burial sites with mounds, statues, and funeral temples. Most exciting to visit are the statues deeper in the countryside. Many can be reached only on horseback as the paths are difficult and often knee-deep in mud, although the landscape is spectacular. Unfortunately, the area is often dangerous; check for up-to-date security information before attempting to visit.

Cradle of liberty

Cobbled street and whitewashed houses in Barichara.

North from Bogotá the rugged eastern cordillera runs for just under 1,000km (620 miles) to the modern industrial city of **Bucaramanga** ⓫, known for

a local delicacy – the *hormiga culona*, an edible species of ant. Before the Spanish arrived, much of this area was populated by the native Muisca people. There is little evidence left of their culture, but the wild, mountainous landscape is arguably the most dramatic in Colombia.

North of Bogotá, the first major city you encounter is **Tunja** ⓬. The Spanish founded the city in 1539, but there was a settlement here long before that. A monument and bridge commemorate the Battle of Boyacá, the decisive battle in the independence struggle, which was fought just south of the city. For a short time after independence, Tunja was the capital of Nuevo Granada. Simón Bolívar referred to it as his "cradle and workshop of liberty." The capital shifted south when a number of important families moved to Bogotá. A measure of Tunja's importance during colonial times lies in the number of churches that were built – anyone interested in religious art should visit the city. The cathedral contains several paintings by Gregorio Vásquez and Ricardo

Acevedo. Also worth visiting, between calles 19 and 20, are the churches of **Santo Domingo** (Carrera 11), with its ornate wooden interior, and **Santa Clara** (Carrera 7), with a 16th-century convent.

Villa de Leyva

Tunja is a good base from which to explore the beautiful villages and towns scattered around the Boyacá highlands. One of the most popular is **Villa de Leyva** which, with cobbled streets lined with low, whitewashed, tile-roofed houses, has become a national monument. The main focus of the town is the wide central square with a museum (daily 9am–6pm) dedicated to the work of a well-known painter and sculptor, and one-time rector of the Centro de Bellas Artes in Bucaramanga, Luis Alberto Acuña (1904–94).

The town is deeply rooted in national history. Antonio Nariño (1765–1824), an intellectual and statesman who led the call for independence at the end of the 18th century, and briefly served as vice-president of the new republic, under Bolívar, lived and worked at No. 19–58, Carrera 9, where he translated Thomas Jefferson's *Declaration of the Rights of Man.*

There are several other buildings worthy of note, including the **Carmelite monastery** and its church opposite in the Plazuela del Carmen. But what makes this town so special is its unhurried atmosphere, particularly during the week. From Villa de Leyva buses and *colectivos* (communal taxis) leave for nearby towns like **Ráquira**, known for its pottery; and **Chiquinquirá**, where pilgrims from all over Colombia converge to visit a painting of the Virgin by Alonso de Narváez – supposedly Colombia's oldest painting. From Chiquinquirá, the lawless emerald mining towns of **Muzo** and **Coscues** can be reached, although be warned that the journey, on an unpaved road, can be arduous in the rainy season.

Heading for the border

From Tunja a twisting road goes northeast for 460km (286 miles) to the Venezuelan border at unattractive **Cúcuta ⑬**. The scenery along the route is quite spectacular and the road passes through several whitewashed towns such as **Málaga ⑭** before arriving at colonial **Pamplona**, which has one of the oldest universities in South America.

Just east of Málaga, Parque Nacional El Cocuy offers fantastic hiking without the crowds found in other Andean national parks. More than two dozen peaks dot the sky. Mountaineering, including rock and ice climbing, along with horseback riding, are other activities in the unspoiled habitat of the Andean spectacled bear.

The main road from Tunja goes north to **Santander**, a coffee province filled with old colonial towns, the most notable of which are **San Gil**, **Barichara**, and **Socorro**, from where the rebel *comuneros* led the first revolt against the Spanish in 1781. This event is remembered in Socorro's **Casa de Cultura** (daily 8am-noon, 2-5.30pm),

THE SEARCH FOR LAW AND ORDER

Success in fighting terrorism and other crime helped to transform Colombia under Uribe, vastly improving safety in the main cities and drawing in billions of dollars in foreign investment. Foreign businesspeople call Bogotá the best-kept secret for expatriates, as they receive high bonuses for living in a supposedly dangerous area, improving an already high quality of life.

After receiving crushing blows, the FARC, the biggest rebel group, are reeling. However, FARC and other groups like the ELN are still present and active in some no-go areas, which visitors should take care to avoid. Organized crime remains a major problem, as right-wing paramilitaries have only partially been demobilized.

While downtowns of major cities including Cartagena and the salsa capital, Cali, are safe, care should be taken in Bogotá's Candelaria area, where armed robberies have been reported. Also, since mid-2012, San Agustín and the Sierra Nevada de Santa Marta national park including the "Lost City," as well as much of the Pacific Coast, are considered dangerous, due to the presence of armed groups and the risk of kidnap. For the latest information, always check the websites of the US State Department (www.state.gov/) and UK Foreign Office (www.fco.gov.uk/) to be aware of last-minute travel security updates.

housed in an 18th-century mansion on Calle 14 near the neo-Renaissance cathedral.

The Caribbean coast

Arriving on Colombia's Caribbean coast from Bogotá seems like stepping into a completely different world. It is as if they are two totally separate countries: one cool and remote, the other tropical and sensual.

A gateway to the coast and to many of the attractions of the north is **Santa Marta** ⓑ, capital of Magdalena province. One of the most pleasant cities in Colombia, it was founded by the Spaniards in 1525, but there are few colonial relics in the popular modern resort town. Visitors come here to loll in the sun along **El Rodadero beach**, considered one of the best in Colombia; to stroll up and down the tourist promenade while being bombarded with salsa; or simply to sit in a pavement bar and enjoy the view across the bay to the rocky island of **El Morro**.

Santa Marta is a good jumping-off point for **Parque Nacional Tairona**, with its string of pristine and often deserted white-sand beaches. This stretch of jungle, once the territory of the native Tairona population, is at the foot of the **Sierra Nevada de Santa Marta**, a pyramid-shaped mountain that drops into the Caribbean Sea. Farther east is the **Santuario de Flora y Fauna Los Flamencos**, a nature reserve which, as the name suggests, is full of pink flamingos.

The Lost City of the Tairona

Santa Marta is also the place from which to reach **La Ciudad Perdida**, the Lost City of the Tairona, that was only "found" in 1975. Larger than Machu Picchu in Peru, the discovery is considered one of the most important of the 20th century in South America, confirming that the Tairona were not just accomplished craftsmen but built one of the largest cities on the subcontinent, with wide boulevards and road links. The city was discovered by *huaqueros* (grave robbers) in the tropical jungle of the Sierra Nevada. Calling it *El Infierno Verde* (Green Hell), they fought over the finds until the government intervened. In the absence of any written records, archeologists can only guess when the city was built – probably during the 13th century – or what disaster led the inhabitants to disappear without trace. Today this legendary city can only be reached by a six-day round-trip trek. Check the security situation before attempting the visit.

García Márquez country

The first image many foreigners have of South America comes from the Caribbean coast of Colombia, thanks to the works of author Gabriel García Márquez. His writings have preserved the life and history of the region, and today the small town of **Aracataca** where he was born and raised – and which he fictionalized as Macondo in his 1967 novel *One Hundred Years of Solitude* – can be visited for a glimpse of coastal life. Aracataca has a plaza with a statue of Bolívar, an old

Beach in Parque Nacional Tairona.

church tower, several shabby billiard halls, and a couple of empty restaurants. Tucked away in a back street is a modest building with the sign "GGM Museum." In a garden full of chickens is the house where Márquez was born in 1928 – wooden, whitewashed, and without a stick of furniture.

A few hours southeast of Aracataca is the city of **Valledupar** . It was founded in the mid-16th century, but there is very little evidence of its colonial past apart from the shady main square, where people sit around a giant mango tree to shelter from the searing midday heat. Every year this space becomes the focus of the country's attention during the festival of the Legend of the Vallenato. For five days at the end of April Colombia's top accordion players battle it out in Valledupar to be crowned King of the Vallenato, a popular style of music that originated here. The festivities are fueled by rum and large quantities of *aguardiente* (fire water).

Cartagena, Spain's New World fortress

Placed on the tropical Caribbean coast, saturated by heat, music, and feverish dreams, the fortress city of **Cartagena de Indias** is a living museum. It is recognized internationally as a World Heritage Site. Just walking its streets recalls the early days of bloodthirsty pirates, galleons full of bullion, and swordfights beneath the palm trees. Founded in 1533 by the first of Spain's scurvy-ridden conquistadors, the town quickly blossomed to become the main colonial port on the Caribbean, and the gateway to the whole South American empire. But as the wealth plundered from the local populations piled up in galleons to be taken back to Cádiz, the city became the target of every pirate and desperado cruising the Caribbean seas.

During the 16th century, Cartagena was besieged five times by buccaneers and cutthroats. The Spanish decided to create fortifications so powerful

that the port would be impregnable. Stone ramparts and battlements were constructed over many decades, the like of which had never been seen in the Americas. The pirate attacks continued, but never with quite the same success – Cartagena was even able to survive several sieges by the English and the French.

Exploring old Cartagena

A highway leading from the airport passes along Marbella beach toward **Las Murallas**, the stone ramparts that still surround the old city. Many small forts, where cannons and other defensive weapons, placed to ward off sea attacks, remain intact. The colonial section of Cartagena is only a small part of the metropolis, but it contains enough places of interest to warrant several days' exploration.

Facing the **Plaza de Bolívar** is the **Palacio de la Inquisición**, one of Cartagena's finest buildings. Its museum recalls the fearful proceedings of the Holy Inquisition, for which a seat was established here in 1610. Twelve people, accused of

An old road running through El Pueblito, Tairona National Park.

Cartagena town center comes alive in the cool of the evening.

heresy, suffered a public auto-da-fé (burning to death) in the plaza. When Cartagena declared its independence, this palace was one of the first places that the angry crowd came to sack.

Adjoining the Plaza de Bolívar is the fort-like cathedral. Three blocks south is the **Plaza de la Aduana**, once used as a parade ground for troops, and now based around a statue of Christopher Columbus (Cristobal Colón in Spanish). Call in at the **Museo de Arte Moderno** (Mon–Fri 9am–12pm, 3–7pm Sat 10am–1pm Sun 10am–1pm 3–5pm) in the former Royal Customs House, then take a stroll under the **Puerta del Reloj** (Gate of the Clock), which once linked the inner walled town to the poorer Getsemaní district by a drawbridge over a moat.

Following the city wall closely around to the south, you will come to the **Iglesia y Convento de San Pedro Claver**, a church and convent named after a Spanish monk who spent his whole life looking after African slaves. Nicknamed the "Slave of the Slaves," St Peter Claver (1580–1654) was the first

Hauling baskets down a Cartagena street.

person to be canonized in the New World. Today the monastery is a haven of solitude and peace, with arched stone patios built around a garden of flowers and foundations.

There are dozens of other colonial houses, churches, and monuments worth visiting in Cartagena. Drop in at the colonial **Casa de la Candelaria** – once a noble's mansion, now a restaurant but also open to non-diners if you just want to have a look around – then stroll around the city walls to **Las Bóvedas**, built two centuries ago as dungeons, with walls 15 meters (50ft) thick. Today they are home to tourist shops and bars.

Barriers of stone

To keep their stolen gold extra secure, the Spanish built even more extraordinary fortifications in key points. Looming over the city from the San Lorenzo Hill is the impregnable **Castillo de San Felipe de Barajas**, a complicated system of batteries, tunnels, and hiding places engineered from massive chunks of stone. The tunnels, which can be visited, were

constructed so that any sound would echo and warn guards of approaching soldiers. If you don't want to go in the tunnels, enjoy the view over the old city from the castle – it is one of the best in Cartagena.

At the entrance to Cartagena Bay is the **Fuerte de San Fernando**, a fort that can only be visited by water. A huge chain was hung between it and another outpost across the bay to prevent surprise attacks. Many films have been shot in its well-preserved interior. On top of a large hill behind the city is the **Convento de la Popa**. The Augustinians built a wooden chapel at the summit in 1607, which was soon replaced by a monastery with an image of the patron of Cartagena, La Virgen de la Candelaria.

Near the Puerta del Reloj is the city's dock area, **El Muelle de los Pegasos**, where you can sit at a juice stall and watch the port life go by. El Muelle is the departure point for tourist boats to the idyllic **Islas del Rosario** ⓲, just 45 minutes away. For a cheap seafood dinner, stroll up **Avenida Venezuela** and call in at one of the *ostrerias*, small booths selling delicious shrimp and oyster cocktails. For more sophisticated nightlife, head for **Bocagrande**, a resort suburb several minutes out of town by taxi, or go to the Old Town and Calle Arsenal.

Around Cartagena

Northeast along the coast is the large port city of **Barranquilla** ⓳, famous for its magnificent *carnaval* held in February. **Mompóx** ⓴, 240km (150 miles) south of Cartagena on an island in the Río Magdalena, is a Unesco World Heritage Site. In the 18th century the Río Magdalena changed course, isolating Mompóx, which had flourished in the Spanish era, as the river provided the most important line of communication between the interior and the north coast. The town has some of the finest colonial architecture in Colombia. Of particular note is the yellow church of **Santa Bárbara**, with its distinctive Moorish octagonal tower. The **Casa de Cultura** (Mon–Sat 7.30am–5pm) stands beside the church of **San Agustín**, where crowds gather during the town's Easter processions.

TIP

Closer to Nicaragua than the South American mainland, San Andrés and Providencía islands are picturesque and popular Caribbean beach resort destinations – expensive by South American standards, with diving and snorkeling along with typical beach sports among their attractions. Providencía, slightly smaller than San Andrés, is less crowded and more hilly, with fine views for hikers.

San Felipe fort in Cartagena.

Watching the fishermen.

View of Los Roques town.

VENEZUELA

This young, vibrant, and varied country, at once Caribbean, Andean, and Amazonian, has fabulous natural treasures for beachcombers and adventurers.

Venezuela, led by its polarizing president, Hugo Chávez, has gained a reputation as a thorn in the side of the United States. Chávez's anti-globalization stance, his romantically socialist vision for Latin America, and his ability to spend his oil revenue freely, have made headlines around the world. However, it would be a shame if the country only gained international attention for its politics. With its diverse geography, ranging from the snow-capped Andes to vast plains with sprawling cattle ranches, from quaint villages to modern metropolitan areas with non-stop nightlife, it offers a huge variety of destinations and experiences. Venezuela has immense natural beauty, with virgin tropical rainforests inhabited by indigenous tribes, the Guayana region straddling ancient rock formations from which gush the world's highest waterfalls, and more Caribbean coastline than any other nation.

Boom and bust

Venezuela is one of the largest oil-producing countries in the world, and petroleum has been a key element in its recent history. During six decades of boom, beginning in the 1920s, money flowed freely. With the seemingly bottomless pot of "black gold," agriculture was virtually abandoned

as people left farms to get a piece of the pie in the principal cities. National industry atrophied as imports soared, and no one took note of corruption or neglect of the country's basic structure. But oil prices began to tumble in the early 1980s and, with the infamous "Black Friday," February 18, 1983, hard reality hit. The value of the national currency was slashed and exchange controls were imposed. The party was over, with the good times only returning in the early 2000s, albeit to a country radically changed.

Main Attractions
Art and history in Caracas
Choroní and Parque Nacional Henri Pittier
Mérida and the Venezuelan Andes
Wildlife tours in the Llanos
Parque Nacional Los Roques
Margarita Island
Angel Falls and Parque Nacional Canaima

In Carupano, fishermen from a community dedicated to artisan fishing prepare their nets and boats.

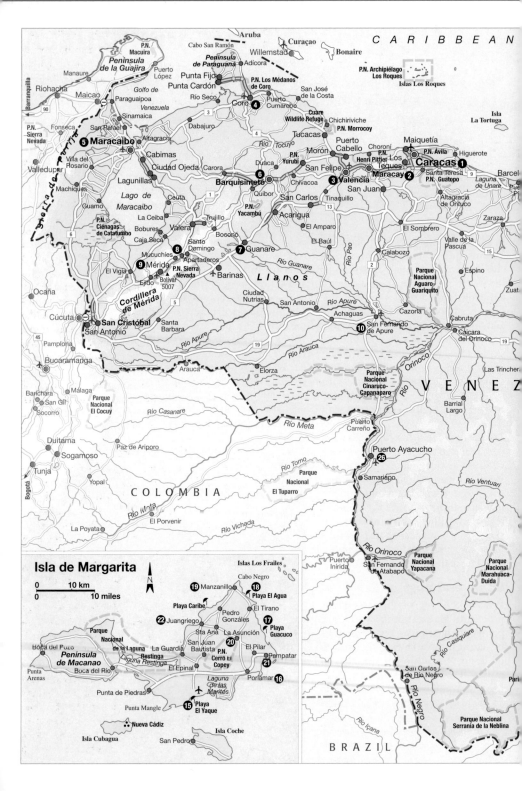

Venezuela

0 50 km
0 50 miles

The real crisis was not felt until Carlos Andrés Pérez returned for a second presidential term in 1989, riding on the popularity from his first time in office in 1974–9. His tough economic measures led to two bloody military coup attempts that year. Pérez survived, but on May 20, 1993, he was indicted on charges of corruption and was convicted in 1996.

Rafael Caldera, president from 1969 to 1974, was re-elected in 1994. Faced with mounting foreign debt, the failure of 17 financial institutions representing nearly half the total of the nation's deposits, massive capital flight, and the public's lack of confidence, the value of the bolívar was slashed and exchange controls imposed from June 1994 to April 1996. The devaluation of the currency hit Venezuelans hard.

Talk rather than action followed promised spending cuts, and the country's public debt increased. Plummeting real earnings and high unemployment have since placed the majority of Venezuelans below the poverty line. Robberies directed against the "haves" have turned them into prisoners of their privilege, living behind guarded doors. Meanwhile, violence among the poor in the barrios of Caracas is rife.

Sweeping changes

In 1998, Colonel Hugo Chávez won the presidential election and overhauled Venezuela's political system, winning a referendum that led to the establishment of a new constitution in 1999. He was re-elected in July 2000 with 60 percent of the seats in a new unicameral parliament, amid claims of vote rigging. Enormous windfalls from the quadrupling in price of Venezuela's oil went to massive increases in both military and social spending, much of it in off-budget "missions" funded by the state oil company PdVSA, Latin America's biggest company, whose management he replaced. Among many of the poor, the benefits from better health services and higher subsidies have won Chávez massive loyalties. The traditional elite has become entrenched and has found little to offer in the decade since Chávez took power, while Chávez on several occasions was able to rule by decree.

Government has not been easy for Chávez. The death of 19 demonstrators in Caracas on April 11, 2002, led to a failed coup attempt by the opposition. His moves against private media, particularly television, sparked student protests, above all when popular RCTV's operating license wasn't extended in May 2007. Extending term limits on his rule, he has battled cancer intermittently, and won a fourth term in office in October 2012. Internationally, he has been at the forefront of OPEC's pricing policies, has created the Venezuela-led ALBA trade block in South and Central America, and has been a vociferous critic of the US and Colombia, which, however, are still by far his country's biggest trading partners.

Caracas: capital of contrasts

The first view of the country for most visitors is El Litoral – the central coast location of Simón Bolívar International Airport. This area was struck by disaster in 1999, when torrential rain turned gentle mountain streams into swollen rivers surging down ravines, picking up ancient trees, giant boulders, and tons of earth as they rushed to the sea. The idyllic landscape was all but ruined. **Caracas** ❶, Venezuela's capital, is 43km (27 miles) away across the coastal mountain range. **Macuto** and **Caraballeda**, some 40 minutes to the east, were obliterated, although both are now recovering.

The mountains of **Waraira Repano** (previously known as Parque Nacional El Avila) form a dramatic backdrop for Caracas, called home by some 5 million inhabitants. The hillsides surrounding the airport road and slopes ringing the metropolis are blanketed with haphazardly constructed *ranchos* (shanty towns), inhabited largely by illegal immigrants and poor rural people who have come to seek their fortune. The central valley and upscale residential areas of the east and south show a modern, dynamic, and affluent side. Miles of trails take hikers through the park, while one can also take a cable car to one of Avila's peaks.

Dominated by sleek but decaying skyscrapers, El Centro is the traditional

View of Caracas backed by Avila mountain.

heart of the city and **Plaza Bolívar** is the core of its historic zone. Its treasures include the 19th-century **Capitolio**, the 17th-century **Catedral** and adjacent **Museo Sacro** (Mon–Sat 10am–5pm). **Casa Natal** was the birthplace of South America's liberator, Simón Bolívar. Next door, there are military memorabilia in the **Museo Bolivariano** (both Mon–Fri 10am–5pm, Sat–Sun 9am–4pm). The **Concejo Municipal** was the site of Venezuela's call for independence. Visit the **Museo de Caracas** (Mon–Fri 10.30am–noon, 2.30–4.30pm) which has a display of miniatures created by Raúl Santana depicting every aspect of life at the end of the 19th century, along with paintings by the Impressionist Emilio Boggio.

Casa Amarilla, formerly a jail and presidential residence, now houses the Foreign Ministry. Facing the northwest corner of the plaza is the **Gobernación**, seat of government of the Distrito Federal. The **Iglesia de San Francisco**, dating from 1575, has walls lined with gorgeous gilded altars and is connected to the **Palacio de las Letras**, the academies of history, language, and science. Several blocks north of the cathedral is the striking pink and gray **Panteón Nacional** (Tue–Sun 9am–noon, 1.30–4.30pm), resting place for more than 130 of the nation's greatest heroes. A newly-built abstract-curved mausoleum for Simón Bolívar at its rear is due to open early in 2013.

The excellent colonial art museum, **Quinta de Anauco** (Tue–Fri 9–11.30am, 2–4.30pm, Sat–Sun 10am–4pm), in San Bernardino, is well worth a visit. Surrounded by lush gardens, this elegant building has been restored with outstanding art and furnishings. **La Candelaria**, east of the Centro, is a Spanish immigrant sector, with many traditional restaurants and *tascas*, bars serving tapas. Shoppers here can delight in the nine-story gold center, **La Francia**, facing Plaza Bolívar, and small shops selling shoes, clothing, and jewelry stretching east from the plaza to the **La Hoyada** metro station.

A few minutes east from the Centro is **Parque Central**. This massive urban renewal project has 53-story twin towers, seven 44-story apartments, and the outstanding **Museo de Arte Contemporáneo de Caracas Sofía Imber**, with a sculpture garden and restaurant. Visitors can go up to the 52nd floor of the East Tower for 360-degree views of the city. There is also a fabulous hands-on museum for children, the **Museo de los Niños**, and the **Museo del Teclado**, a keyboard museum which has weekly concerts. Nearby is the spectacular **Teatro Teresa Carreño** and the **Teatro Rajatabla**, home of a popular alternative theatre group. Other attractions are three great museums (all Tue–Sun): the **Museo de Ciencias Naturales**; the **Museo de Bellas Artes**, with international contemporary art; and the **Galería de Arte Nacional**, showing works by Venezuelan artists. Behind them is the sprawling **Los Caobos Park** and in the background the **Ibrahim bin Abdulazis al Ibrahim Mosque**, the largest mosque in South America.

Enjoying a game of chess in the open air, Caracas.

TIP

Caracas residents are known as caraqueños. The city's name comes from the eponymous tribe that lived just to its north.

Modern east Caracas

Traffic and parking are perennial headaches in Caracas but the cheap subway system, the Metro de Caracas, is the fastest means of getting around. Although a slower option, there is also a non-stop flow of dirt-cheap buses that go everywhere. Decrepit taxis are numerous, but none have meters and few drivers speak English.

Continue on the metro to **Plaza Venezuela**, then walk east to **Chacaíto** along the kilometer-plus *gran avenida* of **Sábana Grande**. This wide pedestrian boulevard is lined with shops, cafés, street vendors, and chess tables, where office workers often spend their lunch hour. It is fun by day, but at night hookers and transvestites take over and the adjacent hotels are primarily rented by the hour.

Middle- and upper-class residential areas include Chacao and Chuao further east, feeding Venezuela's consumption habit with shopping malls including **Centro Ciudad Comercial Tamanaco** (**CCCT**), Sambil, and San Ignacio, the most elegant shopping district. Plaza Altamira is the heart of

Chacao, with numerous nearby restaurants. Las Mercedes also has a large concentration of upscale restaurants.

A little farther east, exit the metro at **Parque de Miranda** to explore the 80-hectare (200-acre) park designed by Brazilian landscape architect Roberto Burle Marx, with a planetarium, a small zoo with a monkey island and large jaguar pen, and an artificial lake. The **Museo de Transporte** (Sun 9am–5pm) facing its east side is connected by a walkway over the busy freeway.

Among the city's other parks, two blocks south of **Plaza Venezuela**, with a giant central fountain, is the **Jardín Botánico** (daily), which has extensive gardens, an arboretum of some 100,000 trees, and sculptures by national artists. Or take the No. 2 spur of the metro from Capitolio west to the **Zoológico** stop to visit the 486-hectare (1,200-acre) "no cages" **Parque Zoológico Caricuao** (Tue–Sun 9am–4.30pm).

West of Caracas

Colonia Tovar, about an hour away by car, is a village high in the mountains

Fishing for sardines off the Isla de Margarita shore.

THE APPEAL OF BASEBALL

Unlike most of the rest of South America, where soccer (football) is by far the favorite sport, Venezuela's most popular game is baseball, which was introduced from the United States in the 1890s and went professional in the mid-1940s. The Caracas Leones (Lions) are the most popular team in the eight-team Liga Venezolana de Béisbol Profesional, and are proud of having had 16 championship titles. Their biggest rivals in domestic baseball are the Navegantes del Magallanes – and rivalry can be quite fierce.

Venezuela has exported players to some of the major leagues in the US and elsewhere. So far, President Chávez has denied all rumors that the government would like to take over the most popular teams.

that was founded in 1843 by Germans from the Black Forest, who transplanted their architecture, language, cultural practices, farming traditions, and cuisine. On weekends, *caraqueños* jam the narrow streets lined with produce and crafts stands. There are numerous cozy hotels and a yearly international chamber music festival in March or April. **Maracay ❷**, 90 minutes west of Caracas via freeway, is the entry point for **Parque Nacional Henri Pittier**, Venezuela's oldest protected environmental zone (since 1937), renowned among birdwatchers for more than 550 species seen here, and by non-birders for its winding scenic routes surrounded by bamboo groves, cloud forests, and mammoth vine-draped trees.

Entry via **El Limón** leads to the beautiful palm-lined arc of **Bahía de Cata**. A short distance before the park is **Ocumare de la Costa**, with various lodging options. Continuing past **Cata**, the beach of **Cuyagua** is a favorite for surfers. Follow the route via Las Delicias to reach the picturesque colonial village of **Choroní** and the coast at the fishing village of **Puerto Colombia**, with many *posadas* (guest houses), a few kilometers on. The broad, palm-shaded swimming beach is about 1km (0.5 miles) to the east. Local fishermen offer boat transfers to the popular beaches of **Chuao** and **Cepe** from Puerto Colombia. Some of the world's finest cocoa is grown there.

From **Valencia ❸**, Venezuela's manufacturing capital, take the road north for a 20-minute mountain drive to the coast, passing the hot springs of **Centro Termas Las Trincheras**. From there, turning east will take you to **Puerto Cabello**, one of Venezuela's most important ports. Here, a beautiful waterfront colonial zone faces **Castillo Libertador**, an impressive fort built in 1732. **Fortín Solano**, the last colonial fortification erected in Venezuela, completed in 1770, stands proudly on a hill in the background.

Turning west at the coast brings you in 40 minutes to **Tucacas**, the first entrance to **Parque Nacional Morrocoy**. Alternatively, continue to another entrance via **Chichiriviche**, with the bonus of a drive through **Cuare Wildlife Refuge** where the flashiest inhabitants are scarlet ibis and a flock of some 20,000 flamingos. The park is also popular for its white-sand, palm-fringed islands and keys, although littering is a problem. Boat shuttles are available from Tucacas and Chichiriviche.

The westbound coastal highway traverses desert plains to **Coro ❹**, declared a World Heritage City by Unesco for its concentration of outstanding colonial structures, including an exceptional **Diocesan Museum**. A side trip north to the windswept **Paraguaná Peninsula** takes you past the towering sand dunes of **Parque Nacional Los Médanos de Coro** to **Adícora**, a windsurfer's paradise, but again, the beach is littered. Fans of colonial architecture can admire houses that demonstrate the Dutch influence of the nearby islands of **Curaçao** and **Aruba**.

Performers from the dance troupe Venezuela Tierra de Encanto, Caracas.

A residential district of Caracas.

WHERE

For a fast route to Táchira, take Highway 6 along the west side of Lake Maracaibo, following signs out of town indicating Machiques.

Source of the black gold

Arriving at the country's westernmost state, Zulia, one encounters **Lago de Maracaibo** (Lake Maracaibo), an almost enclosed ocean bay containing enormous oil reserves and some 40 percent of the country's gas reserves. Cross the **Rafael Urdaneta Bridge**, the longest pre-stressed concrete span in the world at the time of its construction, to reach the sweltering state capital, **Maracaibo ❺**, Venezuela's second-largest city. Maracaibo is the center for the nation's oil industry, and is also populated by thousands of native Guajiro and Paraujano people, the women proudly wearing traditional long flowing dresses.

Near the seven-block-long **Paseo Ciencias** park stands the colonial **cathedral** and the **Casa de Capitulación**. The **Basílica de Nuestra Señora de la Chiquinquirá** honors Zulia's beloved patron saint, nicknamed "La Chinita." **Calle Carabobo** (or Calle 94) is a street of colorful "Maracaibo-style" houses, now mainly shops and restaurants, and a huge municipal market restored

Construction in progress, Caracas.

and converted into the **Centro de Arte de Maracaibo Lia Bermúdez** (Tue–Sun 9.30am–6pm). In the Santa **Contemporáneo del Zulia** (MACZUL; Tue–Fri 9am–4.30pm, Sat–Sun 10am–5pm), the second-largest contemporary art museum in Latin America.

A cheap shuttle boat runs from El Moján to the colonial fort and the extensive beach of **Isla San Carlos**. From nearby **Laguna de Sinamaica**, boat excursions visit communities of Paraujano people who live in houses built on stilts in the lagoon.

Where the Andes begin

The Andean states of **Táchira** and in particular **Mérida** and **Trujillo** are among the most picturesque in the country. Although accessible by air, this area should be visited by car to appreciate the stunning landscapes of glacier-fed lakes bordered by colorful flowers. There are quaint villages with traditional architecture, and wayside restaurants where you can savor trout or smoked cheese on a wheat or corn-flour *arepa* washed down with warm, spiked *ponche andino* or *calentado*.

Take the Trans-Andean Highway from the coast through **Barquisimeto ❻**, with side trips to the weavers' colony in **Tintorero** and to **Quibor**, known for its ceramics and ancient indigenous heritage, and you will enter the area from **Guanare ❼**, in the heart of the central farmlands. Here, you can visit the impressive **Templo Votivo Nacional de la Virgen de Coromoto**, inaugurated in 1996 by Pope John Paul II and dedicated to Venezuela's patron saint.

Alternatively, go via **Boconó**, driving through coffee plantations, or approach from **Barinas** via **Santo Domingo**. Because of their isolation (roads here were not surfaced until the mid-1950s), the church became the center of social as well as religious life for the *andinos*, and this is still evident.

Paso El Águila crowns the highest paved road in the country at 4,007 meters (13,146ft). The surrounding *páramo* (high moorland) is dominated by the tall, otherworldly *frailejón*, with fuzzy silver-green leaves and bright yellow flowers (at their best in October). Near **Apartaderos 8** is the **Observatorio Astronómico Nacional de Llano del Hato**, with four giant telescopes and public viewing.

East of the highway from **Santo Domingo** lies the **Parque Nacional Sierra Nevada**. Principal entrances to its many hiking trails are at **Laguna Mucubají**, the largest of Mérida's 200 glacial lakes (most of them full of trout) and at **Mucuy Alto**.

A rather touristy but nonetheless interesting stop, about 20 minutes north of Mérida city, is **Los Aleros**, a reproduction of an entire Andean village as it would have looked before the highway came through. Along with traditional construction and period artifacts, participants carry out daily chores, and music of the era and even a wedding ceremony are performed daily. The park's creator Alexi Montilla followed up with the all-encompassing **Alexi's Venezuela**

de Antier, between Mérida and the restored colonial village of **Jají**.

From Mérida to the plains

Views of Venezuela's snow capped peaks, the highest of which is Bolívar, at 5,007 meters (16,427ft), can be enjoyed in the year-round spring-like weather of the city of **Mérida 9**. The *posadas* around **Plaza Las Heroínas** (by the cable-car station) are the gathering places for those in search of mountain activities such as trekking, climbing, and paragliding. There are equipment rental, guides, and *toyoteros* – drivers of four-wheel-drive vehicles who take visitors to the remote mountain villages of Los Pueblos del Sur, or to entry points for excursions.

The massive **Catedral Metropolitana** dominates **Plaza Bolívar**. Mérida has the world's highest and longest cable car, along with 43 parks and plazas, including the **Parque Zoológico Chorros de Milla**, with a mini zoo and pretty gardens; and **El Acuario**, which has an aquarium and vignettes with life-size figures showing life in the Andes of the past. Mérida has

Lush vegetation in Parque Nacional Henri Pittier.

Multicolored house window in Maracaibo.

An example of colonial architecture in Ciudad Bolívar.

several art museums, led by the Museo de Arte Colonial (Tue–Fri 9am–4pm, Sat–Sun 10am–5pm) and the **Museo de Arte Moderno** (Mon–Fri 8am–4pm, Sat–Sun 8am–1pm). More interesting for children will be the **Museo de Ciencia y Tecnología** (daily 10am–6.30pm), with dinosaur replicas.

No state more fully epitomizes the unique character of Venezuela's vast *llanos* (central plains) than **Apure**. Huge *hatos* (cattle ranches) covering thousands of hectares, the *llaneros* who work them, *moriche* palms, the traditional *joropo* music and dance, and an incredible abundance of wildlife are its trademarks. Some *hatos* can be reached by road, via the state capital of **San Fernando de Apure** ❿ from the east, or via **Ciudad Nutrias** from the west; others are accessible only by private plane, boat, or four-wheel-drive. Numerous tours are available from Mérida or bookable overseas.

The Eastern Gold Coast

The marine paradise of **Parque Nacional Los Roques Archipelago** is only 35 minutes by air from Caracas, although both day trips and overnight stays are expensive. Along with excellent diving and beautiful (but shadeless) beaches, Los Roques offers unparalleled game fishing. From Caracas you can reach the "Route of the Sun," between Puerto La Cruz and Cumaná, on the eastern coastal highway (avoiding public holidays, when traffic comes to a standstill for hours). While most people head directly to Barcelona and Puerto La Cruz, there are other great beaches en route, including the outer banks of the **Laguna de Unare** (enter via Boca de Uchire) and **Puerto Píritu**.

Barcelona, Anzoátegui state's capital, has a well-preserved historic zone with such attractions as the **Museo de Tradiciones**, along narrow streets bordered by vintage architecture. At the other extreme, beaches along a narrow neck of land lead to the mammoth **El Morro Tourist Complex**. Some 12km (7.5 miles) east along the coast lies **Puerto La Cruz** ⓫. Action never stops along its beachfront boulevard, **Paseo Colón** (but leave swimming until you get to island beaches, since the water here is contaminated). **Pozuelos Bay**, dotted with luxury yachts and traditional fishing boats, and the dramatic rocky islands of **Parque Nacional Mochima**, form the seaward backdrop for the boulevard. A shuttle service is offered by a boatmen's union from the eastern end of the beach to the island beaches, with the best snorkeling and diving spots.

Continuing eastward along the coastal highway, you can stop off at beaches like **Playa Colorada** and **Arapito** on the way to **Cumaná** ⓬, Venezuela's oldest continental city (founded in 1521). A ferry crosses from Cumaná to the **Araya peninsula** ⓭, landing near ruins of a colonial fort and pretty beach. Further east still, you could spend a day relaxing on the fabulous beach of **Playa Medina** near the attractive town of Río Caribe.

To the south, near **Caripe** , is the **Cueva del Guácharo** (officially Monumento Natural Alejandro Humboldt), the country's largest cave, named for the thousands of *guácharos* (night-flying oil birds) that call it home.

Isla de Margarita and the Pearl Islands

Isla de Margarita, less than an hour by air from Maiquetía or 2–4 hours by ferry from Puerto La Cruz, is the main attraction of the three-island Pearl group that constitutes Nueva Esparta state. Water temperature varies from 23°C to 30°C (73°F to 86°F) around the numerous white sand beaches. Activities include water sports, fishing, and horseback riding. The island is a real windsurfing hotspot – **El Yaque Beach** is considered one of the world's top beaches for the sport. With numerous historical sites, a rich tradition of crafts, shopping (the island has more than 2,000 duty-free shops), lodging ranging from intimate *posadas* to luxury resorts, a multitude of restaurants, and lively nightlife, it is

little wonder that Isla de Margarita has become a prime tourist destination.

Spanish settlement of the **Pearl Islands** in 1500 was the first in South America. The colonizers were attracted by the discovery of the first pearls found in the New World in the rich oyster beds surrounding the island of **Cubagua**. However, greed leading to over-harvesting, a devastating storm leveling the stone buildings, and pirates who took whatever the storm had not destroyed, brought an end to the settlement barely four decades later. Pearl fishing continued, but is now permitted only in season (January to April) every other year.

Ruins of the site (along with pristine beaches) on this nearly uninhabited island can be visited on day tours from **Porlamar**, Margarita's largest city. Most of the island's hotels and shops, plus numerous restaurants, nightclubs, and casinos are concentrated in downtown Porlamar. The city also has a ferry service to **Coche Island**, which is just beginning to develop its great tourism potential, with excellent windsurfing and several small resort hotels.

TIP

The dry season (from mid-November to the end of April) is the time to visit Los Llanos, when wildlife is concentrated around shrinking watering holes – the rest of the year, rain is incessant and many places are inundated (or closed), with fauna widely dispersed.

'Nodding donkey' pumpjacks at a Lake Maracaibo oil installation.

The majority of accommodations on Margarita are near the most popular beaches. North of Porlamar, **Playa Guacuco** has some tourist facilities. Farther up the coast, **Playa El Agua** ⑱ is the most popular (a beautiful beach, but with a treacherous undertow). The beaches continue to **Manzanillo** ⑲, near the islands's most northerly point, and down to the west.

The capital city, inland **La Asunción** ⑳, is smaller and more peaceful than Porlamar. Sights in this historical town include the 16th-century colonial cathedral (one of the oldest churches in Venezuela); the **Museo de Nueva Cádiz** (Tue–Fri 9am–4pm), which depicts the history of the town of the same name, destroyed by an earthquake in 1541; and the colonial **Castillo de Santa Rosa** fort (daily 9am–6pm). Some 10km (6 miles) northeast, **Pampatar** ㉑ also has some interesting colonial buildings including a pretty church and fortress.

The town of **Juangriego** ㉒, famed for its sunsets, offers a tranquil beach and nearby communities known for handicrafts. Pottery is made at **La Vecinidad** and **El Cercado**; basketry is the craft at **Pedro González**; hammocks can be purchased at **Tacarigua**; and straw hats at **San Juan**. Within the town of **Tacuantar** is the Taller de Arte Así con las Manos – Tierra, Agua y Fuego artisan village. Contrasting with the bustling eastern half is the island's rugged and scarcely populated **Macanao Peninsula** to the west. **Parque Nacional Laguna La Restinga** lies along the narrow link between the two sections. Boatmen can take you through channels among mangrove swamps en route to the spectacular beach along the outer banks of the lagoon.

The Guayana region: the last frontier

Venezuela's vast southeastern sector (covering Delta Amacuro, Bolívar, and Amazonas states) is known as the Guayana region, named for the Guayana Shield, composed of pre-Cambrian rock, among the oldest on the continent at 1.2 to 2.5 billion years. The unique features in Bolívar

Domes housing the mighty telescopes of the Llano del Hato astronomical observatory.

and Amazonas are *tepuyes*, towering mesas of ancient rock. The most famous are **Roraima – t**he highest in the Guyana region – subject of Sir Arthur Conan Doyle's *Lost World*, and **Auyantepui**, from which Angel Falls drops.

Except for a few roads near the state capitals of **Delta Amacuro** (Tucupita) and **Puerto Ayacucho** (Amazonas), travel is by boat or by air. Difficult access has been the greatest factor in maintaining the mystery, natural state, and allure of the region. The tourism potential in the huge delta of the **Orinoco River**, making up most of Delta Amacuro state, has only recently been exploited. Now some half a dozen rustic tourist camps operate here, and place an emphasis on observation of fauna and visits to the indigenous Warao, the principal inhabitants of this ecosystem. Warao means "the boat people," and their crafts, particularly basketry, are highly prized.

Bolívar, Venezuela's largest state, and one of the most richly endowed, has huge reserves of gold, diamonds, iron, bauxite, hardwoods, and hydropower from its great rivers. On the northern border, **Ciudad Guayana** ㉓ was created in 1961, as the headquarters for development of Venezuela's heavy industry. Mammoth steel, iron, and aluminum plants use electricity generated at **Guri Dam**, one of the most powerful hydroelectric plants in the world, an hour to the southwest, with a visitor center and interesting tours. A recent 3.2 kilometer (2 mile) bridge spans the huge Orinoco here. Tourist attractions include the waterfalls in **Parque Cachamay** and **Parque Llovizna** and ruins of the colonial **Caroní Mission Church**. About an hour away are the 17th- and 18th-century forts, **Los Castillos de Guayana** (Mon–Fri 9am–noon, 1–5pm, Sat–Sun 9am–5pm), overlooking the Orinoco.

An hour west of Ciudad Guayana by freeway is **Ciudad Bolívar** ㉔, the state's capital. Founded in 1764 as Angostura, on the banks of the Orinoco, it became a patriot stronghold, Simón Bolívar's base of operations, and capital of the Third Republic, 1817–21. It was also a gold center, and a thriving river transport hub.

Cowboy at work on the Apure plains.

LOS LLANOS

Los Llanos, the great central plains, are to Venezuela what the Pampas are to Argentina. This vast region has given the country some of its best food and music, and it has also produced several presidents, including José Antonio Páez, whose term ran from 1830 to 1835, and the present incumbent, Hugo Chávez. Seven of Venezuela's 24 states form this hot rural heartland. The Chávez government has funded programs for llanero music, including the *joropo*, Venezuela's most popular form of folk music. Today the plains still teem with wildlife including capybaras, the world's biggest rodents (about 1 metre/yd long and 60cm/24ins high at the shoulder), and anacondas, the world's largest snakes, which you can see on wildlife tours or if you're staying on one of the great *hatos* (ranches).

The opening of the highway joining San Fernando de Apure with the central coast spelled the demise of the river trade and its commercial importance. But evidence of the city's prosperous past can be seen in the impressive architecture, including the colonial **cathedral**, the **Museo Etnográfico de Guayana**, the **Casa del Congreso de Angostura**, and the **Museo Manuel Piar**. Other worthwhile stops are the **Museo de Arte Moderno Jesús Soto** (honoring the city's most famous modern artist) and the **Quinta de San Isidro** (where Bolívar often stayed, and which is now the **Museo Casa San Isidro**). The **Angostura Bridge** can be seen from the riverbanks, the first span across the 2,140-km (1,330-mile) length of the Orinoco (other crossings are by ferry).

The paved road, completed in 1991, linking Ciudad Guayana with **Santa Elena de Uairén**, by the frontier with Brazil, permits even city cars to traverse the length of **Parque Nacional Canaima** and **La Gran Sabana**. Along the highway, observe gently rolling hills of this vast savannah dotted with *moriche* palms; Pemón Indian settlements with thatch-roofed, mud-walled dwellings; and stately *tepuyes* in the distance (among them **Roraima**). There are numerous impressive falls along the roadside, including **Kama Merú** and **Quebrada de Jaspe**. The mission of **Kavanayén** and the stunning falls of **Chinak-Merú** can be visited by four-wheel-drive vehicles.

On a spectacular lake with pink sands fringed by palms and a half dozen waterfalls, **Canaima** ㉕, one of the first areas in Venezuela to be developed for adventure travel, and a major tourist destination, is in the northwest corner of the 30,000-sq km (11,500-sq mile) Parque Nacional Canaima. This sector of the park is only accessible by air, and visitors can take day tours from Maiquetía, Porlamar, or Ciudad Bolívar, or stay overnight. Canaima's principal draw is its proximity to **Angel Falls**, named after the American bush pilot Jimmie Angel, who "discovered" them in 1935. The falls are the world's highest, at 979 meters (3,212ft), of which 807 meters

The cathedral in Ciudad Bolívar, built during the times of Spanish occupation.

(2,648ft) are free fall, and cascade over the edge of **Auyantepui**, the park's largest *tepuy*, which covers 700 sq km (270 sq miles). Weather permitting, visitors may get a look at the falls from the air. Excursions leave from Canaima in the rainy season, May to November, which is also when the falls are at their most dramatic.

Despite fierce opposition, in 2000 Venezuela built electricity pylons and transmission lines through the Parque Nacional Canaima and La Gran Sabana to transport hydroelectric power to Brazil. As well as the irreparable impact on the delicate ecosystems and beautiful scenery of the region, the power lines have encouraged large-scale mining on all the reserve's borders.

A fragile wilderness

Flying over Amazonas state, with a vista of virgin tropical forest, interrupted only by the snaking black lines of rivers, engraves a lasting impression of the vastness of the state and the magnificence of nature it embraces. Although it covers an area larger than Portugal, the Netherlands, and Denmark put together, Amazonas only has about 45,000, mostly indigenous, inhabitants. Paved roads extend only 100km (60 miles) from the capital, **Puerto Ayacucho** ㉖, in its northwestern extreme. The rapids of the Orinoco long prevented extensive penetration. The construction of tourist camps has allowed visitors to savor this extraordinary territory. Independent travelers can reach Puerto Ayacucho by car (or bus) from Caracas via Caicara del Orinoco in about 10 hours, passing through landscapes dominated by enormous sandstone formations called *laja*, and the Panare and Guahibo communities. Do not miss Puerto Ayacucho's outstanding **Ethnological Museum**. Near the capital are the giant petroglyphs of **Tobogán de la Selva**, and the indigenous Piaroa and Guahibo settlements. More distant (and costly) excursions by boat or charter plane include trips to **Autana**, the sacred mountain of the Piaroa, and to visit the native Yanomami (see page 52).

A view of the mountains across the marshes of Isla de Margarita.

A llanero rounding up on the savannah.

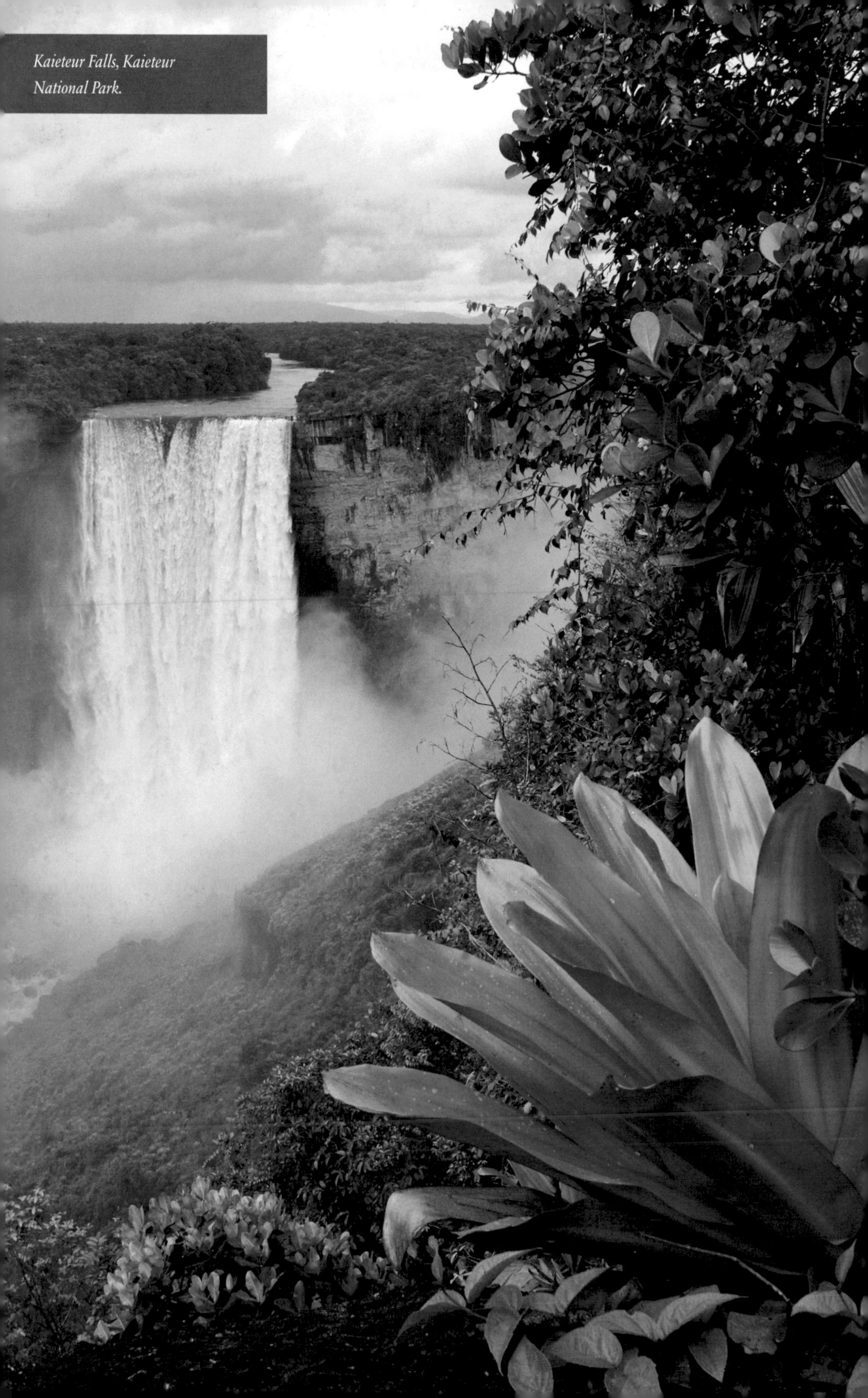

Kaieteur Falls, Kaieteur National Park.

GUYANA

This lush, exotic, and richly forested former British colony is geographically larger than Britain, but has a mere fraction of its population.

uyana means "Land of Many Waters" in a local indigenous language. Life in this country on the northeast shoulder of South America is indeed dominated by its mighty rivers – the Essequibo, Demerara, and Berbice. They act as highways into the rainforests, mountains, and savannahs of the interior, regions which are, in turn, dissected by a network of lesser tributaries and creeks.

Initially colonized by the Dutch in the 17th century, the territories which make up present-day Guyana came under British rule in 1814, and remained so until independence in 1966. The country is populated mainly by the descendants of African slaves and indentured workers from India, together with smaller numbers of Chinese and Portuguese, brought here to work the sugar, coffee, and cotton plantations of the coast. The original indigenous inhabitants now make up just 5 percent.

Because of its colonial history, modern Guyana is South America's only English-speaking country, and is Caribbean in culture and outlook. However, unlike her Caribbean neighbors, Guyana has no palm-fringed powdery sand or limpid waters. Instead, the narrow coastal belt consists mainly of reclaimed swamps, marshland, and deltas of the great rivers, rich in alluvial soil and intensively

cultivated. These areas, and small towns such as **New Amsterdam ①** and **Charity ②**, are protected from the sea by a system of dams and dikes (a practice initiated by the Dutch). Of a total population of 768,000, in a country larger than Britain, 90 percent live on this coastal belt.

Georgetown ③, the capital, lies below sea level on the east bank of the Demerara River. The city is laid out in a grid with wide streets lined with colonial buildings constructed of tropical hardwoods. The skyline is dominated

Main Attractions
Georgetown
Kaieteur Falls
Savannah lodges

Thatched hut in Canaima National Park.

The sheer cliffs of Mount Roraima.

by **St. George's Anglican Cathedral**, said to be the world's tallest wooden church; and by the tower crowning the immense, covered Stabroek Market, where the full pageant of Guyana's ethnic mix barters goods of every conceivable description, from manioc flour to gold. **Georgetown Cricket Club** – the oldest cricket club in the West Indies – and the pan yards where steel bands prepare for the annual carnival, speak loudest of Guyana's Caribbean identity. Georgetown also has comfortable modern hotels and a lively nightlife. However, it is to explore the interior that the great majority of visitors travel to Guyana.

Forest and falls

Kaieteur Falls, the world's highest single-drop waterfall, is at the top of most visitors' lists. It is feasible to journey overland to the falls by driving to **Linden** ④, the bauxite mining town, then continue along a track through the rainforest to join the Potaro River for two days' struggle by boat against the current. It is also just possible, in the dry seasons, to journey

to **Kangaruma** ⑤, near Kaieteur. The easier option is to fly by light aircraft from Georgetown. For about an hour and a half, passengers gaze down at a disk filled to the horizon in every direction with forest, interrupted by glinting threads of water. Occasionally they might be able to identify tiny riverside settlements where solitary gold panners and diamond prospectors sieve for their fortunes. Book ahead as most flights run only on Sundays.

Abruptly, the forest rises about 300 meters (1,000ft) at the point where two folds of the earth's crust overlap. The Potaro River flows calmly through the forest, spills over and plunges down, uninterrupted for 226 meters (741ft) of its 250-meter (820-ft) fall. Airborne tourists are usually treated to a full-frontal vista of the entire falls, before sweeping low over the foaming white cauldron and dropping down on a strip of jungle cleared for a runway. A forest trail leads to the falls, as the gathering roar seems to come from every direction, including below ground. The viewing promontory is just meters away from the falls.

Guyana, Suriname, and French Guiana

A huge volume of black water flows over the lip every second, seemingly in slow motion, turning copper, yellow, and finally a foaming white frenzy.

If this hasn't given you your fill of waterfalls, you can fly for 30 minutes on to **Orinduik Falls**. Here the Ireng River thunders over a series of steps and terraces on a fold of rock that marks Guyana's border with Brazil. Although Orinduik does not offer the full, elemental drama of Kaieteur, the location is stunningly beautiful with views over the rolling, grass-covered Pakaraimae Hills.

Rainforest idyll

A stay at a rainforest lodge is another feature of Guyana's fledgling tourist industry. Close to Georgetown, **Timberhead** is reached by whooshing up the wide, aptly brown-sugar colored Demerara River, then chugging up the oozing Kamuni Creek, its waters blackened by decomposing vegetation. The banks are overhung with undergrowth supported by aerial roots. Enormous blue morpho butterflies flitter about in abundance and troupes of monkeys can be heard crashing through the branches overhead. There are jaguars, pumas, ocelots, and peccaries in the forest, although sightings are more likely farther south in Iwokrama Rainforest Reserve in the heart of Guyana.

Stay at Rock View Lodge (see Travel Tips page 395) at **Annai ❻**, where the savannah meets the Pakaraima mountains. Here you can take boat trips at dawn and dusk to see myriad birds, butterflies, black caiman, and the Victoria Amazonica waterlilies.

Along the upper reaches of the Rupununi River, the landscape changes dramatically into savannah grassland bordered by a ridge of mountains pricking the horizon. Here *vaqueros* (cowboys) ride across the plains, barefoot in the stirrups, rounding up their cattle.

A flight over the rainforest to the airstrip at **Lethem ❼** near the Brazilian border takes you to the heart of the Rupununi. A trip across the savannah by jeep reaches Dadanawa Ranch. From here, visitors ride horses into the mountain foothills, and nights can be spent under the stars. The area is a birdwatcher's and naturalist's dream.

Black caiman inhabit the central Guyana region.

THE WAI-WAI TRIBE

In the 1960s, contact was made for the first time with the Wai-Wai, a tribe living between the Essequibo and Amazon watersheds. The majority live in Brazil, but some 200 (10 percent) live inside the Guyanese borders. Their crafts include pottery, fashioning bows and arrows, and carving flutes from bone. Like other rainforest tribes, they are mainly hunters and gatherers while also practicing limited forms of slash-and-burn agriculture. Despite their remoteness, their way of life has come under threat from logging companies, and from the search for precious metals. To protect their 625,000-hectare homeland and culture, since 2007, they have run their lands as the community-owned conservation area of Konashen, with support from Conservation International. Research; limited travel there is permitted.

SURINAME

This little-known former Dutch colony has a fascinating cultural mix in its sleepy coastal towns and vast swathes of rainforest.

Suriname is the former Dutch Guiana, sandwiched between Guyana (formerly British Guiana) and Guyane, or French Guiana. The Suriname coast was first settled by English and Dutch merchants in 1613, followed by Jews from the Netherlands, Italy, and Brazil. Slaves were shipped from West Africa to work the sugar and cotton plantations. Imports of slaves were banned in 1818, and slavery itself was abolished in 1863. During this period, East Indians, Pakistanis, Chinese, and Javanese from Dutch Indonesia

arrived as indentured laborers. With the indigenous peoples, the result is an extraordinary ethnic cocktail.

Suriname gained independence from the Netherlands in 1975. Relations between the two countries reached a low point in 1982 when dictator Colonel Dési Bouterse had 15 opposition leaders executed. Diplomatic relations were severed for 5 years, until democratic elections were held. Huge numbers of Surinamese emigrated to the Netherlands, leaving a population that today numbers just 500,000. The official language is Dutch, while Sranan Tongo, an English-based creole, is widely used as a lingua franca. While the economy improved under Afro-Surinamese President Ronald Venetiaan of the Nation Party, he was succeeded in July 2010 by former dictator Bouterse. Elected thanks to parliamentary coalitions with former enemies, his government has been dogged by allegations of drugs trafficking, not least in WikiLeaks documents. Although as president he is immune from arrest, Europol has issued an arrest warrant for him.

Suriname's sleepy capital

Roughly 90 percent of the people live in towns strung along the loamy mud flats of the coast. The capital, **Paramaribo ⑧**, is a small, quiet city of faded, peeling wooden buildings arranged in a grid pattern, on the west

The mosque in central Paramaribo.

bank of the Suriname River. It is diffi-cult to comprehend the violence of the 1980s as you wander the sleepy squares.

Suriname is however remarkably free of racial tension. The synagogue stands fraternally next to the mosque. Down the road, Sint-Petrus-en-Pauluskathedraal, the 19th-century Catholic cathedral, may be the biggest wooden building in the Americas. The Hindo Arya Dewaker Temple is also impressive, while the **museum**, in the old Dutch **Fort Zeelandia**, is a modest affair. The **central market** is lively; the aroma of spices brought from India mingles with the smell of fresh shrimp sold by fishermen.

A popular day trip from Paramaribo is to cross the Suriname River to the Dutch fort of **Nieuw Amsterdam** and drive east along the coast, north of the old Jewish settlement of **Jodensavanne** ❾ and through the bauxite-mining town of **Moengo**. The road ends at **Albina** ❿, a thriving little frontier town on the Marowijne, the river bor-der with French Guiana. Another road, westward, passes through the village of **Totness** ⓫. The only other town on the road is **Wageningen**, the rice-growing center, before **Nieuw Nickerie** ⓬, the border town with Guyana at the mouth of the Corantijn River.

Into the forest

The majority of Suriname's territory is covered by dense, virgin rainforest, cut through by great, black rivers. In a government-sponsored scheme in the 1950s a few short airstrips were hacked out of the forest. Near three of these, the Movement for Eco-Tourism in Suriname (METS – owned by Surinam Airways), have built simple lodges where visitors can experience life in the rainforest, inside or adjacent to the vast **Central Suriname Nature Reserve**.

One of them is on Tonka Island in the heart of Saramaccan country. The Saramaccan are a tribe of Cimarrons, descendants of African slaves who escaped to the forests as rebellions swept through the plantations. They speak a hybrid language of West African dialects, with a smattering of English, Dutch, and Portuguese. Many of their practices – drum-playing, dancing, and animist religious beliefs – can be traced directly to West Africa.

A typical visit begins with a light aircraft flight to **Kajana airstrip**, and transfer in a motorized dugout canoe to **Awarradam Lodge** at some impass-able rapids. The double wolf whistles of screaming *piha* and a cacophony of croaks, caws, and the occasional growl of a howler monkey, float over the can-opy. Black caiman crocodiles are often seen lazing by the bank during the all-day canoe trip to **Grandam rapids**. Outsiders are welcomed by the village chief or *Kapiteni* and introduced to vil-lagers who sing as they grate manioc.

Palumeu, the second lodge, is deeper in the interior on the Tapana-hony River. The most stunningly located of the lodges, it has sweeping river views. As eco-travel has become more popular, other attractive jun-gle lodges have been built, including Danpaati on a mid-river island 350km (217 miles) south of the capital.

Central market, Paramaribo.

Working in the garden, Botopasie.

FRENCH GUIANA

Formerly home to a notorious penal colony, this heavily forested *département* of France is today the launch site for Europe's Ariane rockets.

Main Attractions
Kourou Space Center and museum
Îles du Salut former prisons
Les Hattes turtle beach

The small colony of French Guiana (Guyane) has more than 350km (220 miles) of coastline; 80 percent of the 199,000 inhabitants live in the coastal regions. Beyond lies a dense carpet of Amazon rainforest.

Ancient petroglyphs near the village of Kaw bear testimony to thousands of years of human habitation, but European colonization, from the early 17th century, changed the ethnographic make-up of the region. The territory was tenuously held by the French, and when slavery was abolished African slaves, brought in to work the plantations, were replaced by indentured laborers from other parts of the French Empire, notably Indochina.

French Guiana became an overseas *département* of France in 1946. In the 1960s a satellite and space exploration center was established at Kourou, which brought jobs and urban development, but the rest of the country has suffered unemployment and economic stagnation. The population is highly racially mixed, with input from Africa, Europe, native South America, China, and Vietnam. There are many native groups in the rainforest areas, and communities of Noir Marrons, descendants of African slaves, live along the banks of the River Maroni in a traditional African manner with indigenous influences.

Cayenne ⑬, the capital, has some interesting colonial buildings. The **Musée Départemental** (Mon–Fri 8am–1.15pm, Mon and Thur also 3–5.45pm) has an eclectic mix of historical, natural, and archeological artifacts including exhibits on the penal colonies, while the **Musée des Cultures Guyanaises** (Mon–Fri 8am–1pm, 3–5.45pm except Wed am

Devil's Island, where Alfred Dreyfus was imprisoned in the 1890s, falsely accused of treason.

only, Sat 8–11.45am) has ethnological exhibits on native and immigrant communities. The small botanical gardens are adjacent to the university. Other attractions include pleasant squares and markets, including the main market on Place du Coq and the fish market at the old port.

The town of **Kourou** ⓮, 55km (34 miles) northwest of Cayenne, revolves around the **French Centre Spatial Guyanais**, picked for its proximity to the Equator, making it practical for the launch of geostationary satellites. There is a **Musée de l'Espace** (Space Museum; Mon–Fri 8am–6pm and Sat 2–6pm), from where rocket launches can be witnessed.

The modern part of town, with a preponderance of families from mainland France, is very different from the more traditional old village at the mouth of the Kourou River. Boats are available to go to the **Îles du Salut** ⓯, which lie 15km (9 miles) to the north. The infamous **Île du Diable** (Devil's Island), immortalized in *Papillon* by Henri Charrière, is inaccessible due to hazardous landing conditions, but boat trips to Île Royale and St. Joseph are available. The Transportation Camp at **St Laurent du Maroni** ⓰, 250km (150 miles) northwest of Cayenne, was the largest prison in the territory, and can be visited.

Dugout canoes can be hired from the town for trips on the Maroni River. About 40km (25 miles) north of St. Laurent, at the mouth of the Maroni and Mana rivers, is **Les Hattes Beach**, a breeding site for leatherback turtles. The laying season is from April to July and hatching takes place from July to September. The turtles have no shell but a dark blue leathery skin, and measure up to 170cm (67 inches) long when fully grown. Nearby is the indigenous village of **Awala Yalimapo**.

The wild interior

The interior of French Guiana has much to interest naturalists and adventure seekers. Roughly 60km (40 miles) southeast of Cayenne are the **Kaw Marshes**, an area of forest and mangrove swamps, rich in birdlife and inhabited by the rare black caiman. Houseboat accommodations are available in **Kaw** ⓱ village. At **Montsinéry**, 43km (27 miles) southwest of Cayenne, a botanical hiking trail leads to the **Annamite Penal Colony**, where deported Indo-Chinese were detained. Other hiking trails lead to waterfalls and wildlife-infested creeks. The interior can also be explored by *pirogue* (dugout canoe).

South of Cayenne, there is a surprising community. The village of **Cacao** is inhabited by a Hmong community of Laotian descent and here, visitors can sample traditional Hmong cuisine and buy Hmong handicrafts. There are inland jungle expeditions centered around the ancient goldmining village of **Saül** ⓲ and, in the west, **Maripasoula** ⓳, both bordering on the huge **Parc Amazonien de la Guyane** that takes up almost half the French territory.

The white-faced Saki (Pithecia pithecia).

Landscape near Alausi, Avenue of Volcanoes, Ecuador.

A mountainside terraced for agricultural purposes, a relic from Incan times.

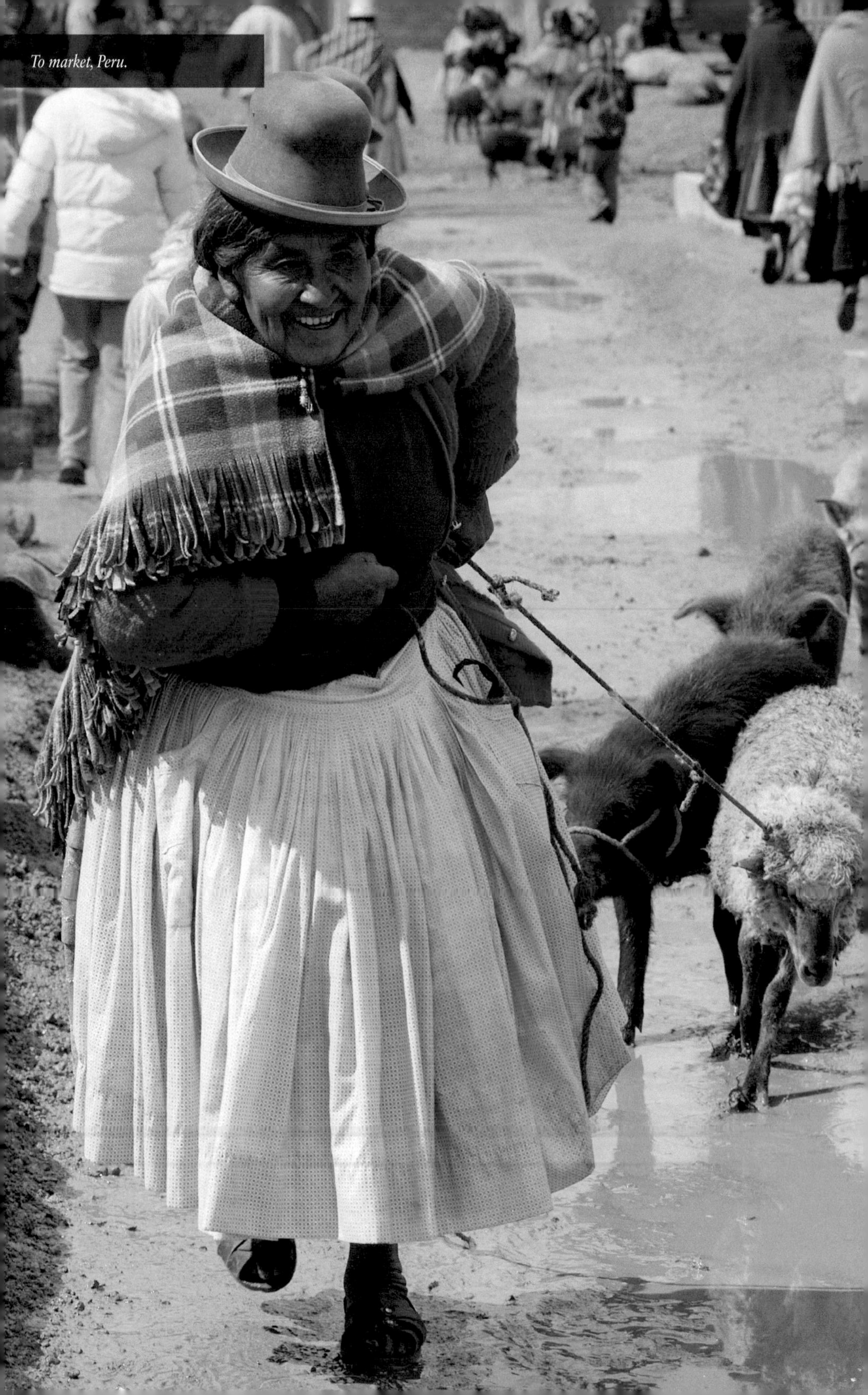
To market, Peru.

THE ANDEAN HIGHLANDS

The ancient heart of the subcontinent, these high-altitude countries continue to fascinate, both for their imperial past and for the rich cultural heritage they proudly maintain.

Adobe wall, Chan Chan.

Clustered around some of the most inhospitable territory in South America are the countries of the Andean highlands: Peru, Bolivia, and Ecuador. The area was home to some of the world's most extraordinary civilizations for thousands of years before being united by the Inca empire in the 14th century. Although the Incas were the most famous rulers of South America, they had a relatively brief moment of glory before the Spanish conquistadors crushed them into submission. The colonists subsequently kept themselves distant from their subjects and to this day the old Inca lands have yet to fully overcome being multiple societies, split into native and African-origin poor, mixed-race middle classes, and a wealthy white elite. But times are changing. Peru and Bolivia have had indigenous presidents, and recognition of indigenous rights has led to a greater, if slow, opening of mainstream society to non-whites.

After being the wealthy center of Spain's South American empire, all three fell behind the Southern Cone countries from the late 19th century. Nevertheless, they outshine their neighbors with their architectural heritage, including Peru's incomparable Machu Picchu, South America's most spectacular ancient city, the baffling Nazca lines, and the adobe city of Chan Chan as

Machu Picchu.

well as Bolivia's Tiahuanaco from before the Spanish conquest. Large and highly varied indigenous communities keep ancient Andean and Amazon traditions alive, as in the Ecuadorian market town of Otavalo. Baroque colonial gems include several Unesco World Heritage Sites, from Quito in the north through Cuenca in southern Ecuador to Peru's Cusco – once center of the Inca empire – and Arequipa to the mining town of Potosí that supplied Spain with silver.

These three countries also share spectacular landscapes, from Andean peaks to steamy Amazon jungles, and are among the most biodiverse countries on the planet. The world's deepest canyons are near Arequipa. Peru and Bolivia share the highest navigable body of water in the world, Lake Titicaca. In the west lie the Pacific beaches of Ecuador, beyond which are the country's pride and joy: the unique Galápagos Islands.

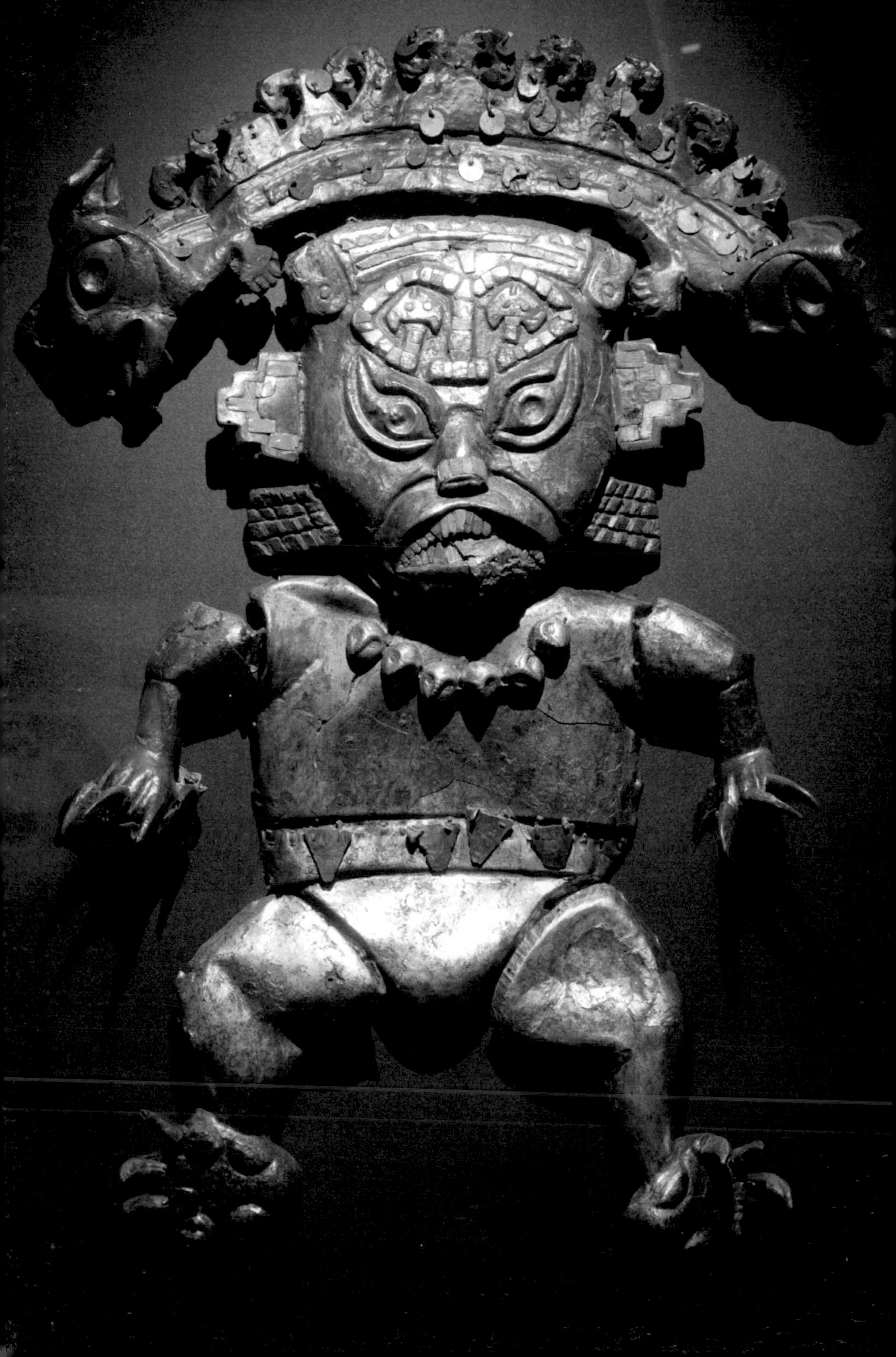

Lord of Sipán tomb artifact.

PERU

The birthplace of ancient empires, Peru has towering mountains, steaming rainforests, and parched deserts. It is the ultimate destination for culture seekers, adventurers, and ecotourists.

No other country in South America has such an astonishing archeological heritage as Peru. Most tourists come to see the monumental citadel of Machu Picchu, while the other big archeological attraction is Nazca, with the mysterious desert lines which can only be viewed from the air. This is a country packed with archeological wonders – the fabulous remains of Inca and pre-Inca civilizations housed in numerous museums, as well as countless pyramids and ruined cities, many still unexcavated.

Then there are the treasures of the colonial period that gild the magnificent cities of Cusco and Arequipa. Lima, the capital, once the center of the Spanish Empire in South America, is an exciting city that moves at a frenetic pace. Many of its colonial buildings have fallen victim to earthquakes and poor urban planning, but it still has some beautiful architecture and an enormous range of museums.

Land of extremes

Peru is an exceptional country even for those who don't have a particular interest in history or archeology. The arid desert in the south and the splendid Pacific coastline, with beaches that attract surfers from around the world, give way abruptly to the snowy heights of the Andean mountain range that edges along the country's coastal belt. Beyond the Andes lies the Amazon basin, a huge rainforest area teeming with exotic plants, insects, birds, and animals.

Tourism is rapidly developing, as this is a country that recognizes the importance of protecting its rich natural and historical heritage. But poverty is still widespread, from the poor indigenous communities eking out a living in the barren Andean plains to the people who inhabit Peru's volatile coastline, which is frequently hit by drought, earthquakes, and by floods

Main Attractions

Lima's historic center
Nazca Lines and Paracas
Cusco, the Sacred Valley and
  Machu Picchu
Lake Titicaca
Arequipa and the Colca Canyon
Manu Wildlife Center
Chan Chan and Lambayeque's
  Brüning Museum

On the Inca Trail.

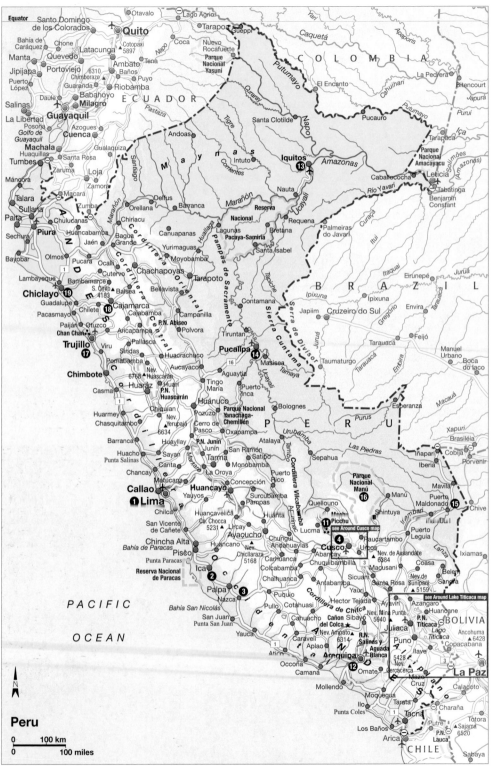

Peru

0 100 km
0 100 miles

brought by the El Niño current. In August 2007, the Ica region was badly affected by an earthquake which killed more than 500 people.

Most areas of tourist interest are safe, although there have been reports of mugging in and around Cusco and Lima – personal effects should not be flaunted. Take care, but don't let such reports spoil your trip – most visitors enjoy the wonders of Peru without encountering any trouble at all.

Peru after independence

José de San Martín proclaimed Peru's independence in Lima on July 28, 1821, although most of the country was still held by the Spanish crown. Simón Bolívar finished the job of freeing the country and, in 1826, the last Spanish troops surrendered. The first years of independence saw few real changes in the way that Peruvians lived. But midway through the century, military leader Ramón Castilla took over the presidency, and under his rule modernization shook the country. Basic services such as water and streetlights were installed in Lima and a rail track – the first on the subcontinent – linked the capital with the nearby port of Callao. Castilla abolished slavery and directed approval of the 1860 national constitution. But setbacks ocurred in the bloody War of the Pacific against Chile, which lasted from 1879 to 1883 and cost Peru its southernmost territory. Even Lima was sacked. Despite these tumultuous changes, life in the 19th century continued much as in the 17th for the bulk of the population – the native peoples living in the highlands; the two worlds of Peru, the Indian and the European, were drifting further apart.

A divided nation

Of all the nations of South America, Peru saw the most violent clash between native and European cultures. Until recently, this conflict provided fertile ground for terrorism. Today, it is more evident in the chaos of Lima,

and in the country's vibrant creativity. Peru has been run by a number of military strongmen. Most intriguing among them was the left-wing dictator General Juan Velasco Alvarado, who, in the 1970s, temporarily turned over the biggest newspaper – *El Comercio* – to a peasant group and renamed all of Lima's streets after national heroes.

Sprinkled among these dictators have been 30 elected presidents, all conservatives until left-of-center Alán García was elected in 1985. The charismatic García drew support from the poor and rural dwellers, who cheered his decision not to pay the foreign debt incurred by past governments. But the cut-off in development aid from the US, economic mismanagement and the unwillingness of businesses to invest in the country, and political maneuvering provoked hyperinflation in 1988 after two years of growth.

The political division and social upheaval accompanying García's presidency opened the way for an independent candidate, Alberto Fujimori, to take over as president. His government waged a savage campaign against

FACT

In 2003, the Peruvian government earmarked US$800 million to compensate victims of the guerrilla war in the 1980s, during which, according to official estimates, more than 69,000 people died, most of them innocent peasants.

Changing of the guards at the Palacio de Gobierno.

the guerrilla group *Sendero Luminoso* (Shining Path), which had taken control of large areas of the countryside and whose activities, as well as causing many deaths, had severely affected tourism in the 1980s. Their leader, Abimael Guzmán, was captured in 1992, and the group collapsed. In December 1996, another Marxist guerrilla group, the Movimiento Revolucionario Tupac Amaru, took hostage nearly 500 guests during a siege of the Japanese ambassador's residence which lasted until April 1997.

Fujimori won a controversial third term of office in 2000, but leaked videos implicating him in bribery forced him to flee to Japan.

Alejandro Toledo, leader of the Perú Posible party and the first Peruvian president of indigenous extraction, formed a government. Toledo's presidency was characterized by civil unrest, strikes by teachers and government workers, and public discontent at the perceived stagnation of the economy. In 2005, he was found guilty of electoral fraud, but Congress voted not to impeach him. Although Toledo began his term a popular leader, by the end of his presidency his popularity rating had fallen to just 8 percent. In 2006 national elections returned Alán García to the presidency. Since then, economic growth has brought relative calm to the country, but many social demands remain unsatisfied, leading to sporadic violent protest and the election of leftwing president Ollanta Humala in 2011 with 51.5 percent of the vote. A former radical, he has moderated his early positions and faced protests against major mining projects.

Lima: capital of the New World

Spanish conquistador Francisco Pizarro considered the site where he founded **Lima ❶** on January 18, 1535, inhospitable: rain seldom fell, earthquakes were common, and winter was a time of gray skies and dreary fog. But his soldiers saw it as the best place for a quick sea escape in the event of a native uprising. Little did they suspect this open plain would become the political and military capital of the New World, seeing the reign of

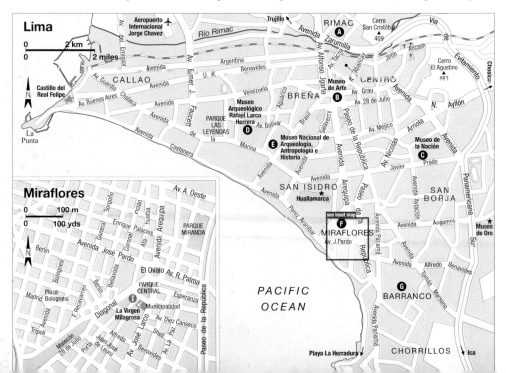

40 viceroys before the "City of Kings" was declared capital of an independent Peru in 1821.

At the heart of the old town, a Unesco World Heritage Site since 1991, the **Plaza Mayor** is where for centuries the power of the new colony was concentrated, and it remains one of the city's most active and attractive squares. At its center are rose gardens, a stone fountain and park benches that draw young couples, shoeshine boys, and families in their Sunday best, posing for photos. The foundations of the **Palacio de Gobierno** (Sat 10am except holidays; free 45-minute guided tour. T; to arrange a tour of the palace reserve at least 24 hours in advance via tel: 01-311 3900, ext. 523; e-mail scuadros@presidencia.gob.pe), date from Pizarro's time, but its facade was changed in the early 1900s. Every day at noon there is a ceremonial changing of the guard, with a band playing, but visits to the interior of the palace have to be pre-arranged at the Oficina de Turismo of the Municipalidad. The best spot for viewing the ceremony is the wide front balcony of the **Palacio Municipal**. The original structure used as a city hall burned down in 1923, but its neoclassical replacement is impressive, with marble stairways, gilt mirrors, and crystal chandeliers. The library, with massive leather chairs, huge wooden tables, and the smell of old books, offers a calming respite from the traffic outside. Its circular stairway was hand-carved from a single piece of Nicaraguan cedar.

Across the square, the **Palacio del Arzobispo** has one of the most beautiful wooden *Mudéjar*-style balconies in the city. Take a peek in the archbishop's patio before heading next door to the **cathedral** (Mon–Fri 9am–5pm Sat 10am–1pm), which contains Pizarro's remains. A block away is the **Museo Banco Central de Reserva** (Mon–Fri 10am–4.30pm), with a small but impressive pre-Columbian collection. Nearby is the splendid **Palacio de Torre Tagle**, constructed in 1735, now used to house the Ministry of Foreign Affairs.

A few blocks to the northeast is the jewel of Lima's old churches, the **Monasterio de San Francisco** (Mon–Sun 9.30am–5.30pm; guided tours). Lovingly repaired after the damage

Plaza Mayor, Lima.

caused by every earthquake in the past four centuries, its cloister features fine mosaic tiles from Seville, frescoes discovered when an earthquake demolished part of an outer wall, and an impressive collection of religious art. Most fascinating are its catacombs, stacked with skulls and bones from the colonial period.

Saints and sinners

Behind the Palacio de Gobierno is the old train station, **Estación Desamparados**, the city's first iron building. Brought in pieces by boat from England and rebuilt here in 1908, it was formerly the depot for all trains out of the capital, but is no longer in operation. Also behind the president's office is the bridge that leads to **Rimac Ⓐ**, one of Lima's oldest neighborhoods, named after the river that flows along its edge. A working-class barrio, where women in doorways chat with their neighbors while children play soccer in the streets, it once was the city's top spot for promenading. Then, the stars were the *tapadas* – seductive women whose skirts shamelessly showed their tiny feet, whose necklines were scandalously low, and whose faces were covered by a veil that bared only one eye. In the afternoons, they were likely to be found on the **Alameda de los Descalzos**, courting and flirting but never lifting their veils to reveal their identities. This promenade, built in 1611, is lined with Italian marble statues representing the months of the year and bordered by lawns and flowers. It leads to the **Monasterio de los Descalzos** (Monastery of the Barefoot Friars; Mon–Fri 9am–12.30pm, 4pm–8pm, Sat 9am–12.30pm), which is well worth the walk to get there.

Lima was home to two of South America's most famous saints: Rosa de Lima and Martín de Porres. Rosa, who died of tuberculosis at age 31, had a fervent following during her lifetime (1586–1617) and was credited with curing thousands, performing innumerable miracles, and even saving the

city from pirate attacks. For Martín de Porres, her near-contemporary, fame came after his death. He lived in the **Santo Domingo** monastery in Jirón Camaná, but was barred from becoming a priest because he was black. His duties included working as the janitor, and statues and paintings of the saint usually show him with broom in hand. Both saints are buried at Santo Domingo, which is open to visitors.

Lima's religious devotion may have been proportional to the terror inflicted by the Holy Inquisition. Chills will run up your spine when you descend into the depths of the **Museo de la Inquisición** (daily 9am–5pm) in Plaza Bolívar. Gruesome tortures were inflicted to obtain "confessions" of heresy, Judaism, and witchcraft. The "guilty" – and few were found innocent – had their property confiscated and were marched off to the Plaza de Armas (now Plaza Mayor) to await their fate, which could range from public flogging to burning at the stake.

Lima's most active square is **Plaza San Martín**, linked to Plaza Mayor by the pedestrian walkway **Jirón de** la Unión. Plaza San Martín is where most of the money-changing houses are located (alongside the Gran Bolívar Hotel). A few hundred meters south of the plaza, the **Museo de Arte** Ⓑ (Tue–Sun 10am–8pm, Sat until 5pm) contains an extensive collection of Peruvian art from the Conquest to the present day. The Filmoteca here is a low-price movie club. It has two auditoriums for concerts, and is surrounded by a pleasant public park.

Outside the city center

Some of the most interesting museums, shops, and beaches are in Lima's suburbs, accessible by bus or taxi from Downtown. Just south of the city center, on Avenida Javier Prado Este, is the excellent **Museo de la Nación** Ⓒ (Tue–Sun 9am–5pm), with artifacts from prehistoric times to the present day (details in Spanish only).

Southwest of the center, in Pueblo Libre, the **Museo Arqueológico Rafael Larco Herrera** Ⓓ (Mon–Sun 9am–10pm) has a fascinating display of pottery spanning 3,000 years, including a huge collection of pieces from the Moche, Sican, and Chimú cultures of northern Peru. There is also an exhibition dedicated to the gold and silver of ancient Peru. A blue line painted on the sidewalk leads to the **Museo Nacional de Arqueología, Antropología e Historia** Ⓔ (Tue–Sat 9am–5pm, Sun 9am–4pm), with pre-Columbian displays and colonial paintings.

In the suburb of San Isidro, bougainvillea grows beside the pre-Inca burial site of **Huallamarca** (Tue–Sun 9–5pm), where there is a small museum of mummies and artifacts.

In **Miraflores** Ⓕ, stomping ground of the children of Peru's wealthy families, you can people-watch at outdoor cafés, shop, or enjoy good meals and music. The pretensions of the Miraflores youths – the *mirafloriños* – are vividly described in the novels of Mario Vargas Llosa. Miraflores is the best place for theaters, trendy boutiques, and nightclubs. Nearby is

Barranco Ⓖ, the bohemian quarter made immortal in Peruvian waltz, and home to the city's best artists, poets, and jazz bars. Here you'll find the lovers' lane, **Puente de los Suspiros** (Bridge of Sighs), lined by fragrant climbing jasmine. It heads down to a lookout point over the Pacific Ocean, and to a steep stairway to the beach. Strolling here at sunset you may hear Peruvian flute music or Argentine tangos wafting from open windows.

The once-popular **Museo de Oro** (Gold Museum; daily 11.30am–7pm) on Avenida Alonso de Molina in the Monterrico district, fell from grace in 1998 with the startling revelation that a large proportion of its artifacts were fakes. After a brief enforced closure it reopened, and claims to have removed all non-authentic items from display. The museum also has a collection of textiles, stone carvings, and ceramics on display.

The most important archeological site near Lima is **Pachacámac**, 31km (19 miles) south of the city and accessible by bus or on a tour from the city center. Rising to prominence

Art for sale in the craft market.

around AD 700, this pre-Inca shrine was later used as an Inca temple for adoration of the sun god, and there is also a reconstruction of the Templo de las Virgenes (House of the Chosen Women), who were also known as *mamaconas*.

South of Lima

Some 220km (135 miles) south of Lima, and worth visiting if you are traveling by road to Nazca, is **Ica ❷**, famous for its vineyards and March wine festival, but especially for the **Museo Regional** (Mon–Sat 8am–6pm), one of Peru's most interesting small regional museums. Exhibits include mummies, ceramics, and skulls from the Paracas, Nazca, and Inca cultures; an excellent collection of Paracas textiles and feather weavings; and a number of *quipus*, the knotted strings that were used by the Incas to keep calculations and records.

Outside Ica, Pisco on the coast has lent its name to the brandy distilled in Peru and Chile from local wines. The Inca Cápac Yupanqui, according to legend, had an aqueduct built to

irrigate the desert area. The Paracas Marine Preserve protects a plethora of species including penguins and hundreds of thousands of migratory birds, while sandboarding has become popular in the nearby dunes.

Cerro Blanco, some 14 km (8 miles) north of Nazca, is purportedly the world's biggest sand dune. Nearby is Laguna de Huacachina, a green lagoon of sulfurous waters that Peruvians claim has medicinal value.

The mysterious Nazca lines

Until the 1930s, **Nazca ❸** was like any other small Peruvian town, with no claim to fame except that you had to cross one of the world's driest deserts to reach it from Lima. Since then, the *pampa* north of the city has become one of the greatest scientific mysteries in the Americas. The Nazca lines are a series of drawings of animals, geometric figures, and birds up to 300 meters (1,000ft) in size, scratched on to the arid crust of the desert and preserved for 2,000 years owing to a complete lack of rain and to unique winds that clean, but do not erase, the *pampa*.

Aerial view of the Nazca lines with hand design clearly visible.

The huge figures can only be properly appreciated from the air.

In 1939, US scientist Paul Kosok, flying over the dry coast, noticed the lines, previously believed to be part of a pre-Inca irrigation system. A specialist in irrigation, he quickly concluded that this had nothing to do with water systems. By chance, the day of the flight coincided with the summer solstice and, on a second flight, Kosok discovered that the line of the sunset ran tandem to the direction of one of the bird drawings. He called the Nazca *pampa* "the biggest astronomy book in the world."

Maria Reiche

However, it was a young German mathematician who became the expert on the lines and put Nazca on the map. Maria Reiche was 35 when she met Kosok, and he encouraged her to study the *pampa*. Reiche devoted the rest of her life to studying the lines, which she measured, cleaned, analyzed, and charted daily from the air and from a 15-meter (49-ft) high platform. She developed the most widely accepted theories on the hundreds of drawings that cover a 50-km (30-mile) belt between Nazca and Palpa, describing them as an "astronomical calendar." For example, she speculated that the drawing of the monkey was the Nazca symbol for the Big Dipper, the constellation representing rain. When rain was overdue – a common occurrence here – the monkey was sketched so that the gods would be reminded that the earth was parched. Because the drawings are only visible from the air there are those who do not accept Reiche's theories, denying that the Nazca people would have drawn something they could not see.

The most damaging theory about the Nazca lines came seven years earlier, when Erich von Däniken published *Chariots of the Gods*, in which he proposed that the *pampa* was part of an extra-terrestrial landing strip – an idea that Reiche discarded impatiently. Von Däniken's book drew thousands of visitors, who set out across the *pampa* on motorcycles and four-wheel-drive vehicles, leaving unerasable marks. Consequently, it is now illegal to drive or even walk on the *pampa*. Reiche used the profits from her book, *Mystery on the Desert*, to pay four guards to keep a constant watch on the plain.

Reiche died in Lima in 1998 and is buried near the Nazca lines, where her former home has been turned into a small museum.

There is a metal ladder and viewing platform at the side of the highway, but the best way to capture the impact of the lines is to fly over them. Tours, including flights, can be booked locally and in Lima. Flights, in very small planes, last from 30 to 45 minutes and can be bumpy. If you want to make the trip more economical, some of the pilots at the Nazca airstrip may be open to offers.

Cusco: capital of the Inca empire

The stallholders in Cusco's market speak Spanish with tourists and Quechua with one another. The

DRINK

Pisco, originating in the late 16th century, is by far the most popular spirit drunk in Peru and Chile, with Peru seeking to impose proprietary use on the name of the liquor. Peruvian varieties include *mosto verde*, distilled from partially fermented must, and *puro*, distilled from a single type of grape. Distilleries around Ica and Moquegua are open to visitors.

Taxis in the afternoon traffic along Cusco's Avenue el Sol.

buildings behind them are colonial, but built on Inca foundations. The elaborately carved facades on the city's churches have detailed scenes of angels and saints – with indigenous facial features. **Cusco** ❹ stands as a living testimony to the fact that the Inca civilization, one of the world's most sophisticated, could not be erased.

Of course, the Cusco of today is dramatically different from the awesome city that Francisco Pizarro and his conquistadors found when they reached the capital of the Inca empire, home to that kingdom's noblemen, priests, and their servants. Five hundred years ago, an estimated 15,000 people lived in the city, which was linked to the rest of the empire by way of *chasquis* – long-distance runners who carried news and messages from the four corners of Tawantinsuyu to its capital. While it today has some 200,000 residents and daily plane and bus services to Lima, it is among the continent's best-preserved Baroque colonial cities.

When the Spanish headed here after executing Atahualpa in Cajamarca (see page 31), they entered the fertile valley where Cusco is located to find a lush, green countryside filled with fields of corn and golden and purple patches where *kiwicha* and quinoa – varieties of amaranth, a high-protein "pseudo cereal" – were planted. Corn was perhaps the most valuable crop in the kingdom. It was used for bartering and as a food staple that appeared in everything from main dishes to the alcoholic *chicha*, prepared by young women who chewed the corn, then spat it into jars where it fermented with their saliva.

The amaranth, which grows well despite extremes in temperature and moisture, nearly fell victim to the Spaniards' attempt to "civilize" the local population. The conquistadors called it the "subversive grain", as it made the natives healthy, and thus harder to enslave. Pressured by the Spanish, the Vatican outlawed its cultivation and consumption. But now, four centuries later, *kiwicha* and quinoa once again flourish in the Sacred Valley, and are used in everything from soup to cookies.

In pre-Columbian times, anyone entering Cusco was greeted with the phrase, "*Ama sua, ama quella, ama lulla*" – "Don't lie, don't steal, don't be lazy" – summing up what was important in this cooperative society. Laziness was a capital offense punishable by death. Everyone in an Incan community – except for royalty and priests – was required to work on projects such as roads, irrigation ditches, and aqueducts, based on a sound philosophy that if everyone participated, they would all take care of the finished product. When the Spanish took control of this country those cooperative projects – known as *mingas* – were replaced by forced labor. But they were not completely erased; today there are still *mingas* in the Andes. Women begin preparing a community meal on *minga* day while the townspeople, regardless of age, set to work.

At its peak, Cusco was a city with sophisticated water systems, paved streets, and no poverty. But its leaders

Backstage at Cusco's Teatro Kusikay.

were not all wise and competent. One Inca chief, Urco, according to legend, perpetrated such atrocities that his name was erased from Incan history and his mention forbidden. Another hung his enemies along the roadsides in the empire's cities. Yet another had the entire population of a nearby city executed for the rape of a virgin selected to dedicate her life to the sun cult. But these excesses fail to overshadow the magnificence of a civilization whose architecture could not be destroyed and whose feats could not be matched.

Walking into the past

The most startling and curious characteristic of Cusco at first glance is its architecture. Huge walls of intricately fitted stone pay testimony to the civilization that, over 500 years ago, controlled much of the South American subcontinent. The Spanish conquerors ended up erecting their own buildings on the indestructible foundations, often using the same huge rocks that had been cut by the Incas. The cathedral in Cusco is made in part from stones hauled from Sacsayhuamán, the Inca fortress outside the city.

To explore this intriguing city, the **cathedral** (daily 10am–6pm, Mass at 10am) is a perfect place to start. It is located on the northeast side of the **Plaza de Armas** which, in Incan times, was known as Huancaypata and, in addition to being the exact center of the empire, was the spot where the most important religious and military ceremonies were held. Although the most spectacular view of the cathedral comes after dark when its lights turn the plaza into a breathtaking sight, its interior can only be seen during the day – and you won't want to miss it.

Built on what was once the palace of Inca Viracocha, the cathedral mingles Spanish Baroque architecture with the stoneworking skills of the Incas, and took a century to build (it was completed in 1654). Its María Angola bell in the north tower can be heard up to

40km (25 miles) away. Made of a ton of gold, silver, and bronze, the bell, which is more than 300 years old, is reportedly the largest on the continent.

Renaissance-style **El Triunfo** (same opening hours as the cathedral), to the right of the cathedral, was built to commemorate a Spanish victory over the Incas, who unsuccessfully tried to burn the thatch-roofed chapel that originally stood on the site. On the other side of the cathedral stands the church of **Jesús María** (irregular opening hours). At only 250 years old, it is regarded as one of historic Cusco's newer structures.

A mingling of cultures

Turn left from El Triunfo and walk one block up to the corner of Calle Hatunrumiyoc, literally "The Street of the Big Stones," and Calle Palacio, to the **Museo de Arte Religioso del Arzobispado** (Mon–Sat 8am–6pm, Sun from 10am; charge). This Moorish building with complicated carvings on its doors and balconies was constructed on the site of the 15th-century palace of Inca Roca,

TIP

An excellent value US$20 ticket allows entry to many highlights of Cusco and the Sacred Valley, including the Regional History Museum, Qenko, Sacsayhuamán, and Pisac.

The gold-leafed Baroque pulpit of Cusco's cathedral.

Powdered pigments for sale in Pisac.

The massive stone ramparts at Sacsayhuamán.

under whose rule Cusco's schools were initiated. The museum displays a fine collection of paintings in the style known as the School of Cusco, which flourished in the 16th–18th centuries – a fascinating mingling of indigenous and Spanish cultures in which archangels are dressed as Spaniards carrying European guns, surrounded by cherubs with native features, and the *Last Supper* shows Christ and his native-looking apostles dining on roast guinea pig and Peruvian cheese. Outside is the **Twelve-Angled Stone**, a tribute to the skill of Inca masons, proving that no piece of granite was too irregular to be fitted without mortar, every piece slotting together like a jigsaw puzzle.

In a city with so many churches, it is an honor to be dubbed the "most beautiful." That is the title given to **La Compañía de Jesús** (daily 9–11.30am, 1–5.30pm; charge), sitting on what was once the palace of Inca Huayna Capac on the southeast corner of the Plaza de Armas. Construction of the church, with its intricate interior, finely carved balconies, and gilded altars, took nearly 100 years, and is a fine example of Andean Baroque. Like the cathedral, the exterior is stunning when illuminated at night.

The street to the side of the church leads to what was the most important place of worship in the Inca empire. The **Iglesia Santo Domingo** (Mon–Fri 8am–5pm, Sat–Sun 2–5pm; charge) was once **El Templo del Coricancha** (or Q'urikancha, Quechua for "golden courtyard") – the Temple of the Sun – and the most magnificent complex in Cusco. Its walls were covered in gold, and its windows were constructed so the sun would cast a near-blinding reflection of golden light from the precious metals inside. Spanish chronicles describe the astonishment of the Europeans when they saw Coricancha's patio filled with life-sized gold and silver statues of llamas, trees, flowers, and delicate butterflies. Current excavations promise to reveal more of the temple's mysteries.

Retrace your steps toward the Plaza de Armas, and on Calle Arequipa you will find another Christian enclave that was formerly an Inca holy place.

This is the **Convento y Museo de Santa Catalina** (Mon–Sat 8am–5.30pm; charge). Now a colonial-style building occupied by Roman Catholic nuns, this was home to the Chosen Women, virgins who were trained to serve their heavenly husband, the sun, or attend to the pleasure of his earthly son, the Inca. The museum contains a fine collection of School of Cusco art.

The valley of ruins

The megalithic fortress of **Sacsayhuamán** ⑤ is a bold example of Inca architectural skills. Constructed from massive stones, this military complex overlooking Cusco has a double wall in zigzag shape. It also marks the birthplace of the river that runs under Cusco, channeled through stone conduits honed by the ancient Incas, invisibly supplying the city with water. Archeologists estimate that tens of thousands of workers labored on this massive structure for more than seven decades, hauling the immense stone blocks that make up its double outside walls and erecting the almost indestructible buildings that made

the complex one of the most wondrous in all the empire. Inti Raymi, the Inca feast of the winter solstice, is celebrated every year on June 24 at Sacsayhuamán, with a procession, a ceremony, and much merrymaking.

Some 7km (4 miles) from Sacsayhuamán, **Qenko** ⑥ is an Inca shrine that has a 5-meter (18-ft) high stone block that *cusqueños* claim looks like a puma. Its name means "labyrinth", and this ceremonial center, dedicated to Mother Earth, has water channels cut into solid rock and a subterranean room. Farther along the road to Pisac is a smaller fortress, **Puca Pucara** ⑦, believed to have guarded the road and the Sacred Valley of the Incas. It has hillside terraces, stairways, tunnels, and towers.

To the north, **Tambo Machay** ⑧ was the sacred bathing place of the Inca rulers and their royal women. A hydraulic engineering marvel, its aqueduct system still feeds water into a series of showers.

From there head down 400 meters (1,500ft) into the valley on the curvy road leading to **Pisac** ⑨ (also spelled

WHERE

Sacsayhuamán is a short hike uphill from the city. Alternatively, you can take a minibus tour, or hire a cab to take you up and wait for you. This is one of the area's most spectacular spots to take photos at dawn. Keep a close watch on your belongings.

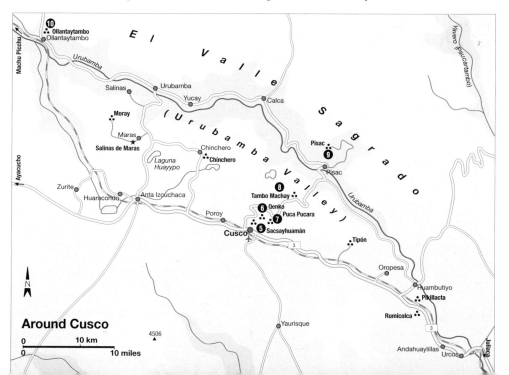

Around Cusco

Pisaq), a friendly village known for its fishing, its Sunday market, and the ruins above the town. To reach the ruins, climb past the mountainside terraces (local children will serve as guides for a small fee). It's a high-altitude hike that may leave your heart pounding. The stones in Pisac's buildings are smaller than those at Sacsayhuamán, but the precision with which they are cut and fitted will amaze you.

If you plan to do a full circuit of the valley, continue to the great fortress of **Ollantaytambo ⑩**, 72km (45 miles) from Cusco. This elegant and intricate granite complex has temples, baths, and impressive military installations. Both Ollantaytambo and Pisac can be visited on the Cusco Visitor Ticket.

The Andes

At 7,200km (4,500 miles), the Andes, the longest mountain chain in the world, forms the backbone of South America. The range stretches from Venezuela down to Tierra del Fuego, and is made up of dozens of parallel mountain ranges known as cordilleras. In Peru, these ranges cluster together,

Vendor at the Sunday market in Pisac, near Cusco.

providing trekkers with easy access to some of the world's highest peaks outside the Himalayas. Except for the most rugged and remote areas, the Peruvian Andes are not an untouched wilderness. Every single piece of arable land, however inaccessible, is farmed by local *campesinos* (peasants).

The formidable Peruvian sierra (mountainous region) was conquered by the Incas, whose terraced system of agriculture enabled large areas of steep yet fertile land to be cultivated. This ancient system is still employed in some areas, and countless remains of ancient terracing give an insight into the productivity achieved by this civilization. Passing through these remote yet populated areas is a bit like stepping back into the past. One- or two-room huts constructed of crude adobe bricks and topped with *ichu* grass have changed little in design since Inca times. There is little electricity, and water is drawn from nearby streams. Small courtyards house chickens and *cuy*, or guinea pigs, which are considered a delicacy in the sierra. Corn and other grains can often be seen drying in the midday sun.

The Inca Trail

Of all the popular treks in South America, the three to five day hike along the Inca Trail (following the course of an old Inca roadway) to Machu Picchu is the best known. The adventure from Cusco begins with a four-hour overcrowded train ride along the Urubamba River, known by the Incas as the **Sacred Valley**. It is no longer possible to walk the Inca Trail independently; you must pre-arrange the trip either before you leave home or in Cusco; this is best done well in advance as there is a limit on the number of trekkers allowed on the trail. If you want to avoid the arduous trekking, the expensive train also stops at Aguas Calientes, 8km (5 miles) from the Lost City, and you can get off there, but you will miss out on some stunning scenery.

Train tickets must also be bought in advance. It's possible to do so from Ollantaytambo, the last stop before Aguas Calientes.

The first 12km (7 miles) of the trail meander through easy terrain of dusty scrub, low-lying hills, and hut dwellings. Then comes the **Huarmihuañusqa Pass**, beyond which lies a wealth of Inca ruins. Struggling to the top of this 4,000-meter (13,000-ft) pass is no small challenge. The hiker soon identifies with its name, which translates as "Dead Woman's Pass." The small guard post of **Runkuraqay**, often shrouded in mist, is the first reward of the Inca Trail. Farther along, the more elaborately constructed ruins of **Sayajmarka** (Dominant Town) perch on top of a narrow cliff. The fine stonework for which the Incas are famous is apparent. An incredible paved highway snakes along the valley below.

Puyapatamarka (Cloud-Level Town) is fascinating for its circular walls and finely engineered aqueduct system, which still provides spring water to the ancient baths. Along the road to **Wiñay Wayna**, a long stone staircase leads into dense jungle. Clinging to a steep hillside, the last set of ruins is the most stunning of all. That something so complex was constructed in a ravine so vertical is almost beyond comprehension.

An hour away lies the jewel in the crown – **Machu Picchu ⓫**. To see it at sunrise, most trekkers stay at the camp beyond Wiñay Wayna, where rainy nights are filled with the howls of campers trying to sleep in leaky tents. The high pass of **Intipunku**, the Sun Gate, provides the first glimpse of the fabled city. Arriving as the Incas did centuries ago, the trekker begins the final descent into Machu Picchu. However, the sheer number of visitors hiking up the trail has caused the tourist board to contemplate controversial changes, such as constructing a cable car from Aguas Calientes to Machu Picchu or even restricting access.

Arequipa: the white city

Although **Arequipa ⓬** was far from Lima and isolated between desert and mountains when the country was young, it was on the route linking the silver mines of Bolivia to the coast. For that reason, the oasis at the foot of the Misti volcano grew to be the Peruvian town with the largest Spanish population and the strongest European traditions. Today, with buildings of white volcanic stone lending it the name "white city," it remains Peru's second most important city.

Arequipa's **Plaza de Armas** is one of Peru's most beautiful. One full side is occupied by the massive **Cathedral** (daily 7.30–11.30am, 4.30–7.30pm), rebuilt twice in the early 19th century after it was destroyed by fire and earthquake. Its clock is the city's unofficial timepiece. Make sure you see the cathedral's organ, brought here from Belgium, and the elaborately carved wooden pulpit, the work of French artist Rigot in 1879. Two-story arcades grace the other three sides of the plaza, with palm trees, old gas lamps, and a fountain set in an English-style garden.

Quinoa, the nutritious staple food of the Incas, is still cultivated and enjoyed in the Andes today.

Pisac market stalls.

Machu Picchu

Machu Picchu, probably still under construction when Spain invaded Peru, is the most important archeological site in the Andes.

The mystery of Machu Picchu did not start in 1911 when archeologist Hiram Bingham stumbled on the snake-infested mountain top citadel hidden by a vast tangle of vines and trees. Earlier researchers, including French archeologist Nicolas Wiener, had in 1875 received notice of possible ruins. But this site on the steep summit overlooking the raging Urubamba River was always a mystery – because only a chosen few in the Inca empire were allowed to glimpse it. To call it a "lost city" is misleading; it was more like a sanctuary.

Machu Picchu means "Old Peak," and the higher Huayna Picchu (Young Peak), stands vigil over it. The site is accessible on the 4-hour bus and train service from Cusco or by hiking the Inca Trail. The area is semitropical, and 900 meters (3,000ft) lower than Cusco.

Machu Picchu was home to priests, high functionaries, craftsmen, and servants and, most importantly, the mamaconas or virgins chosen to dedicate their lives to the sun god. It was a city of streets, of aqueducts where crystal clear waters still run, of liturgical fountains and walkways. The city remained inaccessible until the 1940s, when an archeological expedition working at the site discovered the Inca Trail cutting through the valley.

Disappearing people

The fate of the city's inhabitants remains unknown. Chronicles of the Cusco area make no mention of it. Theories of its demise range from epidemics to suggestions that the occupants were ostracized and forgotten in the bloody political disunity sweeping the empire, or that they simply abandoned a city under construction when the Spanish conquest cut off supplies. Excavations have only added to the mystery. The skeletons of 173 people were found, 150 of whom were women. No gold objects were discovered. At the tomb of the high priestess, as Bingham called it, the remains of a woman and a small dog were found with some ceramic objects, brooches, and woolen clothing. The woman had suffered from syphilis.

The only entrance to the city in ancient times was the narrow doorway at the southwest section of the citadel. The city's cultivated land was farmed on narrow terraces on the steep slopes of the mountain top, and the thousands of steps connecting them have survived for centuries. The city is divided into sections: the cemetery, jails, small dwellings, and temples. The Temple of the Three Windows allows sunlight to pass through its windows to the Sacred Plaza. Higher up is the astronomical observatory and Intiwatana, a curiously shaped stone block believed to have been a solar clock or, as some claim, "the hitching post to the sun," where the sun's rays cast shadows used in planning seasonal activities and religious ceremonies.

Some of the buildings in Machu Picchu were two stories high, originally topped with sharply peaked straw roofs. What amazes architects today is the precision with which building stones were cut and assembled.

A steep and perilous path rises from the site to the top of Huayna Picchu. At the skirt of Huayna Picchu is the construction known as the Temple of the Moon, and from the summit there is an extraordinary view of the ruins and the Urubamba valley. Some 2,500 people a day visit the ruins; Unesco, which has placed the city on its World Heritage list, believes this threatens its long-term preservation, and recommends limiting the number of tourists to 800 a day.

The breathtaking classic view of Machu Picchu.

The city is full of patrician homes built in the 18th century that have withstood its frequent tremors. The one-story colonial structures are replete with massive carved wooden doors, French windows with grilles, and high-ceilinged rooms around spacious patios. The best for visiting are **Casa Ricketts** (daily 9am–1pm, 4–6pm), built as a seminary in 1738 and now used as a bank; the 200-year-old **Casa de la Moneda** or former mint; and the **Casa Moral** (Mon–Sat 9am–5pm), which is named after the venerable mulberry tree on its patio, and has also become a bank.

La Compañía church (daily 9am–noon, 3–6pm) is also well worth seeing. The sacristy's ceiling is covered with miniature paintings and carvings in crimson and gold. The view from the steeple is fabulous, especially at sunset when the fading light gives a rosy glow to the city's white rock buildings.

The most astonishing stop in Arequipa is the **Monasterio de Santa Catalina** (daily 8am–5pm), opened in 1970 after 400 years as a cloister for nuns. Although they lived behind closed doors, the nuns paid little heed to the traditional vows of poverty and silence. During its heyday, this convent's sleeping cells were furnished with soft English carpets, silk curtains, cambric and lace sheets, and tapestry-covered stools. Each nun had her own servant and dined off porcelain plates, using silver cutlery. At the convent's peak nearly 500 nuns were housed here.

When the convent opened its doors again, its anecdotes and scandals were resurrected. But don't believe it when they tell you the story of Sister Dominga, the 16-year-old who entered the convent when her betrothed left her for a rich widow, then staged her own death to escape. This beautiful young woman really did place the body of a deceased native woman in her bed one night, then set the room on fire, but it happened at the **Convento de Santa Rosa** (which is still cloistered).

Another place worth visiting nearby is the **Museo Histórico Municipal** (Mon–Sat 9am–5pm), which is interesting for an overview of the city's history. From here it is only a few meters/

The Ollantaytambo archeological site viewed from the mountainside agricultural terrace.

TREKKING IN THE ANDES

For high-altitude trekking, bring a down jacket and plenty of warm clothes for very cold nights at 4,000 meters (13,000ft) and above. A tent and a good sleeping bag are essential. Equipment can be rented in the major trekking centers, but check the quality. Spend a few days getting used to the thin air around Cusco and Huaraz, or you will quickly become exhausted. If trekking independently (no longer possible on the Inca Trail), stock up on food – you won't be able to buy anything on the way. A lightweight stove for cooking is essential: using up scarce reserves of wood only adds to the serious problem of erosion in the area. Of course, no litter of any kind should be left behind, even if you think it is biodegradable. A local guide can be invaluable – ask around, as competence varies.

yards to the **Iglesia de San Francisco** (daily 9am–noon, 4–5.30pm), the focus of attention every December 8 during the Feast of the Immaculate Conception, when a coach topped with the image of the Virgin Mary is paraded through the streets in a colorful procession. The most interesting museum in the city, the **Monasterio de la Recoleta** (Mon–Sat 9am–noon, 3–5pm), lies across the Río Chili (use the Puente Grau or Puente Bolognesi). The monastery has a vast library of 20,000 books and maps, some dating back to the 15th century.

Independent spirits

Outside Arequipa, set in beautiful countryside, is **Sabandía**, with its nearby flour mill that was restored, stone by stone, in 1973. Three hours away and drawing nearly as much tourist attention as the city itself is the **Colca Canyon**. From the Colca River at its base to the mountains above, the chasm reaches depths of 3,400 meters (11,000ft). Even more remote than Colca, the **Cotahuasi Canyon** is now believed to exceed Colca in depth

Santa Catalina monastery.

(3,535 meters/11,600ft), making it the deepest canyon in the Americas. It is a pristine area of great natural beauty and ideal for both adventurers and nature lovers.

At the Cruz del Cóndor viewpoint you may see a condor, soaring on the warm thermal currents produced in the early morning or the early evening. The Cruz del Cóndor is included in a variety of 1- and 2-day trips, which can be organized in Arequipa. En route, many of the tours take in the **Reserva Nacional Salinas y Aguada Blanca** (at 3,900 meters/12,800ft you'll notice how thin the air is), where groups of delicate vicuñas can often be seen. The area is also accessible from Arequipa, first by bus, then switching to *burros* (donkeys).

To unwind in Arequipa after a hard day's sightseeing, do what the locals do and head to a *picantería* for a cold *Arequipeña* beer and some spicy stuffed peppers, rabbit, or marinated pork.

Puno and Lake Titicaca

Lake Titicaca's great size and breathless altitude, its mysterious antiquity, and even its steamships constitute an exotic legend. At 174km (108 miles) long and up to 64km (40 miles) wide, Titicaca is South America's largest lake (see page 172). The lake moderates the climate and facilitates cultivation around its shores, despite the frosty nights and short growing season. Peru and Bolivia share this lake peacefully, but in bygone times it was at the heart of warring tribalism and imperial ambition. About 1,500 years ago the powerful Tihuanaku civilization built a vast city on the Bolivian shore; its collapse led to centuries of sectarian strife. At Sillustani, the towering tombs of the Colla kings, whose armies fought the Incas, can still be seen. Today, Quechua- and Aymaraspeaking people occupy discrete stretches of Titicaca's shoreline.

You can visit two very different island communities that subsist on the lake. The Uros islanders, dwelling

on spongy reed masses, live on the waters of **Puno** bay. This tourist hub is an old, cold town on the lake shore that has, thanks to the tourism industry, undergone something of a revival. Puno now offers a good selection of comfortable hotels, as well as lively bars and some decent restaurants.

On solid **Taquile**, a traditional way of life manages to survive in spite of the steady flow of fascinated visitors. Taquile is a traditional Quechua-speaking community. The island is best known for its weaving, and two co-ops in the central square sell superb handicrafts. Overnighters should have sufficient time to climb to the highest point on the island. Follow a footpath that turns uphill off the street between the village and the main archway, allowing about 30 minutes to reach the top. Toward the summit there are some tombs dating from pre-Inca times. The summit views of Lake Titicaca, with Amantaní island to the north, are superb. In fine weather you can see a dazzling horizon of snowy peaks, the Cordillera Real, on the Bolivian shore.

The lake's hinterland is a great plateau studded with isolated mountains known as the Altiplano, the high plain. **Juliaca** is its hustling commercial capital, known for its textile and leather goods, while the charming town of Lampa is becoming a tourism center.

The Peruvian Amazon

Three-fifths of Peru is jungle – the Amazon. Despite the encroachment of modern life, this is where adventures can still occur and the exotic reigns. Here the roads are rivers and the vehicles are motorboats and canoes. It is the home of many natural healers, who say that its unique fauna might contain anything from new contraceptives to a cancer cure. The Amazon is the one place the Incas never managed to penetrate. When the Spanish conquistadors arrived, they heard wild tales of a golden city hidden in the heart of the jungle. In their search for El Dorado, they found nothing but disease and hostile tribes, although the legend lives on.

Setting out from Quito, Spanish explorer Francisco de Orellana was the first European to navigate the Amazon River. He named it after the fierce female warriors of Greek legend, possibly mistaking the long-haired Yagua men, who confronted him wearing fiber skirts, for women. A later Spanish expedition was fictionalized in the 1973 Werner Herzog film *Aguirre, the Wrath of God*, about the demonic conquistador Aguirre, who killed for pleasure during his 1560 trek along the Amazon. The search for gold was replaced by missionaries' quest to convert the indigenous population. From the late 1600s to the mid-1700s, thanks to an uprising led by Jesuit-educated Quechua Juan Santos, the jungle was kept free of Europeans, but the missionaries eventually returned. More recently, the Catholic presence in the rainforest has received strong competition from Protestant evangelists.

A llama roaming the slopes of Machu Picchu.

Exploring the ancient Inca ruins of Machu Picchu.

Tour boat on Lake Titicaca.

Sillustani is known for its pre-Incan Chullpas, or burial mounds, on the shore of Lake Umayo.

The rubber barons

The colonization of the Amazon was consolidated at the end of the 1800s with the rubber boom. The period was one of overnight wealth for European and US rubber barons and overnight enslavement for the people of the rainforest. The best-known of the rubber barons was Carlos Fitzgerald, the son of an English immigrant and a Peruvian. Accused of spying for Chile during the 1879 war, "Fitzcarraldo" fled to the Amazon where he made a great fortune in rubber and became obsessed with a plan to travel from the Ucayali River (which flows into the Amazon) through the Madre de Dios River by steamship. (His story was also fictionalized by Herzog in a 1982 film, *Fitzcarraldo*.) Although Fitzcarraldo's quest failed, steamships later made the trip, effectively linking the Atlantic and Pacific oceans – with thousands of natives hauling the ships across the isthmus. Fitzcarraldo and other rubber barons had no cause to miss Europe; they imported every luxury that struck their fancy, from Paris fashions to wines, and European theatre and opera stars regularly performed in the midst of one of the world's densest jungles. But the opulence ended in 1920 when rubber grown in Asia and Africa began to compete on the world market.

Boom towns and exotic wildlife

Peru's most important rubber boom city – and the largest city in the Peruvian Amazon – is **Iquitos** ⑬. The old days of wealth are still evident in the houses covered with Portuguese tiles and, on the **Plaza de Armas**, in the ramshackle two-story metal house designed by Gustave Eiffel for the Paris Exhibition of 1889 and transported to Iquitos piece by piece by rubber magnate Jules Toth. On the waterfront is the colorful **Belén** port, where the houses float on rafts. From here, irregular riverboat services run to Leticia in Colombia and onward to Manaus in Brazil, preserving a taste of the days when air travel was unknown and the only way to reach Iquitos was through weeks of journeying overland and upriver. Although Iquitos is a bustling city of 400,000 people, one only has

to go a short distance on the Amazon, Yanamono, or Manatí rivers to be in virgin jungle. On the way are the wood and palm houses on stilts inhabited by the *ribereños* – mestizos who speak a lilting Spanish reminiscent of Brazilian Portuguese. Exotic birds fly in and out of vine-covered trees, while brilliantly colored butterflies, tapirs, monkeys, peccaries, and pink river dolphins fascinate visitors. Only 100km (62 miles) from Iquitos is the biggest preserve in Peru, the 2 million-hectare (5 million-acre) **Reserva Nacional Pacaya-Samiria**, a wildlife-packed lowland jungle area. Multi-day tours with stays in jungle lodges can be arranged most easily in Iquitos and Lima.

The people in this part of the Amazon live isolated lives, except when they head off in their dugout canoes or hitch a ride on the "river buses" – boats that cruise up and down the river collecting passengers and their cargoes of bananas, yucca, corn, dried fish, and chickens, headed for Iquitos.

Another important Amazon city is **Pucallpa ⓮**, a frontier lumber town and the farthest inland navigable port for ocean-going vessels on the Amazon. It is 9km (6 miles) from **Lago Yarinacocha**, a 22-km (14-mile) body of water luring tourists fascinated by its spectacular sunrises and sunsets, its fishing, and the undisturbed native Shipibo villages along its banks. Its forests are full of cedar, pine, mahogany, and bamboo and serve as home to nearly 1,000 bird species, endless varieties of butterflies, and exotic mammals – including sloths. Local boats called *pekepekes* are available for hire for day trips to some of the isolated villages or to visit the Shipibos and buy their hand-painted pottery and textiles. In nearby **Puerto Callao** you can visit the fascinating artisanal cooperative Maroti Shobo, where high-quality ceramics and weavings made by Shipibo from surrounding villages are displayed and sold, and sent to museums all over the world. Farther south is **Puerto Maldonado ⓯**, just a few hours by river from one of the world's most important wildlife reserves and capital of Madre de Dios, the least-populated, least-developed and least-explored province in Peru.

Colca Canyon viewed from the Cruz del Cóndor.

National Peruvian Marinera Dance Festival parade passing by the cathedral on Plaza de Armas, Trujillo.

At 1.8 million hectares (4.5 million acres), the **Parque Nacional Manu** is one of the largest conservation areas in the world. Founded in 1973, it was declared a Biosphere Reserve in 1977, and a World Natural Heritage Site 10 years later. Parts are accessible only to biologists and anthropologists with permits, one zone is set aside for two local native groups, and the reserve zone is aimed at ecotourists. The excellent **Manu Wildlife Center** allows visitors to meet researchers and scientists on-site. Closer to Puerto Maldonado is another large reserve, the **Reserva Nacional Tambopata Candamo**. Created by the Peruvian government in 1989, this 1.5 million-hectare (3.8 million-acre) zone has been set up both as an extractive reserve (for rubber, Brazil nuts, and other products) and for ecotourism. The reserve encompasses the entire watershed of the **Río Tambopata**, and protects the largest macaw lick in South America, the **Colpa de Guacamayos**, where hundreds of parrots and macaws gather daily. Sadly, the area is under threat from illegal gold mining and a new road to Brazil.

Peru's historical north

Trujillo , the "travelers' resting place" along the Spaniards' route between Lima and Quito, is a graceful coastal city. Founded in 1535 and named after Francisco Pizarro's birthplace in Spain, it soon became worthy of the title "the Lordliest City," and even today its well-preserved Andalusian-style wooden balconies, with decorative grilles, pay testimony to the colonial days.

The city was the first in Peru to declare independence from Spain in 1820, and in the 1920s it was the birthplace of APRA (Alianza Popular Revolucionaria Americana), Peru's longest-standing political party.

The best place to start exploring Trujillo is the **Plaza de Armas**, bounded by the city hall, the bishop's palace, and the cathedral with its marble pillars and gilt hand-carved wooden altars. The colonial building next to the cathedral is now the **Hotel Libertador Trujillo**. Off the main

square, colonial mansions abound, although earthquakes have taken their toll. Most buildings have been elegantly restored by national banks or other private enterprises (most Mon–Fri and Sat am). **Casa de la Emancipación** (Mon–Fri 10am–6pm) is typical of the houses built in the 16th and 17th centuries and contains much of its original furniture. **Casa de Mayorazgo** (Mon–Fri 9.15am–12.30pm), **Casa Urquiaga** (Mon–Fri 9am–3pm, Sat 10am–1.30pm), **Casa Bracamonte** (visits restricted), and **Casa de los Leones** (Mon–Fri 9am–1pm, 2–6pm, Sat 9am–1pm, now an art gallery, also known as the Casa Ganoza Chopitea) are all worth a look. The **Palacio Iturregui** Mon–Sat 8am–10.30am houses the Club Central, with a permanent exhibition of ceramics. Trujillo's pre-Hispanic past is on display at the University of Trujillo's **Museo de Arqueología** (Mon–Fri 8am–2.45pm). The **Museo Cassinelli** (Mon–Sat 9am–1pm, 3–6pm) in the basement of the Cassinelli gas station, holds a fascinating private collection of Moche and Chimu ceramics.

An ancient adobe city

To the northwest of Trujillo are the ruins of **Chan Chan**, which was one of the world's largest adobe cities when discovered by the Spanish. Made up of seven citadels spread over 28 sq km (11 sq miles) and enclosed by a massive wall, Chan Chan was home to the Chimu people, who fished and farmed, worshiped the moon, and left no written records. On the city walls are carvings of fish, sea birds, sea otters, fishing nets, and moons. The Chimus had such a sophisticated irrigation and aqueduct system that they were able to turn the arid wasteland around them into fertile fields of grains, fruits, and vegetables.

About 10km (6 miles) southeast of Trujillo lie **Las Huacas del Sol y de la Luna** (The Tombs of the Sun and the Moon). You can get there by minibus or go on an organized tour. These pyramidal temples were built by the Moche people (100 BC–AD 850). The Huaca del Sol (arguably the largest pre-Columbian building in the Americas) is being excavated, but at the smaller Huaca de la Luna, 15 years

Taking a break at the Museo de Arqueología in Trujillo.

The Pará rubber tree, or seringueira, is named after the Brazilian state.

The ancient adobe citadel of Chan Chan.

of archeological work have unveiled a series of temples superimposed on one another to form a pyramid covered in beautiful, bright murals. Archeology enthusiasts should visit the **Huaca el Brujo**, a recently discovered site a few hours from Trujillo in the Chicama Valley. Ask at the tourist information office for details.

Where the last Inca leader met his fate

Historically, the most important northern city is **Cajamarca** ⓲. This is the city where the Incas and Spaniards had their final confrontation. According to Spanish chronicles, the Inca Atahualpa (see page 30) was taken prisoner after offending the Europeans by accepting a preferred Bible, then tossing it to the ground. To pay the ransom demanded by the conquistadors, people from all over the Inca empire brought gold and silver, filling **El Cuarto del Rescate** (The Ransom Room; Mon–Sat 9am– 1pm, 3–6pm, Sun 9am–1pm), a block from the Plaza de Armas. But the effort was futile and the Spaniards garrotted the last Inca king on the main square.

The **Plaza de Armas** is the hub of this slow-paced city of 120,000 and is ringed by colonial buildings and churches. Opened in 1776, the **cathedral**'s carved wood altars are covered in gold leaf and its facade is of intricately sculpted volcanic rock. The **Iglesia San Francisco**, older and more ornate than the cathedral, is home to the **Museo de Arte Religioso** (Mon– Fri 2–5pm) and some eerie catacombs. Also on the plaza is Restaurante Salas, the place to eat the city's best home cooking. Cajamarca is ideal for exploring the province of **Amazonas**, home of the Chachapoyan, who built several pre-Incan cities, including **Kuélap**, a great walled city perched high above the Río Utcubamba. Minibuses leave in the morning for the village of **Tingo**, from where a road goes to within 15 minutes' walk of the fascinating site.

Digging for the past

The Moche burial area at **Sipán** (Tue–Sun 9am–5pm; guided tours

available), about 30km (18 miles) south of **Chiclayo** ⓳, is the largest tomb excavated in the Americas. Known as the tomb of El Señor de Sipán, it was uncovered in the late 1980s, originally by *huaqueros*, before the excavation was taken over by the director of the Museo Brüning, Walter Alva. He became aware of unusual objects on the black market and realized that a burial site was being ransacked. It is 15 meters (50ft) deep and contained the remains of a high priest or prince wearing a spectacular gold mask with emerald eyes. In his tomb were numerous artifacts including gold and copper, and gilded cotton cloth.

There were also the skeletons of 24 women. The whole burial complex comprises 14 tombs, one of which contained 50 kg (110lb) of gold. The continuing excavation at Sipán promises to provide crucial new evidence about the life of the Moche, a sophisticated pre-Columbian civilization that flourished in AD 100–700.

The nearby **Sicán** site, the first to be excavated using radar, disclosed similar riches from the period betweeen the Moche and Chimu civilizations (9th–10th centuries). The artifacts and remains found are on the same scale as those unearthed in the tomb of Tutankhamun. The site is well worth visiting, but to see the stunning contents of the tomb, when they are not touring the world's museums, you should go to the tiny town of **Lambayeque** nearby to visit the remarkable **Museo Tumbas Reales de Sipán** (daily 9am–5pm), which has Peru's finest publicly owned gold, silver, and ceramic collection, as well as the fabulous finds from the Sipán dig. Significant nearby museums are the Museo Brüning in town and the Museo Nacional de Sicán in Ferrañafe.

One of the most intriguing projects in the area was set up by Norwegian explorer Thor Heyerdahl, whose dig at **Túcume**, near Sipán, brought together a team of European and Peruvian archeologists. Túcume is a plain whose 27 hills are actually pyramids covered by centuries of dirt, and can be explored on a guided tour from Chiclayo.

FACT

Máncora, near Tumbes on the border with Ecuador, has become a surfer's mecca, with reliable waves particularly from November through February and world-class Cabo Blanco beach. Máncora has a laid-back lifestyle, sandy palm-fringed beaches with small beachfront hotels catering to backpackers and local tourists.

Reed boats in the beach town of Pimentel, near Chiclayo.

A REMARKABLE CRAFT

In 1948, a Norwegian expedition led by Thor Heyerdahl embarked on a voyage that would take it from Callao in Peru to French Polynesia in a balsa raft, the *Kon-Tiki*. Heyerdahl's intention was to prove that indigenous people could have colonized the Pacific Islands on balsa rafts, and his expedition launched a whole area of scientific investigation. The raft is now in the Kon-Tiki Museum in Oslo and Heyerdahl's book about his journey became a bestseller. His theory has since been discredited, but interest in the sea-going craft of the pre-Columbian South Americans and Pacific Islanders has increased. Many modern adventurers have their rafts built by Bolivians from the Lake Titicaca region, who are considered the best balsa-raft craftsmen in the world.

When the Spanish first reached the Americas they recorded in detail these craft, which ranged from the *totora* reed-bundle rafts used today by the fishermen of Huanchaco, not far from Trujillo, to huge cargo-carrying varieties. The Spanish chronicler Augustín de Zárate (1514–60) described rafts that could carry as many as 50 men and three horses. In the 17th century, European navigators began to understand the *guara*, or centerboard, a kind of keel used by the native people. Visitors to Peru today can witness the ancient craft in action around Lake Titicaca, or at Huanchaco.

LAKE TITICACA

Surrounded by snow-capped Andean peaks, this lofty expanse of clear, fresh water has fired the imagination for generations.

Linking Peru and Bolivia, the world's highest navigable lake is a large, remarkably clear blue body of water covering more than 8,000 sq km (3,000 sq miles), with more than 30 islands. The lake may look inviting, but bathers beware – at 4,000 meters (13,000ft) above sea level, its waters are extremely cold all year round. Lake Titicaca is full of ancient legends, sacred sites, and living history, as age-old traditions are continued and developed on and around its waters. Ecotours and kayaking are among its newer travel options.

The Isla del Sol, in the middle of the lake, is at the center of the Inca creation myths as recorded by 16th-century Spanish chroniclers. One myth tells of the emergence of four sisters and four brothers from a stone door on the island, two of which were the Incas Manco Capac and Mama Ocllo (or Huaca). Another legend relates that the sun was born on a sacred rock on the island. Ruined Inca temples and sacred sites can be visited on the Isla del Sol and the nearby Isla de la Luna. Folklore holds that before the Spanish reached Cusco in Peru, the Incas took a 1,800kg (2-ton) gold chain of Inca Huascar (whose name means "chain") from Qoricancha, and dropped it into the lake. In 1996 the oldest known temple in South America was found near the lake, occupied between 1500 and 1000 BC, nearly 2,500 years before the Incas. Its discovery adds to the fascination of this remarkable region.

The colorful textile designs of Isla Taquile are not just for decoration but can denote social or marital status, while some are reserved for special times of the year.

A shepherd leads cows down the side of the mountain on Taquile island.

Climbing up to Pacha Pata, an ancient Lake Titicaca religious site.

THE WEAVERS OF ISLA TAQUILE

On the Peruvian side of the lake is Isla Taquile – the island of weavers. Under the Spanish it was a hacienda, and later it became a prison, but the Taquile people have managed to regain ownership. Since 1970 they have been running their own tourism operations to ensure their old traditions are not lost.

There are no hotels, but islanders open their homes to overnight guests, and there are small eating establishments specializing in lake trout.

Tradition has bred a cooperative lifestyle, which has won the islanders their reputation for hospitality. Textiles can be purchased from the weaving cooperatives, most produced from finely spun sheep's wool dyed bright red and blue – the colors and weaves can reveal age, social position, and marital status. More textiles can be purchased at Amantaní, a peaceful island with temples and a carved stone throne on one shore.

Taquile islanders' distinctive clothing, as worn by this young weaver, was in fact imposed by Taquile's colonial owners and adapted from Andalusia.

Drying out the lake's precious reeds for future use, such as in the building of totora reed boats, constructed since time immemorial to sail the vast expanses of the lake.

Lake Titicaca as seen from the Hotel Libertador.

Although the last full-blood Uros died in 1959, modern Uros islanders still use reeds to build not just boats but homes and islands – as well as for food.

A llama farm in Bolivia.

A shepherdess watches over a herd of sheep near Copacabana.

BOLIVIA

Landlocked and isolated, Bolivia rewards intrepid
visitors with its rich cultural heritage and literally
breathtaking mountain scenery.

Bolivia takes you from the heights of the altiplano, the Andean plateau that elevates the northeast of the country, down to the balmy valleys of the subtropical region known as the *yungas* and on to the fertile lowlands of the Oriente. Linking these physically dissimilar territories arc hair-raising zigzag roads that cling to near-vertical cliffs.

Bolivia is noted for its material highs and lows as well, particularly the vast gulf between rich and poor. The poverty is obvious – just look around you on the streets of La Paz, behind the cheerful smiles of the traders and colorfully dressed campesinos (small farmers), or drive past families toiling in the fields early in the morning.

Bolivia's wealth is not so obvious, but it is hinted at in certain genteel cafés in La Paz, the unofficial capital. Much of it, like the riches of the silver and tin mines, was concentrated in the hands of a few, and spirited away to Europe. Additionally, a good deal of the country's physical wealth was taken by Chile in the Saltpeter War. Today, Bolivia is the subcontinent's poorest nation, with about half of its population, of whom many are subsistence farmers, living in poverty, and the highest infant mortality rate in South America. A quarter is still classified as extremely poor. But some progress has come, and economic growth based on natural gas and

mineral exports have lifted the country, according to the World Bank, to the level of a "middle income" nation.

The lust for silver

In 1544 a native named Diego Huallpa discovered silver in the Cerro Rico of Potosí, and from that moment, the country's fate was sealed. For the next two centuries, everything in Bolivia was geared toward extracting this vein of precious metal, the greatest ever discovered. Towns were founded for the sole purpose of supplying Potosí

Main Attractions

Lake Titicaca and Tihuanaco
Yungas valleys
Colonial Sucre
Potosi
The Uyuni salt flats

The Fiesta de la Virgen de Guadalupe in Sucre.

with goods traded from other parts of the empire or to transfer silver back to Europe. Nothing mattered to the Spanish except the ore and its transportation from the freezing wilderness, least of all the fate of the local people. The magnificent Inca systems of terracing and irrigation fell into disrepair, and Christianity was imposed, although the conversion was superficial. More obvious was the imposition of a new form of dress for native women. Layered dresses, derbys (bowler hats), and plaited hair typify the most common tourist view of the Bolivian people today – but this way of dressing actually came about by Spanish decree in the 18th century.

The local populations were theoretically free subjects of the Spanish crown, but in reality they were forced to pay massive tributes, lived at the beck and call of brutal overlords, and were regularly dragged from their farms to work in the mines of Potosí. Native people died by the thousands in the harsh conditions while colonial Potosí grew to match any city in the Old World.

The amount of silver that was taken from Potosí is staggering: 16 million kg (16,000 tons) arrived in Seville between 1545 and 1660, three and a half times the entire European reserves of the day. The wealth was squandered on Spain's futile religious wars, or wasted by the extravagance of its nobles and clergymen, much of it ending up in the coffers of Flemish, German, or English bankers, and thereby triggering inflation in Europe.

The creation of Bolivia in 1825 (see page 36) launched the country on a path in which it was governed by an apparently endless series of military governments, mostly a result of bloodless reshufflings in the palaces of La Paz, with wealth and control being kept in the hands of a small number of families of Spanish descent. Meanwhile, the country proceeded to lose large chunks of its territory in wars with its neighbors.

The only good news seemed to be the discovery of rich veins of tin, in Oruro and Potosí, by a prospector named Simón Patiño. But Patiño amassed a personal fortune from this new boom, becoming one of the 10 richest people on earth by the early 1900s. He left his mark on Cochabamba in the form of the **Palacio de Portales**, built between 1915 and 1925. While Patiño lived in luxury, he kept miners on starvation wages, and he quashed industrial disputes by organizing massacres as he vacationed in Europe.

After the tin boom it was natural gas that replaced silver as Bolivia's main foreign currency earner.

EVO MORALES

Bolivian President Evo Morales is not the first indigenous president in the subcontinent's history, a distinction held by Alejandro Toledo of Peru, but perhaps Morales' left-wing brand of politics makes people forget that he was preceded by the more conservative Toledo, who also had a far more elite education, and received an economics degree from Stanford in the US. During his years in power, Morales has accumulated 20 honorary doctorates, but his background is far more typical of the millions of disadvantaged South Americans, indigenous or otherwise. Of Uru-Aymaran background, he received only basic education, and rose through the ranks as a leader of the lowland coca growers' union, which he joined in his early 20s after being born and raised in an adobe hut in the Altiplano near Oruro.

Moves for change

A period of intense self-reflection followed the lost 1930s Chaco War, creating a movement for change, culminating in the Revolutionary Nationalist Movement (MNR) led by Victor Paz Estenssoro. Winning the elections of 1951, the party was blocked from office by a military coup, and Paz Estenssoro was forced into exile in Buenos Aires. But the miners began an armed revolt and, after heavy fighting, defeated the military. Paz Estenssoro returned to La Paz and the MNR began to put its reforms into action. In the following years Bolivia saw the nationalization of tin mines, the granting of votes to native peoples, and extensive land reform. Unfortunately, the mines were still dependent on foreign capital, and the land given to indigenous peoples was in plots too small to be productive. The economy began sliding and the MNR was ousted in another military coup.

Dictator followed dictator with monotonous regularity. The country's most infamous dictator came to power in 1980 in a coup that cost hundreds of lives: General Luis García Meza sent his tanks into La Paz, shot left-wing leaders, and bombed mining camps in Oruro. He ran an extraordinarily corrupt regime, inviting ex-Nazi Klaus Barbie to help organize his security forces, and selling off national assets to line his own pockets. Finally García Meza was driven from power and in 1982 democracy was restored under Hernán Siles Zuazo, who is unfortunately best remembered for leading Bolivia into one of the world's highest inflation rates, hitting a mind-boggling 35,000 percent a year.

Tin price collapse

In 1985, with the economy on the verge of collapse, Paz Estenssoro returned as president. He embraced the conservative policies recommended by the IMF and, with the collapse of tin prices, sacked 20,000 miners from the state-run COMIBOL company, using the military to head

A Night at the Pena

Among the best-known Andean images is traditional music played with *charangos* and *zampoñas*. Experience it first-hand at a *peña*.

Starting at around 10pm, *peñas* are usually relaxed, informal bars that offer set musical programs. Up to a dozen groups can play on a single night, giving an idea of the range and variety of Andean music; while the rhythms of the altiplano are related, every region has its own unique sound. A group from Potosí is quite different to one from the shores of Lake Titicaca, and different again to one from Cusco in Peru. The musicians are often accomplished mimics and the show generally includes a few comic turns, which can be quite hilarious, even if you don't understand the language.

In La Paz, one of the best *peñas* is the Naira at Sagárnaga 161, a dark and intimate venue with a fine repertory of musicians. Other well-known *penãs* are in the restaurants Los Escudos on

Playing the charango in celebration at a school graduation.

Mariscal Santa Cruz and La Casa del Corregidor on Murrillo 1040.

Instruments

The basic instruments used are the single-reed flutes known as *quenas*, *zampoñas* (deep wooden pipes), drums, and rattles. The famous *charango* is a miniature guitar, sometimes made from an armadillo's shell, with 15 strings with which the player creates a penetrating, tinny sound. Along with the Andean harp, the *charango* is an unusual example of the local culture mixing successfully with the Spanish. Stringed instruments were one of the few cultural innovations that the Andean peoples were glad to accept from Europe. The effect of these instruments is mesmerizing and evokes the loneliness and austerity of the bleak and harsh altiplano. The music is traditionally played without vocal accompaniment, but in recent decades ballads – called *huaynos* – have been added, sung mostly in the Quechua or Aymara tongues, or in a mixture of native languages and Spanish. They often deal with the daily lives of *campesinos*:

Do you want me to tell you
Where I'm from?
I'm from behind that hill
Amid the carnations
Among the lilies.
My sling is of Castilian fabric
And my lasso of merino wool:
Very long-lasting
Very strong.

Popular reception

As an expression of native culture, the music has often had a mixed reception. On radio, it must compete with modern pop, as well as salsa and samba. At its worst, it has "crossed over," producing Western songs on Andean instruments. But as native cultures are increasingly gaining acceptance, the presence of altiplano tunes is definitely growing. The most famous Andean group from Bolivia are Los Kjarkas, who regularly tour the Americas and Europe. One of their songs, *Llorando se fué*, was famously plagiarized in the late 1980s French hit Lambada, leading to a compensation payment. Los Kjarkas' popularity helped set apart Bolivia's particular local music from that of the Andean areas of Argentina and Chile's Nueva Canción. Conversely, Bolivian rock groups like Octavia have incorporated Andean instruments into their music.

off union protests. Inflation ground to a halt, but at the cost of massive unemployment.

Inconclusive results in the 1989 elections led to a congressional vote to elect the president, and center-left Jaime Paz Zamora came to power under an alliance with right-wing ex-dictator Hugo Banzer. Unemployment boosted cocaine manufacture as people looked for new sources of income, and in the early 1990s the US embarked on anti-narcotics programs in Bolivia, tied to aid and trade preferences. Such programs have often provoked violent demonstrations by angry *cocaleros* (coca growers). Many defend their traditional right to grow coca for uses other than drug production, and to grow a crop that is more durable than rice or potatoes and which can be many times more lucrative.

Relative stability under Gonzálo Sánchez de Lozada, ex-dictator Hugo Banzer and Jorge Quiroga ended in early 2003. Bolivia's most violent protests in decades were sparked when Sánchez de Lozada's second government tried to introduce income tax. The police were among those workers who went on strike. The army was called in to restore order but used bullets to control the crowd, resulting in 33 deaths. Income tax proposals were withdrawn, and five ministries were abolished.

Continuing protests over rising fuel prices and the ownership of the country's valuable gas resources, as well as demands for autonomy by resource-rich provinces, make Bolivia a tough country to govern. Sánchez de Lozada was forced to resign in 2003 and was succeeded by Carlos Mesa. Unable to do much better, he too threw in the towel in 2005. One clear leader has emerged from the burgeoning social movements in Bolivia: socialist peasant leader and indigenous coca farmer, Evo Morales. His success in the 2005 elections has been crucial to the indigenous movement of Bolivia, and the country at last has a president who is representative of the majority of the population. Morales has taken a clear stance against US influence in the region and has increased

View of Illimani from the periphery of La Paz.

Food is one of the attractions in La Paz's markets. Street vendors sell papaya milkshakes, spiced chicken and rice, fried trout caught in Lake Titicaca, or pieces of heart with hot nut sauces skewered on a wire. The markets near Plaza San Francisco have a particularly good range of delicacies.

Cholas (indigenous women) selling vegetables in La Paz.

control of the country's gas reserves, which are the second-largest in South America. Almost two-thirds of the voters handed him a second straight term in elections in December 2009, also providing him with a strong parliamentary majority.

La Paz: the highest capital

If you are going to fly to Bolivia's unofficial capital, **La Paz ❶** (Sucre is the official one), try to get a window seat. The views are extraordinary as the airplane sweeps across Bolivia's highest mountain ranges and descends toward the city, which sits in a natural canyon. The one disadvantage is that some travelers arriving in the airport, at an altitude of almost 4,000 meters (13,000ft), are immediately struck by the nausea and headaches of *soroche*, or altitude sickness. However, the city is 400 meters (1,300ft) lower than the airport, and a day or two of taking it easy is a certain cure.

In such a magnificent setting, La Paz at first seems like an ugly blur of orange brick and gray corrugated iron rooftops. But on much

closer inspection, it is one of South America's most unusual and lively cities. The streets of La Paz, made of slippery bricks, are steep and tiring in the thin mountain air. They meet at the **Plaza San Francisco** with its huge stone church containing a statue of Jesus with a blue fluorescent halo.

The snowcapped **Mount Illimani**, at over 6,000 meters (19,000ft), dominates the skyline from most parts of La Paz. The modern city center has a collection of shabby skyscrapers and broad streets, often clogged with traffic. The city's traditional center is the **Plaza Murillo**, where the Italianate **Presidential Palace** is located. It is often referred to as the *Palacio Quemado* (Burnt Palace), because it has twice been gutted by inflammatory crowds since it was first built in the 1850s. Nearby is the modern **Cathedral**. The surrounding streets are the most atmospheric in the city: **Calle Jaén** is still cobbled and without traffic, lined by preserved colonial buildings. Another atmospheric area is behind the church and monastery of

San Francisco, near the upper end of Avenida Mariscal Santa Cruz. Dating from 1549, it has numerous rich and ingenious carvings.

The café of the **Club de La Paz**, on the corner of avenidas Camacho and Colón, is a cultural landmark. This antique wooden retreat has seen innumerable business and political deals, and was probably where many of Bolivia's coups were hatched. It was a favorite hangout of Klaus Barbie before he was arrested in the early 1980s and returned to France for trial as a Nazi war criminal.

Witches and markets

The real attraction of La Paz is the street life. Narrow alleyways stretching up the hillside behind the Plaza San Francisco are generally packed with brightly dressed Bolivian *campesinas* selling blankets, nuts, herbs and – for the *gringos* – woolen sweaters with llama motifs. Near here is the famous **Mercado de Hechicería**, or Witchcraft Market, where elderly ladies sell magic charms for every possible occasion. You can pick up a small

bottle full of colored pieces of wood and oil which, depending on its contents, will give good luck with love, money, or health.

La Paz has an unusual collection of museums, such as the **Museo Murillo** (Tue–Fri 9am–12.30pm, 2.30–7pm Sat–Sun 9am–1pm) on Calle Jaén, in an old mansion once owned by one of the country's greatest heroes, Pedro Domingo Murillo, who led an unsuccessful revolt against the Spanish in 1809 and was hanged for his efforts. There is a good collection of colonial furniture and a room devoted to medicine and magic. In the same street, the **Museo del Litoral** (Tue–Fri 9am–12.30pm, 2.30–7pm Sat–Sun 9am–1pm) has artifacts from the War of the Pacific, which deprived Bolivia of its only access to the sea. A defiant emblem over the cashier's desk reads: "Bolivia Has Not Lost and Will Never Lose Its Right to the Pacific." The **Museo Nacional de Arte** (Tue–Fri 9.30am–12.30pm 3–7pm, Sat 10am–5.30pm Sun 10am–1.30pm), in the 18th-century Baroque palace of the Count of Arana, near the cathedral

Statue in front of the Cathedral on Plaza Pedro De Murillo, La Paz.

Mysterious items for sale at the Witches Market in La Paz.

A hat stall selling the traditional bowler hats.

Waiting outside a guitar shop in La Paz.

at Calle Socabaya 432, has colonial and local paintings, and the **Museo Nacional de Etnografía y Folklore** (Mon–Fri 9am–12.30pm, 3–7pm Sat 9am–4.30pm Sun 9am–12.30pm), in the palace of the Marquis of Villaverde, at Calle Ingavi 916, has some good Ayoreo and Chipaya exhibits.

Beyond the city

La Paz is the perfect base for exploring the Bolivian highlands. The easiest excursion is to the **Valle de la Luna** (Valley of the Moon). Only 11km (7 miles) from downtown La Paz in distance, but light years away in appearance, this is a bizarrely eroded hillside full of pinnacles and miniature canyons. Known technically as "badlands," its desert formations are constantly shifting, and you can spend hours exploring them.

Chacaltaya **B**, an hour and a half by bus from the city center, was once the world's highest developed ski area, but, sadly, the fabled glacier has been melted by global warming. However, the peak still provides some spectacular views of the Andes.

Most visitors to La Paz use the opportunity to visit the Bolivian side of nearby **Lake Titicaca** (see page 172), the great high-altitude expanse of water shared with Peru. One easy excursion is to the small village of **Copacabana** **C**, famous for its miracle-working Dark Virgin of the Lake, the patron saint of Bolivia. An image of the Virgin was taken to Rio de Janeiro in the 19th century and the village later found itself giving its name to a Brazilian beach. The Bolivian Copacabana is a quiet and relaxing place, where visitors can stroll along the lakeside or eat in one of the many fish restaurants. But it comes alive during its fiestas, when the Virgin is paraded through the streets, a copious amount of alcohol is consumed, and new buses and trucks are solemnly blessed by having beer poured over their hoods.

A boat trip to the lush and idyllic **Isla del Sol** **D** (Island of the Sun) is well worthwhile. The sacred rock is where the Incas believed that their founding parents, Manco Capac and Mama Ocllo, emerged from the waters of Lake Titicaca at the call of the sun god. The Inca Utama Hotel and Spa and **Andean Roots Cultural Complex** is an oasis on the lakeshore at Huatajata, which provides a fascinating insight into the culture, lifestyle, and values of the native Andean people.

An ancient civilization

The splendid ruins of **Tiahuanaco** **E**, located on the southern tip of Lake Titicaca, are easily accessible from La Paz. This site is fast becoming one of the most important in South America. Tiahuanaco has a magnificently carved Gate of the Sun, the Acapana Pyramid, and chambers cut from stone with faces staring from the walls. For those who would like to learn more about the ruins, many of the finds are now housed in La Paz, in the **Museo Nacional de Arqueología** (located on the corner of Federico Zuazo and Tiwanaku streets). A few hours south

is Parque Nacional Sajama, a starkly beautiful area on the border with Chile, protecting snow-capped Sajama, Bolivia's highest summit (6,549 metres/ 21,486ft).

Down to the valleys

Sweeping down from the Andean heights near La Paz to Bolivia's steaming Amazon basin is the lush, subtropical region known as the *yungas*. The combination of a warm climate with magnificent mountain views has made the zone a favorite for short visits from the capital and for the growing number of trekkers now flocking to Bolivia.

The *yungas* – the name means "hot valleys" – are in a completely different climatic zone from the Bolivian capital, less than 100km (60 miles) away on the bleak, barren altiplano. The drive from La Paz is one of the most spectacular in South America, going over a high-altitude mountain pass to dive into fertile valleys swirling with tropical mists, lined with ancient Inca terraces, and rich with an abundance of fruit trees.

At 1,500 meters (5,000ft) above sea level, the small town of **Coroico** ❷ is the zone's main commercial center. Coroico itself is little more than a tidy main square surrounded by a few cheap restaurants and hotels. But there are plenty of tranquil walks in the dripping green countryside nearby, beyond the plantations growing coffee, coca, and bananas. The gentle strolls provide spectacular views of snow-capped mountain ranges on the horizon leading to jungle-covered valleys, as well as to several rivers that are good for swimming. The best views of the Cordillera Real are from the little church located above the town, at the top of Cerro Uchumachi. Also worth a visit is the **Mothers of Clarissa Convent**, where the nuns make peanut butter, biscuits, and quite drinkable wine.

The nearby towns of **Sorata** and **Chulumani** ❸ are equally relaxing places to visit, with small guesthouses and good walks. The roads to both places are magnificent and Sorata in particular is said to have the most beautiful setting in Bolivia. A day hike

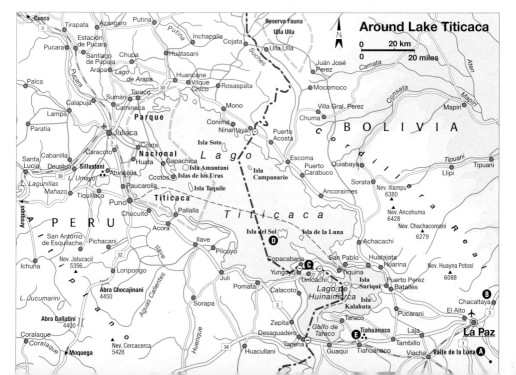

FACT

Gold mining in the Tipuani Valley has major environmental consequences. Deforestation, caused by felling trees for mine shafts, threatens biodiversity through habitat loss and causes landslides and flooding.

from Sorata leads to the bat-filled **San Pedro Cave**; or the more energetic can embark on the Mapiri Trail, a strenuous 8-day expedition. Less adventurous spirits will be content with strolls through the flower-filled valleys that locals insist were the original Garden of Eden.

Bolivia's "Inca Trail"

Coroico is a starting point and a goal for three popular treks, none of which requires any special experience. A four-day hike begins at **La Cumbre**, the highest point of the road from La Paz to the yungas, and follows an ancient Inca road that is in better repair than the path to Machu Picchu in Peru, although it lacks any sites as magnificent as the Inca ruins along the way.

Starting in the freezing and treeless heights, this path quickly descends into the more lush and habitable yungas. Most walkers advance slowly at first, gasping in the thin mountain air and rhythmically plodding over the chilly pass. At this altitude, there are no signs of human habitation.

But farther into the valleys, small villages begin to appear, often inhabited by numerous yelping dogs but few people. More villagers can be seen walking along the path at lower altitudes, usually Bolivian women weighed down with sacks of potatoes or sticks. Finally the Inca path gives way to rough, landslide-prone Bolivian roads, where passing trucks head toward Coroico.

The second trip, a favorite for adrenaline junkies, is the 64-km (40-mile) downhill cycle ride from La Cumbre to Coroico. Following the road that plunges 5,000 metres (16,000ft) provides 5km (3 miles) of thrilling gravity-assisted mountain biking.

The Gold-Diggers' Trail

Another trek begins where the last left off, in Coroico. Taking a road back into the mountains, the trail runs farther down into the **Beni Jungle** along the so-called Gold-Diggers' Trail. It follows the **Tipuani Valley**, a region whose metals were first prospected by the Incas. They exhausted all the surface gold, which

Road into the yungas valley, on the eastern slopes of the Andes.

was used for ornamental purposes in their temples and their art. Today thousands of Bolivians have tossed in their old lives in cities to try their luck in the jungle, and are now digging tunnels in the hope of finding instant wealth.

The trail once again follows an ancient Inca road, this time mossy and crumbling, through a beautiful landscape of jungle-clad mountains and dramatic gorges. Locals still use the trail today as a kind of highway. Residents come panting down the mountainside after trips to the capital carrying portable cassette decks and non-stick frying pans. It passes many small mining communities that can only be reached on foot, like the village of **Fátima**, put together from bamboo and corrugated iron only a few years ago.

The path ends at the hot and dusty town of **Guanay** ❹, a rather insalubrious Amazon outpost. From Guanay there are buses that will take you back to Coroico and La Paz.

Bolivia's most famous fiesta

The town of **Oruro** ❺, 230km (143 miles) south of La Paz, originally came to prominence as a mining town, but its mines are now redundant. Its industrious past is remembered in the **Museo Etnográfico Minero** (Mon–Sun 9am–12pm, 3.15pm– 5.30pm). Other places to visit include the **Casa de la Cultura**, a former residence of tin baron Simón Patiño, the **Museo Antropológico** (Mon–Fri 8.30am–noon, 2–6pm, Sat–Sun 10am– 6pm), an eclectic mix of petroglyphs, mummies and carnival masks, and the **Museo Mineralógico** (Mon–Fri 8.30am–noon, 3–6pm, Sat–Sun by advance request).

Oruro is best known for its carnival, **La Diablada**. Versions of this take place in various parts of South America, but this is the most famous in Bolivia, and is held during the five days before Ash Wednesday.

Ceremonies begin on Friday night, and at dawn on Saturday, eager spectators take their places, huddling against the cold mountain winds. Soon the street vendors are out in force, selling cans of beer. Older people turn up their noses at tinned drinks, preferring a more potent breakfast of *chicha*, the local maize beer. By 10am the crowd is ready for the Devil Dance.

Satan and Lucifer lead a procession of hundreds of dancing devils in fantastic outfits, leaping and pirouetting along the steep roads. Other dancers are dressed as pumas, monkeys, or insects. The lead is soon taken by China Supay, the Devil's wife, who tries to seduce the Archangel Michael with her wiles.

Some dancers dress as Incas, in headdresses shaped like condors, while others appear as black slaves brought over by the Spaniards, clanking through the streets in chains. Bolivian girls in pink and black mini-skirts bounce along the steep streets, dancing with men dressed as giant white bears. The procession ends up at a football stadium, where dancers

Mountain bikers on the road to Coroico.

perform two masques. The first is a re-enactment of the Spanish Conquest, performed, naturally enough, as a tragedy. In the second, the Archangel Michael defeats the forces of evil with his flaming sword, taking on the devils and the Seven Deadly Sins. The result is announced by the Virgen del Socavón, the patroness of miners, and the dancers enter a chapel to chant a hymn in Quechua.

Despite the Christian gloss over the proceedings, the Diablada is a pagan ceremony of thanks to Pachamama, "Earth Mother", to commemorate the struggle between the forces of good and evil. The conquering Spaniards were only able to convert the natives superficially, changing a few names of deities to fit the formulae of the church. The *Diablada* survived and grew during colonial times as an expression of local people's frustration. The Europeans sat on their elegant balconies and looked on, while the subjected peoples were allowed their annual dose of freedom – an act of rebellion that served as a safety valve.

People's parade at the festival of Laja, La Paz.

Central city

Bolivia's fourth-largest city, **Cochabamba** ❻, 160km (100 miles) east of Oruro, lies in a fertile area known as Bolivia's granary, at an altitude of 2,400 meters (9,200ft). This city is an intriguing mix of old entrenched tradition and burgeoning new energy. The heart of traditional Cochabamba revolves around the **Plaza 14 de Septiembre**, with its typical mélange of elegant and imposing edifices, street vendors, busy office workers, and the more elevated personages, defiantly braving the cloying weather in wool and tweed. Notable buildings include the **cathedral** and the colonial churches of **Santo Domingo** and **San Francisco**. In the evening, trendy bars and pizza restaurants around **Avenida España** fill with young people with disposable incomes.

The **Museo Arqueológico** (Mon–Fri 8am–6pm, Sat 8.30am–12.30pm) has an excellent selection of pre-Columbian artifacts dating back to 15,000 BC. Just south of the city center, perched on a hilltop, the impressive **Heroínas de la Coronilla**

monument commemorates the female independence fighters who defended Cochabamba from Spanish forces in 1812. East of the city center, at the end of Avenida de las Heroínas, a statue of Christ stands atop the **Cerro San Pedro**.

There are a number of Inca ruins in the vicinity of Cochabamba, and though none rival Machu Picchu or Tiahuanaco, they are worth visiting. **Inkallajta**, described as the "frontier post of the Inca empire," is an extensive site located on a turn-off from the old Cochabamba–Santa Cruz road. If you don't have your own transportation, you may have difficulty finding someone to take you there; however, there are some guided tours available. **Inka Rakay**, 27km (17 miles) west of Cochabamba, is better known for the wonderful views of the Cochabamba Valley than for the ruins themselves.

Along the Río Mamoré

Puerto Villaroel ❼ is the departure point for boats heading north to Guayaramerín on the Río Mamoré. It's a cozy little village where everyone seems to know everyone else, and from **Ivirgazama** (the last opportunity for river trippers to purchase mosquito nets and hammocks) the road becomes a dirt track. **Trinidad** ❽, in the heart of the Bolivian Amazon, is the capital of Beni province, with airport connections to Cochabamba and La Paz. The **Laguna Suárez**, 5km (3 miles) away, is a popular wildlife-spotting and resting place. Wildlife can also be seen at **Chuchini**, 17km (11 miles) from Trinidad. Chuchini has an archeological museum displaying remnants of the ancient Beni culture. The 300-km (185-mile) trip along the Río Mamoré to **Guayaramerín** ❾ takes three or four days. This bustling frontier town at the northern tip of the country is split by the river. The Brazilian side is known as Guajará-Mirim. The Bolivian side is an incongruous mix of dusty back-streets and brash duty-free shops selling perfume, jeans, and flashy electronic goods.

Riberalta ❿, three hours away by bus, is a pleasant, slow-paced and friendly little town, with a cluster of low-key restaurants grouped around the main plaza, ideally placed for perusing the town's social circuit. Towards dusk, motorbikes begin to trundle around the square. It is possible to catch a boat between Riberalta and **Rurrenabaque** ⓫ along the Río Beni but, as boat traffic has declined since the construction of a road link, you will probably have a long wait. However, the road is unsurfaced and can be a very sticky experience, especially during the rainy season. Rurrenabaque is a very pretty little town that has been enjoying a tourist boom due to its lush rainforest location, which makes it an ideal center for jungle and pampas expeditions and boat trips along the Beni and Tuichi rivers. The town also has some good restaurants and abundant low-budget accommodation.

Devil dancer in the Diablada parade, Oruro fiesta.

Bolivia's official capital

The city of **Sucre** ⑫, 600km (370 miles) southeast of La Paz, is Bolivia's official capital, although much government business is based in the big city on the altiplano. Sucre is a small, elegant city of great historical significance. Notable buildings around the **Plaza 25 de Mayo** include the **Casa de la Libertad** (Tue–Sat 9am–12.15pm, 2.30–6.15pm, Sun 9–11.45am), where Bolivia's declaration of independence was signed, and the **cathedral**, with the nearby **Museo de la Catedral** (Mon–Fri 10am–noon, 3–5pm). The city has many interesting religious buildings, including the churches of San Miguel, San Francisco, and Merced; and the Convento de San Felipe Neri. The Franciscan monastery of La Recoleta and its museum are on top of the Cerro Dalence hill to the southeast of Sucre, and afford excellent views of the city. There is also a natural history museum and the interesting **Museo de Arte Indígena ASUR** (Textile Museum; Pasaje Iturricha 314; Mon–Sat 9am–noon, 2.30–6.30pm), which displays Bolivian textiles woven from llama and alpaca wool. Some 5km (3 miles) south of the city, the **Castillo de la Glorieta** was built in a mixture of European styles by the Argandoña family.

Traditional textiles can be purchased at the typically Andean village of **Tarabuco**, 65km (40 miles) east of Sucre, which is renowned for its weaving. South of Sucre is the Cordillera de los Frailes mountain range, with trekking, rock paintings, and hot springs. Dinosaur bones have been found at **Cal Orko**, 7km (4.5 miles) from Sucre (guided tours to see them can be booked in Sucre).

Potosí, city of silver

Perched at 4,200 meters (13,780ft) above sea level in the shadow of a mountain, **Potosí** ⑬ is located in the southwest of Bolivia, 550km (340 miles) southeast of La Paz. It is the highest city of its size in the world, and was built in this inhospitable location by the Spanish conquistadors for one purpose: silver mining. Today, Potosí is only a shadow of its former self – during the 1600s it was as large as London

The colonial church of San Bernardo, Potosí.

and many times more opulent. Not only is it one of the least-touched colonial cities on the continent and a World Heritage Site, but it symbolizes South America's fate, illustrating that the richest regions in colonial times tend to be the poorest today.

Spain's treasure chest

Appropriately, **El Cerro Rico** (Rich Hill) is always visible from the city's streets. The Incas had known that there was silver in the bare red mountain but did nothing to exploit it. The Spaniards, however, were quick to begin mining, soon discovering that the hill held the largest silver deposit the world had ever seen. A frontier city was quickly created on the bleak mountain side, with conquistadors and missionaries flocking from Spain to win a slice of the fantastic wealth. Local native people were press-ganged to work in the mines, dying by the thousands in horrific conditions.

The city's churches were built with silver altars and the lavish feasts of Spanish nobles glittered with the precious metal. Even the horses were said to be shod with silver in Potosí. When the silver gave out, the city survived for a while on tin mining, but it has now become just a fascinating relic.

Testimony to the former riches are the scattered crumbling villas, stone carved doorways and forgotten abbeys of the city. Ancient houses teeter from both sides to nearly meet in the middle of narrow, winding streets. Potosí is still crowded with masterpieces of colonial architecture and artworks blending the styles of Spain's Golden Age and pre-Conquest South America.

Building funded by silver

Potosí's most impressive building, considered one of the finest examples of Spanish civil construction in South America, is the **Casa Real de Moneda** (Tue–Sat 9am–noon, 2.30–6.30pm, Sun 9am–noon). First built in 1542 and reconstructed in 1759, it was used as a mint by the colonizers. Now a museum, it has rooms full of religious art, collections of colonial coins, and the original wooden minting machines once worked by African slaves.

A Bolivian barge ferry connecting Copacabana to La Paz.

WHERE

As Potosí is more than 4,200 meters (13,780ft) above sea level, it is essential to acclimatize to the altitude with a day or two of relaxation around the city before you expose your lungs to a trip down the mines. Asthmatics should avoid the mines altogether.

Flute-playing in the mountains.

Guided tours (available in English) take up to three hours to work through the many exhibits, which contain anything from altars removed from collapsed churches to relics of Bolivia's foreign wars. One of the prize displays is a pair of iron strongboxes used to transport silver from the New World to Spain, using no fewer than 15 locks to secure them; while a huge gallery makes a valiant, but still incomplete attempt to provide portraits of the country's many presidents. Wear plenty of warm clothes, as the museum is like a refrigerator inside.

Many of Potosí's churches are crumbling into disrepair – in fact, some are dangerously close to collapse. A stroll through the city will take you past **San Francisco**, **La Compañia**, and **San Lorenzo**, as well as the **cathedral** and the **cabildo** (town council) in the main plaza. Wandering through the town, look out for old mansions such as the **Casa de las Tres Portadas** on Calle Bolivar 1092 and the **Crystal Palace** at Calle Sucre 148–56.

A city drained of its wealth

Potosí is much more than a collection of ruined colonial buildings. Many of the indigenous people in the area live in a way that has changed little over the centuries. The city market is a fascinating place to explore, full of women selling produce and butchers carrying whole animal carcasses over their shoulders – usually covered in flies and with the beast's hairy tail still dangling from the meat. But there are few signs of the city's past wealth. The poorest parts of the city, closer to the Rich Hill, were traditionally occupied by miners and their families. A monument to the Bolivian miner has been set up in one of the squares. The mining unions of Potosí and Oruro, once the most powerful force in Bolivian politics, were all but destroyed with the collapse of tin prices in the 1980s. There are few mines in operation these days, and unemployment stalks the streets. The wealth of Potosí proved a curse that is still with the indigenous population today. The city that helped finance the economic development of Europe in

ON THE CHE TRAIL

The ever-growing popular cult over Argentine–Cuban revolutionary Ernesto "Che" Guevara has spawned a tour to La Higuera in the foothills of the eastern Andes, about 150km (95 miles) southwest of Santa Cruz, where his failed attempt to ignite another Bolivian revolution ended in his capture and death. Aged 39, he was cornered in a nearby ravine, lacking supplies. He gave himself up and was executed on October 8, 1967. His body was presented to the media a day later. Che's schoolhouse prison, the hospital laundry where his body was put on show, and the airstrip where he was buried, then disinterred and taken to Cuba 30 years later, can be visited. Che paraphernalia abound in the village, and the Ruta de Che (Che Trail) was inaugurated in 2004. Tours are most easily done from Samaipata.

centuries gone by is deeply mired in Third World oblivion.

Realm of the devil

Deep in the heart of Potosí's Rich Hill, dust-covered miners laugh with the devil. Chewing coca leaves in a candlelit recess full of putrid air, they pay their respects to a small horned statue, the perceived owner of the silver beneath the ground. The miners visit El Tío – "The Uncle" – every day to leave a drink for him or burn a cigarette for luck. The image of the devil in the Incarnación mine was first made 300 years ago by native slaves press-ganged by the Spanish to dig for silver in Potosí.

Shockingly, working conditions in the mines have changed little since those days. The digging is still being carried out in such a primitive and dangerous fashion that many miners accept their work as a kind of death sentence.

Inside a mine in Cerro Rico

There are several private mines still operating, to which guides from the city will bring visitors for a small fee. Most people bring a few packets of cigarettes to share with the miners as they spend the first hour of their day sitting in the cold sun, chatting and chewing coca leaves, in use since long before the Incas to ward off hunger and fatigue.

Visiting a mine is absolutely not for anyone suffering from asthma or for those not acclimatized to the altitude. Claustrophobics won't like it either – you need to crouch just to enter the mouth of the tunnels, while the miners' antique carbide lamps barely dent the darkness.

Ancient wooden shaft supports often sag in the middle. Stalactites hang from the rough walls of the tunnel near its mouth, but as the mine descends into the mountain, polar cold shifts to subtropical heat. Many of the shafts can only be traversed on hands and knees. The air becomes thick and stale. Workers from the previous shift become visible down cracks, stripped to the waist and hacking away with picks. It is not surprising that the devil is reputed to live

Horses in Tupiza.

Coca Leaves

Coca is best known as the raw material for cocaine. In the Andes, it has been part of native culture for more than 4,000 years.

Small green coca leaves are on sale in any mountain town market. Ask at a café for *mate de coca*, and you will get a hot, refreshing drink of coca tea. You may come to appreciate it as the best cure for *soroche* (altitude sickness).

Some three million South Americans chew coca regularly, adding a little bicarbonate of soda or lime to get the saliva going and sucking its juices. It gives energy and dulls the senses against cold. Miners chew up to 1kg (2.2lb) a day.

In Bolivia and adjacent Andean areas, coca is used at every stage of life. Before giving birth, a woman chews the leaves to hasten labor and ease the pain. Relatives celebrate the birth by chewing the leaf together. When a man wants to marry a girl, he offers her father coca. When somebody dies, *mate de coca* is drunk at the wake and a small pile of leaves is placed in the coffin. *Yatiris* (soothsayers)

Coca plants in the Andes near Coroico.

use coca to tell the future, after scattering the leaves over a woolen blanket and reciting a prayer.

Coca was first cultivated in the Andes around 2,000 BC. Three millennia later, the Incas turned its production into a monopoly – just one more way to control the population. Its use was restricted to royalty, priests, doctors, and the empire's messenger runners, known to travel up to 250km (155 miles) a day, aided by chewing the leaves.

By the arrival of the first Europeans, the Incas had relaxed their monopoly on coca and its use had spread beyond their empire. Italian explorer Amerigo Vespucci, arriving in the Caribbean in 1499, noted with distaste that the islanders "each had their cheeks bulging with a certain green herb which they chewed like cattle." But within months of his arrival at Cusco in 1533, Pizarro found some of his own men secretly chewing coca.

The Catholic Church first tried to ban coca chewing, denouncing it as "the delusion of the devil." They quickly changed their tune when it was found that natives needed it to survive the brutal conditions in colonial mines and plantations. To keep the captive labor force under control, the Church then went into the coca business itself.

Coca was almost unheard of in Europe and the United States until the mid-1800s, when Parisian chemist Angelo Mariani marketed a wine made from the leaf. Immensely popular, this Vin Mariani quickly inspired several American soft drink companies to produce drinks based on coca, including Coca-Cola, which used cocaine during the first 20 years of the soft drink's production.

Magical substance

At around the same time, cocaine was first being developed. In 1860, a German chemist, Albert Niemann, earned his doctorate with a dissertation explaining the isolation process for cocaine, and giving the drug its name. It was quickly taken up by such luminaries as Sigmund Freud, who called it a "magical substance." Sir Arthur Conan Doyle wrote of his fictional character Sherlock Holmes regularly partaking of cocaine. But moves were already afoot to ban the drug as its addictive properties soon became obvious.

Scientists agree that there are no dangers in chewing the leaf, nor is it addictive, but because of its association with cocaine, coca leaves are banned in most countries. Taking home just a strip of coca leaf chewing gum or a coca tea bag could get you into trouble. Irrespective of the international prohibition, cocaine trafficking remains widespread and highly problematic.

here – this really does seem like a vision of hell.

There are no power tools and no engineers in these mines. Blasting is done with dynamite bought in the supply store in Potosí, and the miners simply withdraw around a corner as the charge goes off. Each worker keeps the ore he finds himself. Miners on the lowest levels must climb long ladders to the surface with sacks of rocks on their backs.

The real enemy here is silicosis, caused by fine dust gathering in the miners' lungs. Within a few years of entering the pit, many feel a heavy weight on their chests. A few years later they die, coughing blood. Little wonder that tradition holds that the metals of Potosí are the property of the devil, or that the miners give El Tío his daily cigarette for luck.

Group tours lasting four to five hours are organized by recognized guides. Put on your oldest clothes and take a handkerchief to keep the dust from your nose and mouth. A helmet and lamp will be provided. Donations to the miners' cooperative are much appreciated.

The world's biggest salt flats

In the west, near the frontier with Chile, is one of Bolivia's most popular tourist destinations. The **Salar de Uyuni** is the largest salt flat in the world, at 10,500 sq km (4,055 sq miles). It's an eerie sight, lying 3,653 meters (11,985ft) above sea level – bring plenty of warm clothes, as temperatures can plummet at this altitude.

The region is dotted with cactus-filled islands emerging from the expanse of white. The salt flats were formed from great lakes as the Andean plateau rose and rivers and creeks became locked in to these high mountain valleys, unable to flow to the ocean. The desert sun leads to evaporation, and the lakes gradually became flats covered in salt – although their exact form can vary.

Much of Uyuni's surface is relatively flat, while the crust of the Atacama salt flats across the border in Chile is mostly broken and rough. The area also holds large reserves of lithium, a mineral used in cell phone batteries, and possibly to be used in

The rooftops of Potosí.

The miners in Potosí worship a devil god, also called The Uncle, who, as owner of the underground, has the rights of life and dead on the workers.

future batteries for electric cars – yet another opportunity given to Bolivia to acquire wealth from its resources. Don't forget to wear sunglasses as the sun reflection on the salt can burn your eyes. There are accommodations available in the town of **Uyuni** as well as the extraordinary Salt Palace Hotel, which is out on the flats. Not only is it built entirely of salt, but all the furniture and fittings are made of salt as well.

Taking a tour is the best way to go as facilities are few and far between and it is easy – and dangerous – to get lost. Tours of the area can also be arranged from Potosí or Sucre, and most include the option of visiting **Laguna Colorada**, a bright red lake patronized by flocks of pink flamingos who feed on the algae that turns the lake red. It lies 346km (215 miles) southwest of Uyuni. Tours also usually take in another colorful sight, the **Laguna Verde**, a chilly aquamarine lake at 5,000 meters (16,400ft) above sea level.

At one of Cerro Rico's working silver mines.

The lake is surrounded by a beautiful white beach with a backdrop of the cone-shaped volcano Licancabur, which itself has one of the world's highest lagoons in its crater. Scientists from NASA have carried out experiments in the caldera to find out how the organisms there can survive in such a hostile environment. They believe their findings will help them in their search for life on Mars during missions.

Other attractions in the area close to the Chilean border include geysers at Sol de Mañana, and hot springs at Aguas Termales Chalviri. Bus transportation is available here to cross the border to San Pedro de Atacama, as are train trips to Calama via the border town of Ollagüe in Chile. The trip is as grueling as it is spectacular.

Jesuit splendor in the East

Some 500km (310 miles) east of Cochabamba is **Santa Cruz** , Bolivia's biggest city. Its first, short-lived boom came from rubber in the late 19th century. The current growth spurt was encouraged by a government-led "March to the East" from the 1950s and has been powered by natural gas

and tropical lowland crops like soy-beans, sugar, rice, cotton, and coca. Santa Cruz is not a popular tourist destination, although it does have some interesting museums and a rich ethnic mix, due to the numbers of people who swarmed to the city to take advantage of its economic success.

Some two hours west of Santa Cruz in the Andean foothills are the world's largest rock carvings, begun around AD 300 by the Chanes, an Arawak people, close to picturesque Samaipata. Known as **El Fuerte** (The Fortress), an entire hillside of sandstone offering a spectacular view is covered in geometric and animal carvings. The 250-meter by 60-meter (750ft by 180ft) ceremonial center may have been close to the Inca empire's eastern border, and Inca carvings are part of the complex. Carvings include straight east–west lines, and jaguars, and culminate in a series of 48 seats. More than 830 bird species have been counted in nearby Parque Nacional Amboró.

In a broad swath of territory north and east of Santa Cruz known as **Chiquitos** lie ten unique Baroque churches established within Jesuit missions between 1696 and 1760, six of them protected as Unesco World Heritage Sites. Unlike similar missions in Paraguay and Argentina, these far-flung places of worship largely survived. The multi-naved churches have exquisitely carved wooden facades. The extraordinary musical heritage of the missions is celebrated in Renaissance and Baroque music festivals in the local communities on even-numbered years.

The mission town of **San Ignacio de Velasco**, 476km (296 miles) northeast of Santa Cruz, is the last town of any size in the vicinity of the remote, vast Parque Nacional Noel Kempff Mercado. The park, although part of the Amazon basin, includes landscapes varying from savannah to rainforest, leading to an extraordinary variety of flora and fauna. The park is also mentioned among possible inspirations for Arthur Conan Doyle's novel *The Lost World*. Santa Cruz is linked by rail to Brazil and Argentina – a journey best described as an endurance test.

Salt heaps at Uyuni.

Lake Quilotoa crater lake, Avenue of the Volcanoes.

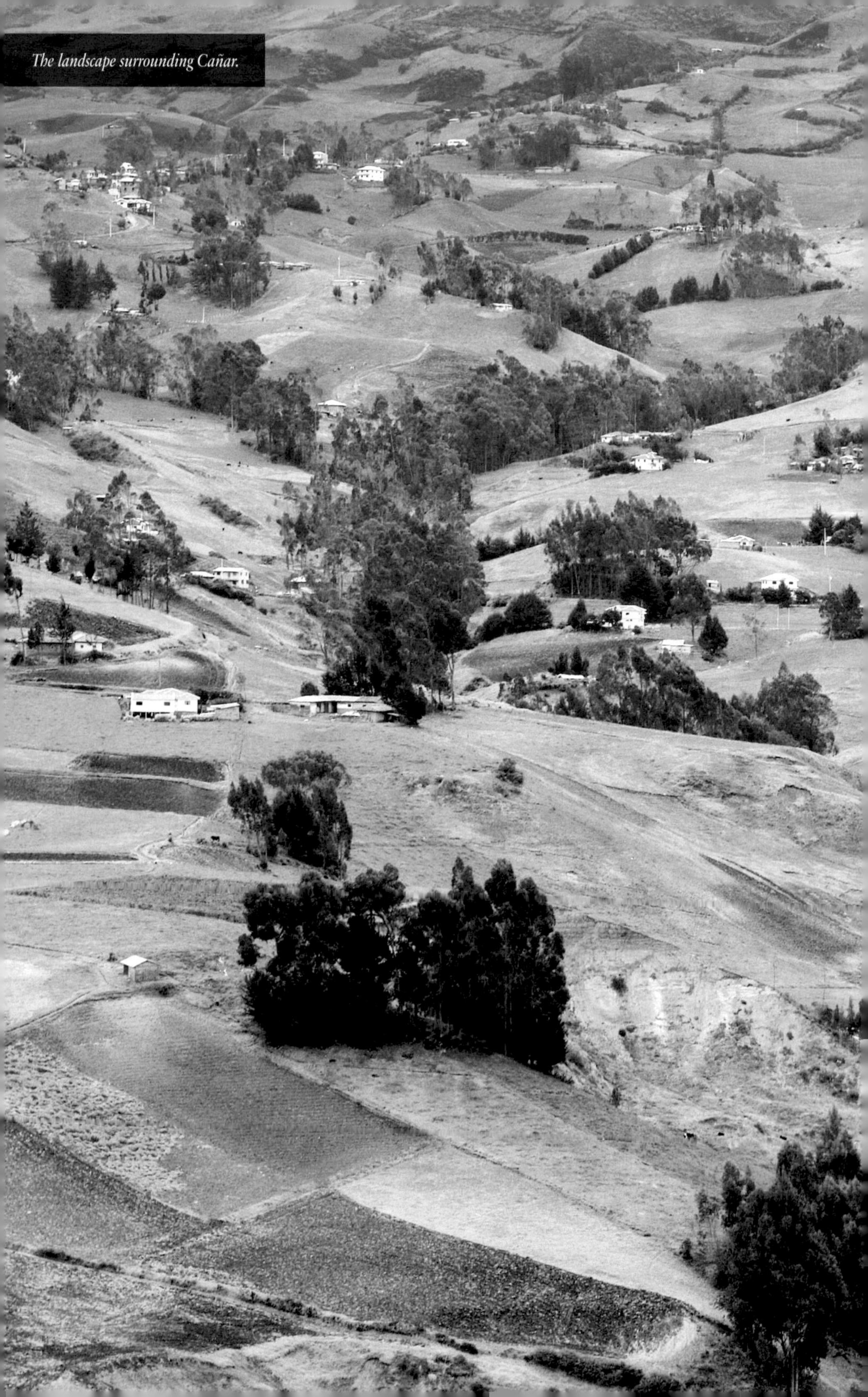
The landscape surrounding Cañar.

ECUADOR

Despite being one of the smallest South American countries, Ecuador has plenty of attractions: smoldering volcanoes, rainforest reserves, native markets and, of course, the Galápagos Islands.

Ecuador is one of the most rewarding countries to explore in all South America. Small but geographically varied, the country's incredible natural diversity has made it the focus of worldwide biological research.

Ecuador has more species of plants (25,000) and birds (more than 1,500) than the United States, which is 34 times larger. Sadly, these precious ecosystems are being degraded by a rate of deforestation higher than any nation in South America (280,000 hectares/692,000 acres per annum). The good news is that the Ecuadorian National Park Service, with the help of national and international conservation organizations, currently protects almost 40 percent of the total landmass in national parks and ecological reserves. In addition, 97 percent of the Galápagos Islands' landmass is protected and a marine reserve protects the waters surrounding them. For a developing nation, these conservation efforts are admirable.

Outdoor activities are Ecuador's biggest tourist draw. Within a day's drive or flight from the capital city of Quito you can experience virgin Amazon jungle, snow-capped peaks, tropical sandy beaches, as well as the Galápagos Islands. Outfitters are set up to organize mountaineering, trekking, jungle canoe trips, mountain biking, rafting, paraskiing, scuba diving, and horseback riding.

A nation in movement

Ecuador is divided into four regions – Sierra (Andes), Coast, Oriente (Amazon), and Galápagos, but people are constantly on the move between these areas. Trucks filled with *plátanos* (green bananas) daily climb the cloud forests of the western slope of the Sierra to stock Quito's cool open-air markets, while sacks filled with endemic varieties of potatoes

Main Attractions
Old Quito
Otavalo
Cotopaxi
Cuenca
Vilcabamba
Parque nacional Yasuni
Galápagos Islands

Puerto López.

FACT

The important Inca sun god Inti is often subtly portrayed in religious colonial art, and in return the Catholic celebration for St Peter is associated with the Inti Raymi festival (winter solstice).

are transported down to the hot and humid barrios of Guayaquil. The Oriente pumps economically vital oil exports through two pipelines crossing the Andes to tankers docked at the port of Esmeraldas. It is not at all uncommon to see a colorfully dressed highland *Otavaleño* on the coast selling woven goods, as well as a coastal *moreno* (Afro-Ecuadorian) on a bus on the Pan-American Highway offering traditional homemade *cocada* (coconut candy).

The majority of Ecuadorians are Catholics but there is a growing number of Protestants (now estimated at around 10 percent). Pre-colonial indigenous religions are rarely practiced in their pure forms except in isolated pockets in the Oriente, but elements are incorporated into modern Christianity.

Pre-Inca civilizations

Ecuador's pre-Hispanic history goes back thousands of years, with only the final decades before the Spanish conquest under Inca rule. At Valdivia on the coast, archeologists have found ceramics dating from around 3000 BC, the oldest in the Americas, while the Cochasquí pyramids north of Quito are witness to the power of the regional fiefs that grew along the spine of the Andes.

Inca Tupac Yupanqui finally completed the conquest of much of Ecuador in a series of bloody wars extending into what is now Colombia. Within few generations however, a northerner, Atahualpa, had become Inca, only to be executed by the Spaniard Francisco Pizarro in 1532 (see page 31). While Pizarro plundered, his lieutenant Sebastián de Benalcázar battled northward to the city of Quito. Arriving in late 1534, he found the city in ruins: Rumiñahui, Atahualpa's general, had destroyed and evacuated it rather than lose it intact to the Spaniards. Benalcázar refounded Quito on December 6, 1534. Rumiñahui was captured, tortured, and executed the following month. Before that however, Rumiñahui may have been able to entomb Atahualpa's mummy in the western Andean foothills.

Monasterio de San Francisco, Quito.

Ecuador was initially ruled by the Spanish as a province of the viceroyalty of Peru, and was the site of the first cultivation of wheat and bananas in South America. Resentment to Spanish administration was felt not just by the oppressed natives but also by the wealthy but relatively powerless locally born elites.

On August 10, 1809, Quito, at the time the second-biggest city in the region, declared a coup against its Spanish officials, one of the first cries for autonomy in Spanish America. It took until 1822 for the area that is now Ecuador to be freed of Spanish rule, and it seceded from Colombia in 1830, retaining the yellow, red, and blue colors it shares with the flags of its northern neighbor and Venezuela.

But already in August, 1809, graffiti in Quito pointedly stated "Last day of despotism – First day of the same." This reflected that while Ecuador's independent history has been turbulent, little changed for the landless and powerless majority. This was true until the mid-20th century.

Turbulent independence

Ultra-Catholic president Gabriel García Moreno ruled ruthlessly between 1861–5 and again from 1869–75, limiting Ecuadorean citizenship to Catholics. Though he offered Ecuador as a protectorate to France, he greatly consolidated a weak state, and started work on a railroad from Quito to Guayaquil, modernized the public administration, and introduced the

Evangelists dance and pray outside Santo Domingo church, Quito.

FACT

Ecuador was the original "banana republic." For many years bananas were its principal export, and the country is still among the world's largest exporters.

telegraph. Resentment of continued conservative repression in 1895 led to the Liberal Revolution led by General Eloy Alfaro, who in 1909 finished the railroad and introduced far-reaching reforms including the separation of Church and State and divorce. Both García Moreno and Alfaro went too far in clinging to power, however, and were assassinated in Quito.

Cash crops, from cocoa to bananas, and, from 1967, the discovery of crude oil, have helped Ecuador achieve some degree of modernization, although most was siphoned off by local elites, including the military, which took control periodically amid frequent political crises. Populist grandstander José María Velasco Ibarra was the dominant political figure of the 20th century, elected to office five times after 1932 only to be toppled by the military on four occasions, the last time in 1972. The military, however, was never able to hang on to power for long and in 1978, Ecuador ushered in South America's generalized return to civilian rule, and for the first time allowed illiterate citizens to vote.

The decades since then have been far from calm. The first 20 years of new democracy saw regular elections and changes of power among social democratic and conservative presidents, but the house came crashing down with the election of populist Abdalá Bucaram in 1997. Flamboyant and blatantly corrupt, he was driven from office by street protests after just 8 months in power. Economic mismanagement and a collapsing price of oil felled Christian Democrat Jamil Mahuad in 2000, as Ecuador introduced the US dollar to fend off hyperinflation. Hundreds of thousands emigrated amid the economic woes, but the economy gradually stabilized and inflation receded.

Colonel Lucio Gutiérrez, a leader of the 2000 coup, was elected in 2003 but fled protesters in 2005 amid corruption and bumbling politics, including allowing Bucaram to return from exile in Panama. Indigenous movements have grown in power and assertiveness but were harmed by their participation in the coup against Mahuad,

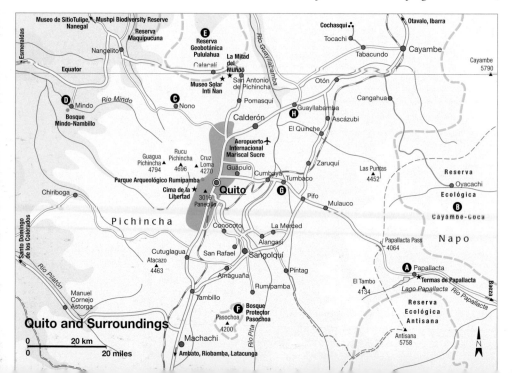

Quito and Surroundings

and their proximity to the unpopular Gutiérrez government.

President Rafael Correa, a left-wing economist who took office in 2007, followed in the footsteps of Venezuela's Hugo Chávez. He has had a new constitution written – Ecuador's 20th – and has promised a radicalization of his "Citizen's Revolution." But while he has spent massively on roads and other infrastructure, his rule has been characterized by the repression of indigenous organizations and freedom of expression.

Quito: Ecuador's expanding capital

Modern **Quito** ❶ spreads north and south into the intra-Andean valley each year, gobbling up rural farms. For its amenities and services, most visitors stay in the **Mariscal** neighborhood, north of **Parque El Ejido**, where old Quito meets new. Hotels, restaurants, and stores bulging with handicrafts line **Avenida Amazonas** and nearby streets. The smarter hotels and boutiques tend to be a bit further north, in the area surrounding the large La Carolina park, but also in the colonial center.

La Casa de la Cultura, housing the **Museo Nacional** (Tue–Fri 9am–5pm, Sat–Sun 10am–4pm), just off Parque El Ejido, is Ecuador's most comprehensive museum, with pre-Columbian treasures and ornate gold, along with republican, colonial, and modern art. Rivaling this is the smaller but excellent **Museo Fundación Guayasamín** (Mon–Fri 10am–5.30pm) in the Bellavista neighborhood. Oswaldo Guayasamín, Ecuador's most renowned painter (see page 67), displays his bold portraits of indigenous people and his collection of pre-Columbian artifacts.

Back down the hill, fast-food joints and shopping malls are proof of the Ecuadorian middle-class fascination with American culture. Quito has a selection of international restaurants, folkloric ballet shows, and salsa bars.

Old Quito: a walking tour

Old Quito displays Spanish colonial architecture at its finest. Walls of brilliant whitewash, deep blue railings, and green tiled rooftops dazzle the eye, and are reminiscent of a period when the city was one of the Spanish empire's cultural hubs. Earthquakes in 1587, 1768, and 1859 caused severe damage to many churches, but nevertheless there are still 87 of them left. In 1978, Unesco declared Old Quito a World Heritage Site. Much of the old town has seen renovations since then, restoring admirable architecture amid the daytime bustle. At night the plazas and churches are illuminated, but like in Bogotás Candelaria, not all areas are safe to walk.

The Spanish past blends with modern cultural migration as members of Ecuador's many ethnic groups make Quito their home. Life on colorful **Calle Cuenca** contrasts with the city's relative affluence. Black women sell tropical fruits, while an indigenous newspaper vendor with a baby at her breast cries "*Comercio*, Hoy!" in a nasal refrain. Above it all stands the church

Pre-Columbian sculpture, Museo Nacional.

Plaza Grande and the Cathedral, Quito.

Metal sculpture outside the Capilla del Hombre museum and cultural center in Quito, designed by Ecuadorian artist Oswaldo Guayasamín.

La Ronda, Quito.

of **San Francisco**, which was the first major religious construction on the continent and is the spiritual heart of the city. The creaking wooden floor contrasts with the spectacular Baroque carvings and the statue of **Our Lady of Quito**, a fine example of the Quito School of Art, deftly blending Spanish and Moorish techniques with the indigenous imagination.

From San Francisco, it is a short walk to **La Merced**, which contains paintings depicting scenes from Quito's past: Antonio José de Sucre riding gloriously into battle, volcanoes erupting, and suspiciously docile indigenous people being converted to Christianity. Two blocks away is the **Plaza de la Independencia**, or Plaza Grande, where the heroes of 1809 are immortalized. Today, *quiteños* sun themselves here, read the morning newspapers, and put the swarming shoeshine boys to work.

The **Palacio de Gobierno** (Presidential Palace), also known as Carondelet, has traditional guards in red, gold, and blue 19th-century-style uniforms, and a mural by Guayasamín

depicting Orellana's descent of the Amazon. The adjacent **cathedral**, finished in 1706, is where Ecuador's illustrious sons, including Sucre, are buried. Among its collection of paintings is the *Descent From The Cross* by Caspicara, perhaps colonial Ecuador's best indigenous artist.

One block south of the church of **San Agustín**, where the first declaration of independence was signed, is the pedestrian thoroughfare **Calle Eugenio Espejo**. Nearby is the magnificent **La Compañía de Jesús** (Mon–Fri 9.30am–5.30pm, Sat 9.30am–4.30pm, Sun 12.20pm–4.30pm), built by the Jesuits between 1605 and 1768. Containing an estimated 7 tons of gold, it is Ecuador's most ornate church. The remains of the *quiteña* St. Mariana de Jesús lie beneath the solid gold main altar, and the walls are covered with colonial paintings, including one that graphically depicts the punishment reserved for sinners in Hell, with the most unpleasant fate reserved for adulterers and fornicators.

From 1828 until his assassination in Colombia two years later, Sucre lived a block from here: his house, the **Casa de Sucre Museo Histórico** (Tue–Fri 9am–5.30pm, Sat 10am–2pm), affords a glimpse of period aristocratic home life. A statue of Sucre occupies the Plaza Santo Domingo, opposite the church of the same name, which is best seen at night when it is floodlit. Inside is an altar to St. Judas, patron saint of desperate causes, where satisfied worshipers have posted "thank you" notices.

One of the best-preserved colonial streets is **Calle La Ronda**, south of Plaza Santa Domingo. A narrow, cobbled lane, it is lined with 16th-century houses with overhanging balconies and heavy grilled doors, many of them now restaurants and pubs popular with local visitors.

Views of the sierra

Far above towers the winged Virgin of Quito at the summit of **El Panecillo**

(Little Bread Roll), with sweeping views of the valley and, on a clear day, the peaks of **Cotopaxi** and **Cayambe**, to the south and northeast respectively. The **sierra** stretching out before you actually comprises two mountain ranges (western and eastern cordilleras) divided by a series of central valleys running north–south. The major highland cities are spaced along the Pan-American Highway in these valleys, 2,000–3,000 meters (6,500–9,800ft) above sea level, and are blessed with temperate climates. This beautiful patchwork of fields is extremely productive, due to rich volcanic soils and little variation in air temperatures. The flat lowland plains are intensely farmed by modern methods, mainly for the huge flower export industry.

The steep hillsides above the valley floor are owned by Quichua indigenous cooperatives, working small parcels of land, which tractors could never till, with hand tools. Their crops of potatoes, carrots, beans, wheat, and corn supply 75 percent of Ecuador's needs. Above are the cold, windswept *páramos* (alpine grasslands), home to grazing horses, cattle, llamas, and sheep. Still higher, the craggy and glaciated volcanic peaks that dominate the skyline are where you may see some of the few remaining Andean condors.

Excursions near Quito

The main road to the Oriente climbs to the continental divide at the headwaters of the Amazon basin. The village of **Papallacta Ⓐ** is located below the pass. Here you will find basic and luxury thermal-spring pools surrounded by lush cloud forest. The area is also known for producing some of the country's best fresh trout, introduced from North American stock. *Quiteños* escape here on the weekends for walks or horseback rides in the nearby **Cayambe-Coca Ecological Reserve Ⓑ**.

Toward the coast, two hours by bus from Quito, are **Nono Ⓒ**, **Tandayapa**, and **Mindo Ⓓ**, villages that are world-class favorite birding spots. Private reserves and lodges have been set up to cater for visitors keen on exploring the forests. To the west beyond Pacto, Metropolitan Touring's unique Mashpi Lodge features an ultra-modern luxury lodge in the midst of protected Chocó rainforest. Closer to Quito is the remarkable **Pululahua crater preserve Ⓔ**, with wooded areas and agriculture. It's past the **overrated Mitad del Mundo** (Middle of the World) monument, which despite its claim fails to accurately mark the equator. **The Bosque Protector Pasochoa Ⓕ** (contact Fundación Natura, at República 481 and Almagro, Quito, tel: 02-503-385, for excursions) is a pleasant nature reserve southeast of Quito. Some of the last intra-Andean cloud forest is protected on the slopes of the ancient volcano. Native trees and plants thrive on the rich volcanic soil and are home to some 120 species of birds. A half-day hike on Ilaló, near the valley suburb of **Tumbaco Ⓖ**, is worth doing for the views of northern Ecuador's main peaks.

Guard at the Palacio Presidencial.

Quito's teleferico (cable car).

North of Quito

The Pan-American Highway heading north, passes through the agricultural town of **Guayllabamba** , several hundred meters lower and much warmer than Quito, and which produces crops of avocado and *chirimoya* (custard apple). Restaurants are full at the weekends with *quiteños* who stop off for the town's specialty of *locro*, a hearty cheese and potato soup with optional avocado and pork skin. The **Zoológico Metropolitano** (Tue–Fri 8.30am–5pm, Sat–Sun 9am–5pm) here houses Galápagos tortoises, jaguars, monkeys, and the Andean spectacled bear.

Farther north, the best equator mark is just off the highway before reaching **Cayambe** ②. This area is historically known for cheese making, but the flower industry has surpassed it in economic importance. These large plantations can be toured, and a dozen long-stemmed roses can cost as little as $1. Cayambe is the jumping-off place for excursions to the climber's refuge on the flanks of **Nevado Cayambe** (5,790 meters/19,000ft), the woodworking indigenous community of **Oyacachi**, with hot springs, and the Inca ruins of **Quitoloma**.

The oldest hacienda (farm estate) in Ecuador, **Guachalá**, built in 1580, is just outside Cayambe on the equator. It used to be a textile factory producing Scottish-style tweed. Several other important haciendas open to visitors are scattered around **Otavalo** ❸, including **Cusín** and **Pinsaquí**, offering a glimpse into the wealth and privilege enjoyed by estate owners in the recent past. Otavalo itself is famous for its beautiful weavings, sold in the Saturday morning market (see page 69). About 5km (3 miles) from Otavalo is an ecologically constructed mountain lodge, **Casa Mojanda**, which has spectacular views from its adobe cottages of the nearby volcano, **Cotacachi** (4,944 meters/16,220ft). Beneath the volcano lies **Laguna Cuicocha**, a collapsed caldera that is now a lake filled with bright blue water.

In the villages surrounding Otavalo the cottage-crafts industry is flourishing. **Cotacachi** is most famous for

Statue of the Virgin, El Panecillo, Quito.

View of Quito and Cayambe volcano.

its leatherwork, **Peguche** and **Agato** for their weaving, and **Ilumán** for its double-sided ponchos and felt hats. To the north, **Ibarra** is a pleasant colonial town with many inexpensive restaurants and hotels, known locally as La Ciudad Blanca (The White City) for its whitewashed walls and red-roofed colonial buildings.

For a challenging but rewarding excursion, climb **Cerro Imbabura** (4,609 meters/15,120ft), just south of town, with views of surrounding villages. This peak was once glaciated, and local people used to harvest ice from the slopes, but climate change has melted away the glaciers. A few hours north by bus, the subtropical **Chota Valley** is the only place in the sierra that is populated by Afro-Ecuadorians.

On the road to San Lorenzo is the **Reserva Cerro Golondrinas** cloud forest. A four-day trek descends from the *páramo* through pristine submontane cloud forest and farmland. Visitors will see the positive effects of the conservation efforts in the area, such as orchid farms, tree nurseries, and reforestation projects. At the Colombian border is **Tulcán ❹**, the provincial capital of Carchi, best known for cypress trees in the graveyard, which are elaborately carved to resemble animals, houses, and geometric figures. At **Reserva Ecológica El Angel**, nearby, you can see the giant *frailejón* plants, members of the daisy family, standing out of the *páramo* vegetation up to 2 meters (6ft) tall. The surreal landscape is something hikers really must see.

South from Quito

Heading south from Quito takes you along the "Avenue of the Volcanoes," with excellent views of all the major peaks. Several haciendas have been converted into hotels, notably **La Ciénega**, steeped in 400 years of history, and **San Agustín de Callo**. The latter was originally built on the site of an important Inca palace and whole chambers in the Inca imperial style remain.

From **Lasso** a dirt road heads up into **Parque Nacional Cotopaxi**, which encompasses the peaks of Cotopaxi, Rumiñahui, and Sincholagua. Cotopaxi is one of the world's highest active volcanoes and attracts thousands of climbers to its 5,897-meter (19,350-ft) summit every year. At its base, **Laguna Limpio Pungo** harbors Andean gulls, Andean lapwings, and the Andean fox. It is one of the best locations to observe páramo vegetation and recent volcanic features.

Just off the Pan-American Highway on Thursdays at dawn, the quiet village of **Saquisilí** comes alive with Ecuador's largest indigenous market. People from outlying communities fill the streets and plazas with their local produce. A little farther south is **Latacunga ❺**, destroyed three times by mud flows from Cotopaxi in the 18th and 19th centuries. In September the streets are alive with processions, dances, and fireworks in honor of the black-faced Virgin Mary, an event known as **La Fiesta de la Mamá Negra**.

TIP

Take a taxi to the summit of El Panecillo – don't walk up as numerous thieves are at work on the way. The giant-winged Virgin Mary at the summit is modeled on a 1732 sculpture.

Fresh produce market, Otavalo.

To the west is the Quichua village of **Zumbahua**, which hosts a colorful vegetable market on Saturdays. An hour's drive away is the starting point for walks to the deep-blue volcanic lake of **Quilotoa**. This area is one of the few places where llamas are still employed as pack animals.

The capital of Tungurahua province, **Ambato**, was leveled by an earthquake in 1949 and rebuilt with concrete buildings that lend a drab feeling to the city. This is an important industrial and fruit-growing area. Between Baños and Ambato lies the Quichua community of **Salasaca**, whose tapestries are sold throughout the country, including at the Saturday Otavalo market. Salasaca's small outdoor market is open on weekends, and you can see artists at work in their homes.

Spectacular train journeys

Rail travel began in Ecuador in 1909, when the line between Quito and Guayaquil opened, reducing to 2 days a former 9-day trek along a mule path. Today, however, only short sections for

Plaza de Ponchos market, Otavalo.

tourist rides survive, although work is underway for a full reconstruction by late 2013.

Currently, the 5-hour train ride south from Quito to Latacunga, past Parque Nacional **Cotopaxi**, offers good views of the Andean peaks and lush farmland before ascending to the high *páramo*. Shorter options are available, including the weekend-only Machachi-Boliche round trip near the park entrance.

The train ride over the Nariz del Diablo (Devil's Nose) from Alausí to Sibambe is a popular day out. New panoramic cars have replaced the adventurous, but potentially dangerous rooftop seating. Trains run on Tuesdays through Sundays for a scenic 2.5-hour return trip. The Devil's Nose switchback is one of the world's most impressive feats of railway engineering.

A short section of railroad from El Tambo farther south to the Coyoctor Inca ruins has also been introduced, as well as a tropical ride from Durán across from Guayaquil to Yaguachi and back. In the north, there are Chiva trips from Ibarra to subtropical El Primer Paso, where there is a swimming pool.

Hot springs and erupting volcanoes

Baños is a very popular destination for Ecuadorian and foreign visitors alike. Named after the thermal springs in town, it is graced with a semitropical climate. However, in August 2006 the **Volcán Tungurahua** (5,020 meters/ 16,470ft) erupted and a number of small surrounding villages were covered in ash and destroyed. There are splendid views of the lava-spewing summit, particularly at night, and many waterfalls nearby. Baños is also a great place to shop for local handicrafts and experience hiking, rafting, jungle trips, horseback riding, and mountain biking.

Farther south, **Riobamba ⑥** sits on the flanks of **Chimborazo**, the highest mountain in Ecuador (6,310 meters/20,700ft) and the farthest spot on the planet as measured from the center of the earth. It is also the starting point for Andean rail trips past the town of **Alausí** ❼. Before the Inca period Puruhá people lived in the region, but during Inca rule they were moved away and people from northern Peru were ordered to move here. Today the region is dominated by different indigenous groups and the variety of hats and traditional dress reflects these strong cultures.

To the west of Riobamba is the expansive and remote Sangay National Park, home to the mountain tapir and Andean spectacled bear, and the daily erupting volcano Sangay (5,230 meters/17,160ft). On the edge of the park is part of an old Inca highway that once ran from Quito to Cusco in Peru. Visitors can hike along the trail from Achupallas as far as the Inca ruins of Ingapirca, built in the 15th century as a ceremonial center.

The Pan-American Highway continues south to **Cuenca** ❽, the third-largest city in Ecuador and formerly the Inca town of Tomebamba. Almost all the Inca stonework was destroyed by the Spanish and replaced by colonial architecture and cobbled streets. Today, patios, plazas, white-washed buildings, and red-tiled roofs as well as a lively cultural scene make Cuenca probably the most attractive Ecuadorian city to visit.

Nearby **Parque Nacional Cajas,** with more than 200 lakes, is a popular retreat for fishermen and hikers. Since Cuenca draws its drinking water from Cajas it is well protected from environmental impacts. South of Cuenca live the indigenous people of **Saraguro** ❾, who have strong cultural pride. Their town has become a center of the indigenous political movement called Pachakutik (New Country). Here, men dress formally with short black trousers and women wear decorative shawls closed with a *tupus* (fastening pin). **Loja**, a pleasant city with some colonial streets, is the gateway to the southern Oriente and the Peruvian border. Quinine, the anti-malaria drug, was first exploited

The Nanda Mañachi musicians' workshop in Peguche, near Otavalo.

Laguna de Cuicocha, near Cotacachi.

from the forests above the city in the 18th century, which sadly led to their destruction.

Farther down the valley, the village of **Vilcabamba** was made famous by the discovery in the 1960s of a large percentage of local people allegedly over 100 years old. Visiting doctors have suggested that a mild and stable climate, low stress levels, simple and healthy diets, and physical labor on small farms help people reach a ripe old age. A number of foreigners have since settled in the region, seeking longevity, and several ecologically sound and health-minded hostels have sprung up as a result.

Also in the vicinity is **Parque Nacional Podocarpus**, with a highland entrance at **Cajanuma** and rainforest entrance at **Bombascara**. There are trails that access the park, and overnight camping is possible. An active environmental movement in Loja has prevented multinational mining companies from moving in and causing deforestation and river poisoning. A spectacular mountain road goes to the town of Macará on the Peruvian

border. This route to Peru is safer and more beautiful than the coastal crossing at Huaquillas.

The Oriente and Amazon

The Ecuadorian east, or **Oriente,** is the upper Amazon basin east of the Andes. It is a place of endless virgin rainforest cut by fast-flowing rivers and inhabited by jaguars, ocelots, anacondas, monkeys, tapirs, fish-eating bats, piranhas, and more than 450 species of birds. Travel in this region is easier than in neighboring countries, as distances are shorter and transportation quite straightforward.

The indigenous inhabitants of the Oriente include the Siona, Cofán, Quichua, Quijo, and Huaorani tribes in the basins of the Napo, Aguarico, and Pastaza rivers to the north; and the Shuars, Ashuars, and Saraguros in the south. Colonization and oil development have affected the lifestyles of the tribes, and many traditions have died, such as those of the Shuar, who until the 20th century would shrink the heads of dead enemies, and among whom the ratio of men to women was

Cotopaxi is one of the mighty peaks forming the Avenue of the Volcanoes.

estimated at one to two, due to constant warfare.

Some of the Huaorani – so fierce that even the Shuar feared them – retain their ancient culture deep in the jungles bordering Peru near the **Río Napo**. They hunt with spears, blowpipes, and poison darts, keep harpie eagles as pets, and make fire by rubbing sticks together. Most of the Huaorani people do not welcome visitors, but some are gradually turning to ecotourism to protect their culture.

Several missionaries, including the Bishop of Coca in 1987, have been killed for attempting to encroach upon the Huaorani culture. Such disturbances of indigenous life date from 1541, when Francisco de Orellana's expedition departed Quito and stumbled upon the headwaters of the Río Napo. Towns such as Archidona and **Macas** ⓫ were soon established as bases for conquest and for conversion to Christianity. Many were subsequently abandoned due to repeated attacks from the indigenous people, but the gold prospectors, driven by desire for profits, and

the Franciscans and Jesuits, driven by fierce faith in their god, gradually pushed back the frontiers.

Oil and tourist booms

The loss of most of the Oriente to Peru following the border war in 1941 stirred the governments' attention, which was rewarded in 1967 with the discovery of huge oil deposits near **Lago Agrio** ⓬. The face of the region has changed drastically since then, with towns constructed overnight to provide services for the booming oil industry, which quickly became Ecuador's main money-spinner. In 1989, Lago Agrio was made the capital of Sucumbíos, Ecuador's 21st province, while in 1998 the new province of Orellana was created to its south.

This influx of people has sent wildlife deeper into the forests. In areas on the edge of the Amazon basin, there is little fauna left apart from birds and insects. For those who are short of time, tours can be organized into the rainforest from the small town of **Misahuallí**. These trips can give a good understanding of how people

Las Piscinas de la Virgen waterfall and baths.

View of Chimborazo volcano from Parque 21st Abril, Riobamba.

FACT

The Spanish chronicler Cieza de Léon visited the largely ruined Cuenca in 1547 and found fully stocked warehouses, barracks, and houses formerly occupied by "more than two hundred virgins, who were very beautiful, dedicated to the service of the sun."

living in the Oriente have adjusted to these outside influences.

The Napo flows on from Misa-huallí to **Coca** ⓭ (officially named Puerto Francisco de Orellana), passing stilt houses with exotic menageries set in rambling banana patches. Farmers load fruit into their dugout canoes and then paddle precariously off to market. The oil town of Coca itself has a somewhat seedy feel, although waterfront cafés provide local people and visitors with a pleasant hangout, and Coca itself is a safer center from which to explore the area than Lago Agrio. Signs of oil development in the area are obvious. Not too far from Coca, however, pure rainforest abounds.

The Río Napo here is ever-widening, bordered on either side by a forest canopy, thickest at the height of approximately 30 meters (100ft), beneath which grows, in damp dimness, an astonishing assortment of ferns and wild lemon trees with tiny edible ants living inside the stems. Above the canopy, the giant kapok tree stands out. The tallest Amazonian species, it can reach up to 60 meters (200ft) high and 40 meters (130ft) around the base of the trunk. Local people on the move often seek shelter at night in the hollows between its roots. Its branches are cluttered with bromeliads, strangler vines, and belladonna.

Hidden in the forest, just off the River Napo, three hours downriver from Coca, is **Sacha Lodge**. An elevated boardwalk heads through the forest, arriving at a piranha-infested lagoon in front of the lodge. Resident naturalists and indigenous guides venture into the forest with visitors on nature walks, canoe floats, or up into the 40-meter (130-ft) -high observation tower to experience forest life high up in the canopy, and maybe spot a sloth lazing atop his tree. Close to Sacha Lodge is **La Selva**, another well-run lodge that offers good excursions to view wildlife.

The rewards of a very early morning boat ride to the edge of **Parque Nacional Yasuní** may be the sight of flocks of macaws and parrots descending onto the cliff by the river to feed on the minerals in the soil. Yasuní is a national reserve created to protect and monitor the incredible biodiversity of this unique rainforest area. The comfortable Napo Wildlife Center is situated in the Yasuní Reserve, operated by the Añangu community. The birding here is excellent and there are also black caiman and giant otters.

The Tiputini River, a tributary of the Napo River, leads to the Tiputini Research Station, where researchers and ecotourists may wake to find groups of monkeys at their cabin windows, exotic birds, and always the unnerving chance of a jaguar wandering through their camp. Amazon cruises operate on the River Napo, aboard the *Manatee Amazon Explorer*, a luxury vessel holding 30 passengers. In the far southeast of Pastaza, Kapawi Lodge is located on the River Capahuari. It was built in partnership with the Achuar community, and is accessible by small aircraft.

Waiting in line at the bank, Alausí.

Coastal Ecuador

The tropical lowland west of the Andes has – along with its inhabitants, who comprise half the nation – been characterized as savage and uncivilized by mountain dwellers, a place to be exploited. It is the traditional source of Ecuador's agricultural exports, based on bananas, coffee, and cocoa. In late 1997 and early 1998, the warm northern current, El Niño, caused serious floods and extensive damage.

Coastal Ecuador begins in the north with **San Lorenzo** ⓮ and its neighboring villages, collections of wooden stilt houses suspended in steamy, timeless isolation amid twisting mangrove channels. It remains a ramshackle tropical town with a Caribbean feel, pulsating with the beat of Colombian salsa. At **La Tola**, on the edge of the San Lorenzo archipelago, the coast road begins – a dusty track through uninhabited swamps bursting with vegetation. Due to the proximity to Colombia, be careful when traveling as the area may be unsafe.

Esmeraldas ⓯, strung along the shore of the river of the same name, exemplifies urban coastal culture. This city is loud and vibrant late into the night. Among a population that is chiefly mestizo and black, mountain *campesinos* in bowler hats sell fruit, Andean panpipes interrupt Caribbean dance music and techno rhythms, and Chinese restaurants serve sweet-and-sour.

Southwest of Esmeraldas are some of Ecuador's finest beaches. The road passes through **Atacames**, a small resort town that in recent years has become a noisy party town; and on through **Sua**, a beautifully situated, friendly fishing village, finally ending at **Muisne** ⓰, with beaches as remote as they are alluring.

Productive regions

The main road south follows the river through cattle farms and plantations of bananas, palm oil, and rubber, rising 500 meters (1,600ft) to **Santo Domingo de los Colorados** ⓱. The Tsátchila natives, who live mainly to the south of town, paint black stripes on their faces and wear their hair dyed red with *achiote*, a plant dye, and cut in

FACT

Esmeraldas, according to legend, took its name from the emeralds found in the river here. The name may also come from the abundant, green vegetation.

New Cathedral, Cuenca.

Boats off Puerto López.

The sprawling Río Pastaza.

a bowl shape. They retain their knowledge of natural medicine but dress traditionally only for special occasions.

Perhaps the most scenic of the lowland routes runs from Santo Domingo to **Manta** ⓲ on the Pacific coast. On **Tarqui beach**, local fishermen unload their catch of shark, dorado, eel, and the odd turtle, which are cleaned and sold on the sand amid an aerial frenzy of seagulls and vultures.

Manta is the gateway to the nearby villages that produce Panama hats. Fine wickerwork furniture and sisal hammocks are also manufactured here. South of Manta lies **Parque Nacional Machalilla**, one of the world's few dry tropical forests. Now protected, it is hoped that this unique forest with its bottle-shaped trees, the skyline dotted with kapok trees and more than 200 species of birds, will survive.

The park entrance is just north of **Puerto López** ⓳, a small fishing town with unspoiled beaches. This is a good base from which to visit the Machalilla park and the Isla de la Plata, an island with some interesting

birdlife. From June through October humpback whales can be seen off the coast, as well. Beaches dot the coast from Cojimíes through Manta to the resort town of Salinas, Ecuador's westernmost point.

Guayaquil, the largest city

South of the central coast, all roads lead to **Guayaquil** ⓴, once the center of the Spanish regional shipbuilding industry and now Ecuador's largest and liveliest city, with approximately 2.8 million inhabitants. New technology and ideas have always come first to Guayaquil, making it Ecuador's main link to the outside world from the early 19th century, and its commercial and banking center through to the present. A pleasant walk goes along the **Malecón Simón Bolívar boardwalk** past **La Rotonda**, commemorating Bolívar's meeting with San Martín, up to **Las Peñas**, the city's only extant colonial district, and scenic **Cerro El Carmen**.

Shrunken heads from the Oriente, pre-Inca ceramics, colonial religious paintings, and a changing modern art

exhibition fill the **Museo Municipal**. The **Parque del Centenario**, where gymnasts and comedians perform, divides Avenida 9 de Octubre, the city's commercial heart. To escape the frenzy, grab a moment of tranquility in the city's botanical garden, **Parque Bolívar**, or in the **Parque Histórico**, a replica of the19th-century city.

The Galápagos Islands

The first sighting by Europeans of the Galápagos Islands was in 1535. It is possible that the ancient Manteños, Incas and even Polynesians visited the islands, which lie 1,000km (600 miles) off the Pacific coast of Ecuador. From their European discovery until their incorporation into Ecuador in 1832, the islands served as a refuge for European and American pirates, whalers and sealers, where they re-stocked supplies of firewood, water, and giant tortoises for meat, which could remain alive for a year in ships' holds.

Just as the islands were beginning to undergo permanent settlement, the HMS *Beagle* dropped anchor in **San Cristóbal Bay** ㉑ and the 26-year-old

naturalist Charles Darwin strode ashore. Previous scientific expeditions had been mounted, but with Darwin's visit, the enormous biological and geological significance of the Galápagos Islands was recognized. Although he stayed for only five weeks in 1835, Darwin made many of the observations upon which he based his theories of evolution and the mutability of species. He noticed 13 types of finch, each with a different beak, designed to collect its particular food.

Darwin recorded encountering a "strange Cyclopean scene" on a San Cristóbal beach – two tortoises munching on cactus. One "gave a deep hiss, and drew in its head", the other "slowly stalked away." Darwin became fascinated with the beasts, noting numerous subspecies.

The islands' romantic appeal was tarnished over the following century, when a penal colony was established on the island of **Floreana**. Conditions were harsh and administrators gratuitously cruel. The original colonists, some 80 soldiers whose crimes of insurrection had been pardoned, fled

Santa Ana hill in the Las Peñas colonial district of Guayaquil.

Hillside houses in Las Peñas, Guayaquil.

A butterfly at Machalilla National Park.

the island, leaving the prisoners to their fate. As recently as 1944, a colony was established on **Isabela** to which increasingly hardened criminals were sent. It was dissolved following a riot and mass escape, and in 1959, the islands were declared a national park.

The archipelago was designated a World Heritage Site in 1979 and a Unesco World Biosphere Reserve 6 years later. In December 2001, in an attempt to stop illegal fishing and in recognition of the conservation issues, Unesco declared the Marine Reserve around the islands a World Natural Heritage Site. Despite efforts to limit visitor numbers, the islands were placed on the UN's list of World Heritage Sites in danger in 2007. Since removed from the list, excessive development remains a danger, despite important efforts to curtail the entry of foreign species.

There are 13 major islands, six small islands and 42 islets spread over an area of 80,000 sq km (30,000 sq miles). The land consists of lava resting on a basalt base, volcanic refuse produced by successive underwater eruptions,

which continue today. The islands have never been connected with the mainland, but emerged from the water individually over a million years.

The violence of the geological past is most evident on **Isabela** with its chain of five volcanoes as high as 1,700 meters (5,600ft). One of them, the **Sierra Negra**, has the second-largest crater in the world, measuring 10km (6 miles) in diameter.

Seeds were transported accidentally by birds and aboard ships. Today the islands support almost 900 plant varieties, the most revered of which is the *palo santo*, found in abundance on **Isla Rábida** ㉒. There are six distinct vegetation zones ranging from low-level desert to the uppermost pampas; a walk up to the old sugar mill on San Cristóbal passes most of them.

On **San Bartolomé**, two sparkling horseshoe beaches are separated by a narrow strip of semitropical forest. From the island's summit, one of the best vantage points in the archipelago, the uninhabited volcanic wasteland of **Santiago** stretches away to the west. Within this desert is a freshwater

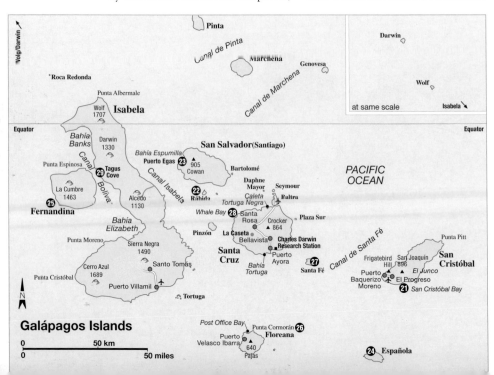

Galápagos Islands

spring. Flamingos dance around the nearby lagoon, and bury each other up to the neck in the coffee-colored sand of **Espumilla Beach**. Near **Puerto Egas** ㉓, fur seals swim through an underwater tunnel between the open sea and two small, clear pools.

Creatures of the sea

Some of the best snorkeling is done off far-flung islands like **Española** ㉔, the only place in the world in which the endemic waved albatross breeds. In **Gardner Bay**, flapping manta rays probably think you are just another sea lion, but the real sea lions know better, and an aggressive bull should be given right of way. The females and young are playful; they can recognize the 290 varieties of fish in the water, but a figure with a mask and flippers is still a curious sight.

The Galápagos are home to the world's only marine iguanas, and the island of **Fernandina** ㉕ holds the largest colony. As inquisitive as the two related land species, they are much more dragon-like, with their scaly skin – which turns from black to blue and red during mating season – and the row of spines along their back. At one time land-dwellers, they can submerge for only a few minutes at a time, searching for algae; and upon resurfacing, snort a salty spray into the air. Watching their antics beneath the smoldering **Volcán La Cumbre**, which erupted in April 2009, is a truly primal experience.

Directly opposite Fernandina is **Urbina Bay**, and one of the few coral reefs in the archipelago. Fish of every color steer clear of the Galápagos penguin, the world's northernmost species. The entrance to nearby **Elizabeth Bay** is protected by a cluster of islands which penguins share with nesting pelicans. En route to Floreana, schools of sperm and killer whales cruise the deep waters, and bottle-nosed dolphins surf the bow waves of boats. At **Devil's Crown**, named after the jagged, truncated volcanic cone rising from the ocean, sea lions glide along strong currents, which can make for very adventurous snorkeling.

The beautiful beach at **Point Cormorant** ㉖ on Floreana is dotted

> **TIP**
>
> The Galápagos Islands are a national park, and all non-Ecuadorian visitors must pay an entrance fee of US$100 (discounts are available for students with ID and children under 12).

Las Frailes beach, Machalilla National Park.

THE FAMOUS HAT

Montecristi and Cuenca are the production centers for the elegant Panama hats, which are woven from the reed *Carludovica palmata*. A top-quality or *superfino* specimen can change hands for up to $1,000, and should be able to hold water when held upside down. It should also fold up to fit into a top pocket without creasing. The hats have always been produced in Ecuador, but were shipped worldwide from Panama, hence the misnomer. Made since pre-Columbian times, they caught on among the conquistadors. Soldiers fighting in the Spanish-American War of 1898 wore the hats, and the export market to the US subsequently took off. They caught on in Europe following the 19th-century World Exposition in Paris. The hats were also a big hit with US prohibition gangsters.

with olivine crystals, while the adjacent lagoons teem with flamingos. Around the point is the **Bay of Sharks** – its ring of pristine white sand is popular with nesting tortoises. The name refers to the white-tipped shark, which is found mainly here and off San Bartolomé. Shark species in the archipelago can be observed safely while scuba diving, including the enormous and equally docile whale shark.

On land, the unchallenged king of the islands is the giant tortoise, which can live for 200 years and weigh up to 300kg (600lb). On rocky, sparsely vegetated islands like Isabela and Española its longer neck and legs and saddle-shaped carapace enable it to reach higher to obtain food – features absent from the more cumbersome species inhabiting fertile islands like **Santa Cruz**.

The **Charles Darwin Research Station** was established on Santa Cruz in 1959, on the centenary of the publication of *The Origin of Species*. One of its most important programs is the controlled hatching of tortoise

eggs, a necessary step since the introduction by early settlers of feral dogs, cats, goats, pigs, and rats. On **Pinzón**, not one young tortoise has been sighted for nearly 50 years. The feral species also destroy vegetation, but have participated in the evolutionary miracle of the islands in at least one respect: the goats on **Santa Fe ㉗**. In the absence of freshwater, they have developed a taste for the sea, and now live on it.

In **Whale Bay ㉘** on Santa Cruz, ceramic fragments conjure images of buccaneer Henry Morgan with a blue-footed booby on his shoulder. Pirates and whalers recorded their passage on the cliff faces of **Tagus Cove ㉙** on Isabela: today the graffiti is seen mainly by flightless cormorants. A more recent ruin is the skeleton of an abandoned 1960s salt mine on Isla Santiago.

The Galápagos Islands are one of the few places in the world where animals still live relatively undisturbed, and nowhere are the forces of evolution more clearly displayed. Visitors should leave no scars.

Sea lions keeping watch in the Galápagos.

The Last Hidden Tribes

Despite legislative protection, the outlook for Ecuador's few isolated Amazon tribes is bleak due to the onslaught of the modern world.

At most, there are 400 tribes believed to be living in Ecuador's northeast Amazon, refusing contact with mainstream civilization. Most of the evidence for these rainforest warriors, clinging to their Stone Age way of life, stems from violent encounters. In 1987, as oil companies encroached on land inhabited by the Tagaeri, a group of Huaorani, Coca's bishop Alejandro Labaka sought to contact them in a last-ditch pitch for their survival. He and Inés Arango, a Colombian nun, gave their lives in the attempt. The ensuing media exposure, however, kept the oil industry at bay.

Nevertheless, conflicts continue. Many Huaroani today work for oil companies or in tourism; some also work with the loggers. Through 2008, poachers of rare rainforest woods were found dead, fatally wounded by the Huaroani's heavy spears. Encouraged by loggers and poachers, in March 2003 a group of Huaroani sought to avenge a Tagaeri "kidnapping" by killing up to 30 forest dwellers, including women and children, who were burned to death inside a large dwelling. But the dead were members of the previously unknown Taromenani who had moved into the jungle building abandoned by the Tagaeri. The judicial authorities did almost nothing to investigate the Taromenani killing.

Members of the two tribes are so few that they fit inside just a few homesteads, each of which can house some 60 people. While these can be widely dispersed in the jungle, pressure from the 21st century is great, both from inside Ecuador and from across the border in Peru.

Protective measures

Aware of the race against the clock to save the tribes, the Correa government set up a half-dozen control posts staffed with police and scientists, to stop access to the "intangible zone" established for their protection in and around the southern part of the Yasuni National Park. The government also says it is doing more to control the boom in the smuggling of hardwoods to the US and Colombia.

Most oil companies demand proof of vaccination and special permits from visitors, in an attempt at protecting the tribes from the common diseases that have eradicated so many other native peoples since the arrival of the first Europeans. Contact with anyone, from tourists to other tribes, could wipe them out in one devastating epidemic. To the exasperation of the government, however, the "intangible zone" means nothing to the Tagaeri and Taromenani, as they roam to hunt, and live in such close proximity to the last outposts of mainstream society that they can steal machetes and axes from nearby tourist lodges and illegal logging camps. Despite their recent "discovery," the modern world has already influenced the Taromenani who now use plastic string and bottle caps to decorate their spears and necklaces.

Environmentalists say that current steps to protect them are too little too late. Some advocate a more aggressive, pre-emptive attempt to vaccinate them against disease before a plague can break out. This, however, would end their isolation, exposing them to the cultural dislocation that has affected other peoples, particularly the Cofán and Huaroani, who also first encountered Western society only a few decades ago. Such is the pressure from the greedy outside world that their traditional way of life will almost certainly end in the foreseeable future, even if they are to survive.

Tsachila Indians at the Complejo Turistico Huapilu cultural center, Santa Domingo.

BIRDS OF THE GALÁPAGOS ISLANDS

From the marbled godwit to the black-necked stilt, the bird life on the Galápagos Islands, which taught us about evolution, is still rich, rare, and rewarding.

Where else but on these small islands off the coast of Ecuador will birds come out to greet you? Life with no native predators has made the birds of the Galápagos fearless, which means that many of them are easy to spot. There are 58 resident species, of which 28 are endemic, as well as about 30 migratory birds. The sea birds are the most often seen: in the dry coastal areas you are likely to spot species of the booby family, the waved albatross (only found on the island of Española) and two flightless sea birds, the Galápagos penguin and the flightless cormorant. The best time to come is October to February, when most migrants are visiting, and birds are reproducing. Then, a serious ornithologist might observe 50 species in a week, and even a novice should be able to spot two dozen. There are dangers in paradise, however: the introduction of domestic animals has been bad news. Some prey on the birds, others destroy or compete for their habitats. Farming on the inhabited islands also destroys habitats, tourist transportation runs over small birds, and a natural phenomenon, the El Niño current, brings mosquito-borne disease and disrupts the food chain.

The blue-footed booby (Sula nebouxii excisa) has a wonderful courtship ritual in which the male ostentatiously displays his brightly colored feet in order to attract a mate. Two or three eggs are laid and both of the parents share the task of incubating them.

The female Galápagos hawk (Buteo galapagoensis) is larger than the male of the species. While the males are monogamous, females will mate with up to seven males per season in order to ensure that breeding will be successful. The female and her males take turns in guarding the nest.

The brown pelican (Pelecanus occidentalis urinator) is a huge, cumbersome bird, which can often be seen following fishing boats in search of food.

THE SECRET OF DARWIN'S FINCHES

The finches of the Galápagos were vitally important in the development of Charles Darwin's ideas about evolution and the formation of species.

When he set off on his voyage around the world on HMS *Beagle* (1831–36), he believed, like most people of his time, in the fixity of species. But on the Galápagos he observed that 13 different species of the finch had evolved from a single ancestral group, and it was this (together with his observations of the islands' tortoises) which led to his contention that species could evolve over time, with those most suited to their natural environment surviving and passing on their characteristics to the next generation.

The main difference he noted between the finches was the size and shape of their beaks, leading him to conclude that the birds which survived were those whose beaks enabled them to eat the available food.

The 13 species of finch are divided into two groups: ground finches (pictured above is the large ground finch, *Geospiza magnirostris*) and tree finches, of which the mangrove finch, found only in the swamps of Isabela island, is the most rare. You are unlikely to see all of them on a short visit, but it's an enjoyable challenge to see how many you can spot.

The vermillion flycatcher (Pyrocephalus rubinus) is an attractive little bird and quite unlike any other to be seen on the Galápagos Islands. It has a high-pitched, musical song and builds a distinctive cup-shaped nest, on which the female incubates the eggs.

The lava gull (Larus fuliginosus) is believed to be the rarest gull species in the world. It roosts on the shores of saltwater lagoons and builds solitary nests along the coast.

The magnificent frigate bird (Fregata magnificens magnificens) and its close relation, the great frigate bird, can be seen near the coasts of many islands. Both males and females have long forked tails and the male is remarkable for the vivid red gular pouch which puffs in the mating season.

View over Rio de Janeiro from the top of Sugar Loaf Mountain.

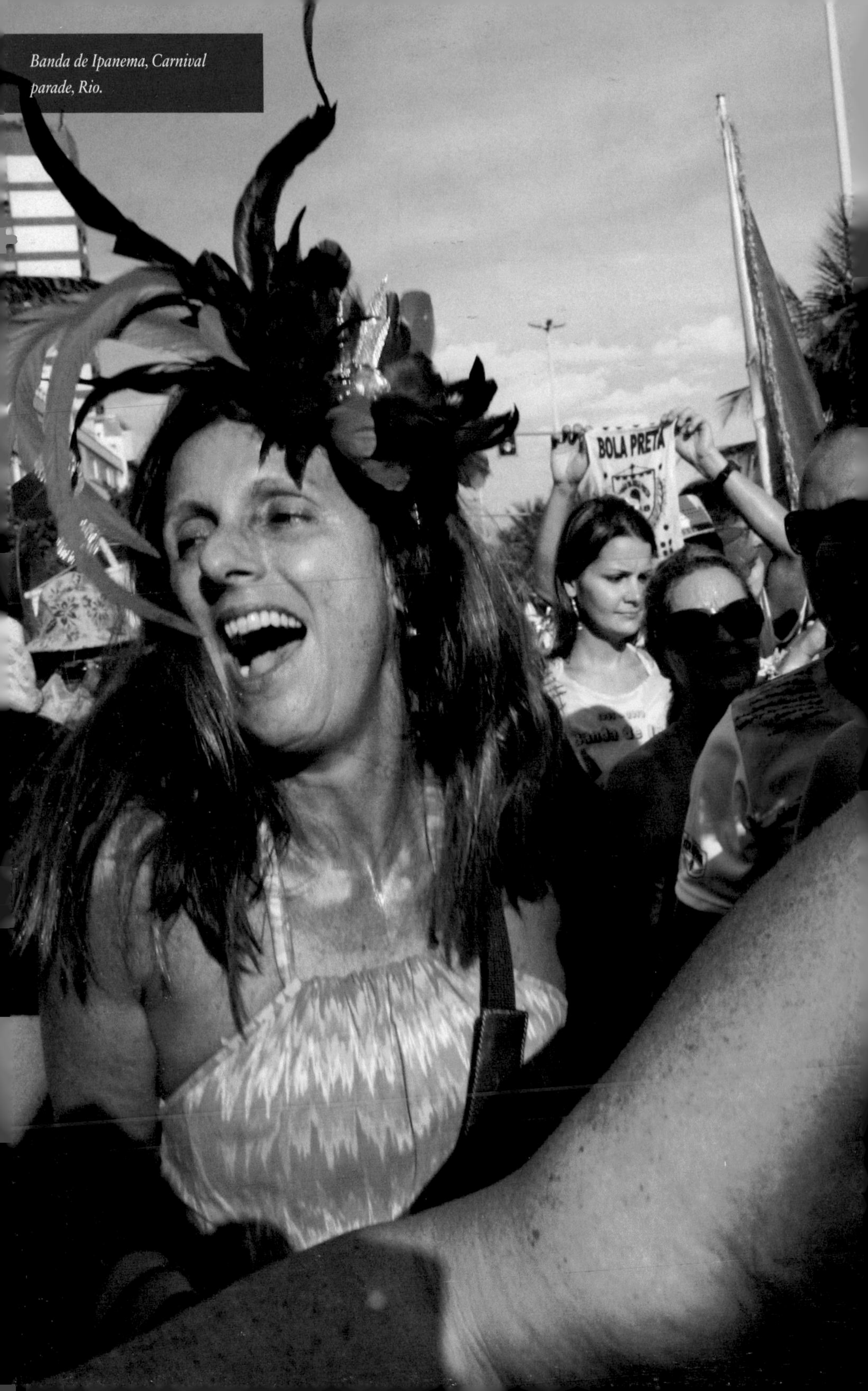

Banda de Ipanema, Carnival parade, Rio.

Lagoa Rodrigo de Freitas, Rio.

THE TROPICAL GIANT

Laid-back tropical paradise, economic miracle,
and home of the hedonistic carnival –
Brazil is a heady mix of them all.

*Bahian woman dressed
traditionally in Salvador.*

Nearly half the South American subcontinent can be described in one tantalizing word: Brazil. Almost as big as the United States and home to 200 million people, Brazil is a world in itself – a sensuous giant that invariably becomes a part of everyone who experiences its pleasures. Brazil the geographic colossus is also a state of mind, one that loosens up even the most cautious of spirits who venture there. That's the power of the Brazilian *jeito*, or way: relax, improvise, and *não esquente a cabeça*: don't get hot-headed come what may.

There is a vibrancy to Brazil unparalleled elsewhere in Latin America; the country's cutting-edge innovations and penchant for fads have led some to call it "the California of South America." But for all its laid-back ethos, Brazil is also an economic dynamo. Fast growth this century has led the world's fifth-largest population to now also produce the planet's number six economy. Cars crafted in São Paulo run on lead-free sugar-cane fuel (home-grown, naturally), and their compact-disc players made in the duty-free Amazon port of Manaus play tunes from the recording studios of Rio de Janeiro.

*Colonial houses in the
historic district of Parati,
Rio de Janeiro State.*

As the major port of entry, Rio is where most visitors get their first dazzling impressions of Brazil, with its beautiful beaches, sensuously rounded peaks, and world-famous *carnaval* ,and investment is pouring in to refurbish the city for the 2016 Olympics. But there's much more to Brazil than Rio. Nearby is South America's and the southern hemisphere's largest metropolis, São Paulo. This is the country's powerhouse, the center of its massive commercial and industrial output. To the northwest lies Brasília, the architectural wonder that sprang from the wilderness to become the capital. In major cities, fabled soccer stadiums are getting upgrades, with some fittingly ultra-modern new venues going up in readiness for the FIFA World Cup 2014.

Beyond are slightly more subdued wonders: the stately colonial cities of Minas Gerais, living monument of the gold and diamond booms; the inviting beaches and rich Afro-Brazilian culture of the northeast; the immense rainforests of the Amazon jungle that still cover more than half the country; the vast marshlands of the Pantanal, a naturalist's paradise; and the enormous, spectacular waterfalls of Iguaçu.

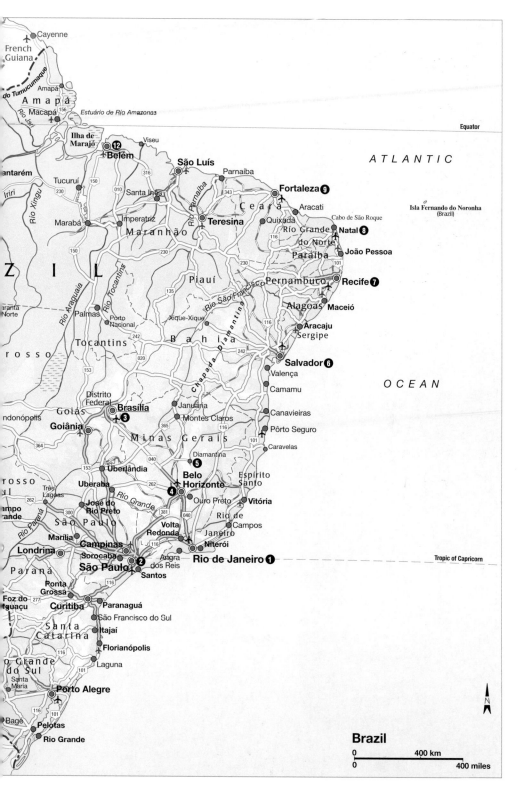

Cayenne

French
Guiana

do Tumucumaque

Amapá

A m a p á
Macapá 156   Estuário de Río Amazonas

Equator

Ilha de
Marajó   Viseu

antarém   **②Belém**   **São Luís**   Parnaíba   A T L A N T I C

Tucuruí   150   316   **Fortaleza ❾**

Iriri   230   010   Santa Inês   343   C e a r a   Aracati

Marabá   Imperatriz   **Teresina**   Quixadá   Cabo de São Roque   Isla Fernando do Noronha
                                                                                    (Brazil)

M a r a n h ã o   Río Grande   **Natal ❽**

Z   I   L   150   230   do Norte

                                              Paraíba   João Pessoa

P i a u í   230   **Pernambuco**   **Recife ❼**

135   Río São Francisco   Alagoas   Maceió

aranā   Palmas   Porto   Xique-Xique   116   **Aracaju**
Norte   Nacional   Sergipe

rosso   T o c a n t i n s   242   B a h i a   242   **Salvador ❻**

                    020   Valença

                153   Camamu

            Distrito   O C E A N
            Federal   **Brasília**   Januária   Canavieiras

ndonópolis   Goiás   **❸**   Montes Claros   Pôrto Seguro

            Goiânia   365   116   Caravelas

364   M i n a s   G e r a i s   101

        153   **Uberlândia**   Diamantina

rosso   **❺**

ul   Três   **Uberaba**   262   **Belo**   Espírito
    Lagoas   **Horizonte**   Santo

ampo   262   **José do**   Rio Grande   **❹**   Ouro Prêto   **Vitória**
rande   **Rio Preto**   300   381   040   Rio de

        São Paulo   Campos

Marília   **Campinas**   **Volta**   Janeiro

Londrina   **Sorocaba**   **Redonda**   **Niterói**

P a r a n á   **❷**   Angra   **Rio de Janeiro ❶**   Tropic of Capricorn
        São Paulo   dos Reis

        Santos

        Ponta
        Grossa   116

Foz do   277   **Curitiba**   Paranaguá
Iguaçu

        S a n t a   São Francisco do Sul
        C a t a r i n a   Itajaí

        116   **Florianópolis**

o Grande
do Sul   101   Laguna

    Santa
    Maria

    Porto Alegre

    116   101

Bagé

    Pelotas

    Rio Grande

Brazil

0   400 km

0   400 miles

Ipanema beach, Rio de Janeiro.

BRAZIL

This vast country pulsates with life, from the rampant fertility of the Amazon to the sensual delights of Rio and the modern sophistication of São Paulo and Brasília.

Visitors can only hope to scratch the surface of this huge land, which still has vast unpopulated areas, and reveals its secrets reluctantly. It's worth making an effort, for there is much to discover, from the excitement of Rio de Janeiro and the gastronomic highlights of São Paulo to the majestic forests of the Amazon, scarred red by twisting rivers; and from the abundant wildlife of the Pantanal to the solitude of the arid northeastern "backlands."

The past comes to life in the once-wealthy gold towns in the south of Minas Gerais, such as Ouro Preto, Tiradentes, and Congonhas. Harder to get to, but well worth the effort, are places like the high plateaux of Bahia state, the Chapada Diamantina, where Brazil's second-highest waterfall tumbles from a mist-clouded plain.

The distance from the Andes to the Atlantic Ocean is almost 4,500km (2,800 miles), and most of Brazil's attractions are a long way from the big cities, as well as from each other: the Iguaçu Falls is thousands of kilometers from torrid Belém in the north. But traveling around Brazil has become easier as infrastructure improves, although fluctuating exchange rates have meant comparatively much higher prices.

Visitors looking for clear, warm waters, white sands, and tropical beauty

Playing music on the streets of Olinda, Pernambuco.

will be overwhelmed by the Brazilian coastline, an endless chain of beaches that can be empty or bustling or anything in between.

Conquering the interior

Brazil's interior was first penetrated by Europeans in the late 1600s. The first pioneers were Jesuits proselytizing to indigenous Guaraní, followed by Portuguese immigrants too poor to acquire land in the sugar-cane dominated coastal regions. These settlers pushed into what is now the state of

Main Attractions
Rio de Janeiro
Costa Verde and Paratí
São Paulo
Colonial towns of Minas Gerais
Salvador de Bahia
The beaches of the Northeast
Olinda
Manaus, Belém and the
   Amazon

São Paulo to raise cattle and plant subsistence crops. Like the wealthy sugar planters whose labor force was mostly black slaves, these farmers also sought bonded workers, so they organized expeditions to abduct the Guaraní people who inhabited the region. The Guaraní sought refuge in the Jesuit missions where indigenous peoples lived in educated, highly productive communities.

Despite their barbaric raids, the *bandeirantes* (so named because of the banners under which they marched), have gone down in Brazilian folklore as brave pioneers who opened up what has become the country's most productive economic region.

One boom after another

Just when the world market for Brazilian sugar started to go soft, around 1700, a new boom shook the country. This time it was gold and diamonds, discovered in the rugged hill country of Minas Gerais. Most of the gold was sent home to the Portuguese crown, but enough remained to build Baroque towns like Ouro Preto, São

João del Rei, and Sabará. The new treasures were shipped to Europe through Rio de Janeiro, putting the backwater port on the map, and by 1763 Rio had become so important that the Portuguese crown moved the capital there from the sugar cane and slave entrepôt of Salvador.

Other booms followed, such as cotton. The biggest and most lasting of the booms, coffee, started in the late 18th century. The state of São Paulo was covered with coffee plantations as the craze for drinking coffee spread around the world. But coffee prices tumbled in 1930, and with them fell the government. Getulio Vargas, governor of Rio Grande do Sul, then seized the presidency and won Brazilians' hearts with his populist rhetoric and championing of organized labor. He established a corporate state loosely modeled on Mussolini's Italian-style Fascism, but he lost support after the fall first of Mussolini, then of Hitler. Vargas resigned in 1945, but returned to office in 1951, before committing suicide three years later.

Candido Portinari's Coffee painting at the Museu Nacional de Belas Artes, Rio.

Eighteen years of constitutional rule and steady economic growth followed, up until the early 1960s. With the number of landless peasants increasing dramatically, land reform became an explosive political issue. The military responded to the growing unrest by seizing power in April 1964.

Birth of the "Brazilian miracle"

The military's crackdown on leftists (many of whom were tortured and killed) together with generous fiscal incentives, combined to attract a flood of foreign investment. The Brazilian economy boomed, mainly enriching those who were already wealthy. Disenchantment with military rule grew as the economy took a nosedive in 1980, crippled by enormous bills for imported oil and public works projects, such as a rarely used Amazon highway. The last of a series of military dictator presidents stepped down in March 1985.

The new government of President José Sarney inherited a foreign debt of more than $100 billion. Sarney, closely allied with the military, quickly lost political support as inflation, which reached 1,000 percent in 1988, continued to ravage the economy.

Economic woes were accompanied by growing street crime. Such anti-social behavior is relatively recent in Brazil, and is widely considered a product of the huge influx of rural Brazilians into large cities since the 1960s. Some were attracted by the hope of finding work, but many arrived as refugees from droughts in the Northeast. With little chance of anything but the most menial employment, and scarce options for accommodations, the newly arrived migrants were clustered together in shanty towns – *favelas* – on the outskirts of the cities, where they formed their own communities.

Progress for the poor is often limited by racial discrimination. Brazil has been called a racial paradise because of the high number of interracial marriages and an absence of open racial conflict, but to be black in Brazil almost always means to be poor, and 40 percent of the country's

In Rio's Rocinha favela.

population is black. But whatever their color, there is little chance of a poor Brazilian becoming a rich one, unless they play soccer well.

From bust to boom

By 1994, inflation was running at more than 3,000 percent a year, when social democrat Fernando Henrique Cardoso became president. He halted the monetary meltdown by introducing a new currency, the real. This set off a chain of events that are still transforming the country. Twelve to 15 million Brazilians joined the consumer society for the first time, causing food sales to surge and the demand for many other goods to explode. Credit, absent for three decades, became accessible, and millions went on a shopping spree, particularly for new cars – but as road building has not kept pace this has contributed to chronic congestion.

In 2002, former metalworker Luis Inácio da Silva, popularly known as Lula, became Brazil's first left-wing president in 40 years. He has followed sensible economic policies while not defaulting on the country's $250 billion public debt. As well as bringing food to 15 million needy people, he continued to meet IMF demands, and secured a series of several hundred billion-dollar loans. Lula was re-elected in 2006, and announced his intention to ensure an annual economic growth rate of 5 percent, while controlling inflation and government spending.

The Northeast has progressed rapidly, as factories have relocated in search of cheaper labor. Stagnant state capitals such as Fortaleza, Recife, and Salvador are being given a new lease on life, and neglected architectural gems are being restored.

Huge natural resources secure the country's future, but they bring responsibilities toward the environment, particularly in the Amazon region, where destruction has occurred on a massive scale. Disturbingly, the Avança Brasil project was announced in 2001. Already well underway, the $40-billion program will include the building of 10,000km (6,215 miles) of highways, hydroelectric dams, and power lines

Cariocas just want to have fun.

in an attempt to industrialize the area. Indigenous peoples, particularly those in the Amazon regions, still suffer daily threats and invasions of their homelands by fire, logging, and from settlers looking for homes away from Brazil's southern cities.

Although Lula and his successor, Dilma Rouseff, have been criticized for a lack of commitment in protecting the rainforest, in June 2004 Lula announced the designation of four new national forests, covering around 400,000 hectares (1 million acres) of threatened land.

Trouble in the rainforest

The conflict of interests over land use is exemplified in the remote western region of Rondônia (see page 257), where settlers are pushing back the rainforest – and the people who have lived there for centuries. Two major factors set off the land rush: first, changes in agriculture in Brazil's prosperous south made many peasants landless in the 1970s. Soaring world prices for soybeans convinced many coffee farmers that it would be more profitable to cut down their bushes and plant soybeans. Peasants who had sharecropped at the edges of the coffee plantations – assuring growers of a stable workforce to harvest the beans – were no longer needed for the mechanized soybean harvest, and were forced to abandon their plots.

Second, the extension of the roadway BR 364 from the coffee regions of São Paulo state to Rondônia, the new Brazilian frontier, put into action the formula for peopling the Amazon that had been enunciated by the Brazilian military, which then governed the country: "A land without people for people without land." Speculators cashed in, buying up enormous tracts for cattle ranches.

Brazil has now become one of the world's 10 biggest economies, with a GDP over $1.3 trillion, and nearly 70 percent of its exports are industrial goods – but the gap between rich and poor is still greater than almost anywhere else in the world. In most cities, unemployment has led to rising crime. Tourists may be targeted, and caution is needed, but things are not as bad as is often made out. A special police force guards tourists on many beaches.

Rio de Janeiro, city of fun

Brazilians call **Rio de Janeiro** ❶ *a cidade maravilhosa* – the marvelous city – and they have ample reason to do so. There's the city's stunning setting: flanked to the east by the enormous **Bay of Guanabara** and to the south by the Atlantic Ocean, Rio sprawls around and even up the sides of enormous granite peaks and down to wide sandy beaches. The result of this topsy-turvy topography is a city sculptured around the whims of nature, giving the urban landscape a look that can only be described as sensuous.

The 6 million people who live in and around Rio are known as *cariocas*, and they epitomize the casual, good-natured disposition associated with Brazilians. Part of the *cariocas*' sunny

Favela in Salvador, Bahia.

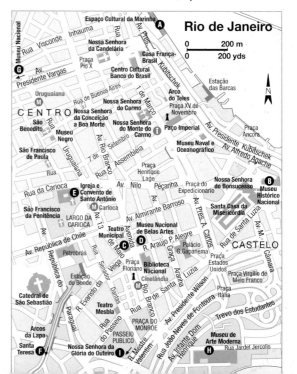

Rio de Janeiro

outlook may derive from the smug satisfaction of living in a place most people only dream of, where it's possible to join the fun on the beaches for the price of a local bus fare. Another reason for their friendliness could be the open social scene of Rio. Unlike other big cities, where exclusivity heightens the appeal of social gatherings, in Rio people of all classes throng to public places for fun. The beaches are the biggest attraction, followed by soccer stadiums and carnivals. In Rio, it's sociable to down a *chopp* (draught beer) and chat with friends on the sidewalk; life is lived in the open air. For all its allure, nobody will deny that Rio has serious problems, epitomized in the record floods of 2011 and the 2012 collapse of downtown high-rises near the municipal theater. The major investments planned for the FIFA World Cup 2014 and the Olympics in 2016 will come none too soon.

Cariocas have a reputation for possessing few inhibitions and tremendous appetites. That image developed in part from the bacchanalian bashes of carnival, in part from the

Soaking up the sun on Ipanema beach.

tantalizingly tiny beach attire favored by both genders. In Rio, you don't have to be gorgeous to be on display – just uninhibited. *Cariocas* are extremely tolerant (gay men seeking open minds flock to Rio from the rest of Brazil) and anyone can indulge in a little exhibitionism. Pleasure became Rio's main moneymaker after 1960, when the seat of government was moved from here to landlocked Brasília.

From the airport to the city center

Most visitors' first encounter with Rio takes place at the sleek complex of Antonio Carlos Jobim International Airport. The airport, also known as Galeão, is located on an island north of Rio, and to the west is a massive swampy area known as the Baixada Fluminense, or fluvial lowlands, a poor, featureless area that is home to two-thirds of the city's inhabitants. The drive into the city from the airport passes Rio's port and the **Espaço Cultural da Marinha** Ⓐ (Avenida Alfredo Agache; Tue–Sun noon–5pm),

one of Rio's principal museums, famous for its detailed model ships. Nearby is the **Museu Histórico Nacional ❸** (Praça Marechal Ancora; Tue–Fri 10am–5pm, Sat–Sun 2–6pm), which holds Brazil's national archives covering the period from 1500 to the proclamation of the republic in 1889.

The main thoroughfare through the heart of the downtown area, **Avenida Rio Branco**, is lined by skyscraping banks, travel agencies, and the ornate 19th-century buildings of the **Teatro Municipal ❸** (which has a splendid ground-floor café with mosaic tiles). Across the street is the **Biblioteca Nacional** (the national library, with neoclassical and Art Nouveau paintings on display) and the **Museu Nacional de Belas Artes ❸** (Tue–Fri 10am–6pm, Sat–Sun 12pm–5pm), one of the country's foremost repositories of classic and contemporary Brazilian art, with around 16,000 works.

One of the best places to watch the action is on the plaza in front of the Teatro Municipal, an area known as **Cinelândia**. Come nightfall it's a mixture of political campaigners, street theater, transvestites, and performers of *capoeira* (a stylized mix of martial art and dance with its own accompanying rhythms and music. On the other side of the Teatro Municipal is a wide pedestrian mall, **Largo da Carioca**, a favorite haunt of all manner of vendors, and artisans working with leather.

For a flavor of what Rio was like before the skyscrapers crowded its skyline, wander down the side streets off Largo da Carioca. Don't miss the stately **Confeiteria Colombo** at Rua Gonçalves Dias 32, with a mirror-lined tearoom downstairs and elegant dining room upstairs. Belle Epoque furnishings evoke the late 19th century, when Rio's intelligentsia used to gather here. Stroll down Rua da Carioca for hearty German food and *chopp* (beer on tap) at the lively Bar Luiz, a downtown fixture for more than a century.

Rising high above Largo da Carioca to the west is the splendid Baroque edifice of the **Igreja e Convento de Santo Antônio ❸** (Mon, Wed–Fri 7.30am–7pm, Tue 6.30am–8pm,

Toucans get their name from tucano, given to them by Brazil's Tupi Indians.

Alberto Guignard's Léa e Maura painting at the Museu Nacional de Belas Artes.

Carnival!

No celebration better reveals the Brazilian love of music, dance, and revelry than its massive Carnival festivities.

Nothing else merits more preparation, more prolonged and devout attention, and a more lavish outpouring of private resources than the annual convulsion that has come to symbolize Brazil, for better or for worse. Extravagance, self-indulgence, exhibitionism, and a kind of gleeful innocence are the basic elements – qualities that color life in Brazil. Streets normally clogged with vehicles are reclaimed by revelers on foot; macho men lasciviously parade in drag; laborers masquerade as 18th-century royalty; mothers dress up like babies; the wealthy watch the poor perform; people stay up all night and sleep all day.

Carnival arrived with the Portuguese, the end-of-winter festivities of Europe tied to Catholic tradition. The celebrations are ostensibly the last shot at merrymaking before the 40 days of Lenten fasting (the name may be a derivation of the Latin

In flamboyant Carnival regalia at Rio's Sambodrome.

carnelevare, farewell to meat). It is celebrated in numerous, mostly Catholic, cities like New Orleans in the US or Cologne in Germany, along with Latin America. Characteristic are parades and floats, and ridiculing of authorities and upper classes, an escape valve for social frustrations for centuries.

Carnival in Brazil began as an aggressive spree of throwing water, mud, and flour at passers-by. This still characterizes Carnival in Bolivia and Argentina, but was banned in Brazil in the 19th century. But the Carnival that Brazil is renowned for did not become a tradition until the 1930s, when neighborhood groups began to compete. Samba has become the signature music of Carnival. Today the competition between samba schools is akin to the rivalry between top sports teams. Most members come from the humblest of Rio's neighborhoods. The schools hold practice sessions for months before Carnival, which are often open to the public. The moment of glory comes at the gates of Rio's mammoth samba stadium, the Sambódromo, designed by Niemeyer and inaugurated in 1984. Some 88,500 spectators can be seated along this kilometer-long strip to watch the samba schools go dancing by; each has about 90 minutes to inch its way down the 700-meter/yd route. If you can't get a ticket, you can see the schools line up outside on Avenida Presidente Vargas. Other cities have similar parade grounds, including Manaus' Bómbodromo and the Sambódromo do Anhembi in São Paulo.

Street dancing

The best street dancing is in Salvador, where carousing hordes follow deafening sound systems mounted on trucks known as trios elétricos. Up to 2.7 million people throng the streets during the revelry. As is the case everywhere, it's best to dress minimally (shorts are good) to blend into the crowds and not attract thieves. Many people prefer Carnival in the Northeast. In Recife the pre-eminent Carnival music is *frevo*, which ignites passions.

Less frenetic are the carnivals held in Olinda and Ouro Preto. Class lines dissolve as revelers hop down the street in camaraderie fueled by generous amounts of beer and cachaça (sugar-cane brandy). Carnival has moved off the streets and into the clubs recently, and this is where the most intense debauchery and exhibitionism goes on.

Not everyone in Brazil is wild about Carnival. Many intellectuals sneer at the kitsch, wanton drinking, and lewdness. But for outsiders, there is probably no better time to see the Brazil of everyone's fantasies.

Sat 7.30am–11am, 3.30–5pm, Sun 9–11am), built between 1608 and 1780. Beside the main church is the lovely chapel of **São Francisco de Penitência** (Mon Fri 9am 1pm). To the south, on the other side of Avenida Republica do Chile, stands Rio's cone-shaped modern **Catedral de São Sebastião** (daily 7am–6pm), finished in 1976.

Neighborhoods off the beach

Nearby is the **Arcos da Lapa**, a towering 18th-century aqueduct that now serves as a bridge for the picturesque trolley cars, or *bondes* (pronounced "bon-jees") – so called because the system was funded by foreign bonds. The trolleys shuttle from a station by the cathedral to the steep streets of **Santa Teresa ❻**, to the west of the center. Known for its precipitous topography and grand views, Santa Teresa is one of the most bohemian of Rio's neighborhoods. Be sure to see the **Chácara do Ceu** (Little House in the Sky; Wed–Mon noon–5pm) on Rua Martinho Nobre. This small museum, set in gardens, has splendid views of the city and a great collection of Brazilian and European paintings, including works by Picasso, Braque, and Matisse.

The area underneath the aqueduct, also called **Lapa**, is one of Rio's best nightlife areas, dotted with bars and music clubs.

Take a detour to the northern suburb of São Cristóvão and the Quinta da Boa Vista Park to visit the **Museu Nacional ❼** (Tue–Sun 10am–4pm), the home of the imperial royal family from 1808 until the monarchy came to an end in 1889. A throne room and reception rooms remain, as does an eclectic ethnographic and natural history collection.

Going south

Much of the shoreline between downtown Rio and the Bay of Botafogo, including Santos Dumont airport, home to the shuttle service to São Paulo, is the result of *aterro* (landfill). Toward the airport, international and Brazilian modern art is also on display in the exciting **Museu de Arte**

· WHERE

The best way to see the elegant 19th-century homes of Santa Teresa is to take one of the yellow streetcars (bondes) that leave from the cathedral. Leave valuables behind, since the open-sided cars are vulnerable to pickpockets.

Copacabana beach in Rio.

Street scene in the Saara bazaar area of Rio.

Guanabara Bay as seen from Sugar Loaf Mountain.

Moderna (Tue–Fri noon–6pm, Sat–Sun noon–7pm), off Avenida Infante Dom Henrique. South of the museum in the Parque do Flamengo is a tall stone monument built to honor Brazilians who died in World War II. Across the road, on a cliff, is the Baroque **Igreja de Nossa Senhora da Glória** (Mon–Fri 1–5pm, Sat–Sun 8am–noon) and adjacent museum.

Emerging like a gigantic granite knee 400 meters (1,300ft) from the waters of the entrance to Guanabara Bay is **Pão de Açúcar** (Sugar Loaf Mountain). Cable cars leave **Praia Vermelha** station every half hour to sweep visitors up the mountain via the Morro da Urca, with restaurant and amphitheater. To the west of Sugar Loaf begin Rio's legendary beaches. The first wide arc spans the neighborhoods of Leme to the east and Copacabana to the west, with Copacabana Fort at the western point. **Leme** is mostly residential and quiet. Rua Princesa Isabel, which divides Leme from Copacabana, is a favorite with prostitutes, and nightlife in the area is rather seedy. **Copacabana**, with 350,000 residents, is Rio's most densely populated neighborhood, and is a lively place to enjoy street celebrations at Carnival and the spectacular New Year's Eve's celebrations. The **Praia de Copacabana** beach is magnificent, and stretches out almost a block to the water. It is floodlit at night, but stay close to the crowds on the sidewalk to avoid getting mugged.

After Copacabana comes **Praia de Ipanema**, which connects at its western end with another beach, called **Leblon**. Both Ipanema and Leblon are much more attractive neighborhoods than Copacabana, and altogether more pleasant areas for tourists to stay. Behind them to the north is the freshwater **Lagoa Rodrigo de Freitas**, a large natural lagoon surrounded by high-rises and restaurants. It is hugely popular with *cariocas*, who make use of the jogging and cycle paths around the lake, take swan-shaped pedaloes out on the water, or hang out at the refreshment kiosks on the lakeside.

South to the most unspoiled beaches

On the west shore of the lagoon are the **Jockey Club** racetrack and the beautifully landscaped **Jardím Botánico**, on the street of the same name, established here by Dom João VI at the beginning of the 19th century. Some 7,000 species of Brazilian plants cover the garden's 100 hectares (250 acres), and the area is rich with birdlife.

Another natural adventure is the ride up the proverbially hunchbacked **Corcovado Mountain** on the impressive steep cog railway that leaves from Cosme Velho. An escalator takes passengers from the station to the summit. At the top, 710 meters (2,330ft) above the ocean, towers Rio's trademark statue of **Cristo Redentor** (Christ the Redeemer). If you are waiting for morning clouds to clear before boarding the little train, pop into the **Museu Internacional de Arts Naïf** (Tue–Fri 10am–6pm) to see a huge collection of Naïve art.

The road down from the statue wends through the **Parque Nacional da Tijuca**, a tropical reserve that includes 100km (60 miles) of narrow, two-lane roads winding through the forest's thick vegetation, and with several breathtaking lookout points.

West of the sands of Leblon, sprawling up the sides of granite slopes, are two *favelas* or hillside shanty towns – **Vidigal** and **Rocinha** (the latter is the largest in South America). Their residents, who number hundreds of thousands, often endure precarious circumstances in order to live close to their jobs on the south side of the city. Rocinha tumbles down into **São Conrado**, a modern beach-side suburb that is the haunt of the city's hangliders and the beautiful Gávea golf course. Farther along the coast, along a two-tier highway, is the start of "new" Rio.

Barra de Tijuca, or simply Barra, is a massive suburb – a little too American for some tastes. Here you'll find the city's largest shopping malls and entertainment complexes sitting between modern, purpose-built condominiums. Barra beach, at over 18km (11 miles), is the city's longest and one of the most

A cobbled street in the historic district of Parati.

Santa Rita church and the harbour, Parati.

FACT

According to a popular joke, there are three great things about Brasília: its cool air, its enormous sky, and its air shuttle to Rio.

popular on the weekends. Beyond Barra are to be found a number of other beaches such as Prianha and Grumari that are relatively unspoiled and that help visitors to understand part of the awesome beauty that gives Rio its enduring magic.

Close to Rio

The coastal route between Rio and São Paulo, a drive of 375 miles (600km), is an attraction in its own right, being one of the planet's most stunning stretches of coastline. The **Costa Verde**, or Green Coast, includes **Angra dos Reis**, a bay with hundreds of tropical islands including the idyllic **Ilha Grande**. There is also the colonial masterpiece of **Parati**, a small coastal town founded in the 17th century, and designated a Unesco National Monument, that hosts one of South America's most important literary festivals, held each year in July or August, which draws major literary figures from all over the world.

Closer to São Paulo are the resort areas of Ubatuba, Caraguatatuba, São Sebastião, Guarujá, and Ilhabela.

Parque Trianon, São Paulo.

The coast to the east of Rio, known as the Costa do Sol (Sun Coast), also holds a number of attractions, most notably the pretty and extremely fashionable village of **Búzios**, that sits on a peninsula 200km (125 miles) from Rio, along with 23 beaches. Búzios is known for beaches, attractive inns, great restaurants, and its exciting and varied nightlife.

The most popular day trip from Rio takes visitors away from the coast and up in to the mountains north of Rio where the imperial city of **Petrópolis** is waiting to be discovered. In the 19th century Dom Pedro II started the fashion for taking to the hills to escape the summer heat, and *cariocas* have been following his example ever since. Take a horse-drawn buggy ride around the town, or visit the **Museu Imperial** (Tue–Sun 11am–6pm) in the splendid building that was once the royal summer residence.

The region is also home to the **Parque Nacional da Serra dos Orgãos**, an area of rich biodiversity that is extremely popular with walkers and trekkers.

São Paulo: Brazil's workhorse

The first thing that strikes most visitors to the city of **São Paulo** ❷ is its sheer enormity. Home to 11 million *paulistas*, as the city's natives call themselves, São Paulo's phenomenal growth shows no signs of abating. Already the city covers nearly 2,600 sq km (1,000 sq miles), and is ringed by mushrooming suburbs with another 9 million people, making it the biggest urban area south of the equator. Two-thirds of the country's industrial goods are produced here, including nine out of 10 automobiles. "São Paulo works so that the rest of Brazil can play," *paulistas* will tell you. Since its foundation in 1554, the city has always attracted self-reliant individualists – it was Brazil's equivalent of the Old West, and today proudly honors its old pioneers, the *bandeirantes*. Those who followed came from all over the world, especially in the 19th century, bringing industrious work habits. More recent immigrants have come from the drought-stricken states of northeastern Brazil. Poorly educated and unskilled, they often end up in the festering slums that house a sizable percentage of the city's population.

São Paulo is not a place to spend your whole vacation, but it is well worth a visit. Its restaurants are as diverse as they are numerous – a reflection of the city's varied ethnic make-up – and the nightlife rivals that of any other major cosmopolitan city.

Paulistas consider themselves trailblazers in the arts as well as industry. The pride and joy of the city is the MASP, the **Museu de Arte de São Paulo** (Avenida Paulista 1578; Tue–Sun 11am–6pm, Thur until 8pm), with nearly 1,000 pieces originating from both ancient Greece and contemporary Brazil, along with changing temporary exhibitions.

Beneath the chaos

The best way to explore São Paulo is by its clean, fast albeit limited subway network. Stop off at **Liberdade**, home to the largest ethnic-Japanese community outside Japan. The Museu da Imigração Japonesa is interesting.

Drinking coffee in Liberdade, São Paulo's Japanese quarter.

Vaca Veja bar and restaurant, Itaim Bibi area, São Paulo.

There are many inexpensive sushi bars in this area, and on Sundays there's a food and crafts fair at **Praça Liberdade**. Neighborhoods such as **Jardim Paulista** and **Jardim America** have tree-lined streets and mansions that provide respite from the downtown rush.

Another favorite oasis is the lovely **Parque do Ibirapuera**, with curving pavilions designed by Oscar Niemeyer. Every even-numbered year (October–December), São Paulo hosts one of the world's largest international art shows, the prestigious Biennial, in a pavilion here. Linked to the pavilion by an undulating walkway is the **Museu de Arte Moderna** (Tue–Sun 10am–6pm), exhibiting work by Brazil's contemporary sculptors and painters. Near the entrance to the park stands the impressive Bandeirantes Monument, a tribute to the country's 17th-century pioneers; and a mausoleum honoring heroes of the 1932 civil war.

Not far away, on Rua do Horto, is the **Horto Florestal** (daily 6am–6pm), founded in 1896. A pleasant place to spend an afternoon, the park has a playground, picnic areas, and the Pedra Grande viewpoint, offering a beautiful view of the north of São Paulo city. Inside the park is the **Museu Florestal Octávio Vecchi** (Tue–Fri 9am–noon, 1.30–4.30pm, Sun 10am–3.30pm) displaying a huge variety of native wood samples.

Whether or not you like snakes, the **Butantan Snake Farm** is a fascinating place. Some 54,000 snakes there are milked for venom daily, and serum is prepared for distribution throughout Brazil and the world. There is a museum as well, at Avenida Dr Vital Brasil 1500, in the Pinheiros district (Tue–Sun 9am–4.30pm).

At night, São Paulo has a wide variety of clubs and cafés in which to while away the hours. Live music is even more plentiful here than in Rio. There's also a counter-culture quarter, the **Bela Vista** (popularly known as **Bixiga**), centered on Rua 13 de Maio. There are few old buildings left in the city, but the **Teatro Municipal**, which has resident opera and dance companies, evokes the elegant days of

Os Candangos or The Warriors sculpture at Praça dos Tres Poderes, Brasília.

ALEIJADINHO

Afflicted by a debilitating disease, Aleijadinho (which actually translates as Little Cripple) sculpted some of Brazil's most beautiful and expressive statuary – in the end, in great pain – with his hammer and chisel strapped to his wrists.

The mulatto artist – son of a Portuguese architect and a black slave – almost single-handedly shifted the esthetics of the Golden Age from the boxish forms of Mannerism to the sensuous curves of Baroque. His particular style made the Baroque of his home region, Minas Gerais, famous throughout Brazil under the name *barocco mineiro*. Aleijadinho's main works include the life-sized sculptures at Congonhas do Campo as well as the church of Sao Francisco de Assis in his home town of Ouro Preto. He never left Minas Gerais during his lifetime (1738–1814).

19th-century coffee barons. The city frequently hosts world-class performers – *paulistas* may be workaholics, but when they stop work they demand the best in entertainment.

Brasília: futuristic capital

Rising out of the great scrubby expanses of Brazil's central *cerrado* woodland savanna, **Brasília ❸** looks more like a gleaming extraterrestrial settlement than Brazil's national capital. Absent are the red-tile roofs, intimate passageways, and harmonious pastel hues typical of Brazilian cities. Brasília is a cool, regimented architectural wonder, a "city of the future" that Brazilians are still trying to reconcile with the present.

At 1,150 meters (3,773ft) above sea level and more than 800km (500 miles) from the coast, Brasília was built precisely because of its isolation from the great coastal cities. When Juscelino Kubitschek was elected president in 1955, he vowed that before he left office Brazil would have a new capital in its unpopulated interior, and he firmly believed that this capital would be a magnet to pull Brazilians away from their beloved coastline.

By 1956, work had already begun on Brasília. The city plan, drawn up by urban planner Lucio Costa, consisted of a central line of government buildings crossed by a curved arc of residential buildings – a layout that resembled the shape of an airliner. The architect chosen to design the structures was the Brazilian Oscar Niemeyer, a student of the great modern Swiss architect Le Corbusier, with whom he collaborated in the design of the United Nations Headquarters building in New York. The project of Brasília was to incorporate all that was new in materials and design. Work proceeded at a furious pace, and by its inauguration in April 1960, the new city already had 100,000 inhabitants. In 1987 it was declared a Unesco World Heritage Site.

Wide thoroughfares sweep through the city, oblivious to the needs of pedestrians. With no sidewalks and few pedestrian crossings, Brasília has the country's highest pedestrian mortality rate. Its grassy knolls are

The National Congress building in Brasília, designed by Oscar Niemeyer.

Brasília's Palacio da Justica.

Church buildings in the town of Mariana, Minas Gerais.

The interior of Catedral Basílica da Sé on Praça da Sé, Mariana.

crisscrossed by red-earth paths created by Brazilians who still depend on their feet to get around.

Modern wonder

Brasília is characterized by the graceful, pristine architecture of its public buildings. Down the hill past the main bus terminal, the **Eixo Monument** (The Monumental Axis) opens onto the **Esplanada dos Ministérios** (Ministries Esplanade). Flanking the end of the Esplanade are Niemeyer's two finest buildings, the **Palácio Itamaratí**, housing the Foreign Ministry, which floats in splendid isolation in the midst of a reflecting pool; and the **Palácio da Justiça** (Ministry of Justice), whose six curtains of falling water on the exterior echo the natural waterfalls around Brasília. At the eastern end of the esplanade is the **Praça dos Três Poderes** (Three Powers Plaza) – a dense forest of political symbols: the **Palácio do Planalto**, the **Supremo Tribunal Federal** (Supreme Court), and the twin towers and offset domes of the **Congresso Nacional** – the building whose silhouette is the

signature of Brasília. On the plaza proper is the small **Museu Histórico de Brasília** (Tue–Sun 9am–6pm). Inside is a series of panels outlining the history of Brasília and the most memorable sayings of Juscelino Kubitschek, whose powers of hyperbole seem to have rivaled his talent for construction.

In front of the Supreme Court is a blindfolded figure of Justice, sculpted by Alfredo Ceschiatti. Facing the Palácio do Planalto are the figures of *The Warriors* by Bruno Giorgi, a tribute to the thousands of workers who built Brasília. A note of whimsy is added to the plaza by Niemeyer's pigeon house, called the **Pombal**.

The most recent addition to the plaza is the **Pantheon Tancredo Neves** – a tribute to the founding father of the New Republic, who died in April 1985 before he could be sworn in as president. Inside the darkened interior is Brasília's most extraordinary and disturbing artwork. The mural, by João Camara, depicts the story of an uprising in the 18th century led by Brazil's best-known

CAPOEIRA

The martial art-dance of *capoeira* is most common in Salvador but can also be seen in Rio and elsewhere. It's an extraordinarily athletic art form, originally brought by slaves from Angola, according to one school of thought, and performed to the rhythm of a tambourine and the throbbing sound of a *berimbau*, whose single steel string stretched across a bowed stick resonates in a hollowed gourd. Two dancers perform highly acrobatic dances within a circle, or *roda*, surrounded by the rest of the group. The most acrobatic jumps are a recent addition to the dance. *Capoeiristas* perform on the street, and request donations, but they also give shows during the evening at a cookery school and restaurant called **Senac** (daily) on Largo do Pelourinho in Salvador, an excellent place to try local food.

revolutionary, Tiradentes (Joaquim José da Silva Xavier). Painted in seven black and white panels (rather like Picasso's *Guernica*), it is heavy with masonic symbolism.

The **Catedral Metropolitana da Nossa Senhora Aparecida**, at the western end of the Esplanada dos Ministérios, is a unique concrete building with a spectacular stained-glass domed roof. Three hundred meters/yds away, on the northern side of the Eixo Monument near the Rodoviária, is the pyramid-shaped **Teatro Nacional** Claudio Santoro (Tue–Sun 9am–6.30pm), where art shows and other exhibitions are held.

Minas Gerais: treasure trove of the Portuguese

Nestled in the steep hills north of Rio de Janeiro are some of Brazil's most beautiful colonial-era cities, in the large state of **Minas Gerais**, a mining region. In the 18th century it was the world's principal source of gold and today more than half the country's minerals and nearly all its iron ore come from here.

Belo Horizonte ❹, today's capital city of Minas Gerais, is neatly planned and a good base from which to explore the region. A hundred kilometers (60 miles) to the south lies the most prized creation of Brazil's Golden Age, the beautifully preserved city of **Ouro Preto**. Its name comes from the gold encrusted with black iron oxide that was discovered nearby, at the beginning of the 18th century.

The find set off a gold rush, and Ouro Preto soon became the colonial capital of Minas Gerais. The gold lasted for more than a century, during which time Ouro Preto and several nearby cities acquired sumptuous Baroque churches and mansions, which proved to be the only lasting heritage of 1,200 tons of gold extracted during that era. Thanks to the Brazilian government's decision to declare the entire city a national monument in 1933, many of its colonial treasures are intact, and it has been made a World Heritage Site by Unesco.

Cobbled streets wend through hilly quarters lined by well-kept colonial homes. Thirteen Baroque churches

The interior of São Francisco de Assis church in Ouro Preto, with ceiling by Athayde.

The colonial charm of Ouro Preto.

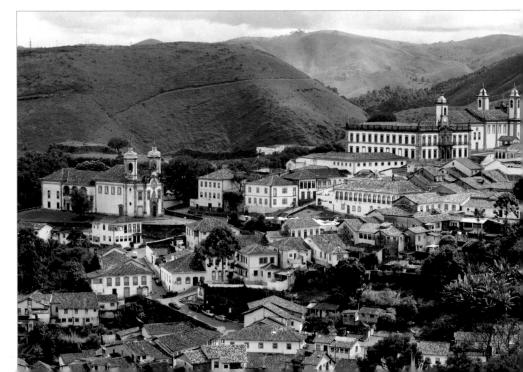

gild the city of 25,000, many displaying the genius of the sculptor and architect Antônio Francisco Lisboa (1730–1814), better known as *Aleijadinho*. The most striking example is the exterior of the church of **Nossa Senhora do Rosario dos Prêtos**, built by black slaves (there were insufficient funds to complete the interior). Nearby is the church of **Nossa Senhora do Pilar**, whose interior is a profusion of Baroque carved angels and gilded walls.

At the center of town is the **Praça Tiradentes**, named after the man who agitated for independence from Portugal and was hanged in Rio de Janeiro on April 21, 1792, a date recognized as a national holiday. The square is fronted by the imposing **Museu da Inconfidência** (Tue–Sun noon–6pm), in which you can see portions of the gallows used for Tiradentes' execution, and a copy of his death warrant.

Just off the square stands the church of **São Francisco de Assis**, an exquisite example of Aleijadinho's artistry and a repository of some of his most moving wood and soapstone figures. More of Aleijadinho's work can be viewed at the impressive **Nossa Senhora do Carmo** church (Tue–Sun 9–11am, 1–4.45pm), also on the plaza, and at the sacred art collection in the nearby **Museu do Oratório** (daily 9.30am–5.30pm).

Ouro Preto has an important mining school, the sprawling **Escola de Minas**, which incorporates a mineralogy museum (Tue–Sun noon–5pm), and there is also an interesting gem museum in the imposing **Governor's Palace** nearby.

Treasures of stone

The colonial town of **Mariana**, just east of Ouro Preto, is another treasure left by gold barons who expressed gratitude for their good fortune by building extravagant churches. Work by Aleijadinho and by Manuel da Costa Athayde, who was born here in 1762, can be found here, as well as a former beating post for slaves, marked by a stone monument to Justice.

Some 30km (20 miles) west of Ouro Preto is **Congonhas do Campo**, the site of Aleijadinho's greatest feat: his hauntingly beautiful soapstone carvings of twelve Old Testament prophets outside the majestic church of **Bom Jesus do Matozinho**, a shrine for pilgrims. There are also 66 expressive carvings in cedarwood of Christ's Passion by Aleijadinho and his students.

Located 100km (60 miles) to the south, **São João del Rei** is a colonial city of 60,000 with three striking 18th-century churches. There is also beautiful pewterware made at a local factory. The train station has been turned into a gleaming museum, the **Museu Ferroviário** (Tue–Sun 9–11am, 1–5pm), a fascinating reminder of old-fashioned rail travel, with locomotives dating from 1880.

Nearby is the silversmith village of **Tiradentes**, named after the national hero. **Sabará**, 22km (14 miles) east of Belo Horizonte, has fine examples of Aleijadinho's work in its church, as well as Oriental influences brought by Portuguese Jesuits.

The least commercialized of all the colonial towns is the World Heritage Site of **Diamantina** ❺, 284km (175 miles) north of Belo Horizonte. Once the center of a diamond boom, Diamantina was the birthplace of President Kubitschek, founder of Brasília. The colorful **Nossa Senhora do Rosário** church was built entirely by slaves, and the woodcarvings of the saints are black. The informative **Museu do Diamante** (Diamond Museum; Tue–Sat noon–5.30pm, Sun 9am–noon), has a back room in which grisly implements of torture used against slaves are kept.

Salvador and the Northeast

Brazil's Northeast is quite different from its prosperous south. The accent is different, the people are different, the food is more fiery, and the barren *sertão* (scrubland) is more like an African savannah than tropical Brazil.

For the essence of the Brazilian mystique, one must go to where it all

began: **Bahia**, the state where Pedro Alvares Cabral established contact between the Portuguese and native cultures in 1500. **São Salvador da Bahia de Todos os Santos** ❻, usually known just as Salvador, was Brazil's first capital and is still the richest source of the country's cultural identity. Salvador is where much of the food, religion, dance, and music that characterize Brazil originated, and where Portuguese Catholic culture blended with the beliefs and esthetics of the slaves who were brought from West Africa to work the plantations.

The 2.6 million inhabitants of Salvador, known as *baianos* (pronounced "bye-*ah*-nooz") are known throughout Brazil for their laid-back, festive temperament. The city is convulsed by street celebrations most months of the year. Carnival is the biggest – it officially begins a day before carnival in the rest of the country. Salvador's carnival is entirely participatory – frenzied hordes of dancers revel behind *trios elétricos* – floats laden with live bands and deafening sound

In the traditional dress of Bahia.

São Joaquim market, Salvador.

A boy dives high into the water at Salvador's old port.

systems. It is not for the faint-hearted, as the crowds often get unruly.

Rich heritage

The backdrop for all this revelry is a city with a rich heritage and a beautiful natural setting. Salvador is built mostly on a high escarpment overlooking a bay; the upper level of the city, where almost all the ancient buildings are found, is known as **Cidade Alta**. The **Terreiro de Jesus** square is home to three of Salvador's most famous churches, the largest of which is the **Catedral Basílica**. Rising majestically from the adjoining square, **Praça Anchieta**, is one of the world's most opulent Baroque churches, **São Francisco**. Its interior is covered from floor to ceiling with intricate carvings encrusted with gold leaf. To the north side of Terreiro de Jesus, the **Museu Afro-Brasileiro** (Mon–Fri 9am–5pm) in the old medical faculty highlights the strong African influence on Bahian culture, including masks and costumes.

The interior of Igreja de São Francisco, Salvador.

The **Pelourinho** neighborhood is full of pastel-colored 17th- and 18th-century colonial buildings, considered by Unesco the best examples in the New World. Visitors will notice numerous women street vendors wearing flowing white lace dresses. They are known as *baianas*, and they sell the spicy and sweet specialties of Bahian cuisine.

A famous Art Deco elevator called the Elevador Lacerda whisks you down from near the Praça Municipal to the **Cidade Baixa** (Lower Town), which has a big handicrafts marketplace called the **Mercado Modelo**. The white, lace-decorated garments sold here are typically Bahian and the market is a lively microcosm of Bahian life. Left from the market is the church of **Nossa Senhora de Conceição de Praia**, which houses the image of Bahia's patron saint and is the site of the annual religious procession held on December 8, one of the most important feast days in Salvador's Catholic calendar. About 10km (6 miles) in the opposite direction stands the famous church of **Nosso Senhor do Bonfim** and another fascinating market, the **Mercado São Joaquim**.

Cidade Baixa is the departure point for schooners taking tourists around the bay, and for passenger boats to small towns in the vicinity, as well as to the island of **Itaparica**, where Club Med built its first installation in Brazil. Most of the island's 20,000 inhabitants make their living from fishing, and the simple restaurants serve delicious seafood. Be sure to try the marinated fresh oysters. Boats also leave from Cidade Baixa for a 2-hour cruise to **Morro de São Paulo**, a stunning series of islands dotted with trendy villages and pristine beaches. Accommodations are in charming and fashionable *pousadas*, the inns of Brazil.

Pristine beaches

Like Rio, Salvador is a city that lives at its beautiful beaches. The most accessible from Downtown is **Barra**, small but extremely popular. Bars near the beach are often jammed, and the fun continues long after sundown. Barra is at the tip of a long, scalloped shoreline of beaches, most of them shaded by palms and with grassy areas. The best are the farthest out from the

city, **Itapoán** and **Piatã**. It's best to hit these beaches on weekends when there are crowds, both for safety and because there will inevitably be live music performed at local alfresco bars.

Some 80km (50 miles) north of Salvador is **Praia do Forte**, an 11km (7-mile) stretch of white-sand beach, bordered by coconut palms, that is very popular with tourists. Also around 80km (50 miles) north of Salvador, is the **Costa do Sauipe** complex, opened in 2001 at a cost of $100 million, a luxury complex of resort hotels and a championship golf course.

Ilheus, a coastal city 390km (240 miles) south of Salvador, is a mixture of modern and ancient architecture. The city is renowned for its lively carnival and for the lovely beaches nearby, and is the center for 95 percent of Brazil's cocoa production. Farther south down the coast is **Porto Seguro**, a tourist hub, where Cabral and his explorers first set foot in Brazil. Other popular resorts along the coast include Itacaré and Trancoso.

Inland from Salvador begins the enormous scrub region called the

Sun-bathing at Praia dos Coqueiros beach, Trancoso.

sertão, frequently parched by drought and a tableau of human misery that has led to revolts and long-running emigration. The heart of Bahia, however, is also where the **Chapada Diamantina** is located, one of Brazil's most beautiful national parks and a major attraction for trekkers. Gateway to the Diamantina Plateau is the colonial town of **Lençóis**, which dates from 1844 when diamonds were discovered in the region.

Beyond Salvador

Bahia is the southernmost part of a nine-state region collectively known as the Northeast, home to a third of Brazil's population. The *nordestinos* have, until very recently, benefited least from Brazil's material progress. Those who live along the coastal regions of Bahia are predominantly of African descent, while those living inland and to the north are a Portuguese/native mixture.

The Northeast has wonderful white-sand beaches where you can still find fishermen using *jangadas*, an ancient precursor to the windsurf board. The

Walking the streets of Olinda by night.

city of **Maceió** has some of the most spectacular beaches. North of Maceió is **Recife ❼**, one of the principal cities of the Northeast, with 1.4 million inhabitants. Recife's beaches are protected by coral reefs, and the most popular beach is in the well-to-do **Boa Viagem** sector of the city. Litter and shark infestation, however, have made them unattractive. Located just to the north is **Olinda**, a beautifully conserved colonial gem designated a World Cultural Monument by Unesco, while to the south lies the popular resort town of Porto de Galinhas.

Farther up the coastline is **João Pessoa**, the easternmost city in the Americas. It's very pleasant and brightly painted, with a wealth of Baroque churches. Huge sand dunes distinguish the beaches of **Natal ❽**, capital of the state of Rio Grande do Norte. Outside the city are other oceanside enclaves, such as delightful **Touros** (95km/60 miles to the north), and to the south, **Praia da Pippa**.

Fortaleza ❾, the capital of Ceará, once drab and utilitarian, has benefited from the huge amount of

capital that has flowed into the region in recent years, using some of it to rebuild the seafront area, which now rivals Recife's Boa Viagem for elegance and liveliness. The city is a popular destination for international tourists, while Canoa Quebrada to the south, and Jericoacoara to the north, of Fortaleza also attract many visitors.

The river ports: Manaus to Belém

The last thing you might expect in the middle of the Amazon jungle, 1,600km (1,000 miles) from the sea, is a thriving port city. But **Manaus** ❿ was cut from the wilderness in the 19th century: where mad conquistadors once searched in vain for gold, Brazilians found a modern El Dorado of rubber. Today, this strange outpost is enjoying a new boom as a tourist destination and through high-tech industries as one of the duty-free capitals of South America. Arriving in Manaus by boat is dramatic, not because of the city, which is spread out on low bluffs – but because it is the meeting place of

two Amazon tributaries at an 8km (5-mile) wide junction. The dark River Negro, which looks like fizzy cola when riverboats churn it up, hits the yellowish River Solimões, and the two powerful currents run side by side without mingling their differently colored waters.

The chaotic bustle of modern Manaus is a dim reflection of its past glory. In 1888 the pneumatic tire was invented, and Amazon rubber suddenly became very valuable. For a brief, dazzling period, Manaus was the richest city in the world. Pioneers flooded into the jungle, creating the boomtown of fast fortunes and grand gestures portrayed in Werner Herzog's film *Fitzcarraldo*.

Thousands of rubber tappers collected latex from isolated trees found deep in the jungle, working as virtual slaves along the sinuous waterways of the Amazon, and the newly rich rubber barons, quaffing champagne and lighting their cigars with $100 bills, earned Manaus a name for extravagance and decadence. When the rubber boom collapsed, Manaus fell into

FACT

The great rubber boom ended almost as quickly as it began: tradition has it that a British gent smuggled rubber seeds out of the country saying they were for Queen Victoria's orchidarium, and soon plantations in Malaya were producing rubber more cheaply than Brazil.

Manaus seen from the water.

SLOWLY DOWN THE AMAZON

Nothing quite matches the romance of taking a slow boat down the world's greatest river. This vast waterway is still plied by hundreds of vessels: from ocean-going cargo ships to passenger boats. Your best bet is to take a half-day trip from Manaus or Belém. Longer voyages are not really geared for tourists and are just a means of getting from A to B, although the intrepid could try it, remembering that the trip from Manaus to Belém takes a little over a week. Smaller, wooden vessels known as *gaiolas*, or "birdcages," after the crowded mid-deck levels where passengers pile over one another in hammocks, still work the smaller tributaries from Manaus to Benjamin Constant, on the border of Colombia, then onward into Iquitos in Peru, and back. Finding one of these boats is largely a matter of patience and luck. The smaller companies have no fixed schedules, and the only way to arrange a booking is to wander around the port, talk to people, and check out the boats for yourself, if possible when they arrive, your best bet at getting an idea of the quality of the transport. It can be relatively comfortable, or crowded, noisy, and somewhat unhygienic. Embark as early as possible to get a decent hammock space. Food is basic, and bottled water should be taken. Stops are made at jungle villages, where the whole population turns out to watch the boat unload beer, pass out a few letters, and take on a cargo of bananas.

a torpor that was only broken in 1967, when it became a duty-free zone.

The most famous and bizarre monument to the boom days is the grand opera house, the **Teatro Amazonas** (tours Mon–Sat 9am–5pm). Materials for this temple of art in the jungle were wholly imported from Europe: white marble from Italy, iron pillars from England, and polished wood from France. The original house curtain remains, painted with Grecian nymphs lolling in the Amazon River. In its heyday, the opera house attracted such greats as the Italian tenor Caruso. Today, fully restored, it can still pull in international names.

The old **port area** of Manaus is thriving. Wooden riverboats dump exotic cargoes while overhead circle black urubu birds. Ramshackle houses have been thrown up around the port on precarious stilts. A more imposing construction is the stone **Alfândega** (Customs House), dating from 1906.

For a glimpse of the lost native cultures of the area, head for the **Museu do Homem do Norte** (Mon–Fri 9am–5pm), at Avenida Sete de Setembro

1385, which gives a good idea of traditional lifestyles. There is even a "beach" near the **Hotel Tropical**, where braver swimmers can prove that the river is free of the piranhas and electric eels that can spoil a holiday.

The majority of visitors to Manaus use the city as a gateway to the Amazon proper. A good selection of lodges are located in the jungle that surrounds Manaus, and the transfer out to a lodge is an attraction in its own right. Most lodge programs cover two or three nights at the lodge and include a number of activities that involve the region's diverse flora and fauna.

Beyond Manaus

Farther down the Amazon toward the sea is the port of **Santarém** ⓫, at the confluence with the Tapajós River. Once a colonial fortress, Santarém today is a kind of Dodge City for half a million jungle gold prospectors, or *garimpeiros*. On the south side of the mouth of the Amazon stands proud, stately **Belém** ⓬, 145km (90 miles) from open ocean. A city of more than

Opera in the jungle: Teatro Amazonas in Belém.

a million inhabitants, Belém retains some of the graceful airs of its rubber-boom heyday. There are colonial-era homes and churches in the old town and there's a fort nearby, now occupied by the Círculo Militar restaurant.

Belém's striking **Catedral de Nossa Senhora da Graça**, built in 1617, contains artworks in Carrara marble and paintings by the Italian artist, de Angelis. Not far away is the dockside municipal market **Ver-o-Peso** (Check out the Weight), where fishermen bring their catches. Another landmark is the **Emilio Goeldi Museum** (Tue–Sun 9am–5pm), with exhibits of native crafts from nearby **Marajó Island**. An interesting addition to the town is the Estação das Docas – imaginatively restored warehouses with tourist facilities and restaurants.

Rondônia: Brazil's Wild West

If you thought the days of the Wild West were over, consider **Rondônia**. At the beginning of the 1970s this Brazilian state was a tree-tangled wilderness on the southern flank of the Amazon jungle, bordering Bolivia. It was home to just a few thousand hardy rubber tappers. Today, settlers have pushed their way pell-mell into almost every corner of Rondônia, hacking down the jungle and frequently enforcing their land claims with the squeeze of a trigger. In the 1980s, nearly a quarter of the Rondônian rainforest was destroyed, mostly by burning, to clear land for planting and cattle pastures. In the dry season, from May to October, a blanket of smoke hangs over the state as forests are incinerated.

With the extension of roadway BR 364 from São Paulo to the capital of Rondônia, the river port of **Porto Velho** ⑬, express buses carry peasant migrants directly to the new frontier. A ride up the highway in one of the local buses provides a revealing view both of frontier life and of rainforest devastation. The road northwest is now paved through Peru and southeast all the way to the Atlantic.

Rubber tapping has been all but abandoned in Rondônia as the trees have disappeared, despite laws enacted

The Pantanal wetland, home to an astonishing faunal diversity.

for their protection. Some 300,000 Brazilians still survive collecting the fruits of the forest – wild rubber, Brazil nuts, and resin. They now live mostly in the state of Acre, west of Rondônia on the borders of Bolivia and Peru. Key to their survival are their isolation and international pressures to protect their benign coexistence with the rainforest. Some protected areas, called extractive reserves, have been established for these jungle harvesters. But as Brazil's population continues to grow faster than new jobs are available, the pressures to clear the forest that have transformed Rondônia are likely to keep moving westward.

The Pantanal: bird paradise

An enormous wetland called the **Pantanal** is perhaps the most exquisite gallery of all for observing Brazilian fauna. Comprising 210,000 sq km (81,000 sq miles) of seasonally flooded swampland east of the Paraguay River on Brazil's western border with Bolivia, the Pantanal is home to more than 650 species of birds, 400 kinds of fish, and an abundance of reptiles and animals as well as 3,500 species of plants. There are white ibises, egrets, blue herons, green parakeets, pheasants, and the 2-meter (7ft) tall white *jabirú* or *tuiuiú* stork.

During the rainy months (October to April) when waters are high in the north, the birds feed on fish in the southern sector. From May until September, they move to the shallower waters in the north. The best time to visit is in the winter months of June, July, and August; January and February are infernally hot and humid. When the waters recede from the northern Pantanal, wide sandy riverbanks are exposed and large alligators, called *jacarés*, like to bask in the sun on the sand. There are also ocelots, pumas, wild boar, jaguars, red lake deer, tapirs, and the world's biggest rodent, the sheep-sized capybara.

Exploring the swamps

Access to the Pantanal's edge is quite easy, but getting around inside is another matter. **Cuiabá** ⓮, capital of Mato Grosso, is an attractive city that once enjoyed a gold boom, though it gets intensely hot here. Some 70km (45 miles) northeast of Cuiabá there are cool waterfalls at **Chapada de Guimarães**, the source of much of the water that enters the northern part of the wetlands. Just south of Cuiabá is **Santo Antônio de Leverger**, on the edge of the marshland. From Cuiabá you can transfer to the lodges and *fazendas* (cattle ranches) within the Pantanal. You can obtain ground transportation, boats, flights, even hot-air balloon trips at these lodges, for observing the wildlife. Fishing is permitted – piranhas are prized for their supposed aphrodisiacal powers but hunting emphatically is not. The main attraction is **Baia Chacorore**, a huge shallow water basin flocked with roseate spoonbills. Its banks literally crawl with alligators.

You can drive into the Pantanal along the partially completed **Trans-Pantaneira Highway**, which starts

The blue-crowned Trogon, found in the Pantanal.

just outside the small town of **Poconé**, 102km (63 miles) from Cuiabá. Vehicles can be rented here. The road is often rough and sometimes flooded, but it crosses many rivers (there are 126 bridges) and provides a close-up view of wildlife. The road ends 145km (90 miles) into the Pantanal at Porto Jofre. Accommodations are available en route and at the port.

Although the Pantanal reaches up to the city limits of **Corumbá** ⓯, a border town on the southwest flank, local tours reveal little – much of the wildlife has fled to more remote areas. The best way to see the Pantanal is to arrange passage on cattle boats that penetrate more deeply into the area, or organize a trip to one of the lodges.

Iguaçú Falls and the Itaipú Dam

The famous falls that link the borders of Brazil, Paraguay, and Argentina, are described fully in the Argentina chapter. The closest Brazilian city to the falls is **Foz do Iguaçu** ⓰, near the junction of the Paraná and Iguaçu rivers. This frontier town has grown

phenomenally in the past decades, due to the construction of the world's largest hydroelectric dam, the **Itaipú** (the name is Guaraní for Singing Rock). It is well worth visiting, and is only possible on a guided tour. Built jointly by Brazil and Paraguay, it is powered by the waters of the Paraná River, which divides the two countries.

The south

The falls at Foz are the main attraction in the Brazilian south, but far from the only one. Others include the beach resorts close to Florianópolis, the capital of Santa Caterina state, especially Santa Caterina Island; the mountain towns of Gramado and Canela, close to Porto Alegre; the German-influenced communities in the interior of Santa Catarina that include Blumenau, with its Oktoberfest; and the scenic train ride between the port of Paranaguá and the model city of Curitiba. The southern coast close to Florianópolis attracts visitors interested in whale watching. The season runs from June through November and involves the southern right whales.

Snappy sunbathers – alligators warming in the sun at Pantanal.

At the aptly named Garganta del Diablo (Devil's Throat), Iguaçu Falls.

THE RICHES OF THE AMAZON RIVER

The world's greatest river and largest rainforest, in the heart of Brazil, is estimated to contain one-tenth of the plant and insect species on earth.

The Amazon River is one of the greatest symbols of Brazil. It rises in the snows of the Peruvian Andes just a short distance from the Pacific Ocean. It then travels across the heart of South America – a distance of 6,570km (4,080 miles) – before it flows out into the Atlantic Ocean at the equator. It has about 15,000 tributaries, some of which, like the Araguaia and the Madeira, are mighty rivers in themselves. Just past Manaus, one of the most spectacular river sights is the meeting of the "black waters" of the Negro River with the "white waters" of the Solimões River, two other Amazon tributaries. The Amazon has a heavier flow than any other river, depositing in the ocean each year about one-fifth of the world's fresh water.

At its mouth the Amazon is 300km (185 miles) wide, a labyrinth of channels and islands, one of which, Marajó, rivals Switzerland in size. The water flows with such force that it is still fresh 180km (110 miles) out into the ocean.

The Amazon's network of dark, dense jungles has often been referred to as The Great Green Hell. In the west of the Amazon basin, it is still possible to fly for several hours and see nothing below but a carpet of tropical forest, broken only by rivers snaking their way through the trees. The Amazon has remained virtually unchanged for the past 100 million years, for it did not pass through the same ice ages that altered other parts of the world's landscapes. Some areas are still inhabited by indigenous groups who have survived through the centuries and have never had contact with the world outside their own jungle.

Amazon region, North West Brazil.

Amazon river turtle in its natural habitat.

Dwelling on a small tropical island a little distance from one of the Amazon's fishing communities.

An Amazon river piranha close up, its razor-sharp teeth exposed and bloodied.

Aerial view of the rainforest being burned, Para. This will clear the land to make pasture for cattle ranching and to grow crops.

DEFORESTATION IN THE AMAZON

Since 1970, more than 600,000 sq km (232,000 sq miles) of Brazil's Amazon has been cut down or burned. Conservation and reforestation programs have so far had no lasting effect in stopping the destruction. In the 1960s and 1970s, in the east of the basin, the government built a vast network of roads, and cattle companies moved in, burning the forest to sow pasture. Agriculture was not successful, for the soil, once denuded of the protective forest cover, quickly became barren.

Foreign lumber companies demand the Amazon's hardwoods, now that many of the world's hardwood forests have been destroyed; and big grain farmers, cultivating genetically engineered soybeans, have moved here from the south of Brazil. But global interest in protecting the forest is on the rise. Eco-friendly travel is one element in the fight to protect the fragile wilderness, now seen as a paradise, not a hell.

Common squirrel monkey in the treetop canopy, close to the Amazon river.

Traveling up the Amazon river.

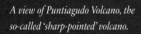
A view of Puntiagudo Volcano, the so-called 'sharp-pointed' volcano.

Musician playing the bandeon in La Boca, Buenos Aires, Argentina.

Northern gaucho riding a horse near Purmamarca, Quebrada de Humahuaca, Argentina.

THE SOUTHERN CONE

The most European part of South America,
this region contains some of its most cosmopolitan
cities and starkly stunning scenery.

The landscape of the Island of Chiloe, Chile.

El cono sur – the Southern Cone of Paraguay, Argentina, Uruguay, and Chile – makes up a geological and cultural unit quite apart from the rest of South America. Sparsely populated in pre-Columbian days by nomadic tribes, these countries today form the most ethnically and climatically European part of the continent.

A cultural island, isolated Paraguay has no access to the sea, but this has not stopped its capital, Asunción, from becoming a bustling duty-free center – although horsedrawn carts still clatter through its streets, beneath statues of longforgotten generals. Half the country is made up of the vast, sparsely populated Chaco.

Squeezed between the Pacific Ocean and the Andes mountains, ultra-narrow Chile covers a huge range of latitudes. Heading south from the Atacama Desert – the driest in the world – you pass through the moderate climate of the capital, Santiago, with its surrounding vineyards, to the snow-covered peaks of the Lake District. Beyond that are the glaciers, cold rainforests, and fjords of Chilean Patagonia.

Asunción cathedral, Paraguay.

Once beacons of progress that attracted millions of European immigrants, tiny Uruguay and giant Argentina fell into deep economic declines after 1945, leaving Montevideo and Buenos Aires, the respective capitals, with an air of faded grandeur. Tourists flock to the elegant beach resorts of eastern Uruguay and northeast Argentina in the European summer months. Bordered by the Andes to the west, Argentina sprawls over every climate zone, with grassy northern plains where gauchos still ride, the subtropical jungle province of Misiones, lush forests around Bariloche, the windswept plains of Patagonia that end on the chilly, mountainous sub-Antarctic island of Tierra del Fuego.

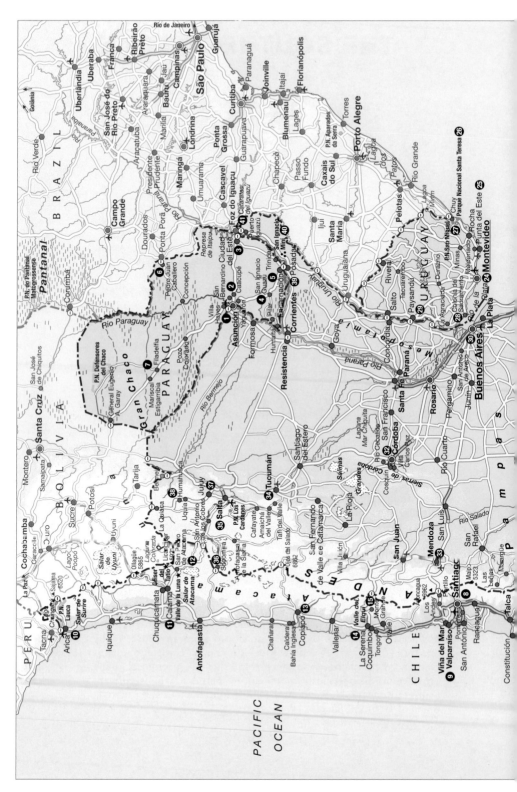

Southern Cone

ATLANTIC

OCEAN

Mar del Plata ③①

Necochea

Bahía Blanca

Río Colorado

Neuquén

Río Negro

Viedma

Golfo
San Matías

Península
Valdés ㊻

Puerto
Madryn

Puerto
Pirámides

Trelew ㊺

Gaiman   Rawson

Camarones

Chubut

Comodoro Rivadavia

Golfo
San Jorge ㊼

Puerto Deseado

Falkland Islands
(Islas Malvinas) (UK)

West Falkland   East Falkland

Port Stanley

Isla de los Estados

Cabo de Hornos

Isla Grande de
Tierra del Fuego

Río Grande

Ushuaia
P.N. Tierra
del Fuego ㉟

Estancia Harberton

Puerto
Williams

Río Gallegos ㊽

Puerto Santa Cruz

Bahía
Grande

R. Santa Cruz

Magallanes

Porvenir ㉘

Punta Arenas ㉒

P.N. Los
Glaciares ㊾

El Calafate

Puerto
Natales ㉑

El Chaltén

P.N. Torres
del Paine

Perito Moreno

Lago
Buenos Aires ㊿

Sarmiento

Cochrane

Tortel

La Junta

P.N.
Queulat ⑱

Puyuhuapi

Puerto
Cisnes ⑳

Coyhaique ⑲

Puerto
Aisén

Puerto
Chacabuco

Bahía
Exploradores

Península
de Taitao

Golfo
de Penas

Isla
Wellington

Campo
de
Hielo
Sur

Lago
O'Higgins

Lago
Argentino

Esquel

El Bolsón

San Carlos
de Bariloche ㊷

San Martín de los Andes

Ingeniero
Jacobacci

P.N. Nahuel
Huapi ㊷

Chaitén ⑬

Chorcha
Quellón

P.N. Los
Alerces ㊹

Futaleufú

Río Grande

Osorno

Valdivia

Puerto Montt

Isla Grande de Chiloé ⑰

Ancud

Castro

Quellón

P.N. Conguillío ⑯

Temuco ⑯

Pucón

Lanín
3747 ▲

Villarrica

Villarrica

P.N.
Huerquehue

P.N.
Villarrica ㊸

Llaima

Los Ángeles

Laja

R. Bío Bío

Concepción

A   N   D   E   S

PACIFIC

OCEAN

N

0   200 km
0   200 miles

see Lake District map

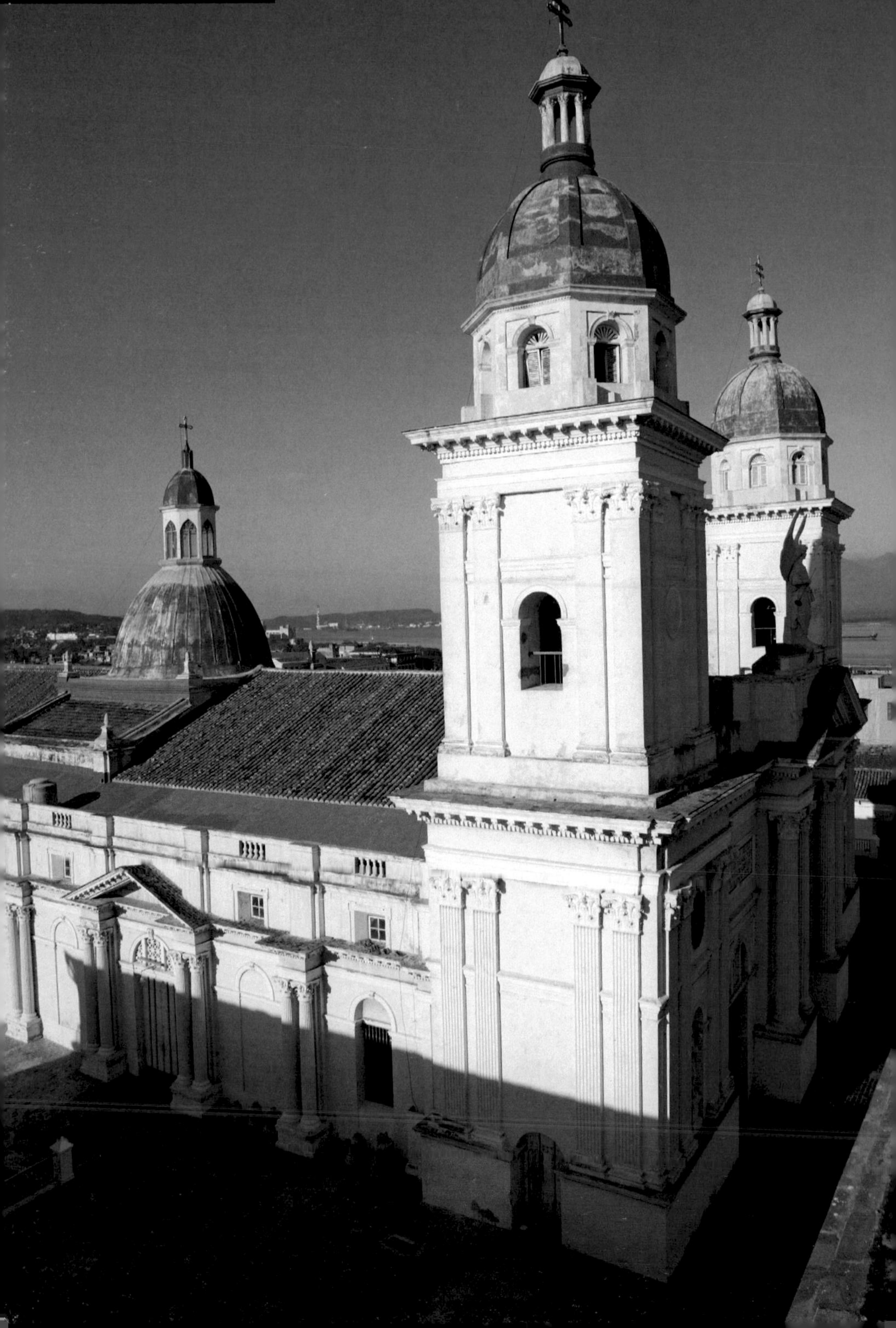

Catedral de Nuestra Señora de la Asunción.

PARAGUAY

This is a land of utopias and experimental communities, where the language of the original inhabitants shares pre-eminence with that of their colonists – and the Gran Chaco is one of the last great wildernesses.

Main Attractions

Asunción and the Circuíto de Oro
Jesuit missions
Parque Nacional Cerro Corá and the Pantanal
The Gran Chaco

Surrounded by Bolivia, Brazil, and Argentina, the small sub-tropical nation of Paraguay lies at the heart of South America. The River Paraguay divides the country into two distinct halves: the lush, fertile east, where most of the population lives, and the barren Chaco tablelands to the west, home to a scattered settlements, Mennonite farmers, and nomadic native tribes. The River Paraguay eventually feeds into the Río de la Plata, linking the country historically and geographically to the other River Plate nations of Uruguay and Argentina.

"An island surrounded by land" is how exiled Paraguayan novelist Augusto Roa Bastos once described his landlocked native country. The phrase refers not only to Paraguay's physical remoteness but to a kind of psychological solitude brought about by wars, dictatorships, and a profound sense of unity. A visitor to the capital, Asunción, can't help noticing the profusion of monuments commemorating military rulers, crushing defeats, and Pyrrhic victories, and pockets of deep poverty. Yet one is also struck by the tropical prettiness of the colonial city, and by the soft-spoken, gentle manners of Paraguayans, reminders that Spanish Jesuits who helped settle this region dreamed not of plunder but of founding an earthly paradise.

In a country where almost everyone is of part-Guaraní descent, schoolbooks devote considerable space to pre-Columbian Paraguay. Mainly farmers, they were also accomplished warriors who bore suffering stoically. Martin Dobrizhoffer, an 18th-century Jesuit missionary, upon his return to Europe wrote a wordy but seminal, early ethnographic description of his work with the now extinct Abipones and Guaraníes. Their language, in the words of one Spanish priest, was "one of the most copious and elegant on

The eyes have it in the case of this owl monkey.

A Bilingual Land

Paraguay is South America's most bilingual country, where children learn Spanish and Guaraní, the language of the original people.

Spanish explorers in Paraguay clashed less with the local population than in other colonies, gradually blending with other European immigrants to form a relatively homogeneous, bilingual society. This was in part because the Guaraní could expect some Spanish support against rival tribes and, particularly, the Incas. It is difficult to say how much the notorious Guaraní "harems" kept by the Spaniards were fact and how much exaggeration, but it was true that a great deal of social mobility was achieved by intermarriage, and that the mestizo offspring were not considered marginal citizens. Resistance from Gran Chaco tribes however was fierce.

Sociologists also cite the relatively high position of women in Guaraní society as a factor in the continuing status of the mother tongue. But perhaps the most decisive element was the missionary work of the Jesuits. Although the Jesuits imposed Spanish

A Guaraní woman.

on the natives, they were impressed by the complexity and musicality of Guaraní, and produced catechisms and hymns in the native language. Ironically, as a result, the Guaraní neglected much of their original music. Nevertheless, Guaraní music still has a distinctive sound. In 1624, Jesuit priest Antonio Ruiz de Montoya created the first Guaraní dictionary and grammar, giving the language a written form and thus a better chance of survival.

During the dictatorship of Doctor Francia (1814–40), marriage between Paraguayans of pure Spanish descent was forbidden. This attempt to dilute the country's ruling class increased contact between the two cultures and their languages. Guaraní was considered a sort of homely argot rather than the speech of educated people, but its use became widespread during the War of the Triple Alliance, as a symbol of national pride and unity. On the battlefields of the Chaco War (1932–5) Spanish was banned and Guaraní was spoken, as a secret language. As a result, many older Paraguayans with little or no indigenous heritage speak Guaraní more fluently than Spanish.

A new generation

In urban areas today, more than 70 percent of the population speak both languages; less than 12 percent speak only Spanish. In rural areas, the use of Guaraní still supersedes that of Spanish; 60 percent of the population speaks only Guaraní. But the reality is more complex than insistence on pure bilingualism would suggest. Wealthier, more educated people speak a Spanish heavily influenced by Buenos Aires, interspersed with some Guaraní phrases. Inversely, many rural farmers speak a form of Guaraní called Jopara, mixed with Spanish phrases.

Before the 1970s it was rare for teachers to use Guaraní in the classroom, but changing ideas have made the new generation not only fluent but literate in Guaraní. Currently, between 4 and 5 million people are estimated to speak the language fluently, making it the second-most spoken indigenous language in Latin America, behind Quechua.

Numerous words from Guaraní and the related Tupí language describing animals and plants have made it into other languages, such as jaguar, tapir, piranha, and capybara, and even the Spanish-sounding maracas. Novels and poetry are published in Guaraní translations; there are also theatre productions, and TV and radio shows. But despite ever-present Guaraní melodies, and the 1981 Law of Native Communities guaranteeing native rights over lands and cultures, the social status of full-blooded Guaraní remains inferior.

the globe," and it was used as a lingua franca throughout the region.

Arrival of the Spanish

Asunción was founded on August 15, 1537, by Domingo de Irala, a man of letters who came seeking refuge from the miseries of the settlement at Buenos Aires and the rigors of the Conquest. The Guaraní, who were also anxious for Inca gold, were eager to form an alliance with the Spaniards and gave them their daughters as tokens of good faith. The lush life in Asunción, far from the sea and the watchful eye of the Spanish crown, plus the discovery that the Incas had already been conquered and plundered by Pizarro, induced Irala and his men to stay. The colonial farms were organized in a feudal manner, although intermarriage evened out the social hierarchy.

Fulgencio Yegros declared Paraguay's independence on May 14, 1811, and ruled along with a civilian lawyer, Dr José Gaspar Rodríguez de Francia. Soon after independence Francia seized power, and Congress named him supreme dictator for life in 1816. To protect Paraguay from the danger of annexation by Argentina or Brazil, Francia closed the borders: no one was allowed in or out during his 24-year reign.

El Supremo, as Francia was called, ruled by absolute decree. A learned man, initially a frugal and honest ruler, he grew deranged by power and isolation. At one point he ordered all the dogs in the country killed; he also decreed that none of his subjects could look at him in the street. At his death in 1840, no Paraguayan priest was willing to say a Mass, and a priest was finally imported from Argentina. Paraguay was plunged into political chaos until the next dictator, Carlos Antonio López, was proclaimed in 1844.

López was an enlightened despot who reopened the country to progress and sent students to Europe to study. But his son and designated successor, Francisco Solano López, led the country to ruin. Fearing that Brazil's intervention in Uruguay's civil war would permanently tip the balance of power against Paraguay, he sent troops through Argentine territory in 1864, triggering war with his two great neighbors and, in the end, Uruguay as well. The War of the Triple Alliance was disastrous for Paraguay. The country was further ravaged by cholera, and López, at this point seriously unhinged, ordered the execution of hundreds of people, including his two brothers and scores of officers. Abetted by his Irish mistress, Elisa Lynch, he also executed his childhood sweetheart and other society ladies who had snubbed Madame Lynch. On March 1, 1870, he was shot by one of his own generals after refusing to surrender. "I die with Paraguay," he exclaimed, which was almost literally true. After the war, more than half the population of 525,000 were dead; of the survivors, only 29,000 were adult males. Paraguay was rebuilt mostly by women, who resigned themselves to a polygamous society as the Catholic Church looked the other way.

19th-century, colonial-era building in downtown Asunción.

Between the fall of Solano López and Paraguay's bloody Chaco War with Bolivia, the country changed presidents 32 times and endured two assassinations of presidents, six coups d'état, two revolutions and eight attempted revolutions. Paraguay won the Chaco War of 1932–5, fought over a piece of barren land that was believed to contain oil and other mineral deposits, but once again the male population was devastated. A succession of dictators followed, until in 1954 the son of a German brewer, Alfredo Stroessner, seized power and ruled with an iron fist for nearly 35 years.

Winds of change

Stroessner played off one political faction against another while providing a sanctuary for fleeing Nazis, and exiling, imprisoning, torturing, and killing rivals and opponents. In the all-pervading climate of corruption, Paraguay became notorious as a haven for smuggling, much of it in narcotics. Human rights activists and some of the country's artists and writers, notably the novelist and poet Augusto

Senate House, Asunción.

Roa Bastos and the artist Carlos Colombino, provided a moral center for resistance. In the 1970s, the construction of a Brazilian–Paraguayan hydroelectric dam at Itaipú in eastern Paraguay stimulated land investment, expanded financial services, and provided thousands of jobs. The giant Paraguayan–Argentinian hydroelectric project at Yacryeta, proposed in 1973, began operating in 1997.

On February 3, 1989, Stroessner was overthrown by General Andrés Rodríguez, his right-hand man and father of his daughter-in-law. Rodríguez promised a free press and a gradual return to democracy after the coup and his Colorado Party was elected into office in 1991. Gleeful Paraguayans took down the photographs of Stroessner, exiled to Brazil, that graced every shop window, changed the names of streets and towns, and decapitated statues of the former president. Since then Paraguay has been experiencing a process of democratic transition, marked by a new constitution, political and press freedoms, and regular elections.

Paraguay has also joined the Mercosur common market, a development that upsets some of the more extreme nationalists but which has opened the country to foreign investors.

Offsetting these achievements are continuing wide disparities in wealth and an absence of land reform, not to speak of a pervasive military presence in national politics that surfaced in May 1996 in an attempted coup by the popular General Lino Oviedo. In 2008, the election of Fernando Lugo, a former Catholic bishop, and his center-left Alianza Patriótica por el Cambio (Patriotic Alliance for Change) ended 60 years of the Colorado Party in power. Though stung by paternity suits, he successfully renegotiated Paraguay's share of earnings from the Itaipú Dam with Brazil, and the country posted remarkable economic growth. But just eight months before the next election, he suffered a lightning impeachment in June 2012 a week after a badly handled conflict between landless farmers and police that left 17 dead.

Elegant Asunción

Today, **Asunción ❶** matches the dynamism of most South American cities while retaining a sleepy elegance, with handsome colonial mansions rubbing shoulders with luxury boutiques, duty-free shops, and neon lights. The **Plaza de los Héroes** is bright with butterflies and birds of paradise. Many passers-by seem to have come directly from central casting: fruit vendors with baskets on their heads, furtive black-market money-changers, the cluster of helmeted military police investigating a broken water pipe.

Gone, sadly, are the bright yellow electric streetcars that Stroessner revived after the oil crisis of the 1970s. Gone too is the neon sign that flashed "Stroessner: Peace, Work, and Well-Being" over the square, but its focal point is still the ornate **Pantéon Nacional de los Héroes**, which was built as a copy of Les Invalides in Paris.

Inside are the tombs of the two López presidents, of two unknown soldiers, and a small urn containing what remains of the dictator Francia. It's said that his bones were dug up and flung into the river by an angry mob.

But no matter how Paraguayans feel about their military governments, this is a country that reveres soldiers; it's not at all unusual for passers-by to stop at this shrine and make the sign of the cross before the heroes' crypts. Diagonally across from the pantheon are shop windows that display Chaco War memorabilia. West of the Plaza de los Héroes, on Presidente Franco, is the **Casa de la Independencia**, where independence was declared in 1811 and which nowadays houses a museum (Mon–Fri 8am–6pm, Sat 8am–1pm) displaying relics from the revolution.

The historic old town

The oldest part of the city can be reached by following Calle Chile down toward the River Paraguay. On a small bluff is the white **Palacio de Gobierno**. It was commissioned in

The Paraguayan capital's Plaza de Democracia.

a neo-Renaissance style by Francisco Solano López, who imported much of the building's beautiful interiors and furniture from Paris. He did not have much time to enjoy the palace, as its construction was interrupted by the War of the Triple Alliance. Farther along El Paraguayo Independiente are the tree-lined **Plaza Constitución**, the **Congressional Palace** with an ultra-modern new parliament building adjacent to its pink former home, now the **Cabildo Cultural Center** (Tue–Sun 10–30am–sunset), and the **cathedral**, which has an excellent museum of religious objects. Opposite the Palacio is the 18th-century **Manzana de la Rivera**, or Casa Viola. Once the headquarters for Stroessner's elite forces, it is now an innovative cultural center incorporating a museum of the history of the city, an art gallery, a library, and a bar. A short distance farther on are the **Aduana** (Customs House), the port buildings and the barracks, naval headquarters, and fortifications that provide eloquent testimony to Asunción's one-time status as a frontier city with only the river separating its inhabitants from the wild lands of the Chaco.

Parks and plazas

East of the Plaza de los Héroes is another large and pleasant square, **Plaza Uruguaya**, which was once the site of a convent and was renamed in tribute to the Uruguayan government when it returned Paraguayan flags captured in the War of the Triple Alliance. There are some interesting bookshops in pavilions in the plaza, which also has stalls selling leather work, paintings, and other crafts. Handicrafts made by the indigenous Macá people in their settlements on the outskirts of the city can be bought here.

A short distance away is the **Estación San Francisco**, a relic of the López years that was designed by Alonso Taylor. Restored courtesy of the Spanish government, the building is a Victorian gem, built largely of wood, but with cast-iron supports and a tower that was once the home of the stationmaster. The station used to be the terminus for the British-run track to Encarnación in southern Paraguay that ultimately linked to Buenos Aires. Nowadays occasional trains run to nearby Areguá on Lake Ypacaraí, pulled by wood-burning locomotives.

Five blocks south of the central Plaza Uruguaya is the religious art museum, the Museo de Arte Sacra (Tue–Sun 9am–6pm) at Domínguez and Paraguarí.

There are also some beautiful old colonial houses with wide verandas and gardens of bottlebrush and banana trees on Avenida España, as well as the American Embassy, the library, and Stroessner's former home, now a museum.

Parque Carlos Antonio López, on the avenida of the same name, provides a good view of the city from the Antonio López and Río Gallegos intersection.

Of Avenida España in the eastern part of Asunción is the attractive modern visual arts center **Museo del**

Uniformed soldier guarding the entrance to Casa de la Independencia.

Barro (Wed–Thur 3.30pm–8pm, Fri–Sat 9am–noon, 3.30pm–8pm) – literally, the "mud museum. Farther north, the **Jardín Botánico**, (7am-5pm daily) with its own zoo, is worth a visit, as are the nearby **Museo de Historia Natural** and the **Museo Indigenista**, (Mon–Sat 7.30 11.30am, 1–5.30pm Sun 9am–1pm) both former residences of the two López presidents.

A reservation of the Macá people, who were brought here from their home in the Chaco as a tourist attraction, is located across the river. They live in rather dismal conditions. Ironically, the best handicrafts are to be found in the middle-class suburb of **San Lorenzo**, along the eastern highway, where the shop of the **Museo Boggiani** (Tue–Sat 9am–5pm) offers authentic and very beautiful artifacts made by the indigenous people of the Chaco.

Traveling east

The Mariscal Estigarribia Highway crosses Paraguay to the Brazilian border town of Ciudad del Este, formerly Ciudad Presidente Stroessner. By express bus the trip takes about 4 hours, but there are interesting stops along the first half of the journey. Trips to resorts and towns in the vicinity of Asunción are known as the Circuito de Oro (Golden Lap). About 20km (14 miles) east of Asunción is **Capiatá**, first settled by the Jesuits in 1640. It has an interesting church, which contains a 17th-century sculpture made by the Guaraní under Jesuit instruction. Some 10km (6 miles) east is **Itagua**, famous for its production of ñandutí, or spiderweb lace, which is woven by hand into handkerchiefs, tablecloths, and hammocks and displayed by the weavers in stalls along Route 2. There is a museum and an annual festival in July.

The resort town of **San Bernardino**, 55km (35 miles) from Asunción on **Lake Ypacaraí**, is a favorite retreat of prosperous Paraguayans and a center for water sports. The lake, immortalized in a hauntingly beautiful Guaraní

song, measures 5km by 24km (3 miles by 15 miles) and is an idyllic spot, surrounded by tropical vegetation. The resort town of **Areguá**, on the southern shore of the lake, and terminus for the short steam-train journey from Asunción, has many shops and stalls selling earthenware. **Caacupé** ❷, 24km (15 miles) down the road from San Bernardino, is another popular resort and religious shrine. On December 8, pilgrims come to this town from all over Paraguay carrying heavy stones on their heads as penance. Nearby are the villages of **Tobatí**, which has pottery and woodcarvings, and **Piribebuy**, with a fine church and an interesting museum. There are some lovely small resorts in the hilly, verdant countryside between Piribebuy and Paraguari near **Chololó**, where bathing is possible in refreshing streams.

Ciudad del Este ❸, on the Brazilian border, has been called South America's biggest late-night shopping center. It's a bustling, rather unattractive city with a makeshift boomtown air. Brazilians arrive by the busload

Detail of Jesuit architecture.

A Jesuit Utopia

Successful while they lasted, the idealistic Jesuit missions were unable to withstand the capitalist pressures from Spain and Portugal.

In colonial times Paraguay encompassed parts of what are now Bolivia, Brazil, and Argentina. Within this vast area the Jesuit order created an administrative unit or province that achieved a semi-independent status. Like the Franciscans who preceded them, the Jesuits' primary mission was conversion. Learning from the mistakes of the first and second generations of conquistadors, they insisted on the human value and dignity of the indigenous peoples and offered an alternative to the Spanish *encomienda* system (see page 32) that sought only to exploit their labor.

The Jesuits' first efforts at conversion started in 1587, one of the fathers being an Irishman, Thomas Fields. The decision to gather the native population into settlements was made at a synod in 1603 and confirmed by Felipe II of Spain in 1609. The following

The imposing remains of the Jesuit mission Santísima Trinidad de Paraná.

year, small parties of Jesuits began to travel into what was still largely unknown territory. In the wild lands of the Chaco the Jesuits did little better than the Spanish military expeditions that occasionally sallied forth from Asunción. With the Guaraní to the south and east of the city, they succeeded.

In the early years the Jesuit *reducciones* (missions) were threatened by the *mamelucos* or *bandeirantes*, slave raiders from Brazil. Many groups of Guaraní quickly grasped the safety afforded by the missions, with whole tribes seeking refuge from the raiders. In 1629 thousands of Guaraní were forced to flee from the upper Paraná, but 12 years later a Jesuit-led army, drawn from the missions, put the *mamelucos* to flight. The missions then flourished and the Jesuit territories became bulwarks against Portuguese advances. Ultimately the Jesuits gathered in around 150,000 Guaraní to 30 missions in a broad belt of territory on either side of the River Paraná, living by theocratic principles and communal ownership of goods that irked the colonial powers. Between 1610 and 1768, 702,086 Guaraní alone were baptized.

By the early 18th century the missions were thriving and acquiring a reputation among European travelers as micro-utopias. The Guaraní were farmers, herding cattle and sheep, and cultivating crops such as *yerba maté* (herbs for maté tea – see page 319). Some developed skills as fine craftsmen and sculptors. The Jesuit priests also found the Guaraní to be highly musical and introduced them to European idioms, to the harp and the guitar. They were, however, subject to large fluctuations in numbers due to periodic epidemics.

Missions

But the grand experiment in communal living was not to last. The Jesuits always had their enemies, and by the mid-18th century these included royal advisers in Madrid. In 1767 the Jesuits were expelled from the country and the Guaraní were left to fend for themselves, at the mercy of the slave raiders, or absorbed into the *encomienda* system. Most of the great Jesuit churches were destroyed or fell into ruin, but the remains of the missions (some still in ruins and some restored) bear testimony to Jesuit achievements. This whole historic episode has been powerfully reconstructed in the movie *The Mission*, starring Jeremy Irons and Robert de Niro. Eight of the missions were in what is now southern Paraguay, with the rest in the neighboring Argentine province of Misiones, *Bolivia*, and Brazil. Paraguay's missions are accessible from Asunción by Route 1 running southeast to Encarnación.

to buy electronics, watches, and other imported goods in the huge air-conditioned malls. The city is also a magnet for con artists, who hawk everything from imitation perfume to "musical" condoms. More impressive is the nearby **Itaipú Dam**, one of the world's largest hydroelectric projects. Ciudad del Este is connected to the Brazilian counterpart city of **Foz do Iguaçu** by the **Puente de la Amistad** (Friendship Bridge), and is a portal to the famous falls of Iguacú (Iguazú in Spanish). There are tours and public transportation to Iguaçu and Itaipú, but the Salto Monday Falls, 10km (6 miles) out of town, are only accessible by taxi.

On the trail of the Jesuits

Most of the Jesuit *reducciones* were set up in the fertile regions of the high Paraná River, southeast of Asunción along Route 1. In **Yaguarón**, 48km (30 miles) south of the capital, there is a Franciscan mission, built in 1640. The church is a jewel of Hispano-Guaraní Baroque. Nearby is a museum dedicated to Doctor Francia (Tue-Sun 9am-3pm). The first Jesuit ruins are at **San Ignacio Guazú ❹**, at Km 226. The **Museo Jesuítico** (Mon–Sat 2–6pm, Sun 8–11am, 2–6pm) houses a fine collection of indigenous art from the missionary period. Route 4 runs west to **Pilar** and ultimately to **Humaitá**, near the junctions of the rivers Paraná and Paraguay, whose garrison held out for three years during the War of the Triple Alliance.

To the northeast of San Ignacio is **Santa María de Fé**, established in 1669. It has a modern church and a museum that houses dozens of Guaraní-made carvings of saints and apostles. Sixteen kilometers (10 miles) south is **Santa Rosa**, founded in 1698. The church was destroyed by fire in 1883, but wooden carvings, a tower, and frescoes remain. These include a figure of the Annunciation, which is one of the great works of Hispano-American Baroque. To reach the Jesuit ruins of **San Cosmé y Damián**, turn

off Route 1 at Km 306 and travel 30km (20 miles) south. Of particular interest is the sundial, which is all that remains of what was once a world-renowned astronomy center, built by Father Buenaventura Suarez and Guaraní laborers.

The city of **Encarnación ❺** was founded by the Jesuits on what is now the Argentinian (southern) bank of the River Paraná, and transferred to the present site on the northern bank in 1621. There is nothing left of the original Jesuit mission of Itapúa. The city, which is close to the **Yacyretá Dam**, is a good center for exploring the **Jesuit missions** at Trinidad and Jesús de Tavarangue. Nearby are Japanese colonies that produce soybeans, vegetables, timber, maté, and cotton. About 30km (20 miles) northeast of Encarnación is Paraguay's most splendid ruin, **Trinidad**. The sheer size of the mission, which has been declared a World Heritage Site by Unesco, gives some idea of the scope of the Jesuit project in the New World. It was founded in 1706, relatively late in the Jesuit era, and the

NEW GERMANIES

The Chaco, like many remote regions, has attracted a number of unusual immigrant communities. Best known are the Mennonites, a strict Protestant Anabaptist sect, who began to arrive from 1927 onwards. They run their own banks, schools, and hospitals, and successful, modern, cooperative farms. Some can be seen in 19th-century dress at markets in Asunción, but many have adopted modern ways. Most speak a variety of German known as Plattdeutsch and, despite being a small minority, produce most of Paraguay's dairy products. Well-educated, they also speak standard German, English, Spanish, and Guaraní.

Less well known is the settlement of Nueva Germania, north of Coronel Oviedo. This was the site of a very different experimental community, founded in 1886 by Elisabeth Nietzsche, the fanatic sister of the philosopher Friedrich Nietzsche, and her equally fanatical anti-Semite husband. Their plan was to found a pure "Aryan" colony, but the venture foundered as the colonists came up against the unforgiving realities of dense vegetation, intense heat, and torrential rains combined with a perplexing absence of ground water. Undaunted either by the rage of the duped colonists or by the suicide of her husband, Elisabeth returned to Germany where eventually she was able to greet Hitler as her true leader. The bizarre story is told in the book *Forgotten Fatherland: The Search for Elisabeth Nietzsche* by Ben Macintyre.

FACT

The 1932–5 Chaco War was fought by a Paraguay seeking oil, at the behest of oil companies, while Bolivia sought access to the Paraguay River to loosen its landlocked status. The war cost 100,000 soldiers' lives – mostly from dehydration and disease – and achieved neither aim, though Paraguay won three-quarters of the disputed territory. It took until April 28, 2009, for a border treaty to be signed.

With its Urunday trees, this is the savannah before the storm, Gran Chaco.

church was only finished in 1760, a few years before the expulsion of the Jesuits. There are many interesting features including a pulpit, carved in great detail. In addition to churches, indigenous houses, and crypts, there is a baptismal font and an impressive carving of the Holy Trinity, which was hollowed at the back so that a priest could hide inside and give an echoing rendition of the voice of God. Ten kilometers (6 miles) along a road north of Route 6 is **Jesús de Tavarangue**, founded by the Jesuits in 1685. Much of the site remains unfinished, as the Jesuits embarked on a massive building program seven years before their expulsion. The most remarkable surviving features are the three arched doorways built by Catalan architects in the Spanish *Mudéjar* style.

Traveling northeast

Less frequently visited than the populous eastern region, the northeast of Paraguay has a number of interesting and remote places to explore. Accessible by taking Route 2 from Asunción to Coronel Oviedo, then heading northward by Routes 3 and 5, is **Pedro Juan Caballero ❻**, on the Brazilian border. Here travelers can cross into Brazil, or travel southwest to **Parque Nacional Cerro Corá**, scene of the last battle in the War of the Triple Alliance and the death of "El Mariscal" López. There are monuments to him in the national park, as well as some caves with intriguing pre-Columbian petroglyphs.

The River Paraguay provides an important route to the north. Some 300km (200 miles) upstream from Asunción is **Concepción**, which is a significant port for trading with Brazil and has a good market. There is boat traffic farther upstream which, depending on river conditions, may be used to reach some of the more remote places. Some of these places are also accessible by four-wheel-drive from the Chaco. The ports on these stretches of the river, such as Puerto Casado and Fuerte Olimpo, can be reached by air or boat, and a ship, *Paraguay Cruise*, allows visitors to explore the **Pantanal** and the **Swamp of Nembucu**. Travelers on a

tight budget should ask for accommodations upon arrival if they wish to visit these intriguing but isolated little towns.

The Chaco

This desolate region, which is extremely hot in summer and waterless for months at a time, covers 60 percent of Paraguayan territory but holds only 4 percent of the population. It was once the preserve of indigenous groups, including the Nivaclé and Lengua people, who now share the region with military personnel, Mennonite colonists, and other assorted migrants. There are a number of Catholic missions and large *estancias* (ranches), for this is cattle-rearing country. Unlike most of the Chaco, the Mennonite areas have good roads and facilities, and accommodations are available in the towns. It is also possible to camp in the Chaco, as long as you take everything with you – especially water. The Chaco is a paradise for ornithologists, with immense gatherings of birds after the rains.

The **Low Chaco**, the region nearest Asunción, is a primeval terrain of marsh and palm forest, used for cattle ranching. It is easily accessible by traveling over the river bridge from Asunción and then up the first few kilometers of the Trans-Chaco Highway to **Villa Hayes**. This small town is named after the 19th-century American president Rutherford B. Hayes, who arbitrated in Paraguay's favor in a territorial dispute after the War of the Triple Alliance.

At about Km 250 is **Pirahu**, which is a good place to stop and find out about road conditions. About 20km (12 miles) farther on is **Pozo Colorado**, the turning for Concepción, and at Km 415, **Cruce de los Pioneros**. About 50km (30 miles) farther along the highway, and off to the right, is **Loma Plata**, largest of the orderly Mennonite towns. Farther on, also off to the right, is the Mennonite town of **Filadelfia** ❼, capital of the

Central Chaco. Farther north along the Trans-Chaco Highway, at Km 540, is **Mariscal Estigarribia**, a military town. The highway is now asphalt and continues all the way to Bolivia, passing the Teniente Enciso national park, which has basic sleeping facilities. Bus travel from Asunción to Santa Cruz is a straightforward possibility, though a bit tiring.

Farther northeast is the **High Chaco**, a desert of thorn forests and military outposts. The roads are unpaved, and the land is rich with wildlife: jaguars, pumas, tapirs, and poisonous snakes, as well as a kind of wild hog, discovered in 1975, which was thought to have become extinct in the Pleistocene Era. The large, remote **Parque Nacional Defensores del Chaco** can be reached by 4x4 vehicle and has basic sleeping facilities but requires some planning as travelers need to bring their own food. Tour operators based in the Mennonite colonies and Asunción offer trips to the remote park and other preserves during the slightly cooler June to September months.

> **FACT**
>
> Like Amazonia, the Gran Chaco, one of South America's last great wildernesses and prime wildlife-watching areas, is under massive threat from the surge in global demand and prices for soybeans. Current deforestation, if unchecked, will destroy it by 2030.

Brothers from a Mennonite community.

Exploring the fjords of Patagonia and Tierra del Fuego – D'agostini Sound.

CHILE

This is a geographically diverse land, where you can experience the blistering heat of the Atacama Desert and chilling Patagonian winds, as well as beaches, lakes, mountains, and city delights.

S naking down the Pacific coast of South America from latitude 18°s to 56°s, Chile covers a huge range of temperatures and landscapes. Squeezed between the Andes and the Pacific, never more than 355km (220 miles) wide, this spaghetti-like strip of land extends over 4,300km (2,700 miles) of coastline. Within its narrow terrain lie the world's driest desert, lush expanses of temperate rainforest and a spectacular array of glaciers and fiords. Stretched directly along the Pacific "ring of fire," Chile also has some 2,085 volcanoes, of which 55 are active. In parts of the country, earth tremors are an almost weekly occurrence, but Chile's hyperactive geology has also produced numerous hot springs.

Earth, fire, and ice

In the north of the country is the mysterious Atacama Desert, rising to more than 4,500 meters (14,760ft) above sea level as it meets the Bolivian altiplano. The north coast is distinguished by a range of expansive Pacific beaches and resorts. Chile's eastern boundary runs along the Andes, which provides a mountain setting for Santiago, the capital, nestled at the foot of the strip. South of Santiago the land becomes cooler, greener, and more alpine. Chile's Lake District has 12 great lakes and most of the country's active volcanoes. Farther south, the coastline

Valley of the Moon, Atacama.

breaks up into islands, the largest being Chiloé, a rainy location steeped in regional folklore. In the far south of the country lie the remote, wild territories of Chilean Patagonia.

This crazy geography hasn't stopped Chile from becoming one of the continent's most developed nations, although beneath the affluent surface are social and economic imbalances waiting to be redressed. Chileans have a reputation for being conservative but there is also a strong artistic streak; and for one of the less populous Latin

Main Attractions
Santiago
Valparaíso
Atacama desert
Portillo ski resort
Villarrica volcano
Chiloé
Torres del Paine

American countries, Chile's cultural output of musicians, poets, and writers rivals that of much larger countries.

Hard left to hard right

Almost from the time of independence, Chile gained a reputation for political stability. However, the country's relatively long democratic tradition, by Latin American standards, didn't make it immune to political polarization, which came to a head in the 1960s and later spilled into violence after the inauguration of Salvador Allende as the world's first democratically elected Marxist in 1970. The narrow margin of victory limited Allende's power, but his reforms to improve the standard of living for the poor initially worked: wages increased, land was redistributed, and jobs were created. But opposition mounted from the middle and upper classes, terrified of revolution, and from the left, who considered Allende too soft on the middle class.

Fearing nationalization, local and foreign capital fled. Production declined while demand increased,

Mexico's City's mayor Marcelo Ebrard and Chile's former President Michelle Bachelet.

spurring rampant inflation, and Allende lost control of radical Marxists demanding the immediate introduction of Communism. The right and the US government plotted to oust Allende, by financing a 1972 truckers' strike. The truckers were soon joined by shopkeepers and professionals.

In the early hours of September 11, 1973, the Allende government fell in a bloody storm as troops surrounded the presidential palace, congress, newspaper offices and party headquarters. Some working-class *barrios* were strafed. The air force bombed the presidential palace, where Allende committed suicide. Thousands of "subversives" were herded into concentration camps, and a military junta took over, declaring a state of siege and declaring that Marxism would be eradicated from Chile. About 3,000 people were killed.

The leader of the coup, General Augusto Pinochet, crushed the left; tens of thousands of dissidents – and many innocents – were imprisoned, tortured, exiled, or murdered. But in 1988 the tide finally turned against Pinochet; a referendum on his presidency was announced for October 5. Voters were registered and exile was abolished. The majority of the 7 million voting-age Chileans voted "No," resulting in a resounding defeat. Pinochet accepted his fate, announcing that elections would be held in 1989.

The new government took office on March 11, 1990, but Pinochet remained head of the army. Confidence and democracy were consolidated slowly, helped by an "economic miracle," which gradually made debt and hyperinflation problems of the past. Events came full circle in 1993 when the center-left Concertación coalition's Eduardo Frei (son of the 1960s president, Eduardo Frei Montalvo) was elected president. In March 1998, Pinochet retired from the army but, as a former president, he was entitled to a life seat in the Senate. However, in October of that year, he was placed under house arrest during a visit to London, pending his extradition to Spain on torture charges. He was finally released in early 2000 on health grounds and allowed to return to Chile. Pinochet died in 2006, unconvicted but accused, and still a divisive force for the foreseeable future.

In 2000, Ricardo Lagos, a socialist, took office as Chile's president, heading the third term of the center-left coalition that has governed Chile since 1990. Lagos aimed to combine economic growth with greater social justice. In 2004, divorce was legalized, despite fierce opposition from the Roman Catholic church, and, a year later, Pinochet's political constitution was reformed, restoring the president's right to dismiss military chiefs.

In 2006, Chile gave South America its first popularly elected woman president, Michelle Bachelet. However, her government had a difficult start as different sectors, encouraged by the high price of copper, Chile's main export, demanded increased social spending and higher wages. This highlighted one of Chile's most important challenges

– to improve an income distribution that, despite almost two decades of solid growth, remains one of the most unequal in Latin America. Bachelet's successor, conservative billionaire Sebastián Piñera, had to deal with the crushing blow of the 2010 earthquake. Most tourism infrastructure was quickly restored, but Piñera has faced massive nationwide student protests as a majority of Chileans clamor for a fair share of the country's wealth.

Chile's sophisticated center

The conquistador Pedro de Valdivia is said to have forgotten his tortuous journey to Chile from Peru when he gazed upon the valley at the point where the Mapocho and Maipo rivers descend from the Andes on their journey to the Pacific Ocean, surrounded by hills and mountains. Today, the conquistadors might not recognize **Santiago** ❽, the smoggy home to 6 million of Chile's 16 million people, but after a winter storm, the view of the snowcapped Andes is spectacular.

Valdivia marked the center of Santiago with the **Plaza de Armas**,

Young Xbox guitar heroes in Santiago.

in 1541. It served as a market and a place of public hangings. Today, this clean, tree-lined square is a haven for old men, shoeshiners, vagrants, and lovers. The neoclassical **Correo Central** (1882) has an impressive iron skylight that illuminates the central corridor. Next door, the excellent **Museo Histórico Nacional** (Tue–Sun 10am–5.45pm) in the Palacio de la Real Audiencia traces Chile's history from its pre-Columbian roots to the present. On the west side of the square is the country's largest church, the **cathedral** (1748–1830), with an impressive Baroque interior.

Two blocks away on Calle Catedral is the **Congreso Nacional**, dating from 1876, a neoclassical structure that was home to Chile's legislative branch until it was closed in 1973 and moved to Valparaíso. The high courts are across the street.

The imposing **Palacio de la Moneda**, built in 1805, is four blocks south on Calle Morandé. Originally a mint, it is now the presidential palace, and it is where Allende died in the 1973 military coup. On the south side of the

palace lies the Plaza de la Ciudadanía and, underneath the square, the **Centro Cultural Palacio la Moneda** (daily 9am–7.30pm), a cement-clad modern arts center.

Paseo Ahumada, a pedestrian precinct linking Plaza de Armas to the **Avenida Libertador Bernardo O'Higgins**, is the heart of Santiago, offering a human collage of businesspeople, bureaucrats, and street vendors. Across the Alameda, the city's major east–west artery, is the imposing, chalkyred **Iglesia San Francisco**. Constructed in 1612, the church has interesting touches of Spanish–Muslim influence, cedarwood choir stalls, and an adjacent museum of colonial paintings.

Alongside is **Barrio París-Londres**, where mansions from the 1920s border sinuous streets. Uptown from Ahumada, three blocks along Calle Augustinas, and past the 17th-century church of San Augustín, is the **Municipal Theater**, opened in 1857 and one of the finest on the subcontinent. Plays, concerts, and other cultural events are held around the small **Plaza Mulato Gil** in the charming Lastarria neighborhood.

Green spaces beneath the Andes

Santiago's founders were careful to include green spaces. Valdivia founded the city while standing atop one of its present-day parks, **Santa Lucía**, a small hill topped with terraces and a replica castle, which offers a view of the downtown area (take identification to register for entry). **Parque Forestal** follows the course of the Mapocho River (corresponding to metro stations from Puente Cal y Canto to Baquedano). Large trees line winding footpaths that betray the park's narrow confines. The **Museo de Bellas Artes** (Tue–Sun 10am–6.30pm) is here, a copy of the Petit Palais in Paris, with a fine collection of works by Chilean artists.

Near Metro Cal y Canto stand Santiago's colorful Mercado Central, famous for seafood (although the

On the campaign trail for Alejandro Navarro, prior to elections.

main restaurants are expensive), and the Estación Mapocho, an old train station converted into an exhibition center featuring concerts, fairs, and art expositions.

The **Parque Metropolitano** covers four hills towering 800 meters (2,600ft) over Santiago. A funicular railway goes to a terrace on the peak, commanding a view of the whole city when the smog is not too thick. There is a statue of the Virgin Mary, two pools, a zoo, a botanical garden, and a wine-tasting center that offers the best of Chile's vineyards. A cable car descends half the length of the hill, to Calle Pedro de Valdivia in the *barrio alto* (high neighborhood).

Bellavista is the cultural heart of Santiago, the nighttime haunt of artists, writers, and people who go to see and be seen. Dimly lit streets are sprinkled with raucous cafés, art galleries, and restaurants, while roving theater troupes and musicians perform, and hippies peddle their work. At night, tables spill from bars along **Calle Pío Nono**, Bellavista's main street. On the side streets, quaint homes with flowering gardens, eccentric details, and sculpted balconies weave an intriguing architectural quilt. **La Chascona** (Mar–Dec Tue–Sun 10am–6pm, Jan–Feb until 7pm, the house where poet and Nobel Prize winner Pablo Ncruda created many of his greatest works, is on Calle Fernando Márquez de la Plata. Other hubs of Santiago's nightlife are near Avenida Manuel Montt in Providencia east, and Barrio Brasil west of the center.

Mercado Franklin, or **Bío Bío** (four blocks east of Metro Franklin), is a weekend flea market that winds for several blocks through large markets and along sidewalks. High fashion is also available in Santiago at a reasonable cost in Calle Bandera's second hand stores. Uptown, the **Alonso de Córdova** area, off Avenida Vitacura, is an affluent neighborhood with several chic boutiques and swanky stores. **Parque Arauco** (Avenida Kennedy 5413) and **Alto Las Condes** (Avenida Kennedy 9001) are shopping centers on the upper east side of the city.

At the eastern end of the city, at the foot of the Andean mountains, is **El**

Colonial architecture in Estación Mapocho, a former train station converted into an exhibition and events center.

Wine Country

Chile has produced wine for centuries but only in the 1980s did the vineyards begin to export, and now it has become world-famous.

The conquistadors introduced vineyards to Chile in the 16th century to supply wine for the Catholic communion. Small wineries were nurtured on haciendas in the Maipo Valley throughout the colonial period by patrons doing their bit for the Church. Today wine is one of Chile's finest products – its purpose rarely spiritual – and an increasingly popular export even to wine-soaked Europe.

The first commercial vineyard was established in 1851 when Silvestre Ochagavía brought French vine stock to the Maipo Valley. Mining magnates built extensive irrigation projects, and the vineyards spread farther from the river banks. The valley's lime-heavy soil, elevation, and dry climate were ideal for producing world-class wines.

Chileans boast that when French vines were destroyed by phylloxera, a grape pest, in the late 19th century, their vines were rushed across the

Vines in Casa Blanca Valley, west of Santiago.

Atlantic to replenish the stricken vineyards. And only here did Carmenère, an old variety of Bordeaux, survive, a grape that is now used in the production of dry red wines.

The larger labels outgrew the confines of the Maipo Valley in the early 1900s and new wineries sprang up near Los Andes and Rancagua. Quality was mediocre, however, as the wealthy preferred to drink whisky and other spirits. It wasn't until the 1980s that Chilean vineyards began to export, and embarked on a process of modernization to adapt their heavy, full-bodied wines – with the strong tannin taste that Chileans were used to – to the lighter and fruitier unblended wines *(varietals)* that are more popular in the US and Europe. Exports expanded rapidly and today there are vineyards from Copiapó on the southern fringe of the Atacama down to Los Angeles near the Biobío River. The Casablanca Valley between Santiago and Valparaíso, discovered as a wine-growing area only 30 years ago, now produces the country's best whites.

The *vendimia*, or harvest, takes place between early March and mid-April – the farther south the vineyard, the later the picking starts. In recent years, the *vendimia* in Santa Cruz, in the Colchagua Valley, has won acclaim for the quality of its tastings and activities. Its Tren del Vino (Wine Train) is a luxurious indulgence, if money is no object. There are also similar festivities in other areas.

Vineyard visits

Many vineyards are open to the public, although off-season visits are usually limited to the bottling plant, the original cellars – some of them, like those of the Santa Rita winery, near Paine, built by the Spaniards in the 18th century – and the grounds of the winery. A number of them, including several in the Casablanca Valley, also have excellent restaurants.

Vineyards close to Santiago include Concha y Toro, Chile's largest wine producer, which has its main center an hour's drive south of Santiago in Pirque, and can also be reached by taking the metro to Puente Alto. A tour of the plant and old family estate might be included in a weekend trip to the nearby Cajón del Maipo, but booking is advisable (tel: 476-5269 or www.conchaytoro.cl). The beautiful Santa Rita vineyard, just off the Pan-American Highway 35km (22 miles) south of Santiago, is well worth a visit. Tours can be booked on tel: 362-2520 or www.santarita.cl. The Cousiño Macul winery, one of the oldest in Chile, is a quiet haven in the Andean foothills and about 45 minutes' drive from the city center. For visits, tel: 351-4100 or www.cousinomacul.cl.

Pueblito de los Dominicos. A creek meanders through the small village, around a cluster of adobe huts with thatched roofs. The sounds of craftsmen at work drift from the workshops where they produce ceramics and leather and metal objects.

Around Santiago

The lofty Andes, the tranquility of rural valley communities, and the cool breezes of the coast are all within a few hours of the capital by car or bus.

Santiaguinos venture to the **Cajón del Maipo** on weekends to take afternoon tea, nibble on *empanadas* and *kuchen* (cake) and relax in little towns and trails along the 60km (38-mile) canyon. A sinuous road leads from **Puente Alto** southeast, against the current of Maipo and its tributaries, to finally reach its source near the 5,000-meter (16,600ft) extinct volcano **El Morado**. Arid peaks with names like **Punta Negra**, **Peladero**, **Lomo del Diablo**, and **Yerba Buena** meld with the changing day's sun, turning from green and brown in the day, to blue, pink, orange, and red before disappearing at dusk.

The narrow valley floor is lush and intensively cultivated with vineyards and pastures. Hiking, swimming, camping, and climbing are practiced in the area, and there are many picnic areas close to the road.

Quaint, colonial **San José de Maipo**, 25km (15 miles) from Puente Alto, was founded in 1791 when miners discovered silver in the surrounding hills. At **San Alfonso** (Km 40) there is hiking and camping at **Cascada de las Animas** (Waterfall of the Souls), a delightful site run by an environmentally conscious family, facing the canyon wall. The road forks at **San Gabriel** (Km 47) where the mountains darken and the air grows thinner. **Lo Valdés** (Km 70) is on the southern fork of the road, a veritable oasis on the semi-arid slopes of the Morado volcano. The Refugio Alemán is a pleasant inn close to extensive trails for exploring the snow-capped peaks surrounding the area. Upriver, **Valle de Colina** has natural hot springs, with baths arranged in smooth, shallow pools, set in a small valley with magnificent views of the Andes and the valley below.

Relaxing in the Valle de Colina thermal springs.

El Morado National Park in the Andes.

South of the capital across the boulder-strewn Maipo River ravine is **Pirque**, a picturesque little town that is the birthplace of Chile's oldest wines. The **Reserva Nacional Río Clarillo** is in the midst of a semi-arid area where the best of indigenous cacti and flora flourish. In colonial times, Spanish aristocrats used to take vacations on the sandy shores of **Laguna de Aculeo**. The lake fills a valley 60km (38 miles) from the capital, in a wooded mountain setting. There are camping facilities, hotels, and several restaurants along the shore, but the lake has become contaminated due to its heavy use for motorized water sports. Twenty years ago the government built a dam where the **Tinguiririca** and **Cachapoal rivers** meet, forming the **Rapel Lake**, which now provides opportunities for water-skiing, swimming, and fishing.

Skiing in the Andes

The omnipresence of dizzying Andean peaks makes Chile one of the finest ski centers in the world, with challenging runs that can be enjoyed from June to September. Three resorts are within sight of Santiago. El Colorado and La Parva are ski villages above El Arrayán, just 50km (30 miles) from Santiago along a sinuous road (access is controlled in winter, with the road one-way up in the morning and down in the late afternoon). Valle Nevado, set in a remote valley above Farellones, is a posh resort built in 1988 by the owners of Les Alpes in France. There are three luxury hotels as well as apartment blocks, and 10 lifts to slopes as high as 3,670 meters (12,000ft) above sea level.

Northwest of Santiago, **Portillo** is one of the most famous resorts in South America, 2,850 meters (9,350ft) above sea level in an Andean pass 7km (4 miles) from the Argentine border at Mendoza. El Arpa offers powdery snowcat-skiing north of the town of Los Andes, with a perfect view of the summit of Aconcagua just across the border.

The Pacific coast

Algarrobo, 140km (87 miles) west of Santiago, became a resort in the late 1800s and is known for its calm seas and elegant vacation homes. It has also become an important yachting center,

Cumberland Bay at the village of San Juan Bautista on Robinson Crusoe Island, part of the Juan Fernández Islands.

JUAN FERNÁNDEZ ISLANDS

The original Robinson Crusoe, a Scotsman named Alexander Selkirk (who inspired Daniel Defoe's novel), was marooned on the Juan Fernández archipelago, 667km (425 miles) west of Valparaíso. The islands have been a Unesco World Biosphere Reserve since 1977. Correspondingly, the two biggest islands of the group bear the names of the fictional and real-life castaways. About 500 people live there now, far removed from mainland Chilean life, with education meaning going to boarding school in Valparaíso. The islands' fabled lobsters (*langostas*) are also exported to the mainland. A German warship was scuttled during a World War I battle with British destroyers and still lies at the bottom of Bahía Cumberland. The islands have been slow to recover from the tidal wave of the 2010 earthquake.

hosting international competitions. Nearby **El Quisco** is a tranquil town with wide beaches complementing a small fishing port and yacht club. **Isla Negra**, 4km (2.5 miles) to the south, is hidden within a cool pine forest, its rocky coast battered by great swells.

Poet Pablo Neruda's home, the inspiration for many of his works, and a delight for anyone interested in his life, is set on a bluff above the sea. It is now a **museum** (Mar–Dec Tue– Sun 10am–6pm, Jan–Feb until 7pm; tours arranged through the Neruda Foundation in Santiago, tel: 777-8741, or at Isla Negra, tel: 35-461284, or it can be visited independently).

The port of **Valparaíso** ❾, 120km (75 miles) west of Santiago, is an enchanting city where wandering is bliss. It is split between the geographically flat port area and 17 *cerros* (hills) that tower above the bay. The picturesque port is host to a bohemian brew of sailors, prostitutes, vagabonds, artists, and tourists. Restoration is cleaning up the beautiful but long-neglected port city. The *cerros* are an impressive maze of colorful homes, winding streets, narrow alleys, rickety *ascensores* (funiculars), hidden plazas, and treacherous stairways that cling delicately to the precipitous slopes. **Muelle Prat**, dating from the 16th century, is the oldest part of Valparaíso's port. To the west, at **Caleta El Membrillo**, fishermen unload their catch near weathered *picadas*, small shacks where the freshest seafood in the city is served. The historic center of the city was declared a World Heritage Site by Unesco in 2003.

Rickety rides

Valparaíso's *ascensores* are the best way to reach the upper city. For a few pesos, these romantic wooden contraptions make harrowing ascents to the neighborhoods high on the *cerros*. Ascensor Artillería, dating from 1893, first ran on coal, and goes to Paseo 21 de Mayo, providing a fantastic view of the bay. **Paseo Yugoslavo** is a promenade that winds along Cerro Alegre, among homes and gardens dating back to the early 1900s. Alegre is reached by the Ascensor El Peral.

Ascensor Concepción (1833) is the oldest elevator, reaching a

TIP

Viña del Mar's annual song and comedy festival, the Festival Internacional de la Canción, takes place in February in the Quinta Vergara, one of Chile's most beautiful parks.

Ski slope at El Colorado, with smoggy Santiago in the background.

Local dolls and tea manufactured from coca leaves make excellent gifts and can be bought in San Pedro de Atacama.

Chungará Lake and Parinacota Volcano, Lauca National Park.

neighborhood dating to the 19th century. Homes along **Paseo Atkinson** are simple wooden structures with zinc facing that creep up the mountainside. **Iglesia Anglicana San Pablo** was built by British immigrants in 1858. The **Ascensor Polanco** on the eastern side of Avenida Argentina, built in 1915 and now a National Monument, is a feat of engineering. Reached by a narrow tunnel, it rises vertically through the heart of the hill, before emerging into daylight at the top of a tower that is connected to the hilltop by a suspended walkway. Muelle Barón juts into the bay, offering great views of the ocean from the bar at its end.

Viña del Mar

Viña del Mar, the garden city, is a cosmopolitan Pacific resort, with a spicy mix of beaches, lush gardens, and nightlife. Viña is taken over in the summer by Chileans and Argentines who crowd the expensive nightspots and bask on its golden, albeit crowded, beaches. A century ago Viña was the retreat for affluent *porteños* (people from the port area) from Valparaíso.

They built mansions with large gardens that later became the city's parks.

The **Quinta Vergara** is Viña's most elegant park, filled with exotic plants from around the world. The **Palacio Vergara** (1908), built by Viña's founding family and today housing the **Museo de Bellas Artes**, is undergoing prolonged restoration from earthquake damage. The **Anfiteatro** hosts a festival of song in February that is well-known in much of Latin America. **La Plaza José Francisco Vergara** is the palm-filled center of old Viña with the neoclassical **Club de Viña** (1910), **Teatro Municipal** (1930), **Hotel O'Higgins** (1935), and the **Casa Subercaseaux**, now a hotel, on its borders.

Pedestrian precinct **Avenida Valparaíso** is a magnet in summer, with cafés, shopping malls, and an artisan fair. At the end of the street is **Cerro Castillo**, a hill sprinkled with late 19th-century mansions and terraces overlooking the bay. Calle Alamos winds up the hill, past Castillo Brunet and the presidential palace. Avenida Peru is a misty promenade following the shore north of the hill. The

EXCLUSIVE ADVANTAGES

The Atacama Desert and the Andes have formed effective barriers that separate Chile from the rest of South America. As a result, the fauna, and particularly the flora, of Chile include some unique species, as well as the Carmenère grape that became extinct in Europe when phylloxera devastated vineyards in the 19th century. Consequently, Chile jealously guards its borders to protect its agriculture from any imported plant diseases. The country's historic isolation has also separated the accent and mentality of Chileans from its Andean and Argentine neighbors, creating a surprisingly homogenous culture over vast distances. Important minorities do exist, however, especially the Mapuche in south central Chile, the Quechua and Aymara in the far north, and the Rapa Nui on Easter Island.

Casino Municipal is the premier gambling house on the Pacific side of the continent, where the rich and not-so-rich play for high stakes. The promenade continues along Avenida San Martín, bordering long beaches that are mobbed by tourists in the summer months.

Reñaca, 8km (5 miles) north, is the chic place to be in high season (January and February). Its mile-long beach lies below a cliffside full of fashionable apartments and smart hotels, which are accessible by little trams and stairways. In contrast, the sleepy fishing village of Horcón is the center of Chile's counter-culture. It is set on a rocky peninsula 40km (25 miles) north of Viña del Mar, in the midst of a eucalyptus forest, with a small wharf and colorful skiffs towed in and out of the water by teams of horses, a fascinating sight when the catch is brought in, and pelicans stand in the water waiting for their share.

Northern deserts

The 2,074km (1,289 miles) from Santiago to Arica seem silent, a landscape sprinkled with whitewashed adobe villages marooned in the Atacama Desert. Tradition bends the rules of Catholicism, and visits by extraterrestrials have found their way into the folklore.

Arica **⑩**, in the far north, is right on the threshold of Peru. The streets are filled with markets and stores catering to Peruvian and Bolivian smugglers. Arica is also known for its beautiful beaches and nightlife. Plaza Aduana provides cool respite from the desert sun. Nearby is Catedral de San Marco (1876), a wrought-iron sanctuary designed by Gustave Eiffel. The Morro de Arica is a huge hill with magnificent views of the city, the Pacific, and the desert. A museum in an old fortress at its top recalls the battle for Arica during the War of the Pacific (1879–83), when the city was won from Peru.

Several travel firms offer trips eastward to Lago Chungará, near Bolivia, a magnificent journey to a height of 4,400 meters (14,500ft). The lake is a Unesco World Biosphere Reserve, where wildlife teems. Flightless

TIP

On a visit to El Tatio geysers, bring aspirin with you and lots of water to drink to ease the effects of altitude – headaches and nausea are common at this height. At the geysers, take great care not to tread on thin ground.

Tres Marias (Three Marys) rock formation in Valley of the Moon, Atacama Desert.

tagua-tagua birds make their nests on reed islands, and the flamingos are perhaps the best-loved inhabitants. On the way up there, giant geoglyphs can be seen from the valley floor. The excursion is best not done as a day trip if you want to avoid altitude sickness. Putre offers a few low- and mid-scale hotels where you can stay and acclimatize.

The emerald lake is surrounded by snowy peaks that rise high above the shoreline. The hamlets of Chungará and Parinacota are located in **Parque Nacional Lauca**, where foxes, vicuñas, vizcachas (big, hare-like rodents), and white geese with black-tipped wings can be seen. Farther south, beautiful little Andean churches typical of the Atacama Desert and the Humahuaca Valley across the border in Argentina dot the arid, high-mountain landscape here and in Parque Nacional Isluga, farther south along the border.

Spectacular landscape

South of Arica are Iquique, a former hub of the saltpeter industry turned beach resort, and Antofagasta, the port through which most of Chile's copper is exported. A large natural arch, La Portada, lies facing the steep cliffs of the Pacific coast just north of the city. Farther east, **Calama** ⓫, 603km (375 miles) south of Arica, is a mining center servicing the massive Chuquicamata copper mine, 16km (10 miles) away. Wisps of sulfur vapor and dust from the mine linger among its bars, cheap hotels, and restaurants. Tours of the biggest open-pit copper mine in the world are available. Due east, **Géiseres del Tatio**, an impressive field of scalding geysers at an altitude of 4,300 meters (14,108ft), are at their most exuberant at sunrise. The easiest way to visit them is in a 4am tour from San Pedro de Atacama.

The pleasant village oasis of **San Pedro de Atacama** ⓬, 93km (58 miles) southeast of Calama, was the most populated Atacamanian town in pre-Columbian times. It was conquered by the Incas in 1450, and by Pedro de Valdivia in 1540. The beautiful **Iglesia de San Pedro** (1641) is constructed of the same white adobe as most of the town. Next door is the impressive **Museo Arqueológico**

Adobe church in San Pedro de Atacama.

Padre Le Paige (Mon–Fri 9am–6pm, Sat–Sun 10am–6pm), founded by a Belgian Jesuit, with a fine collection of pottery, mummies, and ancient native vestments. Nearby is **Pukara de Quitor**, a mountainside stone fortress, and an ancient archeological site has been unearthed at Tulor.

In the distance are lofty volcanoes, including the perfectly cone-shaped **Licancábur**, at 5,916 meters (19,409ft). Not far from the village is the enormous **Salar de Atacama** salt flat, as well as the **Valle de la Luna** (Valley of the Moon), 20km (12 miles) away on a very bumpy road. This mysterious desert valley is purportedly endowed with supernatural qualities and ringed by jagged, white peaks that contrast with the ochre valley floor. At twilight its formations turn brilliant colors.

Other picturesque oasis villages in the area include Caspana and Chiu Chiu, with Chile's oldest church, Ayquina, with elements borrowed from the indigenous culture. To the north, Ollagüe borders with Bolivia near a beautiful desert salt lake.

West of the mining town of **Copiapó** ⑬ are **Caldera** and **Bahía Inglesa**, which comprise three successive bays with long, unspoiled beaches and year-round warm water. Well worth a trip are the remote areas near the border with Argentina, including Ojos del Salado, Chile's highest mountain, and nearby Laguna Verde. Much of the area is inside the Parque Nacional Nevado Tres Cruces. The area is quite remote, however, and independent travelers should calculate carefully how much gasoline they need as there are very few gas stations. The park has a ranger station that accepts visitors.

To the south, **La Serena** ⑭, a colonial city founded in 1543 as a trade link en route between Santiago and Lima, Peru, is known for its 30 distinctive churches. Restored in the 1950s, it is now one of the most attractive towns in Chile. The **Iglesia San Francisco**, dating from 1627, on Calle Balmaceda has a Baroque facade, with interior *Mudéjar* details; and the **Mercado La Recova** has a good selection of regional crafts.

TIP

It is possible to hike to the 2,840-meter (9,318ft) peak of Villarrica Volcano and peer into the steamy crater, but take care, as the weather can turn stormy at a moment's notice.

El Tatio geysers in the Atacama Desert.

TIP

Chile's active volcanism has blessed it with numerous spas, rustic and remote in the arid north and more luxurious, European-style in the south. In places like Chillán, Pucón, or Malalcahuello, winter visits are attractive as the spas offer relaxation after a day at nearby ski resorts.

The clear desert skies in the vicinity have led to the construction of astronomical observatories, several of which can be visited. Most demand reservations well ahead of a tour, but it is one well worth making.

Tongoy (48km/30 miles south of La Serena) is a summer resort on a high peninsula overlooking the Pacific, with expansive, white beaches. Along the Elqui River is the narrow, serpentine **Valle del Elqui**. This lush refuge is famous for its clear blue skies, dry mountain air, steep arid mountains, and intensely cultivated pastures and vineyards that are the source of the national liquor, *pisco*.

Monte Grande ⓯, a small village along the river, is where the Nobel Prize-winning poet and teacher Gabriela Mistral (1889–1957) spent her infancy. Her simple tomb, nearby on the road to Cochiguaz, bears the inscription "It is my wish that my body be interred in my beloved Monte Grande." Her birthplace in **Vicuña** is now a **museum** (Mar–Dec, Tue–Fri 10am–5.45pm, Sat 10.30am–6pm, Sun 10am–1pm, Jan–Feb Mon–Sat 10am–7pm, Sun 10am–6pm. There

Frutillar, in the Lake District, is known for its well-preserved 19th-century German architecture.

are a number of communes in the valley whose inhabitants practice meditation in what is considered to be a focal point of mystical energy.

South to the Lake District

South of Chile's central valley, the Lake District is a land of extreme beauty, a seemingly endless succession of lush alpine valleys, low Andean hills, and snow-covered volcanoes. The outstanding scenery is reflected in the bitter-cold waters of the lakes, which were formed by the abrasive retreat of glaciers that once covered the region. It is hard to believe that access to this natural paradise was once forbidden to outsiders. The Mapuche people wiped out every foreign settlement south of the **Río Biobío** at the end of the 16th century, and remained undefeated until the 1880s.

Concepción ⓰ is Chile's second-largest city (pop. 396,000), set on the banks of the mighty Biobío. It was little more than a garrison town until 1818, when Bernardo O'Higgins, who became the first leader of the independent Chilean state, declared the

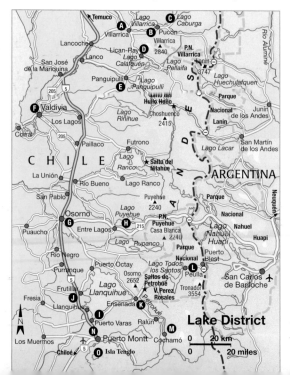

country's independence there. The downtown area is best explored on foot in the streets around the plaza. Four blocks south is **Parque Ecuador**, which winds up **Cerro Caracol** (Snail Hill) for a good view of the city, hard-hit in the 2010 earthquake. To the north is the **Universidad de Concepción**, founded in 1919.

About 15km (9 miles) north of Los Angeles, snuggled deep within a wooded Andes valley, the town of **Salto del Laja** is the gateway to the Lake District. The frigid waters of the Laja River slice through some of the most beautiful scenery in Chile, before plunging 35 meters (115ft) into a deep, rocky canyon, which is eternally bathed in a foggy mist. Within sight of the valley are four volcanoes that rise high above the forest.

The road east snakes through huge pine forests, nearing the mountains as the valley narrows and the terrain becomes semi-arid. Huge lava fields lie nearby, flanked by mountain cypress. **Parque Nacional Laguna del Laja** is located in a narrow valley. In the center is a 200-meter (650ft)-high volcanic cone that holds **Laja Lagoon**, and to the right is the desolate cone of **Laja volcano**. Three of the four lakes in **Parque Nacional Conguillío** (110km/70 miles northeast of Temuco) were formed by the depressions in lava fields spewed out by the **Llaima volcano** (3,125 meters/10,253ft) within the past 50 years. The narrow valley is covered with araucarias, evergreen conifers, up to 1,200 years old, as well as oaks and cypresses.

Turbulent landscape

Villarrica Ⓐ is a major resort on the shore of the 176-sq-km (68-sq-mile) **Lago Villarrica**. Its blue waters change hue as the sun falls low in the sky, reflecting the perfect cone of the **Villarrica volcano**. The lake is scarred by eruptions from the still-active volcano, which glows at night like the end of a giant cigar. The first European colony at Villarrica was beseiged by the Mapuche in 1598, and collapsed without survivors in 1602. The colony was not re-established until 1882. There is a Mapuche museum near the tourist office at Villarrica.

The small, touristy town of Pucón in the middle of the southern Lake District.

The resort village of **Pucón** , farther east along the lake, is a summer haven for affluent Chileans. **Parque Nacional Villarrica**, on the steep slopes of the volcano, is a bizarre mix of untouched forest and barren lava fields that seared through the woods during an eruption. In the winter months there are opportunities for skiing on the slopes of several volcanoes from Conguillío to Villarica.

Slender **Lago Caburga** , 24km (15 miles) to the east, was formed when lava flows were blocked by the precipitous, densely wooded valley. Three pristine lagoons are hidden in the little valley, and several hot springs, fed by volcanoes, gush from the ground.

Lakes Calafquén, Panguipulli, Pellaifa, Neltume, Riñihue, Pirihueico, and, in Argentina, Lacar, are collectively known as the **Seven Lakes**. This little-known area wasn't really settled until the late 1800s, because of its remote setting and harsh winters. **Lican Ray** was built for tourists on a wooded peninsula overlooking Calafquén Lake, with the nicest beach in the area. **Panguipulli** , a small,

Sampling the locally brewed beer at the Kunstmann Brewery outside Valdivia.

picturesque town on the banks of the lake, has an interesting Capuchin mission and church. A road leads to the tip of a wooded peninsula, with sandy beaches on the lake. Nearby, **Salto del Huilo Huilo** crashes down a deep vine-covered gorge into the River Fuy, producing an eternal rainbow.

German settlements

One of the first Spanish settlements in Chile was **Valdivia** , located at the confluence of several waterways in the Valdivia Estuary. The streets follow the sinuous rivers, and **Calle General Lagos** near the waterfront and lively port still has remnants of the architecture that German immigrants brought with them in the 19th century. The **Museo Histórico y Antropológico Mauricio van de Maele** (Mar–Dec Tue–Sun 10am–1pm, 2–6pm, Jan–Feb daily 10am–8pm), on **Teja Island**, chronicles the German migration. Nearby is the **Austral University**, with a large campus. Valdivia was heavily fortified by the Spanish after 1600 to guard against Mapuche invasions. Tours are available to see the forts along the river.

The nearby city of **Osorno** **G**, 990km (615 miles) south of Santiago, is the center of a cattle region. It lies east to west across the Rahue River, surrounded by azure-green pasture-lands nourished by abundant rainfall. The city was settled by German farmers, and its shingled wooden homes and streets with names like Buschman, Amthauer, and Francke are reminiscent of a distant past. **Calle Bulnes** has good river views. Try to catch the morning **Feria Ganadera**, Chile's largest cattle market, where burly *campesinos* haggle over animals.

Lago Puyehue **H** (60km/37 miles east) is a popular fishing and camping spot. The **Casablanca**, **Puyehue**, **Puntiagudo**, and immense **Osorno** volcanoes are all within sight of the lake's waters. Near the eastern shore are the **Puyehue hot springs**, known for their therapeutic qualities. On the road to the Casablanca volcano, through lush virgin forest, is **Aguas Calientes** (which means hot waters).

Picturesque towns creep up to the edge of **Lago Llanquihue** and the perfect cone of the snow-capped Osorno volcano is eternally reflected in its frigid waters. **Puerto Varas** **I**, at the southwest tip of the lake, is an immaculate town created in 1854 to handle lake commerce to Puerto Montt. Today it is a thriving stop-off point for tourists who like to gamble in the casino at **Gran Hotel Puerto Varas** on the shore. **Frutillar** **J**, on the western lakeshore, is filled with German homes with meticulous gardens, and has a peculiar claim to fame: the world's southernmost palm tree. In February it hosts the **Semanas Musicales de Frutillar**, a festival of classical music.

On the eastern shore, **Ensenada** **K** is a tiny village set in the shadow of the Osorno volcano, and surrounded by lush forest cut by lava flows. About 12km (7.5 miles) east, the rapids of the **Río Petrohué** are broken by strange lava formations comprised of thousands of black volcanic stones, reminders of an ancient eruption. Farther east is **Lago Todos Los Santos**. There are daily boat excursions along the length of the lake to **Peulla** **L**, a magnificent journey past shoreline mountains

Maps on pages 268, 298

TIP

When heading to the Lake District, take warm and waterproof clothes. The landscape is so green only because it rains a lot and temperatures drop dramatically as you go south.

Puyehue National Park.

FACT

In Frutillar and other towns around the lakes you will find cozy German cafés where the costumes, coffee, and cakes make you think you are in Bavaria.

covered in dense virgin forest. From here, it is also possible to cross to Bariloche in Argentina. Intriguingly, this allows visitors to cross the Andes by boat (plus short bus rides between lakes). In the high season between December and February, however, the trip becomes crowded and touristy.

The road south from Ensenada to Cochamó is a journey through an area of great wilderness beauty. **Cochamó ⓜ** is a tiny village on the estuary, a branch off to the Pacific through spectacular fiords that rise up to 1,500 meters (4,900ft) straight out of the water. At Cochamó you can hire fishermen to give you a tour of the estuary in a skiff, where it's easy to spot seals, 30kg (70lb) groupers, and even whales.

Puerto Montt ⓝ was founded in 1853 by the adventurer Vicente Pérez Rosales, with a handful of German immigrants intent on settling Llanquihue province. The area mushroomed when the railroad arrived, 60 years later. Today the city is an improving port and the center of the salmon industry, gateway to Chiloé

and the Carrctera Austral. Despite its size, Puerto Montt has a small-town feeling, with many homes of German design: wooden, with pitched roofs, ornate balconies, and shingles well-weathered by the region's eternal drizzle. The cathedral in the central square, the city's oldest building, is made of redwood. Puerto Montt faces the Reloncaví Sound, and a walk along the waterfront is a good introduction to the city.

Angelmó, a contiguous fishing port, is a jewel of maritime activity. Cafés on the pier offer fresh *erizos (sea urchins)*, *locos (abalone)*, and other cold-water seafood, and burly fishermen mend their nets by the skiffs on the shore. The pier is lined with artisan shops that sell a wide selection of woolen goods and woodcarvings. For a small fee, young boys will row you across to **Isla Tenglo ⓞ**, where you can walk around its fishing communities.

The rugged south: Chilean Patagonia

South of Puerto Montt, the land and sea become one as the country breaks into a maze of islands, fiords, rivers with myriad tributaries, lakes, and wooded mountains with trees a thousand years old. Chilean Patagonia is a place of forbidding, intense beauty.

The island of **Chiloé ⓟ** emerges just out of sight of Puerto Montt, a romantic place filled with picturesque villages, 100 tiny enchanted islets, misty waterways, and little wooden homes. Chiloé is steeped in fishing tradition, and the magic of its culture attracts trekkers in search of the customs, legends, and folklore of its friendly people. Here you will find lively dances like the *cueca* and *vals*, local dishes like *curanto*, drinks like *chicha de manzana*, and myriad legends, festivals, and rituals all its own. Somehow it has held on to its oldest traditions.

The island is known for its churches, 16 of which are Unesco World Heritage Sites, because of their

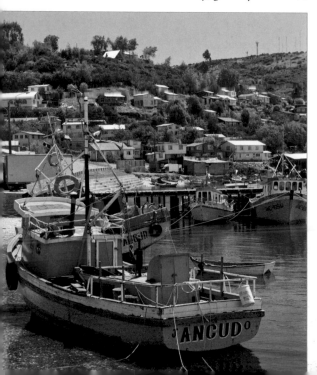
Fishing boats in Ancud, Chiloé.

unique wooden architecture. Many are in poor shape, but are being repaired with international support.

Ancud, with narrow streets packed with wooden commercial buildings from its heyday, is a bustling port. The **Museo Azul de las Islas de Chiloé** (Jan–Feb daily 9.30am–7.30pm, Sat–Sun 9.30am–8pm, Mar–Dec Tue–Fri 10am–5.30pm, Sat–Sun 10am–2pm) contains exhibits on Chilote culture and mythology; and the **Fort of San Antonio**, the last Spanish garrison to surrender to the independent Chilean Republic in 1826, offers a spectacular view on a clear day.

Castro (founded in 1567), on the shores of a protected fiord, is one of the oldest cities in Chile, but risks being disfigured by an oversized downtown shopping mall. Its wooden cathedral, Iglesia de San Francisco de Castro, was finished in 1912. On the outskirts of Castro, the **Museo de Arte Moderno** (daily mid-Jan–mid-March irregular hours; see www.mamchiloe.cl for details) shows some of Chile's best contemporary art in a prize-winning building in the traditional

Chiloé style. In February the Festival Costumbrista Chilote is a marvelous display of island culture. At the waterside, fishermen park their skiffs beside rows of *palafitos*, houses on stilts.

Nearby **Dalcahue** is famous for its Sunday artisan fair, where fine woolen sweaters can be purchased. Day tours of the smaller islands of the archipelago, taking in several fine churches, are worthwhile and can be cheaply booked in Castro.

Chonchi (26km/16 miles south of Castro) is built on a cliff face overlooking the water. There is a nice church among several colorful large houses with well-kept gardens. Heading southward, you reach **Queilén**, a picturesque town on a narrow peninsula with beaches at either end, and elegant old homes dating back to its founding as an immigrant colony in 1900. Ferries leave from **Quellón** (not to be confused with Queilén), the southernmost port. Farther south, the privately owned Tantauco Reserve is being developed to protect pristine forest that comprises almost a quarter of the island.

On the waterfront in Ancud, Chiloé.

The palafitos (houses on stilts) of Castro, Chiloé.

Quellón is famous for its soft, gray ponchos, which are very resistant to the rain because the wool used for making them is raw and still full of natural oils.

South to the end of the world

South of Chiloé lies the remote Aisén (also spelled Aysén) region, where visits still give the sensation of penetrating a new frontier. The Carretera Austral winds through the largely uninhabited far south for almost 1,000km (600 miles). The region is still largely untouched by humans, save a few fishermen and farmers. It is an amazing landscape where rocky cliffs drop into lush river valleys, and dense forests are bordered by glaciers. **Chaitén** ⓭, a coastal ghost town, was wiped out by the volcano of the same name in 2008, forcing the relocation of its residents.

Nearby Futaleufú has become a mecca for rafters. The road continues to **Lago Risopatrón** and **Termas de Puyuhuapi**. Nearby **Parque Nacional Queulat** has amazing views of the *ventisqueros* (glaciers), including one overhanging a cliff, spawning a waterfall that plunges into a lake below. **Puerto Cisnes**, to the south, is a small beachside village that was colonized by Germans and Italians in the late 19th century. Inland, **Coyhaique** ⓳ is a

The Three Towers at Torres del Paine National Park.

good jumping-off point for exploring the region as it is reachable by plane from Santiago. Founded in 1929, it is largely a government and military center. The **Museo de la Colonización** (Tue–Sun 11am–1pm, 3–7pm) in the **Simpson valley,** offers a good introduction to the region's history.

From **Puerto Aisén** ⓴, to the west, boats depart to **Laguna San Rafael**, a pristine bay only accessible after a journey through fiords and archipelagos. The bay is bordered by the **San Rafael Glacier**, which sends huge blocks of 20,000-year-old ice crashing into the water as it makes its way to the sea. A number of companies also offer cruises there from Puerto Montt.

About 120km (75 miles) south of Coyhaique is **Lago General Carrera**, South America's second-largest lake. It juts into Argentina, with views of the vast pampas to the east. On the Chilean side it is bordered by barren, rocky mountains eroded by glaciers. Several towns have lodgings along the shore, including **Puerto Ibáñez** and **Chile Chico**. The Andean landscape is spectacular, particularly around protected

Cerro Castillo and in **Conservación Patagónica**'s *estancia* near Cochrane, which is to be donated as a park to Chile. It is several years from completion but already possible to visit although key facilities are not yet open (for more information visit www.con servacionpatagonica.org/visit.htm).

Farther south, the road continues through temperate rainforest and peat bogs to Tortel, a village entirely on wooden stilts, that snakes along the shore of a minty-green inlet. Road's end is at Villa O'Higgins near the Campos de Hielo del Sur.

Torres del Paine

Down at the far south of the Andes mountain chain, **Torres del Paine National Park**, a Unesco World Biosphere Reserve, is one of the newest nature reserves in South America, a 2,400-sq-km (927-sq-mile) uninhabited wilderness. Aficionados agree that the unique physical formations of the Paine (pronounced *pie-nay*), crowded with glaciers, lakes, and gnarled Magellanic trees, offers the most magnificent walking in the world. The reserve is also home to numerous animals such as *guanacos* (a kind of llama), pumas, and *huemul* deer (an endangered species), along with birds, including the Andean condor and the rare black vulture. The best time to visit the park is between December and April.

The jumping-off point for the national park is **Puerto Natales ㉑**, a small, sleepy town set beside the Ultima Esperanza Gulf, with numerous hotels, and restaurants serving the local specialty, king crab. Tour boats head out from Natales to nearby glaciers. Not far away is a huge cave where the remains of a prehistoric giant sloth were found.

But most people visit Puerto Natales to arrange a trip to the Paine. Several times a week (every morning in summer), vans and buses make the three-hour drive along a rough dirt road to the park. The trail winds through mountain passes before descending to the foot of the Andes, providing the first view of the **Cuernos del Paine** (Horns of the Paine): twisted pillars of gray granite dusted with snow, invariably surrounded by billowing clouds. As with everywhere else this far south,

Magellanic penguins in Torres del Paine National Park.

Guanacos in Torres del
Paine National Park.

weather in the Paine can be unpredictable, even in summer. The famous
Torres del Paine (towers) are even
more spectacular than the Cuernos,
but are often obscured by the harsh,
incessantly windy weather. Expensive
accommodations can be found at
the Hostería Pehoe on a lake and the
Posada Rio Serrano.

Several day trips can be made from
these bases, as well as more ambitious
walks. The park has over 250km (150
miles) of tracks, including a 7-day
circuit. Along the way are *refugios* or
shelters, often scanty wood and corru-
gated-iron structures that barely keep
out the elements – sleeping bags and
cooking gear are essential. Those who
complete the full circuit will, weather
permitting, be rewarded with extraordinary views of snow-covered peaks,
turquoise lakes, and lush valleys. The
trails are lined with the vivid red and
orange flowers of *Calceolaria uniflora*,
known in Spanish as the *zapatito de
la virgen* (virgin's slipper) as well as
several species of orchids. Much of
the park is lushly forested, although a
worm plague killed many trees in the

Virgin's slipper
(Calceolaria uniflora)
thrives in Torres del
Paine.

late 1990s and, more recently, there
was a serious fire. Walks pass the accessible **Grey** and **Dickson glaciers**.

Most routes allow walkers to see
plenty of wildlife, above all guanacos
and culpeo foxes. Although the weather
can turn from fair to foul and back
again within minutes, the memories of
the park will last well after your clothes
have dried. Many people who go for a
day end up staying a week (so go well
equipped in case you decide to do this):
the liberating sensation of being in one
of the most remote and untouched wilderness areas on earth is worth savoring.

Remote Magallanes

The southernmost province of Magallanes is a solitary place with names
like Porvenir (Future) that tries to stop
you feeling you have reached the end
of the world, and Ultima Esperanza
(Last Hope), which suggests that you
have. This is where the tip of South
America has crumbled into myriad
islands as the land, sea, and ice mingle.
The forbidding nature of the territory
is reflected in the names of some of
the islands, like Desolación.

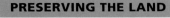

PRESERVING THE LAND

The 1,240km (769-mile) narrow, gravel
Carretera Austral (Southern Highway) is
the result of the Pinochet dictatorship's
effort to tighten links between central
Chile and its far-flung Patagonian territory. The road winds through picturesque villages, along minty-green
rivers and sparkling, aquamarine lakes
rimmed with snow-capped Andean
mountains. Sadly, environmental inju-
ries stemming from the mindlessly
burned forests during early 20th-
century colonization still mar some
parts of the landscape – it's not quite
as virgin as it's made out to be. Private
protection projects and public preserves, however, are proof of a growing interest in preserving the lands,
from the forests of Pumalín to the
Patagonian ice fields, the largest non-
polar icecaps.

Punta Arenas ㉒ is a port city on the rolling hills above the barren, windswept steppe on the Strait of Magellan. This is a peculiar part of the world: the sky looks bigger here, and people seem distant and less open to outsiders, while the sun glares through the damaged ozone layer. Punta Arenas is known for its monuments to the Yugoslav settlers and ranchers who pioneered the region.

The **Museo Regional de Magallanes** (May–Sept daily 10.30am–2pm, Oct–Apr Mon–Sat 10.30am–5pm, Sun 10.30am–2pm), provides a fascinating trip back to the days before the Panama Canal opened, when the city boomed as ships called in on their journeys round the cape. **Cerro La Cruz** has good views of the city and across the straits to Tierra del Fuego.

Tierra del Fuego, an island of inhospitable terrain across the straits, was discovered as Ferdinand Magellan struggled to make the passage to the Pacific in 1520. In the late 19th century the land was settled by a few immigrants from Yugoslavia and England who came to start sheep ranches, and cash in on the 1881 gold rush. The wooded mountains and peat bogs on the western side are cold and snowy in the long winter; the rainforests to the east are warmer and wetter; and the wind never ceases on the treeless pampas facing Punta Arenas. Guanacos, foxes, and condors are among the wildlife most commonly seen.

Little **Porvenir** ㉓ is the largest town on Chile's half of the island. The **Museo Provincial de Porvenir** (Mon–Thur 8am–5.30pm, Fri 8am–4.30pm, Sat–Sun 10.30am–1.30pm, 3.30–5pm) is connected to the municipal buildings on the main plaza, with historical photos and a Fuegian mummy discovered nearby. You can take a ferry across the straits from Punta Arenas to Porvenir docks, though the ferry from Punta Delgada is faster. A road continues to the Argentine side of the island (see page 349) toward the Ushuaia. Just before the border crossing near the bay of San Sebastian, a road branches south to the remote sub-Antarctic forest park of Karukinka, beyond magnificent Lago Deseado.

View across Punta Arenas toward the Strait of Magellan.

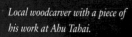
Local woodcarver with a piece of his work at Ahu Tahai.

EASTER ISLAND

This tiny Pacific outpost more than makes up for its remoteness with gigantic, mysterious monolithic figures and beautiful beaches.

PACIFIC OCEAN

CHILE

Santiago

Hidden in the endless wastes of the Pacific, nearly 4,000km (2,500 miles) from the coast of Chile, the small remnant of volcanic rock named Easter Island was once the most isolated place on earth. But in recent decades the huge and inexplicable statues left by the Polynesian culture have drawn attention from around the world. Where once only one ship a year stopped here, today flights arrive six days a week from Santiago. This tiny triangular South Seas outpost measures just 24km (15 miles) across and has a population of only 4,500, but there is a lot to explore. Easter Island has a wonderful raw, unspoiled beauty with windswept coastlines, gentle, treeless hills, and a lush interior. Golden beaches and coconut palms are in short supply.

Archeologists believe Easter Island may have been populated as long ago as AD 400. Norwegian adventurer and archeologist Thor Heyerdahl argued in his book *Aku-Aku* that the inhabitants came from South America, noting resemblances between the island culture and that of Tiahuanaco in Bolivia. But most academics today agree that the first settlers came from Polynesia, bringing sweet potato, sugar cane, and bananas to the fertile soil. Left in total isolation for centuries, the settlement prospered and spread. Its people created not only

Petroglyph of birdman.

the remarkable stone *moai*, but also *rongorongo*, what appears to be a script and what may well be one of only a handful of independent inventions of writing in all of humanity.

The first Europeans arrived on Easter Sunday in 1722, giving the island its name. Dutch Admiral Roggeveen spent a day ashore, recording (unlike later accounts) that the statues were upright, the lands were neatly cultivated, and "whole tracts of woodland" were visible. The population may have been as large as 12,000.

Main Attractions
Rano Raraku crater
Rano Kau volcano
Orongo

Turbulent times

The picture changes in later descriptions. European explorers in the late 18th century noted that many of the statues had tumbled, little land was under cultivation and there were only 1,000 people. The most likely explanation for the island's decline is that the population of Easter Island had outgrown its resources; the food supply failed, the forests were felled and soil began to erode. Without wood for canoes to escape from the island, fighting and cannibalism broke out, and the *moai* were toppled.

The people of Easter Island were to endure further suffering in the 19th century, when whalers and slave traders came to call. Of 1,000 islanders taken as slaves to the guano islands off Peru in 1862, only 100 were released alive, of whom only 15 survived the return journey, bringing smallpox to wreak further havoc in the community. By 1871, only 175 islanders remained. Today, some 5,000 people live on the island, annexed by Chile in 1888, with many being born on the mainland, of Chilean ancestry. The airport, opened in 1967, increased tourism, and in 1988 the landing strip was extended to become an emergency landing strip for the space shuttle, thrusting the island into the technological age. Accessibility has brought problems, with local residents worried about the influx of Chilean residents and more than 70,000 tourists a year. Some even want independence. Rapu Nui is the indigenous name of the island, much of which is a national park and a World Heritage Site.

The mysterious *moai*

No one knows the true story behind the *moai*, but they are thought to have been symbols of gods and ancestors. They were carved from around AD 900, out of the soft volcanic rock forming the sides of **Rano Raraku** crater, where some 400 incomplete pieces remain, many as high as 5.5 meters (18ft) – the largest is 21 meters (69ft) tall. Each probably took a year to complete. Once finished, the *moai* was cut out of the quarry and transported to a family burial platform called an *ahu*, some being given red stone "topknots." The family dead were usually placed in a vault

Moai statues.

beneath the *moai*, which was probably believed to transmit *mana*, or power, to the living family chief. All of the standing *ahu moai* that can be seen now have been re-erected in modern times. In the period of the tribal wars, all the *moai* were toppled, presumably to break the *mana* of the family chief they protected.

The most famous of the *moai* are the standing sentinels embedded in the ground on the southern slope of Rano Raraku. These haughty-looking statues remain eyeless: *moai* were only given coral eyes once they were raised on *ahus*, at which time the *mana* began to work. Most of the sites can be reached by bicycle or horse, but make sure you bring water with you.

The Bird Man cult

The most geologically spectacular place on Easter Island is the volcano **Rano Kau**, with its steep crater and multicolored lake. The ruined village of **Orongo**, sitting on steep cliffs above the crashing sea and three foam-washed islands, is surrounded by rocks with Bird Man carvings: a man's body is drawn with a bird's head, often holding an egg in one hand. Fortunately, we know quite a lot about the Bird Man cult, as it continued up to 1862. It involved a strange rite that probably began in the period of the wars. The basis of the cult was finding the first egg laid by the *Manu Tara*, or sacred bird, each spring.

The chief of each tribe on the island sent one chosen servant to Moto Nui, the largest of the islets below Orongo. Swimming across the dangerous waters, the servants or *hopus* spent a month looking for the first egg. On finding the egg, the successful *hopu* plunged into the swirling waters with the egg strapped to his forehead, swam to the mainland, and climbed the cliffs to Orongo. The *hopu's* master, named Bird Man for the year, would be given special powers and privileges. Today, there are more than 150 Bird Man carvings in the area. Nearby are markings and stones that have been interpreted as forming part of a solar observatory, where on the summer solstice the sun can be seen rising over Poike peninsula – one more mysterious attraction on this beautiful and fascinating island in the Pacific.

TIP

Motorbikes, jeeps, and horses can be rented. Guided tours by four-wheel-drive vehicles are highly recommended. You won't cover every single site in just one day's tour, but you'll see the most important ones.

Fallen moai on the south coast of the island.

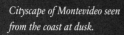
Cityscape of Montevideo seen from the coast at dusk.

The elegant lines of Montevideo's old railway station.

URUGUAY

This tiny nation, wedged in between Argentina and Brazil, has been a pioneer of social reform. It retains flavors of colonial opulence and rural frontier life, as well as elegant beach resorts.

L ong known as the "Switzerland of South America", owing to its size, its democratic tradition, and its dependence on the banking sector, Uruguay and its capital, Montevideo, are often seen virtually as one. This is not so surprising, given that the country covers an area of just 186,000 sq km (72,000 sq miles) and that more than half its 3.5 million people live in greater Montevideo, the rest spread among attractive coastal towns and the interior of the country, dedicated to cattle, sheep, rice, and fruit production.

Colonial occupation devastated Uruguay's indigenous Charrúa population, with the last killed or assimilated in the 19th century; the population today is made up principally of the descendants of Italian and Spanish immigrants who arrived in the late 19th and early 20th centuries, as well as a black and mixed-race minorities descended from former slaves and Brazilian immigrants. Usually seen as less formal than the Argentines, the Uruguayans are of similar ancestry, though as a small and family-based society they are less open in their social relations, in particular with foreign visitors.

Uruguayans tend to use Argentina as a reference point, but there are marked differences between Montevideo and Buenos Aires. One is Montevideo's racial mix: in the 19th century, rumors

of fair treatment attracted emancipated slaves from Brazil and Argentina. The army offered them a familiar regimented life, and many joined the infantry, which considerably reduced their numbers.

Another difference is Uruguay's strong secular tradition. The Catholic church plays no role in government, and holidays all have secular names: Christmas is Family Day and Easter or Holy Week is Tourism Week.

Uruguay claims to host the world's longest Carnival, held in Tourism Week

Main Attractions

Montevideo
Beaches and Punta del Este
Colonia del Sacramento

The lighthouse at Cabo Polonio.

FACT

Montevideo is said to be a corruption of a Galician sailor's cry: "Monte vi eu!" (I saw a hill!), but more likely was named during Magellan's expedition in January 1520.

(Easter) – it's little more sedate than the Rio version, but is a good place to see *candomblé*, which evolved from rituals brought by African slaves. The country also has a long tradition of tango.

Building a nation

The Portuguese were the first Europeans to settle the region, founding the town of Colonia del Sacramento in 1680. Spain established a colony in Montevideo farther east; the two countries battled over the area until Spain won possession in 1726. In 1815, José Gervasio Artigas led Uruguay to independence, becoming leader of the Uruguayan nation, but wars with Brazil postponed full independence for 10 years (see page 36). Artigas was eventually forced into exile in Paraguay. For the next 50 years, civil wars raged between two political forces: the Blancos (Whites) and Colorados (Reds). Initially feuding factions, they would eventually evolve into Uruguay's major political parties. In 1872, in the interest of beef exports, peace was established by ceding the Blancos' influence to the countryside

A watercolour from 1844 depicts soldiers of the Oribe Army in Montevideo.

and the Colorados' to the city, a division that remains to this day.

The social revolution

José Batlle y Ordóñez is usually credited with forging the model of civic order that Uruguay became during the first half of the 20th century. Batlle (pronounced *BA-zhay*) studied in Paris, and returned to Uruguay full of enlightened ideas. He became a political journalist, fearlessly attacking the country's dictators, founded his own newspaper, *El Día*, in 1886, and gradually made his way into politics. He was elected president for the first time in 1903.

On a 4-year sojourn in Europe between presidential terms, Batlle was impressed with the Swiss social legislation and state-operated industries. In his second term, he legalized divorce, abolished the death penalty, and established an 8-hour workday. He also forbade naming public buildings after saints. His 1918 constitution provided complete freedom of the press and the prohibition of arbitrary arrest, and decreed that prisons were for reform, rather than punishment.

By the time he died in 1929, Batlle's reforms had succeeded in liberalizing both parties. The widespread peace and prosperity of the past decades prevented even the conservative moneyed classes from objecting to the advance of social security and workers' rights. A coup d'état in 1933 temporarily halted progress, but a 1942 constitution provided explicitly for universal health, accident, and unemployment insurance, and gave illegitimate children the right to inherit.

End of the welfare state

The collapse of Uruguay's wool and beef economic base in the late 1950s produced a crisis in the country's welfare system and a rise in poverty and unemployment. This in turn facilitated the rise of the Tupamaro guerrillas in the 1960s and, in 1973, the rise of a repressive military government. During 12 years of dictatorship, one in every 50 Uruguayans was arrested at some point for supposed subversive activity. One in every 500 was sentenced to 6 years or more in prison, and some 400,000 fled into

SOCCER

The 1920s through the 1950s were the heyday of Uruguayan soccer, when it won two world championships, the second one against the home team in Rio de Janeiro's fabled Maracaná stadium. The Estadio Centenario in Montevideo was built to host the first FIFA World Cup in 1930. Uruguay's historic top clubs are Peñarol and Nacional, founded in the 19th century. During a 190-day tour of Europe in 1925, Nacional utterly defeated the old contintent's teams, scoring 130 goals and conceding just 30 in 38 games. Since the late 1990s, South American soccer has become increasingly competitive, with Paraguay challenging Argentina and Brazil at the top, and Uruguay in a crowded midfield including Chile, Ecuador, and Venezuela, where anyone can surprise. But recently, many surprises are in Uruguay's favor.

exile. Following the return to civilian government in 1985, Uruguay enjoyed comparatively high living standards and a relatively equitable distribution of wealth. But wedged between giants Brazil and Argentina, the country and its banks remain exposed to its neighbor's crises. Argentina opposes the creation of wood pulp as an industry to offset the declining demand for wool and beef exports.

Jorge Batlle of the center-right Colorado Party was elected head of state and government in 2000. Tax increases, among other measures, were implemented soon afterward in an effort to prevent Argentina's financial crisis from entering Uruguay. In 2005, for the first time in Uruguay's history, the two traditional parties failed to win the presidency. Instead Tabaré Vázquez, a medical doctor, was elected on behalf of the left-wing Broad Front coalition. José Mujica, from the same coalition, succeeded him in 2010. Wiser with the years, the former Tupamaro has been a voice of reason in defending freedom of speech in South America, but is also boldly considering legalizing marijuana in Uruguay.

Montevideo and the coast

To visitors it can seem as if all roads in Uruguay lead to the beach – not so surprising given that the country has one of the most attractive coastlines in the continent. Even **Montevideo** ㉔, the capital, is noted for its long beaches, and virtually all the country's principal tourist destinations are on the coast, linked by the *ruta interbalnearia* (interbeach route) running from Montevideo to Chuy, on the Brazilian border. Visitors who have had enough of the beach may want to head into the country and enjoy a slice of rural Uruguayan life on an *estancia* (ranch), sampling Uruguay's famous beef and wine. Rural activities range from horseback riding to wild boar hunting.

The most pleasant way to travel to Uruguay is to cross the River Plate

FACT

The government of President Tabaré Vázquez, a renowned oncologist, banned smoking in public places in 2006, the first South American country to do so. This was a major public health initiative, in a country where one-third of the people smoke.

from Buenos Aires. There is a choice of hydrofoil, catamaran, or ferry bus, taking 3–4 hours. From the decks, the low hill that gave Montevideo its name comes slowly into view. Landing in Montevideo harbor and walking through the musty customs office may give you the sensation of going back in time. Cobbled streets are jammed with scooters, cyclists, and pedestrians. Uruguay's high import duty on automobiles has filled Montevideo's streets with vehicles that would be considered antiques elsewhere. (Uruguayan auto mechanics are said to be among the best in the world.) The rural air is reinforced every August with a farm show, held in the **Parque Prado**.

With a population of nearly 2 million, Montevideo is the only major city in Uruguay. Economic hard times have given it an elegantly shabby look, although ceremonial occasions such as afternoon tea are as important as they are in Buenos Aires, as is the perpetual ritual of maté (pronounced *"MAH-teh"*) – you'll see people with their maté gourd and thermos of hot water on buses and in bank lines.

The crowded beach at Punta del Este, a popular South American city for vacations.

The best place to begin a tour of Montevideo is at the **Plaza Cagancha** (also called Plaza Libertad) on the main thoroughfare, Avenida 18 de Julio, named after the day in 1829 when Uruguay was finally freed of Argentine and Brazilian control. You'll find the main tourist office on Plaza Cagancha, offering brochures and free city maps. Avenida 18 de Julio runs downhill, past the **Museo del Gaucho** (Mon–Fri 10am–5pm), with its eclectic collection. The street leads to the city's main square, **Plaza Independencia**. To the left is the 1928 eclectic Art Deco skyscraper known as the **Palacio Salvo**, a landmark for Montevideans and once South America's tallest building. To the right is the **Hotel Victoria**, also Art Deco, and in the middle of the square is the subterranean tomb and equestrian statue of General José Artigas. Also worth visiting are the cream-colored **Government House**, now used only for ceremonial purposes, and the jewel-like **Teatro Solís**, an exact copy of the Teatro María Guerrero in Madrid. Now renovated, the theater was established in 1856 and

is still operating, making it one of the oldest in the Americas.

Into the Old Town

The archway at the west end of Plaza Independencia is part of the city wall that once protected Montevideo against its many invaders. It marks the entrance to the **Ciudad Vieja**, or Old Town, a neighborhood of narrow, winding streets and early 20th-century buildings. The heart of the Old Town is **Plaza Constitución**. Here is the old *cabildo*, or town hall. Like the **cathedral**, also in the square, it's been renovated but retains its colonial appearance. The cathedral dates from the early 19th century and is the oldest building in the city. The *cabildo* has a good **Museo de Historia** (Tue–Fri 12.30–5.30pm, Sat–Sun 11.30am– 4.30pm) dedicated to the history of the city, containing clocks, furniture, and portraits. **La Bolsa** (Stock Exchange), the **Banco de la República**, and the imposing **Aduana** (Customs House) are all north of the plaza and worth a look. Also intriguing is the **Palacio Taranco**, on Plaza Zabala, the former home of a wealthy merchant who imported every stick of furniture and even the marble floors from France.

Following Calle Piedras down to the waterfront leads to the **Mercado del Puerto**, a lively market with a series of open-air restaurants at one end. The market is only open in the afternoon; it's as much about atmosphere as about the produce on sale, and Saturdays are particularly lively.

From the old town there is a view across the port to the **Cerro**, the 139-meter (456ft) hill that gave the city its name, and is topped with a lighthouse and fort.

A city of beautiful beaches

If the weather is good, try to visit one of the city's clean white-sand beaches. It also has two lovely parks of historical interest. The **Prado** is located northwest of downtown (follow Agraciada north from 18 de Julio) in a neighborhood where some of Uruguay's grand old houses still stand. It was once the property of a 19th-century financier, José Buschental, who built a 40-hectare (100-acre) estate here and married

Souvenir maté gourds for sale.

SHARING A MATÉ

Everything stops for maté in Uruguay – in fact, so important is this stimulating brew that many Uruguayans carry their own maté kit around with them the whole morning and sometimes later. This usually consists of a drinking gourd known as a *culha* or maté, sometimes decorated with silver, containing *yerba* (dried leaves); a *bombilla* (drinking tube), which has a strainer at one end; and a thermos bottle filled with hot water.

Maté, or *yerba* maté, is brewed from the leaves of an evergreen plant, *Ilex paraguariensis*, which is related to the holly and grows wild in Paraguay and southern Brazil. The drink was popular with the Guaraní people in pre-Columbian times, and the leaves were first cultivated on a large scale by the Jesuits.

Maté is still an integral part of the culture of Uruguay, Paraguay, and Argentina, with the gourd often shared between friends or family, though its consumption has declined in other countries where it used to be popular. Each guest drinks from the gourd and passes it back to the host to be refilled in turn. Maté is usually drunk plain, but sometimes lemon juice, sugar, or even milk are added. Iced maté is also very popular. *Yerba* maté has diuretic and anti-rheumatic properties, and maté teabags are available in many northern-hemisphere health shops.

Tango dancers in Plaza Fabini, Montevideo.

the niece of Brazilian Emperor Dom Pedro II. He brought fish from Asia and exotic plants and animals from around the world. There is a statue of Buschental, and 800 varieties of roses. **Parque Rodó**, just behind the city's **Playa Ramírez** beach, is resplendent with palms, eucalyptus, and native *ombú* trees. It was named after José Enrique Rodó, one of the most prominent 19th-century South American writers, whose most famous work, *Ariel*, influenced a generation of intellectuals.

Fashionable suburbs

The metropolitan beaches stretch east as far as **Carrasco**, a fashionable suburb with streets shaded by large trees, and houses that belong to the few well-to-do people left in Uruguay. Montevideo's international airport lies just beyond Carrasco, 14km (9 miles) from the city center.

Beyond Carrasco, the highway turns inland, but smaller roads branch off to the beaches. At Km 42, shortly before Atlántida, is the **Fortín de Santa Rosa**, an 18th-century fortress

Lighthouse in Colonia de Sacramento.

converted into a hotel with a virtually private beach and an excellent restaurant. **Atlántida**, 45km (28 miles) from Montevideo, is surrounded by a windbreak of cypress and eucalyptus. The beach also has a casino, golf course, and tearoom. Just beyond Atlántida is **Piriápolis**, a pretty town on a curving bay with an old-fashioned promenade dominated by the imposing Argentino Hotel, a 1920s spa with mineral baths, stained-glass windows, and an elegant solarium where you may sip the curative sulfur-flavored water.

The most famous beach on the Uruguayan coast is **Punta del Este** ㉕, a jetset-studded peninsula that attracts well-heeled Argentines as well as a fair share of international celebrities and European royalty. Prices at "Punta" make this primarily *porteño* resort an exclusive one. The peninsula has two long and beautiful beaches: the Atlantic one is more windswept than the tranquil bay side. Those who don't share the Argentine herd instinct might find Punta more attractive off-season, when hotel rates go down and cool autumn breezes clear the sand of body-to-body sunbathers.

North of Punta del Este, the Uruguayan Atlantic coast is rich with gorgeous seascapes and deserted white-sand beaches. Along the coastal highway toward Brazil, it is worth stopping at the 18th-century Portuguese fortresses of **Santa Teresa** ㉖ and **San Miguel** ㉗, now beautiful national parks and popular bird sanctuaries; and **Punta del Diablo**, an attractive fishing village where a number of small restaurants offer excellent seafood.

European communities

West of Montevideo are some interesting European settlements. **Colonia Valdense** was settled by Waldensians from the Piedmontese Alps, and **Colonia Suiza** is a small Swiss enclave, also known as **Nueva Helvecia**. Some 50km (30 miles) west of Colonia Valdense is the 17th-century Portuguese town of **Colonia del**

Sacramento ㉘. Colonia retains more of its original flavor than most cities in the region, partly because little has happened here since the Portuguese founded it as a rival to Buenos Aires in 1680, although in recent years many Argentines have bought land and houses here.

Sights to see in the old quarter include the **Museo Español** (closed for renovation, otherwise Fri–Wed 11.30am–5pm), in a restored 18th-century viceroy's mansion; the **parochial church**; and the **Museo Portugués** (Thur–Tue 11.15am–4.45pm), which has an excellent collection of mahogany and Cordoban furniture, and military uniforms. Also, **Museo Indígena** (Tue–Wed, Fri–Sun 11.15am–4.30pm) exhibits artefacts found in Colonia, belonging to various Indian cultures including arrowheads, stone tools and ceramics. Narrow cobbled streets lead toward the river, where you can walk along the promenade to the remains of the colonial fortifications. A couple of miles farther out stands a grandiose bullring, which has not been used since Uruguay outlawed bullfighting

in the early 20th century. A hydrofoil connects Colonia with Buenos Aires.

Along the Río Uruguay

The small, tidy villages along the Uruguay River were at one time the crucibles of Uruguayan independence. About 30km (18 miles) upriver from Colonia is **La Agraciada**, where the famous "Trienta y Tres Orientales" (33 Patriots) landed from Argentina and organized a battalion to expel the Portuguese. A statue to General Lavalleja, the patriots' leader, is on the beach.

The port of **Fray Bentos** commemorates revolution of a different kind in its **Museo de la Revolución Industrial** (daily Apr–mid-Dec 9.30am–5pm, mid-Dec–Mar until 7pm. Fray Bentos was the site of the country's first meat extract factory. **Paysandú ㉙**, farther upriver, is the town where Artigas led his followers when they fled Spanish rule in Montevideo. Today it's a popular spot for stalking the delicious *pez dorado* game fish. North of Paysandú are the remedial hot mineral springs of **Termas de Daymán** and **Arapey**.

FACT

In summer, many Buenos Aires political news articles are datelined Punta del Este, Uruguay – Argentina's movers and shakers are all at the beach.

This Sunday street market is a local tradition in the Aguada and Cordon neighborhoods of the capital.

Harvesting grapes at a vineyard in Luján de Cuyo, Mendoza.

Portait of a northern gaucho on horseback near Purmamarca, Jujuy province.

ARGENTINA

From its glaciers to its subtropical jungles
to cosmopolitan Buenos Aires, vast Argentina
is a perfect destination.

Main Attractions

Buenos Aires
Salta and the Humahuaca Valley
Iguazú Falls
The Lake District
Península Valdés
Patagonian glaciers

It is the second-largest country in South America and the eighth-largest in the world, but geographical magnitude is not the only grand aspect of Argentina. The country is characterized by large cities, large ranches, large open spaces, even large steaks. In the early 20th century, Argentina was one of the world's richest nations and seemed set to become a world leader. But instead, the country became notorious for political drama and military dictatorships.

Argentina has always been heavily oriented toward its capital, Buenos Aires, with the city sometimes described as a giant's head on a dwarf's body. Most of the country's economic, political, financial, and industrial activity is focused on the Buenos Aires area, implying that the distribution of wealth and resources is extremely skewed. Despite periodic economic and political crises, many Argentines live well, enjoying restaurants, museums, and theaters. Throughout the country, the urban middle class has its nearby beach, lakeside resort, ski center, or mountain village retreat.

From jungles to glaciers

Argentina covers a range of latitudes, from the subtropical northeast, with Jesuit ruins and the imposing Iguaçú Falls, to the Andean northwest, changing abruptly from barren mountains to lush greenery, with the colonial architecture of Salta and the sugar-producing province of Tucumán. Central Argentina is characterized by spectacular mountain scenery, vineyards, and impeccable urban planning in Mendoza; green mountains and lakes in Córdoba; and attractive beach resorts in Buenos Aires province. In the south, bleak oil towns coexist with Welsh communities, pseudo-Tyrolean architecture, pretty towns surrounded by snow-capped mountains and lakes, and magnificent glaciers in the far

Carnival time in Buenos Aires.

south. All have a well-developed tourist industry with good transportation links, plenty of accommodations, and excellent food.

The people of Argentina

Argentines are known for strong localist tendencies and a disdain for those from the rest of the subcontinent, tempered by a genuine instinct to be hospitable. While the *porteños* (inhabitants of Buenos Aires – literally "people of the port") see their city as more sophisticated and cosmopolitan than the rest of the country, many provincial cities – Tucumán, Mendoza, and Córdoba – have large populations of second- and third-generation descendants of European and Arab immigrants, and are far enough away from the capital to have developed an exciting cultural, artistic, and academic life of their own.

Very few indigenous peoples remain, with small groups of Guaraní, Colla, Toba, and Wichi in the far north and Mapuche in the south, marginalized by the so-called "European" culture.

Porteños, gauchos, and caudillos

In the 18th century, when Buenos Aires was thriving as a smuggling center, fortunes began to be made in cattle hides and mule breeding, and indigenous people were forced off the pampas. Huge tracts of land were set aside by a few Spanish families, whose names would recur again and again as the power brokers of Argentina. For 70 years after independence was declared in 1816, civil wars raged, with Buenos Aires trying to impose central rule over local strongmen (*caudillos*) and their armies of gauchos – mestizo horsemen from the pampas. The most famous caudillo was Juan Manuel de Rosas, who rose from the chaos of civil war in 1829 to become governor of Buenos Aires province and de facto ruler of Argentina. Rosas is remembered for his reign of terror, enforced by secret police, and his nationalist policies, enabling Argentine goods to compete against foreign trade. After 23 years, he was thrown out and his supporters massacred. His protective tariffs were dismantled, and the country

Gauchos in the streets of Mercedes, Corrientes Province.

was flooded with foreign goods, while the civil wars resumed.

It was not until 1886 that the final step toward nationhood was made, when Buenos Aires was separated from its province and declared the capital of Argentina. The country's leaders were eager to appear cultured and urbane, notably Domingo Sarmiento, who divided the world into "civilization" – represented by all things European – and "barbarity": the caudillos, gauchos, and natives. Codes were introduced to control the gauchos. General Julio Roca embarked on a "Conquest of the Wilderness" in the 1870s to open up the pampas and Patagonia. He punished brave resistors with death, the rest herded into reservations. Cultivation of the pampas exploded to keep up with the new demand for beef. Railroads were laid and Argentina was soon outstripping its rivals, Australia and Canada, in agricultural advances.

The immigrants arrive

Thousands of laborers were needed to keep the boom going. Before 1880, only a trickle of foreign workers stayed in Argentina. Overnight this became a flood. Most were poor peasants from northern Italy, with the next-largest group coming from Spain. But Argentina's boom wealth was not shared among these new arrivals, and Argentina remained the property of around 200 close-knit families known as "the oligarchy." The result was a distortion in ownership that has stunted the country's growth and political life.

As the economy expanded, the new-found importance of Buenos Aires allowed it to shed the Hispanic colonial atmosphere and become an expression of all things French. The 16th-century street plan was cast aside and streets widened into grand avenues lined with marble footpaths, cafés, and jacaranda trees. But political and economic inequalities began rising to the surface. Protest movements against the oligarchs' grip produced the middle-class Unión Cívica Radical, forerunner of today's party of the same name.

While tensions grew in the 1920s, Buenos Aires became the cultural

---

FACT

To the disgust of the Argentinian old wealth, the most famous occupant of the Recoleta cemetery in Buenos Aires is the daughter of a provincial nobody – Eva Perón. Thousands visit her tomb every year, in a crypt of black marble which has a single rose laid before it.

Eva and Juan Perón.

A LASTING LEGACY

Rather than fading after he guided Argentina into the Third World, Juan Domingo Perón's legacy surged in the 1980s and continues to dominate Argentine politics. One reason for this is that Peronism's broad, malleable ideology of social justice appeals to the millions of socially disenfranchised low-income Argentines, which has allowed politicians as different as Carlos Menem and Néstor Kirchner to claim allegiance to Peronism. Several political movements lay claim to the label, with intense personal rivalries between the Kirchners and other self-proclaimed Peronists of the early 21st century – Eduardo Duhalde, Carlos Reutemann, and Francisco de Narváez. Conflicts have periodically erupted in violence, infamously at Perón's 1973 arrival from his exile in Spain, when 13 people died.

Poster of Evita Perón at the Evita Museum in Buenos Aires.

mecca of South America. The rich indulged in tango parties and balls rather than worry about social ills. Then the Great Depression hit. Nobody was surprised when, on September 6, 1930, the Argentine military marched into the presidential palace to take power under General José Uriburu. It was the first of many such interventions.

The age of Perón

The military handed power over to a series of conservative governments in the 1930s, allowing the oligarchy to run the country as if nothing had changed in 40 years. Then, in 1943, a group of young army officers staged a successful coup. One of the figures in the new government was a man who founded a movement that still dominates Argentine politics: Juan Domingo Perón.

Perón had joined the army at the age of 16, and later became an ardent admirer of Benito Mussolini while serving as military attaché in Italy. Perón took the post of Secretary of Labor and started to organize trade unions and to champion

disenfranchised and unprotected workers. He was joined by a beautiful actress, Eva Duarte. The daughter of a peasant, Evita shocked high society but was worshiped by the working class for her passionate speeches on their behalf. Thanks to her, women got the vote and a public health service was developed.

Perón became president in 1946, nationalized industries, and started social welfare programs, while Eva toured Europe in jewels and couture dresses as if she were royalty. She died of cancer in 1952 at the age of 33, but the Vatican resisted calls for her canonization. The Perón magic quickly began to wear off: the cost of living surged, government spending went out of control, and corruption was rife. When it was rumored that Perón would distribute arms to the trade unions, the military struck, bombing the presidential palace and forcing Perón to flee on a Paraguayan gunboat. His supporters were purged from every level of government, and even mentioning Perón's name in public was banned.

Mural showing Che Guevara in the San Telmo neighborhood, Buenos Aires.

The "dirty war" and war with Britain

Despite the repression, Peronism lived on through 18 years of equally incompetent military and civilian rule. When full democratic elections were allowed in 1973, Peronist candidates won easily – and invited the aging founder back from exile in Spain to become president once again. Returning in triumph to Buenos Aires, Perón promptly died, leaving the presidency to his third wife, a cabaret dancer known as Isabelita. Argentina's economy nosedived again, guerrilla fighting began in the mountains in Tucumán, and terrorists began letting off bombs and kidnapping prominent figures. The military let the situation drag on until they had popular support for a coup in 1976. Then they began a "dirty war" to purge Argentine society of everyone suspected of left-wing sympathies. As many as 30,000 people were kidnapped, tortured, and secretly executed in the campaign.

But in 1982, with inflation reaching record levels and poverty growing, President Leopoldo Galtieri decided to distract attention by taking the Falkland Islands (Islas Malvinas to the Argentines). The possession of these windswept rocks had been contentious since the British annexed them in 1833. After a brief, bloody war (during which British Prime Minister Margaret Thatcher rejuvenated her own electoral prospects on the back of her zeal to counterattack) the Argentines were defeated and the humiliated military were forced to call democratic elections in 1983.

Radical candidate Raúl Alfonsín won the presidency and guided the country into a new democratic era. In 1989 the Peronist party's candidate, Carlos Menem, won the presidential elections by a landslide. Menem imposed a series of draconian economic reforms and reformed the constitution to allow for his re-election.

Recession and poverty

In 1998, Menem proposed farther reforms to allow himself a third term, despite repeated allegations of corruption, but in October 1999 his 10-year tenure as president ended when Fernando de la Rúa, representing the Unión Cívica Radical, was elected. The recession rapidly worsened and poverty and unemployment rose sharply, with jobless rates at 25 percent, and around half the population below the poverty line. One in four children was suffering from malnutrition in a country capable of feeding 10 times its population.

The country was on the verge of imploding financially, politically, and socially. Bank accounts were frozen, and in December 2001 President Fernando de la Rúa resigned after 27 people died in food riots. Three days later Adolfo Rodríguez Saa was named interim president; he resigned a week later. On January 1, 2002, congress elected Peronist senator Eduardo Duhalde as caretaker-president. Days later, the government devalued the peso, ending 10 years of parity with

FACT

The economy of Argentina, the only country that has fallen from the First to the Third World, proceeds in great lurches and busts tied to the price of its agricultural exports. Inflation in the 1980s led to a collapse followed by a boom in the 1990s, only to slide into a recession and yet another bust in 2001. While it has since recovered, there are few signs that the latest recovery will finally be lasting.

Kids playing in Humahuaca, Quebrada de Humahuaca.

Beef and Wine

You will have heard that Argentina is a carnivore's paradise but you may know less about the wine they produce to go with it.

Steak preparation is regarded as an art, and the *parrillas* (steak houses) on every corner in Buenos Aires can seem more like temples to beef than restaurants. The most extravagant have meat in their windows being cooked in the traditional gaucho fashion, with whole carcasses crucified on metal crosses around a mound of coals. Others have stuffed cows flanking the doorways, and over the tables are posters illustrating the cuts. The most expensive and leanest cut is the *bife de lomo*, roughly equivalent to a sirloin steak in other countries. The popular *bife de chorizo* is cut from the rib near the rump, while a *bife de costilla* is a T-bone.

In a class of its own is the *tira de asado*, which is a strip of rib roast usually large enough to feed two. The *parrillada* is often served at restaurants on a small grill of mixed cuts – for the most committed carnivores. Besides beef, these start off with

Steak and wine at Don Julio parilla restaurant, Palermo Soho.

different types of sausages including *morcilla* (blood sausage) and may also include tripe, kidneys, and possibly chicken.

Vacio comprises the bottom part of what in the US is designated as sirloin, porterhouse, and the flank, and is the juiciest of all cuts. *Matambre* is shaped like a Swiss roll with a vegetable and hard-boiled egg filling. Often served cold, it can be an appetizer, or eaten inside French bread.

If you like your beef rare, order it *jugoso*; medium is *punto*; and well done is *bien hecho*.

Steaks at an Argentine restaurant are unlikely to be sullied by vegetables, gravy, or sauces. The most common accompaniment is a salad, which can vary from lettuce and tomato to a giant mixed extravaganza with artichokes and eggs. For those whose taste buds require a little more than salt and flesh, order the salsa *chimichurri*. This oregano and spice mix is traditionally a gaucho's favorite. The flavor is considered so strong that asking for it often gets a grunt of respect from the most sombre waiter – although the spices are unlikely to surprise most foreign palates. In Patagonia, beef is often replaced by lamb, barbequed on a rack shaped like a St Andrew's cross.

Fine wine

Until recently Argentina's fine wine was one of the country's best-kept secrets, with little being exported, despite being the world's fifth-largest producer. Today, Argentina's wines are being appreciated on dinner tables worldwide. Taken together, a cut of beef with a bottle of red are both a simple meal and part of a gastronomic ritual that goes to the heart of the country's traditions.

Argentina is the sixth-largest consumer of wine in the world and has a wine growing tradition nearly 500 years old. Grown in a long swath east of the Andes from the drier stretches of the north near Salta down to Mendoza and into Patagonia's Río Negro province, wines are both cheap and amazingly good. *Vino común*, served in jugs, is at the rougher end, but you will appreciate any of the inexpensive bottled *vino fino* on the wine list. Around 50 types of wine are produced; many European grapes are used, but Malbec and Torrontes are the local varieties, and the best whites are from Cafayate. One positive thing to come out of the recent economic collapse is an increase in exports from the chief wine-growing region: Mendoza, which has close to 145,000 hectares (360,000 acres) of grapes under cultivation, followed by San Juan to the north. And the United States is one of the biggest foreign consumers.

the US dollar. Three months later, banking and foreign-exchange activity were suspended. Argentina seemed close to economic meltdown.

In 2002, the country defaulted on a $800m debt repayment to the World Bank, after failing to secure IMF aid. Peronist governor Néstor Kirchner won the presidential run-off vote in 2003 when his rival, former President Carlos Menem, withdrew from the race. Accusations of fraud forced Menem to flee to Chile – a familiar South American scenario – but he returned in 2004 when arrest warrants were canceled.

Under Kirchner, Argentina regained its political and economic stability. The country paid off short-term IMF loans, and settled with many of its foreign creditors. Kirchner adopted more trad-itional Peronist policies, expanding state influence over the economy. At the end of 2007, Kirchner stepped aside to leave his wife Cristina Fernández de Kirchner as the Peronist candidate for the presidency. She won the election by a wide margin in the first round, and in December 2007 became Argentina's first elected female president. Her popularity has ridden a roller coaster, waning amid tax disputes with farmers and high inflation that has made Argentina an expensive destination once again. Progressives have applauded her investments in education and for permitting same-sex marriages in 2010. Re-elected in 2011 after her husband's death, in 2012 she seemed increasingly desperate to remain in control of an economy that after a booming decade once again appeared on the brink of a bust.

Sophisticated Buenos Aires

Few countries are so gripped by their capital cities as Argentina is by **Buenos Aires** ㉚. Everyone and everything that passes through Argentina must at some stage come to "the Paris of South America." Sprawling over the flat, empty pampas, by the shores of the muddy Río de la Plata (River Plate), Buenos Aires flaunts its European heritage. It is a city of immigrants who always intended to return home, but still find themselves, somewhat uncertainly, in a remote land. But it is also a city with a creative energy that can almost put New York to shame. In good times or bad, you can see people of all ages enjoying a meal in a restaurant, lining up for a movie, or in deep discussion in a café.

Porteños are a special breed, renowned for their contradictions. Obsessed with style, they turn their city into an open-air fashion parade. They are in love with the theatre, public debate, and the spectacle of politics. Privately, the dramas of the mind exert an endless fascination: Buenos Aires has more psychiatrists per head of the population than Manhattan.

A slice of Europe

Buenos Aires was founded more than 400 years ago, but it was virtually re-created at the end of the 19th century. Riding the beef boom of the 1880s,

Fountain in the Plaza del Congreso.

Sitting at an outdoor café in Palermo.

FACT

Global demand for soybeans has transformed Argentine agriculture. Area cultivated for soybeans more than doubled to 53 percent by 2007 when 10 years earlier, it had been 26 percent. Among other crops, Argentina's fabled wheat production has fallen the most, dropping to 18 percent in 2007 from 30 percent a decade earlier.

the city's Hispanic colonial buildings were leveled and replaced in the image of Paris. It was a time of tremendous wealth: Buenos Aires was a world center of fashion and high art, the cultural mecca of the Americas. But cracks were already appearing, and no sooner was the city built than the decline began. This sense of faded grandeur makes it a fascinating place to wander through. Buenos Aires is not so much a city of sights as of atmospheres, where the main pleasure is to stroll through the neighborhoods, stop for a coffee, stroll on again and absorb the everyday flavor of a city that seems to exist in a world of its own.

El Centro

The center is carved up by wide avenues, lined by jacaranda trees and magnificent buildings that nobody has ever had the money either to knock down or to restore. Bulbous cupolas protrude from roofs, windows are framed by statues of Greek gods, and hidden inside are chandeliers and marble stairways.

The natural spot to start is at the pedestrian walkway of **Florida**, which is crammed at every hour of the day with *porteños* trying to catch glimpses of themselves in window reflections as they pass. It is lined with boutiques selling Argentina's famous leather goods, although shoppers should try to control themselves until reaching the cheaper **Avenida Santa Fe** at the **Plaza San Martín**, where a dramatic statue commemorates one of the only heroes in Argentine history who commands universal respect (see page 36). The better shops in Florida are also at this end, between Avenida Córdoba and Santa Fe. Intersecting Florida is another pedestrian mall, **Lavalle**, with movie theaters, bingo and video-game halls, restaurants, and bargain stores, and which can get clogged with people at night.

The presidential palace is called the **Casa Rosada Ⓐ** (Sat–Sun 10am–6pm) , the Pink House for the tint of its masonry. It stands in the **Plaza de Mayo Ⓑ**, where guards in blue uniforms strut and parade, surrounded by schoolchildren. White headscarves painted on the ground commemorate the Madres de la Plaza de Mayo, who for many years after 1980 marched here every Thursday to demand information from the authorities about their "disappeared" children.

To the east of the Casa Rosada are the recycled 19th-century brick warehouses of the old port of Buenos Aires, now the smart area for working and eating out. An oasis of sun and silence at the edge of the bustle of the banking district, the **Puerto Madero Ⓒ** dockland development is an ideal, if pricey, place for a late afternoon drink on the promenade overlooking the water.

At the other end of the plaza is one of Buenos Aires' few colonial buildings, the **Cabildo**, housing the **Museo Histórico Nacional Ⓓ** (Wed–Fri 10.30am–5pm, Sat–Sun 11.30am–6pm), once the office of the municipal authorities. Inside this whitewashed

Avenida de Mayo, Buenos Aires.

edifice, the city's independence from Spain was declared in 1810. Next door is the **Catedral Metropolitana** , where General José San Martín is buried. The grand **Avenida de Mayo** stretches from here to the **Palacio del Congreso** ❺ (Mon–Tue and Fri 11am–5pm), which looks like the White House in Washington DC. On the way, it crosses the **Avenida 9 de Julio**, which, despite being the widest avenue in the world, manages to be clogged with traffic at most hours of the day. The street's crowning glory is the **Obelisco** ❻, a rather tasteless phallic object around which the city revolves.

The nearby **Avenida Corrientes** is the show-business heart of Buenos Aires, lined with bright lights, Art Deco theaters, and movie-theater palaces dating from the 1920s. Argentines prefer to eat dinner very late, and the restaurants along this street can be packed until 2am, while on Saturday night, the last movie session does not even begin until 1.30am. Corrientes is also noted for its dozens of bookstores, which are crowded with browsers until the early hours of the

morning. The **San Martín Cultural Center** ❼ (daily 8am–9pm) hosts art exhibitions, film festivals, and photographic displays.

A few blocks northeast, on Plaza Lavalle, is the sumptuous **Teatro Colón** ❽, one of the world's great opera houses. If you can get tickets, a performance here should not be missed, if only for the experience of sitting back in wooden armchairs with plush velvet padding, looking out over six gilded tiers and gallery boxes. Guided tours are given daily of the theatre's three floors of underground workshops and the small museum commemorating appearances by such greats as Melba, Nijinsky, Pavlova, and Caruso.

Café society

To understand Buenos Aires, try to do as the *porteños* do: spend as much time as is humanly possible in the *confiterías*, or cafés, of the city, watching the world go by. To the *porteño*, Buenos Aires is mapped out not by streets, landmarks, or barrios, but by key places to sit, write, think, and observe.

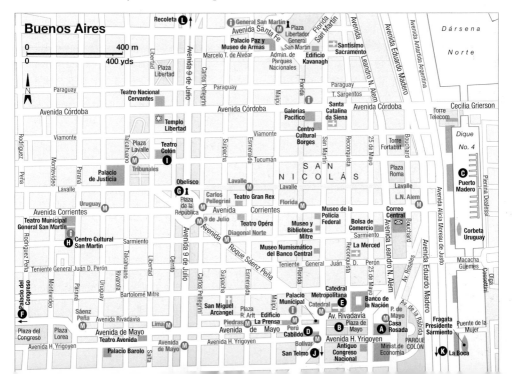

Dance of Passion

The music of sailors and immigrants, tango is undergoing a renaissance both traditional and fused with electronic pop music.

Loneliness and despair, jealousy, and homesickness – all are themes of tango, the most famous musical tradition of Argentina and Uruguay. The accompanying dance is a demonstration of strutting Latin machismo: passionate, erotic, and flamboyant. So closely associated with the history of Argentina (despite strong roots in Montevideo), tango is said to be a distillation of the national character. Where Brazil has the exuberant samba, *porteños* listen to the melancholy tango. Tango lingers like a perfume from another age.

The origins of tango can be traced to the slums of Buenos Aires at the end of the 19th century, where cultures from around the world were meeting – discharged soldiers from Argentina's civil wars, descendants of African slaves, and boatloads of Italian and Spanish immigrants. Overwhelmingly male, the new arrivals gathered in the bars and

Argentinians demonstrate the tango.

brothels. They shared the loneliness of exiles, mixing their national music to create the haunting tango sound. The dance was invented before lyrics were introduced, usually performed by two males waiting in line at the local bordello.

Before long, the tango was gaining popularity among the *porteño* working class. By the early 20th century, the wheezing sound of the *bandoneón* (concertina) had been added to the guitar, flute, violin, and piano of tango ensembles. Writers even began putting their names to tangos.

When the tango reached Europe, mothers in Edwardian England tried in vain to stem the popularity of the sensual dance, with its thrusting hip movements and intertwined limbs. In most of Europe, tango was the rage. And once the dance had succeeded there, the Argentine upper crust accepted it wholeheartedly, agreeing with the French that it must be the very essence of Latin style. A decade later than in the Old World, Rudoph Valentino popularized tango in the US in 1921. The ballroom dances that followed in North America and Europe depart somewhat from the Argentinian original.

Tango renaissance

In 1917, the little-known singer Carlos Gardel recorded the tango *Mi Noche Triste*. Almost overnight, the handsome figure became the first great tango star whose voice was heard around the world. Although arguments continue as to whether Gardel was born in France or Uruguay, he is remembered in Argentina as *El Pibe del Abasto* – the kid from the Abasto district of Buenos Aires. He became a movie star in Argentina, his place in the local pantheon assured when he was killed in an airplane accident in 1935 – as though Gardel were living out a tango himself. Today, new techniques are used to improve his old recordings, and in Buenos Aires they say: "Every day he sings better."

Tango declined in the 1950s until it was pushed in new directions by *tanguistas* like Astor Piazzola. Trained in classical and jazz music, he led a revival with his new, energetic arrangements. In the 21st century, tango is enjoying an extraordinary renaissance. At the beginning of the 1990s, it was danced by aging locals in half-empty venues. Today, it is exciting and fashionable, practiced by trendy youths in steamy, underground dancehalls. Fused with the beats and rhythms of electronic music, it has also been transported into the post-techno age. Groups like Gotan Project and Bajofondo Tango Club lead the charge and tour in other parts of Latin America and in Europe.

Two of the city's oldest and most venerable *confiterías* are located within walking distance of this area. The Ideal, on Suipacha, near Corrientes, was where the once sizable British community in Buenos Aires met for high tea every afternoon. These days you can still have tea and cakes surrounded by polished wood, brass, and marble pillars. Possibly the most famous of the *confiterías* is the Tortoni, on Avenida de Mayo and Piedras. In the 1920s it was the hangout of bohemians such as the writer Jorge Luís Borges, listening to tango music, experimenting with cocaine, and debating politics. Its red leather chairs, sparkling mirrors, and chandeliers have changed little since that time, and every Friday night older patrons gather in a back room to hear the tango again.

Remnants of the colonial city

For a taste of Buenos Aires as it used to be, head for the artistic barrio of **San Telmo** ①, south of the Plaza de Mayo. During the 1700s it was the riverside hub of the city, with one-third of its population black. Its cobbled streets are lined by low buildings, tango bars, and antiques shops.

The most surprising thing about the working-class suburb of **La Boca** ⓚ is the sudden splash of vibrant color. Coming to life in the mid-19th century as the home for Genovese dock workers, this barrio by the river is famous for its houses of corrugated iron, all painted in different dazzling tones. The 20th-century Argentine painter Benito Quinquela Martín was a leading influence in the suburb's use of color, and his home has been turned into a gallery for his paintings of workers. By night, La Boca has a series of gaudy restaurants where bands play renditions of kitsch classics.

The city's upper crust fled to the **Barrio Norte** in the 1870s when yellow fever hit Buenos Aires. Today it is the most elegant and refined of *barrios*, where old ladies in mink coats sit under oak trees at outdoor cafés, and businessmen in European suits arrogantly order waiters about. The neighborhood is built around a

TIP

San Telmo's major event is the Sunday antiques and crafts market that spans several blocks including the main square. Here you can scour hundreds of stalls for unique memorabilia of Argentina's past while live jazz is played in nearby cafés and buskers tango in the streets.

Outdoor refreshments on Plaza Serrano.

giant walled cemetery, the **Recoleta ⓛ**. Hundreds of ornate marble crypts contain the remains of the city's wealthiest families, with giant angels and grim reapers adding to the unsettling effect. The nation's great leaders, as well as their enemies, are buried here. The neighborhood is also home to the city's range of *albergues transitorios* – hotels where rooms are rented out by the hour. Here, overlooking the Recoleta necropolis, local denizens can steal a few hours of sensory gratification.

Taking a break

When the urban rush becomes too much and you feel the need for a view and fresh air, head for the **Costanera Norte**. A promenade runs along the brown Río de la Plata. Fashionable *parrillas* (grillhouses) line the road on the other side of the walkway, for when the exercise loses its charm. In October or November, a classic day can be spent watching polo by heading out to **Palermo** playing fields.

An alternative day-trip venue is the **Tigre Delta**, a weekend refuge for *porteños* of all ages for more than a century. Trains and buses are plentiful from central Buenos Aires, taking passengers to the quiet, tree-lined rivers and canals within an hour. Wooden ferries leave for destinations farther into the delta, where French restaurants and guesthouses retain the genteel atmosphere of the 1930s.

Popular resorts

About 5 hours' drive from Buenos Aires are the Atlantic coastal resorts of Mar del Plata, Villa Gesell, and Pinamar. **Mar del Plata ㉛** is also accessible by air in about 30 minutes from the city. By far the largest of the country's seaside towns, it has an enormous number of hotels at all prices, all of which fill up from mid-December to mid-February.

This very attractive city is the country's most popular resort, and has a long *rambla* (pedestrian promenade) along the coast, beginning at its famous casino. The beach becomes heavily overpopulated in summer, but suburban areas are reasonably peaceful throughout the year. There are numerous *confiterías* and restaurants serving excellent seafood, and a good variety of movie theaters and nightclubs.

Farther north on the coast, **Villa Gesell** and **Pinamar** are much smaller and more peaceful. Both towns have open spaces and wooded areas, in addition to their beaches, Pinamar being the more exclusive of the two, with more nightlife.

Córdoba and its environs

The city of **Córdoba ㉜**, some 700km (435 miles) northwest of Buenos Aires, is one of the country's cultural and religious centers, known for the number of lawyers' offices and seminaries it houses. The university is one of the oldest and most distinguished in Argentina, and the city offers some well-preserved colonial architecture – especially in religious buildings – and an active modern urban life, though parts of the city are decaying.

San Telmo's Sunday flea market.

The lakeside resort of **Villa Carlos Paz**, a former German enclave that still slightly resembles a Bavarian village, lies 36km (22 miles) west, in the green sierras of Córdoba. Villa Carlos Paz is often crowded with visitors in summer and is famous for its busy nightlife. Here, there is a wide range of hotels and restaurants, as well as beautiful scenery and access to the sierra. To the north are **Cosquín**, a smaller town, which hosts the National Folklore Festival every January; and **Río Ceballos**, a quiet place to enjoy the mountains and rivers, and to walk in the Córdoba range, which is less rugged than the Andes. All these towns are easily reached by excursions from Córdoba city.

To the land of wine and sun

Southwest of Córdoba, on the Chilean border, **Mendoza 33** is more a tribute to hard work and ingenuity than to Argentina's natural scenery. An arid province at the foot of the Andes, Mendoza attracted Italian and French settlers in the late 19th century. With encouragement from the progressive provincial government they installed irrigation methods that allowed the province to become one of Argentina's principal agricultural zones. Known as "the land of sun and good wine," Mendoza is the country's principal area of wine production and vineyards, although its prosperity is also based on its significant oil reserves.

Mendoza is not as architecturally interesting as cities like Córdoba, due to earthquake devastation. However, it is by far the cleanest and tidiest city in Argentina, and full of trees planted to dispel the desert image. To the west of the city is the huge **Parque San Martín**, with hillside views of the city, a lake, horse-drawn carriage rides, a local university, and a monument to national hero José San Martín, whose famous Andes crossing to Chile began at Mendoza. Public buses and organized tours go to the bodegas (wineries).

From the central plaza an attractive pedestrian precinct leads past the provincial legislature to **San Martín**, the main street. The attractive **Plaza**

Gaucho at Estancia La Paz, Córdoba province.

Houses in vivid shades in the Caminito area of La Boca, Buenos Aires.

TIP

An excellent way to pass an evening in Salta is at a local *peña*, where traditional food is served and folk music is performed live by local musicians. Among the city's best are El Boliche de Balderrama and La Casona del Molino.

The countryside at Estancia Los Potreros, Córdoba province.

España was donated to the city by the Franco government in the 1940s and displays a beautiful collection of Spanish tiles, as well as an example of the Mendozan obsession with fountains, lawns, and trees. Mendoza is the base for a number of outdoor activities, including pony trekking and skiing, although the most exclusive center for skiing is the **Las Leñas** resort, roughly 400km (250 miles) southwest of the city. Mendoza is also the place to which committed mountaineers come to explore the high peaks of the Andes, with Aconcagua (6,962 meters/22,840ft) the highest of all.

Northern traditions

The north is the only part of this huge country where indigenous people still survive in significant numbers. The region gives visitors a fascinating glimpse into Argentina's colonial past and the Andean countries just across the border. It was here that the first Franciscan monks settled, coming south from Peru and building white-washed chapels in the desert.

Tucumán ❹, 90 minutes from Buenos Aires by air or about 16 hours by bus, is known as the "cradle of independence," because Argentina's freedom from Spain was declared here in the **Casa de la Independencia** (Mon–Sun 10am–6pm) in 1816. Nightly son et lumière shows are held here. On the **Plaza Independencia** is the neo-French style government house and the **cathedral**. Nearby stand the churches of **San Francisco** and the **Virgen del Rosario**. Near the main plaza, on and around Avenida 24 de Septiembre, are various crafts shops and a number of restaurants offering excellent regional specialties. The tourist office and the **Museo Folklórico** (Mon–Fri 8am–1pm, 4.30–7.30pm, Sat–Sun 9.30am–12.30pm) are also on Avenida 24 de Septiembre.

Leaving Tucumán by bus or car for Tafí del Valle, the road winds through mountainous terrain with subtropical foliage, rivers, and waterfalls, as well as the El Cadillal reservoir near Tafí, an attractive mountain village favored by *tucumanos* for summer holidays. To the north of Tafí, the mountain landscape

becomes dry and moon-like before you reach Quilmes, the expansive remains of a pre-Hispanic village and fortress (daily 8am–6pm) dating back to the 11th century.

Some 20km (12 miles) farther north is Amaicha del Valle, one of the few villages in Argentina where indigenous people hold the title to their ancestral lands. The Fiesta de la Pachamama (Mother Earth Festival) is held here in February. Santa María, 10km (6 miles) away, is an attractive place turned boom town by the nearby Bajo La Alumbrera gold and copper mine. About an hour beyond Santa María is Cafayate, a pretty town surrounded by wineries. The arid mountainous scenery between Tucumán and Cafayate (about a 6-hour drive) is among the most breathtaking and varied in Argentina.

Colonial Salta

Salta ❸❺ is an open, relaxed and very Andean town that can be used as a base to explore the surrounding provinces. Neo-colonial buildings line the straight streets that head toward the mountains, often little more than outlines obscured by dust. The center of town is an unexpectedly green plaza with well-preserved Spanish and Italian-style buildings. Most of the city's best colonial buildings are on La Florida and Calle Caseros, including the **Casa Uriburu** (Tue–Fri 9am–7pm, Sat 9am–1.30pm), housing a colonial-era museum; the Iglesia de San Francisco; the Convento de San Bernardo; and the **Cabildo** (city hall), which now houses the **Museo Histórico del Norte** (Tue–Fri 9am–7pm, Sat–Sun 9am–1.30pm, 3–7pm). Most of the rooms are devoted to European–Argentine heroes from the Wars of Independence, with paintings of their deeds alongside medals, vests, and gloves. Much better for pre-Hispanic art and archeology is the modern **Museo de Arqueología de Alta Montaña** at Mitre 77 (Tue–Sun 11am–7.30pm). For an altogether

different view of the city, take the cable car up to Cerro San Bernardo.

Although the north of Argentina is saturated by religion, visitors to Salta may be surprised by the number of churches and statues dedicated to San Francisco. But the town's pride and joy, housed in the **cathedral,** does not relate to St Francis. The Virgin and Cristo del Milagro (Virgin and Christ of the Miracle), are statues carved in the 16th century and credited with miraculous powers. The ship carrying them from Spain was wrecked, but the figures were washed up on the Peruvian shore. Then, in 1692, an earthquake in Salta was dramatically halted when the statues were paraded in the streets. The simple, almost childlike figures are almost lost in the huge Baroque altar. Across the aisle, the faithful pray before a life-sized effigy of Christ fresh from the cross, complete with vast holes in his chest and a virtual fountain of fake blood. Depictions of suffering in colonial religious art had to be horrific if they were to impress indigenous people as being worse than their own lives.

Tempting empanadas (turnovers) at Salta's famous Doña Salta restaurant – which specializes in the cuisine of Salta and the Northwest region.

Vineyard employee during harvest time, Mendoza.

The Train to the Clouds

For a change of pace, one of the most exciting trips from Salta is to take *el Tren a las Nubes* – the Train to the Clouds. Due to the height at which the train travels it is quite common to see clouds underneath its bridges. Fully equipped with a dining car, this poetically named service leaves Salta for a spectacular journey through nearby mountains. It climbs through the barren **Quebrada del Toro** across steel span bridges past the high-altitude indigenous desert town of **San Antonio de los Cobres**, to its highest point at **La Polvorilla** at 4,200 meters (13,780ft). The whole trip takes almost 17 hours, crossing 29 bridges, 13 viaducts, and two zigzags in all and is available throughout the year outside the January to February rainy season.

To the Bolivian frontier

A highway heads north from Salta to **Jujuy** ❸❼. The population becomes more indigenous the closer you get to the Bolivian border, while the road gets rougher, the houses poorer, and the religious imagery stranger. Tiny chapels can be seen in the most remote villages. One of the most curious, in **Uquaia**, contains the *Angeles Arcabuceros*: a painting of angels dressed as 17th-century musketeers.

The road climbs to over 3,000 meters (9,800ft) and the countryside dries out completely along the *quebrada* (gorge) of the **Río Grande**. Odd land formations appear: some mountains are sharp triangles, others seem to spill like molten lava, while still others look like decayed ants' nests. The sides of the gorge range in color from purple to yellow: near the village of **Purmamarca** is the famous "hill of seven colors," while nearby **Tilcara** has a pre-Columbian fortress and is home to numerous potters and weavers. The town of **Humahuaca** ❸❽ is almost in Bolivia. In early afternoon it becomes an empty dust bowl, with winds sweeping in from the valleys to cover everything with orange powder. The only sound comes from the 16th-century church. The town has several guesthouses and restaurants, and is not far from the extensive archeological

Portrait of a young Quechua girl, Humahuaca, Jujuy province.

Iglesia Catedral, Salta's main church on 9 julio square.

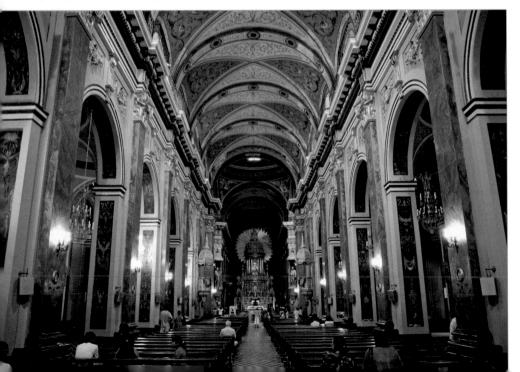

site of **Coctaca**, whose mysteries are still being unraveled.

Humahuaca is dominated by a huge iron monument to Argentina's 19th-century War of Independence. An artistic sleight-of-hand has given native faces to the fierce figures staring down over Humahuaca.

Misiones and Jesuit ruins

Sticking out like a crooked finger from the northeast of Argentina, the subtropical province of **Misiones** boasts some unexpected associations. Graham Greene used its wet and steamy towns as the setting for his atmospheric novel *The Honorary Consul*, where expatriate Britons and South American revolutionaries accidentally meet. The award-winning 1986 movie *The Mission*, which was shot in the area, publicized the province's 18th-century Jesuit empire.

A visit to the region usually begins in the provincial capital, **Posadas** ❸❾, which is accessible from Buenos Aires by daily flights. The town has a Paraguayan handicrafts market and

several museums. A highway escapes north from the town into the rich green countryside, which is kept lush by regular downpours. The road follows the flood-prone **Río Paraná**.

It was in this same region in the 1600s that teams of Jesuit priests began setting up their mission stations (see page 278). At their height in the 18th century, they housed 100,000 of the local Guaraní people, studying, growing grain, and carving musical instruments which became renowned in the finest courts of Europe. Today, the ruins of the greatest Jesuit mission at **San Ignacio Miní** ❹⓿ (Mon–Fri 7am–7pm, with a nightly son et lumière show), just a 2-hour drive from Posadas, are announced by the unfortunate marriage of a piece of Jesuit art caught in a concrete military bridge, designed by a former province governor. The grounds themselves are more tastefully kept. Busloads of visitors wander among the old Jesuit living quarters and cathedral, decorated with indigenous carvings of celestial beings and stars. Outside, the priests' gravestones

The landscape from the Camino de los Colorados trail around Purmamarca.

WHERE

The Argentine Andes has a series of ski resorts from Mendoza in the center of the country down to the forested slopes of Cerro Castor near Ushuaia on Tierra del Fuego. Most are centered around Bariloche, with the ski season running from early July to late September.

bear simple messages: "Here Lies Father Juan, a good man."

Other Jesuit ruins can be found nearby, mostly overgrown by jungle. Sitting among these shattered relics of their religious empire, it is difficult to imagine the experiment that flourished here for more than 150 years. While indigenous people in the rest of South America were being brutally exploited on plantations, here they were working and learning in a system that has earned the praise of many modern socialist writers. The Jesuit priests distributed grain according to need, and arranged indigenous armies to keep out slave traders.

Only when the Jesuits were expelled in 1767 was the fatal flaw of the system revealed. The priests had ruled a paternalistic order, and never trained the natives to run it themselves. With the Jesuits in exile, slave traders were more successful in their incursions, the crops failed, and the Guaraní people fled back into the jungle. Today, many of their descendants have returned to the ruins – selling trinkets and feathers to tourists.

*Market in
Purmamarca.*

Iguazú Falls

The other great attraction of Misiones is a few hours farther up the highway to the border with Brazil: the magnificent **Cataratas del Iguazú ㊶**. The falls can be reached from the commercial center of **Puerto Iguazú**. (A linguistic note: we have used the Spanish spelling, Iguazú, but on the Brazilian side the Portuguese Iguaçu is used.) This spectacle is one of South America's most extraordinary sights. Vast torrents of water thunder over the various cascades with such force that most visitors wear waterproof raincoats for protection from the violent spray. The falls are divided between Brazil and Argentina – while the Brazilian side is most spectacular, the Argentine side is more pleasant to explore – but to see them properly one must visit both sides. If attempting to do so in a day (which is possible, with some effort – and don't forget your passport), it's best to start out on the Brazilian side. Although more removed from the falling waters, the Brazilian vantage point gives a far more panoramic view of the immense cascade. The light there is best in the morning for photographers.

The Brazilian side also gives the best views of the most spectacular section of the falls, the roaring **Devil's Throat**. Fourteen falls combine forces in their 100-meter (330ft) fall, pounding the water below with such force that there is constantly a huge rainbow-spanned cloud of spray hovering above them. Swallows make their nests under the roaring waterfalls. A catwalk on the Brazilian side, reached by a winding foot trail and an elevator, gives more intimate views. Helicopter rides are also available, but they do disturb the local wildlife.

A stop at the Argentine interpretive center can provide much useful information about the falls and the surrounding flora and fauna. A train service takes visitors to the start of two walking trails, which explore the Argentine falls, including one that takes visitors over the water rushing into **Devil's Gorge**. It is also possible to climb down a series of trails and stairways to the river below, where a short (highly recommended) boat trip takes visitors to the island of San Martín, making a pass close to one of the falls. The climb back up is strenuous, and should be attempted only by those in good shape.

The Argentinians have created a national park adjacent to the falls, where there is a jungle trail posted with information, and a bird hide overlooking a swamp. A trek through the park can take most of the day. In the evening, catch a bus to **Puerto Canoas**, where the day's dying light heightens the beauty of Devil's Gorge as swallows dive into their nests in the walls behind the tumbling water.

Iguazú Falls are best visited in fall and spring – summers are intensely hot and the busiest time for tourists, while the water level drops considerably in winter. There are hotels on both the Brazilian and Argentine sides. Near the falls a marker shows the point at which Paraguay, Brazil, and Argentina all converge.

The only sight capable of crowning the Iguazú experience is **Moconá Falls**, where the River Uruguay falls into itself in a fault more than a kilometer (0.5 miles) long, not far from the Brazilian town of **Tenente Portela**. For a panoramic view, take a ferry to Brazil from the Argentine town of **El Soberbio**. Boat trips are on offer in the same town for those craving a close-up white-water view.

Bariloche: Switzerland in the Andes

Strategically placed between the towering Andes and the plains of Patagonia, for 6 months of the year **San Carlos de Bariloche** ⓮ is a booming vacation resort with an unusual alpine flavor. Summer – from December to March – brings hordes of travelers here to enjoy walks among the lush forests, spectacular glaciers, and mountains of the surrounding Lake District. Later, the winter snows (June to September) bring South America's select set of affluent skiers to the Andean slopes, filling Bariloche's restaurants by night with raucous fireside carousing. The

Viewing platform over the Iguazú Falls.

The Gaucho

Proud gauchos, South America's famous cowboys, still herd cattle on vast estancias from grasslands in southern Brazil to Patagonia.

Scattered through the *estancias* of the Argentine hinterland are horsemen wearing a uniform from the distant past: black Spanish hats, woven native-style shawls, and baggy pants known as *bombachas*, and carrying deadly knives called *facones*. They are the last descendants of a breed of South American cowboys, the gauchos.

From the early days of Spanish settlement, individuals disappeared to the countryside and mixed with the local population. Fleeing criminals, escaped slaves, and deserting militiamen lived at the fringes of society and were known as *la gente perdida*: the lost people. They developed their own harsh, nomadic lifestyle on the pampas, taming feral horses to ride and slaughtering escaped cattle, while learning how to hunt with the skillful use of lassos and *boleadoras* or bolas: three or more balls connected by ropes that, when thrown, could

Gauchos herding cattle at the Huechahue Estancia, Patagonia.

wrap around the legs of any running target – weapons used by the native Tehuelches.

From the early 19th century, they became known as gauchos – the name may have derived from the Quechua word huacho (orphan) or from the Mapudungun word *cauchu*, meaning vagabond. They gained a reputation for gambling, horsemanship, and knife fighting. Women, called *chinas*, were often kidnapped from settlements and raised children in small huts indistinguishable from those of the indigenous population.

During the wars for independence, gauchos fought against the Spanish. But in the late 19th century, large tracts of pampas land was distributed to prominent *porteños*. Fences were put up in the grasslands and gauchos were seen as little better than cattle thieves. Many grudgingly signed up as ranch hands, working for subsistence wages on the lands they once roamed.

When the British took Buenos Aires in 1806, many gauchos were pressed into the army. After independence, they joined up with the private armies of provincial caudillos, who allowed them to indulge in their usual drinking, gambling, and knife fighting. But as the era of civil wars drew to a close, the days of the gaucho were numbered. New codes were introduced to regulate their movements, dress, drinking habits, and diet.

Soon the gaucho was a symbol of the backward, chaotic Argentina that the statesmen of Buenos Aires wanted to destroy. Barbed-wire fences hindered their movements still farther – the gaucho was being eliminated as a distinct social grouping.

A lost culture

As this was happening in the 1870s, José Hernández wrote in two parts his classic epic poem, *The Gaucho Martín Fierro*, which lamented the passing of the wild frontier past.

By 1926, when the second great literary work on gauchos appeared, *Don Segundo Sombra* by Ricardo Güiraldes, the gaucho was little more than a literary memory. This does not mean to say that there are not glimpses of their lost culture in the Argentina of today. In the farthest reaches of the country, on remote farms in Salta and Patagonia, ranch hands still wear traditional gaucho dress – even if they are as likely to be driving a pickup truck as riding a horse. Throughout the pampas and Patagonia, rodeos – often drawing participants from as far away as Chile and Brazil – still offer fascinating glimpses into their lifestyle, and powerful displays of horsemanship and camaraderie.

remaining neglected months of the year are perhaps even more delightful: in spring, the valleys of the **Lake District** are filled with flowers and greenery, while fall brings the slow shift of the forest colors to red, orange, cinnamon, and ochre.

The alpine atmosphere attracted Swiss, German, and Austrian settlers at the end of the 19th century. Today, the town itself is a reproduction of a Tyrolean skiing village. Many of the buildings are designed like chalets, while the streets are full of chocolate shops and restaurants offering Swiss fondue, trout, and roast venison. But the real attraction is the surrounding countryside. Bariloche's setting, by the shores of **Lago Nahuel Huapi**, surrounded by jagged brown mountains, is spectacular. In the distance you can spot the towering **Cerro Tronador**, the highest peak in the region at 3,554 meters (11,660ft).

It's a good idea to begin your visit by going to the **Patagonian Museum** near the **Civic Center** (Tue–Fri 10am–12.30pm, 2–7pm, Sat 10am–5pm). It relates the region's history from the days when indigenous nomads roamed the countryside, covered from head to toe in animal grease for warmth, to the arrival of the first European pioneers. Outside in the square is a statue of General Roca, leader of the desert campaign that led to the virtual extermination of local tribes.

Dozens of tour companies offer visits to the surrounding attractions – alternatively, you can hire a car in Bariloche to explore the dirt roads and byways of this magnificent region on the border of Chile. The *circuito chico* or "short circuit" runs out along Lago Nahuel Huapi to the Hotel Llao Llao. Refurbished and reopened after years of neglect, it reflects the glory of its 1940s heyday. Boats run from the docks of Bariloche to **Isla Victoria**, whose myrtle forests are said to have inspired some of Walt Disney's advisers when drawing backgrounds for

Bambi. Continuing around the circuit is the path to **Cerro López**. In summer, the peak can be climbed to a refuge run by Club Andino, where hikers can stay overnight. On a clear day the summit offers spectacular views over the lakes and mountains of the region to Chile. Day trips can also be taken from Bariloche to **Cerro Tronador**, **Cerro Catedral**, **Cerro Otto**, and the waterfalls of **Los Cesares**. The region is world-famous for its trout fishing from November to March, and in summer there is sailing and windsurfing on the lakes.

The wild countryside

Also passing through some of the world's most magnificent scenery is the so-called Ruta de los Siete Lagos (Route of the Seven Lakes), which winds along the border with Chile. It leads to the small town of **San Martín de los Andes** ⓭, a fashionable and more upscale tourist destination than Bariloche, often used as a base for hikes, camping trips, and skiing, and where mountain bikes are available to rent. The return trip over the **Córdoba**

FACT

The great icefields of the Patagonian Andes spawn a series of glaciers that, on the Argentine side, end in great azure lakes. Several are protected in the 24,280-hectare (600,000-acre) Parque Nacional Los Glaciares, notable above all for the Perito Moreno glacier, one of few worldwide that is still growing.

Toucan in the forest in the Iguazú area.

TIP

Recent fossil discoveries have made Argentina a mecca for paleontologists. Little Trelew, near the Península Valdez National Park, has a modern museum exhibiting some of the latest finds, including Argentinosaurus, one of the biggest ever found. The Museo Paleontológico Egidio Feruglio also runs a dig site near Gaiman, showing fossilized remains of seagoing mammals. Another impressive paleontological museum is the Museo Municipal Carmen Funes in Plaza Huincul, Neuquén.

View over Lanin volcano, Lanin National Park, Patagonia.

Pass runs through the lower regions of Neuquén province, much drier and closer to the Patagonian wastes. Fingers of stone protrude from thorny expanses, in what one English traveler in 1920 compared to the prehistoric *Lost World* imagined by Scottish novelist Sir Arthur Conan Doyle. Many of the *estancias* or ranches of the region are still run by the descendants of foreigners and worked by Chilean peons (farmhands) or weather-beaten gauchos, whose ponchos, knives, and *bombachas* are not worn just for tourists.

For a longer excursion, an overnight trip can be made to **El Bolsón**, once a hippy refuge of the 1960s, now a tourist and fishing resort with a twice-weekly handicrafts market. Farther south, a road cuts through the serene **Cholila Valley** to **Esquel** ㊹. First settled by the Welsh, it is now the base for visiting **Parque Nacional Los Alerces** and the gateway to the **Chubut Valley**. The national park, dotted with lakes and crossed by streams, features walking trails and horseback riding opportunities. Standing by the shores of the lake is the **Estancia Nahuel Huapi**,

founded by a Texan cowboy named Jared Jones in 1889. The house, which is still standing, was a refuge for Butch Cassidy and the Sundance Kid, on the run from the Argentinian authorities, having brought their Wild West ways to the new frontier of Patagonia in the early 1900s.

South to Patagonia

Way down at the chilly southern end of South America, Patagonia has for centuries been a byword for the remote and the strange. But today Patagonia is linked to Buenos Aires by daily flights, and by bus for those with enough time to fully appreciate the size of this flat, empty plain that takes up one-third of the country's landmass. Heading south, the rich cattle country dries out and becomes divided into sheep stations. As recently as the 19th century some of these ranches were bigger than small European countries, with their owners ruling like royalty.

First stop is the city of **Trelew** ㊺, surrounded by dry bluffs and dusty scrub. Thousands of Welsh colonists

came here after 1865, fleeing their homeland, where their culture and language were being repressed by the English, to set up a "Little Wales" in the middle of nowhere. Despite some early disasters, the colony began to succeed. The Welsh used their irrigation skills to make the desert bloom, and soon Patagonian wheat was winning prizes at international shows. Welsh was spoken in the streets and taught in the schools. But by the beginning of the 20th century, things were going awry in Trelew. The Argentinian government had imposed its authority on the town and many Spanish-speaking immigrants, attracted by the Welsh success, had arrived with their families. Floods devastated the area's crops. Many settlers left for Canada or Australia, but the core of the community stayed on, their Welsh nationalism slowly being diluted by intermarriage with Spanish speakers.

Today, Trelew looks much like other provincial Argentinian towns, although the street signs are still in Welsh. Echoes of its origins can be found in the old Hotel Touring Club, with cracked windows and an antique wooden bar full of old men playing chess on quiet afternoons. Many of the town's elders still speak in their native Welsh to one another, using Spanish when necessary. The city today sports Argentina's best paleontological museum, **Museo Paleontológico Egidio Feruglio** (Sept–Mar daily 9am–7pm, Apr–Aug Mon–Fri 10am–6pm, Sat–Sun 10am–7pm) with a world-class collection of fossilized dinosaur bones. For a taste of the Welsh colony as it once was, take a half-hour bus ride to the village of **Gaiman**. Built around the irrigation canals that converted the desert into an oasis, Gaiman has a number of Welsh teahouses serving Welsh cream pastries to passing visitors. A small museum located in the old train station is well worth a visit.

Whales and frontier towns

Easily reached from Trelew is the famous **Península Valdés** ㊻, which contains some of the world's most spectacular wildlife. Charles Darwin spent weeks here on his famous

Trekking expedition past the icy walls of Perito Moreno glacier, in the El Calafate area.

View over Nahuel Huapi Lake and the Llao Llao Hotel, near Bariloche.

TIP

Ushuaia is the closest town to the Antarctic Circle, making it a hub for cruise ships that travel to the southern-most continent during the October–April summer months. Shorter cruises to Cabo de Hornos (Cape Horn), the Chilean tip of South America, are also available.

journey in the *Beagle*, and today tourists come to watch the sea lions and sea elephants yawning by the rocky shore, and hundreds of penguins wandering in orderly lines to the sea. During September and October, enormous right whales can be seen throwing up their tail fins as they mate dramatically offshore, while killer whales hunt seals. Inland, groups of *guanacos* and the hare-like *maras* can be seen. At Punta Tombo, south of the beach resort of Puerto Madryn, some 250,000 penguins make their nests. Puerto Madryn itself has a fine, modern museum of the sea, the **Ecocentro** overlooking the bay just south of the center (daily 10am–7pm). It also has a separate **Museo Oceanográfico y de Ciencias Naturales** (July–mid-Sept Wed–Mon 3–7pm, mid-Sept–mid-Dec Wed–Mon 3–8pm, mid-Dec–Feb Wed–Mon 5–9pm).

Traveling south from Trelew, the Patagonian plain below looks increasingly desolate. Towns like **Comodoro Rivadavia** ㊼, once the center of an oil boom, and **Río Gallegos** ㊽, 3,000km (2,000 miles) south of Buenos

Perito Moreno glacier.

Aires, are devoid of rural charm. Unfortunately, because most flights pass through here, many travelers end up spending a night. Nothing much has happened since 1905, when Butch Cassidy and the Sundance Kid held up a bank on the main street.

Changing to a small propeller-driven plane in Río Gallegos, a one-hour flight cuts west across the plains to the foothills of the Andes and some of the most magnificent scenery in South America. The village of **El Calafate** ㊾ is surrounded by snow-capped mountain peaks and sits next to **Lago Argentino**, which looks as if it is full of turquoise milk rather than water. This remote village is enjoying a boom as the stepping-off point to the huge blue glaciers wedged in the forest-covered countryside nearby.

The most famous of these is **Perito Moreno** ㊿, in a national park of the same name, a 50-meter (160ft) high wall of ice that cuts through a lake. It cracks and growls throughout the day, with enormous chunks of ice regularly falling from its side to send waves of water thundering to the shore. The

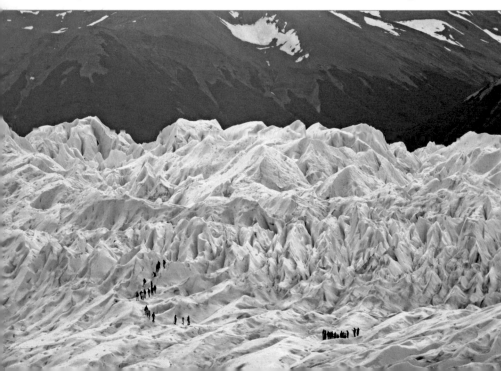

glacier is still advancing in 4-year cycles. Blocking off part of the lake, the water level rises until the glacial wall collapses in a spectacular scene lasting several hours.

From Calafate you can visit the sheep *estancias* of Argentina's deep south, where the occasional gaucho figure still works. Sheep-raising is a key industry in Patagonia, and between October and January, traveling teams of workers arrive for the shearing season. **La Anita** became notorious in 1921, when the whole of Patagonia was paralyzed by a strike of farmhands, known as *peones*. The organizer was a young Spanish anarchist named Antonio Soto, who had wandered through the country from Buenos Aires to Patagonia. The mostly British *estancieros* called on the government for help, and the army ended the strike, with bouts of shooting followed by mass executions. One of the biggest of these was at La Anita – although it has since changed hands, and hardly anybody remembers where the 200 or so workers are buried.

Located a few hours from Calafate is the **Parque Nacional Fitzroy**, where you can pass from the windswept plains to lush and wet forest among the snowcapped Andes. Hikes through the park cross mountain streams and landscapes reminiscent of Scottish moors. Clouds are constantly billowing overhead, but on a good day you can often catch a glimpse of Mount Fitzroy, a sheer knife of granite that is a favorite with fearless mountaineers.

Tierra del Fuego

It is the forbidding image of Tierra del Fuego that paradoxically lures travelers to the southernmost tip of South America. It was named "Land of Fire" by Magellan, who saw mysterious fires glowing in the darkness when he first passed the island – probably the campfires of the indigenous inhabitants. For centuries afterwards, Tierra del Fuego was feared by sailors for the icy Antarctic winds that blew their ships

toward jagged rocks. Few of them considered **Ushuaia** 🔂, the world's most southerly city, an attractive refuge from the storms. Over the years it progressed from a primitive whaling station to a prison colony where Russian anarchists lived out their last days. Today, the land at the end of the world can be reached by daily flights from Buenos Aires and, in summer, from Chile. Ushuaia is no longer the wild and wooly outpost it once was, but more a blend of modern tourist center, duty free manufacturing, and the gateway to one of the world's last great wilderness areas.

The northern half of the island is flat sheep-farming land – much like the rest of Patagonia – but the south is rugged and thickly forested. Surrounded by snowcapped mountains, great Lago Fagnano stretches east to west for 100km (60 miles) from the village of Tolhuin, jutting just inside Chile. Approaching Ushuaia by plane is a suitably dramatic arrival, since the town is surrounded by snowcapped claws of granite. The dominating peak, **Mount Olivia**, would suit

Horseback riding at Estancia Peuma Hue, Patagonia.

a Walt Disney wicked witch, with its mist-shrouded and triangular appearance. The weather lives up to Tierra del Fuego's reputation: even during the 20 or more hours of summer daylight, it shifts erratically from cold drizzle to perfectly cloudless skies, with the only constant being a gusty southern wind.

Ushuaia itself, Argentina's only city on the other side of the Andes, is a picturesque, albeit slightly ramshackle pioneer town with sweeping views of the mountains, the sea, and almost uninhabited Chilean islands to the south. It is home to a large naval base, government offices, and stores for imported and outdoor goods. Houses with decorative cornices, built by prisoners, are still scattered in the older part of town and have a somewhat Russian flavor. They are intermingled with modern concrete structures, imported Swedish prefabs, and hundreds of small, wooden houses. Usable land is in short supply in this area, hemmed in by mountain and sea; new houses climb the mountainsides and many people live

Ushuaia, capital of the province of Tierra del Fuego.

in mediocre conditions. Nevertheless, subsidized building and improvements are going on everywhere. The main street is like an open-air department store, with duty-free electronic goods being offered. One of the town's claims to fame is the Bank of Tierra del Fuego, which is the world's first financial institution to have a branch in Antarctica.

Housed in a former prison, the **Museo Marítimo y Presidio de Ushuaia** (daily 10am–8pm) provides an interesting glimpse into the town's role as a penal colony and the early days of settlement. The **Beagle Channel**, on which the town sits, was named after the ship that carried Charles Darwin here in the 1830s for his famous wildlife studies. Boat trips can be taken on the channel past mountains dropping sheer into the water, circling islands populated by penguins and sea lions. Museo Yámana (daily Oct–Apr 10am–8pm, May–Sept noon–7pm) describes the origins of the indigenous Yámana people and their customs and meetings with European explorers through models and photographs.

Windswept wilderness

Parque Nacional Tierra del Fuego is the main attraction of Ushuaia because of its easily accessible wilderness area. The walking here is simply magnificent, following the spectacular coastline to lakes and glaciers. The park preserves the sense of being at the end of the world, with paths that wind around spongy moss oozing cold water, past tough shrubs and thorny bushes and trees that the wind has bent 45 degrees. The path to **Bahia Ensenada** passes an encouraging altar to the Virgin of Luján, Argentina's patron saint of travelers. There is a camping ground at the rocky beach, where you can breakfast on sweet calafate berries. A boardwalk leads to **Bahia Lapataia**, the end of the road for Argentina. A picturesque narrow-gauge train will take you into the national park along a route formerly used to transport prison inmates to cut lumber for houses.

Almost 30km (18 miles) east of Ushuaia, in a broad, forested valley, is Cerro Castor, Argentina's most modern ski resort. Cross-country skiing and dogsledding are also available in the winter season from June to September, along with the only full-sized ice rink in South America. Three hours' drive from Ushuaia along a winding dirt road is **Harberton**, the first *estancia* on Tierra del Fuego. Founded by the Rev. Thomas Bridges in 1888, it is open to tourists, with guides in English and Spanish. Harberton is worth visiting not just for its history but for the beauty of its setting. Surrounded by trees and flowers, perched above the blue Beagle Channel, it seems like the calmest place on earth.

Back in Ushuaia, shops are full of books on the Fuegian native peoples – Yaganes, Selk'nam or Onas, Haush, and Kawéskar – who lived in the area. In them you can read about the way of life of these very different, seafaring or *guanaco*-hunting nomads, and the violent extinction they suffered at the hands of European (mostly British), Argentinian, and Chilean colonizers at a shockingly late date: the early 20th century. The final certainty of the destruction of these tribes is that the fires now burning in Tierra del Fuego are gas flares from its oil production.

FACT

The Portuguese explorer Ferdinand Magellan, the first European to see Patagonia, reported it to be full of dog-headed monsters and natives with steaming heads.

Stained glass window at Nuestra Señora del Nahuel Huapi Cathedral, Bariloche.

A GRISLY PAST

The good Reverend Thomas Bridges, an Anglican missionary who set up a mission in Tierra del Fuego, spent much of his time in Harberton in the late 19th century working with the Ona people and compiling a dictionary of their complex Yaghan language. To his dismay, he could see before his death that the lists of words would soon be the only monument to those who spoke them. As the British writer Bruce Chatwin noted, Darwin's theory of "survival of the fittest" was put into brutal practice here in the 1890s. The indigenous people of the area, who had lit the fires that Magellan saw, occasionally killed and ate the sheep brought onto their land by European settlers. The newcomers decided to remove this "pest" en masse. Official records show that most of these people died of disease, but the folk memory persists of active resistance, battles, and massacres.

The most grisly tale is of white bounty hunters being paid £1 sterling for each pair of "Indian" ears they took. Old-timers tell of such gruesome characters as the Scotsman Alex MacLennan, nicknamed the Red Pig, who was infamous for his drunken ravings about killing indigenous people. The Englishman Sam Hyslop, who is (dis)credited with gunning down 80 members of the Ona tribe, was caught by natives and flung from a cliff.

Beached boat on the Falkland Islands coastline.

THE FALKLAND ISLANDS

These windswept islands in the South Atlantic were at the center of a war in the 1980s. Still an archipelago of sheep pastures and penguin colonies, they remain a bone of contention.

Main Attractions
Port Stanley
Bluff Cove

Rockhopper penguins (Eudyptes Chrysocome) on Pebble Island, West Falklands.

Some 500km (300 miles) off the coast of Argentina, the Falkland Islands (Islas Malvinas in Spanish) offer treeless, windswept, austerely beautiful landscapes. Attempts have been made to plant trees with little success. The islands offer four seasons in one day, with sun, wind, and rain coming and going in a matter of minutes. There are southern desert-like landscapes, tall grass, and wild flowers, though in places the scenery is marred by signs warning of minefields left over from the 1982 war

(some 17,000 mines remain in certain areas hidden beneath sandy beaches).

The islands have an area of some 12,000 sq km (4,633 sq miles), and a population of around 3,500 *kelpers* (residents, universally of British origin), with 500,000 sheep, plus penguins, geese, whales, elephant seals, and sea lions for company. Some 1,500 *kelpers* live in the capital, **Port Stanley** (Puerto Argentino). The few hundred youngsters who don't live in the capital attend school by radio; teachers visit for 2 weeks a year. There's a monthly mail service to and from Britain.

Disputed territory

Exchanging hands frequently since 1764, Britain has controlled the Falklands and South Georgia Islands since 1834, although Argentina has steadfastly demanded sovereignty, never wavering from its claim that "*Las Malvinas son Argentinas.*" Their name In Spanish however comes from the French Îles Malouines, after the Breton port of St. Malo. Still remote, they do have strategic importance as a base for claims both to Antarctic territory and to offshore oil deposits that have become increasingly exploitable with modern technology.

The 1982 war between the UK and Argentina followed an invasion first of South Georgia then of the Falklands by troops sent by Argentine dictator Leopoldo Galtieri. The war brought about the deaths of 655 Argentines

and 255 British soldiers. Thereafter, the attitude of the *kelpers* to Argentine sovereignty claims hardened still further, with distrust of Argentine politicians reaching new heights. Communications with Argentina were cut off, and it was only in July 2000 that a joint declaration between Argentine and British governments was enforced, permitting Argentines to visit the islands – only relatives of fallen soldiers were previously allowed occasional visits to Darwin Cemetery.

Despite the traumatic experience of the invasion and the emphatic rejection of post-war Argentine overtures by the *kelpers*, who now have British passports, economic life improved after the war, not just because of oil exploration. A permanent garrison of some 2,000 troops has been based in Mount Pleasant since then, an airport, hospital, and secondary school have been installed, and average annual income is around US$20,000, a 700 percent increase over pre-war levels. Economic life centers on fishing – this includes fishing licenses to foreign ships operating in the islands' 240km (150-mile) exclusion zone; agriculture;

and services, especially tourism, which benefits from the spectacular wildlife. Agricultural lands were subdivided and sold by the Falkland Islands Development Corporation after the war, and are now in the hands of local farmers.

One private sheep farm has developed an award-winning museum, Bluff Cove, an hour's 4x4 drive from Stanley, with several thousand penguins on the beach. The museum hosts live music and home baking, rounding out the displays on the Falklands' rural way of life.

Port Stanley is a picturesque, very English, town, with neatly painted houses framed by lawns and flowerbeds, and three churches. It offers various types of accommodations, including two hotels, and a few guesthouses, lodges, and vacation rentals. There are restaurants and bars, too. It also has virtually the only trees in the islands, brought from abroad and laboriously protected from the constant high winds. The port, with its windbreak hill backdrop, steadfastly faces the treacherous Southern Ocean and the still visible wreckage of old fishing vessels.

British telephone box alongside a house in Port Stanley.

INSIGHT GUIDES TRAVEL TIPS
SOUTH AMERICA

ARGENTINA
BOLIVIA
BRAZIL
CHILE
COLOMBIA
ECUADOR
FALKLAND ISLANDS
FRENCH GUIANA
GUYANA
PARAGUAY
PERU
SURINAME
URUGUAY
VENEZUELA

OVERVIEW

GENERAL TIPS ON TRAVEL IN SOUTH AMERICA

Accommodations

South America offers accommodations of all types, from seedy and ramshackle to ultra-luxurious. Very remote destinations tend to have options on the extreme ends of the spectrum, including luxury hotels or jungle lodges, along with dodgy oilmens' hangouts where you won't want to take the kids. In very many places you will be expected to drop toilet paper in a waste basket, not the toilet itself, because the plumbing can't cope. Major cities, particularly the capitals, will tend to have accommodations of the greatest variety, including hostels popular with overseas travelers, along with luxury hotels catering to business travelers. Quality in most countries except Venezuela is improving, and many small hotels will offer guests wireless internet for free – something luxury hotels should do as a courtesy as well. Note that throughout South America, "motels" are establishments that rent out rooms by the hour.

Climate and When to Go

In South America, temperature depends greatly on altitude above sea level, and temperate climates can be found among mountain landscapes away from the coast. Hot temperatures tend to prevail throughout the year in the lowlands, mainly along the coast.

What to Pack

Take light summer clothes if you are heading for tropical zones. Note that shorts and very skimpy tops are frowned upon in churches. In the highlands, a sweater should suffice in the evenings. Take plenty of layers of warm and waterproof clothing if you are heading up into high mountain areas. Good hiking boots are an essential investment for trekking. Pack some high-factor sunscreen and lip salve, and bring or buy a hat. A money belt is handy so that you can avoid carrying all your money in one place. Don't forget rechargeable batteries and a recharger for any electrical equipment, perhaps taking along a multi-outlet charging strip for rooms with just one outlet. Note the differences in electrical current from country to country, with the Andean countries using 110 volts and US-style plugs and the Southern Cone using 220 volts and European-style plugs, with Brazil a mixture of the two. Adapters can be bought easily in major cities and at airports or even on flights.

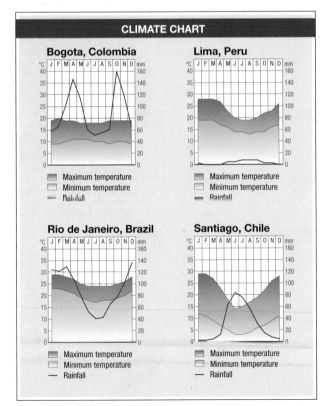

CLIMATE CHART

Bogota, Colombia

- Maximum temperature
- Minimum temperature
- Rainfall

Lima, Peru

- Maximum temperature
- Minimum temperature
- Rainfall

Rio de Janeiro, Brazil

- Maximum temperature
- Minimum temperature
- Rainfall

Santiago, Chile

- Maximum temperature
- Minimum temperature
- Rainfall

Crime and Safety

The crime rate is generally high in South America, but risks can be minimized by taking a few basic precautions. Jewelry should not be worn and large amounts of money and expensive watches should be kept out of sight. Scam attempts abound, including soiling clothes with all manner of substances. Ignore offers of help by passersby and clean up in a safe place. Wear a money belt when traveling. Keep an eye on your possessions at all times and use hotel safes whenever possible (but take a verified list of what you have deposited). Do not leave valuables in cars. Avoid walking alone and in deserted areas after dark. Never carry packages for other people without checking the contents. Radio taxis are safer than curbside taxis after dark.

Traveling alone after dusk is not advisable. Don't hitchhike. For journeys overland choose well-known and established bus companies. Carry your passport at all times – and leave a photocopy in your hotel. For specific inquiries, contact your embassy.

The US State Department and the British Foreign Office both publish detailed information on all South American countries and offer advice to travelers. Their websites are, respectively:

US: http://travel.state.gov
UK: www.fco.gov.uk

Embassies and Consulates

The US and UK have embassies and consulates throughout South America. Ireland has consular services in nearly all the countries. Canada and Australia share embassy and consular services in some smaller countries like Ecuador. For directories of diplomatic services, see the following web pages: US: www.usembassy.gov; UK: www. fco.gov.uk; Canada: www.international. gc.ca; Australia: www.dfat.gov.au; Ireland: www.dfa.ie; New Zealand: www.mfat.govt.nz.

Entry Requirements and Customs Regulations

Visas

Residents from major English-speaking countries rarely need visas to travel in South America, as long as passports are valid for more than six months. US citizens need visas for Bolivia and Brazil. A yellow-fever vaccine at least 10 days before departure is a good idea as it may be requested if traveling between Andean and tropical countries,

A couple at the textile market in Otavalo, Ecuador.

including Brazil. Some countries charge travelers entry fees for visas if their citizens are charged, and the amounts will be similar. It is essential to **check current entry requirements** well in advance of departure.

Customs

In many countries, luggage is X-rayed as it passes through customs, and it is illegal to introduce food and plants. In general, if you are taking $10,000 or more in currency it must be declared. Check with individual country regulations for the introduction of pets. As narcotics smuggling is a problem throughout the region. Be prepared for frequent checks. If you are coming to live in South America, the entry of household goods is likely to be a time-consuming affair in most of the region.

Etiquette

South Americans appreciate courtesy and will be offended by someone who is incapable of saying a simple *"buenos días/bom dia"* (before noon) or *"buenas tardes/boa tarde"* (later in the day), when starting a conversation. Locations such as churches and restaurants may refuse entry to improperly dressed people. Visitors should, in any case, show respect for local sensibilities by not wearing skimpy clothing in inappropriate situations. Visitors should remember that most people they encounter will have had fewer advantages in life and should treat them with the appropriate respect. At the same time, be firm as well as polite when being approached and always ask for prices in advance of any services.

Health and Medical Care

Consult your local public health service before leaving home and be sure to get a certificate for any vaccination you have. The most common illnesses are picked up from contaminated food and water, so you should pay particular attention to what you eat and drink. Be particularly wary of street food.

The quality of tap **water** in much of South America is unreliable. You are advised to drink only bottled or boiled water, or to take purifying tablets.

Hepatitis, picked up from contaminated food and water, is common, and all travelers should get immunized against the disease.

Malaria occurs in jungle areas of South America, so you should take anti-malaria tablets if you are visiting any part of the Amazon, and always wear long-sleeved tops to avoid mosquito bites.

Yellow fever, transmitted to humans by mosquitoes, is prevalent in the whole of South America except Chile, Argentina and Uruguay. You are therefore advised to seek immunization. A yellow-fever shot protects you for 10 years, but is effective only after 10 days, so plan ahead. You may need to show your yellow-fever vaccination certificate if arriving from a country where yellow fever is endemic or risk being denied entry.

Your physician or, in the UK, the Medical Advisory Service for Travellers Abroad (MASTA), tel: 0906-822-4100; www.masta-travel-health.com, will advise you about other tropical diseases that may be endemic in the area you are visiting – such as dengue fever and Chagas disease. All travelers should check that they are inoculated against tetanus, typhoid, and polio.

You should take some form of remedy for **stomach upsets** and **diarrhea**, which is likely to be the main complaint of most travelers. Imodium is a useful travel companion, but note that this medication treats the symptoms rather than the cause. Sipping water with a pinch of salt and sugar added can help rehydrate you after a bout of diarrhea.

ARGENTINA BOLIVIA BRAZIL CHILE COLOMBIA ECUADOR FALKLAND ISLANDS FRENCH GUIANA GUYANA PARAGUAY PERU SURINAME URUGUAY VENEZUELA

The other main cause of illness is the **heat**. Have respect for the power of the tropical sun: wear a hat, use high-factor sunscreen, and be sure to drink plenty of fluids.

Travelers planning to spend time in the Andes should be aware of the dangers of **altitude sickness** (*soroche*). Anyone arriving by air in La Paz, for example, is likely to need several days to acclimatize. Coca tea is a good and legal natural remedy.

Acute mountain sickness (called *puno*) is totally unpredictable – even the fittest people can be affected – and the only solution is to go back to a lower altitude as fast as you can. If you must continue, rest for a few days, drink lots of fluids but do not smoke or consume any alcohol.

Lost Property

Be careful with your property as theft is a problem in many cities and on domestic bus routes. Do not necessarily expect lost property to be returned, but a quick return or telephone call to your hotel or the restaurant you were eating in may well help you recover that misplaced camera lens or trekking jacket.

Money

Changing money. You can change money in banks, *casas de cambio* (exchange bureaux) and larger hotels; *casas de cambio* usually give the best rate of exchange. US dollars are the most convenient foreign cash but avoid denominations greater than $50 notes because they may not be accepted for fear they could be counterfeit or drug money. Also bring only notes in good condition as some exchange bureaux can be sniffy about old ones. It is worth using a calculator or mobile phone, as some rates of exchange run into the thousands.

The Chilean unit of currency is the peso ($ or CHP).

Cash. You will always need to carry some local cash with you, of course, and should think ahead if you are traveling into a rural area for some time, but try not to exceed the amount covered in your insurance policy. It is also advisable to hoard coins and small notes when you get them, as exact change is often in short supply, especially outside the cities.

Credit and debit cards are also widely accepted, with ATMs (cash machines) located in most cities. In Brazil, cards are more convenient to use than traveler's checks. Before leaving home, memorize your PIN number, and check handling fees and cover in the event of loss or robbery. Many establishments also add their own supplementary charges.

Traveler's checks in US dollars have lost much of their convenience with the spread of ATMs. While generally safe and acceptable all over South America, they may not be the best option as there may be high fees and time involved in cashing them. Sterling and euros are not worth bringing unless you are only staying in one of the major cities or the Falkland Islands and French Guiana, respectively.

See the separate Money section under each country for more detailed information.

Finally, it is worth remembering the much-quoted advice: pack half the clothes you think you'll need, but twice the money.

Photography

Digital photography has taken over most of South America, just like the rest of the world, and there are places to print photos or record them onto a CD in most shopping centers and downtown areas of larger cities and tourism hubs like Aguas Calientes near Machu Picchu or Ushuaia in Patagonia. Film is still available in larger centers,

although it can be expensive.

Note that it is forbidden to photograph military sites (including ports, transport terminals, and bridges). It is best to ask permission if you are unsure.

Many people, particularly from indigenous cultures, are sensitive about having their photo taken, so always ask permission first. Others, especially children, are happy to pose but will ask for a tip (*propina/ponta*).

Shopping

Many of South America's best bargains are still to be found in the local markets, particularly in the Andean countries, where prices are low and the choice of goods extensive. Jewelry, textiles, sweaters, ponchos, and leather goods are all widely produced. A certain amount of haggling with traders is expected but be careful not to go too far; think of your income compared to theirs.

Telecommunications

South America has gleefully participated in the global boom in mobile telecommunications, particularly as many state-owned telephone companies were woefully slow to extend service. In most countries, it is possible to buy GSM SIM cards for use with unlocked mobile phones; nevertheless, check to see if your phone runs on the right bandwidth; quad-band phones are the best option.

Access to the internet is common through numerous internet cafés, though it is often painfully slow outside the main towns. Many budget and mid-range hotels also offer wireless internet access. Hotel rates for telephone calls are typically very high in international hotel chains, but there are plenty of kiosks offering telephone services sometimes right on the street. Rollout of 3G networks allows you to use VOIP for long-distance calls.

Tourist Information

While ever-increasing travel information is available on the internet, tourist offices at airports and large bus terminals in the major cities will also have information on accommodations and sights to help you when you arrive. Smaller destinations that have a fair number of tourist arrivals – like Bariloche, Coyhaique, or Cuenca – also have tourism offices in town. Better first-hand information will often be available at smaller hotels catering to foreign visitors than in the more anonymous establishments geared to the needs of businesspeople.

Tour Operators

In the US

South American Explorers' Club, a non-profit organization, publishes monthly updates to travel information across the subcontinent and has clubhouses in Buenos Aires, Cusco, and Quito. There is a yearly member-ship fee of $60 ($90 for couples.) 126 Indian Creek Road, Ithaca, NY 14850, tel: 607-277-0488; www.saexplorer.org. **Exito travel**, specializes in airline tickets to Latin America, 108 Rutgers Ave, Fort Collins, CO 80525, tel: 800-655-4053 from the US, 800-670-2605 from Canada, www.exitotravel.com. **Inka's Empire Tours**, luxury tours to Peru, also Brazil, Chile, Ecuador, 2345 Broadway, Suite 638, New York, NY 10024, tel: 212-787-0500, www. inkas.com. **Latin Discover**, tours from the Amazon to Antarctica and most South American countries, self-driving tours in Chile, 6703 NW 7th St, Miami, FL 33126-6007, tel: 800-791-6520, www.latindiscover.com.

In the UK

Latin American Travel Association, produces a useful guide to South America and lists all the main travel companies who operate there. Tel: 020-8715 2913, www.lata.org. **Dragoman Overland**, adventure group tours. Camp Green, Debenham, Suffolk IP14 6LA, tel: 01728-861 133, www.dragoman.com. **Exodus**, adventure group tours. Grange Mills, Weir Road, London SW12, tel: 020-8675 5550, www. exodus.co.uk. **Explore Worldwide**, adventure group tours. Nelson House, 55 Victoria Road, Farnborough, Hampshire, GU14 7PA, tel: 0845-291 4542, www. explore.co.uk. **Journey Latin America**, flights, tailor-made itineraries, escorted tours, and adventure trips. 12–13 Heathfield Terrace, Chiswick, London W4 4JE, tel: 020-3582 8754, www.

Airlines

The names of the main airlines flying to each country are given in the appropriate section. Check their websites for departure airports and other details. Most flights from Australasia involve a stopover in the US.

journeylatinamerica.co.uk. **STA**, specialists in student and under-26 fares, tours, and hotels, with 400 branches worldwide. Tel: 0871-230 0040, www.statravel.co.uk. **Trailfinders**, long-haul flights and tailor-made holidays. 194 Kensington High Street, W8 7RG, tel: 0845-054 6060, www.trailfinders.com. **Trips Worldwide**, specialists in tours to the Guyanas. 14 Frederick Place, Bristol BS8 1AS, tel: 0117-311 4400, www.tripsworldwide.co.uk. **Western and Oriental**, flights and tailor-made itineraries. Layden House, 76–86 Turnmill Street, London, EC1M 5QU, tel: 020-7666 1260, www. wandotravel.com.

In Australia

STA, specialists in student and under-26 fares, tours, and hotels. 841 George Street, Sydney 2000, NSW, tel: 02-9212 1255, call center 134-783, www.statravel.com.au.

In Canada

Canoe.ca, Canadian online travel service that organizes trips to many parts of South America, 333 King Street, Toronto, ON, M5A 3X5, http://travel.canoe.ca.

In Ireland

Trailfinders, long-haul flights and tailor-made holidays. 4/5 Dawson Street, Dublin 2, tel: 01-677 7888, www.trailfinders.com.

In New Zealand

STA, services as above. 130 Cuba Street, Wellington 6001, tel: 0800 474 400, www.statravel.co.nz.

Transportation

Getting There

The normal way of arrival in South America is, of course, by plane. The main hubs for flights here are Madrid in Europe (where UK passengers join flights booked from London or other UK airports), and Miami and Houston in the US. There are flights to Buenos Aires, Sao Paulo, Santiago and other South American destinations from Sydney, Australia, Wellington New Zealand, Johannesburg, South Africa, and Toronto, Canada. Numerous cruise ships however also call from the Caribbean coast to Tierra del Fuego and the Falkland Islands on the way to Antarctica. Some freighters will also take on a few passengers. There is no way to arrive directly by road as none has been built to cross the Darien Gap between Panama and Colombia.

Getting Around

Sadly, long-distance rail travel has largely fallen into disuse in the region except for a handful of tourist trains. Most travel is done by overland bus or plane, with riverboats playing a great role in the Amazon and the Guyanas. Safety along the main lines has improved much since the 1970s, though irresponsible bus and truck drivers are a problem, particularly in the Andean countries and Venezuela. Car rental is generally quite expensive in countries outside the Southern Cone and Brazil. Driving is relatively straightforward if one is careful to expect the unexpected and drives defensively.

What to Read

Wines of South America by Jason Lowe and Monty Waldin. Comprehensive look at emerging wine-producing regions. **Around South America: By Ship** by Charles R Dillon. A journey through the Panama Canal to every major city on coastal South America. **Where to Watch Birds in South America** by Nigel Wheatley. Excellent reference guide for birders. **The South American Table: The Flavor and Soul of Authentic Home Cooking from Patagonia to Rio De Janeiro** by Maria Baez. Comprehensive cookbook that also touches on culture and geography. **The Explorers of South America** by Edward J. Goodman. Colorful look at nearly 500 years of exploration, with personal accounts.

Other Insight Guides

In the *Insight Guide* series, South America is covered by books on *Argentina, Brazil, Chile, Ecuador, Peru,* and *Venezuela.* There are also *Berlitz Pocket Guides* to *Buenos Aires* and *Rio de Janeiro.*

Women Travelers

While Latin American courtesy dictates a certain deference to women, machismo and prejudice about "liberal" attitudes may easily make some men think that foreign women – particularly those traveling alone – are easily seduced. Advances can be irritating but are rarely aggressive. If politeness fails, it is perfectly fine simply to leave. In the street, refusal to acknowledge "chat-up" attempts usually works, except with the most persistent. It is normally easy and safe to join other travelers on the backpacking circuit.

ARGENTINA BOLIVIA BRAZIL CHILE COLOMBIA ECUADOR FALKLAND ISLANDS FRENCH GUIANA GUYANA PARAGUAY PERU SURINAME URUGUAY VENEZUELA

ARGENTINA

ESSENTIAL TRAVEL TIPS TO HELP YOU GET THERE AND GET AROUND

FACT FILE

Area 2,780,400 sq km (1,074,000 sq miles)
Capital Buenos Aires
Population 40 million
Language Spanish
Currency Argentine peso
Weights and measures Metric
Electricity 220 volts
Time zone GMT -3hrs
Dialing code 54 (Buenos Aires +11)
Internet abbreviation .ar

TRANSPORTATION

Getting There

By Air

From Europe: Aerolíneas Argentinas, Air France, Alitalia, British Airways, Iberia, KLM, Lufthansa.
From/via US: Aerolíneas Argentinas, American Airlines, United.
From Canada: Aerolíneas Argentinas, United, Air Canada, LAN.
Check the airlines' websites for details of departure airports.

Getting Around

From the Airport

Ezeiza International Airport (**EZE**), officially called Pistarini Airport, is the arrival point for all foreign travelers from the US, Europe, Australasia, and Canada. It is about 40 minutes from downtown Buenos Aires. There are buses to the center of the city every 30 minutes, and plenty of taxis, as

well as the **Manuel Tienda tel: 4314-3636** minibus service.

By Air

Local airlines include **Aerolíneas Argentinas, LAN Argentina** (www.lan. com), Sol (www.sol.com.ar) for central Argentina and Uruguay, and **Lineas Aereas del Estado** (LADE; www. lade.com.ar), which serves mostly Patagonian destinations. Airlines in Argentina operate a two-tier pricing structure, which means that foreign travelers pay up to three times as much as locals Jorge Newbery Airport (Aeroparque) is Buenos Aires' airport for domestic flights and Uruguay. Confirmation 24 hours before your flight is strongly recommended. There is a departure tax of around $18 on leaving the country, which will mostly be charged in cash.

By Bus

Bus services are available from Chile, Bolivia, Paraguay, Uruguay, and Brazil, with connections to other countries as far away as Venezuela. Large air-conditioned buses are usually used for long-distance overland travel, but travelers must remember to be vigilant to ensure personal safety.

By Sea

Few cruise ships call at Buenos Aires. Traveling to Uruguay on the ferry is pleasant and inexpensive and, considering travel times to airports, competitive. Options between Buenos Aires and Montevideo are either direct ferries or bus and ferry combinations. **Buquebus** (www.buquebus.com) and **Seacat** (www.seacatcolonia.com) have direct services. Colonia Express (www.coloniaexpress.com) offers bus connections from Colonia to Montevideo. Through the picturesque

Tigre delta from the Buenos Aires suburb of the same name, **Cacciola** (www.cacciolaviajes.com) has departures to Carmelo, while **Líneas Delta** has a service to Carmelo and Nueva Palmira departing at 7:30 a.m.

By Rail

Long-distance passenger services are limited to the **Tren Patagónico** that crosses Patagonia east to west from Viedma to Bariloche (www. trenpatagonico-sa.com.ar) and to Mar del Plata and Bahía Blanca.

Local Buenos Aires trains run to the suburbs. There are four main terminals in the city: **Retiro**, for services to the northern suburbs, San Isidro, Tigre, Capilla del Señor, Zarate, Campana, San Pedro, San Nicolás y Rosario with TBA (Mitre line) tel: 0800-333-3822; www.tbanet.com.ar. **Once**, serves the western part of Buenos Aires, also operated by TBA (Sarmiento line), goes to the western suburbs, Moreno, Mercedes and Luján. **Constitución**, services the southern suburbs, La Plata, Mar del Plata and Bahía Blanca via Ferrobaires tel: 4304-0028; www.ferrobaires.gba.gov. ar. For local trains, **Federico Lacroze**, tel: 4555-1616 or 0800-555-1616.

The journey from Olivos to Tigre on the **Tren de la Costa** (tel: 4002-6000; www.trendelacosta.com.ar) offers great views of the River Plate. Note that service is generally poor and some severe accidents have happened.

By Road

Traveling by car is easy as most of the main roads are paved, but cautious driving is absolutely essential. In Patagonia, headlights must be on at all times on the highways.

The **Automobile Club of Argentina**, in Buenos Aires on Av.

ARGENTINA ◆ 363

ARGENTINA
BOLIVIA
BRAZIL
CHILE
COLOMBIA
ECUADOR
FALKLAND
ISLANDS
FRENCH
GUIANA
GUYANA
PARAGUAY
PERU
SURINAME
URUGUAY
VENEZUELA

Libertador 1850, tel: 4808-4000, is very helpful and can provide maps and useful information.

Hertz, Avis, Travel Rent a Car, and Localiza all have offices at the airport and in Buenos Aires itself, and there are many other rental companies; check www.welcomeargentina.com/ciudadbuenosaires/car-rental.html for a full list. You will need a credit card to be swiped as a deposit.

In Buenos Aires

By Bus

Buses in Buenos Aires are usually prompt and inexpensive, but avoid them during the rush hour. The number and destination are clearly marked on bus stops. Long-distance travel on buses is common. A huge, modern bus terminal is located in Retiro. Information on destinations throughout Argentina can be obtained there from the different companies.

By Taxi

Taxis are black with a yellow roof. The meter registers the fare. Be careful when paying and make sure you receive the correct change.

Remise taxis, or *remises*, are private cars that can be rented, with a driver, by the hour, day, or any other time period. Fares normally work out cheaper than those charged by ordinary taxis. A list of *remise* offices can be found in the telephone directory, and staff at your hotel should be able to provide information too.

By Subway

The subway, or Subte, is the fastest and cheapest way to get around Buenos Aires, and is the oldest in South America, built in 1913. Trains run daily 5am–10pm and tickets cost US$0.57 flat fare per journey. The rides take no more than 25 minutes, and the waiting time is 3–15 minutes.

A–Z

Accommodations

Inflation and an overvalued official exchange rate mean Argentine prices have surged. In addition to hotels, there are also *hosterías*, *hospedajes*, and *pensiones*, which offer more basic but usually clean rooms at cheaper prices. Many of these places are found near bus stations which, although they may be noisy, are convenient. Ask for a room at the back *(en el interior)* if the hotel is on a particularly busy street.

Outside the cities, there are numerous *estancias* (ranches) for those wishing to sample rural life and gaucho culture.

During the summer, in **Pinamar, Villa Gesell,** and **Mar de la Plata,** the huge beach hotel complexes are fully booked and discos and bars everywhere are packed until sunrise. Quiet, undeveloped beaches are only to be found further south near **Bahía Blanca. Mar del Sur,** below Miramar, is a peaceful haven with 40km (25 miles) of sandy beach. Book in advance during the summer months (December through March) and around Easter. Tourist information offices and the websites provide hotel listings.

Arts

Theaters and Concerts

The theater season in Buenos Aires opens in March. Open-air concerts, held in city parks, are very popular on hot summer evenings. South America's premier theater is the **Teatro Colón.** This magnificent theater has a capacity for 3,500 people, with about 1,000 standing. The acoustics are considered to be nearly perfect. Opera and ballet are two of the favorite programs for the season. A guided tour can be arranged by calling tel: 4378-7100. Tours: daily 9am–5pm. Tickets are for sale at the box office on Calle Tucumán. **San Martín Theatre,** Calle Av. Corrientes 1530, tel: 4371-0111, offers plays and musicals, and free music performances and exhibitions in the foyer.

Tango can be enjoyed in venues all over Buenos Aires, and elsewhere. The main art museums are the **Museo de Arte Latinoamericano de Buenos Aires,** for modern and contemporary Latin American art, and the **Museo Nacional de Bellas Artes,** with Argentine and European classic and modern art. Opening times for the major museums are given in the text; most charge an entrance fee.

Budgeting for Your Trip

The following prices should be taken as an approximate guide. The peso may fluctuate strongly against the dollar.

Airport Transfer: an authorized taxi or *remise* from Ezeiza airport into the center of Buenos Aires: $42. Manuel Tienda León bus service from Ezeiza into the center of Buenos Aires: $17.
Car Rental (international company):

Small car: $65 per day. 4x4 pick-up: $161 per day (prices include insurance, mechanical assistance, and value added tax). Insurance must be bought for cars entering from a foreign country before passing through customs.
Gasoline: 95¢ per liter.
Accommodations: The north of Argentina offers by far the cheapest accommodations in the country – around $50 per night for a 3-star double room. In Buenos Aires and the south, accommodations are more expensive and a similar room will set you back $100.
Food: Most restaurants are very reasonably priced. A three-course meal, including wine, at an upmarket establishment will cost around $40 for two people.
Museums and Attractions: Most charge a small entrance fee but some have a free day, and there is often no charge for children.

Children

Good attractions for children include the Atlantic beaches, Iguazú Falls, Patagonia's wildlife – particularly the Península Valdes, the Andean ski resorts, and the Lake District during both winter and summer. Trelew's paleontological museum is also a good place to take children.

Climate

Most of **Argentina** lies within the temperate zone of the Southern Hemisphere. The northeastern part is very humid and subtropical, the northwest is dry and spring-like except for its hot tropical valleys. The pampas are temperate while

Dancers in Buenos Aires.

the southern part of the country gets progressively colder. Tierra del Fuego, however, isn't any colder than Scotland. While traveling light is very useful, South Americans tend to be amused by those tourists who dress as if going on a remote expedition while walking downtown.

Crime and Safety

Argentina is a safe destination in general. Beware of pickpockets and tricks such as spraying someone with ketchup or more disgusting substances in an attempt to lift the victim's wallet. Use caution when withdrawing cash at ATMs. In major cities, you should also be careful when in an unfamiliar area at night; and order a radio taxi rather than picking one up on the street.

Disabled Travelers

In Argentina, airports, large bus terminals, major museums, and international hotel chains have modern access including automatic doors and wheelchair ramps. Many important sites like Iguazú Falls and Perito Moreno Glacier are also at least partially accessible in wheelchairs.

Eating Out

What to Eat

Breakfast includes café con leche (coffee with milk) and medias lunas (croissants, smaller and denser than the French variety). Other types of pastry (facturas) are usually also on offer. Breakfast is usually available from 8am.

Argentina is best known for its beef. The typical meal will begin with empanadas (meat pastries, although the filling will vary according to the region), chorizos (pork and paprika sausages) or morcilla (pork-blood

sausages), and an assortment of achuras (sweetbreads). For the main course, excellent meat dishes such as bife de chorizo (T-bone steak) or tira de asado (grilled ribs) are the most popular choices, accompanied by various salads. To finish off, try a flan (custard), topped with dulce de leche and some whipped cream. Restaurants often offer parrilladas – miniature barbecues – that will feature all of the above. In Patagonia, beef is generally replaced by lamb, while Andean cuisine has a strong influence from Salta northwards.

Restaurants

Practically all towns of interest for tourists have a restaurant district popular with locals and visitors alike. Some of the best asado is served in Buenos Aires. Restaurants open for lunch at noon, and for dinner around 8pm. But no one dines out in the evening before 9pm, with restaurants really coming alive between 10pm and 11pm. At weekends, restaurants stay busy long after midnight. A 10 percent tip is usual; restaurants in more touristy areas may add this to the bill in the form of a service charge.

Embassies and Consulates

The following are in Buenos Aires:
UK
Calle Luis Agote 2412, Recoleta, tel: 4808-2200, ukinargentina.fco.gov.uk/
US
Av. Colombia 4300, tel: 5777-4533, http://buenosaires.usembassy.gov.
Australia
Calle Villanueva 1400, tel: 4779-3500, www.argentina.embassy.gov.au.
Canada
Calle Tagle 2828, tel: 4808-1000, www.dfait-maeci.gc.ca/argentina.
Ireland
Av. del Libertador 1068, 6th floor, tel: 5787-0801 www.embassyofireland.org.ar.

Emergency Numbers

Police 101 (can advise about other emergency services in the area)
Ambulance service 107

New Zealand
Carlos Pellegrini 1427, 5th floor, tel: 4328-0747, fax: 4328-0757, www.nzembassy.com/home.

Entry Requirements and Customs Regulations

Visas

Visitors to Argentina must have a valid passport and return ticket; a visa is not necessary for citizens of the EU, US, Canada, Australia, and New Zealand, who can stay for three months, but passports must be valid for at least six months. Those wishing to extend their trip past the 90-day limit can try leaving the country and returning to get a fresh stamp. This usually works, but is frowned upon if done regularly, and the provision of a stamp is at the discretion of the border guards.

Customs

Duty-free imports include $300 in gifts, 400 cigarettes or 50 cigars, 2 liters of alcohol, 2 bottles of perfume. Travelers under 18 may import half these totals.

Etiquette

In a business environment, handshaking is prevalent. Among friends and acquaintances, women greet other women as well as men with a kiss on each cheek. Among male friends, kisses on the cheek are also common in Buenos Aires. Argentines have what could be called a relaxed attitude towards punctuality.

Festivals

January

Festival Nacional del Folklore, Cosquín, Córdoba province. Annual folk festival. **Fiesta del Lago** Villa Pehuenia, Neuquén province. Celebration of the anniversary of Villa Pehuenia. Parades, sports activities, cultural shows, and concerts.

February

Carnival, celebrated mainly in Buenos Aires and in Gualeguaychú and Corrientes in Misiones in the northeast. There is also a colorful

La Poesía bar and restaurant, San Telmo, Buenos Aires.

Shrove Tuesday procession in Salta.
Festival de Tango, Buenos Aires.
Concerts, tango shows, and classes in venues throughout the city.

March
Festival de la Vendimia, Mendoza. Grape harvest festival culminating in an extravaganza of lights, music, and dancing in an amphitheater set in the Andean foothills.

April
Festival Internacional de Cine Independiente, Buenos Aires. Interesting independent film festival which is helping new talent gain recognition.

May
Arte BA, Buenos Aires. Contemporary art fair hosted by galleries throughout the city.

July
Festival Internacional de Tango, La Falda, Córdoba province. Tango aficionados from all over the world come to this tango festival.

October
Semana Musical, Llao Llao, Río Negro. Held in the beautiful Llao Llao Hotel, this festival brings classical music to the Andes.

November
Día de la Tradición. A celebration of traditional culture with gaucho displays of horsemanship and enormous *asados* throughout Argentina. The largest festival takes place in San Antonio de Areco.

December
Campeonato Abierto Argentino de Polo, Campo Argentino de Polo, Palermo, Buenos Aires. Spring polo season championship.

Gay and Lesbian Travelers

Argentina is rightly considered one of the most gay-friendly countries in South America. Buenos Aires has become a major global destination for gay and lesbian visitors in recent years. The city offers many services and activities directed towards gay and lesbian travelers, including themed circuits of the city, and gay tango and *milonga* nights.

The rest of the country does lag behind a bit and prejudice may be more prevalent in smaller towns and the countryside. For a gay guide to Argentina, visit www.guiag.com or www.thegayguide.com.ar.

Health and Medical Care

Health care in Argentina is good. Hospitals have trained personnel who have studied at home and abroad, and there are excellent specialists in most of the medical fields. Medical equipment is very costly, but all efforts are coordinated in order to maximize benefits. In some sections of the country, the hospitals may not have up-to-date equipment, but what is available is adequate for an emergency. For medical emergencies in the Buenos Aires area, you can contact the following:
British Hospital, Calle Perdriel 74, tel: 4309-6400.
Children's Hospital Pedro Elizalde, Calle M. Oca 40, tel: 4363-2100.
Ricardo Gutiérrez, Calle Gallo 1330, tel: 4962-9247.
Hospital de Clínicas, Calle Córdoba 2351, tel: 5950-8579.

Media

The main local newspapers are *La Nación* and *Clarín*, which are good for Buenos Aires cultural listings. The English-language newspaper is the *Buenos Aires Herald* and there's a free tourist information paper, the *Buenos Aires Times*. There are newspaper and magazine stands in downtown areas of all major cities, selling the major Argentine papers. In Buenos Aires, some foreign papers and international magazines are available.

Money

Casas de cambio will usually accept traveler's checks. ATM dispensers are fairly widespread and major credit cards are widely accepted. US dollars, in cash, may be accepted in small denominations. It is always useful to have some change on hand. Buying dollars is limited by government regulations, leading to a black market where dollars are close to 30 percent more valuable than at the official rate.

Nightlife

Buenos Aires is often labeled the city that never sleeps, but the same applies to most large towns outside the capital. Argentinians are creatures of the night – it is customary for them to have their evening meal between 10pm and midnight and then go out to socialize. Most restaurants do not close until after 2am, while some in the bigger cities are open all night. Movie theaters are also open late, with the last showings at around midnight. In Buenos Aires, the nightlife centers around the San Telmo, Puerto Madero, and Palermo areas. If you are sampling the bar and club scene be prepared to begin your night at 2am and carry on partying until daylight. Lots of the best DJs from around the world come and play Buenos Aires.

Opening Hours

Offices open Mon–Fri 9am–6pm, and banking hours are Mon–Fri 10am–3pm. Stores normally open Mon–Fri 9am–8pm, but are often closed around 1–4pm.

All government agencies and banks close on public holidays.

Postal Services

The main post office in Buenos Aires is on Calle Sarmiento 189, and operates Mon–Fri 8am–8pm. Hotels are the best source of stamps. Check www.correoargentino.com.ar for locations throughout the country.

Public Holidays

January 1 New Year's Day
March/April Good Friday
May 1 Labor Day
May 25 Commemoration of First Government
June 10 Malvinas Day
June 20 Flag Day
July 9 Declaration of Independence
August 17 Death of San Martín
October 12 Columbus Day
November 10 Día de la Tradición
December 8 Annunciation Day
December 25 Christmas Day

Shopping

Argentina offers a wide variety of craftwork, from silver and leather to alpaca wool ponchos.

Buenos Aires
The best-known, and the most touristy, shopping street in the Argentinian capital is **Florida**, with Avenida Santa Fe coming a close second. You'll find the most expensive boutiques in **Recoleta**, the most exclusive part of Buenos Aires, primarily along **Av. Alvear**, **Quintana**, **Ayacucho**, and small side streets. Trendy clothes and design stores are common in Palermo.

For antiques, try **San Telmo**, which has a fair every Sunday. The plaza is surrounded by stalls that sell an array of objects, from cheap to outrageously expensive. Around the plaza are many antiques stores.

Alternatively you could go to one of the many shopping malls (known simply as *shoppings*). **Patio Bullrich** in Recoleta (Libertador 750) offers a selection of chic stores, whilst the enormous **Paseo Alcorta** (Salguero 3172), **Alto Palermo** (Av. Santa Fe 3253), and **Solar de la Abadía** (Acre 940) offer a vast range of shops, from high end to cheap.

Sport and Activities

Many summer and winter sports played in the Northern Hemisphere are also played in Argentina. Team sports include soccer, basketball, and volleyball. The Andes, Patagonia and *estancias* are excellent destinations for horseback riding. Biking is possible in most of the country, and tours are available. The Lake District and Atlantic beaches offer water sports, including surfing, kite-surfing and windsurfing. Hiking and mountain climbing are best in the Andes along almost the entire western border of the country. Winter sports include downhill, snowboarding, and (rarer) cross-country skiing. There are ski resorts in Mendoza, Bariloche and Ushuaia. In winter, there is ice hockey in Ushuaia.

Attendance at a major soccer game, particularly Boca vs River Plate, is a must for a serious fan, but check the security situation beforehand.

Telecommunications

Telephones

There are three cellular phone companies in Argentina: **Movistar**, **Personal**, and **Claro**. All charge about the same. The cheapest way to use a cellphone, if coming from abroad, is to bring your own phone and buy a SIM card once in Argentina.

Domestic calls can be made from public phone boxes using coins or cards. In main cities the **Centros de Llamadas** or *Locutorios* offer telephone and fax services. In Buenos Aires you can make international calls and send faxes from the communications office at Av. Corrientes 705, which is open 24 hours.

Internet

Internet can be accessed at internet cafés (*cibercafés*) all over Argentina.

Tipping

A 10 percent tip is usual in restaurants. In more touristy areas this may be added to the bill. Taxi drivers also expect a small tip.

Tourist Information and Agencies

There are *casas de turismo* (tourist offices) in most big towns. Buenos Aires has the following offices and services:

The **National Tourist Office** is at Calle Santa Fe 883, tel: 4312-2232, www.turismo.gov.ar. Open Mon–Fri 9am–5pm. Other tourist information centers are found at: Diagonal Norte/Florida, Galerias Pacifico, Retiro Bus Station, Ezeiza International Airport, and Jorge Newbery Airport. In these booths travelers can obtain maps of the city and a bilingual (Spanish and English) tourist information newspaper, the *Buenos Aires Times*; it offers complete listings of what is happening.

The provinces of Argentina have offices in Buenos Aires offering tourist information and a ready supply of pamphlets about events, attractions, hotels and restaurants, etc. All the offices in other cities are located in the center of town and can be easily located.

Travel Agencies

ASATEJ, Calle Florida 835, 3rd floor, Office 320, Buenos Aires, tel: 4114-7528, www.asatej.com. Primarily aimed at students, but there's no age limit. Bright and cheerful office with noticeboard brimming with items for sale, travel news, travelers seeking companions.

Eurotur, Calle Viamonte 486, Buenos Aires, tel: 4312-6077, www.eurotur.com. Tours, transport and accommodations for individuals and groups. English spoken; highly professional and recommended.

Kallpa Tour, Calle Tucumán 861, 2nd floor, Buenos Aires, tel: 5270-0010, www.kallpatour.com. Specialists

in trekking, horseback riding, and cultural tours.

Swan Turismo, Cerrito 822, Buenos Aires, tel: 4129-7926, www.swanturismo.com.ar. Long-established, high quality, specialist travel agency, which organizes trips throughout the country.

Websites

www.welcomeargentina.com, comprehensive guide for travel throughout the country.
www.liveargentina.com, in six languages, and easy to use.
www.bue.gov.ar, the government's official website for tourist information in the capital.
www.museos.buenosaires.gov.ar, comprehensive guide to the museums in the capital.
www.interpatagonia.com, excellent guide and listings for the whole of Patagonia

What to Read

The Argentina Reader: History, Culture, Politics by Gabriela Nouzeilles and Graciela R. Montaldo. Comprehensive introduction to history, culture, and society.
In Patagonia by Bruce Chatwin. Chatwin's classic journey.
Buenos Aires: A Cultural and Literary Companion by Jason Wilson. Explores the history of the city.
Motorcycle Diaries: A Journey Around South America by Ernesto "Che" Guevara. The entertaining story of 23-year-old Che Guevara's road trip.
The Perón Novel by Tomás Eloy Martínez. A novel by one of Argentina's top writers depicting the rise and tragedy of Perón's rule in Argentina.
The History of Argentina by Daniel K. Lewis. Covers entire history from pre-Columbian times to 2001.
Insight Guide Argentina. An illustrated in depth guide to the country and its culture.

Boca Juniors football match at the Bombonera stadium, La Boca.

BOLIVIA

ESSENTIAL TRAVEL TIPS TO HELP YOU GET THERE AND GET AROUND

FACT FILE

Area 1.098.581sq km (424,200 sq miles)
Capital Sucre is the official capital but La Paz is the effective capital.
Population 10.4 million
Languages Quechua, Aymara, and Spanish
Currency Boliviano
Weights and measures Metric
Electricity 110 volts in La Paz, 220 volts elsewhere. Check first.
Time zone GMT -4hrs, EST +1hr
Dialing code 591 (La Paz +2)
Internet abbreviation .bo

TRANSPORTATION

Getting There

By Air

From Europe: BoA, LAN, TAM. There are no direct flights to Bolivia from Europe.
From/via US: American Airlines, BoA, Taca.
Most flights involve a stopover in Miami. Check the airlines' websites for details of departure airports.

Getting Around

From the Airport

El Alto, at some 4,000 meters (13,000ft) above sea level on the altiplano above La Paz, is the highest international airport in the world. Taxis to the center take about 30 minutes and currently cost $8. **Cotranstur**

minibuses also go to various points downtown, for about US50¢, but allow about an hour because of all the drop-offs.

By Air

Domestic airlines **TAM**, **Aerocon**, **Boa** and **Amazonas** cover routes between most major towns and cities. Fares are fairly cheap and, if time is short, it is worth flying to avoid a back-breaking bus journey, especially from La Paz to Potosí (you can fly to Sucre then take the 4-hour bus journey to Potosí). **Crillon Tours** offers a comfortable minibus connection that can be arranged in La Paz – their office is at Av. Camacho 1223, tel: 233-7533, www.titicaca.com.

By Bus

The bus network in Bolivia is extensive, being the main form of public transportation for most Bolivians. The quality of service, however, depends on the conditions of roads (of which only some 5 percent are paved) and the terrain covered. Luxury services run between La Paz, Cochabamba, and Santa Cruz; there are quite rough services to Potosí. A wide choice of services are available to Coroico and Copacabana. Toilet stops are few and far between, and the facilities very basic: take toilet paper and hand-wash gel.

Most overland travelers enter Bolivia via Lake Titicaca in Peru. Many firms offer minibus connections between Puno and La Paz. Crillon Tours offers a luxury hydrofoil service both ways across the lake, with a stopover on the Island of the Sun, a meal in Copacabana, and a visit to the Museum of the *altiplano*, with audiovisual displays, which gives an

excellent introduction to Bolivia. If you are taking this route, you may have to change buses at the border.

It is also possible to travel from Argentina by land, crossing the frontier at La Quiaca and continuing by bus or train – a slow but fascinating journey. Reliable, comfortable bus service from Arica in Chile to La Paz takes 4 hours through spectacular scenery.

By Train

Trains run from Oruro to Villazón and Potosí. This is a long journey, so worth paying for a pullman seat if available. Tickets can be bought in advance but schedules change frequently and delays are common.

From Brazil, the so-called **Tren de la Muerte** (Death Train) comes up from Corumbá on the edge of the Pantanal to Santa Cruz. Tickets can be up to 50 percent cheaper at the station than from a travel agent, despite agents' scare tactics. It is advisable to board the train as soon as it is possible to do so.

The train is not particularly comfortable and can take anything from 12 to 40 hours to reach its destination. There are similarly tough rail links to and from Ollagüe in Chile and La Quiaca in Argentina.

In La Paz

By Taxi
For longer distances within La Paz, taxis are probably the best way to get around, either privately, by which you can go anywhere in the city for about $1.70, or caught as *colectivos*, sharing with other passengers along a fixed route for about US25¢ each. It can be very cramped but does save some money.

ARGENTINA

BOLIVIA

BRAZIL

CHILE

COLOMBIA

ECUADOR

FALKLAND ISLANDS

FRENCH GUIANA

GUYANA

PARAGUAY

PERU

SURINAME

URUGUAY

VENEZUELA

A–Z

Accommodations

While Bolivia is the cheapest destination in South America, hotel accommodation here is also more basic than in other countries of the region, and the star ratings system is unreliable. Many small hotels impose curfews as early as 9.30pm in small towns. Rooms in less expensive hotels are rarely heated. Low water pressure is a frequent problem, even in areas now popular with tourists, like Uyuni, so ask in advance about the availability of hot water. Hotels must display prices. More expensive lodgings are called *hoteles*, mid-range accommodations *residenciales*, and at the bottom of the price scale are simple *alojamientos* or *posadas*. There is at least one two-to-three-star quality hotel in all larger cities, and there are modern jungle lodges in the Amazon north as well as a handful of resorts on the shores of Lago Titicaca. La Paz, Cochabamba, Potosí, and Sucre have some lovely hotels in restored colonial buildings. The better hotels in the *yungas* valleys have swimming pools. Book ahead for travel during religious holidays, especially if attending the Carnival in Oruro. It is also a good idea to arrive as early in the day as you can because hotels can fill up quickly.

Arts

La Paz continues to be Bolivia's main cultural hub. Opera, ballet, and classical music concerts are held at the **Teatro Municipal Alberto Saavedra Pérez** on Sanjinés and

Indaburu, with a smaller stage at the adjacent **Teatro Municipal de Cámara**. On Plaza San Francisco the **Casa Municipal de la Cultura Franz Tamayo** and the **Palacio Chico** on Ayacucho and Potosí host exhibitions. The latter also offers concerts. A Baroque music festival is held in the Jesuit missions of eastern Bolivia on even-numbered years.

Budgeting for Your Trip

The following prices should be taken as an approximate guide. The boliviano rate is loosely pegged to the dollar. Budget travelers should expect to pay about $30 a day for two people traveling together.
Airport Transfer: an authorized taxi from El Alto to the center La Paz: $8.
Accommodations: Rates at cheap *posadas* are as inexpensive as $2–5 a night, while mid-range hotels cost $20. Luxury hotels run to over $80. Check to see if the prices include a 20 percent tax and service surcharge.
Food: Most restaurants are quite cheap, but a 23 percent surcharge for tax and services may be added to the bill. A relatively expensive meal will cost $20 for two people. Also expect to pay a 3 percent surcharge when paying with a credit card.
Museums and Attractions: Most charge a small entrance fee. Some have a free day mid-week and most have reduced rates for children.

Children

The extreme altitude of La Paz and the Bolivian *altiplano* means some care must also be taken to allow children to get used to the thin air. Make sure they drink plenty of bottled water and are properly hydrated. Bolivian food tends to

be on the spicy side, which many children won't like. Sunblock and a hat are also essential items, along with insect repellent for warmer climates. Interesting destinations for children include Lake Titicaca, Tiahuanaco, and the resorts of the *yungas*. Many parks in several cities have attractions for children. Older children will enjoy the tropical lowlands of the north.

Climate

In **Bolivia**, the average temperature in the highlands – the most popular area to visit – is 10°C (50°F). Rain falls heavily in summer (November through March) here, but winter (May through November) is very dry. The average temperatures in La Paz are 6–21°C (42–70°F) during summer and 0–17°C (32–63°F) in winter. Warm clothing is a daily essential.

Crime and Safety

Bolivia in general is a safe destination for travelers. Beware of pickpockets in markets and other crowded places frequented by tourists. They may use all kinds of tricks to distract you while they attempt to lift your bag or wallet. Use caution at ATMs. Looking lost and frightened always heightens the risk of drawing attention to yourself. Hiking in most areas should be done in groups. In Santa Cruz, use caution when in an unfamiliar area at night and order radio taxis. Strikes may occur at unexpected times in much of the country, particularly in the eastern half from Beni to Tarija. Travelers planning overland trips should consider that these strikes can force them to stop or turn back at any time. The National Tourism

Dancers at the Oruro Carnival, Bolivia.

Emergency Numbers

Police 110
La Paz Tourism Police 222-5016
Ambulance 118
Firemen 119

Police are posted in the larger cities, with officers that can assist tourists with the filing of documents in emergencies. Some Tourist Police officers speak English, but don't assume that they will.

Disabled Travelers

Impoverished Bolivia is the least-equipped country in the region to provide services for travelers with disabilities. It is strongly recommended that wheelchair-bound travelers book trips through specialized tour operators as few facilities or establishments offer any kind of help.

Eating Out

What to Eat

Bolivian food varies by region. Lunch is the main meal of the day and many restaurants offer an *almuerzo completo* or three-course fixed menu. Staple foods of the highlands are potatoes, bread, and rice. Meats are highly spiced. Trout from Lake Titicaca is excellent. *Picante de pollo* is a spicy chicken dish, *fritanga* is a substantial pork stew, and a delicious dessert is *helado de canela* (cinnamon ice cream). *Salteñas*, sold on the streets rather than in restaurants, are pastries filled with meat and potatoes.

Lunch usually begins between noon and 2pm; dinner starts from 8 or 9pm.

Drinking Notes

The usual tea, coffee, and soft drinks are readily available in restaurants and cafés, as is the *maté de coca* in tea bags.

Bolivian beer, brewed under German supervision, is good, particularly Paceña. The favorite drink of everyday Bolivians is *chicha*, the potent maize liquor produced near Cochabamba. The local spirit *singani* is diluted with lemonade to make a very drinkable *chuflay*. Do keep in mind that altitude intensifies the effects of alcohol – both the intoxication and the hangover. Also remember that many Bolivians drink to get drunk.

Embassies and Consulates

The following are all in La Paz.
UK (also represents New Zealand)
Av. Arce 2732, tel: 243-3424, ukinbolivia.fco.gov.uk/es/
US
Av. Arce 2780, Consulate on Av. Potosí, tel: 216-8000, http://lapaz.usembassy.gov.
Australia
Av. Arce 2081, Edificio Montevideo Mezzanine, Office 2, tel: 297-1339, (mobile/cellphone) 591-7061-0626.
Canada
Victor Sanjinés 2678, Sopocachi, tel: 241-5141.
Ireland
Pasaje Gandarillas No 2667 and Macario.Pinilla, Sopocachi, tel: 241-1873.

Entry Requirements and Customs Regulations

Citizens of most European countries do not need visas and may stay for up to 90 days as tourists; Australians and New Zealanders can stay for 30 days under the same terms. US citizens need visas, which can be obtained at the border and on arrival at La Paz airport. For US citizens, the cost of the visa is $135, and it is valid for several entries over a period of 5 years. The office for visa extensions is at Av. González 240 in La Paz.

Customs

You may bring the following into the country duty-free: 400 cigarettes and 50 cigars or 500g of tobacco; 3 liters of alcoholic beverages; new articles up to the value of US$1,000.

Festivals

January

Alacitas (24). In La Paz, this festival is dedicated to Ekeko, the god of plenty. Craftsmen sell miniatures of the objects worshippers hope to be able to get in the coming year, ranging from cars to houses, diplomas, or airline tickets. They must be blessed by a Yatiri (priest) in order to be effective.

February

Virgen de la Candelaria (2). A festival celebrated throughout Bolivia, but most specially in Copacabana on Lake Titicaca, with dancing and bullfights along with processions and fireworks.

February–March

Carnival. This is celebrated most famously in Oruro's traditional indigenous La Diablada extravaganza. Hundreds of revelers parade and dance in elaborate costumes and masks. In Santa Cruz, it is a Brazilian-style celebration.

May–June

Festividad del Señor del Gran Poder. A religious celebration during which thousands of dancers form processions in La Paz and elsewhere.

June–August

Fiesta de la Virgen de Urkupiña. At varying dates, this 4-day festival is celebrated near Cochabamba in Quillacolla, with dancers in masks and costumes.

September

Spring equinox (21). The equinox is celebrated by indigenous groups in Tiahuanaco as the rays of sun shine on the main portal of the Kalasasaya Temple.

October

International arts festival in Potosí and Sucre (dates vary throughout the month), featuring musical and theatrical performances from international participants, along with presentations of contemporary art, literature, and films. **Celebración de la Vírgen del Rosario** in Tarabuco, Yamparáez province. The biggest festivity in Tarabuco is celebrated with the procession of the Virgin of Rosario, patron saint of music and dance.

Gay and Lesbian Travelers

Bolivia is among the less gay-friendly countries in South America, and conservative attitudes are prevalent even in La Paz and Santa Cruz, more so in rural areas. It is recommended that you take these prejudices into consideration and act accordingly, by exercising discretion.

Health and Medical Care

Gastrointestinal problems are common with travelers, usually from contaminated food and water. Drink only bottled or boiled water and be careful with street food. Medical standards are generally low. Make sure you have medical insurance that will provide you with private medical cover if needed. The main health threat in the *altiplano* is altitude sickness. Though illegal in the US, coca tea is a good, natural remedy. In northern and eastern Bolivia, dengue fever has been a problem, most recently in early 2009. Yellow-fever vaccinations are highly recommended.

Major hotels have doctors on call. The **Clínica Alemana** in La Paz (Calle 6 de Agosto 2821, tel: 243-3676), and the **Clínica del Sur**, Avenida Hernando Siles and Calle 7 No. 3539, Obrajes. tel: 278-4003 are both competent and well-run.

Media

In La Paz, Spanish speakers can choose from the conservative daily *El Diario*, the independent dailies *Hoy*, *Los Tiempos*, *Ultima Hora*, or *La Razón*. Otherwise you will be dependent on the weekly English-language publication the *Bolivia Times*. Other cities have their own local papers.

Money

Exchange your money in either banks or hotels as there is a lot of false currency in circulation and changing of cash in the street is never a good idea. Ask for low-value Bolivian bank notes and only carry small amounts with you. Try to accumulate small change as it is often in short supply. Credit cards are not always accepted outside of major hotels and restaurants so always check in advance if you are hoping to use one. Visa cash advances are possible from the Banco de La Paz in the capital, and most banks in cities have ATMs.

Nightlife

La Paz and the other cities of the highlands are nowadays the best places in South America to experience traditional Andean music in *peñas* (folk clubs), with several located in central areas. More current pop and rock clubs, as well as bars frequented by affluent young people, are along **20 de Octubre** in La Paz and near the zoological garden in Santa Cruz, where the action rarely gets going before midnight. The clientele tend to be quite young.

Opening Hours

Most businesses are open Mon–Fri 9am–noon and 2–6pm, but banks generally close at 4.30pm.

Postal Services

The main post office in La Paz is at Av. Mariscal Santa Cruz and Oruro,

open Mon–Fri 8am–8pm, Sat 8am–6pm, Sun 9am–midnight. The outbound mail is quite efficient. The poste restante *(lista de correos)* will keep letters for three months. Don't forget to take your passport if you are collecting mail.

Public Holidays

January 1 New Year's Day
February/March Carnival
March/April Good Friday
May 1 Labor Day
May/June Corpus Christi
August 6 Independence Day
November 2 All Souls' Day
December 25 Christmas Day

Shopping

Bolivia produces a wide range of interesting craftwork, including tapestries, woolen clothing, and wooden sculptures.

Where to Shop

The **artisans' market** in La Paz is on Calle Sagarnaga, between Mariscal Santa Cruz and Isaac Tamayo, and has a vast selection of craftwork. Most shopping takes place in markets. Vendors will give you a price but they expect a bit of gentle haggling.

Sport and Activities

Considering the altitude, visitors are unlikely to engage in very athletic activity during a visit to the *altiplano*. Tours on mountain bikes are available from La Paz, but you should always check the equipment carefully before you start off. Bolivia is a paradise for hikers and mountaineers alike, with numerous high summits to conquer. If you would rather watch than participate, soccer is by far the most popular spectator sport and a visit to a match is fun.

Telecommunications

Telephones

Telephone calls can be made by satellite to the US and Europe. You can call from your hotel, which is by far the most expensive option, or the **Entel** offices in La Paz, Edificio Entel, Calle Ayacucho 267.

Public telephones, found in all major cities, are the cheapest option. Phone cards can be bought in various denominations. Cellular phones work on the 850 and 1900 MHz bands. The three mobile operators in the country

are Entel, Nuevatel (Viva), and Tigo. Wireless modems can be used in larger cities.

Internet

Internet access is widespread, although not always reliable, and can be very slow.

Tipping

Foreigners are expected to tip about 15 percent in a restaurant (along with the surcharge which is usually added). Tipping is rare in other situations, but taxi drivers will be happy if you give a small amount.

Tourist Information and Agencies

Most tour companies offer trips all over the country. For information on trekking and lists of recommended mountaineering guides, contact: **Andean Summits**, Edificio Luisa No 1009, Muñoz Cornejo and Sotomayor, Sopocachi, La Paz, tel: 242 2106 for trekking and adventure tours. **Andes Expediciones**, Av. Camacho 1377, Edificio Saenz, 3rd floor, Oficina 1, La Paz, tel: 231-9655 is a recommended specialist agency.

Websites

www.bolivia.com, comprehensive information, in Spanish only. www.bolivia.travel/ www.boliviaweb.com, tourist information in English. www.titicaca.com, created by Crillon tours, information in four languages.

What to Read

Marching Powder by Rusty Young. The bizarre world of Bolivian prison life portrayed by an English drug smuggler
Bolivian Diary by Ernesto "Che" Guevara. Weighty narrative of the last, doomed, 11 months of the revolutionary.
Bolivia in Focus: A Guide to the People, Politics, and Culture by Paul Van Lindert.
The Incredible Voyage: A Personal Odyssey by Tristan Jones. The author's account of sailing a small craft from the Dead Sea to Lake Titicaca.
We Eat the Mines and the Mines Eat Us: Dependency and Exploitation in Bolivian Tin Mines by June Nash. As the title suggests, a book on life and death in the Bolivian tin mines.

BRAZIL

ESSENTIAL TRAVEL TIPS TO HELP YOU GET THERE AND GET AROUND

FACT FILE

Area 8,514.877 sq km (3,285,600 sq miles)
Capital Brasília
Population 192 million
Language Portuguese
Currency Real (plural, reais)
Weights and measures Metric
Electricity Mostly 127 volts; 220 volts in Brasília, Florianópolis, Fortaleza, Recife, and São Luis; 110 volts in Manaus
Time zone Major cities and eastern half of country GMT -3hrs (EST +2hrs); Mato Grosso and the north GMT -4hrs (EST +1hr); Acre and western Amazonas GMT -5hrs (EST)
Dialing code 55 (Brasília +61, Rio de Janeiro +21)
Internet abbreviation .br

TRANSPORTATION

Getting There

By Air
From Europe: Air France, Alitalia, British Airways, GOL, Iberia, KLM, Lufthansa, Swiss, TAM, TAP, Turkish Airlines.
From/via US: American Airlines, Delta, GOL, TAM, United.
From Canada: Air Canada (non-stop to São Paulo), United
From South Africa: South African

By Sea
It is possible to travel between the US and Europe and Brazil at the start and end of the Brazilian

cruise season when the ships are relocating. The high season for cruising is December through March and the main ports of call are Rio de Janeiro, Manaus, Recife, Salvador, and Búzios.

Getting Around

From the Airport
Most visitors arrive via São Paulo or Rio de Janeiro. The easiest and safest way to get from the airport to your final destination is to take an official airport taxi, for which you pay a fixed rate in advance according to your destination. You can pay by credit card or cash. If you do choose to take a regular taxi, it's a good idea to first check out the fares posted for the airport taxis, because if your flight coincides with rush hour, there is every chance the airport taxi will be cheaper. Brazilian airports are connected to their city centers and main hotels by regular bus services – both executive air-conditioned buses and standard ones. They are efficient but frequent drop-offs can make the journey a long one.

By Air
Brazil has a good network of domestic flights provided by established companies such as **GOL** (www.voegol.com.br) and **TAM** (www.tam.com.br), as well as budget and regional airlines including **Azul** (www.voeazul.com.br), **Avianca** (www.avianca.com.br), **Trip** (www.voetrip.com.br), **Web Jet** (www.webjet.com.br), and **Pantanal** (www.voepantanal.com.br). All of the larger lines fly extensive routes throughout the country and have ticket counters at the airports and ticket offices in most cities.

There are extensive shuttle services between Rio and São Paulo (with flights every half hour), Rio and Brasília (flights every hour) and Rio and Belo Horizonte (usually about 10 flights per day). Despite the frequency of flights, a reservation is still a good idea.

By Bus
Comfortable and punctual bus services are available between all major cities, and to neighboring countries. While it is a good way to see the countryside, distances are huge, you sit in a bus for several days and nights, and the landscape is not continuously fascinating. Buses on longer routes will stop for meals at regular intervals. Some luxury (leito) overnight services are available between large cities that include on-board service and blankets. On some long routes, there may be only one bus a day or just one or two a week. International service is available from Argentina Bolivia, Paraguay, Uruguay, and (to Manaus) from Venezuela.

By City Bus
The larger cities have special air-conditioned buses connecting residential areas to the central business district, including routes from airports and bus stations that pass by many of the larger hotels. You will be handed a ticket as you get on. Take a seat and an attendant will come around to collect your fare.

Regular city buses are entered through the back door (often quite a high step up) and after paying the cobrador, who will give you change, you move through the turnstile.

Theft is common on crowded buses, particularly in Rio and São

Paulo, even in daylight hours. Avoid the rush hour if you can, don't carry valuables, keep shoulder bags in front of you, and your camera inside a bag. Avoid attracting attention by speaking loudly in a foreign language.

By Boat

Amazon River boat trips last from a day up to a week or more. These range from luxury floating hotels to basic accommodations. Boat trips can be taken on the São Francisco River in the northeast and in the Pantanal marshlands of Mato Grosso, popular for wildlife safaris and for angling.

By Rail

In the southern state of Paraná, the Curitiba–Paranaguá railroad is famous for spectacular mountain scenery. A return trip can be done in a day. Bear in mind that you may not see much on a cloudy day.

In Minas Gerais, antique steam locomotives haul passengers between São João del Rei and Tiradentes on Friday, weekends, and holidays. In the state of Rio de Janeiro, the Mountain Steam Train runs between Miguel Pereira and Conrado every Sunday.

By Taxi

Taxis are the best way for visitors to get around. Radio taxis are slightly more expensive, but safer and more comfortable. In major cities, there are two metered rates. Rate 2 is higher and charged after 9pm and on weekends. Make sure the driver activates the meter before you start, and charges the right rate. Some drivers try to make money from tourists by refusing to put the meter on. If a driver tries to agree a fixed fare in advance, he is probably overcharging you. Insist on the meter being used, or take another cab.

By Car

Car rental facilities are available in the larger cities. The main chains are **Avis** (tel: 011-2155-2846; www.avis. com.br), **Hertz** (tel: 0800-602-7525 toll-free; www.hertz.com.br), and **Localiza** (tel: 0800-979-2000; http:// www.localiza.com). You can rent a car with your regular driver's license. For a relatively modest additional fee you can hire a driver with the car.

The excellent Quatro Rodas (Four Wheels) *Guia Brasil*, available at many newsstands, has maps, city and regional itineraries, and hotel and restaurant listings (in Portuguese). Speeding fines can be high (several hundred dollars).

In Rio de Janeiro and São Paulo

Rio and São Paulo both have good, although not extensive, subway services. Lines radiate from the city centers and are extended by bus links. Maps in the station mean you can find your way without needing Portuguese.

A–Z

Accommodations

Tourist offices can provide visitors with comprehensive lists of hotels in all price ranges.

There is no shortage of excellent hotels and decent hostels in Brazil. The larger cities and resort areas, especially, have hotels run to international standards, with multilingual staff. At all grades, rooms are usually clean and the staff is polite. A Continental-style breakfast is usually included in the price, and sometimes a lavish buffet-style breakfast with fresh tropical fruit and eggs among other things.

In the Santa Teresa district of Rio there is a bed-and-breakfast association called Cama e Café that offers accommodation in attractive homes. The Roteiros de Charme is a small group of hotels and *pousadas*. They are of a very high standard and usually in historical buildings. Attractive, intimate, and with good food, these establishments are likely to offer the most memorable accommodation of your trip. For more information tel: 21-2287-1592; www. roteirosdecharme.com.br.

It is always best to book well in advance, especially if you are visiting during Carnival or a major holiday. Hotels are then full of Brazilian tourists as well as visiting foreigners. Travelers from colder climates often

come to Brazil to get away from the Northern Hemisphere winter, and Brazilians also travel more during the school holidays in the summer months of January and February, and in July. Even if you are traveling to an area that you think is off the usual tourist route, local facilities may be saturated with Brazilian vacationers during these peak months. Hotels can also be unexpectedly full because of local festivals or events at various times of the year.

Campgrounds: If you are interested in camping, contact the Camping Clube do Brasil. Its national headquarters is located at Rua Senador Dantas 75, 29th floor, Rio de Janeiro; tel: 21-2532 0203; www. campingclube.com.br.

Arts

Music and Dance

Brazil has exerted great influence on musical styles abroad, especially jazz. It is easy to buy Brazilian music abroad, but there is much more to discover on the spot.

A huge variety of musical forms have developed in different parts of the country, many with accompanying forms of dance. Bossa nova, samba, *choro*, and *seresta* are popular in Rio and São Paulo, for example. And if you are visiting at Carnival, you will see and hear plenty of music and dancing in the streets, mostly samba in Rio and *frevo* in the northeast. There are also shows all year long that give tourists a taste of Brazilian folk music and dance.

The classical music and dance season runs from Carnival through mid-December. One of the most important classical music festivals in South America, which takes place in July each year, is the Campos do Jordão International Festival in the state of São Paulo.

Carnival parade at the Sambodrome, Rio.

Chaika restaurant in Ipanema, Rio.

Budgeting for Your Trip

The exchange rate for the real has fluctuated wildly since 2002. When oil is expensive, so is Brazil.

Accommodations: Allow $80 upwards per day for two people for accommodation, starting at the hostel or "cheap and cheerful" level.

Food: Budget for $20 per person per day for basic meals in snack bars and inexpensive restaurants, without alcohol; obviously meals in better restaurants cost a lot more, as does ordering wine with your meal.

Local transport: Allow around $15 per person per day for getting around Rio or São Paulo, based on one taxi ride and the rest by bus or Metro.

Museums and Attractions: Most charge a small fee, some have reductions for students and children.

Children

Brazil's vast distances can make travel rather tedious for children. Consider this when planning your itinerary. Remember to take insect repellent, sunblock, and a hat. Taking a child seat with you is a good (if cumbersome) idea if you are going to be renting a car as they may not be available. Good destinations for smaller children include Iguaçú, Rio, and of course the many beaches, particularly Buzios and those of Bahia and the Northeast. Older children will enjoy wildlife-watching adventures on the Amazon and in the Pantanal.

Climate

In Brazil's jungle region, the climate is humid equatorial, with high temperatures and humidity, and heavy rainfall all year round. The eastern Atlantic coast of Brazil, from Rio Grande do Norte to the state

of São Paulo, has a humid tropical climate, but with slightly less rainfall than in the north, and with summer and winter seasons. Most of Brazil's interior has a semi-humid tropical climate, with a hot, rainy summer from December to March and a drier, cooler winter (June to August).

Part of the interior of the northeast has a tropical semi-arid climate. Most of the rain falls during March–May. The average temperature in the northeast is 24–27°C (75–80°F).

Brazil's south, below the Tropic of Capricorn and Rio de Janeiro, has a humid subtropical climate. Rainfall is distributed regularly throughout the year and temperatures vary from 0–10°C (32–40°F) in winter, with occasional frosts and snowfall (but the latter is rare) to 21–32°C (70–80°F) in summer.

Crime and Safety

Brazil has a bad reputation for violence and organized crime, but most of it involves local gangs and drug deals and does not affect tourists. However, while more than a million visitors travel to the country annually without encountering problems, there is reason to be careful. Pickpockets tend to frequent markets and crowded tourist areas, so take care of your bags and wallets, and never leave anything more valuable than a towel lying on the beach. It's a good idea to leave your passport in your hotel safe and just carry a photocopy with you. As elsewhere, use caution at ATMs, and be watchful in an unfamiliar area at night. When driving, it may be better not to wait at red lights after dark to avoid robbery; some major cities like Recife turn red lights to flashing yellow at night for this reason. In Salvador, beggars can be very pushy but are not aggressive.

Disabled Travelers

Airlines provide free wheelchair reception for passengers with disabilities who request it in advance. Laws in Brazil require public places to be wheelchair-friendly, but not all of them are. Many major city centers are gradually equipping all crossings with curb ramps, and some more modern city buses can accommodate wheelchair entry and exit. Some elevators in more modern buildings have Braille numbering for buttons. Travelers with disabilities should expect to encounter difficulties, but can also expect friendly help.

Eating Out

What to Eat

A country as diverse as Brazil naturally has regional specialties. In parts of the south, the cuisine reflects the influence of a German community, while Italian and Japanese immigrants brought their skills to São Paulo. Some of the most traditional dishes are adapted from African or Portuguese foods.

The staples for many Brazilians, however, are rice, beans, and manioc. Although not a great variety of herbs is used, Brazilian food is tastily seasoned. Many Brazilians enjoy hot pepper (*pimenta*), and the local *malagueta* chilis range from pleasantly nippy to infernally fiery.

The most unusual Brazilian food is found in Bahia, where a distinct African influence can be tasted in the *dendê* palm oil and coconut milk. The Bahianos are fond of pepper, and many dishes call for ground raw peanuts or cashew nuts and dried shrimp. Two of the most famous Bahian dishes are *vatapá* (fresh and dried shrimp, fish, ground raw peanuts, coconut milk, *dendê* oil, and seasonings thickened with

Brazil's National Dish

Considered to be Brazil's national dish, *feijoada* consists of black beans simmered with a variety of dried, salted, and smoked meats. Originally made out of odds and ends to feed slaves, nowadays the tail, ears, feet, etc. of a pig are thrown in. *Feijoada* for lunch on Saturday is an institution in Rio de Janeiro, where it is served with white rice, shredded *couve* (kale), *farofa* (manioc-root meal toasted with butter), and sliced oranges.

ARGENTINA
BOLIVIA
BRAZIL
CHILE
COLOMBIA
ECUADOR
FALKLAND ISLANDS
FRENCH GUIANA
GUYANA
PARAGUAY
PERU
SURINAME
URUGUAY
VENEZUELA

bread into a creamy mush); and *moqueca* (seafood in a *dendê* oil and coconut milk sauce). Although delicious, the palm oil together with the coconut milk can be a rich mixture to digest.

Popular all over Brazil is the *churrasco* or barbecue. Most *churrascarias* offer a *rodizio* option: for a set price diners eat all they can of a variety of meats.

Dishes found in the Amazon include those prepared with *tucupi* (made from manioc leaves and having a slightly numbing effect on the tongue), especially *pato no tucupi* (duck) and *tacacá* broth. There are also many varieties of fruit that are found nowhere else. The rivers produce many fish, including piranha.

There is a wide variety of delicious tropical fruits available.

Drinking Notes

Café is roasted dark, ground fine, prepared strong, and taken with plenty of sugar. Coffee mixed with hot milk *(café com leite)* is the traditional breakfast beverage throughout Brazil. Other than at breakfast, it is served black in tiny *demitasse* cups.

While beers are good (*cerveja* is bottled beer; draft beer is *chope*), Brazil's unique brew is *cachaça*, a strong liquor distilled from sugar cane, a type of rum, but with its own distinct flavor. Each region has its locally produced *cachaça*, also called *pinga, cana,* or *aguardente*. Some delightful mixed drinks are concocted with *cachaça*. Most popular is the *caipirinha* – a simple concoction of *cachaça*, crushed lime – peel included – and sugar topped with plenty of ice.

Many of the tropical fruits are crushed to make refreshing juices.

Where to Eat

Lunch time is usually noon–3pm, although some restaurants stay open all afternoon. For local people, this is the heaviest meal of the day. Dinner is 7pm–midnight (locals tend to eat late), but some restaurants stay open until 1 or 2am. Many restaurants in Brazil are closed Sunday evening and/or Monday. It is advisable to make reservations for the more expensive restaurants. A portion is usually enough for two people. It is perfectly acceptable to ask for a doggy bag. *Comida a kilo* restaurants (meaning food by weight) are great, cheap places to get a wide choice of quality dishes.

Embassies and Consulates

UK
Brasília: SES, Sector de Embaixadas Sul, Quadra 801 Conjunto K, tel: 61-3329-2300.
Rio de Janeiro: Praia do Flamengo 284, 2nd floor, tel: 21-2555-9600.
São Paulo: Rua Ferreira de Araújo 741, 2nd floor, Pinheiros, tel: 11-3094-2700.

US
Brasília: Av. das Nações Unidas, Quadra 801, Lote 3, tel: 61-3312-7000.
Rio de Janeiro: Av. Pres. Wilson, 147, tel: 21-3823-2000.
São Paulo: Rua Henry Dunant 500, Chácara Santo Antônio, tel: 11-5186-7000, www.embaixada-americana.org.br.

Australia
Brasília: SES Quadra 801, Conjunto K, Lote 7, tel: 3226 3111, visa information: tel: 1905-280-1437.
São Paulo: Alamenda Santos 700, tel: 11-2112-6200.

Canada
Brasília: SES, Av. das Nações Unidas 16, Quadra 803, Lote 16, s1. 130, tel: 61-3424-5400.
São Paulo: Av. das Nações Unidas 12901, 16th floor, Torre Norte, tel: 11-5509-4343.
Rio de Janeiro: Av. Atlantica 1130, 5th floor, tel: 21-2543-3004.

Ireland
São Paulo: Alameda Joaquim Eugênio de Lima 447, Jardim Paulista, São Paulo/SP, tel: 11-3147-7788

New Zealand
Brasília: SHIS QI 09, conj. 16, casa 01, 71625-160, tel: 61-3248-9900.
Sao Paulo: Alameda Campinas 579,15th floor 01404-000, tel: 11-3141-4169

Entry Requirements and Customs Regulations

Visas

US citizens must apply for a visa in advance; European Union citizens do not need one for up to 90 days.

If you do not need a visa in advance, your passport will be stamped with a tourist visa upon entry. This usually permits you to remain in the country for 90 days. If you apply for a visa in advance, you have up to 90 days after the issue date to enter Brazil.

Emergency Numbers

National (free) numbers
Ambulance 192
Police 190
Fire 193
Civil Defense 199

São Paulo
Women's police station (specializing in crimes against women, staffed by female officers) 11-3976-2908 and 180
State highway police 11-2795-2300

Rio de Janeiro
Women's police station 21-3399-3690 and 180
Coastguard (Salvamar) 21-2253-6572
State highway police 21-3503-9000

Customs

Duty-free imports include: 400 cigarettes or 25 cigars, a maximum 2 liters of alcohol, and gift articles with a total value not exceeding US$500 or equivalent in other currency.

Festivals

Besides national holidays, many religious or historical events are commemorated locally. Each city celebrates the date on which it was founded and the day of its patron saint. Many villages and neighborhoods stage their own regional folk celebrations – usually with music, dancing, and stalls selling food and drinks traditionally associated with the event. Some of the most important festivals are listed below.

January
Bom Jesus dos Navegantes. A 4-day celebration in Salvador starts with a spectacular boat parade.

February
Iemanjá (2) festival in Salvador. The Afro-Brazilian goddess of the sea corresponds with the Virgin Mary.

February/March
Carnival celebrated all over Brazil on the 4 days leading up to and including Ash Wednesday. Dates vary depending on the date of Easter. Most spectacular in Rio, Salvador, and Recife/Olinda.

March/April
Good Friday Colonial Ouro Preto puts on a procession; Passion play staged at Nova Jerusalem.

June

Amazon Folk Festival (15–30)
Held in Manaus. **Festas Juninas**
Street festivals in June and early July
in honor of saints John, Peter and
Anthony, featuring bonfires, dancing,
and mock marriages.

June/July

Bumba-Meu-Boi Processions and
street dancing in Maranhão are
held in the second half of June and
beginning of July. This has become a
huge, spectacular event.

August

Festa do Peão Boiadeiro In Barretos,
São Paulo state. The world's largest
annual rodeo, also country music.
**Festival Literaria Internacional
Parati (FLIP)** International literature
festival in Parati (sometimes held in
July).

October

Oktoberfest in Blumenau, staged by
descendants of German immigrants.
Cirió religious procession in Belém.

December

New Year's Eve (31) Millions gather
on Rio de Janeiro beaches to watch
the fireworks, and to offer gifts to the
goddess Iemanjá.

Gay and Lesbian Travelers

Brazil is a generally tolerant country,
and both Rio and São Paulo have
gay parades that have become
major annual events with a Carnival
atmosphere, attracting people of all
kinds of minorities. Gay and lesbian
travelers will not feel discriminated
against in major city centers. However,
as in most countries, the more remote
rural areas tend to be conservative.

Health and Medical Care

If you need a doctor while you are in
Brazil, your hotel should be able to
recommend reliable professionals.
Many of the better hotels even have
a doctor on duty, who will probably
speak English. Your consulate can
supply you with a list of physicians
who speak your language. Make
sure you have adequate health
insurance before traveling and
check that your plan will cover any
medical service that you may require
while abroad.

No vaccinations or health
certificates are required before
entering Brazil, but if you are going to
the Amazon region or the Pantana you
should have a yellow-fever shot (these

protect you for 10 years, but are only
effective after 10 days).

Most common health problems
suffered by tourists are upset
stomachs and too much sun. Drinking
bottled water will help you avoid the
former, and being sensible about the
length of time you spend in the sun
and the degree of sunscreen you use
will help with the latter. Always wear a
hat in the heat of the day, as well, and
don't get dehydrated.

Media

The Miami Herald, the Latin American
edition of the *International Herald
Tribune*, and the *Wall Street Journal*
are all available on many newsstands
in the big cities, as are magazines like
Time and *Newsweek*. If you have a
smattering of Portuguese, the weekly
magazine *Epoca*, along with *Veja*
and *Isto E* are good sources of local
information.

Money

Using ATMs is generally the easiest
way to obtain foreign currency, and
they are found in cities throughout
Brazil. You can exchange foreign
currency at banks, hotels, and
tourist agencies. If you can't find
one of these, some travel agencies
will change your currency, although
this is, strictly speaking, an illegal
transaction. The few hotels that
exchange traveler's checks generally
give a poor rate. Banks other than
Banco do Brasil will not exchange
reais or traveler's checks into
foreign currency. Stores in major
shopping areas and most hotels
and restaurants accept Visa and
MasterCard/Cirrus cards. Most hotels
will also accept traveler's checks.

Nightlife

The legal drinking age in Brazil is
18, and some bars and clubs may
ask young people for ID. Carry a
photocopy of your passport rather
than the real thing. Many nightclubs
will not allow you to enter if wearing
shorts. Prostitutes frequent many
establishments – particularly those
popular with tourists.

Brazilians love partying so even
in smaller towns there is often a
club staying open later at weekends,
but beware – away from the tourist
routes, people tend to go to sleep
earlier, particularly during the week.

Some bars with live music charge
for entry, typically $5–10 for a popular
attraction, while others may set a

similar minimum spending limit per
person *(consumação mínima)*.

Live music in bars is most
frequently some strain of Brazilian
– samba, *choro*, *frevo*, *pagode*,
sertanejo (country music), and the
ubiquitous MPB, the latter standing
for Popular Brazilian Music, and
covering a host of styles including
"tropicalized" rock'n'roll.

For information on nightlife in the
main cities, see the relevant chapters
in the Places section of this book. But
beware, what is hot and happening
one week can be deserted the
following week.

Opening Hours

Business hours for offices in most
cities are Mon–Fri 9am–6pm. Lunchtime closures may last several hours.
Banks open Mon–Fri 10am–3pm.
Currency exchange offices usually
operate 9am–5.30pm.

Postal Services

Post offices generally open Mon–Fri
9am–5pm, Sat 9am–1pm. In large
cities, some branch offices stay open
until later. The post office in the Rio de
Janeiro Airport is open 7am–7pm.

Public Holidays

January 1 New Year's Day
February/March (movable) Carnival
March/April (movable) Good Friday
April 21 Tiradentes Day.
May 1 Labor Day
September 7 Independence Day
October 12 Nossa Senhora de
Aparecida
November 2 All Souls' Day
November 15 Day of the Republic
December 25 Christmas

Music at Rio Scenarium club.

Shopping

If you're looking for a number of different gemstones, **Brazil**'s tremendous variety is unmatched, and prices are low. If you're not an expert gemologist, it's wise to buy from a reliable jeweler.

The leading jewelers operating nationwide are H. Stern and Amsterdam Sauer, but there are other reliable smaller chains. The top jewelers have shops in the airports, shopping centers, and in most hotels. Leather goods, especially shoes and bags, are another good buy in Brazil; the finest leather comes from the south.

Sport and Activities

Beach sports, from volleyball and soccer in the sand to swimming, kite-surfing, windsurfing, and plain old surfing are wildly popular in the country with South America's longest coastline. Diving is possible near Rio, though best on Fernando de Noronha. Hiking and horseback riding are common in the national parks of the interior like the Chapada Diamantina. Soccer of course is the top spectator sport, followed by Formula 1 racing. Tours and attendance at games in Rio de Janeiro's fabled Maracaná stadium can easily be organized by hotels and travel agents in the city.

Telecommunications

Telephones

Pay phones in Brazil use phone cards (cartão de telefone), which are sold at newsstands, bars, or shops. An orange sidewalk telefone público is for local or collect calls; blue is for direct-dial long-distance calls within Brazil. As elsewhere in the world, the explosion in the use of cellphones has led to a fall in the number of public

pay phones. Several companies offer short-term rentals to visitors that can be picked up at the international airports or delivered to your hotel. Visitors will also be able to use their own cellphones in Brazil as long as their handset is at least tri-band or preferably quad-band. Eight mobile operators work in Brazil. Claro, Oi, TIM, and CTBC, use GSM networks.

Internet

Brazil is very well connected with internet services, and internet cafés are found throughout the country. Connections are slower and more expensive when you get away from major cities.

Tipping

Hotels and the more expensive restaurants will automatically add a 10 percent service charge to your bill, but this doesn't necessarily go to the individuals who served you and were helpful to you. Don't be afraid of overtipping – most employees earn a pittance and rely on the generosity of tourists.

Tipping taxi drivers is optional; most Brazilians don't but drivers will appreciate it if you do. And if your driver has been especially helpful or waited for you, you should reward him appropriately. At the airport, tip the last porter to help you – what you pay goes into a pool.

A 10–20 percent tip is expected in barbershops and beauty salons. Gas station attendants, the men who shine your shoes, etc. should be tipped a small amount, again, depending on the level of service provided.

Tourist Information and Agencies

Embratur is the international arm of the Ministry of Tourism, but mainly

deals with the travel trade, so is not very useful for tourists. Its only interface with the public is its website, www.braziltour.com, which is quite helpful.

Each state and major city has its own tourism bureau, most with staff who speak fairly good English.

Websites

www.brasil.gov.br Brazilian government.
www.brazil.org.uk. Brazilian Embassy in London.
www.brasilemb.org. Brazilian Embassy in Washington.
In Portuguese only:
www.estado.com.br. Estado de São Paulo (newspaper/links)
http://oglobo.globo.com. O Globo, Brazil's most popular newspaper.
www.ipanema.com. Comprehensive information about Rio de Janeiro's attractions.

What to Read

Futebol: The Brazilian Way of Life by Alex Bellos. Wonderful, entertaining combination of history and anecdote that will fascinate even those who have no interest in football.
Pelé Autobiography of the world's greatest and most famous soccer player.
A Concise History of Brazil by Boris Fausto. Covers 500 years of Brazilian history.
City of God: A Novel by Paulo Lins. The book on which the award-winning film was based – life and violence in a Rio slum.
Dona Flor and Her Two Husbands by Jorge Amado. Colorful novel by Brazil's favorite author.
Tropical Truth by Caetano Veloso. The John Lennon of Brazil explains how Tropicalismo revolutionized the country's culture and politics.
Eat Smart in Brazil by Joan and David Peterson. Recipes and vocabulary to help you get the best out of Brazil's food, from abacaxi (pineapple) to patinho de carangueijo ao vinagrete (marinated crab claws).
Brazil: Amazon and Pantanal by David Pearson (Academic Press, 2001). Written by professional biologists, but accessible.
Insight Guide Brazil. An illustrated in-depth guide to the country and its culture, complete with hotel and restaurant listings.
Berlitz Pocket Guide Rio de Janeiro. A short, informative guide to the city and its top attractions, plus a useful listings section.

Fashion boutique in the Jardins area, Sao Paulo.

CHILE

ESSENTIAL TRAVEL TIPS TO HELP YOU GET THERE AND GET AROUND

FACT FILE

Area 756,626 sq km (292,134 sq miles)
Capital Santiago de Chile
Population 17 million
Language Spanish
Currency Chilean peso
Weights and measures Metric
Electricity 220 volts
Time zone GMT -4hrs, EST +1hr
Dialing code 56 (Santiago +2)
Internet abbreviation .cl

TRANSPORTATION

Getting There

By Air

From Europe: Aerolíneas Argentinas, Air France, Iberia, KLM, LAN.
From/via US: American Airlines, Delta, LAN.
From Australia and New Zealand: LAN, Qantas.
From Canada: Air Canada have direct flights; LAN and United indirect ones.

Getting Around

From the Airport

Santiago's main airport for international and domestic flights is **Arturo Merino Benítez Airport**, 26km (16 miles) west of the city. There are frequent buses from the airport for about $1.50, and shuttle buses, which cost around $12. If taking a taxi, use the official service, which has a desk close to the arrivals

exit. A taxi to the center of town should cost around $20.

By Air

Flying long distances in Chile is rather expensive, although cheap offers may be available. Domestic flights are operated by **LAN** (www.lan.com; tel: 600-526-2000), **Sky** (www.skyairline.cl; tel: 600-600-2828), and **PAL** (www.palair.cl; tel: 2-651-0600).

By Bus

Chile's private intercity bus services are generally good. In Santiago, check which terminal your bus leaves from, as there are several, all on the main subway line. During off-peak times, you can bargain for a cheaper fare; always ask before you pay full fare. Book well ahead of long weekends and major holidays, during which prices may double.

By Train

The remaining services cover only destinations between Santiago and Temuco in the south and a few suburban routes. All trains leave from Santiago's Estación Central.

Train timetables can be obtained and bookings made by calling 600-585-5000/585-5990, or in person at Estación Central, Av. B. O'Higgins 3170, Mon–Sun 7am–10.30pm, or at the railway office in the Universidad de Chile metro station (tel: 585-5494), Mon–Fri 9am–8pm and Saturday 9am–2pm.

In Santiago

By Bus and Metro

Santiago's bus routes run on short feeder routes that connect with trunk routes along major arteries, served by larger articulated buses, and the

metro. Fares are paid using a prepaid smartcard which can be purchased at metro stations and many shops. One fare, currently around $1.30, covers up to three connections (only one of which can be to the subway), within a 2-hour period. Avoid the crushing rush hours.

By Taxi

Black taxis with yellow roofs can be flagged down in the street, and all run on meters. It is good to have a map as drivers are often not particularly knowledgeable. Women on their own at night should call a radio taxi. Tipping the driver is not customary, but it is usual to round up the fare. Collective taxis (*colectivos*) have a fixed route similar to buses and may carry up to five passengers. The fare is displayed on the windshield.

A–Z

Accommodations

Chilean hotels are relatively expensive for South America and quality varies as hotel ratings aren't obligatory. Hostels with public kitchens are most common in southern Chile. The busy seasons are the summer months (December–March) and the week around the Independence Day holiday, on September 18. You will find establishments called *hosterías*, *hospejades* and *residenciales*: There's not much difference between *hosterías* and hotels, but *residenciales* are more basic affairs. At an *hospedaje*, you'll get a room in a private house, but

Le Filou de Montpellier Restaurant, Cerro Alegre, Valparaíso.

standards vary a lot. Hotels on Easter Island are both expensive and mediocre. Many local families also rent out cabins or rooms; these are best chosen on arrival (and after inspection) from among the many offers touted at the airport. Non-residents are freed from paying Chilean value-added taxes in hotels.

Arts

Santiago

The best theaters are the traditional **Teatro Municipal** in downtown Santiago (though it doesn't have a resident symphony orchestra; international artists perform here sporadically), the **Centro Cultural Matucana 100**, **Teatro La Comedia**, and **Teatro Antonio Varas**. The main fine art museums are in Parque Forestal and near La Moneda. There are several art galleries in the wealthy Vitacura neighborhood on Alonso de Córdova and on Nueva Costanera.

Budgeting for Your Trip

The following should be taken as an approximate guide. The peso may fluctuate strongly against the dollar and Chile is relatively expensive by South American standards.
Accommodations: Budget hotels and hostels cost around $18–25, mid-range hotels approximately $40. Foreign tourists don't have to pay the

18 percent value-added tax charged at mid- to higher-range hotels.
Food: An inexpensive lunch in downtown Santiago will cost about $5 per person, while you can easily pay $25 per person in more expensive places, the same as a moderately expensive dinner. Beer will cost about $2, pisco sour or a glass of moderately expensive wine $5.
Transport: Taxis from the airport to downtown cost $20 and close to $30 for eastern Santiago. Airport transfers take more time but cost approximately half the price of the taxi. Car rental prices vary, with the major brands competing with local outlets and a small car costing $300 per week. Gasoline costs approximately $1.6 per liter but becomes much more expensive away from the main towns.
Museums and Attractions: Budget for these to each cost a couple of dollars, although some are free.

Children

A child seat is obligatory for children in cars, but as a relatively recent rule it is only gradually being enforced. Good destinations for smaller children include the Lake District and the Pacific coast beaches. Santiago has several large parks including the **Parque Intercomunal** in the La Reina neighborhood and the largest, **Parque Metropolitano**, on a ridge overlooking downtown Santiago and Providencia that has a funicular, cable car, zoo, and two outdoor swimming pools. Booking a hotel with a swimming pool can be a good investment.

Climate

Chile's central valley, including Santiago and the central coast (Valparaíso, Viña del Mar), have a Mediterranean climate with hot summers (January–February) and mild winters. It can feel quite cold as housing isn't well-heated or insulated from cold. Smog can be a serious problem in Santiago, particularly in winter, while the Andes become covered in snow.

In the Atacama Desert, the days are very hot and the nights extremely cold. In March, a phenomenon known as the Invierno Boliviano (Bolivian winter) can lead to rain and flash flooding.

The Lake District has a pleasant temperate climate, but winds can be chilly. The mountains are cold and it rains a lot. Patagonia is almost always cold. Fog, rain, and high winds are not

uncommon even in the summer. The weather changes almost constantly.

Crime and Safety

While generally a safe country in which to travel, opportunistic petty crime is rampant in central Santiago and the capital's poor suburbs are no-go areas for tourists. Do not walk around alone at night in mining cities like Antofagasta and Calama. Do not leave bags, backpacks, or other potentially tempting objects in plain sight in cars, and always try to park in well-lit streets or parking lots after dark. When traveling with a car, choose hotels with parking lots. Follow warnings and ask local advice about minefields in the Atacama Desert and southern Patagonia.

Disabled Travelers

Although progress is slowly being made, Chile can be difficult for visitors with disabilities, especially outside Santiago. Most large hotels present no problems, and neither does the metro, Santiago's subway, but not all public buildings have access facilities. New buses in Santiago have pavement-level access but, in other places and on intercity services, the steps are high (although help will usually be provided). Before booking an air ticket, check the airline's policy; there have been cases in which disabled passengers have not been allowed to board on grounds of lack of mobility or self-sufficiency.

Eating Out

What to Eat

Lunch is the main meal of the day in Chile, and restaurants have lunch menus for as little as $1. It starts with a simple salad, followed by a hot bowl of *cazuela* (soup with meat, chicken or seafood) or *empanadas* (pastries stuffed with meat, onions, a boiled egg, and an olive). In summer don't miss *humitas*, seasoned puréed corn wrapped in corn leaves, or *pastel de choclo*, a corn and meat pie. Seafood is a favorite in Chile. Try *jaiva* (crab), *locos* (abalone) or *ceviche* (marinated fish or seafood). The main course usually consists of rice with chicken, meat or fried fish. Lunches are less expensive than dinners and there are plenty of inexpensive restaurants selling hearty meals in downtown Santiago. More trendy restaurants are in Bellavista, Providencia and in the Borderío complex in Vitacura. Note that a *vegetariano* is a mixed salad served with your choice of chicken, ham, or tuna.

Drinking Notes

Wine is by far the best alcoholic drink in Chile. *Concha y Toro, Carmen, Santa Rita,* and *San Pedro* are among the oldest and most reliable names. They are all worth sampling and most are inexpensive (see page 290 for more details). Pisco is the national liquor, best enjoyed as a frothy, lemony pisco sour. Leading quality brands include Alto del Carmen and Artesanos de Cochiguaz.

Embassies and Consulates

UK
El Bosque Norte 0125, 3rd floor, Las Condes, Santiago, tel: 370-4100, ukinchile.fco.gov.uk
US
Av. Andrés Bello 2800, Las Condes, Santiago, tel: 330-3000, chile. usembassy.gov
Australia
Isidora Goyenechea 3621, 13th floor, Las Condes, Santiago, tel: 550-3500, www.chile.embassy.gov.au/
Canada
Nueva Tajamar 481, Piso 12, Torre Norte, Santiago, tel: 652-3800, www. canadainternational.gc.ca/chile-chili
Ireland
Isidora Goyenechea 3162, Piso 8, Las Condes, tel: 245-6616.
New Zealand
Isidora Goyenechea 3000, Piso 12, Las Condes, tel: 616-3000, www. nzembassy.cl.

Entry Requirements and Customs Regulations

Visas

Only passports and tourist cards (not visas) are required by citizens of Australia, Canada, Ireland, New Zealand, South Africa, the UK, and the US. The cards are handed out on planes and at entry points, including harbors and airports. However, there is an entry tax for citizens of the US ($160), Canada ($132), Australia ($95). Tourist cards valid for 90 days can be renewed for a further 90 days for a small fee at the immigration office on Calle San Antonio in

Emergency Numbers

Police 133
Ambulance 131
Fire brigade 132

Santiago. To stay longer than 180 days, the quickest method is to go to a border country and return rather than go through the bureaucratic application procedure.

Customs

Bags may be searched for agricultural products that may harbor disease, so food should be eaten or disposed of. Duty-free items include those from duty-free stores up to a value of $500, 400 cigarettes or 500g of tobacco or 50 cigars and 2.5 liters of alcohol.

Festivals

January

Semanas Musicales de Frutillar Classical music festival on the shores of Lago Llanquihue.

February

Festival International de la Canción International Song Festival in Viña del Mar.
Semana Valdiviana A week-long festival on the Calle-Calle River in Valdivia.
Regata de las Mil Millas 1,600km (1,000-mile) nautical race starting from Viña del Mar.

March

Fiesta de la Vendimia de Santa Cruz Recognized celebration of Colchagua Valley wine.

April

Campeonato Nacional de Rodeo Chilean rodeo championships, Rancagua.
Fiesta de Cuasimodo (Easter) Religious and folkloric festival, Santiago.

July

La Tirana (16) Native and religious festivity east of Iquique, reminiscent of Oruro's carnival in Bolivia.

September

Independence Day (18) A national holiday.
Army Day (19) National holiday, military parade.

December

Fiesta de la Virgén de Andacollo (23–27) Religious festivity near La Serena drawing thousands to a small, picturesque village.

Gay and Lesbian Travelers

Chile's ultra-conservative reputation is somewhat exaggerated. Attitudes

among young people are changing rapidly, but older men particularly can be homophobic. However, there are an increasing number of gay and gay-friendly bars, restaurants, and discotheques in Santiago, especially in the Bellavista area, and in Valparaíso.

Health and Medical Care

Chile is among the healthier destinations in South America. Service is by far the best in central Chile. **Pharmacies** in Chile are usually well stocked with medical supplies, and most products are available without a prescription. Many pharmacies remain open until midnight, and some operate round the clock.

While it's best to avoid unwashed salads and dodgy fast food places, the tap water in Santiago is safe to drink. In the Atacama Desert and on Easter Island, the heat can cause serious exhaustion and sunburn. Don't overestimate your skin's resistance, and always wear proper sunscreen on the beach or in the Andes, and wear a broad-brimmed hat. Two Santiago clinics are:
Clinica Alemana Av. Vitacura 5951, Vitacura, tel: 210-1111
Clinica Arauco Av. Kennedy 5413, Parque Arauco, Las Condes, tel: 299-0000

Media

The Santiago Times is a good English-language newspaper, which can also be read online at www. santiagotimes.cl/santiagotimes. For Spanish speakers there's *La Tercera* or the more conservative *El Mercurio*.

Money

Changing money on the streets is not advisable anywhere. ATMs, called *Redbanc*, are prolific, even in quite small towns. They accept most major credit cards and bank cards, although not in remote areas. Hotels, restaurants, and shops generally take most credit cards.

Nightlife

Nightlife starts late – bars begin to fill up at about 10pm; and don't even think about going to a nightclub before midnight. Note that drinking on the street is forbidden and can be strictly enforced. For bars, try the area around the junction of Manuel

Montt with Providencia and along nearby **Santa Beatriz**. On **Manuel Montt** itself, you'll find the famous **Liguria**, but there are plenty of other options. Calle Suecia in Providencia, however, has lost its attractiveness and is unsafe. Drinks are cheaper in bars around **Plaza Ñuñoa**, which attract a younger crowd. Bars abound in the **Bellavista** and **Barrio Brasil** neighborhoods and many new bands play there. In Valparaíso, the bar scene centers around Cerro Concepción and Cerro Alegre down to Plaza Aníbal Pinto.

Opening Hours

Business hours change somewhat from city to city. In Santiago they are as follows: Mon–Fri 9am–1.30pm, 2.30–6.30pm. Banks open Mon–Fri 9am–2pm. Exchange houses (casas de cambio) generally open Mon–Fri 9am–6pm, and Sat am.
Stores open Mon–Fri 10.30am–7.30pm, Sat 9.30am–1.30pm. Malls usually open on Sunday.

Postal Services

Most post offices open Mon–Fri 9am–6pm, and Sat until noon. The postal system is fairly reliable. Poste restante services in Santiago are available in the main post office on Plaza de Armas.

Public Holidays

January 1 New Year's Day
March/April Easter

Silverwork for sale.

May 1 Labor Day
May 21 Navy Day
June Monday closest to St Peter and St Paul
July 16 Day of the Virgin of Carmen (Chile's patron saint)
August 15 Assumption
September 18 Independence Day
September 19 Army Day
October 12 Discovery of America
October 31 Lutheran Holiday
November 1 All Saints' Day
December 8 Immaculate Conception
December 25 Christmas Day

Shopping

Chile produces some fine copper ornaments and lapis lazuli jewelry.
Santiago's most exclusive shopping street is **Alonso de Córdova**, off Av. Vitacura, but the **Alto Las Condes** and **Parque Arauco** malls (both on Av. Kennedy) also offer a wide range of local and imported goods.
On Av. Apoquindo 9085, **Alba Pueblito de los Dominicos** is a collection of old-style buildings housing 200 shops where more than 300 craftsmen and women work and sell their goods.

Sport and Activities

Many summer and winter sports played in the Northern Hemisphere are also played in Chile. Team sports are dominated by soccer, while the elite crowd plays rugby and polo. The Andes, Patagonia, and haciendas in central Chile are excellent destinations for horseback riding. Biking is possible in most of the country, and tours are available. The Lake District and Pacific beaches offer water sports, including surfing, kite-surfing and windsurfing. Pichilemu is one of South America's premier surfing spots. Note that the waters of the Pacific are very cold. Hiking and mountain climbing are best in the Andes, and attractive from the desert north to Torres del Paine, South America's top hiking destination. Rafting is most famous around Futaleufú in Patagonia. Winter sports include downhill and (in Chillán) cross-country skiing as well as snowboarding.
Spectator sports: Attendance at a major soccer game is interesting, particularly Colo Colo versus Universidad de Chile, the premier sporting event. Check the security situation beforehand however. Consider attending the horse races at the beautiful Club Hípico. Chilean-

style rodeos in the Central Valley are colorful events.

Telecommunications

Telephones

Calls overseas can be made directly from public phones and from call centers. Cellular phone networks run on the 1900 MHz band. Companies are Claro, Entel, and Movistar, and 3G and 3.5G networks are being rolled out in major cities. Santiago cafés and many small hotels throughout the country have free wireless internet. Check details before using prepaid cards for internet access via wireless modems.

Tipping

About 10 percent is usual in restaurants. Taxi drivers don't expect a tip, but it is usual to round up the fare rather than ask for change.

Tourist Information and Agencies

The National Tourist Service (Sernatur) has an office at the airport, tel: 601-9320, in Santiago at Calle Providencia 1550, tel: 731-8336, and in all the major city centers.

Websites

The following all have useful general information for visitors.
www.sernatur.cl.
www.visit-chile.org.
www.turismochile.com.
www.gochile.cl.
www.chilecontact.com.
www.chipsites.com.
www.thisischile.cl

What to Read

My Invented Country: A Memoir by Isabel Allende. Autobiographical account from Chile's acclaimed novelist. Allende reflects fondly but clear-sightedly on the idiosyncrasies of her home country.
Between Extremes: A Journey Beyond Imagination by Brian Keenan and John McCarthy. Travels along South America's backbone by the former Beirut captives.
Travels in a Thin Country: Journey Through Chile by Sara Wheeler. Lone woman's travels along the longest mountain range on earth.
Insight Guide Chile. An illustrated in-depth guide to the country and its culture, complete with hotel and restaurant listings.

COLOMBIA

ESSENTIAL TRAVEL TIPS TO HELP YOU GET THERE AND GET AROUND

FACT FILE

Area 1,141.748 sq km (439,600 sq miles)
Capital Bogotá
Population 46 million
Language Spanish
Currency Colombian peso
Weights and measures Metric
Electricity 110 volts
Time zone GMT -5hrs (EST; no daylight savings time)
Dialing code 57 (Bogotá +1)
Internet abbreviation .co

TRANSPORTATION

Getting There

By Air

From Europe: Air France, Alitalia, Avianca, Iberia, Lufthansa.
From/via US: American Airlines, Avianca, United.
From Canada: Air Canada.

By Sea

Close to 100 cruise ships dock in Cartagena annually. Colombia's San Andrés and Providencia islands are also regularly served by cruise ships.

Getting Around

From the Airport

Bogotá's international airport is at **El Dorado**, about 12km (7 miles) from the city center. Registered yellow taxi services will take you to the city center. The rate will be determined at the Taxi Registration Point and the address will be registered and handed to the taxi driver. Airport buses run to and from the airport from 5am to 11pm during the day but luggage space is very limited.

It is recommended to only take the bus when traveling lightly.

By Air

Traveling by air is generally the safest way to travel within Colombia. Correspondingly, there are numerous domestic destinations, including the remote east and Amazon regions. Arrive at large airports at least 90 minutes ahead of your flight because of intense security. Domestic routes are served by Avianca (www.avianca.com), Aerorepública (www.aerorepublica.com), Easyfly (www.easyfly.com.co), LAN Colombia (www.lan.com), and Satena (www.satena.com), which has the most extensive network and flies to several towns in Colombia's Amazon region.

By Bus

Bus transportation between the main routes is generally good, with modern buses and luggage ticketing, but it deteriorates when heading into the more remote areas. The alternative on main routes is a *buseta* (minibus) or *colectivo* (a shared taxi that is more expensive but much quicker). It is strongly

Play Safe

Because of safety issues, renting a car during your stay is not recommended.

recommended to travel only during daylight hours.

From Ecuador, buses go to and from the border at Tulcán/Ipiales; the route from Lago Agrio is prohibitively dangerous. From Venezuela, you can choose between the coastal route from Maracaibo to Santa Marta, or the highland route from Caracas and Mérida to Cúcuta via San Cristóbal. From Brazil, the only way to enter is via Leticia on the Amazon and then fly to Bogotá.

By Taxi

In main cities, taxis are cheap and relatively reliable. Every taxi has to use a meter. It is advisable to order a taxi by phone (especially at night) on 01-311-1111 or 01-411-1111 (the operator will give you the car number and the key code). Always lock the door once inside the car.

In Bogotá

Bogotá's Transmilenio (www.transmilenio.gov.co) rapid-transit system has exclusive bus lanes on major arteries, allowing it to run faster than normal buses. There is no subway. Outside rush hour, it is the fastest way to get around. The system uses single- and multiple-use cards. There are also cheap shared taxis (*busetas*) that stop on demand. Taxis are fairly cheap but insist that meters are used. The meters indicate a scale of tariffs rather than price. Each driver must have a copy of the tariffs list, as well as full identification. Drivers are generally not tipped.

Medellín, Colombia's second largest city, has a metro train service, with a cable car, MetroCable, that ascends to the city's poorer northeast.

A–Z

Accommodations

Colombian hotels range from small *casas de huéspedes* (guesthouses) to huge 5-star resorts. It is advisable to choose hotels recommended by the official Colombian Hotel Association (COTELCO), which grades establishments with star ratings (Carrera 11a nº 69-79, Bogotá; tel: 742-7766 to make reservations; www.cotelco.org). Cartagena and the beach resorts of San Andrés and Providencia are packed during summer holidays and in the week before Easter and between Christmas and New Year, so reserve well ahead during those times. There are campsites in national parks. The main tourist destinations have youth hostels along with hostels catering to backpackers.

In addition to hotels, there are also *hosterías*, *hospedajes*, and *pensiones*, which offer more basic but usually clean rooms at cheaper prices. It is worthwhile paying a little bit more for safety.

Arts

Bogotá has literally dozens of museums, from art to historic, along with numerous art galleries. The two top museums are the **Museo Botero**, featuring impressionist and modern art as well as 120 works by Fernando Botero himself (the figurative artist born in the city in 1932); and the excellent **Museo del Oro** (Gold Museum). Colombia's top theatre and concert hall is Bogotá's historic **Teatro Colón** at Calle 10 5-32 in the old-town Candelaria neighborhood, with opera, concerts, ballet, and drama. **The Cinemateca Distrital** on Carrera 7, 22-79, has showings of foreign films. North Bogotá has the largest concentration of art galleries.

The main centers of art and culture beyond Bogotá are Medellín, which has a downtown **Palacio de Bellas Artes** for expositions and an annual jazz festival in September; Cali; and Cartagena. In late January to February Cartagena holds its version of the international Hay Festival of Literature and Arts, the **Mapfre Hay Festival Cartagena de Indias**. Along the Cali River is the **Museo de Arte Moderno La Tertulia** west of downtown.

Budgeting for Your Trip

The following prices should be taken as an approximate guide. Be aware that the peso may fluctuate strongly against the dollar.

Accommodations: Travelers will be wise to pay a little more for accommodation for the sake of security. Expect to pay close to $20 for a budget-range double room and $25–35 for a mid-range option.

Food: Most restaurants are very reasonably priced. A set lunch will cost about $4, although the evening meal will be more expensive. A three-course meal, including wine, at an upmarket establishment will cost around $40 for two people.

Transport: An official taxi is the safest way to journey. From the airport to the center of Bogotá, it will cost around $9, and rates within the cities are also reasonable.

Museums and Attractions: Visiting museums in Colombia is inexpensive. The Museo de Oro, for example, charges $3.00 and is free on Sunday (and every day for children and those over the age of 60).

Children

Bogotá's theater festival has numerous children's events and the cable car to Monserrate is usually a favorite. As travel destinations, Colombia's long Caribbean beaches, including San Andrés and Providencia, are attractive. Parque Explora in Medellín is an interactive technology park holding Latin America's biggest freshwater aquarium, which is usually a hit with children. As elsewhere in South America, always ensure that children wear high-factor sunscreen, and a shady hat.

Climate

Colombia's Andean highlands have moderate weather all year round. Be prepared for cool weather – particularly at night – and for surprise downpours. The coffee-growing areas to the northwest, and both Cali and Medellín, are much warmer than Bogotá. Microclimates in the Andes vary dramatically, hence wet and dry seasons are not the same everywhere. The Pacific and Caribbean coasts are sweltering and tropical year-round. December through March tend to be the driest months.

Crime and Safety

Colombia is the source of a major drug-smuggling route, so it is particularly important that you do not carry packages for other people, ever. Be guided by advice before you leave home about which areas are safe, and those in which overland travel is discouraged. Although most

Forever in bloom at a South American artificial flowers stall.

Colombians are honest and friendly, theft occurs in the larger cities, and visitors should look after valuables at all times. The **Tourist Police Office** at Calle 28 No.13A-15, 1st floor, Bogotá, tel: 606 7676 Ext.1371, is open daily 8am–5pm. In case of theft or loss of documents or valuables, call the national police number **(112)** or ask for the nearest police station. Use ATMs only inside protected spaces like shopping malls, and use caution here, too. Beware of two men approaching you closely on motorcycles at the same time – they may be after your valuables. And while friendliness should not be discouraged, be careful with approaches that are too friendly. The security situation in Colombian cities has, however, improved dramatically over the years – although Cali remains less safe than other big cities. There is reason to be careful but not to be paranoid.

Disabled Travelers

Wheelchair ramps, while mandatory in public buildings, are only gradually being installed. They are mainly available in newer public buildings and shopping malls. Services are otherwise limited, particularly outside Bogotá, Medellín, Cali, and Cartagena. Both the Bogotá Transmilenio and Medellín Metro have facilities for passengers with disabilities and wheelchair users. For the Transmilenio, buy the "Propio" prepaid card. Contact airlines at least 48 hours before a flight in case you need assistance. Policies towards disabled passengers vary from one airline to another.

Eating Out

What to Eat

Colombian cuisine is Andean in the central highlands and with a strong infusion of Afro-Caribbean flavors along the coasts. Like most South American countries, there is a great love of beef, and Colombia shares a love for *arepas* – a maize pancake

Emergency Numbers

Bogotá

Police 112
Fire Department 119
Red Cross 132
Report Traffic Accidents 127

Cali

Police 123

whose infinite possibilities of toppings (chicken, beef, vegetables, sauces) are what makes it most tasty, as an alternative to a burger. Another alternative snack or breakfast is chocolate *santafereño*, hot chocolate accompanied by cheese and bread.

Vegetarian food is limited to the larger cities, but there's always plenty of rice, vegetables, fruit, or pasta available. On the coast, try *cazuela de mariscos* (seafood stew) and *arroz con coco* (rice cooked in coconut oil). In the Andes, for a hearty meal try *bandeja paisa*, a dish of ground beef, sausages, beans, rice, plantain, and avocado. *Ajico* is a spicy soup of chicken, potatoes, and other vegetables.

Where to Eat

The least expensive meals are *comidas corrientes* (which means "ordinary meals"), set lunches consisting usually of a piece of fried meat served with beans and rice. Practically all towns of interest to tourists have a restaurant district that is popular with locals and visitors alike. In **Bogotá,** these areas include the "M" zone in the Macarena neighborhood downtown, the "G" zone in the financial district, along with the north and the Usaquén neighborhood. In **Cartagena,** the old town and Bocagrande have the best restaurants. Restaurants open for lunch at noon, and for dinner around 7pm, though Colombian patrons rarely show up before 9pm. At weekends, restaurants stay busy long after midnight.

Embassies and Consulates

UK
Carrera 9 No. 76-49, 8th–9th floor, tel: 01-326-8300, ukincolombia.fco.gov.uk/
US
Carrera 45, No 24B-27, Bogotá, tel:01-275-2000, bogota.usembassy.gov
Australia
Carrera 18, No. 90-38, Bogotá, tel: 01-218-0942.
Canada
Carrera 7, 114–33 13th floor, Bogotá, tel: 01-657-9800. www.canadainternational.gc.ca/colombia-colombie/
Ireland
Av. de las Americas 56-41 Bogotá, tel: 01-446-6114.
New Zealand
Postal address: Santa Fe de Bogotá, tel: 310 230 7795 (cellphone/mobile).

La Catedral Primada, Bogotá.

Entry Requirements and Customs Regulations

Visas

All visitors to Colombia need a passport but currently do not require a visa. Check, however, since regulations may change. Visitors are given a 60- or 90-day stay on arrival. Stiff fines are imposed if passports are not stamped on arrival and if stays exceeding 60 days are not authorized by the Colombian Immigration Agency (Migración Colombia, tel: 511-1150 in Bogotá). Extensions of 15 days for a maximum 6-month period may be applied for.

Exit stamps are necessary on departure. Foreigners pay $35 departure tax when leaving Colombia by air unless staying short-term, which means less than 24 hours. Make sure that your documentation is stamped on arrival, to avoid paying double the exit tax on departure. Note that you should be at the airport 3 hours before an international flight, as security checks are lengthy.

Customs

Duty-free allowances include 200 cigarettes or 50 cigars or up to 500 grams of tobacco and two bottles of alcoholic beverage. It is illegal to transport more than $10,000 in cash and any amount in excess of that will be confiscated.

Festivals

January

Carnival de Negros y Blancos (Carnival of Blacks and Whites) **(4–6)** in Pasto near Ecuador, stemming from

ARGENTINA
BOLIVIA
BRAZIL
CHILE
COLOMBIA
ECUADOR
FALKLAND ISLANDS
FRENCH GUIANA
GUYANA
PARAGUAY
PERU
SURINAME
URUGUAY
VENEZUELA

a colonial festivity in which blacks were allowed to pretend they were white and their masters showed their approval by painting their own faces black. Revelers put on black face paint on January 5 and whiten their faces a day later, a day with numerous parades and floats.

February/March

Carnival (varying dates) particularly attractive in Barranquilla, which is less commercial than the celebrations in Brazil, but similarly lively.

March/April

Caribbean music and **film festivals** (two separate events) in Cartagena. **Semana Santa** processions in Popayán in the week before Easter. On even-numbered years: **Festival Iberoamericano del Teatro**, Bogotá, Latin America's biggest theater event (www.festivaldelteatro.com.co).

April

Festival de la Leyenda Vallenata, Velledupar. Huge festival of *vallenato* music, one of Colombia's most popular musical forms.

June

Providencia carnival, with Caribbean music styles fusing calypso, *soca*, and reggae.

June/July

Rock al Parque. This is the second largest rock festival in Latin America, after Rock in Rio. The event is held in Simón Bolívar Park in Bogotá.

August

Medellín flower festival (first week). The festival includes a procession of *silleteros*, traditional flower sellers bearing flowers on their heads and backs in a chair-like harness, and an enormous procession of horses and riders

October

Bogotá International Film Festival. Celebrating Colombian film production since 1984.

November

El Piraracú de Oro An international Amazonian folk music festival held in Leticia.

December

Cali Fair (25th–New Year's Eve), this event is famous for marathon salsa concerts played by renowned salsa bands. The fair also includes bullfights and parades of riders on horseback.

Gay and Lesbian Travelers

Colombia is the most gay-friendly country in the Andes, making Bogotá the third most important gay hub in South America after Rio de Janeiro and Buenos Aires. The center for gay-oriented bars, clubs, and gyms is trendy North Bogotá. Medellín also has a fair-sized gay scene.

Health and Medical Care

Make sure you have valid health insurance before you travel as, in an emergency, hospitals will almost certainly demand payment before treatment. Service in major cities is good, but much poorer in rural areas. As in neighboring countries, visitors should take precautions against tropical diseases as well as avoiding strenuous activities at high altitudes before becoming acclimatized. Take the usual precautions with drinking water and food hygiene, and be wary of sunstroke.

Some travelers coming to Colombia seeking cheap cosmetic surgery have suffered grave complications and even death from operations carried out in badly run and inefficient clinics.

Medical centers in Bogotá include: **Cruz Roja Colombiana**, Carrera 68 No. 68B-31, Bogotá tel: 437-6300. Emergency, tel: 132. **Hospital San Ignacio**, Carrera 7 No. 40-62, tel: 594-6161, call centre: 651 3910. **Clínica del Country**, Carrera 16 No. 82-57, tel: 530-0470 or 530-1270.

Media

Newspapers

If you speak some Spanish you may interested in the main Colombian newspapers: *El Tiempo*, *El Espectador*, and *La República*, all from Bogotá. The English-language *Latin American Post* appears weekly. US and European newspapers are available in Bogotá at Librería Luvina, Carrera 5 No 26C-06, La Macarena.

Money

There are some legal *casas de cambios* (exchange bureaux) but it is best to exchange cash and traveler's checks (in US dollars) at a bank. Since a photocopy of your passport is often required, you can speed up transactions by taking a supply of spare photocopies with you from home. Do not change money on

the street and avoid carrying large amounts of cash. Keeping a supply of small change is useful for cab fares.

Credit cards (Visa, MasterCard, American Express) are widely used, but often accepted only in high-priced establishments in bigger cities. Debit cards (Cirrus or Maestro) can be easily used at ATM machines in cities. Avoid withdrawing money after dark and try to do so in enclosed spaces such as shopping malls.

Nightlife

As usual in South America, the nightlife gets going late, though it is usually a bit earlier on Thursdays. North Bogatá, particularly the **Zona Rosa**, is the center of nightlife, along calles 81 and 84, carreras 11 and 14, or in the **Parque de la 93**, Calle 93, Carreras 11A and 13.

Though **salsa** is danced everywhere, Cali is its epicenter. In Cartagena, there are numerous bars in the old town near Santo Domingo. The **Bocagrande Hotel** and beach zone is where the Caribbean city's main discos are. There is a lot of nocturnal activity around Cali's **Parque del Perro** and in Medellín's **El Poblado** district and on Carrera 70 in the **Laureles** neighborhood.

Opening Hours

Bogotá: generally Mon–Fri 8am–5pm. Banks are open Mon–Fri 9am–3pm; some branches open additionally 5–7pm and on Saturdays.
Outside Bogotá: Mon–Fri 8am–noon and 2–4pm, Sat 10am–4pm.

Postal Services

There are two national postal systems in Colombia, The more reliable and efficient one consists of private companies (eg Deprisa and Servientrega). They have many offices in most large cities. The other system, Adpostal, is state-run, cheaper but less reliable and used in small towns and rural areas as well as for international post.

Public Holidays

1 January New Year's Day
6 January* Epiphany
19 March* St Joseph's Day
April Maundy Thursday and Good Friday
1 May Labor Day
13 May* Ascension
3 June* Corpus Christi

30 June* Sagrado Corazón (Sacred Heart)
3 July* St Peter and St Paul
20 July Independence Day
7 August Battle of Boyacá
15 August* Assumption
12 October* Day of the Discovery of America
1 November* All Saints' Day
11 November* Independence of Cartagena
8 December Immaculate Conception
25 December Christmas Day
Holidays marked * are moved to the nearest following Monday if they fall on a Saturday or Sunday.

Shopping

Besides good woolen Andean clothing and leather goods, Colombia specializes in jewelry and emeralds. Take care to buy from a reputable jeweler to avoid fakes. Colombia, particularly Medellín, is also one of South America's centers of fashion.

Where to Shop

For Colombian **handicrafts**, the best place to shop in Bogotá is **Artesanías de Colombia**, which has outlets at Carrera 3 No. 18A-58 and Carrera 11 No. 84-12. **Emeralds** can be bought in the *joyerías* in La Candelaria Centro, plus **Palacio de la Esmeralda**, Calle 16 No. 5-24, tel: 283-3578 or **The Emerald Center**, corner of Av. Jimenez and Carrera 5. For an exclusive collection of **Colombian jewelry** visit **L.A. Cano**, Centro Andino, Carrera 11 No. 82-51, Local 210, tel: 610-1175 (note that "local" means the shop or unit number).

Sport and Activities

Even if you are not headed to Colombia for a particularly active holiday, consider cycling through Bogotá. On Sundays and holidays, 121km (75 miles) of the capital's main streets are closed to vehicle traffic for cyclists, skaters, and pedestrians. Cycling is one of Colombia's preferred sports, and one of the best places for mountain biking is Parque Natural Los Nevados in the center of the country.

In the Andean national parks, hiking and mountaineering is first-rate and is now accessible again because of the improved security situation, though some permits may be necessary from the park service's visitor services and ecotourism office (Carrera 10 No. 20–30, 1st floor, Bogotá; tel: 353-2400).

Birdwatching is excellent, as would be expected in the country harboring the most species anywhere in the world (1,876).

Whale watching is possible July through October from Bahía Solano, Nuquí, and Parque Nacional Gorgona near Buenaventura.

Rafting and kayaking are attractive on the Río Negro and in the Chicamocha Canyon. Beach and water sports, of course, are available on the Caribbean coast.

Diving is best at the Islas del Rosario, Parque Nacional Tayrona, and around San Andrés and Providencia. Surfing tours are the best way to ride the waves of the Pacific coast.

Cali's draw for foreigners wishing to learn to dance salsa has led to the establishment of salsa academies.

Soccer and, in January, bullfighting are the most popular spectator sports. The most important soccer rivalry is between Santa Fe and Millionarios, for which tickets should be bought well in advance.

Telecommunications

Telephone

Telephone systems are automated and phone cards can be purchased. People on the street offer cheap cellphone calls to local, national, or any other cellphone (mobile) number in Colombia. Movistar offices in most cities have international call facilities.

Cellphone operators Tigo, Movistar, and Claro are all rolling out 3G and 3.5G services. Cellphones work on the GSM850 and 1900 networks. Make sure of all details before attempting to use mobile internet access with prepaid cards.

Tipping

Colombians are among South America's stingiest tippers. In small restaurants, some people tip 1,000 pesos or less (about US$0.50, or at most 2,000 pesos (about US$1). In more expensive restaurants, customers usually tip about 10 percent. Increasingly the better restaurants spare you the dilemma by adding another 15 percent onto the bill as a service charge, with no additional tip expected. Tipping taxi drivers is rare.

Tourist Agencies

Bogotá: Panamericana de Viajes, Carrera 11A No. 93A-80, Oficina 104, tel: 01-650 0400 or Fundación Colombiana de Caminantes Sal Si Puedes, Carrera 7 No. 17-01, Oficinas 640, tel: 01-283-3765.

Santa Marta: Turismerk, Calle 20 No 3-73, Centro Histórico tel: 5-431 0892, can arrange trips to Ciudad Perdida, Parque Tayrona, Cabo de la Vela, and the Guajira Peninsula.
Cartagena: There are many tourist agencies in Bocagrande, the modern beach resort.

Tourist Information

Tourist Offices

There are several tourist information offices in Bogotá, including:
Bogotá Turismo, Carrera 8 No. 9-83, tel: 283-7115
Unicentro, Av. 15 No. 123-30, 1st floor, main entrance, tel: 637-4482. Limited information is also available at the Edificio Centro de Comercio Internacional, Carrera 13 No. 26-62, tel: 286 2248. All the major cities also have centrally located tourism offices.

Websites

www.colombia.travel/en is Colombia's official tourism site. It also has a mobile guide at http://m.colombia.travel.
www.bogotaturismo.gov.co or www.culturayturismo.gov.co are the official Bogotá sites.
www.cotelco.org or www.reservas hoteleras.com.co (online bookings)
www.parquesnacionales.gov.co information on Colombia's National Parks.

What to Read

The Making of Modern Colombia: A Nation in Spite of Itself by David Bushnell. Remarkable examination of a country that is so much more diverse than its stereotype suggests.
My Cocaine Museum by Michael T. Taussig. An imaginative look at south Colombia's impoverished communities.
Colombia: Fragmented Land, Divided Society by Frank Safford and Marco Palacios. Most comprehensive single source on Colombia's history.
More Terrible than Death: Massacres, Drugs, and America's War in Colombia by Robin Kirk. Compelling narrative by human-rights investigator on effect of US role in drug war on Colombian lives.
One Hundred Years of Solitude by Gabriel García Márquez. Classic work of magical realism by Nobel Prize-winning author.
News of a Kidnapping by Gabriel García Márquez. Chilling, journalistic account of kidnapping of prominent journalists.

ECUADOR

ESSENTIAL TRAVEL TIPS TO HELP YOU GET THERE AND GET AROUND

FACT FILE

Area 283.561 sq km (104,500 sq miles)
Capital Quito
Population 14 million
Languages Spanish and Quichua
Currency US dollar
Weights and measures Metric
Electricity 110 volts
Time zone GMT -5hrs (Galápagos Islands -6hrs)
Dialing code 593 (Quito +2)
Internet abbreviation .ec

TRANSPORTATION

Getting There

By Air

From Europe: Iberia, KLM, LAN.
From/via US: American Airlines, United, LAN.

Getting Around

By Air

Domestic flights are run by AeroGal (www.aerogal.com.ec), LAN Ecuador (www.lan.com), and TAME (www.tame.com.ec). AeroGal and TAME run regular services to the Galápagos.

Ecuador has international airports at Quito and Guayaquil. From Quito's **Mariscal Sucre Airport** there are buses to the old and new city centers, and taxi fares are around $6. A new international airport, 20km (13 mile) east of Quito, is

slated to open early 2013. Taxis from Guayaquil's **José Joaquin de Olmedo Airport** to the city cost $4–5, and buses are also available.

By Bus

Buses in Ecuador are cheap, plentiful, and reach even remote destinations. The quality is often poor, however, some drivers appear suicidal, and landslides are common in mountainous regions during wet seasons. Some air-conditioned, luxury buses (*autobús de lujo*) cover the most popular routes. Always carry your passport when traveling by bus.

Buses from Quito: Long-distance buses heading south leave from the Terminal Terrestre in Quitumbe. There are about 24 bus companies with offices at the terminal. Buses north to Otavalo and beyond, including Colombia, depart from the northern terminal in Carcelén. Regional buses to the northwest around Mindo leave from La Ofelia, also in northern Quito. There are also companies that operate more comfortable buses from terminals in the Mariscal district, including Ormeño, which has connections to Venezuela and Argentina and countries in between. Rutas de América runs a direct bus service to Lima and one to Bogotá via Ibagué.

In Quito

Local city buses are frequent and inexpensive, Destinations are shown on the front of the buses. The Ecovía and Trolebús are north-south express buses. Beware of pickpockets when buses are crowded.

A–Z

Accommodations

Five-star luxury accommodations can be found in Quito, Guayaquil, Cuenca, the Royal Palm and Red Mangrove in Santa Cruz, Galápagos, and the resort areas of Esmeraldas and Santa Elena. There are first-class jungle lodges in the Oriente and around Mindo west of Quito, including the Mashpi Lodge. Most other areas rely on basic but clean country inns (*hosterías*), pensiones, or residenciales. Ecuador has two high seasons for travel (June–September and December–February), and reservations should be made early for those seasons, as well as for weekends in Otavalo at any time of the year as this is popular with local people and tourists for the weekend market.

A double room in a luxury hotel might cost up to $150–200 or more a night, in a first class hotel it would be $80–100, while a double room with private bath in a perfectly clean and comfortable residencial can be had for around $20. Decent backpacker hotels with shared bathrooms can generally be found for $3–6 per person in even the remotest areas.

In most places service (10 percent) and taxes (12 percent) will be added to the bill. It is often cheaper and easier to arrange accommodation as a package through a tour operator or local travel agency

Camping is a cheap and popular option in many coastal areas, and most campsites provide access to bathrooms and running water. On the

Galápagos, there are three sites on the island of Santa Cruz.

Arts

Quito, Guayaquil, and Cuenca are the arts hubs of the country. Quito's main venues are the **Teatro Sucre, Teatro de Variedades**, and **Teatro Bolívar** in the old town, and the nearby **Teatro México**. The **Casa de la Cultura** and its **Teatro Prometeo** are near the Mariscal district, while the largest center for classical music, **La Casa de la Música**, is in the northeast. The museum and art gallery of **Oswaldo Guayasamín** is in the Bellavista neighborhood in northern Quito, where most of Quito's art galleries are. There is a growing arts scene in the Cumbayá suburb.

Guayaquil's museums are concentrated around the modern waterfront, Malecón Simón Bolívar. Cuenca's **Museo de Arte Moderno**, home to Ecuador's main contemporary art exposition, the Bienal (held during odd-numbered years), is at Sucre 1527 and Coronel Tálbot on the western fringe of the historic center.

Budgeting for Your Trip

Ecuador falls in the middle when comparing prices with other Latin American countries.
Accommodations: As mentioned in the Accommodations section, in the large cities and major tourist destinations budget accommodation will run from as little as $6 per night to several hundred dollars a night for a luxury hotel, but $25 is an average price. In small, rural villages it is easy to find accommodation in hostels and *hospedajes* for just a few dollars per person. In the Oriente, lodges tend to be rather expensive, starting at around $50 per day, although this usually includes food and activities.
Transportation: By bus the cost averages about $1 per hour, depending on the level of comfort. Within cities, taxis are cheap and ubiquitous, and rarely will a ride within a city, even Quito or Guayaquil, cost more than a few dollars. Some locations in the Oriente, as well as the Galápagos, can only be reached by airplane, which can be expensive. A round-trip plane ticket to the Galápagos, for example, will cost about $350.
Food: The cost of food varies greatly. In large cities, and especially in the Galápagos, rarely will you be able to eat at a restaurant for less than $5

Fruit and vegetable stall at a Colombian market.

per person, but you can pay as much as $60 per person for a meal in a top restaurant. In rural areas, small local restaurants will serve menus, usually including several hearty courses, for just over a dollar. It may be the only option in town.
Museums and attractions: There is a small entrance fee (around $2) for many museums, but most of the lovely colonial churches are free.

Children

Small size and ease of travel makes Ecuador a relatively easy destination to visit with children. As in most places of South America, care should be taken to apply sunscreen and you should ensure they take it easy at high elevations. The creatures of the Galápagos are children's favorites, but apart from these, and beaches, Quito and Guayaquil have attractive parks including the Parque Histórico in Guayaquil, which has a small zoo. Quito's zoo is in Guallabamba, a small town north of the city itself. In the Andes, children will enjoy the hot springs destinations like Papallacta and Baños.

Climate

Ecuador's regions each have a distinct climate. The coast is hottest and wettest from January to April. The northern Andes are driest and clearest between June and September, and in December; Cuenca is damper. The Oriente is usually inundated with rain between June and August, followed by a drier season until December. As on the coast, however, a torrential downpour is never out of the question.

Crime and Safety

With the exception of Guayaquil, Ecuador has long been known as one of the safest countries in South America. The situation has, however, improved in Guayaquil's protected areas around the waterfront and Las Peñas. Unfortunately, the situation in Cuenca and particularly in Quito has deteriorated despite the urban renewal of the capital's historic old town. Visitors should not walk to El Panecillo overlooking the old town, and should be careful when hiking to the summit of Pichincha from the cable car. Pickpockets are a problem in the Trolebús system and robberies in the Mariscal district. Avoid traveling to the area around San Lorenzo in Esmeraldas near the Colombian border without detailed security information.

Disabled Travelers

In large cities and tourist areas, most large hotels and attractions are equipped with ramps and/or elevators. Elsewhere there are few services available. The Galápagos Islands tend to be quite untouched by development for conservation reasons and therefore lack proper facilities for wheelchair users. Consult a tour operator to see what types of activities may be accessible.

Eating Out

What to Eat

Ecuador has a varied cuisine; while sharing many dishes with its Andean neighbors, has numerous regional differences. Esmeraldas in the northwest has the strongest African influence, using plenty of coconut with fish and seafood in *encocados*. Manabí on the coast is known for its variety of fish and seafood, including grilled shellfish and lobster in beer sauce. Food in the Andes is heartier, with guinea pigs *(cuy)* a favorite from the southern Andes, while fried pork *fritadas* and potato patties called *llapingachos* are popular in the north.

Where to Eat

Quito's best restaurants are spread in a long swath from the historic center to the **Mariscal** district and northern Quito, and some in the suburban valleys. Some of the capital's hotels, such as **Hotel Colón** and **Hotel Oro Verde** have excellent restaurants. In Cuenca, **La Esquina** is a good restaurant; in Guayaquil, they are concentrated in the north of the city and the **Via Samborondón**.

Embassies and Consulates

UK
Edificio Citiplaza, Av. Naciones Unidas and República de El Salvador, Quito, tel: 02-297-0800/0801, ukinecuador. fco.gov.uk

US
Avigiras N12-170 y Eloy Alfaro, tel: 02-398-5000, http://ecuador. usembassy.gov.

Australia
Rocafuerte 520, 2nd Floor, Fundación Leonidas Ortega Building, Guayaquil, tel: 04-601 7529.

Canada
Av. Amazonas and Unión Nacional de Periodistas, 3rd Floor, Edificio Eurocenter, Quito, tel: 02-245 5499, www.quito.gc.ca.

Ireland
Calle Yanacona N72-64 y Juan Procel, Condado, Quito, tel: 02-357-0156.

Entry Requirements and Customs Regulations

Visas

Visas are not required for anybody for a stay of up to 90 days. Longer-stay visas cost $230 and stays can't top 180 days. To enter the country, you will need a passport valid for 6 months, a return ticket, and proof of sufficient funds for your stay.

Customs

Duty-free allowances include 300 cigarettes or 50 cigars or 200g of tobacco, 1 liter of alcohol, and gifts and personal effects worth up to $200 (for stays of up to 7 days) or $300 (for stays of 8 days to 6 months).

Festivals

There are huge numbers of festivities celebrated in Ecuador from rural hamlets to the big cities.

April/March
Carnival, most celebrated in Guaranda and Ambato

June
Festival of San Juan (23–24) Otavalo, Tabacundo, Guamote
Corpus Christi, Cuenca

July
Celebrations for the foundation of Guayaquil (23–25)

August
Independence Day festivities (3–5) Esmeraldas

September
Yamor festivities (2–15) Otavalo

October
Independence Day festivies (9–12) Guayaquil

November
Independence Day festivities (3) Cuenca
Mama Negra festival, Latacunga

December
Pase del Niño procession and parade **(24)** Cuenca
Año Viejo (Old Year) **(31)**, throughout Ecuador, celebrates the end of the year by the burning of straw-filled effigies of popular figures and politicians

Gay and Lesbian Travelers

Homosexuality is often shunned, but in large cities, particularly Quito, gay communities have developed, and homosexuality is slowly becoming more tolerated. The Mariscal district of Quito is the center of the gay scene. For more information visit: www.quito gay.net, www.gayecuador.com.

Health and Medical Care

Make sure you have valid health insurance before you travel as hospitals may ask for payment before treatment. Service in major cities is good but much poorer in rural areas. As in neighboring countries, visitors should take precautions against tropical diseases (get advice about vaccinations before you leave home), avoid strenuous activities before acclimatization at high altitudes, and be sensible about food hygiene and drinking water.
Main hospitals include
Hospital Metropolitano
Av. Mariana de Jesús s/n and Nicolás Arteta, Quito, tel: 399 8000

Emergency Numbers

Fire 102 (911 in Quito)
Police 101 (911 in Quito)
Ambulance/Red Cross 131

Clínica Kennedy
Av. Del Periodista and Callejón 11-A, Guayaquil, tel: 228-9666/228-6963.

Media

The most important newspapers are Quito-based *El Comercio* and *Hoy* and Guayaquil's *El Universo* and *Expreso*. There are no Engllish-language newspapers published in Ecuador.

Money

Major credit cards are accepted widely in cities and ATMs are common. Master Card and Diners Club are more convenient to use than Visa, which may be blocked without notice.
Traveler's checks and credit cards are more widely accepted than debit cards and in rural areas it is best to travel with small denomination notes. On Sundays and holidays, when banks and *casas de cambio* are shut, you can change money in the larger hotels. Traveler's checks can be changed almost as easily as cash.

Nightlife

Nightlife in Ecuador often involves bars with astonishingly loud music. In Quito, the **Mariscal** has its share of clubs and pubs.
In Guayaquil, many all-night clubs play the latest American and Latino tunes, and some good Colombian salsa. They are not places for the faint-hearted. Cuenca's nightlife is concentrated on the **Calle Larga**. Otavalo has a couple of *peñas* which are lively at the weekend.

Opening Hours

Government offices in Quito are open to the public Mon–Fri 8am–4.30pm. In Guayaquil, hours are Mon–Fri 9am–noon and 3.30–6pm.
Banks are open Mon–Fri 9am–6pm with some also open 9am–1pm on Sat. Stores are generally open Mon–Fri 9am–1pm and 3–7pm, and Sat 9am–1.30pm, with many now staying open during lunchtime. Shopping centers and supermarkets stay open until 8pm. Drug stores (*farmacias*) are open Mon–Fri 9am–8pm and some are

listed "on duty" 24 hours a day (see local newspapers for the daily roster).

Postal Services

It is worth having your letters certified (*certificado*). The main post office in Quito is at Calle Japón No 36-153 and Av. Naciones Unidas. Guayaquil, Aguirre 301 between Chile and Pedro Carbo.

Public Holidays

January 1 New Year's Day
February/March Carnival
April Good Friday and Easter Sunday (date variable)
May 1 Labor Day
May 24 Battle of Pichincha
August 10 Independence Day
October 12 Columbus Day
November 2 All Souls' Day
December 25 Christmas Day

Shopping

Ecuador is renowned as the home of the Panama hat and also for its colorful balsa wood carvings, as well as tapestries, leather goods, and embroidered textiles from Otovalo market and other outlets.

Where to Shop

There are dozens of *artesanías* stores and kiosks in Quito, especially in the **Mariscal** area. Several have outstanding selections of high-quality folk art and clothing. **Otovalo market** (daily June–August, Wed and Sat rest of year) is well worth the 30-minute bus journey from Quito. It is famous for hand-knitted clothing, jewelry, woodcarvings, tapestries, leather goods, and textiles, and offers the best buys in Ecuador, but there are also stores in Quito, Guayaquil, Cuenca, and Baños where similar goods are sold at good prices. **Cuenca** is the best place to buy **gold and silver jewelry**. Ecuador (*not* Panama) is also the place for **Panama hats**, which are made by hand in Montecristi and Cuenca but sold all over the country.

Sport and Activities

Quito's old town is pedestrianized and several main thoroughfares are closed to vehicle traffic for **cycling**. Mountain bike tours are organized from Quito and Cuenca. The Andes are a paradise for **hiking** and **mountaineering**. **Birdwatching** is excellent in the area around Mindo and in Amazon lodges and of course

Bertha Pachay Mero panama hat shop and factory, Montecristi.

on the Galápagos. **Whale-watching** is possible from Puerto López. There are numerous **kayaking** and **rafting** opportunities down Andean rivers headed for the coast and the Amazon. Montañita beach in Manabí is Ecuador's top **surfing** spot. **Soccer** is wildly popular, and attendance at a match is a safer experience than in many other countries.

Telecommunications

Ecuador's phone network is run by CNT and Etapa, and a couple of private companies; one of the best places to make calls is at the phone company's office in each town.

Hotels add hefty surcharges, usually with discounts after 7pm.

There are numerous internet cafés in Quito, Guayaquil, and Cuenca, many of which also offer a cheap internet phone service. Porta and Movistar run mobile telephone services and are rolling out 3G and 3.5G networks. Cellphones run on the 850 MHz band. Make sure of all details before using mobile internet access with prepaid cards.

Tipping

In many restaurants 22 percent service and tax is added to the bill, but some cheaper establishments will leave it to your discretion, in which case leave 10 percent. Airport porters should be tipped about US$0.50. Taxi drivers do not expect a tip.

Tourist Information and Agencies

The Ministry of Tourism has an excellent website (www.vivecuador. com), and its **iTur** tourist offices can be found throughout the country. In Quito they are at El Telégrafo E7-58 between Ultimas Noticias and El tiempo, tel: 399-9333.

Bookings for the Galápagos Islands cruise aboard the *Santa Cruz* can be made at Metropolitan Touring in Quito or Guayaquil, or their US agents Adventure Associates (tel: 800-527-2500; www.adventure-associates. com).

The *Eclipse* is a luxurious, medium-size vessel, holding 48 passengers. It is operated by Ocean Adventures, tel: 02-246 6301, www. oceanadventures.com.ec. There are dozens of yachts operating cruises around the islands, most of which work out of Puerto Ayora, with a growing number based in Puerto Baquerizo Morena. They can take from 6 to 20 people on board.

Galápagos Sub-Aqua, Av. Charles Darwin, Puerto Ayora, Isla Santa Cruz, tel: 05-526-350, www.galapagos-sub-aqua.com, offers scuba-diving tours and instruction.

In the UK, many operators feature Galápagos cruises, including **Select Latin America**, tel: 020-7407-1478, www.selectlatinamerica. co.uk; and **Journey Latin America**, tel: 020-3432-1504, www. journeylatinamerica.co.uk.

What to Read

Galápagos: A Natural History Market by Michael Jackson.
The Voyage of the Beagle 1835–1836 by Charles Darwin. Darwin's epic voyage around the coasts of South America which led, 20 years later, to his theory of evolution by natural selection.
Eight Feet in the Andes: Travels with a Donkey from Ecuador to Cusco by Dervla Murphy. An Andean adventure.
Ecuador: A Climbing Guide by Yossi Brain.
Insight Guide Ecuador. An illustrated in-depth guide to the country and its culture, complete with hotel and restaurant listings.

THE FALKLAND ISLANDS

ESSENTIAL TRAVEL TIPS TO HELP YOU GET THERE AND GET AROUND

FACT FILE

Area 12,173 sq km (4,700 sq miles)
Capital Port Stanley
Population 3,140
Languages English
Currency Falkland Islands pound
(fixed on par to pound sterling)
Weights and measures Metric
(imperial measures widely used)
Electricity 240 volts AC, 50Hz
Time zone GMT -4hrs (summer GMT
-3hrs)
International dialing code 500
Internet abbreviation .fk

TRANSPORTATION

Getting There

By Air

There are Royal Air Force flights twice
weekly from Brize Norton in the UK,
with some seats open to civilians.
Book well ahead.
From Punta Arenas, Chile, LAN
flights arrive and depart Saturdays.
LAN passengers pay a £22 ($36)
departure tax.

By Sea

Cruise ships from about four dozen
lines call at Stanley in season.
Most visitors reach the islands on
cruises.

Getting Around

By Air

The Falkland Islands Government Air

Service (tel: 27219) has daily flights
to settlements and offshore
islands in the archipelago, with a
capacity of eight passengers per
flight to the hamlets' grassy airstrips.
Departure and arrival times are
announced nightly by radio. Internal
flights go through the small Stanley
airport. Airport bus transfers are
available.

By Sea

Cruise ships often call at Stanley
during the Antarctic cruise season.
Day-long boat trips may be chartered
from Stanley and elsewhere on the
islands.
Some settlements offer landing
vessels or other craft to reach outlying
islands. Check with tour operators in
the capital.

By Road

Overland travel is difficult and
vehicles can frequently get bogged
down, hence 4x4 vehicles are
essential. There is one asphalt
road linking Stanley, the Mount
Pleasant airport, and Goose Green,
and an all-weather graded track
linking Mount Pleasant with various
hamlets in the north of East
Falkland as far as Port San Carlos.
On West Falkland, a similar track
links settlements there.
The best option for sight-seeing
is to hire a guide in Stanley (see
Tourist Information and Agencies,
page 391).

Stanley

There is no public transportation
system and walking is the easiest
way to get around. There are two taxi
services: Bonners, tel: 51126, and
Town, tel: 52900. Agree fares before
you start.

A–Z

Accommodations

Accommodations on the islands
include bed and breakfasts,
guesthouses, and small hotels. There
are also lodges at Pebble Island, Port
Howard, San Carlos, and Sea Lion
Island. Compared with mainland
South America, lodging in Stanley is
expensive, and you should book in
advance. If you are on a strict budget,
camping is a cheaper option. Ask for
permission outside of Stanley and
take care because of the threat of fire.

Budgeting for Your Trip

Prices are similar to the UK, with some
imported goods more expensive.
Accommodations: range from about
$30 to $200 (for the top-category
executive suite at the Malvina House
hotel). Add about $10 for guesthouses
and lodges offering full board.
Tipping: In restaurants, add 10
percent to the bill if no service charge
has been included.

Children

Except for the chilly weather, the
Falklands are a great destination for
children because of the fascinating
wildlife and good safety record.

Climate

The climate is temperate and very
windy. Wear windproof clothing and
solid hiking boots for excursions.
Sunblock is necessary due to the
proximity of the ozone hole. October

Emergency Numbers

All emergency services: 999

through March are the best months to visit. Winters are relatively mild.

Crime and Safety

The islands are a very safe destination.

Disabled Travelers

Stanley is easy to get around; however, assistance is necessary for travel elsewhere on the islands.

Eating Out

Falklands cuisine is a mixture of hearty British food – including fish and chips and afternoon tea – with seafood of the type served in Argentina and Chile. "Smoko" is a term for tea or coffee served with home-baking. Specialties include local lamb, mutton, and pork.

Entry Requirements and Customs Regulations

Visas

Passports are required, but no visas are necessary if no visa is required for entry into the UK. Proof of accommodation may be requested upon arrival.

Customs

Visitors may bring in duty free 200 cigarettes or 50 cigars or 100 cigarillos or 250g of tobacco, 1 liter of alcoholic beverage over 38.8 percent or 2 liters up to 22 percent proof and 2 liters of wine and 10 liters of beer or cider.

Health and Medical Care

Medical care is free to visitors whose country has a reciprocal National Health Service agreement, and the appropriate documentation with them. Otherwise, medical insurance is highly recommended, including travel insurance that can cover a medical evacuation by airlift to a third country, worth at least $200,000. The well-equipped King Edward VII Memorial Hospital in Stanley is the only hospital on the islands.

Media

Newspapers

The *Penguin News* is published weekly in Stanley and all British national newspapers are also available. The *Falkland Islands Gazette* is a government publication.

Money

Exchange facilities are available in Stanley at the Standard Chartered Bank, which has no ATM. The Falklands' currency cannot be exchanged anywhere outside the islands. Both sterling bills and dollars are accepted in most places, and carrying some dollars is useful in case a flight is diverted to the continent. In Stanley itself, MasterCard and Visa are widely accepted, but rarely elsewhere, while American Express and Diners Club are less commonly accepted. Sterling traveler's checks are more useful than dollar checks.

Nightlife

Nightlife is largely limited to the handful of pubs in Stanley and to dances at the Stanley town hall.

Opening Hours

Public offices are open Mon–Fri 8am–4.30pm, private offices a half hour longer. Stores stay open at least until 6pm, including Saturdays, less commonly on Sundays.

Postal Services

Stanley's town hall serves as the post office.

Public Holidays

1 January New Year's Day
2 April Good Friday
21 April Queen's Birthday
14 June Liberation Day
6 October Spring Holiday
8 December Battle Day
25–28 December Christmas

Shopping

Shops in Stanley offer typical British products that would be found in a similarly sized town in the home country. Local goods include wool sweaters from Falklands sheep, along with jewelry made from local semi-precious stones.

Sport and Activities

The Falkland Islands have several clubs for team sports including soccer, cricket, hockey, and volleyball. There are also facilities for clay-pigeon shooting and several of the southernmost golf courses on the planet. The archipelago is excellent for fishing and sailing, and of course for wildlife watching.

Telecommunications

UK mobile service operator Cable & Wireless provides GSM service on the 900 MHz network. There are good satellite telephone links to the Islands.

The Cable & Wireless office is open Mon–Thur 8.15am–noon and 1.15 4.30pm (Fri until 4.15pm), and sells phone cards for use in the international telephone service booths situated in the office. Payphones are available throughout Stanley and Mount Pleasant. Some accept coins but most require pre-paid telephone cards which can be bought at stores.

Tourist Information and Agencies

In Stanley, the **Falkland Islands Tourist Board** at Jetty Visitor Centre, tel: 22215, offers information on island travel and sights. Shipping agent **Stanley Services' Falkland Islands Holidays** offers bookings for tours and accommodations. Also see other operators in the flowing links:

Websites

www.falklandislands.com Official tourist board site.
www.falklands.info General local information site.
www.falklands.net Critical local environmental group website.
www.falklandstravel.com International Tours and Travel.
www.falklandislandsholidays.com Falkland Islands Holidays
www.discoveryfalklands.com Discovery Falklands.

What to Read

The Battle for the Falklands by Max Hastings and Simon Jenkins. Excellent account of the war and the political events that led to it. **Razor's Edge: The Unofficial History of the Falklands War** by Hugh Bicheno. Visceral, up-to-date depiction of the fighting. **A Falkland Islander Till I Die** by Terence Severine Betts. A personal account of a father living in Stanley during the Argentine invasion and of the locals' debate on who the islands should belong to, Britain or Argentina. **Falling Off a Horse in the Falkland Islands** by Edward John Colgate. First-person account of an English teacher's experiences in remote parts of the islands during the 1960s.

FRENCH GUIANA

ESSENTIAL TRAVEL TIPS TO HELP YOU GET THERE AND GET AROUND

FACT FILE

Area 91,000 sq km (35,135 sq miles)
Capital Cayenne
Population 236.250
Languages French (official language), French Guianese Creole and English
Currency Euro
Weights and measures Metric
Electricity 220 volts
Time zone GMT -3hrs, EST +2hrs
International dialing code 594
Internet abbreviation .gf

TRANSPORTATION

Getting There

By Air
From Europe: Air France, Air Caraïbes.
From/via US: Air France (via Paris), Air Caraïbes (via Dominican Republic), Surinam Airways (via Miami and Paramaribo).
From Australia: Air Austral, Quantas.
From Canada: Air Canada (connecting with Air France).

Getting Around

From the Airport
Cayenne-Rochambeau airport is 16km (10 miles) from Cayenne. There are no airport buses; taxis currently cost $25 (more at night).

By Air
Air Guyane (www.airguyane.com) has regular services to Maripasoula and Saül from Cayenne. Brazilian airline TAF (www.voetaf.com.br) may offer flights to Belem on the Amazon and Macapá in the adjacent Brazilian state of Amapá. Book well ahead for domestic flights.

By Boat
Visitors can reach the interior of French Guiana by boat. *Pirogues* (dugout canoes) are equipped with outboard motors. Wooden *pirogues* can carry up to 14 passengers. Tours can be arranged; the average journey time is 5–6 hours. Contact local tour agents in Cayenne or Kourou for details.

There are ferries to cross the border at Albina/Saint Laurent du Maroni from Suriname.

By Bus
Ground transportation on buses is grouped into 30 lines providing regularly scheduled transportation throughout the northern half of the country, from Saint Laurent du Maroni to Saint-Georges-de-l'Oyapock on the Brazilian border.

By Car
It is possible to hire cars in French Guiana but, while it can be convenient, it will be stressful unless you are used to driving in developing countries. Driving along dirt tracks is dangerous in the rainy season and 4x4 vehicles are necessary.

In Cayenne
Cayenne and its suburbs are served by a regular bus network. Buses do not run on Sunday. Routes and schedules are available from SMTC, 3 place des Palmistes, tel: 314-566. The official tourism site has transport information, including numbers for local taxis. Central Cayenne is quite compact and best visited on foot.

A–Z

Accommodations
No hotel has more than three stars. The quality of accommodations is mixed and lodgings are expensive compared with the rest of South America. Breakfast is normally not included in the room price. Several bed and breakfasts and rental homes have been registered with quality rental services Clévacances (www.clevacances.com/EN) and can be booked online, while some rural hostels and guesthouses are available that have been certified by Gîtes de France (www.gites-de-france.com). Accommodations in Amazonia can be as simple as a hammock.

Arts
French Guiana's arts scene is concentrated in Cayenne and Kourou, though there are government efforts to hold cultural events in the interior. The main museums are the very eclectic **Musée Départemental Franconie** and the **Musée des Cultures Guyanaises** in Cayenne. In July and August, open-air movies are shown in some rural locations reachable only by plane or *pirogue*.

Budgeting for Your Trip
Prices in French Guiana are European rather than South

American, and the strong euro makes it more expensive.

Accommodations: Hotels generally cost $45 and up for a double room, but cheap places to sling a hammock can cost as little as $8 a night. For multi-day stays, renting a vacation house can be a cheaper option.

Food: Budget for $20 per person, although you can pay a lot more. It isn't easy to find a meal for under $10; many Asian places – which tend to be the cheapest – offer menus for around $12.

Transportation: Car rental starts at about $50 a day, $400 a week.

Museums and Attractions: Entrance fees vary but are more in line with European charges.

Children

By tropical standards, French Guiana is a relatively easy destination to travel with children as health and food standards are high. Good destinations are the Kourou Space Center and Space Museum (see Sports and Activities, page 394) as well as *pirogue* trips into the interior. The former prisons, too, are interesting as there is wildlife including monkeys and agoutis. There is also a zoo at Montsinéry, west of Cayenne, open Wed–Sun 9.30am–5.30pm, with canopy walks.

Climate

The best time to visit French Guiana is August through October; the rest of the year there is heavy rain, though there can be a comparatively dry period in February and March. The climate is hot and tropical in all parts of the country and the humidity rarely drops below 80 percent.

Crime and Safety

Cayenne has seen some increase in violent crime, including robberies, and petty crime occurs in many towns. Travelers should keep valuables out of sight, particularly when they are left in a car. Ask at your hotel or at the tourist office about which streets to avoid, and always travel by taxi at night.

Disabled Travelers

The quality of services is somewhere between the low standards of South America and the higher ones of France. The colony's government is expanding wheelchair access to public transportation for the bus

Emergency Numbers

General emergency number for Police, Ambulance and Fire: 112

services in Cayenne and along the coast, and to public buildings, but much remains to be done.

Eating Out

What to Eat

French Guiana has an extremely varied cuisine of a high, French standard in the main towns. Beyond French and Creole food, Vietnamese, Indonesian, and Chinese food are common. Fish and seafood – including local giant shrimp – are also among local delicacies, accompanied by local rice, red beans, or *couac* (similar to the Brazilian *farofa* made of manioc). A typical cocktail is the Ti-punch, made of rum, cane sugar syrup – sometimes flavored with vanilla – and a slice of lemon, mixed and drunk without ice.

Where to Eat

Cayenne

Relatively inexpensive Javanese and Creole cafés and food stalls are on the Canal Laussant south of downtown Cayenne, though be watchful of cleanliness, and remember that the area is unsafe at night. A large number of restaurants are concentrated in the area between Malouet and Canal De L'Est streets in the center of town.

Embassies and Consulates

UK

British Honorary Consulate, 16 Rue Monerville, Cayenne, tel: 311-034.

US

The US Embassy in Suriname provides consular services. Dr Sophie Redmondstraat 129, Paramaribo, tel: (011) 597-472-900.

Entry Requirements and Customs Regulations

Visas

For a stay of up to 90 days, visitors from the US and EU, Australia, and New Zealand only need passports, a return ticket, and a yellow-fever vaccination received at least 10

French Guiana's annual Carnival in Kourou.

days before entry. US journalists on assignment need a visa.

Customs

Duty-free allowances for visitors outside the EU include 200 cigarettes or 50 cigars or 100 cigarillos or 250g of tobacco, 1 liter of spirits over 22 percent or 2 liters of alcoholic beverages up to 22 percent proof, 2 liters of wine, 50g of perfume and 250ml of eau de toilette, 500g of coffee or 200g of coffee extract, 100g of tea or 40g of tea extract, and other goods up to the value of €255 or €130 for children under 15.

Festivals

January–February/March

Carnival, beginning on the weekend after Epiphany, culminating in the five days before Ash Wednesday. Traditions differ from Brazilian and Caribbean carnivals. Women don full-length disguises and call themselves *Touloulous* on the Saturday before Ash Wednesday, and men must not refuse requests to dance. Parades are held the next day in central Cayenne. Vaval, the festival's devilish soul, is burned at Place des Palmistes on Mardi Gras to officially end the celebrations, while mourners wear black and white in parades the next day.

September

La Biennale du Marronnage at Matoury near Cayenne, during even-numbered years. African music festival, also including seminars and presentation of typical food.

Gay and Lesbian Travelers

There is no gay scene in French Guyana and attitudes are more conservative than in France.

Health and Medical Care

Standards are high, though yellow-fever vaccination is mandatory and medical insurance is advisable. There are few healthcare facilities outside Cayenne, Kourou, and Saint Laurent du Maroni. Tap water in the main towns is safe to drink, though bottled water is advised. There are three hospitals and 21 public health clinics throughout French Guiana. In Cayenne, contact the **Centre Hospitalier André Rosemon**, Rue des Flamboyants, tel: 395-050. In Kourou, contact the **Red Crossís Centre Médico-Chirurgical de Kourou**, Av. des Iles, tel: 327-676.

Media

La Presse de la Guyane is the local daily newspaper. *France-Guyane-Antilles*, a weekly, has up-to-date tourist information. Maison de la Presse at 14 Av. Général de Gaulle sells mainland French newspapers.

Money

Dollars or traveler's checks are easily exchangeable for euros in banks and exchange bureaux in Cayenne. Major credit cards are widely accepted, and visitors can get cash advances from ATMs at post offices. There are two ATMs at the Cayenne airport.

Nightlife

Outside of Carnival, Cayenne's nightlife is relatively quiet. There are numerous little bars in which to escape the heat with a cold beer. Cayenne, Kourou, and Saint Laurent du Maroni each have movie theaters presenting French-language cinema. The three cities also have discos. In Cayenne, there are two on Av. Charles de Gaulle in the center of town: **Club 106** and **Number One**, charging an expensive cover of about $20.

Opening Hours

Shops open Mon–Fri 8am–1pm and 4–7pm, Sat 9am–12.30pm. Banks open Mon–Fri 7.45–11.30am and

3–5pm. Supermarkets stay open until 8.30pm and open Sundays 9am–12.30pm.

Postal Services

There are five post offices in Cayenne. The main branch is at Route du Baduel outside the city center, open weekdays 7am–6.15pm and Saturdays 7am–noon.

Public Holidays

1 January New Year's Day
February/March* Mardi Gras and Ash Wednesday
March* Mi Carême (mid-Lent)
March/April Easter Monday
1 May Labor Day
8 May Victory in Europe Day
13 May Ascension
24 May Whit Monday
10 June Abolition of Slavery
14 July Bastille Day
15 August Assumption
15 October* Cayenne Festival
1 November All Saints' Day
2 November* All Souls' Day
11 November Remembrance Day
25 December Christmas Day
*regional

Shopping

Crafts carved from wood, Hmong embroidery, and rum are the main handicrafts produced here.

Sport and Activities

The interior holds numerous routes for canoeing and **kayaking**. **Jet-skiing** is popular on the Montsinéry River. **Wildlife watching** including birding is possible in the interior, along with fishing. The best area from which to visit the jungle is Saül in the center of the colony, around which numerous well-marked trails run. Tours are available. Observation of **sea turtle-hatching** is most accessible at Les Hattes beach. There is a **golf** course in Kourou. Visits to the **Kourou Space Center** are free but should be booked several days in advance at tel: 326-123 (www.cnes-csg.fr).

Telecommunications

As in France, public telephones use prepaid cards that can be used for international calls. Internet and cellphone access is available from the border with Suriname to the area around Cayenne, but spotty towards the east and nonexistent in the

interior. Mobile service providers are Digicel and Orange Caraïbe, the latter with the broadest service. Cellphones work on the 900 and 1800 MHz bands. 3G services are available in Kourou and Cayenne.

Tipping

Virtually none. At hotels and restaurants the service charge is included. Taxi drivers are very rarely tipped.

Tourist Information and Agencies

There are nine tourism offices in French Guiana, including the **Syndicat d'initiative** at 19, rue Léon Gontrand Damas in Cayenne. The **Comité du Tourisme de la Guyane** (French Guyana Tourism Board) at 12, rue Lallouette, has comprehensive information on hotels, transportation, and other activities. The Chambre de Commerce et d'Industrie de Guyane has information at the international airport on tours and hotels. Also see other tour operators in the following links:

Websites

www.tourisme-guyane.com/en.html Official tourism site with comprehensive listings, not fully in English.
www.espace-amazonie.com Espace Amazonie, highly recommended local operator.
www.jal-voyages.com Jal Voyages, long-established operator.
www.guides-guyane.com Association of nature guides (in French) with links to many attractive trips through the interior, including the Amazon national park.
www.parc-guyane.gf Website for the Amazon national park (in French).

What to Read

Mad White Giant by Benedict Allen. Account of his 2,400km (1,500-mile) journey from the mouth of the Orinoco to the mouth of the Amazon in 1983, and his time with the Wai-Wais.
Papillon by Henri Charrière. Classic story of Charrière's daring escape from penal colony in French Guiana to Colombia, Guyana, and eventually to Venezuela.
Space in the Tropics: From Convicts to Rockets in French Guiana by Peter Redfield. A cultural history of the colony, reviewing France's struggles in deciding what to do with its remote territory.

GUYANA

ESSENTIAL TRAVEL TIPS TO HELP YOU GET THERE AND GET AROUND

FACT FILE

Area 215,000 sq km (83,000 sq miles)
Capital Georgetown
Population 800,000
Language English (official language), Creole, Hindi, Urdu, and several indigenous languages
Currency Guyana dollar
Weights and measures Metric (imperial measures widely used)
Electricity Some 220V in Georgetown; 110V is most common throughout the country
Time zone GMT -4hrs, EST +1hr
International dialing code 592
Internet abbreviation .gy

TRANSPORTATION

Getting There

By Air

From Europe: Caribbean Airlines, British Airways, or Virgin Atlantic connecting with LIAT.
From US: Delta Airlines, Surinam Airways.

Getting Around

From the Airport

Chedi Jagan International Airport is 40km (25 miles) from Georgetown at Timehri. Minibuses (No. 42) to the center cost $1, and will take you to your hotel for a small fee; taxis cost $20–25 (more at night, use official taxis; it is cheaper to book a seat on

a minibus on arrival). Departure tax is G$4,000 ($20).

By Air

Internal flights are the easiest way to get around Guyana. **Trans Guyana Airways** has scheduled flights from Georgetown to Lethem. Charter companies include Trans Guyana Airways, Roraima Airways, and **Air Services Ltd**. The airport at Ogle, about 20 minutes from the center of Georgetown by road, is used for domestic charter flights. Book early and reconfirm as flights are commonly overbooked. Baggage on domestic flights is limited to about 10kg (20lbs); check with the airline as this may vary.

By Bus and Taxi

Minibuses and collective taxis run along the coast and to many destinations inland. This form of transport is cheap but slow. Taxis have an "H" in their number plates. There are long-distance bus connections to Lethem on the border with Brazil, for which tickets should be bought at least 24 hours in advance.

By River

Guyana has over 965km (600 miles) of navigable waterways. There are frequent services but they tend to be erratic. *Ballahoos* are six-seater boats; *corials* are four-seater boats.

By Car

Most of the main roads are in the coastal area. There is a highway between Lethem in Guyana and Boa Vista in Brazil. Driving is on the left, as in the UK.

In Georgetown

Cramped minibuses are the main

way of getting around the capital. There are also collective taxis that travel on set routes with fixed fares. The main departure points are Stabroek and Avenue of the Republic. Taxis are cheap and plentiful and the safest way of traveling after dark.

A–Z

Accommodations

Most of the luxury and business hotels are in Georgetown; quality ranges from good to reasonable. Note that cheap hotels are often of the type that rent by the hour. The city has several quaint hotels in colonial houses.

Jungle and Savannah Lodges

There are many lodges and camps in the tropical forest interior, catering for the ecotourism market. These establishments, whose facilities range from basic to upmarket, usually run their own nature safaris. Recommended are Timberhead (www.timberheadguyana.com), Arrowpoint Nature Resort, and Emerald Tower Rainforest Lodge, all near Georgetown. Dubalay Ranch on the Berbice River is to the southeast. Shanklands is to the west on a bluff topping the Essequibo. Rainbow River Safari is on the Mazaruni River at Marshall Falls. In the southern Rupununi Savannah are the vast Dadanawa Ranch (www.dadanawaranch.com) and Karanambu Ranch (http://karanambu.com). The Rock View Lodge (www.rockviewlodge.com) is at the meeting point of the savannah and the Amazon forest in the center of the country.

Arts

Georgetown is the country's cultural hub. Near the botanical gardens, east of downtown, is **Castellani House**, which holds the National Art Collection, and the Cultural Centre, Guyana's largest theatre. The other main theatre is the **Playhouse Theatre** on Parade Street, two blocks from the Atlantic Ocean.

Budgeting for Your Trip

Accommodations: Expect to pay $11–25 for decent budget hotels with fans, and from $40 for rooms with air conditioning. Jungle and savannah lodges cost $100 and up. It is a good idea to book tours, to save time.
Food: Food is relatively cheap, with inexpensive meals costing just $2–4, and a meal at one of the better restaurants costing about $20 per person.

Children

The lodges of the interior are a good destination for children, due to the outdoor activities and possibilities for wildlife viewing, as are those near Georgetown for swimming and other activities. Insect repellent and sunblock are essential.

Climate

The temperature remains warm with equatorial humidity all year round, but is not excessively hot. The climate varies from north to south. In the north, there are two wet seasons, May–June and December–January, and the best time to visit is in the July–November dry season. The south and the Rupununi region have one May–July wet season. The dry season is better to see the wildlife, but Kaieteur Falls is most impressive during the rainy season.

Crime and Safety

Georgetown is a colorful and attractive city but you should take care in some areas (avoid Tiger Bay and Albouystown in particular) and do not walk around the streets at night. Violent crime on the streets and highways is common, and there are many beggars, although most are harmless.

Disabled Travelers

Services for travelers with disabilities are as yet practically nonexistent. Check with tour agencies for travel opportunities.

Eating Out

What to Eat

Guyanese cuisine is good and varied, combining influences from the Caribbean, Africa, Europe, North America, and Asia, as well as indigenous cooking. Seafood is particularly tasty. Interesting Creole dishes include the traditional Christmas dish, pepperpot (meat cooked with hot spices and cassava juice); cow-heel soup, and saltfish. There is a wide range of tropical fruits (often served as refreshing drinks in some excellent juice bars) and vegetables. Locally produced rum is the favored tipple. The best are Demerara Distillers' 12-year King of Diamonds and 15-year El Dorado. The beer, Banks, is quite palatable.

Where to Eat

The most formal restaurants are found in the best hotels; shorts are not permitted. There are numerous restaurants of all kinds in the downtown area, particularly **Middle Street** and **Main Street**. Rum shops are the cheapest, most raucous bars. Cheap restaurants are close to **Stabroek Market**. Many restaurants close on public holidays; cheaper places are often open only for lunch.

Embassies and Consulates

UK
High Commission, 44 Main Street, Georgetown, tel: 226-5881–4.

US
100 Young Street, Georgetown, tel: 225-4900.

Australia
Services provided by the embassy in Santiago, Chile: Isidora Goyenechea 3621, Santiago, tel: 550-3500, www.chile.embassy.gov.au.

Canada
Corner of High Street and Young Street, Georgetown, tel: 227-2081.

Ireland
10 Bel Air Springs, Georgetown City, Georgetown, tel: 2269-339.

Emergency Numbers

Police 911
Fire 912
Ambulance service 913

Entry Requirements and Customs Regulations

Visas

Visas are not required by visitors from the US, Commonwealth, and non-East European EU countries. Proof of return travel is necessary.

Customs

Visitors aged 16 and older are allowed to bring in duty free 200 cigarettes or 50 cigars or 225g of tobacco and spirits and wine not exceeding 750ml.

Festivals

February

Mashrami (23), on Republic Day, is similar to carnival, celebrated elsewhere in the region around this date. Parades of decorated floats, costume competitions, and dancing in the streets to calypso music.

March/April

Easter, celebrated in part by flying kites.

August

Wats Hott is a popular music festival in Georgetown and Essequibo.

September

Guyexpo trade show, Georgetown, accompanied by concerts.

October

Diwali, Hindu festival of lights. Many houses, mandirs (temples), and streets are lined with rows of lights and there is a nocturnal parade.

Gay and Lesbian Travelers

There is no gay scene as such in Guyana, but the atmosphere is tolerant and bars and clubs tend to be welcoming and gay-friendly.

Health and Medical Care

Standards are mediocre and sanitary conditions in some treatment centers are poor. Medical insurance is strongly recommended. Tap water isn't suitable for drinking, though its brownish color is from

tannins, not pollution. Seek advice on malaria prophylaxis when traveling to the interior and take insect repellent. Yellow-fever vaccination is recommended when traveling outside Georgetown (it takes 10 days before it is effective). Bring essential medicine as it may not be available locally – certainly not in the remote interior.
The main clinics are:
St. Joseph Mercy Hospital, 130–2 Parade Street, Georgetown, tel: 227-2073-5.
Prasad's Hospital, 260 Thomas and Middle streets, tel: 226-7210/9.
Davis Memorial Hospital, 121 Durban Street Lodge, tel: 227-2041-3.
Georgetown Public Hospital, New Market Street, tel: 227-8232/8204–9.

Media

The main newspapers are *The Chronicle* (daily), *The Mirror* (weekly), and *The Stabroek News* (daily).

Money

The value of the Guyanese dollar (G$) is revised weekly. Most banks and *bureaux de change* (known as *cambios*) buy only US or Canadian dollars and UK sterling. It is possible to change traveler's checks at the larger stores and travel agents in Georgetown. Scotia Bank and Republic Bank branches have ATMs. It's not worth the risk of changing money on the black market. Credit cards are not widely accepted.

Nightlife

Georgetown's nightlife is quite lively. **Sheriff Street** outside the center is the hot spot, with numerous bars and late-night restaurants. In the center, **Camp Street** and **Middle Street** have several bars and discos. Beyond rock, some clubs offer jazz and Indian music. Clubs include the Blue Note on Camp Street.

Opening Hours

Stores are open Mon–Fri 8.30am–5pm and Sat 8am–noon. Supermarkets generally open Mon–Fri 8.30am–6pm, Sat 8.30am–7pm, while markets open at 7am except for Stabroek and Bourda, which are open round the clock. Office hours are 8am–noon and 1–4.30pm.

Postal Services

Postal services are good and cheap. The main post office is on North Road in Georgetown.

Public Holidays

January 1 New Year's Day
February 23 Republic Day and Mashramani Festival
March/April Phagwah (Hindu religious holiday), Good Friday, Easter Monday; Eid-ul-Azha (Muslim holy day) is moveable as it follows the lunar calendar
May 1 Labor Day
May 26 Independence Day
July 1 Caricom Day
August 1 Freedom Day
December 25 Christmas Day
December 26 Boxing Day

Shopping

Georgetown's markets are colorful and attractive places to shop for local crafts, and this is where most locals do their shopping. Take care in the Stabroek Market and don't take valuables with you. Other markets include Bourda, La Penitence, and Kitty. There can be good offers on gold jewelry, but it's dangerous to buy it on the street. Local handicrafts include hammocks, baskets, woodcarvings, leather goods, and objects made out of a resin called *balata*. The main shopping districts are around Regent Street and Charity Village.

Sport and Activities

Guyana's most popular sport is **cricket**. The Georgetown Cricket Club at Bourda is one of the most famous grounds in the Caribbean. The Providence Stadium was built specifically for the World Cricket Cup in 2007.
The coastline is not ideal for water sports, but there are some good opportunities in the interior for **trekking** and **river-rafting**, which can be arranged by local tour operators.
The Essequibo River provides an excellent arena for **water sports**. Enjoy sunfish sailing, kayaking, water skiing, and tubing. Less strenuous activities such as croquet, mini-golf, and volleyball can be played on the lawns and beaches.

Telecommunications

International direct dialing is available in most main towns

and cities. GT&T offers cellular service on the 800 MHz band, rival Digicel Guyana on the 900 MHz band.

Tipping

Some restaurants add a 10 percent service charge. Tipping is not generally expected, but is appreciated, so if you are pleased with the service add a 10 percent tip (in Guyanese dollars in the interior as there are no exchange facilities).

Tourist Information and Agencies

Guyana's Tourism Authority, National Exhibition Centre, Sophia, Georgetown, tel: 233-6351, is the best source of local information on accommodations and activities of all kinds.

Specialist Tour Operators

Wilderness Explorers, Cara Suites, 176 Middle Street, Georgetown, tel: 227-7698, www.wilderness-explorers.com.

Websites

www.guyana-tourism.com The tourism authority's website.
www.kaieteurpark.gov.gy Official information on traveling to Kaieteur Falls.
www.iwokrama.org Information on the Iwokrama conservation project in central Guyana.

What to Read

Three Singles to Adventure by Gerald Durrell. The witty British naturalist's autobiographical account of his experiences while living in Guyana.
Jungle Cowboy by Stanley Brock. A description of ranch life and wild animals in Guyana.
Guyana Fragile Frontier: Loggers, Miners and Forest Peoples by Marcus Colchester. The book's title indicates its contents – it's a serious look at the environmental challenges the country faces and the threats to the survival of its indigenous people.
The Ventriloquist's Tale by Pauline Melville. Set in Georgetown and the Guyanese savannah, the author jumps from the 1920s to the present in describing the follies of colonialism and its aftermath, along with the perils of forbidden love affairs.

PARAGUAY

ESSENTIAL TRAVEL TIPS TO HELP YOU GET THERE AND GET AROUND

FACT FILE

Area 406,752 sq km (157,000 sq miles)
Capital Asunción
Population 6.6 million
Languages Spanish and Guaraní
Currency Guaraní
Weights and measures Metric
Electricity 220 volts
Time zone GMT -3hrs in east, -4hrs in the west (EST +3hrs, EST +1hr)
International dialing code 595 (Asunción +21)
Internet abbreviation .py

TRANSPORTATION

Getting There

By Air

From Europe: Aerolíneas Argentinas, Iberia.
From/via US: TACA, TAM.
From Australia: Qantas, LAN.
From Canada: Delta, United.
From New Zealand: TAM.

Getting Around

From the Airport

Asunción's **Silvio Pettirossi Airport** is 16km (10 miles) from the city center; taxis can be reserved at agencies' desks, and cost approximately $18; buses to the center cost US$0.50, but luggage space is limited.

There is an international departure tax of around $40 (it is cheaper to pay

in guaranís). Punta del Este's airport also has air traffic to and from Brazil.

By Air

At time of printing, no reliable scheduled domestic air traffic existed in Paraguay.

By Bus

Buses are the main means of transport within Paraguay. The main bus terminal is a 20-minute cab ride from the center of Asunción at Av. Rep. Argentina and Fernando de la Mora, tel: 551-740/1. "Executive" buses vary according to the company but overall offer the highest quality and fastest service.

There is a luxury international bus service that serves Asunción and Ciudad del Este, Pedro Juan Caballero and Encarnación by way of Argentina, Uruguay and Brazil. Bus service to Bolivia through the Chaco is available, though buses are prone to breakdowns, which can mean very long trips. Take food and water.

By Car

Gasoline is cheap and car rental fairly inexpensive; contact **Touring y Automóvil Club Paraguayo**, 25 de Mayo and Calle Brasíl, tel: 210-550 for further information on car touring in Paraguay.

In Asunción

Inexpensive buses barrel through Asunción. The service runs 6am–midnight, most bus lines however shut down by 10pm. Most of the main sites are easily seen on foot as they are in a relatively compact area and close to the main hotels. Taxis use meters and are plentiful. One main taxi stand is in front of the Hotel Guaraní on the Plaza de los

Héroes; or call RadioTaxi, tel: 550-116/311-080.

By River

There are several boats that sail up the Paraná River to Concepción every 2–3 weeks, a journey of 27–30 hours. An irregular passenger boat service shuttles downstream between Buenos Aires and Asunción. The journey takes 5 days but may be suspended during the dry winter months. The trips are rustic: take essentials like sleeping bags, food, water, toilet paper, and insect repellent.

A–Z

Accommodations

Paraguay has a broad selection of mid-range hotels with showers, private bath, and breakfast, with fewer good basic lodgings. Book well ahead during the popular July August travel months. Hotels tend to offer two rates, one for rooms with air conditioning, the other without. Some sites allow camping, including one adjacent to the botanical gardens in Asunción. There are rural estancias that have been turned into hotels; see the rural tourism association for more information, www.turismorural.org.py.

Arts

Paraguay's main art museums are the centrally located **Museo Nacional de Bellas Artes** and the **Centro de Artes Visuales** at Isla de Francia away from the center in Asunción. The latter holds the native and contemporary art museum **Museo del Barro**. Plays are performed at the 700-seat **Teatro Municipal Ignacio A. Pane**, also in the center of town, completed in 1889 and renovated in 2006. Paraguayan music is unique in the region in the dominance of guitar and harp. In Asunción the following foreign cultural institutes hold events: the **Centro Cultural Paraguayo-Americano** on España 352, the **Asociación Cultural Paraguayo Británica** on Juan de Salazar 391, the **Alianza Francesa** at Mariscal Estigarribia 1039, and the **Instituto Cultural Paraguayo Alemán – Goethe Zentrum** at Juan de Salazar 310.

Budgeting for Your Trip

Paraguay is cheaper than Argentina and Brazil.
Accommodations: There are numerous decent mid-range hotels in a price range between $20 and $30, but most hotels with pools charge at least $80 per room.
Food: Dinners in more expensive restaurants average $20–35 per person but you can eat for considerably less.
Museums and Attractions: Budget for a couple of dollars per person for entrance fees, none are expensive.
Transportation: Taxis are inexpensive, averaging $2 per journey in Asunción. Minimum charge is about US$0.80; 30 percent more at night. Buses are very cheap.

Children

Paraguay's extremely hot summers mean that care must be taken to keep children hydrated, and use lots of sunblock. Central Paraguay and the waterfalls of the east are good destinations for children. Many resorts on the Golden Circle central tour have swimming pools, and Aregua still has a running steam-powered train.

Climate

Paraguay has a subtropical climate. Summer (December–February) is very hot and humid; spring and fall are milder. In winter (June–August)

Emergency Numbers

Ambulance, Fire, Police 911

temperatures can drop to just a few degrees above freezing but it never snows. While rain can occur at any time, it's heaviest from October through April.

Crime and Safety

While safer than its neighboring countries, Paraguay has registered an increase in crime, including theft but also robbery and mugging in Asunción, Ciudad del Este, and San Lorenzo. It is advisable not to resist armed assault. Travel by taxi at night in cities and avoid night-time overland travel by car. Take care when crossing streets as pedestrians are ignored by buses and cars alike.

Disabled Travelers

Even by South American standards Paraguay offers limited services for travelers with disabilities. Check with specialized tour operators for tour opportunities.

Eating Out

What to Eat

Paraguayan specialties include *surubí*, a tasty fish dish; *sopa paraguaya*, a rich cornbread made of ground maize and cheese; *soyo*, a beef and vegetable soup; *empanadas*, and fresh tropical juices. Paraguayan beef is superb. Immigration has also led to a profusion of good-quality restaurants including Japanese, Korean, Chinese, and German. There are also a number of excellent Brazilian restaurants with succulent barbecue-grilled meats and large self-service buffets.

Drinking Tips

Paraguayan beer is made according to German methods and is extremely refreshing. The local sugar-cane liquor, *caña*, is popular and many liquors are imported at low prices. Also try non-alcoholic *tereré*, a local ice-cold drink made from maté; it's like the iced tea version of the hot maté drunk in Argentina and Uruguay.

Where to Eat

Most of the better restaurants are inside or in the vicinity of more upscale hotels around Estados Unidos and Colón in central Asunción and, increasingly, east of downtown in Recoleta and Villa Morra.

Embassies and Consulates

UK
Honorary Consul, J. Eulogio Estigarribia and Bogarin 4846, Asunción, tel: 210-405.

US
Av. Mariscal López 1776, Asunción, tel: 213-715, www.spanish.paraguay.usembassy.gov.

Australia
Accreditation through the embassy in Argentina: Calle Villanueva 1400, Buenos Aires, tel: 4779-3500, www.argentina.embassy.gov.au.

Canada
Accreditation through the embassy in Argentina: Calle Tagle 2828, tel: 4808-1000, www.canadainternational.gc.ca/argentina-argentine.

New Zealand
Accreditation through the embassy in Argentina: Carlos Pellegrini 1427, 5th floor, tel: 4328-0747, www.nzembassy.com/argentina.

Entry Requirements and Customs Regulations

Visas

UK and Irish citizens don't need visas; visitors from the US, Canada, Australia, and New Zealand need to obtain a visa from a Paraguayan embassy before entering the country.

Customs

"Reasonable" quantities of alcohol, tobacco, perfume and electronic items for personal use are admitted to the country duty-free.

Festivals

February

Fiestas de San Blas (3). Throughout Paraguay. Street dancing and floats, merging with carnival, which has moveable dates.

June

Festival de San Juan (24). Throughout Paraguay. It is celebrated with bonfires and walking over hot coals.

July

Fiesta de la Virgen del Carmen (16). It is celebrated with religious processions and school parades, traditional food and games of Paraguay.

September

La Virgen de la Merced (24). Puno. A festival of great religious significance.

Gay and Lesbian Travelers

Paraguay's machismo, which is more prevalent than elsewhere in the region, makes the country less welcoming for homosexual travelers. It is recommended that you exercise discretion and act accordingly. Nevertheless, there is a relatively well-known gay and lesbian club, Trauma, located on 25 de Mayo 760.

Health and Medical Care

Travelers should have vaccinations against hepatitis, typhoid fever, and tetanus. Tap water is considered safe but bottled water is widely available. Vegetables should be eaten cooked and peeled. Meat – while generally good quality – and fish should also be well-cooked, and eaten while still hot.

Health insurance is necessary. A satisfactory ambulance service is not available; it's best to transport a patient by private means or taxi. Have someone phone the hospital, stating the nature of the problem and asking that a doctor receive the patient in the emergency room.

For emergencies, contact any of the Asunción emergency rooms:
Hospital de Clínicas, Av. Dr. Montero and Lagerenza, Asunción, tel: 420-982/983.
Hospital Bautista, Av. Rep. Argentina and Campos Cervera, Asunción tel: 600-171/607-944.

Money

It is almost impossible to exchange guaranís outside the country, so only change what you will need. *Casas de cambio* will accept traveler's checks. Best exchange rates are in Asunción, with many on Palma and Estrella. ATMs are fairly widespread, and major credit cards are widely accepted. MasterCard is easier to use than Visa.

Nightlife

A typical evening's entertainment is a restaurant floor show, with Paraguayan harp and guitar music, and sometimes the (indescribable and unmissable) bottle dance. Prices vary according to the quality

of the show, but are generally about US$10 per person. Recommended spots in Asunción include: **Casino de Asunción Av. España and Av. Sacramento, open 9pm–6am**, and **Sky Lounge & Resto Av. España and Malutin, Paseo Carmelitas, tel: 600-940**. There are popular pubs and discos on Cerro Corá. Asunción's most important street for nightlife is Brasilia, drawing young crowds. Ciudad del Este and Encarnación have casinos.

Opening Hours

During the hot season (December–February), a long midday siesta is observed and many shops and offices open Mon–Sat 6.30am–noon and 3–7pm. Banks tend to be open Mon–Fri 7.30–11am, although some stay open for longer hours. Dinner is served somewhat earlier than in neighboring countries, that is, around 8.30–11pm.

Postal Services

The mail system is expensive and inefficient. Send important letters by registered mail. All mail must be deposited at a post-office counter. The main post office is on El Paraguayo Independiente in Asunción.

Public Holidays

1 January New Year's Day
1 March Battle of Cerro Corá
March/April Good Friday, Easter Monday
1 May Labor Day
15 May Independence Day
12 June Peace of the Chaco
15 August Founding of Asunción
29 September Battle of Boquerón
8 December Immaculate Conception
25 December Christmas Day

Shopping

Paraguay is famous for its *ñandutí* (*guaraní* for cobweb) lace, used to decorate bedcovers, tablecloths, blankets, etc. Other good buys are guitars and harps, gold and silver filigree jewelry, tooled leather, and ponchos of cotton and wool.

Where to Shop

In Asunción, the **street market** in Calle Palma is pedestrianized on Saturday morning and has a variety of goods; leather and lace are great value. Nearby, several streets have numerous good crafts shops: Pettirossi, Estrella, and Colón. Stores

may grant up to 15 percent discounts for cash payments.

Sport and Activities

Wildlife-watching, including birding, is excellent in the Chaco and Pantanal and best done through an organized tour. **Soccer** is the most popular sport, and Paraguay has produced important international stars such as striker Roque Santa Cruz.

Telecommunications

Long-distance calls can be made from COPACO office on Oliva and 15 de Agosto. Telex and fax services are available. International calls are *ordinario* or *urgente*, urgent calls costing twice as much. Cellphone services are from Claro Paraguay, Vox, Tigo and Personal. The first two use the 1900 MHz band and have 3G services. Personal runs on the 850 and 1900 MHz bands and offers 3.5G services.

Tipping

Tip waiters 10–15 percent, unless a service charge is included. Taxi drivers should be tipped a similar amount.

Tourist Information

The **Dirección General de Turismo Paraguayo** is at Av. Palma 468, Asunción, tel: 494-110/441-530. Information is also available at the Touring & Automobile Club at Calle 25 de Mayo and Brasil.

Tours

Inter Express, Calle Yegros 690 and Herrera, Asunción, tel: 490 111, email: iexpress@interexpress.com.py
Martin Travel, Perú 436 and España, Asunción, tel: 211-747, email: incoming@martintravel. com.py.

Websites

www.senatur.gov.py Official government tourism website.
www.paraguay.com Excellent information on Paraguayan culture.

What to Read

I, the Supreme by Augusto Roa Bastos. Novel by the great Paraguayan author depicting the life of the enlightened despot José Gaspar Rodríguez de Francia.
At the Tomb of the Inflatable Pig by John Gimlette. Humorous and in-depth travel account that doesn't gloss over the darker aspects.

PERU

ESSENTIAL TRAVEL TIPS TO HELP YOU GET THERE AND GET AROUND

FACT FILE

Area 1,285,212 sq km (496,100 sq miles)
Capital Lima
Population 30 million
Language Spanish and Quechua
Currency Nuevo sol
Weights and measures Metric
Electricity 220 volts
Time zone GMT -5hrs (EST)
Dialing code 51 (Lima +1)
Internet abbreviation .pe

TRANSPORTATION

Getting There

By Air

From Europe: Air Europa, Air France, Alitalia, Iberia, LAN, Lufthansa, KLM.
From/via US: American Airlines, Delta, United, LAN, TACA.
From Australia, New Zealand: Qantas, LAN.
From Canada: Air Canada.

Getting Around

From the Airport

The most reliable bus service to and from **Jorge Chávez International Airport** is **Shuttle Bus Urbanito**, Calle Manoa 391, Breña, tel: 424-3650/425-1202. The fare to central Lima is $6, and to Miraflores or San Isidro, $8–10.
Reliable taxi services include:
Taxi Green, tel: 484-4001, email: taxigreen@peru.com; **CMV Taxi**

Remisse Ejecutivo, tel: 422-4838; **Mitsui Taxi Remisse Ejecutivo**, tel: 261-7788; and **Taxi Seguro**, tel: 241-9292. A taxi fare to the center of Lima is $10–15, and to Miraflores or San Isidro, about $20. *Ejecutivo* taxis charge a little more. On leaving, note that when booking for departures, the airport departure tax (TUUA) is now included on international flights.

By Air

LAN (www.lan.com), and **TACA** (www.taca.com) serve most cities in Peru. **Star Perú (www.starperu.com) offers charters in Peru and also for some countries in South America** .

By Boat

Crillon Tours, Av.Camacho 1223, La Paz, Bolivia, tel: 591-2233-7533, www.titicaca.com, runs several hydrofoil services across Lake Titicaca.

By Bus

Numerous transport companies operate morning and evening departures from Lima to most cities. Reliable companies include **Cruz del Sur** (www.cruzdelsur.com.pe), **Tepsa** (www.tepsa.com.pe) and **Ormeño**, tel: 472-5000, www.grupo-ormeno.com.pe, offers a good quality international service from Caracas to Buenos Aires and points in between, as well as La Paz. From Bolivia, efficient minibus services take you from La Paz to Puno, from where other buses operate. It is cheaper to switch to domestic buses when crossing borders.

By Rail

PeruRail operates three daily services from Cusco to the ruins at Machu Picchu: the luxury *Hiram Bingham* train, the *Vistadome* service, whose panoramic windows offer passengers spectacular views, and the no-frills *Backpacker* service. Tickets can be purchased at the PeruRail office in Cusco (Av. Pachacutec, tel: 581-400) or through their website: www.perurail.com. There are other rail operators on this route as well. The Lima–Huancayo passenger service, the world's highest train journey, is operated by **Ferrocarril Central Andino S.A.** (tel: 226-6363, www.ferrocarrilcentral.com.pe). See also www.incasdelperu.org for up-to-date information on this service. Passenger trains run several times a week from Arica in Chile through the desert to Tacna in southern Peru. Buy tickets at the station 24 hours before the trip. The voyage is short but rustic.

In Lima

Lima's transport system consists mainly of thousands of chaotic standard and mini-sized buses that are cheap but overcrowded and full of pickpockets. Taxis are cheap but fares need to be negotiated in advance. Dedicated Metropolitano bus lines traverse the city including downtown, Miraflores, and Barranco, while Tren Eléctrico rail service runs along its eastern fringe from the central Grau station.

A–Z

Accommodations

Accommodations in Peru range from the smartest five-star hotels imaginable to village home-stays where bed is a mattress on an earthen floor. In between there's

ARGENTINA BOLIVIA BRAZIL CHILE COLOMBIA ECUADOR FALKLAND ISLANDS FRENCH GUIANA GUYANA PARAGUAY PERU SURINAME URUGUAY VENEZUELA

a plethora of sleeping options, from colonial mansions to simple and welcoming hostels. For longer stays, many cities now offer rental apartments. Some of the loveliest places to stay in Peru are the country haciendas and lodges, away from the big towns. Most hotels in Peru are clean, efficient, friendly, and surprisingly good value. Hot water is not always reliable, however (even in the smarter places), so it's worth checking whether the taps run warm 24 hours a day. Most hotels include continental breakfasts in their rates and many, particularly in Lima and Cusco, offer a free airport pick-up and internet connection.

Arts

From music and song to a huge spectrum of handicrafts, Peru has one of the most diverse arts scenes in South America.

You can't leave without spending an evening at a *peña* (see Nightlife, page 403), where you'll experience some of the country's hundreds of musical genres. In Lima's theaters, you'll find everything from plays of Inca origin to distinctly avant-garde productions. Check the Cultural section of *El Comercio* newspaper for performances and exhibitions. The main theatres are the **Teatro Larco**, Av. Larco 1036, Miraflores, **Teatro Británico**, Bellavista 527, Miraflores, and the central **Teatro Municipal**, Ica 377. The best art and antique establishments are in the areas of San Isidro, Miraflores, and Barranco. The **Philharmonic Society** in Lima presents celebrated international orchestras and soloists from April to November.

Budgeting for Your Trip

You can get by in Peru on $30 a day – but that would be just getting by at rock bottom prices, and why would you want to stint when there's so much enjoyment to be had? A more reasonable budget is $60 per day for an enjoyable holiday. If you stay in four- and five-star hotels and eat in restaurants designed for tourists, your budget will need to be several hundred dollars per day.
Accommodations: Mid-range comfortable accommodations cost $25–50 a night.
Food: Meals at less touristy restaurants are amazingly cheap. The best value is the daily *menú*, which rarely costs more than five soles.
Museums and Attractions:

Individually they are not very expensive, but as there are so many of them, prices can add up. You can save money by purchasing the Cusco ticket, which for $49 gives you access to many highlights of Cusco and the Sacred Valley.

Children

In Lima and the bigger cities there are parks with children's playgrounds, and older children will enjoy many of the regular tourist attractions. Máncora and Paracas are excellent family destinations. Be very careful with the food your children eat. Avoid uncooked vegetables, salads, and unpeeled fruits. Make sure all water is bottled, filtered, or at least well boiled. Children become especially tired at high altitude: take it easy. Peruvian children's clothes and shoes are beautiful and cheap.

Climate

Peru's coastline has warm average temperatures, while in the highlands – or Sierra – it is normally cold, sunny, and dry for much of the year. The rainy season in the Sierra is from December to May. The jungle is hot and humid year-round. Lima alone suffers from the climatic condition the Peruvians call *garúa* – a thick wet fog that covers the city without respite from April through November.

Crime and Safety

Petty crime is rife in the urban centers of Peru. Pickpockets and thieves are common in Lima and Cusco and are amazingly adept at slitting open shoulder bags, camera cases, and knapsacks. Officials also warn against dealing with anyone approaching you in your hotel lobby or on the street, allegedly representing a travel agency or specialty shop.

A special security service for tourists has been created by Peru's Civil Guard, recognizable by a white braid across the shoulder of their uniforms. In Cusco, all police have tourism training.

Disabled Travelers

Peru has few facilities for disabled travelers. Hotels, except for luxury categories, normally don't have accessible rooms or bathrooms. In Lima, **Pro Peru Travel**, Av Jorge Basadre 399, San Isidro, tel: 421-5510, specializes in tours for travelers with disabilities.

Eating Out

What to Eat

Peru's cuisine ranges from scrumptious seafood to potatoes and guinea pig *(cuy)* – featured in a variety of highland dishes – to tropical fruits from the Amazon jungle. Immigrant cuisines – particularly Chinese – have contributed to its development. Recommended dishes include *ceviche*, raw fish and/or shellfish marinated in lemon juice and onions. Besides numerous fruit juices the soft drink *chicha morada*, made with purple maize, is popular. *Chicha de jora* is a home-made alcoholic brew known throughout the Andes, that could best be described as an acquired taste. The national **cocktail** is *pisco sour*.

Where to Eat

Lima has become South America's culinary capital, with several extremely good international restaurants. Most of the better restaurants are in **Miraflores**, **Barranco**, and **San Isidro**. Arguably South America's most renowned restaurant is Astrid y Gastón, which has opened branches in other South American capitals. In Lima, it is at Cantuarias 175, tel: 242-5387, 242-4422.

Other top Miraflores restaurants include Huaca Pucllana, General Borgoño Cdra 8 s/n, tel: 445-4042, and Rafael, at San Martín 300, tel: 242-4149. There are dozens of good *chifas* – Chinese restaurants – particularly in the Barrios Altos part of the old town.

Embassies and Consulates

UK
Torre Parque-Mar, 22nd floor, Av José Larco 1301, Miraflores, tel: 617-3000, http://ukinperu.fco.gov.uk/en.

Emergency Numbers

Police 105
Ambulance 470-5000
Fire 116
Tourist Police in Lima 423 3500 (Lima north) or 243 2190 (Lima south).
The tourist information service **Iperú** can assist in contacting police to report a crime: 24-hour hotline, tel: 574-8000.

US

Av. La Encalada s/n, cuadra 17, Surco, tel: 618-2000, http://lima.us embassy.gov.

Australia

Víctor A. Belaúnde 147, Edificio Real 3, Of. 1301, San Isidro tel: 222-8281.

Canada

Bolognesi 228, Miraflores, Lima 18, tel: 319-3200.

Ireland

Miguel Alegre Rodríguez 182, Lima, tel: 449-6289.

New Zealand

Leonidas Yerovi 106, Office 42, San Isidro, Lima, tel: 627-7778

Entry Requirements and Customs Regulations

Visas

Citizens of the EU, US, Canada, Australia, New Zealand, and South Africa do not require tourist visas. With a valid passport, citizens of these countries receive a tourism card which is usually valid for 90 days.

A 30-day extension is available upon payment of $20 and presentation of a return travel ticket. Contact the **Dirección General de Migraciones** in the Oficina de Migración, Av. España 730, Breña, tel: 200-1000.

Customs

Duty-free allowances include 400 cigarettes or 50 cigars or 250g of tobacco, alcoholic beverages not exceeding 2.5 liters and gifts or new articles for personal use up to a value of $300. It is illegal to take archeological artifacts out of the country.

Festivals

January

Anniversary of the founding of Lima (18). In Lima, with concerts, dancing, and fireworks.
Festival de la Marinera (end Jan). In Trujillo, with traditional dances and competitions.

February

Virgen de la Candelaria (early Feb). Puno. "La Mamita Candicha," the patron of Puno, is honored with parades, dances, fireworks, and music.

Carnival (mid-Feb). Puno and Cajamarca.

March

Fiesta de la Vendimia (early Mar). Ica. A celebration of the grape harvest.

June

Corpus Christi (mid-June,) Cusco. Procession of the Consecrated Host.
Inti Raymi (24) (Festival of the Sun), Cusco. This ancient festival is staged at the Sacsayhuamán fortress, and involves Inca rituals, parades, folk dances, and contests.

July

La Virgen del Carmen (15–17). Festivities are held throughout the highlands and are especially colorful in Paucartambo, 255km (160 miles) from Cusco.

August

Arequipa Day (15). The city's most important annual event. Festivities include folkloric dances and handicraft markets, and climax with a fireworks display in the Plaza de Armas.

October

El Señor de Luren (17–20). Ica. Thousands of pilgrims pay homage to the town patron.
El Señor de los Milagros (18, 19 and 28). Lima. A massive procession in honor of Lima's patron saint, on the 18th.
Unu Urco Festival (19). Urcos and Calca (near Cusco). Ceremonies, Andean music, dancing, and parades.

November

Puno Jubilee Week (1–7). Puno celebrates its founding by the Spanish, followed by a re-enactment of the emergence of the legendary founders of the Inca empire, Manco Capac and Mama Ocllo, from the waters of Lake Titicaca.

Gay and Lesbian Travelers

Homosexuality is rarely openly talked about or revealed in Peru. Gay men are derisively called *maricón* or *mariposa* (butterfly), and lesbian women are barely heard of. That said, there is a gay community, particularly in Lima, and information on gay venues in the city can be found at www.gayperu.com (in Spanish). The same organization runs a travel agency operating tours to major tourist destinations: www.gayperutravel.com.

Health and Medical Care

Standards in rural areas are low. Drink bottled or boiled water. Malaria prophylaxis and yellow-fever vaccinations are necessary for travel in tropical areas, and medical insurance is strongly advised. Take care with the altitude in Cuzco and Puno. In Lima, contact **Clínica Anglo-Americana**, Calle Alfredo Salazar 350, San Isidro, tel: 616-8900; **Clínica Internacional**, Jr Washington 1471, tel: 619-6161; **Clínica San Borja**, Av. Guardia Civil 337, San Borja, tel: 702-4300; or **Hospital de Emergencia José Casimiro Ulloa**, Av. Roosevelt 6355, Miraflores, tel: 204 0900.

Media

The cultural section of *El Comercio* is worth checking for listings. The English-language Peruvian Times, founded more than a century ago, has now gone online, and is worth a look (www.peruviantimes.com).

Money

Lima has legal, green-jacketed money exchangers on downtown Plaza San Martín. Travel agents accept payment in some foreign currencies and exchange small amounts. Banks and exchange bureaus otherwise exchange currency, and there are ATMs in most towns throughout Peru. It is convenient to carry some US dollar cash in addition to as traveler's checks, and credit and debit cards.

Nightlife

Lima is full of colorful *peñas* where there is non-stop folk music and dancing into the early hours. Aim to arrive about 9pm to get a good seat. Try **Brisas del Titicaca,** Jr. Héroes de Tarapacá 168, tel: 715-6960, an authentic *peña* with Peruvian dance shows. Popular with the locals and cheap. Also **La Candelaria Av. Bolognesi 292**, Barranco, tel: 247-1314. In the heart of Barranco, La Candelaria has live music and a lively folkloric floorshow every weekend from 10pm and serves exotic cocktails and snacks .

Miraflores and Barranco are home to the best bars and nightclubs.

Opening Hours

In Lima office hours are Mon–Fri 9am–5pm with a noon lunch break. Shops are open from 10 or 11am until 8 or 9pm. Banks are generally open Mon–Fri 9am–6pm. Outside Lima, shops and banks usually close at lunchtime. Most banks are open on Saturday. *Casas de cambio* open 9am–6pm, while money changers are on the streets nearly 24 hours a day.

Postal Services

The central post office in Lima, operated by **Serpost** (www.serpost. com.pe), at Av. Tomás Valle s/n, Los Olivos, opens Mon–Sat 8.15am–1pm, 2–7.30pm, Sun 8am–1pm.

Public Holidays

1 January New Year's Day
March/April Holy Week
1 May Labor Day
29 June St. Peter's and St. Paul's Day
28–29 July Independence Day
30 August St. Rosa of Lima Day
8 October Angamos Battle
1 November All Saints' Day
8 December Immaculate Conception
25 December Christmas Day

Shopping

Each region has its own distinctive crafts, but you will also find most of them in Lima. **Las Pallas**, Calle Cajamarca 212, Barranco, tel: 477-4629, sells selected crafts and collectors' pieces. **Figuras Peruanas, Copernico 179, San Borja, tel: 459-2175**, is a market with stalls containing a great variety of traditional crafts.

Peru Artcrafts, Larcomar Mall, Miraflores, has top-quality arts, crafts, and clothing, while **Alpaca 859**, Av. Larco 859, Miraflores, tel: 447-7163 is best for alpaca and Pima cotton garments. Peru is also known for its bargain gold, copper, and silver items. A good range can be found in the artesanías markets in Lima.

Sport and Activities

Climbing and trekking are excellent in many areas of the Andes, particularly Huaraz and around Cusco. It is not possible to hike the **Inca Trail** independently: you must pre-book with a tour operator, and arrange it well in advance of your arrival in Cusco. The dry season, May–September, offers the best views and finest weather. For safety reasons and for greater enjoyment, parties of three or more should hike together. Groups are easily formed in Cusco, and the tourist office on the Plaza de Armas provides a noticeboard for this purpose. In Huáraz, contact Explorandes, Av. Agustín Gamarra 835, tel: 428-071.

Mountain-biking and **horse riding** are also available, and **rafting** and **kayaking** from Cusco and Arequipa. Year-round **surfing** and **swimming** is good on the Tumbes area beaches; elsewhere December–April. **Birdwatching** is excellent in the Amazon, Colca Canyon, and around Paracas.

Telecommunications

Local, national, and international calls can be made from public phone boxes using coins or phone cards, available from newsstands. Alternatively, calls can be made from a *locutorio* (call center), where you pay for the call after you have made it. *Celulares* (cell/mobile phones) are ubiquitous and relatively inexpensive, and signal coverage is good. Claro and Nextel mobile phones work on the 1900 MHz band, Movistar on the 850 MHz band. All offer 3G or 3.5G service. Check details with providers before attempting to use wireless modems. Internet cafés are common and several locations in Lima, with free or paid-for wireless internet access.

Tipping

Hotels and restaurants sometimes include service charges of up to 30 percent. Tipping isn't expected, but you can leave a few soles. It's not customary to tip taxi drivers, but give a few soles to people who help you with your luggage and those who have serviced your hotel room. At the end of trekking, climbing, and other outdoor adventure activities, it's usual to leave a generous tip for your guide.

Tourist Information and Agencies

Lima: Jorge Chávez International Airport (24 hours), tel: 574-8000. Jorge Basadre 610, San Isidro, tel: 421-1627. Larcomar Entertainment Center, Module 10, Plaza Gourmet, Miraflores, tel: 445-9400.
Cusco: Main office: Velasco Astete Airport, tel: 237-364. Plaza de Armas, Portal de Arinas 177, tel: 252-974
Also worth visiting is the **South American Explorers' Clubhouse**, Calle Piura 135, Miraflores, Lima, tel: 445-3306, www.saexplorers.org.

Websites

www.limaeasy.com. Practical information on the capital.
www.peru.info. National tourist site.
www.perulinks.com. Links to Peru-related sites in Spanish and English.
www.peru-hotels.com. Hotel listings and bookings, and transport and flights information in English.
www.andeantravelweb.com/peru. Excellent travel site with many useful Peru links.

What to Read

Aunt Julia and the Scriptwriter by Mario Vargas Llosa. Entertaining novel set in Lima about a young writer's affair with his aunt
Lost The Bridge of San Luís Rey by Thornton Wilder. An acclaimed, somber tale, by Pulitzer Prize-winner, about a bridge that collapses in 18th-century Peru.
City of the Incas by Hiram Bingham. Bingham's enthusiastic account of the discovery of Machu Picchu – a treasure.
The Conquest of the Incas by John Hemming. Authoritative description of the Spanish conquest and its aftermath,
Go and Come Back by Joan Abelove. Tale of Peruvian jungle village for people of 12 years of age and older.
Insight Guide Peru. An in-depth guide to the country and its culture.

Artifact from the archeological site at Sechín Bajo, outside the city of Casma.

SURINAME

ESSENTIAL TRAVEL TIPS TO HELP YOU GET THERE AND GET AROUND

FACT FILE

Area 163,265 sq km (63,037 sq miles)
Capital Paramaribo
Population 480,000
Language Dutch (English widely spoken)
Currency Suriname dollar
Weights and measures Metric
Electricity 110/220V AC, 60Hz
Time zone GMT -3hrs, EST +1hr
International dialing code 597
Internet abbreviation .sr

TRANSPORTATION

Getting There

By Air
From Europe: Surinam Airways, Caribbean Airlines, KLM.
From/via US: Surinam Airways, Caribbean Airlines, Insel Air.
From Canada: Caribbean Airlines.

By Boat
Ferries transport passengers and cars from Guyana and French Guiana.

Getting Around

From the Airport
All international flights land at **Johan Adolf Pengel Airport** (also known as Zanderij) which is about 50km (32 miles) south of Paramaribo. There are several minibus companies, which charge about $5 to the center, or taxis costing around $35.
Departure taxes are $35, plus an additional $10 terminal fee, which is normally included in the airfare.
    The airport at **Zorg en Hoop** in Paramaribo is used for domestic flights. Airlines include Surinam Airways (www.slm.nl), Blue Wing Airlines (www.bluewingairlines.com), and Gum Air (www.gumair.com).

By Boat
There is a daily 4-hour journey up the Commewijne River. A ferry travels between Paramaribo and Meerzorg on opposite sides of the Suriname River, and smaller boats travel between Leonsberg (5km/3 miles north of Paramaribo) and New Amsterdam. Or you could try exploring the rivers in *korjaals* navigated by highly skilled Maroons.

By Road
There are no major roads in the interior except for the east–west highway that runs from Albina in the east to Nieuw Nickerie in the west. Buses operate on the coastal highway but they are a very uncomfortable way to travel. It is also possible, and not too expensive, to use taxis around the coastal regions. Remember that driving is on the left.

In Paramaribo
In Paramaribo, public transport consists of overcrowded buses and minivans, with a lot of pushing and shoving to get aboard. Check fares carefully to avoid being overcharged. Taxis don't have meters so agree on the fare beforehand.

Emergency Numbers

Ambulance, Fire, Police 115

A–Z

Accommodations
Hotels are largely concentrated in Paramaribo and a few lodges outside. Paramaribo hotels are generally relatively expensive compared with other South American destinations and limited options mean rooms should be booked ahead. There are relatively few mid-range and decent budget options: check with the tourism office. It is also possible to rent furnished apartments. There are campsites at Blaka Watra, Cola Kreek, Republiek, and Zandery.

Arts
The country's main museum, the **Surinaamse Museum** in Fort Zeelandia, on the eastern tip of downtown, also has temporary exhibitions. Paramaribo has several art galleries, and the **Academie voor Hoger Kunst- en Cultuuronderwijs (Academy for Arts and Cultural Education)** has temporary exhibitions. The Nationale Kunstbeurs, an art fair, is held annually in Paramaribo in late October.

Budgeting for Your Trip
Accommodations: Budget $10–20 for cheaper accommodations, $20–30 for mid-range hotels, and $45 and upwards for three-star and higher category hotels. Hotels tend to add a 10–15 percent service charge. House or apartment rental can be cheap, around $200 a week.

Food: Restaurants are inexpensive, with cheap meals costing under $5, and "expensive" restaurant meals costing from $10.

Children

Surinamese food is on the spicy side for children's palates. Remember that the sun is fierce, and cover them in sunscreen. Don't forget the insect repellent, either. An interesting spot to take children is Fort Zeelandia. On Sundays and holidays, people take their songbirds to parks and plazas for songbird contests, which children will probably like. Excursions children will enjoy are to Brownsberg Nature Park, with numerous monkeys and waterfalls, Galibi Nature Reserve, with wildlife ranging from sea turtles and dolphins to monkeys, and Boven Coesewijne Nature Reserve, with giant otters and birdlife.

Climate

Suriname's climate is humid and tropical, but frequent breezes from the northeast bring cooler air. Cloud cover is frequent and it can rain at any time of the year – particularly in the interior. There are four seasons: moderately rainy November–February, moderately dry February–April, main rainy season April–August, and main dry season August–November.

Crime and Safety

While generally safe, some degree of criminal activity exists in Paramaribo and other coastal towns. Travelers should therefore not wear expensive or flashy jewelry and should not display large amounts of money in public. Changing money in the street is dangerous, too. Don't walk long distances from lodgings at night and avoid the Palm Garden area after dark. Public minibuses should be avoided, due more to the irresponsible driving and maintenance of the units than to risks of pickpocketing. It is preferable to book trips to the interior through a tour agency because of the very limited infrastructure.

Disabled Travelers

Suriname has few facilities for travelers with disabilities. Hotels, except for luxury categories, normally don't have wheelchair-accessible rooms or bathrooms. Check with tour operators for those offering services for disabled travelers.

Eating Out

What to Eat and Drink

The standard of food in Suriname is high, with Asian food having a much greater influence than Dutch. The local cuisine matches the rich ethnic mix of the Surinamese people, and can be very good. Indonesian dishes such as *bami* (fried noodles) and *nasi goreng* (fried rice) are spicy, and served in cheap and cheerful food stalls. Manioc (cassava), sweet potato, plantain, chicken, shrimp, and fish feature prominently in Creole cuisine; while Hindustani specialties include *roti* (mixed curried vegetables and chicken wrapped up in a fried pancake) and *phulawri* (fried chickpeas). Chinese cuisine is plentiful and good value. The locally beer, Parbo, is quite drinkable and cheaper than imported brands. The most popular spirit is rum.

Where to Eat

Blauwgrund is the neighborhood for Indonesian restaurants, while plenty of Javanese food stalls crowd the **Waterkant** street along the Suriname River. There are several restaurants on **Keizerstraat, Wilhelminastraat,** and **Rust-en-Vredestraat**.

Embassies and Consulates

UK
Honorary Consulate, c/o VSH United Buildings, PO Box 1300, Van't Hogerhuysstraat 9–11, Paramaribo, tel: 402-558.

US Embassy
PO Box 1821, Dr. Sophie Redmond-straat 129, Paramaribo, tel: 472-900.

Australia
Consular assistance provided by the Consulate in Trinidad and Tobago: PO Box 4640, St. James Port of Spain, tel: +1 (868) 628 0695.

Canada
Wagenwegstraat, 50 Boven, Paramaribo, tel: 424-527.

Entry Requirements and Customs Regulations

Visas

Visas are required for visitors from Australia, New Zealand, and South Africa and can be obtained at Surinamese embassies and consulates, including Cayenne in French Guiana and Georgetown in Guyana. For most nationalities, they cost $45, for US citizens $100, but the latter are valid for 5 years. Since November 2011, $25, 90-day tourist cards are available upon arrival for UK, US, and Canadian visitors at the international airport.

Visitors from the UK can contact the Honorary Consulate of Suriname, 33 Pier House, 31 Cheyne Walk, London SW3 5HN, email: ajethu@honoraryconsul.info.

Visitors from the US can contact the Surinamese Embassy at 4301 Connecticut Avenue NW, Suite 460, Washington DC 20008, tel: 202-244-7488, www.surinameembassy.org. Visa forms can be downloaded online.

Customs

Duty-free allowances include 200 cigarettes or 200 cigarillos or 20 cigars or 500g of tobacco; 1 liter of spirits, 4 liters of wine, and 8 liters of beer; 50 grams of perfume and 1 liter of eau de toilette, lotions and eau-de-cologne, and other goods for personal use up to the value of $500. There is no limit on the amount of local or foreign currency that can be imported, but amounts over $10,000 should be declared on entry. The export of local currency is limited to 1,000 Surinamese dollars. Customs agents can be quite thorough.

Festivals

February/March
Carnival (dates vary). Throughout Suriname.

March
Holi Phagwa. Hindu festival of color marking the start of spring.

March/April
Avond Vierdaagse (weekend after Easter). Parade of participants in various traditional costumes performing ethnic dances and songs.

July
Keti Koti (1). Commemoration of the abolition of slavery (1863), with cultural events all over Suriname.

October
Jazz Fest (23–25). Paramaribo.

December–January
Surifesta (December 15–January 7), year-end cultural festival with shows, street parties, and flower markets; www.surifesta.com.
Eid al Fitr (end of Ramadan) is also

celebrated, but has not been included in the above as the dates change every year, according to the lunar calendar (see Public Holidays page 407).

Gay and Lesbian Travelers

Suriname is not yet tolerant of open homosexuality, particularly in the case of men. Behind closed doors, lesbian relationships *(Matis)* are accepted, particularly among Afro-Surinamese. Paramaribo has a small gay community centering on Café XPO, a gay bar and restaurant on the western edge of Downtown.

Health and Medical Care

Paramaribo tap water is comparatively safe to drink, but outside the capital, drink boiled or bottled water. Eat well-cooked vegetables, meat and fish, preferably served hot. Fruit should be peeled. Ask for advice before swimming in rivers and lakes because of poisonous fish. Note that Suriname has a high HIV/Aids rate.

Health insurance is strongly recommended. Medical care is limited: there is only one emergency room in Paramaribo and there are few hospitals or health care facilities in outlying areas.

Hospitals in Paramaribo include: **Academisch ziekenhuis**, Flustraat 1, tel: 442-222.

Diakonessen ziekenhuis, Zinniastraat, tel: 499-644.

Sint Vincentius ziekenhuis, Koninginnestraat 4, tel: 471-212.

Media

Suriname's newspapers are in Dutch. They include *De West* and *De Ware Tijd*, which has some articles in English (www.dwt.net).

Money

ATMs are not widespread, and the Royal Bank of Trinidad and Tobago (RBTT) is the only bank whose ATMs reliably dispense cash to foreign-issued cards. It is difficult to buy Suriname dollars abroad, so most travelers take US dollars into the country. The best place to change money is at banks or *cambios*. MasterCard and American Express are accepted in most large hotels and tourist restaurants and shops, but Visa and Diners Club are not widely used. To ensure hassle-free purchases during your trip, let your credit card company know you will be traveling to Suriname.

Nightlife

Nightlife in Paramaribo includes bars, dance clubs, and casinos. Dancing gets going late, not before 1am on weekends. One of the main spots is the area of the Torarica Hotel along **Wilhelminastraat** just east of downtown. **Starzz** is the main disco in this area, while **Touché** is close to the US embassy. Note that Brazilian prostitutes frequent some nightclubs. The Torarica has a **casino**, as do the Ambassador and Plaza hotels.

Opening Hours

Banking hours are Mon–Fri 9am–2pm. Shops and businesses are open Mon–Fri 9am–4.30pm, Sat 9am–1pm.

Postal Services

Compared with most of South America, the postal service is efficient and cheap. Post office hours are brief, however: Mon–Thur 7.30am–2.30pm and Fri 7.30am–2pm. The main post office is located at 1, Kerkplein in Paramaribo, tel: 477-524.

Public Holidays

January 1 New Year's Day
March (movable) Holi Phagwa
April 2 Good Friday
April 5 Easter Monday
May 1 Labor Day
July 1 Abolition of Slavery Day
November 25 Independence Day
November (movable) Deepavali
December 25–26 Christmas
Muslim holidays are also celebrated, but the dates vary considerably, according to the lunar calendar.

Shopping

What to Buy

Interesting local goods are crafts of indigenous and Cimarron origin, along with jewelry.

Where to Shop

The highest concentration of good crafts shops is on Neumanpad and Nieuwe Dominee Straat. There is a handicrafts market on the riverfront.

Sport and Activities

While attractive, **kayaking** and **rafting** for the most part need to be done on craft brought in by travelers themselves as there is little equipment available for rent. Experienced **divers** can dive

in the man-made van Blommenstein Meer. **Horseback riding** and **mountain biking** are options for tours in the interior, including to old plantations.

Telecommunications

International direct dialing is available. There are no area telephone codes. Offices of **Telesur**, the national phone company, throughout the country can be used to send telegrams. Cellphone networks work on the 800 and 1900 MHz networks. The three mobile operators are Digicel, Telesur, and UTS.

Tipping

Leave around 10–15 percent in restaurants, unless a service charge is added to the bill. Taxi drivers appreciate a 10 percent tip.

Tourist Information and Agencies

Specialist Agencies

Access Suriname Travel, Prinsessenstraat 37, Paramaribo, tel: 424-533, http://www.surinametravel.com/en

METS Travel and Tours, Dr J.F. Nassylaan 2, Paramaribo, tel: 477-088, www.surinamevacations.com

Oetsi Tours, Parijsstraat 40, Munder, Paramaribo, tel: 441-488, www.oetsitours.com

Tourist Organisations

Official tourism information is at the **Suriname Tourism Foundation**, PO Box 656, Dr J.F. Nassylaan 2, Paramaribo, tel: 410-357, www.suriname-tourism.org. Contact **Stinasu** (the Nature Preservation Foundation of Suriname) for information and inexpensive guided tours, Cornelis Jongbawstraat 14, PO Box 12252, Paramaribo, www.stinasu.com

Websites

www.surinametourism.com. An online tourist guide in English.
www.suriname.org. Swiss site with eco-travel links.

What to Read

The Riverbones: Stumbling After Eden in the Jungles of Suriname by Andrew Westoll. Personal account of a young Canadian primatologist traveling around Suriname off the beaten track.
Tails of a Shaman's Apprentice by M.J. Plotkin. A botanist learns about Amazon rainforest flora from a Surinamese shaman.

ARGENTINA BOLIVIA BRAZIL CHILE COLOMBIA ECUADOR FALKLAND ISLANDS FRENCH GUIANA GUYANA PARAGUAY PERU SURINAME URUGUAY VENEZUELA

URUGUAY

ESSENTIAL TRAVEL TIPS TO HELP YOU GET THERE AND GET AROUND

FACT FILE

Area 176,215 sq km (68,000 sq miles)
Capital Montevideo
Population 3.4 million
Language Spanish
Currency Uruguayan peso
Weights and measures Metric
Electricity 220 volts
Time zone GMT -3hrs, EST +2hrs
International dialing code 598
(Montevideo +2)
Internet abbreviation .uy

TRANSPORTATION

Getting There

By Air

From Europe: Iberia, TAM.
From/via US: American Airlines, Copa, Delta, LAN, TACA,
From Canada: Copa, United, LAN.

Getting Around

From the Airport

Montevideo's airport is at **Carrasco**, 30km (18 miles) away. It's 30 minutes by taxi, and costs about $51, but agree the price beforehand; you can pay in dollars or pesos. Various bus services to the city center charge $1–4. The trip takes up to 55 minutes. International departure tax is $40 (except for flights to Buenos Aires, for which $19 is charged).

By Boat

A catamaran *(buquebus)* connects

Buenos Aires with Montevideo. It takes 3 hours and sails several times a day each way. Fares and schedules are available from www.buquebus. com. Also from Buenos Aires, there are daily ferries to Colonia (about 160km/100 miles to the west of Montevideo).

There is a connecting bus service to Montevideo, which takes about 3 hours. There is also a twice-daily bus-and-boat service with Cacciola (www. cacciolaviajes.com) from Montevideo via Carmelo and Tigre near Buenos Aires.

By Bus

Long-distance buses depart from the modern **Tres Cruces** bus terminal, about 3km (2 miles) east of downtown Montevideo. There is a daily bus service from Buenos Aires to Montevideo. The terminal's Spanish-language website, www.trescruces. com.uy, has exact departure information.

By Road

All long-distance buses depart from the Tres Cruces terminal in Montevideo. The bus system is extensive throughout the country and the service is good. For information on driving in Uruguay, contact the Automóvil Club de Uruguay, Av. Libertador 1532, tel: 1707, www.acu. com.uy (in Spanish only).

In Montevideo

Taxis are cheap though not always plentiful. The city bus system is a mixture of old British Leyland buses and ancient electric trolleys. *Remise* taxis, or *remises*, are private cars that can be rented, with a driver, by the hour, day, or any other time period. A list of *remise* offices can be found in

the telephone directory, and staff in your hotel should be able to provide information too.

A–Z

Accommodations

Hotels are concentrated in Montevideo and the beach resorts around Punta del Este. Quality ratings range from one through five stars. Hotels should be booked ahead of time for the December 15–March 15 and Carnival travel seasons, during which prices are higher. Service charges and value-added tax add another 14 percent and 23 percent to the hotel bill, respectively. The online reservation system at www.visit-uruguay.com is free and some hotels offer discounts for bookings made through the service. Stays at rural *estancias* can also be booked. There are campsites throughout the country.

Arts

Montevideo runs two main exhibition centers. The **Centro de Exposiciones** is in the Palacio Municipal on Soriano. The **Salón Municipal de Exposiciones** is underneath the Plaza del Entrevero. The **Museo Municipal de Bellas Artes Juan Manuel Blanes** at Millán 4015 features paintings by Blanes, a 19th-century local artist, and also has temporary exhibitions. The **Museo Nacional de Artes Visuales** at Tomás Garibaldi 2283 has contemporary sculpture. The neoclassical **Teatro Solís** on Reconquista and Bartolomé Mitre is the main theatre. Plays in English are presented at the **Teatro**

Millington Drake in the Anglo-Uruguayan Cultural Institute. The **Cinematica** at Lorenzo Carnelli 1311 has international art films.

Budgeting for Your Trip

If traveling on a tight budget, one can get by on around $40 a day, half of that going to a stay at a budget hotel. **Accommodations:** Mid-range hotels cost $25–40, high-end $100 and up. **Food:** A cheap set lunch at a *confitería* will cost around $4, while a more expensive dinner will cost about $25 per person – but much more in Punta del Este, where it could easily cost $65 per person.
Museums and Attractions: Many museums and gallerias are free.
Transport: Bus and taxis fares are very reasonable.

Children

Uruguay is an excellent family destination. In Montevideo, the Parque Rodó has a lake with rowboat rentals and an amusement park. The Cerro (summit) from which the city gets its name has a good view of Montevideo, and cannons of an old fort, now a military museum. Rural visits allow for excellent horseback riding with the gauchos. The beaches stretch from Montevideo past Punta del Este, where Playa Mansa on the bay side is best for children. There are two large aquatic parks near Salto, Acuamanía and the Parque Acuático, part of the Termas de Guaviyú spa.

Climate

The climate is Mediterranean. Winter (June–August) can be quite cool and damp. Spring (September–November) and fall (March–May) are pleasant; summers (December–February) are hot but tempered by the cool Atlantic breezes.

Crime and Safety

Uruguay is one of South America's safest destinations, but while criminals tend to be non-violent, they may resort to violence if victims resist. More likely, tourists will attract petty criminals if toting cameras or backpacks – take care when slinging a purse over a chair in a restaurant.

Emergency Numbers

Ambulance, Police 911, Fire 104

Fishing in the Rio del Plata at Colonia del Sacramento.

Some parts of the old city aren't safe for individuals or couples after dark.

Disabled Travelers

Uruguay has few services for disabled travelers, but Uruguayans are helpful.

Eating Out

What to Eat

Uruguayan food consists of two staples: beef of exquisite quality, and pasta, but good seafood is also available. Breakfast consists of coffee and croissants; lunch is the main meal, served 1–3pm. Portions are often enormous; it is acceptable to order one dish for two people.

Drinking Notes

Uruguayan wines are made of unusual grapes including Tannat and Albariño. Medio y medio – a mix of sparkling and white wine – is surprisingly good and goes well with red meat. Beer is made with spring water and is also very good, especially Norteña.

Where to Eat

In Montevideo's old town, fine beef sandwiches are available around Plaza Zabla, but the highlight is the **Mercado del Puerto**, with numerous good restaurants. Montevideo favorites are *confiterías*, large bars offering meals at any time. Dining in **Punta del Este** is excellent, and there are many restaurants on the peninsula itself, but they are quite expensive.

Embassies and Consulates

UK
Calle Marco Bruto 1073, Montevideo, tel: 622-3630, www.ukinuruguay.fco.gov.uk.

US
Calle Lauro Muller 1776, Montevideo 11200, tel: 418-7777, http://uruguay.usembassy.gov.

Australia
Cerro Largo 1000, tel: 901-0743.

Canada
Plaza Independencia 749, Office 102, Montevideo, tel: 902-2030, www.canadainternational.gc.ca/uruguay.

New Zealand
Miguel Grau 3789, Montevideo, tel: 622-1543.

Entry Requirements and Customs Regulations

Visas

Tourists traveling to Uruguay from the UK, Western Europe, the US, Canada, or Australasia do not require a visa. The stamp on passports is usually good for 90 days and can be extended at the **Oficina de Migraciones**, Calle Misiones 1513, Montevideo, tel: 916-0471.

Customs

Travelers may import the following items into Uruguay duty-free: 400 cigarettes or 50 cigars or 500g of tobacco, 2 liters of alcohol, 5kg of foodstuffs, and two items of the following equipment: portable radio, photo camera, movie camera, movie projector. Allowances are half of this for people under 18 years of age.

Festivals

February/March

Carnival (varying dates). Montevideo. Uruguay's *candomblé* replaces the Brazilian samba.

ARGENTINA · BOLIVIA · BRAZIL · CHILE · COLOMBIA · ECUADOR · FALKLAND ISLANDS · FRENCH GUIANA · GUYANA · PARAGUAY · PERU · SURINAME · URUGUAY · VENEZUELA

March/April

Semana Criolla (Easter week). Towns all over Uruguay celebrate traditional customs. The main events are held in Parque Roosevelt in Montevideo and include displays of horsemanship and traditional clothing and crafts.

Gay and Lesbian Travelers

Uruguay is one of South America's most gay-friendly destinations after Buenos Aires and Rio de Janeiro. In 2005, it unveiled the subcontinent's first monument to sexual diversity, on Policía Vieja between Plaza de la Constitución and Plaza Independencia at the edge of Montevideo's old town. Beyond the capital, Carmelo and Colonia and, above all, Punta del Este, can be considered gay-friendly.

Health and Medical Care

Health services are above the South American average. Tap water is safe to drink in cities and towns. For emergency service in Montevideo contact the **Hospital Británico,** Av. Italia 2420, tel: 487-1020.

Money

Most banks and exchange offices (casas de cambio) make a small charge for cashing US dollar traveler's checks into dollars (rather than pesos). Changing money in the street is an unnecessary risk. Credit cards and traveler's checks are widely accepted in Montevideo and Punta del Este, but not elsewhere. A 10 percent surcharge for credit card use is common. ATMs on the Cirrus network are widely available in Montevideo and Punta del Este.

Nightlife

Bars and Nightclubs

After Buenos Aires, Montevideo is the main center for tango; try **Living de Tango**, Edil Hugo Prato. The most popular nightclubs are **Makao**, on Mar Artico 1227, which serves good food and plays 1970s and 1980s music, and **Luna Gaucho**, on Motivos de Proteo and Rambla. There are numerous bars and dance clubs near Plaza de la Constitución. Punta del Este discos charge expensive covers and rarely get going before 2am.

Opening Hours

Most shops open Mon–Fri 9am–noon and 2–7pm, Sat 9.30am–12.30pm. In Montevideo, banks are open Mon–Fri 1–5pm.

Postal Services

Uruguay's mail service, **Correos del Uruguay** (www.correo.com.uy), is slow and unreliable. There are post offices (correos) throughout the country and some pharmacies also accept mail service and are open 24 hours.

Public Holidays

1 January New Year's Day
6 January Epiphany
February/March Carnival
March/April Easter
19 April Landing of the 33 Patriots
1 May Labor Day
18 May Battle of Las Piedras
19 June Birth of General Artigas (Día del Nunca Más)
18 July Constitution Day
25 August Independence Day
12 October Día de la Raza
2 November All Souls' Day
25 December Christmas Day

Shopping

Montevideo's old town is a good area to look for antiques and to buy semi-precious stones. For the latter, head to **Calle Sarandí**, where they are sold at Cuarzos del Uruguay and Benito Sityá. There are several craft shops around Plaza Independencia, including the Montevideo Leather Factory. Cheaper prices are at two handicrafts markets, both open daily: the **Mercado del los Artesanos**, Plaza Cagancha 1365 downtown, and **Mercado de la Abundancia** at San José 1392. There are several weekend street markets, including at Tristán Narvaja near Plaza Cagancha and on Plaza de la Constitución.

Sport and Activities

Biking is possible in most of the country, and tours are available. The Atlantic beaches offer **water sports**, including surfing, kite-surfing and windsurfing. Huge dunes along the Atlantic shore from Chuy to Punta del Este allow for sandboarding. **Horseback riding** is possible on the numerous estancias of the interior. There are nine **golf courses** in Uruguay. **Wildlife watching** includes observation of huge numbers of sea lions and, in season, of whales and sea turtles. **Soccer** is hugely popular and attendance at a major soccer game, particularly Peñarol vs Nacional, is fun. Check the security situation beforehand. **Horse racing** is held four days a week at the Las Piedras track.

Telecommunications

State-owned **Antel** operates telecentros in most towns. Payphones require tokens (fichas) which can be bought at Antel or at newsstands. International rates are discounted Mon–Fri 10pm–7am, Sat 1pm–midnight, and all day Sunday. There are three mobile telephone service providers, Claro on the 1900 MHz band, Antel on the 1800 MHz band, and Movistar, using the 850 and 1900 MHz bands. All offer 3G service. Montevideo's area code is 02, Punta del Este 042.

Tipping

Despite the tax and service fee on restaurant bills, a small tip is expected. If a service charge isn't added, waiters are tipped about 10 percent, as are taxi drivers.

Tourist Information and Agencies

The main tourist office on **Plaza Fabini** (Entrevero) offers free maps, hotel information, etc. There are also tourist offices at the Tres Cruces bus terminal and the Carrasco airport. **Estancias Gauchas** at Cecilia Regules Viajes, Bacacay 1334 in Montevideo, tel: 916-3012, is a recommended tour operator. Montevideo **city tours** run daily from the Palacio Municipal.

Websites

www.estancias-uruguay.com Information on rural hotels/estancias in English.
www.welcomeuruguay.com Travel information, hotels, and services.
www.visit-uruguay.com An online hotel information and reservation system.
www.turismo.gub.uy Web site of the Ministry of Tourism, with some English.

What to Read

The Shipyard by Juan Carlos Onetti. Existentialist 1960s novel portraying a shipbuilder's life in Montevideo – almost foreshadowing the author's later imprisonment and exile.
Only in the Meantime & Office Poems by Mario Benedetti. Bilingual edition of Benedetti's observations on daily life in Montevideo.

VENEZUELA

ESSENTIAL TRAVEL TIPS TO HELP YOU GET THERE AND GET AROUND

FACT FILE

Area 916,442 sq km (352,143 sq miles)
Capital Caracas
Population 24 million
Language Spanish
Currency Bolívar (Bs)
Weights and measures Metric
Electricity 110 volts
Time zone GMT -4hrs, EST +1hr
International dialing code 58 (Caracas +212)
Internet abbreviation .ve

TRANSPORTATION

Getting There

By Air

From Europe: Air Europa, Air France, Lufthansa, Condor, Alitalia, Avianca, Iberia, KLM, TAP.
From/via the US: American Airlines, Santa Bárbara, Delta.
From Canada: Air Canada.

Getting Around

From the Airport

The **Simón Bolívar International Airport** is in Maiquetía, 28km (17 miles) from Caracas. The international and domestic terminals are very close to each other and there are shuttle buses every 10 minutes between the two. Shuttle buses also run to Caracas with stops by the Gato Negro Metro station (use this stop only during daylight hours)

and at their terminal two blocks west of the Bellas Artes Metro station (Calle Sur 17).

The black Anfitriónes de Venezuela taxis charge fixed prices (around $35 to the center of town). Otherwise, the **taxis** that park near the departure area have a monopoly and charge nearly double the going rate. To avoid paying over the odds, call Tele-taxi on tel: 753-4155/9122 (pre-paid phone cards are sold in dispensers next to the banks of phones in the terminal). Do not get into unlicensed taxis, as foreign visitors are sometimes mugged by these drivers.

By Air

Domestic airlines include **Aeropostal** (www.aeropostal.com), **Avior** (www.avior.com.ve), **Santa Bárbara** (www.sbairlines.com), and **Conviasa** (www.conviasa.aero). Airport departure tax should be included in your ticket.

Every state has at least one airport for commercial flights, except for Delta Amacuro. Travelers wishing to reach this state by air will have to fly in to Monagas's Maturín airport, then use public transportation or rent a car to reach the delta.

By Bus

Cheap transportation is found virtually everywhere. From Caracas, long-distance eastbound bus lines operate from the **Terminal del Oriente**, Av. General Antonio José de Sucre, on the eastern outskirts. Westbound buses leave from **La Bandera**, at the junction of Av. Nueva Granada and the El Valle *autopista*, near Los Próceres, near La Bandera Metro stop. The quality of most buses is poor; breakdowns and delays are frequent.

By Ferry

There are ferry services between Puerto La Cruz and Cumaná and Isla Margarita, as well as Cumaná to Araya.

There is a very inexpensive passenger-only service between Chacopata (on the Araya peninsula, Sucre state) and Coche Island, continuing to Margarita (landing in Porlamar, by the shopping area).

By Car

While gasoline is about the cheapest in the world, driving in Caracas is chaotic, slow, and potentially dangerous. It is less stressful to book tours. Driving in the interior is pleasant, and the roads are of good quality, apart from the potholes. In many areas, driving is the only way to appreciate landscapes, explore villages, and mingle with local people. A little Spanish will go a long way.

Driving at night is not advisable since lighting, lane markings, and warnings of obstacles are poor to nonexistent, and there are frequently animals in the road.

In Caracas

Caracas is one of South America's most congested cities, so the subway (Metro) is the fastest way of getting around (single and multiple tickets are available) and the air conditioning mostly works. Taxis are often old jalopies and don't have meters so you must negotiate fares ahead of travel. It is advisable to take radio taxis at night. For the brave and reckless, there are also motorcycle taxis. Buses are the above-ground form of transport, but the heavy traffic makes them a slow way of getting around the city.

ARGENTINA BOLIVIA BRAZIL CHILE COLOMBIA ECUADOR FALKLAND ISLANDS FRENCH GUIANA GUYANA PARAGUAY PERU SURINAME URUGUAY VENEZUELA

A–Z

Accommodations

Venezuelan hotels have for years underinvested and, at the official exchange rate, are ridiculously expensive, particularly considering the awful state many of them are in. It is advisable to book ahead from outside the country and pick hotels belonging to major international chains, though this makes budget options difficult to find other than on the internet. When calling hotels for reservations, ask for special packages, which may have major discounts.

It is also better to seek bargains on Isla Margarita through travel agents. Thus, you should check out offers with them rather than booking directly with a hotel. In Margarita, a free port, the 16 percent value added tax does not apply, but in some areas a 3 percent municipal tax in addition to standard 1 percent national tax for tourism promotion is applied for most accommodations.

With the emphasis on business travelers, decent mid-priced lodging is difficult to find. Though dozens of these hotels are found in the Plaza Venezuela to El Rosal area, surrounding the popular Sabana Grande Boulevard, they are almost exclusively by-the-hour places frequented by prostitutes and their clients (with *por ratos* – meaning just for a while – rates clearly posted). Hotels in central Caracas are likewise not recommended because of the high degree of insecurity at night.

Arts

Caracas has a dynamic cultural agenda. To find out what's going on, check *The Daily Journal* (English-language) with a daily calendar of events. The Bellas Artes zone in Los Caobos concentrates the main theaters, including **Ateneo de Caracas**, **Rajatabla**, and **Teatro Teresa Carreño**; and museums, including **Museo de Arte Contemporáneo de Caracas Sofía Imber**, tel: 573-8289, daily 9am–5pm, **Museo de Bellas Artes**, tel: 578-1816, Tue–Fri 9am–5pm, Sat–Sun 10am–5pm and the **Galería de Arte Nacional**, tel: 578-1818, Tue–Fri 9am–5pm, Sat–Sun 10am–5pm. The greatest concentration of private galleries is found in **Las Mercedes**, with Sunday (roughly 11am–2pm) the principal day for openings.

On **Isla Margarita**, the best source of information about special activities is the local press, especially El Sol de Margarita. **Museo Casa de la Aduana** in the Fodene building, facing the colonial fort on the main street passing through Pampatar, has hanging exhibits of contemporary art; Mon–Fri. **Museo de Arte Contemporáneo Francisco Narváez**, Calle Igualdad at Calle Díaz, Porlamar, tel: 261-8668, has a permanent exhibition of the works of its namesake along with temporary exhibitions; Mon–Fri 8.30am–3.30pm, Sat 9am–2pm.

Budgeting for Your Trip

It is highly recommended that you seek advice from local acquaintances or travelers on internet forums about budget trips well ahead of arrival. At the official exchange rate, Venezuela is very expensive, irrespective of cheap flight offers to Margarita from Europe.

Accommodation: It is hard to give an average price as rates vary so widely. It is best to book as many overnight stays and activities from outside the country as possible – or from an online account while inside Venezuela.

Food: Meals at upmarket restaurants can be very expensive but it is possible to eat cheaply with lunchtime set 'specials.'

Museums and Attractions: Museums are reasonable, and often free, but families can spend quite a lot on attractions.

Children

Most lodging facilities offer discounts for children. One of the best destinations for children is the Mérida area, since there are numerous places to let them run around, along with many attractions that are geared specifically to them, such as Valle Hermosa, tel: 0274-789-3226, or that are as enjoyable for children as for adults, such as the reconstructed old Andean village, Los Aleros, or the science museum in Mérida. The beaches and attractions of Margarita are also a good place to take children. Diverland, Via Porlamar–Pampatar road on the island, is a large amusement park, which also includes Waterland (with an excellent dolphin show), open daily 6pm–11.30pm; admission price is for unlimited use of all the rides; happy hour for kids under 9; free entrance 6–7pm. Also on Margarita, Parque El Agua, between Av 31 de Julio and Playa El Cardón, tel: 263 0710, is a water theme park with five enormous water slides, a "river" with built-in current to float effortlessly through the park in inner tubes, swimming pools, playgrounds, food and beverage services, and lockers; in high season, open daily 10am–5pm; low season Wed 10am–5pm Thur–Sun 10am–6pm; flat fee for full day use of about $35 per adult/$28 for kids. In general, camps, *hatos* (ranches), and other adventure and ecotourism destinations are not appropriate for younger children. Some places refuse to admit children under a certain age, either for safety reasons or out of consideration for other guests, especially when observation of fauna is involved and boisterous kids can scare the wildlife off.

Climate

Venezuela has a tropical climate with average temperatures. Four climatic zones are represented within its boundaries: hot, mild, cool, and, in the high Andes, cold.

The rainy season lasts from mid-May until the end of October, but showers may fall in December or January. In Caracas, the tropical heat is tempered by its altitude of 1,000 meters (3,000ft).

Crime and Safety

The crime rate in Venezuela, particularly in Caracas, is very high. Don't take expensive items or jewelry to Venezuela, and take care with cameras. Avoid deserted streets even during the day, both in and outside Caracas. You should not walk alone in narrow streets in downtown Caracas after dark. Use radio taxis after dark. Beware of two men approaching on motorcycles– they may try to grab your bag or camera. It is strongly recommended that you do not travel by car at night, particularly in the countryside where, should you have an accident or breakdown, the risk of robbery and other crimes is much greater.

Disabled Travelers

There is very little consideration for the disabled in Venezuela, even in the capital; in the interior, it is virtually nonexistent. One notable exception to the rule is in the **Sala Braile (Braille)** of the

Museo de Arte Contemporáneo de Caracas Sofía Imber. In this special unit, they offer guided visits (where participants can appreciate sculptural pieces by touch, with accompanying explanations by the guides, and they even have paintings with overlay of Braille), directed reading (in a Braille library focusing on topics related to art), workshops in Braille, and special vacation plans that are geared to the needs of non-sighted art lovers.

Eating Out

What to Eat

Pabellón, the national dish, combines rice, black beans, shredded beef, and *tajadas* (fried ripe plantains). The Andes is known for *pisca* (a rich broth with eggs and bread), trout, and smoked cheese. Coro is famous for *tarkari de chivo* (curried or roasted goat) and goat's milk cheese. Zulia state has delicious coconut-based specialties like *conejo en coco* (rabbit cooked in coconut milk). The coastal region is known for *consomé de guacucos* (clams) and *empanadas de cazón* (shark-meat pies), lobster, and fish such as grouper.

At Christmas, *hallaca* (a stew of chicken, pork, beef, spices, olives, raisins, and capers, wrapped in banana leaves and steamed) is the most traditional dish.

A typical and very popular Venezuelan dish is *mondongo* (tripe stew with chickpeas). *Arepa* is traditional flat round bread made from corn meal or wheat flour. The beef is excellent throughout the country.

Where to Eat

In Caracas, **Las Mercedes** and the **Altamira–Los Palos Grandes** zone offer a huge variety of restaurants and trendy, more upscale dining spots; **Av. Francisco Solano**, between Chacaíto and Av. Las Acacias, has a large concentration of Italian restaurants; **Candelaria** (recommended only for daytime visits) is popular for Spanish food and *tascas*.

Embassies and Consulates

The following diplomatic missions are located in Caracas:

Emergency Numbers

The nationwide emergency telephone number, **171**, is for police, fire, and ambulance.

UK
Torre La Castellana, Piso 11, Av. La Principal de la Castellana, La Castellana, tel: 263-8411, http://ukinvenezuela.fco.gov.uk/en.

US
Calle F and Calle Suapure, Colinas de Valle Arriba, tel: 975-6411, http://caracas.usembassy.gov.

Australia
Quinta Yolanda, Av. Luis Roche, between 6th and 7th transversals, Altamira, tel: 263-4033.

Canada
Av. Francisco de Miranda and Altamira Sur, Altamira, tel: 600-3000, www.canadainternational.gc.ca/venezuela.

Ireland
Torre Clement, Piso 2, Av. Venezuela, El Rosal, Caracas, tel: 951-3645.

Entry Requirements and Customs Regulations

Visas

Entry is by passport and visa or passport and tourist card. If arriving by air, tourist cards (valid for 90 days) can be issued to citizens of the UK, the US, Canada, and Australia. Tourist visas are supposedly necessary to enter overland from Colombia and Brazil, but regulations sometimes change overnight, so double-check in advance with your nearest Venezuelan Consulate.

It is a good idea to carry your passport with you at all times (be sure to have photocopies of all documents in a separate location in case of loss) as the police mount spot checks and anyone without ID may be detained.

Customs

The following items may be imported into Venezuela duty-free: 200 cigarettes and 25 cigars, 2 liters of alcoholic beverages, four small bottles of perfume, and gifts up to a value of $1,000.

Festivals

February
Virgen de la Candelaria (2). National. Masked processions and dances.
Carnival (variabale dates). National.

March/April
Semana Semana Santa (week before Easter). National. Processions.

June
Los Diablos Danzante (Corpus Christi Day). San Francisco de Yare (Miranda) and Chuao, Caracas.
Los Tambore de San Juan (24th). Caracas. Wild drumming and dancing mark both of these June festivals.

October
El Hatillo Music Festival (late Oct). Folk, jazz and rock festival. There are many others – keep an eye out for announcements in the local media.

Gay and Lesbian Travelers

Caracas is relatively tolerant by South American standards. While there are gay and lesbian bars in several neighborhoods, they are most common around Sabana Grande and Av. Abraham Lincoln.

Health and Medical Care

No vaccinations are needed, but a yellow-fever certificate is recommended if you intend traveling in the jungle: Venezuela is an endemic area for yellow fever, although this applies mainly to the upper Orinoco near La Esmeralda and Parima in Amazonas. Don't drink tap water anywhere. The **Centro Móvil de Medicina Permanente** in Caracas is an emergency service with doctors who can make 24-hour house calls, tel: 483-7021/6092.

Two useful addresses are: **Hospital de Clínicas Caracas** (HCC), Calle Alameda con Av. Panteón, San Bernardino, tel: 508-6111; and Instituto de Clínicas y Urologia Tamanaco, Sector San Román, Ca. Chivacoa, Las Mercedes, tel: 999-0111.

Media

The English-language *Daily Journal* has a daily calendar of events.

Money

US dollars can be exchanged for bolívars upon arrival at the airport and at *casas de cambio* in major cities, and ATMs dispense bolívares at the artificially inflated official exchange rate. Credit-card fraud is rife, even at large, well-known establishments. For a realistic market exchange rate check http://dollarparalelovenezuela.com or www.lechugaverde.com and ask travel agents or budget hotel staffers. Travel agents and

Harvesting coffee beans in Buenavista, in the state of Lara.

shopkeepers may exchange money at an acceptable rate, but don't change money on the street as this is dangerous.

Nightlife

Caraqueños usually eat at home around 8pm, or between 9pm and 11pm when they go out to restaurants; the partying goes on until well into the early hours of the morning. There are many small clubs, restaurants, and bars on **Plaza Altamira Sur** and along the **Sabana Grande Boulevard**. Restaurants are often so full that patrons must wait in line outside.

Opening Hours

Generally Mon–Fri 8am–noon and 2–6pm. Most shops open Mon–Sat 9am–1pm and 3–7pm, but in high season, Mon–Sat 9am–7pm, Sun 9am–1pm.

Postal Services

The Venezuelan postal system (IPOSTEL) is extremely inefficient, but much better for international than domestic mail. For Europe or the US, mail takes 10 days to three weeks. For a small extra charge, you can have your letter certified *(certificado)* or ask for a return receipt *(con aviso de recibo)*.

Public Holidays

1 January New Year's Day
February/March Carnival
April/March Holy Thursday, Good Friday
19 April Independence Day

1 May Labor Day
24 June Battle of Carabobo
5 July Independence Day
24 July Birth of Simón Bolívar
12 October Day of Indigenous Resistance
25 December Christmas

Shopping

Venezuela's craftsmen hold a prestigious position because of the variety and quality of their workmanship. Outstanding Quibor ceramics have pre-Hispanic origins, molded using styles and techniques handed down through the generations. Baskets, hammocks, hats, and other products made from vegetable fibers can be found in the towns and villages along the east coast. Beautifully woven ponchos, colorful blankets, and caps are sold by the Andean people while craftsmen of the *llanos* (prairies) sell four-string guitar-like musical instruments called *cuatros* as well as harps and mandolins.

Where to Shop

In the Caracas area, **Hannsi** in El Hatillo has the widest selection of Venezuelan arts and crafts in the country, with items for every budget. The most exquisite objects are found in **Casa Caruba**, Av. Andrés Bello between 1st and 2nd transversals, Los Palos Grandes. The **Sabana Grande Boulevard** is an excellent commercial artery with numerous boutiques and assorted stores.

Sport and Activities

Venezuela is an excellent destination for numerous sports ranging from **aquatics** to **mountain climbing**. **Surfing, windsurfing** and **kite-surfing** are possible along most of the beaches, particularly on Isla Margarita and the Península Adícora. There are several **golf courses**. **Trekking** and **mountaineering** are best in the Andes around Mérida and in the vast Parque Nacional Canaima that includes Angel Falls and Roraima. **Horseback riding** is excellent in the llanos. **Baseball** is the most popular spectator sport.

Telecommunications

Telephone

Most numbers are seven digits. To make national calls, add a zero before the area code. Dial 122 for the long-distance operator. Mobile

phone providers use the 850, 900, and 1900 MHz bands. Companies include Digitel, Movistar, and the government's Movilnet, which has the largest number of customers.

Internet

Internet cafés are common but the computers are generally very old and connections slow.

Tipping

A tip of 10 percent is normally added to restaurant bills. Even so, it's customary to leave 5–10 percent extra. Taxi drivers aren't usually tipped unless they carry bags or perform some special service.

Tourist Information and Agencies

Inatur www.inatur.gov.ve (in Spanish) is the national tourism body for Venezuela. There are no tourist information kiosks in Caracas; there is a booth at Maiquetía airport but the opening hours are irregular.

Websites

www.eluniversal.com/english Leading independent newspaper's English-language site.
www.explorandorutas.com Interesting site with information on routes of beaches, jungles, mountains and ecotourism.
www.venezuelatuya.com A useful search facility for finding accommodations.
www.guia.com.ve Information from culture and arts to health and transport .

What to Read

Hugo Chávez: The Bolivarian Revolution in Venezuela by Richard Gott. Excellent account of the Bolivarian revolution.
The Hacienda by Lisa St. Aubin de Terán. Lively and often tragic account of the author's time in 1970s Venezuela.
In Trouble Again by Redmond O'Hanlon. Erudition and hilarity as O'Hanlon travels up the Orinoco.
Personal Narrative of Travels in the Equinoctial Regions of America 1799–1801 by Alexander von Humboldt. Pick up Vol. II for Humboldt's marvelous descriptions of Venezuela.
Hungry Lightning: Notes of a Woman Anthropologist in Venezuela by Pei-Lin Yu. Journal of the Pum way of life.

LANGUAGE

UNDERSTANDING THE LANGUAGE

Making Contact

Whether you need to know what time the next bus leaves or how to book a hotel room, making yourself understood in the local language will really help you get the most out of your stay in South America. The good news is that you can get by in the whole continent with just two languages: Spanish and Portuguese (with the obvious exceptions of the Guyanas).

While people in many tourist establishments will speak English, once you are off the beaten track, hardly anyone will, and just making the effort to speak a few words will be appreciated, as well as making life easier. There are idiomatic differences from one country to the next, but you will soon pick these up as you go.

It would be impossible for us to give a complete language guide here, but the following are some useful words, phrases, and tips that will hopefully ease understanding.

Spanish

There is a colorful variety of local idioms throughout Spanish South America. In Argentina and Uruguay, the Spanish "**ll**," as in "*llanos*," comes out like something between a **j** and **zh**, whereas elsewhere it is more like "**y**," as in Spain; while the familiar "*tu*" is replaced by the archaic sounding "*vos*." In Chile, they are notorious for dropping the ends off their words, particularly those that end in "–ado," which become "ao" instead, and for speaking at breakneck speed.

In the Andes, *indígenas* generally speak Spanish but you will hear Quechua (also spelled Quichua) words that have crept into the language:

wambras translates as "guys," and *chévere* means "cool" from Venezuela to Peru.

In many parts of South America the word "súper" is used, as in "súper bien" to mean very good.

Berlitz publishes an excellent *Latin American Spanish Phrase Book and Dictionary*, containing vocabulary and phrases for every situation.

Pronunciation
Vowels
a as in cat
e as in bed
i as in police
o as in hot
u as in rude
Consonants are approximately like those in English, the main exceptions being:
c is hard before **a**, **o**, or **u** (as in English), and is soft before **e** or **i**, when it sounds like **s** (as opposed to the Castilian pronunciation of **th** as in think). Thus, *censo* (census) sounds like "senso".
g is hard before **a**, **o**, or **u** (as in English), but where English **g** sounds like **j** – before **e** or **i** – Spanish **g** sounds like a guttural **h**. **G** before **ua** is often soft or silent, so that *agua* sounds more like "awa", and Guadalajara like "wadalajara".
h is silent.
j sounds like a guttural h.
ll sounds like y.
ñ sounds like ny, as in the familiar Spanish word *señor*.
q sounds like **k**. *¿Qué quiere usted?* is pronounced "Keh kee-ehr-eh oostehd?"
r is often rolled.
x between vowels sounds like a guttural **h**, eg México.
y alone, as the word meaning "and", is pronounced **ee**.

Note that **ch**, **ll**, and **ñ** are sometimes still considered separate letters of the Spanish alphabet; if you're looking in a phone book or dictionary for a word beginning with **ch**, you may find it after the final **c** entry; **ll** after the **l** entry, and **ñ** after **n**.

Greetings
Hello! *¡Hola!*
Hello (Good day) *Buenos días*
Good afternoon/night *Buenas tardes/noches*
Goodbye *Ciao/¡Adios!*
My name is… *Me llamo…*
What is your name? (formal) *¿Cómo se llama usted?*
Mr/Miss/Mrs *Señor/Señorita/Señora*
Pleased to meet you *¡Encantado(a)!*
Do you speak English? *¿Habla inglés?*
How are you? (formal/informal) *¿Cómo está? ¿Qué tal?*
Fine, thanks *Muy bien, gracias*
See you later *Hasta luego*

Getting Around
Where is…? *¿Dónde está…?*
Which way is it to…? *¿Cómo se va a…?*
Yes *Sí*
No *No*
Thank you *Gracias*
You're welcome *No hay de que/ De nada/ Por nada*
Alright/Okay/That's fine *Está bien*
Please *Por favor*
Excuse me (to get attention) *¡Permiso!/¡Por favor!*
Excuse me (to get through a crowd) *¡Permiso!*
Excuse me (sorry) *Perdóneme, Discúlpeme*
I need… *Necesito….*
I'm lost *Estoy perdido(a)*
I'm sorry *Lo siento*

I don't know *No sé*
I don't understand *No entiendo*
Slowly *despacio/lentamente*
What? *¿Qué?/¿Cómo?*
When? *¿Cuándo?*
Why? *¿Por qué?*
Who? *¿Quién(es)?*
How? *¿Cómo?*
Which? *¿Cuál?*
How much/how many? *¿Cuánto?/¿Cuántos?*
How long? *¿Cuánto tiempo?*
big, bigger *grande, más grande*
small, smaller *pequeño, mas pequeño/chico, más chico*
I want…/I would like…/I need… *Quiero…/Quisiera…/Necesito…*
Where is the lavatory? *¿Dónde se encuentra el baño?*

Shopping

What time do you open/close? *¿A qué hora abren/cierran?*
Open/closed *Abierto/cerrado*
I'd like… *Quisiera…*
Do you have…? *¿Hay…?*
How much does it cost? *¿Cuánto cuesta?*
smaller/larger *más pequeño/más grande*
It's too expensive *Es demasiado caro*
Do you have something less expensive? *¿Tiene algo más económico?*
Anything else? *¿Quiere algo más?*
a little more/less *un poco más/menos*
That's enough/no more *Está bien/no más*

At the Hotel

Do you have a vacant room? *¿Tiene una habitación disponible?*
I have a reservation *Tengo una reservación*
I'd like… *Quisiera…*
a single/double (with double bed)/a room with twin beds *una habitación individual/una habitación matrimonial/una habita-ción doble*
for one night/two nights *por una noche/dos noches*
Could you show me another room, please? *¿Puede mostrarme otra habitación, por favor?*
I would like to change rooms *Quisiera cambiar de habitación*
How much is it? *¿Cuánto cuesta?*

At the Restaurant

Waiter *Garzón/mozo*
I'd like to book a table *Quisiera reservar una mesa, por favor*
Do you have a table for…? *¿Tiene una mesa para…?*
I have a reservation *Tengo una reservación*
breakfast/lunch/dinner *desayuno/almuerzo/cena*
I'm a vegetarian *Soy vegetariano(a)*
menu *la carta (or el menú)*
wine list *la carta de vinos*
fixed-price menu *menú fijo*
special of the day *plato del día*
mineral water still/carbonated *agua mineral sin gas/con gas*
with/without ice *con/sin hielo*
coffee *un café*
tea *té*
beer *cerveza*
soft drink *bebida/refresco*
a glass of red/white wine *una copa de vino tinto/blanco*
pollo **chicken**
cerdo/chancho **pork**
pescado **fish**
arróz **rice**
azúcar **sugar**
huevos **eggs**
mantequilla **butter**
pan (tostado) **bread (toast)**
queso **cheese**
sal **salt**
arróz **rice**
azúcar **sugar**
mantequilla **butter**

Time

morning *la mañana*
afternoon *la tarde*
evening *la noche*
last night *anoche*
yesterday *ayer*

today *hoy*
tomorrow *mañana*
now *ahora*
early *temprano*
late *tarde*
a minute *un minuto*
an hour *una hora*
half an hour *media hora*
a day *un día*
a week *una semana*
a year *un año*

Days of the Week

Monday *lunes*
Tuesday *martes*
Wednesday *miércoles*
Thursday *jueves*
Friday *viernes*
Saturday *sábado*
Sunday *domingo*

Months of the Year

January *enero*
February *febrero*
March *marzo*
April *abril*
May *mayo*
June *junio*
July *julio*
August *agosto*
September *septiembre*
October *octubre*
November *noviembre*
December *diciembre*

Numbers

1 *uno*
2 *dos*
3 *tres*
4 *cuatro*
5 *cinco*
6 *seis*
7 *siete*
8 *ocho*
9 *nueve*
10 *diez*
11 *once*
12 *doce*
13 *trece*
14 *catorce*
15 *quince*
16 *dieciséis*
17 *diecisiete*
18 *dieciocho*
19 *diecinueve*
20 *veinte*
21 *veintiuno*
25 *veinticinco*
30 *treinta*
40 *cuarenta*
50 *cincuenta*
60 *sesenta*
70 *setenta*
80 *ochenta*
90 *noventa*
100 *cien*
101 *ciento uno*
200 *doscientos*

Sign in Junin de Los Andes, Patagonia, Argentina.

300 *trescientos*
400 *cuatrocientos*
500 *quinientos*
600 *seiscientos*
700 *setecientos*
800 *ochocientos*
900 *novecientos*
1,000 *mil*
2,000 *dos mil*
10,000 *diez mil*
100,000 *cien mil*
1,000,000 *un millón*

Portuguese

Although Portuguese, and not Spanish, is the language of Brazil, a knowledge of Spanish will certainly prove useful: you will recognize many similar words, and some, although not all, Brazilians will understand you if you speak in Spanish. Be aware, however, that words that look very similar when written may sound totally different when spoken. The Berlitz *Portuguese Phrase Book and Dictionary* is an excellent guide to the language, with a comprehensive guide to the rather complex pronunciation rules, and includes Brazilian variants.

First names are used a great deal in Brazil. In many situations in which English-speakers would use a title and surname, Brazilians often use a first name with the title of respect: *Senhor* for men (written *Sr* and usually shortened to *Seu* in spoken Portuguese) and *Senhora* (written *Sra*) or *Dona* (used only with first name) for women. If *João Oliveira* or *Maria da Silva* calls you *Seu John*, rather than Mr Jones, then you should correspondingly address them as *Seu João* and *Dona Maria*.

There are three second-person pronoun forms in Portuguese. Stick to *você*, equivalent to "you," and you will be all right. *O senhor* (for men) or *a senhora* (for women) is used to show respect for someone of a different age group or social class or to be polite to a stranger. As a foreigner, you won't offend anyone if you use the wrong form of address. But if you want to learn when to use the more formal or informal style, observe and go by how others address you. In some parts of Brazil, mainly the northeast and the south, *tu* is used a great deal. Originally, in Portugal, *tu* was used among intimate friends and close relatives, but in Brazil, it's equivalent to *você*.

If you are staying longer and are serious about learning the language, there are of course Portuguese courses for non-native speakers,

easily found in the larger cities. Meanwhile, here are some of the most essential words and phrases.

Greetings

Tudo bem, meaning "all's well," is one of the most common forms of greeting: one person asks, "*Tudo bem?*" and the other replies, "*Tudo bem.*" This is also used to mean "OK," "all right," "will do," or as a response when someone apologizes, meaning, "that's all right, no worries." Other forms of greetings are:
Good morning (good afternoon) *Bom dia (boa tarde)*
Good evening (good night) *Boa noite*
How are you? *Como vai?*
Well, thank you *Bem, obrigada/ obrigado*
Hello (to answer the telephone) *Alô*
Hello (common forms of greeting) *Bom dia, boa tarde* etc.
Hi, hey! (informal greeting also used to get someone's attention) *Oi*
Goodbye (very informal and most used) *Tchau* (similar to the Italian Ciao)
Goodbye (literally "until soon") *Até logo*
My name is (I am) *Meu nome é (Eu sou)*
What is your name? *Como é seu nome?*
It's a pleasure *É um prazer*
Pleased to meet you *Prazer*
Yes *Sim*
No *Não*
Good! Great! *Que bom!*
Cheers! *Saúde*
Do you speak English? *Você fala inglês?*
I don't understand (I didn't understand) *Não entendo (Não entendi)*
Do you understand? *Você entende?*
Please *Por favor*
Thank you (very much) *(Muito) Obrigado* (or *Obrigada*, for a woman speaking)
You're welcome (literally "it's nothing") *De nada*
Excuse me (to apologize) *Desculpe*
Excuse me (taking leave or to get past someone) *Com licença*

Getting Around

Where is the...? *Onde é...?*
beach *a praia*
bathroom *o banheiro*
bus station *a rodoviária*
airport *o aeroporto*
train station *a estação de trem*
post office *o correio*
police station *a delegacia de polícia*
marketplace *o mercado*
embassy (consulate) *a embaixada (o consulado)*

currency exchange *uma casa de câmbio*
bank *um banco*
pharmacy *uma farmácia*
(good) hotel *um (bom) hotel*
(good) restaurant *um (bom) restaurante*
bar *um bar*
snack bar *uma lanchonete*
bus stop *um ponto de ônibus*
taxi stand *um ponto de taxi*
subway station *uma estação de metrô*
service station *um posto de gasolina*
newsstand *um jornaleiro*
public telephone *um telefone público*
hospital *um hospital*
taxi *taxi*
bus *onibus*
car *carro*
airplane *avião*
train *trem*
boat *barco*
A ticket to... *Uma passagem para...*
I want to go to... *Quero ir para...*
How can I get to...? *Como posso ir para...?*
Please take me to... *Por favor, me leve para...*
Please call a taxi for me *Por favor, chame um taxi para mim*
I want to rent a car *Quero alugar um carro*
Where are we? *Onde estamos?*
How long will it take to get there? *Leva quanto tempo para chegar lá?*
Please stop here (Stop!) *Por favor, pare aqui. (Pare!)*
Please wait *Por favor, espere*
What time does the bus (plane, boat) leave? *A que horas sai o ônibus (avião, barco)?*
Where does this bus go? *Este ônibus vai para onde?*
Airport (or bus station) tax *Taxa de embarque*

Shopping

Do you have...? *Tem...?*
I want... please *Eu quero... por favor*
I don't want... *Eu não quero...*
I want to buy... *Eu quero comprar...*
Where can I buy... *Onde posso comprar...?*
film *filme*
a ticket for... *uma entrada para...*
this (that) *isto (aquilo)*
something less expensive *algo mais barato*
shampoo *xampu* or *shampoo*
soap *sabonete*
toothpaste *pasta de dente*
sunscreen *filtro solar*
aspirin *aspirina*
I need... *Eu preciso de...*
a doctor *um médico*
a mechanic *um mecânico*

transportation *transporte*
help *ajuda*
How much? *Quanto?*
How many? *Quantos?*
How much does it cost? *Quanto custa? Quanto é?*
That's very expensive *É muito caro*
money/cash *dinheiro*
Do you accept credit cards? *Aceita cartão de crédito?*

At the Hotel

I have a reservation *Tenho uma reserva*
I want to make a reservation *Quero fazer uma reserva*
a single room (a double room) *um quarto de solteiro (um quarto de casal)*
with air conditioning *com ar condicionado*
I want to see the room *Quero ver o quarto*
suitcase *mala*
bag or purse *bolsa*
key *chave*
the manager *o gerente*

At the Restaurant

Waiter! *Se faz favor!*
I didn't order this *Eu não pedi isto*
The bill, please *A conta, por favor*
Is service included? *Está incluido o serviço?*
I want my change, please *Eu quero meu troco, por favor*
cardápio **menu**
carta de vinhos **wine list**
café da manhã **breakfast**
almoço **lunch**
jantar **supper**
especialidade da casa **house specialty**
água mineral com gás **carbonated mineral water**
água mineral sem gás **still mineral water**
café **coffee**
chá **tea**
cerveja **beer**
vinho branco/tinto **white/red wine**
um refresco (suco) **soft drink (juice)**
gelo **ice**
sal **salt**
pimenta **pepper**
açúcar **sugar**
um tira-gosto **an appetizer**
um lanche **a snack**
porco **pork**
frango **chicken**
peixe **fish**
camarão **shrimp**
carne **beef**
bem passado **well done**
aô ponto **medium rare**
mal passado **rare**
verduras **vegetables**
salada **salad**

fruta **fruit**
pão **bread**
manteiga **butter**
torradas **toast**
ovos **eggs**
arroz **rice**
batatas (fritas) **(fried) potatoes**
feijão **beans**
sobremesa **dessert**

Time

hour *a hora*
day *o dia*
week *a semana*
month *o mês*
When? *Quando?*
What time is it? *Que horas são?*
Just a moment please *Um momento, por favor*
What is the schedule? (bus, tour, show, etc.) *Qual é o horário?*
How long does it take? *Leva quanto tempo?*
At what time? *A que horas?*
At one o'clock *A uma hora*
(two, three…) *(duas,três…)*
An hour from now *Daqui a uma hora*
Which day? *Que dia?*
yesterday *ontem*
today *hoje*
tomorrow *amanhã*
next week *a semana que vem*

Days of the week

Monday *Segunda-feira*
Tuesday *Terça-feira*
Wednesday *Quarta-feira*
Thursday *Quinta-feira*
Friday *Sexta-feira*
(Monday to Friday are often written as 2a, 3a, 4a, 5a)
Saturday *Sábado*
Sunday *Domingo*

Months

January *Janeiro*
February *Fevereiro*
March *Março*
April *Abril*
May *Maio*
June *Junho*
July *Julho*
August *Agosto*
September *Setembro*
October *Outubro*
November *Novembro*
December *Dezembro*

Numbers

1 *um*
2 *dois*
3 *três*
4 *quatro*
5 *cinço*
6 *seis*
half a dozen *meia*
7 *sete*
8 *oito*

9 *nove*
10 *dez*
11 *onze*
12 *doze*
13 *treze*
14 *quatorze*
15 *quinze*
16 *dezesseis*
17 *dezessete*
18 *dezoito*
19 *dezenove*
20 *vinte*
21 *vinte e um*
30 *trinta*
40 *quarenta*
50 *cinqüenta*
60 *sessenta*
70 *setenta*
80 *oitenta*
90 *noventa*
100 *cem*
101 *cento e um*
200 *duzentos*
300 *trezentos*
400 *quatrocentos*
500 *quinhentos*
600 *seiscentos*
700 *setecentos*
800 *oitocentos*
900 *novecentos*
1,000 *mil*
2,000 *dois mil*
10,000 *dez mil*
100,000 *cem mil*
1,000,000 *um milhão*

Send Us Your Thoughts

We do our best to ensure the information in our books is as accurate and up-to-date as possible. The books are updated on a regular basis using local contacts, who painstakingly add, amend and correct as required. However, some details (such as telephone numbers and opening times) are liable to change, and we are ultimately reliant on our readers to put us in the picture.

We welcome your feedback, especially your experience of using the book "on the road". Maybe we recommended a hotel that you liked (or another that you didn't), or you came across a great bar or new attraction we missed.

We will acknowledge all contributions, and we'll offer an Insight Guide to the best letters received.

Please write to us at:
**Insight Guides
PO Box 7910
London SE1 1WE**
Or email us at:
insight@apaguide.co.uk

CREDITS

Insight Guide Credits

Project Editor
Alexia Georgiou

Series Manager
Carine Tracanelli

Art Editor
Lucy Johnson

Map Production
Original cartography Berndtson &
Berndtson, updated by
Apa Cartography Department

Production
Tynan Dean, Linton Donaldson and
Rebeka Ellam

Distribution

UK
Dorling Kindersley Ltd
A Penguin Group company
80 Strand, London, WC2R 0RL
customerservice@dk.com

United States
Ingram Publisher Services
1 Ingram Boulevard, PO Box 3006,
La Vergne, TN 37086-1986
customer.service@
ingrampublisherservices.com

Australia
Universal Publishers
PO Box 307
St Leonards NSW 1590
sales@universalpublishers.com.au

New Zealand
Brown Knows Publications
11 Artesia Close, Shamrock Park
Auckland, New Zealand 2016
sales@brownknows.co.nz

Worldwide
Apa Publications GmbH & Co.
Verlag KG (Singapore branch)
7030 Ang Mo Kio Avenue 5
08-65 Northstar @ AMK
Singapore 569880
apasin@singnet.com.sg

Printing
CTPS-China

INDEX

Main attractions are in bold type